THE ENCYCLOPEDIA OF FISH COOKERY

THE ENCY

fis

DESIGNED BY ALBERT SQUILLACE | PRODUCED BY THE RIDGE PRESS

CLOPEDIA OF

sh

COOKERY

by A. J. McClane

photography by
Arie deZanger

HOLT, RINEHART AND WINSTON | NEW YORK

Published simultaneously in Canada by Holt, Rinehart & Winston of Canada, Limited.

Library of Congress Catalog Card Number: 77-72781
ISBN: 0-03-015431-6

Printed in the United States of America
10 9 8 7 6 5

Edited by Inez M. Krech

Prepared and produced by The Ridge Press.
Art Director: Albert Squillace
Production: Arthur Gubernick
Art Associate: David Namias
Art Production: Doris Mullane

All photographs are by Arie deZanger except those on the following pages: 20: Donald E. McAllister, National Museums of Canada. 22: California Department of Fish and Game. 31: A. J. McClane. 55: State of New Hampshire, Department of Fish and Game. 58: State of New Hampshire, Department of Fish and Game. 82: State of New Hampshire, Department of Fish and Game. 100: (center and bottom) Robert J. Learson, National Oceanic and Atmospheric Administration, Gloucester, Mass. 113: A. J. McClane. 118: Bob Stearns. 129: Donald E. McAllister. 136: Patti McClane. 148: (left) T. F. Pletcher. 149: Donald E. McAllister. 172: (center and bottom) A. J. McClane. 175: (bottom, both) A. J. McClane. 177: Dennis Opresko. 178: A. J. McClane. 228: Patti McClane. 237: State of New Hampshire, Department of Fish and Game. 243: A. J. McClane. 248: (both) A. J. McClane. 262: (top and bottom) T. F. Pletcher; (center) State of New Hampshire, Department of Fish and Game. 301: Lennert Borgstrom. 332: T. F. Pletcher. 356: A.J.McClane. 363: (bottom) T. F. Pletcher. 395: A. J. McClane. 398: (bottom) State of New Hampshire, Department of Fish and Game. 399: (both) State of New Hampshire, Department of Fish and Game. 400: (top) State of New Hampshire, Department of Fish and Game; (bottom) A. J. McClane. 401: State of New Hampshire, Department of Fish and Game. 414–415: A. J. McClane. 416: (top) A. J. McClane. 416–417: (bottom) T. F. Pletcher. 417: (top) State of New Hampshire, Department of Fish and Game. 419: State of New Hampshire, Department of Fish and Game. 420–421: A. J. McClane. 425: Patti McClane. 468–469: A. J. McClane. 474: Albert Squillace. 475: State of New Hampshire, Department of Fish and Game.

The illustrations on pages 74–75, 171, and 249 are by F. McK. Watkins.

ISBN 0-03-015431-6

Contents

Foreword

Man has captured fish as a food ever since he has been on earth. His technical skill in harvesting the seas is very ancient. Bone fishhooks, 5,000 years old, differing little from our modern design, were found in the Skipshelleren Cave of Straumen, Norway, the site of a fishing village during the Stone Age. Historically, the importance of fish in various cultures is evident in mythology, the arts, medicine, politics, the rise and fall of empires and religions. The Greek word for fish ('Ιχθύs) is an acronym for that biblical phrase "Jesus Christ, Son of God, Savior," a connotation used as a divine symbol among the terrorized Christians of Roman times. In the Resurrection appearance at the Sea of Tiberias in Galilee, Jesus instructed His disciples where to net fish, after none had been caught. The netted fish were then prepared on a charcoal fire. This meal had eucharistic significance; thus even a crude drawing of a fish was a "sign" among people who lived precariously in the pagan world of Caesar.

Yet, from an even earlier time, the mummified bodies of Nile perch have been found in the tombs of ancient Pharaohs. It is likely that divine status was accorded to fish from earliest times, as a symbolic sacrifice between heaven and earth from an alien aquatic world. Even today man knows less about the 328 million cubic miles of water he calls the "sea" than he does about the moon. Fish was a Lenten denial food and a monotonous experience for many Catholics each Friday, until Pope Paul VI issued his 1966 apostolic decree. This was perhaps less demanding than the 145 fast days of Elizabethan England, but neither regimen did anything to put fish in an exuberant culinary perspective.

In the pharmacopoeia of ancient times the organs of various fish were believed to hold great curative powers. For a toothache, both Pliny and Galen advised that the brains of a shark boiled in oil provided relief when rubbed on the painful member, and this mixture was also an antidote against the bite of a rabid dog. Dioscorides found salted tuna meat "useful against viper bites," while its blood, spleen and liver—collectively *depilatorio*—would remove unwanted hair. In speaking of pike, Gesner observed that "the heart and galls is very medicinal to cure agues and abate fevers," and in the reign of Charles II, the heart of the pike was "a remedy against febrile paroxysms and the gall of much use in the affections (sic) of the eyes." The ashes of a cremated pike were used "to dress old wounds." Pike nostrums were approved by the Royal College of Physicians. Of course, the gonads of some species, and especially the testes of salmon, were considered an

aphrodisiac, a role later usurped by the oyster—after civilized man learned to eat an oyster. The roe of herring is still paramount to the nuptials in a Buddhist ceremony when a Japanese bride is served *kazunoko*, a verbalized play on the words for "many children." The ultimate discovery of cod liver as a valuable source of vitamins A and D was simply part of the naturopathic curiosity of early-day fishermen who first used cod-liver oil on hands made painfully raw by howling gales of the winter fishery. The vile-tasting liquid was introduced orally by some brave soul who correctly surmised that "if it cures one thing, it will cure another," and the world prospered with the first specific remedy for rickets, a bone-destroying disease of the nineteenth century. Then the even larger livers of shark were found to be vitamin rich. However, the medicines of fact and fancy bear little importance when compared to the food value of most aquatic organisms. The nutrient composition of fish itself is one healthy reason to become an ichthyophile—but sheer enjoyment is foremost, and the concern of this volume.

Any work that aspires to be an encyclopedia must present facts to the extent that we know them, but the author humbly apologizes for taking his hobbyhorse on a brief canter at certain points, as facts do not provide a personal opinion. The fact that pompano, for example, always commands a high price in the market and is a gustatory tribute at table is of no consequence unless comparable and less expensive options are known. I bear no grudge to the pompano, but other species are similar in texture and flavor and many fish are superior, particularly if the pompano has been frozen—a mind-boggling consistency in the vernacular of restaurants who believe that "fresh" means recently thawed. Whether our tastes agree or not, at least I have announced the existence of my prejudices beforehand. In a lifetime dedicated to piscatorial matters, I have enjoyed every fish, bivalve, mollusk and crustacean described or mentioned in this book, plus many others too far removed from modern kitchens to warrant inclusion.

My career in the kitchen is in part a hobby and to some extent a matter of "self-defense." As Fishing Editor of *Field & Stream*, and subsequently Executive Editor, I have enjoyed 30 years of wandering in remote places of the world from the Arctic to Tierra del Fuego, the jungles of Africa and the wilds of the upper Orinoco, the central Amazon and Matto Grasso—where cooking was often pertinent to survival. It became apparent early in the game that one could dine splendidly outdoors, as my good friend Charles Ritz so capably demonstrated. Many years ago while making a film on the Stamp River for the

National Film Board of Canada in British Columbia, at our lunch break, he produced grilled salmon steaks in a sauce provençale made over an alderwood fire with the same attention to detail that it would have received in the Ritz Hotel. The fresh tomatoes and cream were no extra burden to our grub box in this location. It was simply a matter of anticipating the meal, much as one would bring along ketchup and relish for a hamburger. To me, there is no finer food than a fish taken fresh from the water and prepared with a totality of concept, usually simple in form but accompanied by vegetables or fruits of the season and fresh garden herbs in honest sauces—when sauces are required. Although a thousand fish dinners have passed since that day on the Stamp, it's easy to remember most of them in the context of location, companions, and the always delightful experience of new flavors which are infinite to a true ichthyophile. There are at least 25,000 species of fish in the world and far more mollusks and crustaceans than one could sample in a lifetime.

While writing this book I traveled to many lands, visiting markets and restaurants and talking with suppliers, chefs and the fishermen themselves. Almost every meal consisted of seafood in one form or another, yet over a period of a month on any one trip I seldom felt the "need" for the beef or other animal meats we generally accept as essential to the American diet. There is no end to the imaginative variety possible in fish cookery, but as an art or, if you prefer, a discipline, this cookery suffers in our country for the lack of hard information, not in the sense of kitchen technique but in understanding the raw materials. Although this book does not deal with fishing in any technical sense, fishing remains one of two sports that allows the average man to harvest his own food, a game that some 60 million people in the U. S. enjoy; in this context many fish, crustaceans and mollusks go unutilized as they are not recognized as being edible.

The consumption of seafood in the U. S. when last compiled (1973) was the highest since the Federal Government began keeping records in 1909. According to the National Marine Fisheries Service we consumed 2.6 billion pounds (edible weight), a figure which does not include the very substantial quantity caught by sport fishermen; in edible weight this would be an additional 630 million pounds taken in saltwater and more than 300 million pounds from freshwater sources. However, other nations such as Japan depend on seafood for more than 50 percent of their diet despite the postwar boom in animal protein. It's estimated that the Japanese consume well over 7 billion pounds annually. The Soviet Union and the People's Republic of China are close behind. Thus, com-

mercial fleets of these and other nations operate in all the world's seas; despite the myriad international agreements on annual quotas and territorial limits, demand far exceeds supply. Many species of fish that we once considered abundant and cheap are both scarce and expensive today. At the present rate of human population growth, our oceans and freshwaters will be exploited to a greater extent than ever. A fish dinner may well be an occasion of great celebration, an irony in view of our history, as various fish dinners *were* festive occasions in centuries past.

The common and scientific names used in this book are those recognized by the American Fisheries Society. In the case of fish species not indigenous to North America, the names used are those appearing in international fishery statistics.

NOMENCLATURE

A universal problem in seafood cookery is the profusion of common names in many languages which has no counterpart in other foods. The semantics of a pork chop, for example, are limited, and few cooks could confuse one with a sirloin steak. Aquatic products, however, are often a mystery, not solely to the amateur chef but to the *garde-manger* of some of the world's best restaurants. Although it's not practical or even gastronomically stimulating to use Latin names in a cookbook, I have made an attempt to "screen" the various possibilities that a common name may present. Many fish species in American waters go unutilized, yet they are the same regional specialties celebrated in other cuisines. The ubiquitous searobin, for example, which American anglers consider a nuisance and ignore completely, is the *grondin* of *bouillabaisse* fame, and the *fogas* around which a cult of Hungarian dining has been built is generically the same fish we call, perhaps too graphically, the walleye. Thus, the foreign names of each fish are appended to major entries, where pertinent, in six or more languages according to their occurrence in other cuisines.

For ease in relating different recipes to fish of the same family the entry names such as COD encompass all members of that group such as haddock, hake, pollock and tomcod, which are individually treated under the main heading. You need not be an amateur ichthyologist to determine which fish belongs to what family, simply look up the name you know in the index and you'll find where it's located. This has a two-fold purpose: to place correctly misleading market or common names such as "green cod" or "blue cod," which are not related to the true cods in taxonomy or kitchen methodology, and to focus your attention on groupings of fish which have similar qualities as a food, or those which are exceptions to the rule.

NUTRITIONAL VALUE

The popular "fat, medium, lean," concept of individual species is a broad generalization at best. A trout, for example, can be fat *or* medium *or* lean depending on a variety of factors which will become apparent. The oenophile and the ichthyophile have much in common: both must learn to read behind the labels. The term "Burgundy" is no more revealing than the catchall "sole"; we are talking about numerous products of many origins which have good seasons and poor, and either subject demands qualitative judgments. The variations within any single species in the amount of fat present depend on the kinds of food the fish eats (a trout that feeds mainly on insects will be leaner than one taken from a population whose diet is dominated by smelts, for example, due to the high oil content of this forage), and the time of the year (just prior to spawning the fat content of most fish reaches its highest level and during spawning its lowest level). A cod, for instance, may lose about 20 percent of its fat with a parallel increase in water and water-solubles during spawning. Fat is only one of four major components of fish flesh; it's composed mostly of water and water-solubles (a complex mixture of free amino acids, mineral salts, vitamins and various nitrogenous bases), and protein. These seasonal variations also differ according to the size of the fish, with larger individuals showing greater amplitude than smaller ones. The terms "fat" and "oil" are used interchangeably in the sense of a solid as it exists in the live fish or liquid form as it is rendered in cooking.

Fish oil contains a high proportion of polyunsaturated fatty acids (more so than beef or pork) and low amounts of cholesterol. These factors tend to suppress the blood cholesterol level in man and diminish the risk of atherosclerosis. Most fish and shellfish have a low oil and a high protein content, such as the various rockfishes, pollock, haddock, whiting, cod, shrimps, scallops and lobster. These foods are ideal for inclusion in a weight-reduction diet. Although other species have varying ratios of fat to protein, comparatively few show a high fat to low protein content (more than 15 percent fat and less than 15 percent protein), but bear in mind, they also contain relatively high levels of polyunsaturated fatty acids; fish in this category would include herring, mackerel and certain lake trout.

Since the advent of the low-sodium diet, it may be important for some readers to know that no species of fish contains as much sodium in an average serving as the maximum permitted level (100 milligrams per 100 grams of food). Saltwater fish have no more sodium in their flesh than freshwater species, even though they live in a highly saline environment. Naturally in fishery products with introduced sodium chloride, such as smoked fish of any kind, or salt cod, the sodium content will be high. In general, however, all fresh fish contain less salt than beef. Oysters and soft clams are low in sodium, but hard clams and lobster contain higher levels and are not recommended for the dieter.

Fish and shellfish provide relatively large amounts of phosphorus, potassium and iron. Saltwater species are also a rich source of iodine. In addition to flouride other trace minerals include copper, zinc, manganese, cobalt, molybdenum and selenium, which are especially abundant in fish roes and in shellfish.

QUALITY

There is a vast difference between fish markets. You only have to walk into a shop like Nickerson's in Chatham on Cape Cod or any of his counterparts the world over and the whole concept of quality becomes immediately apparent. From the moment you enter the first impression is a fragrant, almost sweet smell of prime seafoods. It is a small market with only seasonally available fish displayed, and these shine like jewels nestled in beds of shaved ice. The bold black stripes of the striped bass are vivid against its silvery scales, the delicate orange pectoral fins of the weakfish look as if they belong in a formal Japanese garden, and the green backs of the mackerel are as emerald as the Ring of Kerry. Mr. Nickerson *knows* his seafood; like any reliable fishmonger, he takes pride in his products. Compared to so many markets with overpowering odors, where slack-skinned fish of a uniform dull color are piled often one on top of the other, it requires little expertise on your part to evaluate the source of supply. Just as a quality butcher shop reveals itself to the beholder, so does the fish market. Unfortunately, in a meat-oriented nation such as ours the average buyer has no preconceived standards, and this is really where seafood cookery begins.

Fish and shellfish are our most perishable foods. In an unfrozen form but properly iced most fish have a shelf life of about 5 days if caught within 48 hours before delivery. Seafood is sometimes 10 days or more in transit before reaching the market, and only the cleanest boats with proper chilling procedures can land "fresh" fish within that period. Frozen fish (processed aboard) can, of course, tolerate extreme time lapses but must be kept at storage temperatures below 10°F. at the retail food cabinet.

The ideal fresh fish are those you catch yourself, just hours out of the water. Anglers often sacrifice quality for convenience by not taking the time to dress and chill their catch. To keep a fish in prime condition, gut it, and drain off as much blood as possible. Removal of the intestines, liver, heart and gills means elimination of the largest source of bacterial contamination. The digestive enzymes in most fish are extremely powerful, and these "gastric juices" quickly attack the walls of the body cavity if the fish is not dressed immediately. The only exceptions to this rule are nonfeeding anadromous fishes such as salmon and steelhead, whose stomachs atrophy after returning to freshwater; without the production of digestive enzymes there is little or no spoilage. In cold regions such as Labrador or Iceland whole fish are often left buried in the permafrost for several days before utilization with no apparent spoilage. Obviously these are exceptions to the rule. Whenever possible, keep an ice chest on board to store your catch. Chips of ice, or flake ice, or scale ice, are better than a cake of ice because the smaller pieces have a more intimate contact with all surfaces, thereby increasing the cooling rate which in turn prolongs keeping quality.

On the stream you should use a wicker creel which allows free circulation of air. Separate the fish by packing them in grass or ferns to permit some circulation of air. However, at temperatures over 70°F. conditions are most favorable for the growth of spoilage bacteria. Fish should not be kept in a creel for more than 3 to 4 hours on warm days. Do not put fish in jacket pockets or expose them to the sun.

Stringers kept in the water are also of limited value. Hardy specimens such as bass, walleye and bluegills may remain alive for hours, but an animal killed instantly will be in better condition than one that dies slowly, struggling and being bruised in the process. At ordinary, warm surface temperatures fish may spoil even before they are removed from the stringer.

When buying fish at the market there is, of course, some element of chance in finding a perfectly fresh product, although a reliable shop can often provide better quality than an amateur angler. Evaluation is really quite easy if you use the following checkpoints for a whole fish, drawn or in the round:

(1) When pressed with your finger the flesh will be firm and elastic; it must not feel so soft that your finger leaves an indentation.

(2) The fish's eyes should be clear and full, not milky and sunken.

The eyes are an excellent test for freshness.

The gills of a fresh fish are bright red.

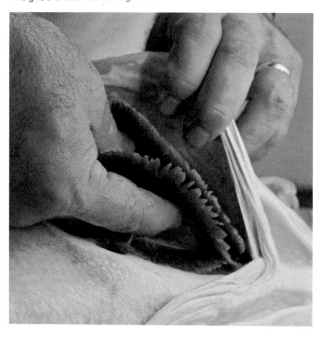

(3) Its gills should be bright red rather than a muddy gray.

(4) It will have a clean, often cucumberlike odor.

(5) Its characteristic skin color should be unblemished by any reddish patches along the ventral area.

In fillet or steak form the flesh must have a clean-cut appearance and a firm moist texture. There should be no leathery traces of yellowing or browning around the edges. At an unfamiliar market, you should have these cuts custom made from a fresh fish, drawn or in the round.

FLAVOR

The terms most often applied to describing the flavor of a fish are sweet, fishy, bland, mossy and oily. A fresh fish will taste sweet. Likewise, a correctly frozen product should never taste "fishy." A strong or rancid flavor indicates that the raw material was improperly handled before or during the freezing process, or it was kept in protracted storage. Rancidity is caused by an oxidation of the fish oils which produces bitter-tasting carbonyl compounds. This is a more common problem with some species of fish than others. As a rule, aquatic animals containing only a small quantity of oil keep better than those which have a high oil content. Mackerel, lake trout, herring and smelt, for example, are more susceptible to rancidity than cod, yellow perch, halibut or sole. However, there are notable exceptions; of the 5 species of

Pacific salmon, the lean pink salmon becomes rancid and discolored in less than one tenth of the time required by the king salmon, which has the highest oil content.

It also is possible that a particular kind of fish may be highly palatable in one geographic location and inferior in another due to environmental conditions such as various types of pollution, the presence of certain algae in the water, and the foods consumed by the fish in a particular area.

TERMINOLOGY

In common with all wild game, a fish is "dressed," not cleaned. To clean implies that it's in less than a pristine state, which a fresh fish is not. In fact, various parts of the body in many species are highly edible, such as the gonads, liver, cheeks and tongue. Some fish are eaten whole, such as the component species of whitebait. Fish are dressed in many different ways according to their size, shape, skeletal structure, and the intended method of cooking. The terminology used in this book with respect to the raw material is as follows:

CENTERCUT A centercut is taken from that portion of the fish past the pectoral fin to a point before the body narrows. When sliced out in one piece, it's commonly called a **LOIN CUT.** The loins of large fish such as salmon, blackfin tuna, albacore, wahoo or lake trout are usually deboned and used for poaching or baking. Loins may also be skinned and glazed for decorative presentations. The remaining parts of the fish can be reserved for other purposes.

DRAWN A whole fish which has been scaled, with the gills, long gut and stomach removed. The head and fins are intact and the gonads left in the body cavity. This is a common practice in marketing herring; as applied to herring it's properly called a **GIBBED HERRING;** if the head is also removed, it's known as a **NOBBED HERRING.** Smelts and small trout are frequently drawn.

FILLETS The sides of a fish cut lengthwise free of the backbone. The rib cage can also be eliminated by making a wide angular cut from the gillcover to the vent, or by slicing it from the fillet; either way it's called a **NAPECUT FILLET.** The skin may or may not be left on depending on the species and recipe requirements. The fish may also be cut along both sides with the two pieces remaining joined along the back; in this style it is known as a **BUTTERFLY FILLET;** this is the traditional and proper form for small haddock in making Finnan Haddie. If filleted by cutting along the back with the two pieces remaining joined along the belly, it is known as a **KITED FILLET;** this is particularly suitable because of its natural envelope for a recipe such as **Trout Stuffed with Crab Meat** *(which see)*. Flatfish like the flounder or sole can be filleted in two pieces to obtain **CROSSCUT FILLETS,** but if each of these is cut out in two pieces, as in the case of a large fish, they are known as **QUARTERCUT FILLETS.**

The dividends after filleting—head, skin and bones—should be reserved for making stocks and sauces.
FINGERS The fish is filleted with skin removed, then cut into finger-length strips by slicing vertically across the grain, usually in ½-inch-wide pieces. Fingers are designed for deep-frying with a suitable batter *(see COOKING METHODS)* but they may also be used in pickled form in a preparation such as **seviche** *(see under PICKLED FISH).*
PAN-DRESSED A fish which has been scaled and gutted with head and fins removed. Pan-dressed fish are usually sautéed or deep-fried. When deep-frying brook trout, sunfish, dabs, smelts, yellow perch and other small fish, do not remove the tail. The tail lacks spines and becomes very crisp and nutlike; eating it will be like eating a potato chip.
SCORED Either a drawn or whole-dressed fish with a varying number of vertical cuts (on a dorsal to ventral axis). Scoring expedites heat penetration and is mainly used when deep-frying, although it may be necessary for uniform brining in preparing smoked fish, or when barbecuing or baking a large fish. Fillets may also be scored for deep-frying as in the Chinese preparation of Sweet-and-Sour Fish *(see under ROCKFISH).* Crisscross cuts expedite cooking time without loss of flavor or moisture.
SASHIMI Sliced fish to be served raw. There are 4 basic cuts according to texture: these are flat, cubed, threadlike, and paper-thin *(see under SASHIMI).*
SKINNED Some species of fish are necessarily skinned rather than dressed such as catfish and eels. For methods see under individual entry.
SPLIT A whole fish cut along the underside lengthwise from gillcover to tail. Depending on its size, this usually requires more than one cut to be done neatly. The knife blade should be pressed against the backbone and the fish sliced in two. The fish is then gutted and scaled, and the gills removed. The backbone may or may not be removed according to the recipe, but about 2 inches should be left at the tail for support when cooking if the fish is deboned. The head is usually left on. Fish are split for exotic interior seasoning or stuffing before baking and are often served *en croûte*, wrapped in a puff pastry.
STEAKED Large round-bodied fish may be steaked. The fish is scaled, gutted, then cut into crosswise pieces from 1 to 1½ inches thick. Each portion includes a piece of the backbone; in most species this should not be removed

as it supports the musculature while cooking. However, according to taste, it may be desirable to excise the bone and surrounding bitter, though nutritious, dark meat in fishes belonging to the tuna family such as albacore, king mackerel and school bluefin. Certain large flatfish, notably the halibut and turbot, can also be cut into steaks. Steaks are usually poached, broiled, baked or sautéed. Marination and basting are important elements when cooking over direct heat.
STICKS Different from fingers; a stick is a uniform rectangular cut mitered commercially from a block of frozen fish fillets. Fish sticks are sold in frozen form, usually breaded, and either precooked or uncooked. It's often difficult to judge which species is involved, and the culinary possibilities are severely limited.
WHOLE-DRESSED A whole fish which has been scaled, the gills removed, and gutted. The head and fins are left intact. Any edible organs such as the roe to make caviar, or the white roe to add to a sauce or to an integral part of the recipe, are reserved for subsequent use. Whole-dressed fish are usually baked, poached, barbecued or, if reasonably small (1½ to 2½ pounds), deep-fried. There is no need to cut off the fins. It's easier to pull these out *after* cooking, as the basal bones below the skin will then come free, intact.

READING THE RECIPES

Aquatic foods are not as readily obtained in their full spectrum as meats, for example, and seafood cookery begins with what has been harvested or what is available. With reasonable certainty one can order a 6-pound leg of lamb or 3 pounds of veal cutlets from the local market, but our supplies are both seasonal and often exotic. Too, the form in which they arrive in the kitchen—whole, filleted, steaked, fresh, smoked, precooked, *ad infinitum*—immediately expands or limits the number of recipes that may be suitable. It is time-consuming to read down a long list of ingredients (which you may have) only to discover that the subject is a whole-dressed 15-pound lake trout, or a dozen fresh lobsterettes, which you do not have. Seafood cookery often demands a number of primary ingredients—**bouillabaisse, paella, suquillo** or **cioppino** are good examples—as well as secondary ingredients such as a pound of dried fennel twigs or a quart of fish stock. So in this book the first ingredients listed will be the fish or shellfish. If these primary subjects are not available, then read on to the next recipe. Other ingredients will be listed in order of use, but be sure to read all the ingredients before you begin, because the secondary ingredients may not be at all routine.

Anatomical Terms Used In This Book

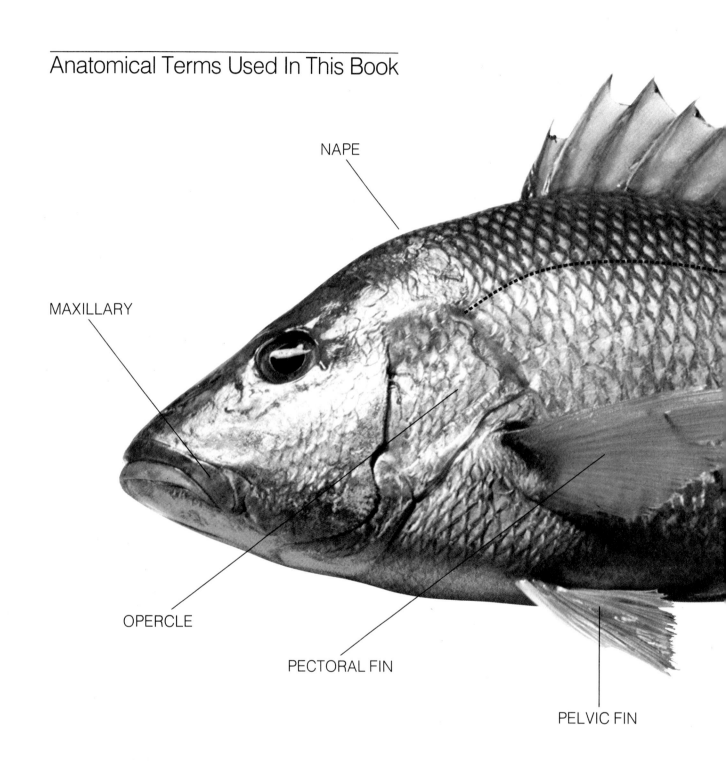

NAPE

MAXILLARY

OPERCLE

PECTORAL FIN

PELVIC FIN

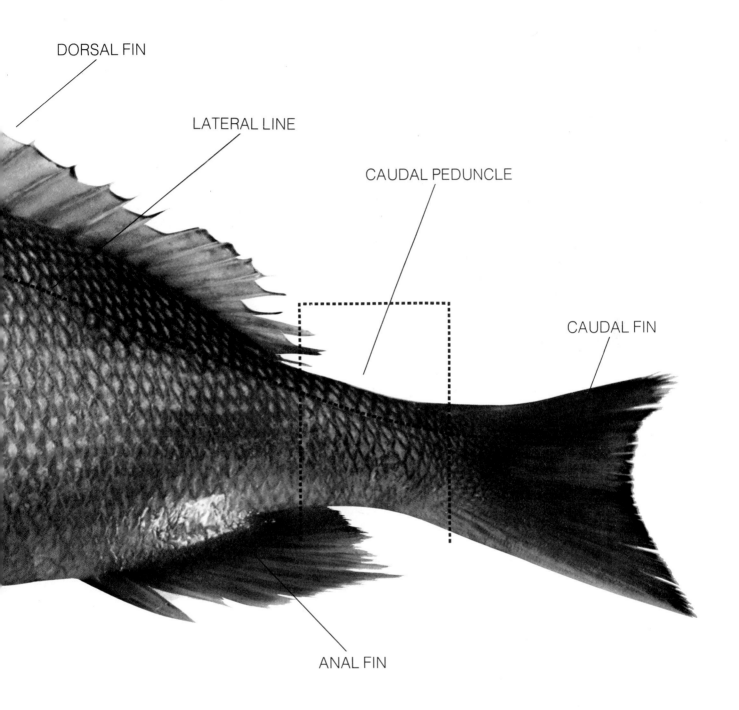

DORSAL FIN

LATERAL LINE

CAUDAL PEDUNCLE

CAUDAL FIN

ANAL FIN

HOW TO DRESS A ROUND FISH

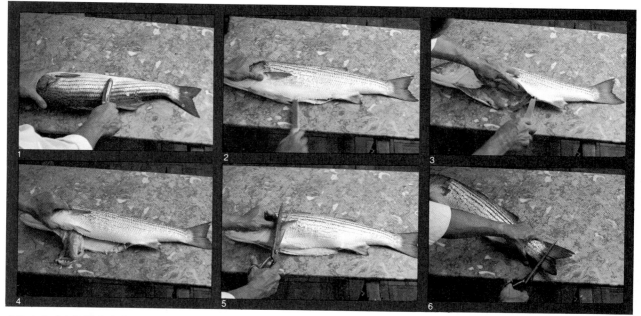

1. Scale the fish. **2.** Slit the belly
without breaking into the entrails. **3.** Cut
the opening toward the head, then toward
the anus. **4.** Remove entrails. **5.** Cut off
fins. **6.** Cut off tail.

HOW TO STUFF A ROUND FISH

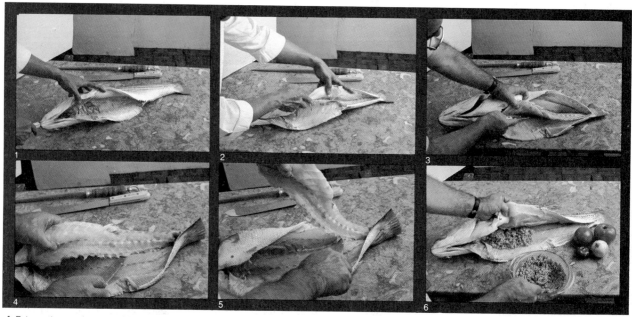

1. Enlarge the opening toward the head.
2. Slide the knife down the upper side of the backbone
and rib cage; **3.** then along the lower side.
4. Loosen the bony cage from the flesh.
5. Cut the backbone at both ends and detach
it. **6.** Stuff the fish in the cavity.

HOW TO FILLET A ROUND FISH

1. The area of the fillet outlined.
2. Cut off the head back of the gills. 3. Slide
the knife along the backbone from nape to tail. 4. Split
the fish. 5. One half will contain the whole backbone.

6. and 7. Slide the knife under the
backbone from nape to tail, and remove the
backbone. 8. and 9. Holding the knife
at an angle, cut off the bony edges and fins.

HOW TO STEAK A ROUND FISH

1. Cut down to the backbone to mark off
the steaks. 2. Holding the knife in place, use
a mallet to tap the knife through the
backbone. 3. Each steak will contain a piece
of the backbone.

HOW TO DRESS A FLAT FISH

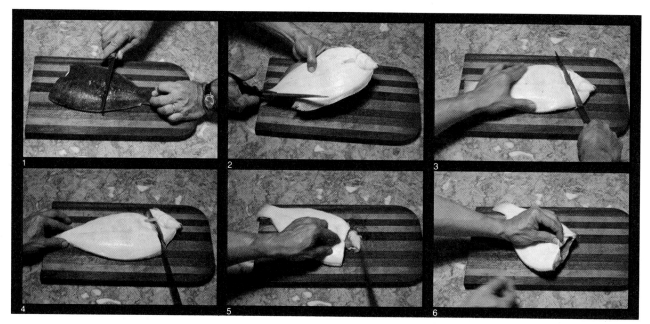

1. Scale the fish. **2.** Cut off fins.
3. and **4.** Cut off the head. **5.** and **6.** Press the
fish gently to empty the viscera.

HOW TO STUFF A FLAT FISH

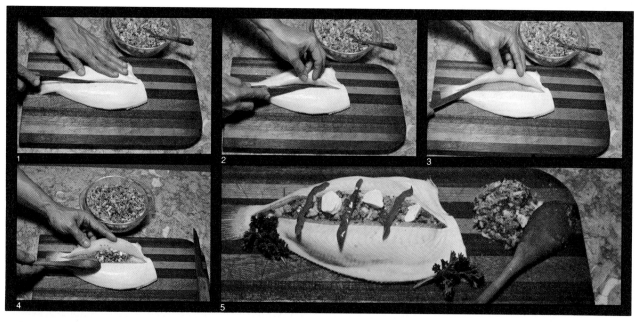

1. Cut down to the backbone. **2.** and **3.** Slide
the knife blade along the backbone on each side
to open up a space; the backbone
remains in the fish in a thin-bodied flat fish.
4. Spoon stuffing into the cavity. **5.** Press
edges together over the stuffing, and garnish.

HOW TO FILLET A FLAT FISH

1. The area of the fillet outlined.
2. Cut down to the backbone just back of the head. 3. Cut from nape to tail, sliding the knife along the backbone on one side.
4. Slide knife along the other side to release the fillet. 5. A boneless fillet removed.
6. With skin side down, cut flesh from the skin.

HOW TO QUARTERCUT A FLAT FISH

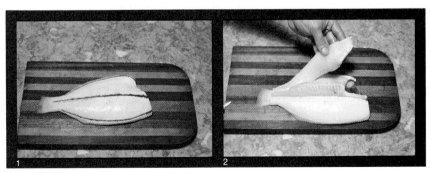

1. Outline of quarterfillets.
2. Cut each fillet into lengthwise halves to give 4 quartercuts.

a

Aalmutter

Literally "eel-mother" as a common name (Germany) used in the Baltic fishery for eelpouts of the family Zoarcidae. Eelpouts are not related to true eels. There are numerous species in the Atlantic and Pacific Oceans, eighteen of which occur in North American waters; they are generally called "sea pout" or "ocean pout." An attempt was made to market eelpout fillets in U.S., partly as a war measure, but demand fell by 1948. The name *Aalmutter* is of mythological origin, from an ancient attempt to explain the origin of eels. *See EEL; OCEAN POUT.*

Abalone

This large univalve mollusk looks like a human ear in shape, and thus its generic name *Haliotis* comes from two Greek words meaning "sea ear." A univalve has a shell that protects the animal's body yet permits the muscular foot to maneuver along the bottom or cling with great suction to a holdfast. There are other univalves utilized as food such as the conch, whelk and limpet, but none has the culinary status of an abalone. There are many species of abalone occurring in various parts of the world, from the Indo-Pacific region along the coasts of Asia and Africa to the Mediterranean, in the Channel Islands between England and France, along the Pacific Coast of Mexico to Chile; wherever they are found the resource has been thoroughly exploited. The inner shell with its opalescent greens and blues or iridescent pinks and pearl has long been a source of jewelry from primitive to modern man. The paua shell *(H. iris)* of the Maori people was used to great effect as inlay in their wood carvings and also fashioned into spoon shapes, providing one of the earliest artificial lures for fishing. In the 1870s when vast quantities of abalone were being shipped to China and Japan from California, the shells commanded twice the price of the dried meats.

There are about 100 species of abalone in the world's seas, of which eight occur along our Pacific Coast; the largest is the red abalone *(H. rufescens)*, which grows to a foot in length and may weigh 8 pounds; while the average is half this size, the shell contains a very substantial meat. In addition one can find the green, the pink or corrugated, the black, threaded, northern green, Japanese or pinto, and the white abalone. There is one extremely rare species in our Florida Keys *(H. pourtalese)*, known only to shell collectors although very few specimens exist. This deepwater (200 to 600 feet) univalve would have no culinary value even if it were more available, as it apparently does not exceed 1 inch in length. Otherwise our Atlantic Coast is bereft of abalones.

While 16,000 metric tons are taken annually in Japan, we land only 2,800 metric tons in the U.S. Much work and money has been expended on developing techniques for artificial cultivation of this univalve, notably in Japan. We may succeed along these lines when work at Ensenada, California, begins to advance.

These univalves are strict vegetarians, feeding with tiny rasplike teeth only on seaweeds. They are not filter feeders such as the bivalves and as a result the abalone is immune to red tides and does not build up concentrations of bacteria in polluted water. Between man and the sea otter, who swims through forests of kelp in an endless search for the succulent abalone, our stocks have dwindled to the point that prying the univalve loose is strictly regulated, for man at least. California does not permit the canning of abalone, nor the shipping of fresh or frozen abalone out of state. Small quantities are imported here from Mexico in frozen form; the canned product, either minced or in cubes, usually originates in Japan. A dried product, which is made by brining, smoke-cooking, and sun-drying until the abalone meat is reduced to 10 percent of its original weight, is sold shredded as **kaiho** or in powdered form as **meiho.**

As in all univalves the meat of a fresh abalone is rubbery, indeed tough, but once tenderized the delicate white steaks have an unforgettable flavor. Simply pry the meat away from the shell, discard the viscera, trim off the dark mantle along the edges, then remove the dark skin from the lower part of the foot. Slice the steaks out across the grain with a thin-bladed sharp knife. The cuts should be made parallel to the bottom of the foot, with each steak about 3/8 inch thick. Place the steaks on a wooden board and pound with a rolling pin or mallet. The pounding should be gentle, just forceful enough to soften the meat and release its fragrant white juice.

The paramount rule in abalone preparations is to avoid overcooking. This is true of all seafoods but even more so with mollusks. If the steak is to be sautéed in butter, for example, it requires no more than 45 seconds on each side. Bear in mind that it's perfectly edible in its raw state after tenderizing, and that the more heat you apply the tougher it will become.

Abalones are also called **Oreille de mer** (France), **Orecchia marina** (Italy), **Orejas de mar** (Spain), **Orelhas** (Portugal), **Petrovo uho** (Yugoslavia), **Haliotis** (Greece), **Seeohren** (Germany), **Soore** (Denmark), **Havsora** (Sweden), **Zee oor** (Holland), **Paua** (Maori of New Zealand), **Awabi** (Japan).

ABALONE SALAD
(Enrique Carillo)

1 pound cleaned abalone meat, simmered, or canned abalone	¼ cup olive oil chopped green chili pepper
3 medium-size tomatoes	minced fresh orégano
1 medium-size onion	lemon or lime juice
¼ cup ketchup	salt and pepper

Cut abalone into small cubes. Chop tomatoes and onion. Mix together with ketchup and olive oil. Add minced chili, orégano, lemon or lime juice, and seasoning to taste. Add more ketchup and olive oil if you like. Makes 4 servings.

CHINESE ABALONE

1 pound abalone steak	5 water chestnuts, sliced
5 large dried Chinese mushrooms	1 tablespoon each of soy sauce and sherry
1 cup chicken stock	2 teaspoons potato starch or cornstarch
4 scallions, sliced	
½ cup slivered celery	

Soak the mushrooms in hot water for 3 hours, then drain and cut into strips. In a skillet or wok heat the chicken stock. Add scallions, celery, water chestnuts and the mushroom strips; cook for 5 minutes. With the flat side of a cleaver, flatten and tenderize the abalone. Cut abalone into strips and add them to the vegetables. Add soy sauce and sherry. Dissolve starch in 2 tablespoons water and stir into the mixture. Cook, stirring all the while, until sauce is clear and thickened. Serve at once, with rice. Makes 2 or 3 servings.

ABALONE À LA MEUNIÈRE

2 large abalone steaks	¼ pound unsalted butter
salt and pepper	juice of ½ lemon
flour	2 tablespoons chopped parsley
2 eggs, beaten	lemon wedges and fried parsley
⅓ cup olive oil	

left, Black abalone; right, White abalone

Tenderize abalone steaks and flatten to ¼ inch thick. Cut into halves. Season pieces with salt and pepper and dredge with flour. Shake off excess, dip into beaten eggs, dredge again with flour, and again dip into egg. Heat the oil and half of the butter in a skillet, and in it brown the abalone steaks on both sides; do not overcook the steaks lest they become tough. Remove steaks to a serving platter. Pour off fat from the skillet and put remaining butter in it. Cook the butter until it becomes nut brown, then add lemon juice and chopped parsley. Pour over abalone and serve at once, garnished with lemon wedges and fried parsley. Makes 4 servings.

Akule

The Hawaiian name for the bigeye scad *(Selar crumenophthalmus)*, a small member of the jack family. This fish occurs in tropical and subtropical seas around the world. While it has no commercial value in mainland U. S., the akule is a highly valued foodfish in Hawaii, where it's split, salted and sun-dried.

Alaska Pollock

A market name for the walleye pollock, a member of the cod family. *See under COD.*

Alga

A number of kinds of marine algae, commonly called "seaweeds," are used by man as food, such as **kelp, Irish moss, dulse.** Although chiefly popular in the Orient, marine algae are utilized as a food to a lesser extent in the Western world, where derivative products such as the colloidal extract agar, and an organic compound alginic acid, are used as food stabilizers and jelling agents. *See also SEAWEED.*

Anchovy

There are 16 species of anchovy in American waters. These small silvery fish with the big eyes are more commonly used as bait than as food in the U.S. Although the ancient Greeks considered anchovies superior to herring, probably because of their abundance in the Aegean Sea, few people take the time today to catch anchovies and enjoy them fresh. A component member of many whitebait dinners, this fish otherwise rarely appears at table in the form of an entrée. I can catch them by the hundred off our beach with a small seine, and there's hardly a strand on the East or West Coasts of the U.S. that won't produce one species or another. Anchovies travel in densely packed schools, frequently mingling with silversides and the so-called green fry of young herring, and *voila* whitebait! On a larger commercial scale anchovies are marketed in salted form, canned, smoked, dried, in butters, cream and paste. Their distinctive rich flavor is widely used as a garnish to other foods such as veal, eggs, fowl, vegetables and blander species of fish.

The anchovy's oldest claim to fame is in the making of **garum**, a fermented sauce popularized at Roman banquets, made by mixing ungutted whole fish with concentrated brine and exposing the mixture to the sun. There are many similar completely autolyzed and liquefied fish sauces found throughout the world, particularly in Southeast Asia where a spicy condiment is welcome in bland rice dishes. Fermentation results from the action of enzymes in the fish flesh and entrails in the presence of salt. The wet fish and salt are mixed in the proportion of 1 part salt to 3 parts fish. This is allowed to ferment under anaerobic conditions for periods of up to 1 year. A similar product is made on the French Mediterranean from silversides *(which see)* but when this species is used the sauce is known as **poutine.** In Greece the anchovy fermentation process is accelerated by adding the hydrolyzed livers of mackerel, in which case the end result is called **gáros** rather than **garum.**

The anchovy product familiar to most Americans is the canned fillet packed in oil. Its red color is not the natural white of a fresh anchovy but is created by packing the fish in barrels of salt and allowing them to ripen for about 4 months until the flesh is cured to a deep red. These fillets are sold flat or rolled. The rolled anchovy, balanced on a lemon slice, is the classic topping for Schnitzel Holstein; the German penchant for all forms of **Sardelle** transcends that of the Mediterranean cultures. **Sardellenbutter, Sardellencreme** and **Sardellenpaste** figure prominently in many German recipes. In Sweden,

Northern anchovy

where anchovy is known as **sardel,** the similar word **anchovis** means sprats and small herring and excludes the anchovy.

Also known as **Anchoa** (Spain), **Anchoveta** (Peru and Chile), **Camiguana** (Venezuela), **Acciuga** (Italy), **Brgljun** (Yugoslavia), **Antjúga** (Greece), **Hamsi** (Turkey), **Katakuchiiwashi** (Japan), **Ansjos** (Denmark and Norway), **Ansjovis** (Sweden and Holland), **Anchois** (France), **Sardelle** (Germany).

Arctic Char

A member of the family Salmonidae; for individual description *see under TROUT.* As related to other char species *see under CHAR.*

Ark Shell

See PEPITONA under CLAM TERMINOLOGY.

Aspic

A jellied flavored liquid used as a coating for cold dishes, or as a means of molding small pieces of fish or shellfish in a container. Most aspics are transparent, although they may be colored by their ingredients—tomato juice, red wine, etc. However, jellied mayonnaise and *chaud-froid* are also aspics, and these of course are not transparent.

Aspic is used to keep the surface of food from drying, very useful for buffet service. It can be used simply to give a smooth gleaming finish to the food, and it is the ideal way to attach decorations.

An aspic for a fish dish can be made from any good fish stock as in the recipe for **White-Wine Fish Aspic** that follows. However, it is sometimes useful to make a small amount of aspic quickly, and for this procedure

chicken stock or broth is useful. Another possibility is a mixture of clam broth and white wine, but the intense flavor of clam broth and its saltiness does not make it suitable for every dish. For a basic pattern see the recipe for **Quick Aspic;** this method can be used with other liquids, with wine in place of Cognac, and with other flavorings in place of lemon juice.

It is necessary to add gelatin to fish stock to make an aspic that will jell firmly or hold its shape when unmolded. Use unflavored gelatin, which comes in packets that weigh ¼ ounce or 7 grams. Each packet will jell about 2 cups liquid; you need enough to make an aspic that will set, but not so much that it will become rubbery, so the amount should be carefully measured. Before adding the gelatin to hot stock, soften it in cold liquid; use ¼ to ½ cup water, or use part of any cold liquid in the recipe. Add the gelatin during the clarifying process as in the recipe that follows, or separately, after stock is strained and clarified. If added separately, stir the aspic over low heat until the gelatin is completely dissolved.

Instead of white or red wine, which can be used as part of the liquid in cooking the stock for aspic, fortified wines such as Madeira, port or sherry, or other liqueurs, can be added toward the end, but be sure to add any flavoring ingredient before clarifying, or the aspic may become cloudy.

WHITE-WINE FISH ASPIC

1 pound fish bones, heads and skins	1 teaspoon dried thyme
4 cups water	½ teaspoon salt
1 cup dry white wine	6 peppercorns, bruised
1 medium-size onion, chopped	2 envelopes unflavored gelatin
1 tablespoon chopped fresh tarragon	¼ cup cold water
2 bay leaves	3 egg whites
	3 tablespoons white vinegar

Place fish bones, heads and skins in the water. Add the white wine, onion, tarragon, bay leaves, thyme, salt and peppercorns. Bring to a boil and boil for 2 minutes; then reduce heat and simmer for 30 minutes, stirring occasionally. Soften gelatin in the ¼ cup cold water. Combine egg whites with vinegar and beat until whites are stiff. Add this to the unstrained fish stock with the softened gelatin. Bring stock again just to a boil and simmer until mixture is clear. Strain through a cloth-lined sieve. Makes about 4 cups liquid aspic.

Fishing boats, Madeira

Trout in white-wine aspic

RED-WINE FISH ASPIC

Follow the recipe for white-wine fish aspic, but use red wine instead of white. Or make **Red-Wine Fish Stock** *(see under STOCKS)*, strain it, clarify it, and add gelatin.

QUICK ASPIC

Sprinkle 1½ envelopes of unflavored gelatin on ½ cup cold water; set aside. In a saucepan combine 2 cups chicken broth and ¼ cup Cognac; heat but do not boil. Add the softened gelatin and stir until dissolved. Add 1 tablespoon lemon juice. Cool aspic until syrupy.

TO TEST FOR JELLING

Place about 2 tablespoons of the liquid mixture on a flat plate and place in the refrigerator. The liquid should be set in about 20 minutes. If it is still soft, your liquid will need more gelatin. Measure the amount carefully in relation to the amount of liquid and the natural gelatin it already contains; use part of a packet if that's all you need.

TO CLARIFY STOCK FOR ASPIC

Strain stock to remove all coarse pieces. Chill it to allow any fat to rise to the surface. Lift off and discard fat. For 4 cups liquid use 2 egg whites with the egg shells. Beat egg whites until well mixed but not stiff; crumble the shells; add both to the stock. Bring stock to a boil, stirring all the while. Reduce heat to keep liquid barely simmering for about 30 minutes. With a skimmer lift off the egg-white and shell foam on the top and discard it. Ladle the stock through a strainer, lined with a moistened cloth or several layers of cheesecloth, into a clean pot.

For a more intense flavor, add 1 cup chopped fresh fish, matching your stock, and ¼ to ½ cup flavoring vegetables (leeks, celery, parsley, etc.) with the egg whites. These will also be discarded, but the stock will be flavorful like a *consommé double*.

TO COAT FISH WITH ASPIC

This procedure is described in the recipes for **Glazed Salmon** *(which see)*. Of course it can be used for other whole fish. The fish should be chilled and the aspic should be cold and syrupy, on the point of setting. If it becomes too stiff to pour, place over low heat until it is liquid again. Spoon aspic over fish, a little at a time. Several thin layers, each jelled in turn, will make a smooth glossy coating, but a thick layer will run off and jell unevenly. For some recipes you may find it easier to brush on the aspic with a clean pastry brush. Decorations should be dipped into liquid aspic before being placed on the fish. Let them set in place before adding more aspic.

Some cookbooks advise placing the food on a cake rack for this coating, but it isn't easy to transfer a fish to the serving platter afterward, especially a large fish, so unless you are coating small steaks or fillets, easy to lift on a broad spatula, it's better to coat the fish on the serving platter. Use a spoon or pastry brush, don't pour the aspic over, and if you're careful you can do this without letting a lot of excess drip down on the platter.

FISH STEAKS IN ASPIC

This basic method can be varied by using other garnish, other sauce, even aspic flavored in some particular way.

Pour 1 inch of aspic into a serving platter and let it set completely. Place poached fish steaks on top of aspic. Decorate the fish with capers, olives, sliced hard-cooked eggs, etc. Spoon one third of the remaining aspic over fish; let it set completely. Pour the rest of aspic over fish and let set. Serve with a cold sauce (**Dill Sauce, Green Mayonnaise**).

TO COAT A MOLD WITH ASPIC

Chill the mold thoroughly. Ideally it should be set in a container filled with cracked ice, but the procedure works well with chilling in the refrigerator. Spoon cold syrupy aspic into the mold and immediately turn the mold around to let aspic reach the entire inside; it should stick to the cold mold and set almost at once. Chill again. Add 2 more layers to make a stable coating, adding each in the same way.

If the mold is to be decorated—these decorations will be on top when the dish is unmolded—add these, each dipped into aspic, after the first layer has set, and let them chill thoroughly before adding the second and third layers.

ASPIC DIAMONDS

Pour liquid aspic into a flat shallow pan, making a layer ¼ to ½ inch thick. Chill until firm, then knife-chop into dice. These glittery aspic diamonds can be arranged around a whole fish or fish steaks or fillets on a serving platter.

A thin layer of aspic can also be cut into shapes with truffle cutters.

JELLIED MAYONNAISE

For 1 cup mayonnaise use 1 packet (7 grams) unflavored gelatin softened in ¼ cup cold water. When gelatin is softened, heat over hot water until completely dissolved. Stir thoroughly into mayonnaise.

CHAUD-FROID BLANC

Make **velouté sauce** using fish stock, or **béchamel sauce** or **cream sauce,** in the usual way but make it fairly thick. Soften 1 packet unflavored gelatin in ¼ cup cold water, then stir it into 1 cup of the sauce which is simmering. Stir and simmer until the gelatin is thoroughly dissolved. Stir in ½ cup heavy cream and let it become hot, but do not let the sauce boil. Since this needs to be absolutely smooth, strain it through a fine sieve into a metal bowl. If you need it at once, set the bowl in a larger container of crushed ice and stir until the sauce is cold and on the point of jelling. Spoon over the food quickly. If decorations are used with *chaud-froid*, dip them into clear aspic to attach them, and coat the finished preparation with a final layer of clear aspic.

Atka Mackerel

A member of the family Hexagrammidae, or greenlings. This is not a mackerel. There are several species of greenlings found in Pacific waters of the U. S., the most important being the lingcod *(which see)*. The Atka mackerel is highly esteemed in Japan where it's known as **kitanohokke.**

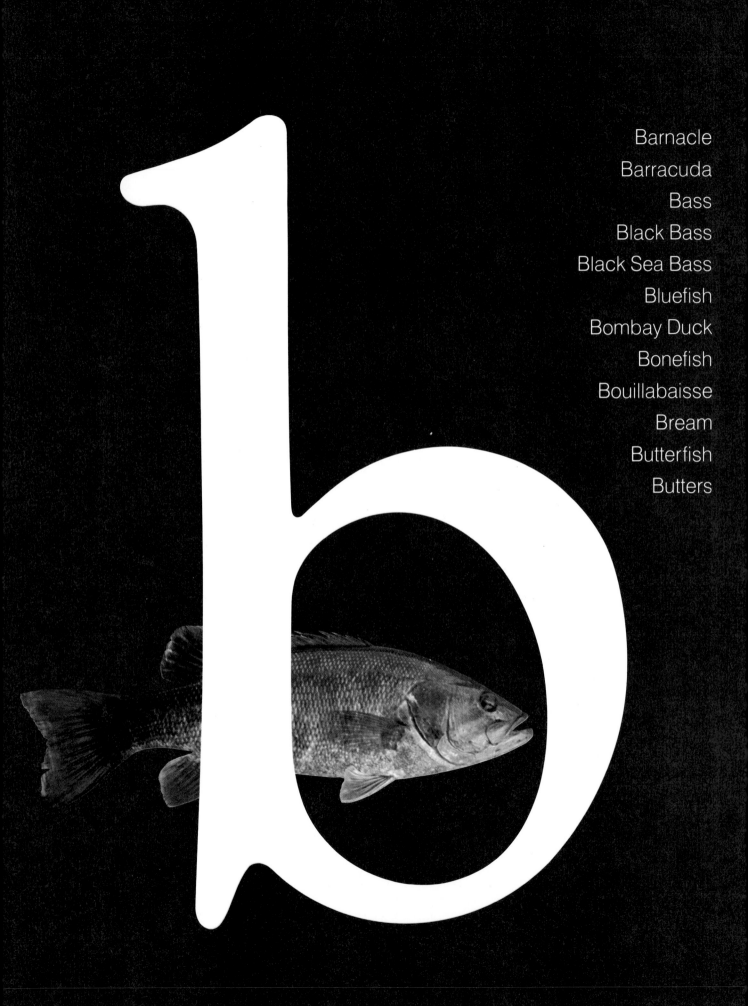

Barnacle
Barracuda
Bass
Black Bass
Black Sea Bass
Bluefish
Bombay Duck
Bonefish
Bouillabaisse
Bream
Butterfish
Butters

b

Barnacle

Barnacles are crustaceans, related to crabs, shrimps and lobsters. Most species have a hard limy shell and live attached to rocks, logs, seaweeds, turtles, manatees, whales, crabs or various mollusks. They fasten themselves tenaciously to their substrate by rootlike projections. They feed by continuously waving filamentous legs through the water and straining out minute plankton organisms. Most barnacles are of the "acorn" type, with a flat base and a cylindrical or paraboloid body. These are commonly observed encrusting boats, wharves, pilings, hawsers and the like, especially between tide lines, and the rate at which the young colonize a smooth area is amazing. Acorn barnacles are not edible.

A second group, the "stalked" barnacles, are characterized by a leathery "neck" at the end of which is the flattened animal. These are pelagic, attaching themselves to floating objects such as logs, seaweed and other flotsam. The term "goose barnacle" is used for this group, for ancient naturalists believed that young geese were brought forth from these crustaceans. Goose barnacles are a very popular seafood in Portugal where they are known as **perceve,** in Spain as **bellota de mar** or **percebe,** and in Italy where they are called **balani** or **pico.** These barnacles can be eaten raw but they are usually steamed and dipped into melted butter or grilled with butter. Unlike the steamer clam, it is the stalk and not the body that is consumed. The tough outer skin will slip off easily when the barnacle is cooked. On our side of the Atlantic, I have rarely found them big enough to be worthy of cooking, but that is a variable.

A third group known as "rock" barnacles contains some rather large Pacific species which may weigh 3 pounds or more. These barnacles attach themselves to submerged rocks rather than ships or floating objects. Various kinds are found from the Aleutians to Chile. Although collected by a small coterie of seafood addicts in Washington and Oregon, the resource is largely unutilized. In Chile, however, the **pico** is considered a great delicacy and is marketed in fresh form and as a canned product. Steamed barnacles was a specialty of the Res-

taurant Escorial in Santiago during its halcyon days only a decade ago.

Barracuda

To write in a seafood cookbook on a topic that I would rather bury in a footnote is embarrassing to the author. However, there are more than 20,000 species of fish in the world and we can't expect all of them to be edible. There are plants, fungi and meats which are toxic to man, predictably and unpredictably, as there are fishes, and we need this knowledge. The average reader will not have access to a barracuda, although it's a common fish in Florida, and apparently enough are consumed to provide statistics—unpleasant statistics. I must emphasize that our subject is the great barracuda of the western Atlantic. Our Pacific species is not only edible but, historically, it has been a valuable and highly esteemed food in southern California. The great barracuda, however, is often toxic and there's no way of distinguishing the "good guys" from the villains.

Ciguatera poisoning is not common in Florida, but its incidence increases through the Bahamas and eastern Caribbean, particularly in the Virgin and Leeward Islands, probably because more barracuda are consumed in these areas. This poison is not the result of bacterial decomposition but a distinct toxin which produces unpleasant symptoms, with a fatality rate of about 12 percent. It is generally accepted that fish under 5 pounds in weight are safe to eat, as the ciguatoxin has only been known to occur in large fish, which apparently acquire the poison through their food chain (the causative organism is thought to be a benthic alga). So despite the fact that people do eat barracuda in the western Atlantic, there is little point in extolling its merits. Due to the fact that other fish species have been involved in ciguatera poisonings, notably the blackfin snapper, misty grouper and amberjack, hotel owners in the Virgin and Leeward Islands generally import frozen fish from the U.S. rather than gamble on the local product. Ciguatera also occurs in the western Pacific from Hawaii to Japan, but again this involves the great barracuda *(Sphyraena barracuda)* rather than our perfectly safe Pacific barracuda *(Sphyraena argentea).*

The Pacific barracuda has been caught from southern Alaska to Baja California, but its occurrence north of Monterey in California is sporadic as this is essentially a warmwater fish. The U.S. commercial landings depend on warming ocean temperatures when large numbers of barracuda migrate northward from Mexico.

facing page, Smallmouth bass, a black bass

Thus, there is a considerable fluctuation in the annual catch, ranging from as little as 50,000 pounds to more than 4 million pounds. Barracuda school close to shore and are taken in quantity by sport fishermen from jetties, docks and boats, beginning in April; they remain available until late September, with their peak season during the summer months. Pacific barracuda seldom weigh more than 12 pounds and the average is less than half that size. Barracuda has a firm meat of distinctive flavor. It is sold fresh in California markets. A minor quantity is smoked and also sold as a specialty pack in the form of fish cakes. The popular cooking methods are to oven-broil the fillets or steaks, or barbecue them with an appropriate basting sauce.

Bass

This name covers a number of unrelated fishes. The early form of the word, "barse," is from the Teutonic root *bars* which means to bristle. This is descriptive of many spiny-rayed species. In fact, most fish called bass are really something else. The true sea basses include the groupers, hamlets, hinds, jewfish and the more common, in our cuisine, black sea bass. These differ greatly as far as recipes are concerned from the various black basses of freshwater, striped bass, giant sea bass, kelp bass, and totuava or white seabass. The only fish bearing the singular name "bass" is found in Europe and is most popular in French cuisine as the **loup** or **bar commun.** *See BLACK BASS, BLACK SEA BASS, GIANT SEA BASS (under STRIPED BASS), KELP BASS, STRIPED BASS, WHITE SEABASS (under DRUM).*

Bellyfish

A market name for the goosefish *(which see).*

Black Bass

The black bass, and more particularly the smallmouth species, was first mentioned in literature by Pierre Boucher in his magnum opus *Histoire véritable et naturelle . . . de la Nouvelle-France* in 1664. The early French colonists in the St. Lawrence River valley called the fish **achigan,** the Algonquian word for "ferocious," a somewhat exaggerated description when one considers the aggressive and multitoothed pike found in these same waters. The northern Indians, including the Hurons, evidently made some use of bass as a food, as did the Creek and Hitchiti speakers of Florida. William Bartram, the

naturalist, in his *Diary of a Journey through the Carolinas, Georgia, and Florida* in 1765 described how the Seminoles caught largemouth bass with lures made of deer hair. Although the bass may have provided a fashionable cookout under the live oaks at that time, it's of little interest to the modern generation of Seminoles which eschews all fish except the easily caught gar. A gar has the texture of cotton and about as much flavor. I doubt if the black bass was significant in centuries past, as aboriginal man sensibly harvested those fish that were hugely abundant, readily captured, and of a size that made the effort profitable. The sturgeon, salmon and striped bass were more typically American Indian foods. If the black bass has a culinary genesis it evolved through sport fishing during the nineteenth century when the fish were widely transplanted from Maine to California by railroad. In fact, few other species have been so globally introduced to Central and South America, Europe, Africa, Asia and Oceania. True, the bass has not thrived everywhere but its overall success has been remarkable—from the Po River valley of Italy to the Clanwilliam drainage of South Africa.

The various black bass are not true bass but members of the sunfish family, Centrachidae. They are not related to the black sea bass nor to the striped bass, and recipes for one will seldom work for another. These freshwater fish are very lean and the meat has a delicate texture in comparison to other "bass." But don't let that disturb you as these American gamefish are not purveyed by commercial markets so there's little chance of confusion when you have to catch your own. Black bass are readily available in 49 states. While opinions differ on their eating qualities, the largemouth, smallmouth, spotted and redeye species can be prime table fare in the hands of a competent chef. In fact they can be made into a classic dish as we shall see later on.

The skin of all black bass has a mossy or weedy flavor which most people find objectionable. However, when shucked of its skin a bass fillet has a subtle flavor and aroma and lends itself to many forms of cooking; it can be pickled in the form of *seviche*, deep-fried in tempura style, baked, broiled, poached in wine, served cold in aspic, made into an excellent chowder, or simply dusted with cornmeal and sautéed. Some of the greatest campfire meals I've ever enjoyed consisted of fillets of smallmouth bass taken from the cold clear lakes of southeastern Maine, and fried in butter and bacon drippings in a skillet until they curled, crisp and golden. With a boiled potato and a tossed green salad one can't help but go back for seconds, and thirds. Even the largemouth bass in our south Florida ponds, which feed very heavily on freshwater shrimps, are firm and sweetly flavored. The smaller fish are better eating than big bass; for the table I never keep a fish over 3 pounds, despite the fact that we catch many good-sized largemouths, as the heavier fish are coarse in texture; releasing them provides more fun for somebody else. In various taste panel studies made over the years the results indicated that water source was a major factor in creating unpleasant flavors in fish; a common problem is waste matter from industrial plants such as the effluent from a paper mill. This applies particularly to bass, walleye and northern pike, as they are often found in polluted waters.

A traditional *quenelle de brochet* made from pike is the classic fish course in many a formal meal, but most restaurants use substitutes such as snapper or sole, as pike, which arrive in our markets from Canada, are so often in short supply. Unfortunately, not all restaurants identify the fish used if it is not pike, but several have made a reputation for their *quenelles* made with yellowtail flounder or walleye.

At the 1973 dinner for the Chevaliers du Taste-vin at the Breakers Hotel in Palm Beach, we used freshwater bass for the *quenelles*. Even in the context of a magnificent dinner, the *quenelles* of black bass won the main event.

BLACK BASS TERMINOLOGY

GUADALUPE BASS This is a rather isolated species *(Micropterus treculi)* of black bass, being limited to a few watersheds of central Texas, notably the Guadalupe River system. It resembles the spotted bass in appearance but seldom attains a length of over 12 inches. Because of its small size, the Guadalupe bass is usually treated as a panfish in cooking, i.e., panfried or deep-fried in whole form or as skinned fillets.

LARGEMOUTH BASS The most widely distributed bass *(Micropterus salmoides)* in the U.S., the largemouth is dark

Largemouth bass, a black bass

greenish in color fading to white ventrally with a black lateral band along the midline. This bass attains weights to 20 pounds although the average size is much smaller and varies according to geographic locale; a Florida subspecies grows larger than the northern forms. The largemouth thrives in weedy lakes, often with soft muck bottoms, as well as in sand- or gravel-bottomed ponds; these environments produce flavor differences of varying quality, with the poorest product coming from muddy waters or lakes where blue-green algae are common. The skin of the largemouth has a pronounced "mossy" taste; however, a skinless fillet can be very bland or even faintly sweet.

REDEYE BASS This species *(Micropterus coosae)* is limited to river habitats (it will not spawn in standing water) of the southern U.S., from Tennessee through Georgia, Alabama and into northern Florida. The redeye is an olive brown in color dorsally, with dark vertical bars fading to white along the belly. Its lower fins are brick red and the eyes are bright red. This bass is most common in clear, fast-flowing upland streams where it feeds primarily on insects. It seldom attains a weight of over 1 pound but is an excellent panfish with firm white meat. The redeye is often called "mountain trout" in the southern hill region due to its superior quality at table.

SHOAL BASS The taxonomic status of this bass *(Micropterus spp.)* is uncertain; until recently it was considered a race or subspecies of the redeye; however, it grows to 6 pounds or more. It has a very limited range and is only found in a few drainage systems of Georgia and Alabama. Unlike the redeye, the shoal bass feeds heavily on crayfish; this diet combined with its fast water habitat and greater growth produces a prime foodfish of local importance.

SMALLMOUTH BASS The smallmouth bass *(Micropterus dolomieui)* is almost as widely distributed as the largemouth, occurring in both rivers and lakes having rocky or gravel substrates. The smallmouth is olivaceous or bronze in color with its sides mottled by dark diffused bars or blotches fading to a dusky white on the belly. The maximum size is about 12 pounds but the usual catch is closer to 2 pounds. When taken from clear flowing rivers or lakes the smallmouth is comparable to the redeye or shoal bass in quality.

SPOTTED BASS At first glance the spotted bass *(Micropterus punctulatus)* generally resembles a largemouth in coloration, but it has numerous dark blotches (usually diamond shaped) along its back and rows of small spots extending laterally below the midline. The spotted bass occurs from Ohio south to the Gulf states and west to Texas, Oklahoma and Kansas. There are 2 subspecies, one

preceding pages, The largemouth bass is America's most popular gamefish.

of which is the Alabama spotted bass. The Alabama bass reaches a weight of 8 pounds but the usual size taken by angling is 1½ to 2 pounds. This species occurs in both lakes and rivers but is not as tolerant of cold water as the largemouth or smallmouth. As a foodfish it ranks on a par with the largemouth.

SUWANNEE BASS In common with the Guadalupe bass, the Suwannee *(Micropterus notius)* is very limited in distribution and small in size. It is found only in the Santa Fe, Withlacoochee and Suwannee River watersheds of north Florida. This fish is very striking in color with an olivaceous back that fades into a distinctive turquoise blue below the midline; it is marked with dark bronze lateral blotches. The Suwannee bass seldom attains a length of over 12 inches. This is a tasty little panfish but of very local interest.

NOTE: Black bass are on rare occasions subject to parasitic infestations which occur in the flesh, from the yellow grub *(Clinostomum marginatum)* and the black grub *(Uvulifer ambloplitis)*. These are larval trematodes which originate in snails or aquatic birds with the bass as an intermediate host. Trematodes are easily recognized as the encysted yellow grubs are somewhat wormlike in appearance and the color distinctive from the surrounding white muscle; the black grub is immediately evident as numerous black "dots" in the meat. These parasites are more common in waters that support large bird rookeries or an abundance of snails, and they do not occur with great frequency. Neither trematode is known to be harmful to man when the fish has been cooked. However, aesthetically a parasitized bass has little appeal and should be discarded. When in doubt, it's best to convert all bass into skinless fillets to check for normal quality.

ORANGE STEAMED BLACK BASS

2 pounds skinned black bass fillets from one or more
  fish of over 4 pounds live weight
juice of 1 orange
1 can (8 ounce) mandarin orange segments
2 tablespoons soy sauce
2 tablespoons dry sherry
1 tablespoon sesame or peanut oil
2 tablespoons shredded peeled fresh gingerroot
1 bunch of scallion tops, cut into 2-inch lengths

Cut the bass fillets crosswise into ½- to ¾-inch-thick slices. Arrange slices on a heatproof platter side by side so they re-form a fillet shape, excluding thin tail pieces according to size of platter. Sprinkle with fresh orange juice. Drain juice from mandarin oranges into a small bowl, add the soy sauce, sherry, oil and gingerroot, and mix thoroughly. Pour over the fish. Arrange the scallion pieces decoratively on top.

Place platter on the rack in a steamer with water within 1 inch of the rack. Bring water to a rolling boil, cover steamer, reduce heat, and maintain steam for 12 to 15 minutes.

Serve bass on the platter, surrounded with orange segments. Accompany with steamed rice and a well-vinegared salad. Makes 4 servings.

BARBECUE-STEAMED BLACK BASS

4 black bass fillets,	2 tablespoons lemon or
6 to 8 ounces each	lime juice
4 lemon or lime slices	1 tablespoon minced garlic
4 tablespoons finely	½ teaspoon salt
chopped green onion tops	¼ teaspoon dry mustard
6 tablespoons butter	1 tablespoon chopped parsley

Place black bass fillets on individual sheets of heavy-duty foil. Center 1 lemon or lime slice on each fillet and sprinkle with green onion. Melt butter in a saucepan with remaining ingredients, mixing thoroughly; drizzle some of the butter mixture over each fillet. Fold the foil and seal securely. Place packets on grid of charcoal grill 8 to 10 inches from firebed, or in the oven heated to 350°F. Cook at exact heat for 20 minutes. Packets can be made ahead of time and stored in refrigerator until ready for use. Makes 4 servings.

QUENELLES OF BLACK BASS
(Louis Sussey, The Breakers, Palm Beach)
PANADE À LA FRANGIPANE

8 egg yolks	dash of white pepper
9 ounces all-purpose flour	dash of grated mace
6½ ounces butter, melted	2 cups milk
1 teaspoon salt	

Beat the egg yolks only until blended, then mix in everything else except milk. Heat milk to the boiling point, then stir in the other ingredients and simmer gently for 5 to 7 minutes, stirring constantly. Place the *panade* in the refrigerator for at least 6 hours, until thoroughly chilled.

QUENELLES

1 pound black bass fillets	2 egg yolks
8 ounces beef suet	1 teaspoon salt
(from around the kidneys)	dash of white pepper
8 ounces chilled panade	

Grind bass fillets and suet, then mix well with *panade*, egg yolks and seasoning. Put the whole mixture through the grinder twice and mix to make a completely homogeneous batter. Pinch off a small amount at a time and roll into *quenelles* of thumb size and shape. Poach gently in boiling water for 5 to 7 minutes. Cool in ice water. Makes about 36 *quenelles*.

BAKED BLACK BASS

1 smallmouth bass,
   or (optionally) largemouth
   bass from clear
   water, 4 to 5 pounds,
   with head on
juice of 1 lime or lemon
celery salt
pepper
9 tablespoons melted butter
1 bunch of green onions,
   chopped

½ pound fresh mushrooms,
   sliced
1 teaspoon dried rosemary
½ cup bread crumbs
paprika
½ cup dry Madeira wine
2 tablespoons minced parsley
lime or lemon wedges

Gut and gill the bass, and scale until skin puckers. Wipe the dressed bass inside and out with lime or lemon juice. Sprinkle with celery salt and pepper.

Heat 4 tablespoons of the butter in a saucepan; add green onions, mushrooms and rosemary. Simmer for 5 minutes. Add bread crumbs and mix well. Season with more celery salt and pepper. Spoon this stuffing mixture into body cavity of bass and close with small metal skewers or wooden food picks. The stuffing will expand so do not pack tightly. Sprinkle paprika liberally on both sides of bass.

Cut off a sheet of heavy-duty foil large enough to cover baking pan, allowing about 3 inches extra on two sides which will be used later to lift out fish intact. Brush foil on pan bottom with 1 tablespoon melted butter. Place bass in pan and cover tightly with a second sheet of foil. Cook in preheated 350°F. oven for 20 minutes. Remove the top foil sheet and add Madeira. Bake uncovered for an additional 10 to 15 minutes, splashing with remaining melted butter to brown.

Lift bass from pan by holding foil overlaps, and slide fish onto a serving platter. Sprinkle with minced parsley and surround fish with lime or lemon wedges.

When portioning fish at table make first slice from nape to tail along back to halve. Then cut vertically, but not through backbone, into pieces of suitable size. When top half is removed, grasp tail and lift out backbone and rib cage before slicing lower half.

Serve with cold Mustard Sauce *(see under SAUCES)* and buttered tiny potatoes. Makes 6 servings.

PAUPIETTES OF BLACK BASS FLORENTINE

6 skinless fillets of black bass
   (2½ to 3 pounds fish)
celery salt
pepper
2 packages (10 ounces each)
   frozen chopped spinach
6 tablespoons butter
1 medium-size onion, chopped fine
3 teaspoons dried thyme
1 cup Sauce Mornay (p. 287)
grated Parmesan cheese
12 thin pimiento strips

Bass fillets should not be too thick, nor too wide. Do not use any portion from rib cage. Sprinkle bass fillets with celery salt and pepper and lay them flat on a countertop. Thaw spinach and press out as much liquid as possible. Melt 2 tablespoons of the butter in a pan and sauté the onion until it wilts and cooks, but do not brown it. Turn off heat and mix the spinach with onion. Divide the spinach evenly among the fillets and sprinkle each with thyme. Roll up the fillets like jelly rolls; begin rolling at nape or widest end to have a tapering end to secure. Fasten the ends with skewers or wooden food picks. Place the paupiettes in a greased baking pan. Melt remaining 4 tablespoons of butter and brush some on each paupiette. Cover pan with foil. Bake in a 350°F. oven for 20 minutes. Remove foil, coat each paupiette with Mornay sauce, and cook uncovered for an additional 6 to 8 minutes, until the sauce becomes flecked with brown. Sprinkle lightly with grated Parmesan cheese. Decorate each paupiette with 2 crossed strips of pimiento. Makes 6 servings.

BLACK BASS PUDDING

1½ cups flaked cooked bass, free from skin and bones
3 tablespoons butter, softened
3 eggs, separated
1 cup light cream
½ cup cracker crumbs
1 teaspoon onion juice
1 teaspoon Worcestershire sauce
1 teaspoon lemon juice
pinch of grated nutmeg
salt and white pepper

Work the flaked fish and butter to a cream. Beat the egg yolks with the cream and add to fish with cracker crumbs. Add the flavorings, with salt and pepper to taste. Sample the mixture, as the success of the dish lies in getting it well flavored; add more seasoning if necessary. Beat egg whites very stiff, and gently fold them into the mixture. Pour into a buttered 6-cup mold, allowing room for the rising. Cover the mold, with the cover well buttered on the inside, or with buttered parchment paper tied around the mold. Set the mold on a rack in a kettle, and pour in enough water to come halfway up the mold. Cover the kettle. Steam for 2 hours. Add more boiling water to the kettle if it boils away, but open the kettle as little as possible. Put the mold into a warm oven to dry out, so contents may be easily removed.

Remove the cover and turn out the pudding onto a platter; garnish in any preferred manner. Serve hot with a good rich sauce, or cold with Sauce Tartare *(see SAUCES)*.

This pudding can be baked in the oven: set the mold in a larger pan with hot water around, and bake at 375°F. for 40 minutes. Makes 4 servings.

Similar puddings can be made with other kinds of fish, and the seasonings can be adjusted accordingly.

Black Cod

A market name for the sablefish *(which see)*.

Blackfish

A common name (Eastern U. S.) for the tautog *(which see)*.

Black Sea Bass

One of the more historical fishing grounds out of New York Harbor lies about 12 miles south from Ambrose Channel Lightship. Until the year 1832, commercial fishermen who supplied the Fulton Market seldom had need to venture beyond Sandy Hook Light to catch smack loads of sea bass; with a demand exceeding the supply, resourceful skippers began seeking more productive locations. A certain Captain Harris of New London dropped anchor on a rocky underwater plateau of several miles in length that September, when sea bass are at their fattest, and quickly filled the hold of his ship. New York City was suffering from an epidemic at the time, and in the way of seafaring superstition the ground was named Cholera Banks. This and the nearby Middle Grounds and Angler Banks required skilled navigation to get a fix, as land ranges could only be used in clear weather and steering by compass alone on hazy days was no guarantee of success. The city became less visible in its own smoke during the following decade while Manhattan burned off the last of its forests, so ships often missed the banks only to discover new ones. Party boats already in vogue (the first record is of President George Washington chartering a boat to fish the banks off Sandy Hook) became so popular that woodcut posters were distributed around New York depicting men carrying great strings of sea bass. In those days sea bass fishing was a total adventure; the police steamer *Patrol* found it expedient to meet the craft on their return from the banks "in order to gather in the wounded and their assailants without undue loss of time." Fortunately the "plug-ugly of primitive New York has disappeared from the sea." (*Deep Sea Fishing Grounds*, F. Weidner Printing and Publishing Company, Brooklyn, New York, 1930.)

Although our black sea bass (*Centropristis striatus*) is not a very distinguished-looking fish, it has firm white meat with a delicate flavor derived from feeding chiefly on crabs, shrimps and mollusks. It can be cooked by any method and is one of few fish that's difficult to ruin by a lack of culinary skill, an endowment that compensates for its otherwise bland appearance.

The black sea bass occurs from the vicinity of Cape Cod to Florida but in catchable numbers only from New York to North Carolina. This is a true sea bass of the family Serranidae and has 3 closely related species in its genus, the southern sea bass, bank sea bass and rock sea bass; for our purposes these can all be regarded as the same fish. Culinary confusion only comes about in the use of the common name "blackfish" which is also applied to the tautog *(which see)* found from Cape Cod to Delaware Bay. The tautog is a fine table fish, but with its even firmer musculature it is clearly at its best in chowder form. Sea bass at market usually run from 1½ to 3 pounds, but fall fish may weigh up to 5 pounds. New York's Chinese restaurants use great quantities of small sea bass whole as deep-fried presentations in the "fire basket" or as squirrel

Black sea bass

fish **(Sung-shu-yu)** and in steamed form served with fermented black beans **(Tou-shih-cheng-hsien-yu).** The sea bass is also a favorite in Italian restaurants as in both cuisines it bears a great resemblance to their homeland sea bream.

STEAMED SEA BASS

2 pounds sea bass fillets	minced fresh dill
with skin, scored	soy sauce
1 tablespoon chopped leek	1 garlic clove
1 teaspoon shredded fresh	1 tablespoon peanut oil
gingerroot or ground ginger	2 teaspoons sesame oil
½ teaspoon salt	

Combine leek, ginger and salt; rub into fish. Sprinkle fish lightly with dill; add a few drops of soy sauce. Place fish skin side down in a wok or steamer and steam for about 20 minutes. Crush the garlic clove into the peanut and sesame oils; cook over high heat until garlic is slightly browned. Strain oils to remove garlic. Brush oils over fish, just prior to removing from heat. Makes 4 servings.

SEA BASS LISBON STYLE

4 pounds sea bass fillets,	1 tablespoon chopped parsley
cut into chunks	¼ teaspoon crushed
½ tablespoon olive oil	dried marjoram
or clarified butter	1 bay leaf
2 tablespoons chopped onion	½ teaspoon salt
4 large ripe tomatoes,	¾ cup dry red wine
peeled, seeded and chopped	½ cup light cream
1 garlic clove, minced or	1 tablespoon butter
crushed	1 tablespoon flour

Heat the oil in a heavy ovenproof skillet, then in it sauté the onion, tomatoes, garlic, parsley and marjoram gently for 5 or 6 minutes. Bury the bay leaf in the vegetables, then lay the bass pieces on top. Sprinkle with the salt. Combine the wine and cream and pour it into the skillet. Cover, and cook in a preheated 325°F. oven for 20 minutes. Transfer the fish to a warm platter, then remove the vegetables with a slotted spoon, allowing the juices to drain back into the pan. Arrange the vegetables around the fish on the platter; discard the bay leaf. Bring the juices to a gentle simmer in the pan. Knead the butter and flour to a smooth paste, then drop bits of it into the juices, stirring until each bit has dissolved before adding another bit. Let the sauce simmer for at least 5 minutes after the last bit of butter and flour has been added, then pour it over the fish pieces. Makes 4 to 6 servings.

SEA BASS CHOWDER

4 pounds sea bass fillets,	3 medium-size onions, chopped
cut into chunks	4 cups chopped tomatoes,
6 cups cold water	with all juices
½ teaspoon salt	2 tablespoons dry vermouth
½ lemon, cut into thin slices	1 cup medium-dry sherry
3 tablespoons butter	1½ tablespoons lemon juice
4 potatoes, cut into ½-inch cubes	

Put the fish in a deep pan, cover with 6 cups cold water, and bring it to a boil, skimming the froth. Reduce heat to a simmer, add the salt and lemon slices, and continue simmering for 15 to 20 minutes. The fish need not be completely done, but should flake in large pieces. Reserve the fish in a warm bowl.

Spread 1 tablespoon of the butter on the inside of a deep kettle or saucepan. Put in the pieces of fish, the potatoes, onions and tomatoes, then strain the cooking juices over them. Cook at a gentle simmer for 20 minutes, or until the potatoes are tender. Stir in the vermouth, sherry and lemon juice, and cook for 2 or 3 minutes longer. Remove from the heat, stir in remaining 2 tablespoons butter, and serve in soup bowls. Makes 6 to 8 servings.

Bloater

(1) In Europe, specifically the U. K., a large fat salted herring, usually whole and ungutted, then cold-smoked to a pale gold color. *See under HERRING.*
(2) In the Great Lakes (U. S.) a name used for one of the ciscoes. *See under WHITEFISH.*

Bluefish

In 1928 when Governor Alfred E. Smith of New York was running for President against Herbert Hoover, he went fishing for "snappers" in Hampton Bays. That is to say, he made some slaps at the water with a bamboo pole. This demonstration was for the benefit of the press as Smith, unlike his opponent, had no credentials as a sportsman. I happened to be sitting on the dock; hardly a day passed when I *wasn't* sitting on that dock, only a mile from my grandfather's house. Never having seen a head-of-state, least of all a cigar-smoking dandy in a tailored suit with polished shoes peeking from under a pair of spats and wearing a brown derby while fishing—it boggled my six-year-old mind. His angling technique was recalled many years later by a postcard that Charles Ritz sent to me when Dwight D. Eisenhower was running for President.

An uncompromising expert, Ritz had taught the General how to fly-cast, a skill that requires considerable dexterity. The maestro reported, "I believe he will make a good President but unfortunately he doesn't know how to use his left hand." In any event, Governor Smith knocked his bait can off the dock and all the gunk in his bait can splashed on his spats. He lost my vote on footwork alone.

Snappers, or juvenile bluefish, were one of those ubiquitous species such as the cunner, porgy and blowfish that took up the slack in many American stomachs during the depression years. They could be collected around any coastal pier or for that matter in the Hudson and East Rivers in the summer months. You'd see people shouldering soggy burlap bags of fish on the trolley cars and subway trains in Manhattan, and the Long Island Railroad began its weekly "Fisherman's Special" to Montauk, which was always jammed to the doors. Although called "snappers" because their razor-sharp teeth click like castanets, they bear no relation to the true snapper family which is distinctly different at table. A baby bluefish (under 1 pound in size) is soon known by another euphemism—"chopper"—which describes its lusty adult existence. In his *Report to the United States Fish Commission* in 1874, Professor Spencer F. Baird drew a portrait of the fish which does not exaggerate its character:

The Bluefish has well been likened to an animated chopping-machine, the business of which is to cut to pieces and otherwise destroy as many fish as possible in a given space of time. Going in large schools, in pursuit of fish not much inferior to themselves in size, they move along like a pack of hungry wolves, destroying everything before them. Their trail is marked by fragments of fish and by the stain of blood in the sea, as, where the fish is too large to be swallowed entire, the hinder portion will be bitten off and the anterior part allowed to float away or sink. It is even maintained, with great earnestness that such is a gluttony of the fish, that when the stomach becomes full the contents are disgorged and then again filled. It is certain that it kills more fish than it requires for its own support.

The feeding frenzy of bluefish is a phenomenon that has no parallel in the marine world. Even sharks must be stimulated by some unnatural condition such as the presence of a chum slick or quantities of fish caught in a net before blindly pursuing their prey *en masse*. An extract from the *Gloucester Telegraph* on June 4, 1870, describes what must have been a mother lode of blues during a period of cyclic abundance:

ABUNDANCE OF FISH IN NEW JERSEY
Accounts from New Jersey say that the Bluefish came in at *Barnegat Inlet last week, sweeping through the bay, over flats as well as through the channel, driving millions of bushels of bunkers before them and filling the coves, creeks, ditches, and ponds in the meadows full. At Little Egg Harbor Inlet they drove shad on shore so that people gathered them up by wagon-loads. Fish lie in creeks, ponds, etc., along the meadows two feet deep, so that one can take a common fork and pitch them into a boat or throw them on the bank. In some places they lie in windrows on the meadows where the tide has taken them, so they take large woodscows alongside and load them.*

It almost seems ludicrous that so savage a fish could be the subject of a romantic idyll, but John J. Brown comments in *The American Angler's Guide* (1849) that bluefishing is a mode of piscatorial amusement, for the inhabitants of Connecticut, New York and Long Island.

It is usually performed in a good-size sail-boat, with a guide who knows the ground, or by casting from the shore, and drawing in alternately. The former method is most practiced, and being highly approved of by the fair sex, who often compose the best part of a fishing party, of course stamps it at once with perfection. To those ladies who unfortunately have to be placed on the list as invalids, and can endure the delightful and bracing summer breeze and gentle south wind, a few days' sport in the Sound, with a bluefishing party, will amply repay them for their exertion.

Robert Barnwell Roosevelt in his *Gamefish of the Northern States of America* (1862) was particularly fond of Fire Island Inlet; he described how on a summer day one could see the white sails of 50 boats tossing about in the roll of the breakers. He advised the reader to land on Racoon Beach at noon "and either cook his fish by a fire built from the wraiths of the sea, or get a fashionable dinner from Dominy or t'other man that keeps a hotel there."

The dynamics of bluefish populations are not understood. It's possible that Nature imposed some balancing gene in its most predacious marine organisms (as well as in those numerically abundant such as the weakfish) to compensate for any overactivity such as the almost lemminglike population of 1870. According to Zaccheus Macy in his account of Nantucket (*A Short Journal of the First Settlement, etc.*) bluefish were very abundant around that island from the first settlement of the English in 1659, and were taken in immense numbers from June until mid-September. The fish disappeared, however, in 1764 and didn't arrive *en masse* again until 1800. A Dr. Samuel L. Mitchell states that bluefish were entirely unknown about New York prior to 1810, but they began to be taken in small quantities along the wharves in

1817, and became abundant in 1825. Huge schools appeared off the coast of New Jersey in 1841. Throughout the history of this fishery, highs and lows occur in a totally unpredictable pattern. Since 1970 the landings by sport fisherman alone have exceeded 100 million pounds annually in the area from Cape Cod to Cape Hatteras.

SOURCE AND SEASON

The bluefish is common off our Atlantic Coast from Florida to Cape Cod and in warm years north to Nova Scotia. Within this range they migrate from south to north in our spring and summer, and from north to south in the fall and winter months. Evidently spawning occurs mainly in northern waters as the young summer fish or "snappers" are only known in the Chesapeake Bay to New England area. So the season for fresh bluefish is variable, beginning in December in Florida and finishing by April, and beginning in May and ending by October in New York waters.

Bluefish occur in other parts of the world, along the entire East Coast of South America and from the Azores to Portugal and south to the Cape of Good Hope in Africa. Migrations also appear in Mediterranean North Africa and the Black Sea. They are also abundant around Australia.

Also known as **Anjóva** (Spain), **Anchôva** (Azores and Portugal), **Enxova** (Brazil), **Pesce serra** (Italy), **Tassergal** (France), **Strijelka skakuša** (Yugoslavia), **Gofári** (Greece), **Lüfer** (Turkey), **Tailor** (Australia and southeastern U. S.), **Amikiri** (Japan), **Elf** (South Africa), **Anchoa** or **Pez azul** (Venezuela, Uruguay, and Argentina).

FACTORS AFFECTING QUALITY

When dining out, I would never order bluefish except at seaside restaurants where freshness is guaranteed—assuming the proprietor is credible. At its best, it's very good, soft textured of long flake, and mild tasting in smaller sizes. Although there is no hard evidence to back me up, I think our southern bluefish in Florida are of better flavor than northern stocks. Bluefish will consume literally any species available, but the most abundant forage in any region is their obvious first choice. In southern waters bluefish feed chiefly on mullet, false pilchard and anchovies, whereas the very oily and strongly flavored menhaden or "mossbunker" becomes a chief item of bluefish diet as the schools progress north. During peak years in the bunker cycle blues are definitely below par. The young snappers, on the other hand, are always sweetly flavored as they feed on crustaceans, mollusks and various small inshore fishes, notably the silverside which gourmets know as "whitebait."

As in all highly predacious fish, the digestive enzymes of the bluefish are extremely powerful and the meat will spoil quickly, within a few hours of being caught, if left ungutted without ice. A bluefish must be dressed as soon as possible after being taken from the water. Since the meat has a high oil content it does not travel well unless icing is continued. For the same reason be sparing in the use of oils or fat in creative recipes; the best recipes contain neutralizing acids in the form of vegetables such as tomatoes or onions, or citrus fruits such as lemon or lime. In common with other fast-swimming pelagic species such as the tuna or mackerel, bluefish have a large amount of muscle hemoglobin in the form of a dark strip of meat which can be removed from the fillet. Although extremely nutritious it's perhaps too "fishy," even slightly bitter to some palates, when served hot, yet it's perfectly delicious when cold.

Small snapper blues are ideally panfried. Fresh from the water, gutted and scaled, they have a delicate flavor. In common with many other species, however, the larger this fish grows, the less flexible it becomes in the kitchen. Blues up to 6 or 8 pounds are the perfect size for baking and broiling in fillet form. Bluefish are a poor species for poaching or making into chowders as the musculature shreds into fine pieces. Perhaps the best method for very large whole fish of 10 pounds or more is to bake over charcoal in a covered cooker, then chill and skin to serve cold with a sour-cream and lemon dressing the next day. This is a good way to prepare a bluefish in the 15- to 20-pound class; such a fish can be presented in much the same fashion as a cold salmon in aspic. Fish of all sizes can be hot-smoked, and this is truly a superior product. Unfortunately it's not widely known.

BROILED BLUEFISH

Fillets of bluefish are ideally broiled. Skin them, then remove the dark midline meat with a sharp, thin-bladed knife; make a shallow V-cut the length of the fillet on both sides of the dark center without penetrating the opposite side. Lift out this strip. Before broiling wipe the outside (the former skin side) with vegetable oil to prevent sticking to the pan or foil. Always cook with the outside down to keep the musculature intact. Do not turn.

BASIC BROILED   The simplest and perhaps tastiest way of preparing a truly fresh small to medium-size bluefish fillet. Prepare as above, then liberally sprinkle with lemon or lime juice about 30 minutes before cooking. Salt and pepper to taste, then dot with pats of butter. Add more butter at the halfway point in cooking, and color the fillet with sweet paprika (paprika crystallizes and becomes bitter if exposed too long to direct heat). Cook under low heat for 5 minutes and under high heat for an additional 6 minutes, or until fork tender. Serve with a garnish of chopped parsley and wedges of citrus.

BASIC MEDITERRANEAN   A variety of additives under the catchall labels "Italian," "Portuguese," "Spanish" or "Greek" are added to butter-broiled bluefish, but the basic ingredients are thin slices of onion and tomato cut into rounds and lapped over the top of the fillet. This is not only decorative but does enhance the flavor of larger bluefish, those exceeding 6 pounds total weight. Strips of green pepper can be inserted crosswise between the rounds. Optionally, depending on individual taste, one may drizzle the vegetable-garnished fish with olive oil rather than butter. In either case, herbs are added, either one or several, usually orégano, basil, thyme, rosemary, tarragon and minced garlic; these are generously sprinkled over the fillet. Decorate with chopped parsley before serving.

BASIC BARBECUE   The only difference in preparation when cooking on charcoal is that the fillet should be scaled but *unskinned*. The dark midline strip should still be removed. The oiled skin side laid against the grid will keep the fish intact. Make several shallow crosswise incisions in the skin to prevent "puckering" as the musculature of a fresh fillet will contract to some extent. The barbecued fillet can be treated according to the basic broiled style or the Mediterranean. However, it should be cooked under cover over low heat. The addition of wet hickory chips to the firebox greatly enhances its flavor.

BARBECUED BLUEFISH BUFFET STYLE
(Mary Coucens)

1 bluefish, 8 to 10 pounds or larger	1 tablespoon lemon juice
vegetable oil	4 tablespoons capers
1½ cups sour cream	4 tablespoons minced dill
½ cup mayonnaise	white pepper
1 tablespoon prepared horseradish	1 cherry tomato
	lemon slices

This is a cold dish served in the manner of a whole poached salmon. It's best cooked the day before serving. Dress the bluefish, leaving its head and tail intact, and scale. Wipe the entire fish with vegetable oil and place on a grid over a low charcoal fire; use a covered charcoal cooker. The fire should be at least 10 inches from the fish. Depending on the heat intensity and size of the fish it should require 45 minutes to 1 hour or more as it must be

Bluefish

cooked slowly. Add wet hickory chips at intervals to maintain smoke. Remove the bluefish from the grill with large spatulas, retaining its whole shape, and arrange on a suitable serving platter. When cool, carefully peel off the skin but do not remove the underlying dark meat (as in salmon preparations). Refrigerate overnight or for at least 6 hours to firm.

Before serving blend the sour cream and mayonnaise with horseradish, lemon juice, capers and dill. Season with white pepper to taste. Spread this mixture evenly over the body of the fish with the flat edge of a knife. Substitute a cherry tomato for the eye, and decorate the fish with thin lemon slices. Keep cold until ready for the table. Makes 8 to 10 servings.

NOTE: If grill is too small to accommodate a whole bluefish, a loin cut can be used in this recipe.

BAKED NORTH FORK BLUEFISH

1 bluefish, 8 to 10 pounds	¼ cup olive oil
2 cups seasoned fine bread crumbs	1 pound canned or fresh tomatoes, chopped
½ teaspoon dried orégano	1 teaspoon sugar

Place the cleaned fish in a large baking pan lined with aluminum foil. Mix the bread crumbs with orégano and olive oil, and spread over the fish. Pour tomatoes over the entire dish and sprinkle with the sugar. Bake at 400° to 425°F. for 1 hour. Test with a fork for firmness, whiteness and flakiness as indications that fish is ready to serve. This recipe can be used successfully with large bluefish in the over-10-pound range; increase ingredients in proportion. Makes 8 servings.

BLUEFISH WITH ALMONDS

1 pound bluefish fillets	5 tablespoons melted butter
1 cup milk	1 cup silvered almonds
salt	2 tablespoons lemon juice
½ cup dried bread crumbs approximately	

Combine the milk and 1 tablespoon of salt. Dip the fish fillets into the milk, then into bread crumbs. Place in a greased baking dish; add no water, but sprinkle with 1 tablespoon of melted butter. Brown quickly in a 500°F. oven for 10 to 20 minutes.

Lightly brown the almonds in remaining butter. After the almonds are brown, pour off butter into a cup and add the lemon juice and a pinch of salt; stir until well blended. When ready to serve spread the almonds over the fish and pour the butter and lemon juice over all. Makes 2 generous servings.

Bombay Duck

A split, boned, and dried fillet of fish *(Harpodon nehereus)* caught in the Indian Ocean. This is served as one of the accompaniments to a curry dinner. Enthusiasts of Indian food do not consider a curry presentation authentic without a few strips of Bombay duck. It has a delightful pungent aroma and crisp texture. I sometimes use it broken into small pieces for oil-based salad dressings, and, after lightly sautéing in butter, as a component of sauce meunière to be served over a bland poached fish such as cod. Obtainable in specialty shops.

Bonefish

This marine gamefish is highly prized by American sport fishermen but is generally regarded as inedible. Nearly all bonefish that are caught by angling are released. However, the enigmatic *Albula vulpes* is extremely good eating and highly esteemed among people who have more popular options in East Africa, Hawaii, the Bahamas and throughout the Caribbean. The bonefish is the only living member of its genus and belongs to a family of primitive fishes which date back to the Cretaceous Period about 125 million years ago. It occurs in tropical and semitropical seas throughout the world, but on our coasts is only found in abundance from Miami, Florida, southward.

The bonefish is a bright silvery fish with a piglike snout which is effectively used for rooting in sand and marl. It feeds in very shallow water, often with its tail in the air as it burrows in the bottom. Due to its exposure to predation under these circumstances the bonefish is also a tremendously fast swimmer when alarmed. The average fish taken by anglers in Florida and the Bahamas weighs from 4 to 6 pounds, and somewhat smaller fish are caught in Mexican and Central American waters. Bonefish in excess of 20 pounds occasionally enter the markets in Mozambique, where large individuals are caught in deep water. Other names for the bonefish are **Banane** (West Africa), **Kondo** or **Kpole** (East Africa), **Macabi** or **Raton** (West Indies and South America), and **'O'io** (Hawaii).

The meat of bonefish is white, rich, and nutlike in flavor. Bonefish consume sea urchins at times and to some extent small fishes, but they are primarily mollusk and crustacean feeders and their flesh reflects this

Bonefish

HOW TO DRESS BONEFISH

1. Cut down the back from nape to tail. **2.** Cut along
both sides of the dorsal fin. **3.** Cut on both sides of the tail
and twist it loose. **4.** Make parallel cuts on both
sides of floating ribs. **5.** Backbone, rib cage and viscera
can be lifted out. **6.** Dressed bonefish, stuffed and baked.

well-defined diet. The roe of female bonefish is also excellent to eat and can be prepared like shad roe. This fish is exceptionally good when smoked, and after it firms under refrigeration the bones can be lifted out quite easily. Bonefish may be fried, broiled or baked, but the latter method is much the best; I wouldn't suggest frying at all and broiling tends to dry out the fish. Baking in this case is a long, low-heat process with the fish wrapped in foil. A 6- to 8-pound fish should be in the oven at 175°F. for 6 hours. I will only give one recipe for cooking bonefish. While it can be baked at high heat for a short period the results are not the same. Any variation in seasonings is a matter of individual preference. It's pointless to cook a bonefish under 6 pounds in size, and preferably you want an 8- or 10-pounder, as with this species the bigger the better. It is extremely bony, comparable to a shad in having "floating ribs" or Y-shaped intermuscular bones, but large fish provide substantial chunks of nearly boneless meat.

HOW TO DRESS BONEFISH

Bonefish can be made almost boneless with very little practice. Cut the fish down the back along both sides of the dorsal fin from nape to tail, but do not cut through the rib cage. Cut down on both sides of the tail to free it from the meat, and twist it loose. Run the knife forward from the tail to penetrate the interior but do not cut through the skin along the underside; work the blade around the rib cage to keep it intact. The backbone, rib cage and viscera can now be lifted out. There is a short series of small floating ribs lying forward dorsally on both sides of the fish, the tips of which are easily seen; these can be removed by making parallel cuts above and below each strip.

A bonefish dressed in this fashion is usually "stuffed" by spreading a layer of bread crumbs, finely chopped celery, green pepper, tomato slices and onion rings over the meat, then covering with several slices of bacon. Bake a fish prepared this way on foil, uncovered, in a preheated 350°F. oven for 30 minutes. However, time permitting, the slower marination method described in the following recipe is worth the effort.

BAHAMIAN BONEFISH

1 bonefish, 6 pounds, scaled and butterflied	1 green pepper, diced
	3 tablespoons peanut oil
12 Key limes (preferably), or lemons	1½ cups tomato sauce
	¼ cup Worcestershire sauce
freshly ground black pepper	1 teaspoon dried thyme
salt	crushed red pepper
2 medium-size onions, diced	4 tablespoons minced parsley

Lay bonefish, skin side down, on a piece of foil large enough to be folded over the fish later. Place foiled fish in baking pan. Slice limes and squeeze juice over flesh side of fish, rubbing some of the pulp on it until the fillets are thoroughly soaked. Sprinkle with pepper and salt to taste. Store the fish in refrigerator overnight to marinate.

When ready to cook, sauté onions and green pepper in peanut oil in a large skillet until onions are transparent. Add tomato sauce, Worcestershire sauce, thyme, and crushed red pepper to taste; let simmer until flavors blend. Spoon sauce over entire fish, sprinkle with parsley, and fold the foil over to cover. Place fish in oven and cook at 175°F. for 6 hours. Serve hot or cold. Makes 6 servings.

Bouillabaisse

This Bouillabaisse a noble dish is—
A sort of soup or broth, or brew,
Or hotchpotch, of all sorts of fishes,
That Greenwich never could outdo;
Green herbs, red peppers, mussels, saffern,
Soles, onions, garlic, roach, and dace;
All these you eat at Terré's tavern,
In that one dish of Bouillabaisse.
The Ballad of Bouillabaisse,
William Makepeace Thackeray

There is a school of gastronomy which holds that *bouillabaisse* cannot be prepared beyond the environs of Marseilles, and what masquerades elsewhere under that noble name is merely a fish soup. The argument, simple and ingenuous, is predicated on the conviction that *bouillabaisse* requires 12 different kinds of fish native only to the Mediterranean. In truth, collecting all twelve would baffle a working ichthyologist.

To the gourmet whom education has made articulate, the lack of these fishes has hobbled *la bouillabaisse.* The consumption of this dish has for 2,600 years been a *massaliote* preoccupation. Yet, even when that great *chef de cuisine* Charles Janon is faced with whatever the morning's market has to offer he does not hesitate to simmer a substitute to brothy perfection.

The great truth is that *bouillabaisse* never demanded anything more than the local fishing would yield. After frequent tours of the bistros along Le Canebière down to the Old Port, it seems obvious that the hometown lads improvise. The stews were simply a blend of whatever *le patron* could obtain fresh. A *bouillabaisse* is essentially an artistic presentation of seafoods, and even Alexandre Dumas *père* didn't hesitate to brew a pot because one or two of the preferred fish were lacking. In this country we cannot make a *bouillabaisse véritable comme l'on fait à Marseilles,* but on the other hand neither can the *massaliote* make one *à la Florida* or any place else in the world.

The members of this gastronomic wedding are often simply hiding behind Gallicisms, and upon examination prove to be world citizens, as, for example, the **rouget,** or goatfish. This blushing reef dweller with the chin-whiskery barbels is found in all tropical and semitropical seas and at least one species wanders as far north as Cape Cod. The **merlan** is simply a whiting. The **Saint-Pierre** is our John Dory. Others, such as the **grondin,** hide in the trash barrels of our professional draggers, who find them too grotesque for commerce. Monsieur Grondin, a winged nightmare that makes young men faint and old men scream, is better known to American fishermen, who promptly throw them back, as a searobin. The **lotte** or **baudroie** is identical to our goosefish, another ugly bottom dweller that nobody would think of eating on this side of the Atlantic although it is extremely delicious. As for the **rascasse,** this is one of several Scorpaenidae which Californians can find as "sculpin" and Easterners as red scorpionfish. The **vive** is a member of the weever family, which does not occur in our waters but differs little from the searobin. The **congre** is the conger eel, which we have in abundance. In brief, the classic ingredients of a Mediterranean *bouillabaisse* can be duplicated to a large extent if one demands authenticity, but I question whether it's worth the effort.

To me, improvisation is one of the delights of *bouillabaisse.* The best I have ever enjoyed was made by Chef André Sarat, in the days when Axel Wenergren owned the Lighthouse Club on Andros Island in the Ba-

BOUILLABAISSE (prepared by Chef Charles Janon, Inter-Continental Hotel, Paris)

1. The ingredients, counterclockwise: langoustine; grondin, Saint-Pierre, tomato concentrate and green herbs; lotte, rascasse, rouget; vive, and the baguette; congre; tomatoes and fennel. 2. Dress the various fishes and cut into appropriate portions. 3. Pour olive oil into a heavy pot. 4. Add shredded onions, and let cook for 15 minutes without browning. 5. Mash garlic with flat side of a heavy knife. 6. Add garlic to onions. 7. Add quartered peeled tomatoes; 8. then bouquet garni (thyme, bay leaf, parsley stems, peel of 1 orange, tied in fresh fennel ribs). 9. Simmer until vegetables are translucent and juices evaporated. 10. Layer fish in the pot. 11. Add boiling water to reach 1 inch above level of fish. 12. Season with coarse salt, 13. then with ground white pepper. 14. Add tomato concentrate and saffron. 15. Simmer for 15 minutes, then add langoustines and cook for 7 minutes longer, until all ingredients are cooked. 16. Transfer cooked fish and langoustines to a serving platter. 17. Reduce the broth, then strain into a soup tureen. 18. Completed bouillabaisse. Serve over toasted rounds of baguette (thin French bread) in individual bowls.

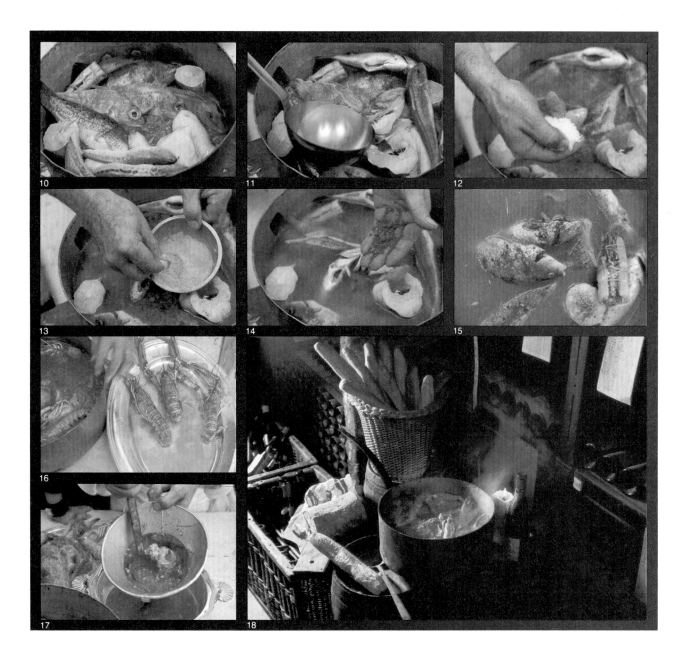

hamas. Sarat concocted a *bouillabaisse* with grunts, cow-fish, snappers, Spanish mackerel, grouper, spiny lobster and shrimps. The cowfish is a magnificent addition; we seldom get cowfish at home in Florida, but it is common throughout the Bahamas and the West Indies. Coastal South America calls it **el toro** because of its horns and tough, leathery body. Ordinarily, the whole fish is flamed under a broiler, so that the skin cracks off like slate. Those species which the native commercial fisherman can't obtain, Chef Sarat personally collected with his casting rod off the club dock. Monsieur Sarat was adamant on three points concerning *la bouillabaisse:* it must be started with a rich fish stock made by simmering the bones and heads, never in plain water; a dry white wine must be added to the stock; finally, saffron must be generously used.

Like holy matrimony, a *bouillabaisse* should not be entered into lightly or unadvisedly. There must be lean fish and fat fish, large ones and small ones. The largest should be cut into crosswise chunks and the very small left whole. Fish such as mackerel and mullet, which have a high oil content, should be used sparingly, since you are charged with marrying the flavors and not divorcing them from the entity. Do not hedge on your first adventure; invite at least 4 people to dinner, otherwise you can't economically get enough variety in seafoods without being burdened by a mountain of leftovers. No flower wilts more quickly than yesterday's *bouillabaisse.* As the fish must come fresh from the water, so must the stew come fresh from the fire, steaming with the passion of sudden union. In fact, I prefer to gather 8 hungry neighbors at the groaning board and commence with 8 pounds of ocean-fresh fish plus 1 pound of eel. I might also suggest at least 4 species as a base: the flounder, striped bass, whiting or sea bass, and halibut or cod, if you are an Easterner; a sole, salmon, halibut or sculpin, and rockfish, if you live in the West; pompano, red snapper, grouper or seatrout, and Spanish mackerel in the South. While there is dissension on Mediterranean shores concerning the use of lobster, shrimps or any bivalve, I would include these and mussels or clams as well. The more textures and flavors you incorporate, the better the *bouillabaisse.*

It's difficult to make a *bouillabaisse* of fresh-water fishes. Generally there is not a sufficient variety of species available in any one region for the angler, although some delectable soups and chowders can be made with a day's catch. I have made *bouillabaisse* by adding supplements from the market, particularly crustaceans and mollusks, but, basically, most freshwater fish are lean and when caught in the same habitats there is a similarity in flavors and textures. An ideal combination, and I am

speaking now of fish that can be obtained at market, would include whitefish, yellow perch, walleye (yellow pike), and lake trout or salmon. These make a good contrast and include both fat and lean species. The only freshwater crustacean capable of keynoting a *bouillabaisse* is the crayfish. Any of our American species which grow to an edible size are worthy additions. However, some of the ingredients must be of ocean origin, either fresh or frozen, and marine and freshwater fishes can be mixed with happy results.

HOW TO MAKE BOUILLABAISSE

Before venturing into the recipe that follows, I will describe my own method for the sake of procedure. The sequence of arranging various items in the pot is important; you will want large and heavy chunks of lobster, for example, on the bottom and over these rough-edged clams and mussels in order to avoid breaking the pieces of fish when it comes time to serve. The most delicate fillets or small whole fish should be on top. Bear in mind that a chunk of lobster will cook more slowly than a thin fish fillet or shrimp, whereas a halibut or grouper steak will be intermediate in timing. Separate ingredients according to slow, medium and fast; never add them to the pot all at once, but in sequential order. If the lobster has been at simmer for about 4 minutes, then it's time to introduce the halibut or cod and, given another 4 minutes, the more fragile cuts of fish.

I adhere to the Sarat principle and begin with a rich stock, either one reserved in our freezer or made for the occasion. You will need at least 2 pounds of heads, bones and skins to 1 gallon of water. Place these in a large pot, preferably cast iron; add 1 peeled onion studded with 8 to 10 cloves and 2 chopped celery ribs with a handful of greens. Bring the water to a boil, and continue boiling for about 2 minutes. Turn the heat down and simmer for 1 hour to reduce the liquid by one third. Mash the fish heads with the back of a wooden spoon, then strain the stock carefully into a second pot (any kind will do), removing all solids, and reserve the stock. Wash out the residual froth in the cast-iron pot. Pour in 1 cup olive oil; add 1 cup minced onion, 1 tablespoon minced fresh fennel (or 1 teaspoon dried fennel), and 1 teaspoon minced fresh thyme (or ½ teaspoon dried thyme); simmer over low heat but do not blond the onion. Next add 4 large quartered and peeled tomatoes and 6 minced garlic cloves, and continue to simmer, allowing the liquid from the tomatoes to evaporate. Then add a 6-ounce can of tomato paste, 1 teaspoon of grated orange rind and a generous pinch of saffron. Pour 2 cups of dry white wine into the pot and stir until thoroughly mixed. Season judiciously with salt and pepper, then slowly pour in the reserved fish stock, stirring, and return all to a simmer.

With a flat strainer or slotted spoon submerge the pieces of lobster; in 4 minutes add the clams, mussels and eel, then the firmer cuts of fish and the shrimps over the bivalves. Cook for another 4 minutes and introduce the delicate fish fillets. These may only require 2 or 3 minutes of additional cooking time; when they reach the color and consistency of a boiled egg white, the *bouillabaisse* is complete.

We have an optional choice in serving *bouillabaisse*. Most chefs at this point pour the broth into a deep tureen over slices of toasted *baguette* rubbed with garlic, and serve the fish on a separate platter. I much prefer to spoon the liquid into large individual bowls, then carefully add various pieces of seafood, and provide a basket of oven-moist but crisply crusted French or Italian bread for sopping up the juices. I keep the remainder warm in a covered tureen to ladle out more broth or fish as required. Either way it must be accompanied by finely chopped parsley and a **Sauce Rouille** (p. 289), without which *no bouillabaisse is authentic. See also FISH SOUPS AND STEWS.*

BOUILLABAISSE
(Hotel Inter-Continental, Paris)

3 pounds whole undressed grondin (searobin)

3 pounds whole undressed congre (substitute eel)

2½ pounds whole gutted rouget (goatfish)

2½ pounds rascasse (rockfish), 8 fillets

2½ pounds Saint-Pierre (John Dory), 8 fillets

2 pounds whole undressed lotte (substitute burbot)

2 pounds whole undressed vive (substitute tautog)

8 langoustines (lobsterettes)

1 cup plus 2 tablespoons olive oil

2 pounds onions, shredded

7 garlic cloves, peeled

1½ pounds fresh tomatoes, peeled

2 celery ribs, chopped

bouquet garni (thyme, bay leaf, parsley stems, peel of 1 orange)

5½ ounces fresh fennel

coarse salt

white pepper

6 tablespoons tomato concentrate

½ ounce saffron

French bread (baguette)

⅔ cup grated Parmesan cheese

1½ cups Sauce Rouille (p. 289)

Dress fish and cut into appropriate pieces. Use fillets of John Dory whole, cut rockfish into large pieces, skin eels and cut into 3-inch sections, and so on. Use a deep, wide, heavy kettle. Pour in 1 cup of the oil, then the fine onion shreds. Simmer over low heat, stirring now and then, for 15 minutes; onions should be translucent but not browned. Mash 5 garlic cloves with flat side of a large knife; quarter the tomatoes. Add these with celery to the kettle. Tie the herbs and orange rind with the fennel ribs to make a *bouquet garni,* and add to the vegetables. Simmer for 15 minutes longer, until moisture from tomatoes has evaporated. Layer fish in the kettle on top of vegetable mixture. Add boiling water to reach 1 inch above the fish. Season with coarse salt and ground white pepper. Add tomato concentrate and saffron. Simmer the stew for 15 minutes. Add lobsterettes and continue to cook for only 7 minutes.

Remove kettle from heat. With a skimmer or flat strainer remove fish from kettle and arrange each kind together, with the lobsterettes on top. Reduce the broth in the kettle by one third; it will thicken. Force through a fine strainer into a soup tureen. Rub crust of *baguette* with remaining whole garlic cloves. Cut bread into about 16 rounds and place in a shallow earthenware dish. Sprinkle with remaining 2 tablespoons oil, and brown lightly in oven or broiler. Sprinkle hot toast with 2 tablespoons or more grated cheese.

Thin the Sauce Rouille with some of the broth, and stir in a little of the grated cheese. Serve the soup over toast in individual bowls, or serve toast separately. Serve the fish and lobsterettes, remaining cheese, and the Sauce Rouille. Makes 8 servings, or more.

Bream

(1) In Europe the common freshwater bream is a member of the carp family (Cyprinidae) although this is a very minor market item and chiefly limited to Germany as **Brachsen** or **Brassen.** *See CARP.*

(2) In Europe a widely used market name for various members of the porgy family (Sparidae) collectively known as sea bream. *See PORGY.*

(3) In the U.S. a regional name for various freshwater sunfish sometimes called "brim" which are caught by sport fishermen only. *See SUNFISH.*

(4) In the Orient and Indo-Pacific region to South Africa a widely used common name for various members of the porgy family (Sparidae) collectively known as sea bream. *See PORGY.*

Buffalofish

There are 3 species of buffalo found in North American freshwaters. These are members of the sucker family Catostomidae. *See under SUCKERS.*

Butterfish

A small, deep-bodied fish found along the Atlantic Coast from Nova Scotia to the Gulf of Mexico. There are several genera in the butterfish family, Stromateidae, but the most common commercial species are the butterfish *(Peprilus triacanthus)* and the harvestfish *(P. alepidotus);* one Pacific member, *P. simillimus* or Pacific "pompano," also appears in markets. Butterfish are of some importance in northeastern U. S., both in fresh and smoked form. The fish gets its name from its normally high fat content; its musculature is mostly dark-meated but of excellent flavor. The annual landings fluctuate but some 10 million pounds are sold in peak years, mainly in Boston and New York. The season for fresh butterfish is during our summer months, but it may appear until late fall. There are several European members of the butterfish family where they are generally known as **pomfret**.

Butterfish seldom exceed 10 inches in length. The scales are so fine that they can literally be rubbed off; the fish is best cooked with the skin intact by splitting, then broiling or baking. It can be prepared following any mackerel recipe.

Butters

Butter alone is useful in fish cookery, as you will see in the recipes, but butter can be changed by heating or by combining with other ingredients to make sauces or sauce additives. A compound butter can be shaped into a roll to be refrigerated or frozen. These rolls can be sliced to add to a finished dish. Or they can be served in a soft lump, or added to other sauces to give flavor and glossiness.

CLARIFIED BUTTER

Clarified butter has a higher burning point because the milky residue has been removed. It is that protein residue (casein and whey) that burns when unclarified butter is heated for cooking. To eliminate it, melt desired amount of butter in a saucepan over very low heat until the milky residue sinks to the bottom. Skim off the foam and pour off the oil, leaving the residue behind. Strain the butter oil through cheesecloth.

Large amounts of clarified butter can be pre-pared and stored in the freezer. The process works with both salted and unsalted butter.

BEURRE MANIÉ

A mixture of uncooked butter and flour, used for thickening a sauce or the liquid in a soup or chowder. It is not usually made with equal parts of butter and flour, as a roux is made, but rather with 2 parts butter to 1 part flour. However, different proportions are possible. Use room-temperature butter, and knead with flour into small balls. Add as required. After adding it, the sauce must be cooked, of course, to avoid a floury taste, but it is better not to let the mixture boil. *Beurre manié* can be made ahead and stored in the refrigerator for up to 2 weeks.

ROUX

A mixture of fat and flour that is cooked before being combined with liquid. Clarified butter is the ideal fat. (Other fats or oils can be used; the process is the same.) Heat the clarified butter in a heavy pot until it no longer foams. Remove from the heat, add the flour and combine thoroughly, then return to very low heat. Cook, stirring often, until the flour is cooked and the roux reaches the color you need. For pale sauces, 2 to 4 minutes (longer time for a larger amount of roux)—white or *blond* roux. For darker sauces, 4 to 8 minutes—golden roux. For brown sauces, 8 to 12 minutes—brown roux. Off the heat, add liquid of the same temperature as the roux, whisking constantly. Return to low heat and cook until sauce is thickened.

BROWN BUTTER (BEURRE NOISETTE)

Add desired amount of butter to pan over medium heat. (Optional: when the butter melts and foams, add a little lemon juice.) When the butter starts to turn pale hazelnut brown, it is ready to serve.

BLACK BUTTER (BEURRE NOIR)

In a saucepan over high heat melt 4 ounces butter, and cook until it begins to brown. (Optional: add at once 2 tablespoons each of chopped parsley and capers and 1 teaspoon wine vinegar.) Bring to a dark color but not really black. (With the addition of herbs and vinegar, it makes a classic French sauce for poached skate.)

WHITE BUTTER (BEURRE BLANC)

In a saucepan combine ¼ cup wine vinegar, ¼ cup dry white wine, 5 shallots, minced almost to a purée, 1 table-spoon minced parsley, and a little salt and white pepper. Simmer the mixture until the liquid is reduced to hardly more than a damp spot in the pan. Over *very* low heat gradually beat in ½ pound of unsalted butter, about 1 ounce at a time, whisking constantly, and never allowing the butter to melt. If it seems about to melt, lift the pan from the heat, but continue to whisk. When the emulsion is complete, the mixture will be almost white, and foamy. Serve at once.

LEMON BUTTER

Place ½ pound butter in a heavy saucepan over an asbestos pad, or in the top part of a double boiler over hot water. Try to control the heat so the butter doesn't really melt, as in White Butter. Using a wooden spoon or a whisk, beat in the juice of 2 lemons (about 6 tablespoons juice). This can be flavored with a few drops of onion juice, paprika, Italian seasoning, ground cuminseed, etc. Serve at once in a soft lump, or chill to serve cold, or melt and serve hot.

MAÎTRE D'HÔTEL BUTTER

For each 4 ounces of butter add 1 tablespoon of lemon juice, 1½ tablespoons of minced parsley and ¼ teaspoon each of salt and pepper. Serve melted, or chill and serve as a soft lump.

COLBERT BUTTER

Make Maître d'Hôtel Butter, and add 1 tablespoon chopped fresh tarragon (or 1 teaspoon dried) and 1 teaspoon *glace de viande*. Always served in soft form.

ANCHOVY BUTTER (BEURRE D'ANCHOIS)

For each 4 ounces of butter add 1 tablespoon of anchovy paste. Mix thoroughly over low heat. Chill.

GARLIC BUTTER (BEURRE D'AIL)

For each 4 ounces of butter add 1 tablespoon of minced or pressed garlic. Simmer until the garlic turns *blond*. Strain or not as you prefer, and let it chill.

GREEN BUTTER (BEURRE VERT)

Use 10 spinach leaves and 10 watercress leaves. Pull leaves from stems and ribs. Add 1 tablespoon minced parsley and 1 tablespoon minced fresh tarragon, or mixed tarragon and chervil. Drop all the greens into a large pot of boiling water and keep just at the boiling point for 5 minutes. Pour through a very fine strainer, then plunge into cold water and strain again. Let greens dry, then mash them to a paste. Beat in ½ pound butter, salted or unsalted. Push butter through a fine sieve, then chill until ready to use. Good alone or as an addition to other sauces.

PARSLEY BUTTER

This name is sometimes given to Maître d'Hôtel Butter, but it can be made differently. Follow the method for Green Butter, but use only parsley. For 4 ounces butter use 3 tablespoons minced parsley..Or use uncooked parsley if the butter is to be used at once; cream the butter in a warm bowl and beat in the parsley. Chill until ready to use.

MUSTARD BUTTER (BEURRE DE MOUTARDE)

In a saucepan melt 4 ounces of butter. Remove the pan from the heat and add 1 teaspoon lemon juice and ¼ teaspoon salt. Beat in gradually 2½ teaspoons prepared mustard, and continue beating the sauce until it is thick and cool. Serve slightly chilled.

TARRAGON BUTTER (BEURRE D'ESTRAGON)

For each 4 ounces of butter add 1 tablespoon of minced fresh tarragon, 1 teaspoon minced parsley and a dash of lemon juice. Beat together until well mixed. Chill.

Other herb butters can be made following this method.

SHELLFISH BUTTER

This recipe is based on shrimps *(beurre de crevettes)*, but the method is the same for crayfish butter *(beurre d'écrevisses)* or lobster butter *(beurre de homard)*. Crayfish butter is an essential element in **Sauce Nantua** used for pike quenelles or mousse *(see under PIKE)*, but shellfish butter can be added to other sauces to give color and flavor.

Shell 2 pounds shrimps. Use the shrimp meat for something else. Barely crisp the shells in a hot oven, and chop them into small pieces. Melt ½ pound butter in the top part of a double boiler with ¼ cup water and the chopped shells, and cook for 10 to 12 minutes without allowing the butter to boil. Pour off the liquid through a strainer. Add a little boiling water to the shells remaining in the pot and pour that off through a strainer. Pour the combined liquids through a cloth-lined sieve into a bowl of ice water. Set the bowl in the refrigerator until the butter hardens on the top. Skim off the butter, pack it into a jar, and cover. Store in the refrigerator.

DRAWN BUTTER

In the top part of a double boiler, over hot water, melt 4 tablespoons butter; stir in 4 tablespoons flour until well mixed, then add 2 cups boiling water or light fish stock and stir and cook until the sauce is thick and about to boil. Remove from the heat but keep over hot water. Just before serving put the pot again over heat and beat in ¼ pound butter, cut into little bits. Season with salt to taste. If you like, add about 2 tablespoons freshly squeezed lemon or lime juice. Makes about 3 cups.

Cabezon

The cabezon is a large Pacific marine sculpin found from Mexico to British Columbia. It reaches a weight of 25 pounds. The color of the fish varies from green to cherry red and the flesh often shows similar variations, most often having a greenish cast. It is an excellent foodfish with a delicate flavor; however, the roe is poisonous to man.

Cabezon should not be confused with a smaller fish (*Scorpaena guttata*), commonly called "sculpin" on the West Coast, which is correctly known as the California scorpionfish. Scorpionfishes are also fine table fare, and this particular species is very popular in San Francisco under the "sculpin" label. Two very similar species are found in the Mediterranean and are popular in French cuisine as the **Rascasse rouge** and **Rascasse noire.**

Cabio

See COBIA.

California Sheephead

A member of the wrasse family, Labridae, found in Pacific waters only and no relation to the sheepshead of the Atlantic, which is one of the porgies (Sparidae). The California sheephead (*Pimelometopon pulchrum*) is found from Monterey Bay south to the Gulf of California, Mexico. This is a distinctive-looking fish with a deep body and slight hump on its head that slopes to thick lips and a heavy jaw; the adult female is reddish to rose in color while the male has a purple to bluish-black head and tail with a red midsection. The sheephead reaches a weight of 30 pounds but 4 to 5 pounds is more common. It is caught only by hook-and-line, or taken by spear fishermen, and chiefly during the late fall or winter months. Thus the annual commercial landings are very minor. The sheephead feeds on lobsters, abalone and other shellfish, and this diet is reflected in its flavor. The flesh is white and firm, similar to the related tautog (also a wrasse) of the Atlantic. The sheephead can be cooked according to any cod or rockfish recipe. It makes a good chowder, and it can be poached and flaked, then turned into a salad.

Carp

The carp may not be a spectacular food, but a fat winter fish, preferably taken from a clear flowing stream, is certainly worthy of your attention. It's excellent when pickled or smoked and is considered by many Jewish mothers as an essential ingredient to gefilte fish. I will dispute the latter claim *(see GEFILTE FISH)*, but the carp, when stuffed and baked, broiled or panfried, has a loyal following. Carp roe, which is sometimes used as a caviar substitute, is of fine flavor. I suppose the one thing to know about a carp is that its mass of dark meat differs biochemically from the other musculature and has contractile properties which make it tough and unappetizing. When this dark meat is cut away, the lighter-colored flesh can be used in many recipes. Izaak Walton called the carp "the Queen of the Rivers: a stately, a good, and a very subtle fish . . ." which may be a very apt description.

An ancient food of Asia, the carp was pond-cultured in China 500 years before Christ. It was subsequently transplanted to Europe, being mentioned by Aristotle as early as 350 B.C., where it flourished on aquatic farms beginning in the eleventh century. The carp offers many advantages to the fish culturist: it is tolerant of high water temperatures—to 96°F. for a 24-hour period, yet equally capable of withstanding temporary freezing. The fish can also absorb atmospheric oxygen, and in drought-prone countries it's the last organism to expire in a drying pond. Above all, the carp is a cheap source of protein with a yield greater than that of prime cattle in a lush pasture. Carp can be raised on land too barren to support other crops by the simple act of digging a hole and providing water. Amid much fanfare the carp was sent to America from Germany in 1876; a small number had arrived in New York a decade earlier but these had not yet made a dent on the market. Historically, it was an unwise introduction. The carp is not only a prolific breeder, but because of its bottom-grubbing style of feeding which muddies the water, thereby destroying sunlight-dependent aquatic plants and plankton, it soon ruined the fertile habitats of our native gamefish. No study had been made of the carp in 1876, and the *wunderkind* touted as "a cheap but sumptuous food" became a textbook example of the dangers of exotic species.

The U. S. Fish Commission placed 345 adult carp in its breeding ponds at Druid Hill Park in Baltimore, Maryland. Their numbers increased so rapidly that in the

Carp. Finials on bench ends in Jakobikirche (St. James Church), Lübeck, on the Baltic, are a reminder of the original occupation of James the Apostle, who from a fisherman became a fisher of men.

politically oriented environment of nearby Washington, D. C., a scheme arose to make every voter a carp farmer. Any Congressman could bestow a few carp on his constituents, and in 1883 alone 260,000 fish were distributed to 298 of the 301 Congressional Districts. These were transported on special refrigerated cars and the inevitable population explosion of carp was phenomenal. The fish found their way through broken dams and by indiscriminate stocking to waters that held bountiful supplies of trout, pike and bass. The adaptable carp took over. Eradication of carp populations through netting and eventually chemical treatment became more important than carp production. Against this publicity the carp never found a widely receptive kitchen in America, except by people of Central European origins. Since its introduction, however, the carp has become widely distributed from coast to coast and in southern Canada. It is most abundant in our Mississippi River drainage where 16 to 17 million pounds are caught and sold each year; our overall commercial harvest in the U. S. runs at slightly less than 30 million pounds annually. Although it thrives under a wide range of conditions, the carp prefers warm streams and lakes with an abundance of organic matter; many algae produce a mossy taste in fish flesh, and especially carp, during summer months and for this reason winter is their prime season.

There is only one carp *(Cyprinus carpio)* that appears in various guises for culinary use. These are selectively bred strains with different body shapes and scale patterns, characteristics which have become stabilized in centuries-old experiments to develop a faster-growing fish. The typical wild carp is three times as long as its body is deep and is fully scaled; it grows slowly and matures late in life. Selectively bred varieties are known as "king" carp to distinguish these from the wild strain. There are two recognized king body shapes: the longer, thick-bodied Lausitz, Bohemian, and French strains; and the shorter, deep-bodied Galician and Israeli strains. These domesticated carp may have scales like the wild fish, or they may be the singularly endowed "mirror" carp which have scales distributed in one row along each side, called Israeli Carp, or they may have scales spread haphazardly over the body, which the Russians describe as *ramchatyi* (framelike). Mirror carp have been stocked in some American waters and are caught from time to time in our southern and central states. The third strain is completely scaleless and is called a "leather" carp. Selective breeding has been pursued for other reasons. The Russians, for example, have produced a cold-resistant strain for stocking in sub-Arctic waters, and the Chinese a **Hi-goi** or golden carp which is both ornamental and supposedly more attractive to the consumer. Despite a profusion of names the quality of a carp, gastronomically speaking, depends on the season and the quality of the water it was taken from.

If you catch your own carp the fish should be killed and bled immediately by cutting through the body from the back of the head to the rear of its gills. The dorsal or "back" fin can then be cut out and the scales and outer skin removed by a process known as "flensing." This requires a very sharp, thin-bladed knife. Grasp the carp by the tail and shave both the scales and skin off in strips by working the knife toward the head but without cutting the flesh. The body cavity is then split from back to front, care being used to avoid cutting into the viscera which may then be removed as a whole. The head is then cut off back of the front fins, and the tail and other fins cut away. The fish is then thoroughly cleansed in cold water.

A simpler operation which removes the entire skin is to plunge the fish (or its fillets) into boiling water, allowing it to remain for about 25 seconds after boiling starts again. The skin may then be easily rubbed off while the fish is hot, and the flesh rinsed in cold water. If the boiling is continued too long, the flesh may break up.

BASIC PREPARATION

After dressing, the carp should be treated with a dry marinade which will greatly improve its flavor. Cover the dressed fish or fillet with a mixture made in the following proportions:

1 cup salt	1 teaspoon black pepper
1 cup ground onion	⅛ teaspoon grated mace
2 tablespoons vinegar	

Grind the onion by passing through the finest plate of a food chopper, saving all the juice. Mix the ingredients thoroughly. Place the fish in a deep plate, cover all surfaces with the mixture, and allow it to stand for 1 hour. Thoroughly rinse the fish and discard the mixture. Wash the fish in a pan of cold water for about 1 minute to remove any traces of salt on its surface.

FRIED CARP

Prepare fish following basic preparation. Split or fillet to about ⅝-inch thickness. Wet in cold water and roll in a mixture of cornmeal and flour or crumbs as desired. Do not use additional seasoning. Fry the fish by the same methods used for other fish.

BROILED CARP

Prepare the fish according to basic preparation. Split, or fillet, to about ⅝-inch thickness. Broil without additional salt or pepper.

BAKED CARP

Prepare the fish according to basic preparation. Bake whole with stuffing, or bake flat in slices, but without additional seasoning. Add sliced onions, stewed tomatoes or other suitable vegetables if desired; or serve with Creole, white or other sauces. For an excellent dish dip the slices of fish into unsalted milk, roll in sifted bread crumbs, and pour 1 teaspoon of cooking oil over each serving portion of fish. Place the fish in an oiled pan and bake in a preheated oven at 550° to 600°F. for 10 minutes.

BOILED CARP

Prepare the fish according to basic preparation. Boil in salted water for 8 minutes, allowing 1½ tablespoons salt to each quart of water. Any desired sauce may be served with the fish. Extra portions can be used for flaked fish dishes.

PAPRIKA CARP IN THE HUNGARIAN MANNER

4 pounds carp	1 tablespoon paprika
1 teaspoon salt	(Noble Sweet)
2 medium-size onions, minced	½ pound green peppers
1 tablespoon oil	1 medium-size tomato
1 tablespoon butter	1 teaspoon flour
2 tablespoons water or fish stock	3 tablespoons sour cream
	rings of yellow, green and red peppers

Clean the carp; cut it into 12 to 15 pieces, and season them with salt. Fry onions in mixture of oil and butter (or use 1 heaping teaspoon of lard). Remove from heat and add the water or fish stock and the paprika. Cut green peppers to ½-inch pieces. Peel and dice the tomato. Add to onions and bring to a slow boil. Cover and cook for 20 to 22 minutes. Place pieces of the carp in the vegetable mixture and cook for 5 to 7 minutes, or until done. Transfer 2 large spoonfuls of the liquid to a separate container; add flour and sour cream. Mix, and return to the rest of the mixture. Decorate with pepper rings. Makes 6 servings.

Catfish

On the basis of availability the U. S. leads all other nations in the consumption of catfish. Literally millions are caught here each year, particularly in our southern and central states. The sport catch is augmented by a commercial industry involving hundreds of thousands of acres of ponds in 34 states under the leadership of the Catfish Farmers of America. This profitable wet crop yields up to 2,000 pounds per acre. Catfish are marketed through modern processing plants under rigid state and federal controls. Some of the larger operations purvey 10,000 pounds of fresh and frozen catfish per week. Their major buyers include supermarkets, restaurants and over-the-counter dealers.

While the prime sales have so far been below the Mason-Dixon Line, the demand in the North now exceeds the supply. Such disparate enclaves as San Francisco, Chicago and New York have discovered that catfish are a gastronomic delight. When less good, it's rarely a matter of flesh quality but often the inability of the chef. The popular method is deep-frying, which requires careful attention to detail. In this respect the catfish is one of the most abused foods I can think of; in many "family-style" restaurants along the cornmeal circuit, the volume, age and temperature of the oil is as predictable as Halley's Comet; even the hush puppies resemble lead sinkers. When prepared by an honest craftsman, catfish becomes a noble dish, one for which I have seen people spurn a prime steak, when both arrived at table.

There are 28 species of catfish in North American waters, varying in size from the inch-long madtom to our giant blue catfish which may weigh up to 120 pounds. The largest catfish in the world are found in the Amazon Basin and in European rivers east of the Rhine, where they have been recorded to over 600 pounds. The largest known catfish was caught in the USSR: the fish was 16½ feet in length and weighed 660 pounds. This is the wels catfish *(Siluris glanis)*. In the U. S. the three most popular species are the channel, white and blue catfish. Among aficionados, half-pounders that can be crisped and eaten like corn on the cob are the ultimate. In sophisticated southern cities large catfish dominate the market. The reason is that a city like Atlanta, for example, is conditioned to steaked and filleted saltwater fish. The crosscuts taken from a large channel or blue catfish find a more receptive audience in restaurants where free-style finger-licking is the custom.

There are about 10 freshwater catfishes of the family Ictaluridae, and 2 marine species in the family Ariidae that enter U. S. kitchens. The remaining members of our North American group consist principally of very small "madtoms" which have no value except as bait. The edible varieties include certain bullheads which are true catfish. While regional names are both numerous and confusing, a rule of the thumb is that any species which achieves pan size is worthy of rolling in cornmeal. There are qualitative differences, to be sure, but all catfish have a comparatively simple skeletal structure that provides boneless eating; the meat can be prepared by every cooking method. While it's true that deep-fried catfish is a classic, these fish can be turned into a chowder, aspic, *étouffée*, *quenelle* or just about any other form of presentation. Smoked catfish is marvelous but, unfortunately, a very local product. Most catfish, with the exception of the brown bullhead and yellow bullhead, have a good shelf life. The frozen packages at market (which consist mainly of channel catfish and to some extent the white and blue) are generally of prime quality.

Of the many South American catfishes which are taken commercially and appear in restaurants on that continent, the **surubi** or giant river catfish *(Bagre giganticus)* is most popular, but probably because of its large size. I have seen 6-foot-long fillets drying on jungle beaches. From a market standpoint the sheer quantity of boneless meat is appealing, however, I find the product both dry and "cottony" in texture. Even at a classic little *hosteria* in Corrientes on the Paraná River, where the food was excellent by any measure, a **surubi** in aspic prepared with great skill could only be described as a culinary debacle. The **rayado** or tiger catfish *(Pseudoplatysoma fasciatum)*, on the other hand, is in the class of our channel catfish, moist but firm with a delicate river flavor. The name **bagre** is rather widely used in South America to encompass catfish in general, and it's difficult to say what will arrive at table as there are hundreds of species. One can only decide after sampling it whether the local kind is worth repeating at subsequent meals.

When dining in Europe one must make a distinction in the use of the name "catfish." The extremely large and only member of the family found in Europe is *Siluris glanis*, more commonly known as the **wels.** The name **Katfische** in Germany, for example, is applied to the marine wolffish. In Europe the wels occurs from the Rhine River eastward, including tributaries to the Black, Caspian and Aral Seas. The wolffish, on the other hand, is a North Atlantic member of the Anarhichadidae and totally unlike a catfish in texture or flavor *(see WOLFFISH)*. In the U. K. it's often marketed as "ocean catfish" or "sea cat"; however, the wels catfish occurs in some of England's lakes.

HOW TO DRESS CATFISH

Catfish have skin similar to that of an eel, which is thick, slippery and strong. Regardless of size all catfish should be skinned, even the larger ones which can then be cut into fillets or steaks. However, catfish must be handled carefully as they have very sharp spinous rays on the leading edge of their dorsal and pectoral fins. These rays have a locking mechanism which enables the live fish to hold them erect as a defense weapon. In some catfish these needlepoint spines have a poison gland at their base; if they puncture your hand the toxin produces a paralyzing sensation much like a severe beesting. Both the sea and walking catfish can maneuver their pectoral fins and should be handled with extra caution.

There are various ways of skinning catfish; while some methods are quicker than the one I will describe, these require more experience and could result in a punctured amateur hand even when the fish is dead. The easy method is to drive a heavy nail through a board, using the nail point to hold the catfish firmly in place. Lay the catfish belly down on the board; grasp the fish on top of the head between thumb and forefinger and make a cut through the skin just in back of the head, bringing the blade around and behind each pectoral fin to circle the nape. Next, impale the head of the catfish on the nail; grasp the incised skin with pliers and peel it off as you would skin an eel. Catfish skin varies in density; a thin-skinned species like the yellow bullhead is more difficult to "peel" than the thick-skinned brown bullhead. The skin should come free in one piece with a bit of practice, but if it does divide along the back simply repeat the process. Cut off the head, slit the belly, and remove entrails.

The only catfish that poses a unique problem in dressing is the armored catfish. These members of the family Loricariidae were accidentally introduced to Florida from South America, and some specimens have been caught north of Miami and in the Tampa Bay area. As the name implies, armored catfish are covered with heavy bony plates instead of scales and are virtually impossible to penetrate with a knife. Although I doubt if the average person would care to eat one if he caught one, Amazonian Indians simply toss them in a fire whole and after roasting they crack the "shell" to pry the meat loose.

CATFISH TERMINOLOGY

BLACK BULLHEAD This species is found from the St. Lawrence River west to North Dakota and south to Northern Mexico. The black bullhead *(Ictalurus melas)* has a nearly square tail and jet-black fin membranes. It frequents warmwater ponds and sluggish streams and is extremely tolerant of both pollution and turbidity. This is the "horned pout" of our eastern and midwestern states; it's readily caught by angling. The black bullhead is edible when taken from clear, unpolluted waters, but due to its small size the fish is of no commercial importance. The maximum weight is about 2 pounds, but fish of ¼ to ½ pound are the usual run.

BLUE CATFISH Found in large rivers from Minnesota and Ohio southward to northern Mexico. Introduced to eastern U. S. and the second most important species in commercial fish farming. The blue catfish *(Ictalurus furcatus)* has a deeply forked tail and is readily identified by its color, a silvery pale blue dorsally to a milk-white below. The blue prefers clear, swift streams with a rock, gravel or sand substrate. It has been recorded to 150 pounds, but most large specimens weigh from 20 to 30 pounds. An excellent table fish, the blue is eagerly sought throughout its range.

The blue catfish was an important commercial species before the turn of the century. The industry was centered at Morgan City, Louisiana, where in the short period from May to September, more than 2 million pounds were processed from the Atchafalaya River alone. The catfish were delivered in live boxes towed by tugboats, then dressed, iced, and shipped all over the U. S.

This catfish is considered the very best by many gourmets; it has firm, sweet snow-white meat. It is a large fish when marketed and should be steaked or filleted.

BROWN BULLHEAD The brown bullhead *(Ictalurus nebulosus)* is a small slender catfish, usually yellowish brown to chocolate brown in color, with dark mottlings on its back and a yellow to white belly. It's found from Maine to the Great Lakes and south to Florida and Mexico. It reaches a maximum weight of about 7 pounds but is more

Brown bullhead, a catfish

commonly caught at less than 1 pound. The meat of this bullhead is pink to red in color and is often marketed as "red cat." It does not keep as well as other catfish and should be iced as quickly as possible.

CHANNEL CATFISH Our most important American catfish is found from the Great Lakes south to Virginia and west to Mexico. It has been widely introduced elsewhere in North America. This species *(Ictalurus punctatus)* is recognized by its deeply forked tail and scattered black spots along its sides; the spotting disappears with age and old fish become inky black. Although mainly a stream fish, the channel catfish also occurs in some large lakes. It is valuable to both the sport and commercial fisheries and is intensively farmed in the southern U.S. Not tolerant of pollution, it requires well-oxygenated water and is reliably an excellent foodfish. The smaller channel catfish of up to 3 pounds, often called "sharpies" or "fiddlers," are most desirable, but the species does attain weights to 60 pounds. The flesh is firm and white, and of delicate flavor.

Albino channel catfish or "golden cats" have recently become popular in the restaurant trade because of their eye appeal. Albinos are rare in a natural habitat but these mutations can be culled and propagated under hatchery conditions. Albino fish of any kind may be white but are just as frequently yellow in color and with black eyes rather than red.

FLAT BULLHEAD Found from the Roanoke River in Virginia southward to the Altamaha River in Georgia. This species *(Ictalurus platycephalus)* has an emarginate or slightly forked tail, a flattened head and a narrow black margin on all median fins. It is usually brown in color and is often called "brown cat." In some watersheds the body may have a strong yellowish coloration, so it is sometimes confused with the yellow bullhead. However, the lower third of its dorsal fin has a prominent black band or blotch. The flat bullhead occurs in streams, lakes and ponds with soft muck, mud or sand bottoms. Only a small poundage of this species is taken commercially, but its flesh is comparable to that of the channel catfish. Maximum size is about 2 pounds, but it averages less than 1 pound.

FLATHEAD CATFISH Found in large rivers from the Mississippi River system east to Pennsylvania and south into Mexico. Easily recognized by its broad, flat head, large adipose fin and projecting lower jaw. This species *(Pylodictis olivaris)* favors long, deep pools with slow currents especially around logs and down timber. An omnivorous feeder with a preference for other fish and crayfish, the flathead is largely nocturnal and angling is most effective at night. The flathead attains weights up to 100 pounds but averages 3 to 4 pounds. Fish of 20 to 30 pounds are fairly common. Commercially important because of its large size, it is also known regionally as the goujon or yellow cat.

GAFFTOPSAIL CATFISH Found along the Atlantic Coast through the Gulf of Mexico and south to Panama. This catfish *(Bagre marinus)* occurs in brackish waters in bays and estuaries; like the sea catfish, it lacks nasal barbels; it has 4 barbels, whereas the sea catfish has 6 barbels. Both the dorsal and pectoral fins end in long striated filaments. The gafftopsail feeds chiefly on crabs and other crustaceans. It is susceptible to cold-kills, and large numbers die in unseasonable weather. Maximum weight about 8 pounds with a ½-pound average. Contrary to popular belief, it's a good table fish and a substantial poundage enters our Gulf States commercial fishery.

GREEN BULLHEAD Found from Cape Fear, North Carolina, to the St. John's River in Florida. This species has an emarginate caudal fin, an inferior mouth with decurved snout and a flattened head. Although the body coloration is generally uniform, it's sometimes spotted and occasionally mottled. The green bullhead *(Ictalurus brunneus)* occurs in streams and rivers with a moderate to swift current over gravel or rock bottoms. It's usually caught in pools below riffles and dams or in deep channels. Good eating but of little commercial value due to its small size. Maximum weight about 1½ pounds, but averages ¼ pound.

SEA CATFISH Found along the Atlantic Coast from Cape Cod to Texas and the West Indies. The sea catfish *(Galeichthys felis)* prefers higher salinities than the gafftopsail, but the young fish occur in brackish waters. Distinguished by absence of nasal barbels and the presence of 4 barbels on its chin. Maximum weight about 3 pounds, but averages ½ pound.

SPOTTED BULLHEAD Found from northern Florida to southern Georgia and westward to southeastern Alabama, the spotted bullhead has a very limited range. This species *(Ictalurus serracanthus)* has a flattened head, and is readily distinguished by its spotted body and the strong serrations on its pectoral fins. This bullhead occurs in large streams and rivers with moderate currents and in impounded lakes within its range. Relatively abundant in limited areas, it may outnumber the white and channel catfish in certain locations. A mollusk feeder, it is commonly called "snailcat." Rarely taken with nets but commonly in commercial slat traps and on hook-and-line. Edible but small, its maximum weight is probably about 1 pound with the average in Suwannee, Ochlockonee, and Apalachicola Rivers running ¼ pound.

facing page, Panfried channel catfish at Chez Helene, New Orleans

Yellow bullhead, a catfish

WALKING CATFISH Accidentally introduced to Florida from Bangkok in 1966 and now found in a discontiguous range in the Tampa Bay area and from Lake Okeechobee south to Miami. The walking catfish *(Clarias batrachus)* can breathe air; this coupled with ability to migrate over land and thrive in brackish water makes its ultimate range unknown. Only the lethal temperature zone (from 41° to 48°F.) has kept the species from invading other states; it is often found on Florida roads after a rain. Edible, but it's difficult to remove the thin, foul-smelling skin. Use extreme caution in handling, as pectoral spines cause severe pain.

WHITE CATFISH Found in coastal streams from the Chesapeake Bay region to Texas, the white catfish has been widely introduced elsewhere in U. S. waters. This species *(Ictalurus catus)* has a slightly forked tail, and a more rounded head than the channel catfish with which it is sometimes confused. Basically prefers slow currents but also occurs in brackish estuaries. An imported sport and commercial species because of its firm white flesh, the white catfish is popular in "pay" lakes. Maximum size about 15 pounds but averages 1 pound. This catfish makes extensive random migrations in rivers and is known to occur near the surface of very deep lakes.

YELLOW BULLHEAD Found from New York to Florida and west to North Dakota. This species *(Ictalurus natalis)* has a rounded tail and sharp serrations on its pectoral spines. The lower jaw barbels are whitish and distinguish the yellow from the brown bullhead with its black barbels. Of some importance commercially, the yellowish flesh is palatable but doesn't keep well; it must be served fresh. Maximum size is about 3 pounds but averages less than 1 pound.

BAYOU CATFISH

6 pan-dressed skinned catfish	2 tablespoons lemon juice
1 cup dry white wine	2 tablespoons chopped parsley
½ cup melted fat or oil	2 teaspoons salt
½ cup chopped fresh mushrooms	¼ teaspoon crushed bay leaf
¼ cup chopped green onions	¼ teaspoon pepper
	¼ teaspoon dried thyme

Cut 6 squares of heavy-duty aluminum foil, 18 inches each. Grease lightly. Place a fish on half of each foil square. Combine remaining ingredients. Pour sauce over fish, using approximately ⅓ cup sauce for each fish. Fold other half of foil over fish and seal edges by making double folds in the foil. Place packages of fish on a barbecue grill about 6 inches from moderately hot coals. Cook for 20 to 25 minutes, or until fish flakes easily when tested with a fork. To serve, cut a big crisscross in the top of each package and fold the foil back. Makes 6 servings.

SESAME CATFISH

6 pan-dressed skinned catfish	4 tablespoons lemon juice
½ cup melted fat or oil	1 teaspoon salt
½ cup sesame seeds	dash of pepper

Basting with this simple sesame-seed sauce enhances the flavor and adds a crunch to each bite. Place fish in well-greased, hinged wire grills. Combine remaining ingredients. Baste fish with sauce. Cook about 4 inches from moderately hot coals for 8 minutes. Baste with sauce. Turn and cook for 7 to 10 minutes longer, or until fish flakes when tested with a fork. Makes 6 servings.

Caviar

In this modern age when writing about caviar one has the feeling that it should be in the form of an obituary, as the world supply has dwindled to a trickle and its price has risen to such heights that it can no longer be classed as a mere fishery product. Caviar has been made in the Soviet Union (it is known in Russian as **ikra**) since the thirteenth century. Due to primitive methods of trade and transport, other countries only learned of this delicacy at a much later date. The word "caviar" is a corruption of the Turkish *havyar*. It is the roe of various sturgeons whose eggs range in color from pearly gray to pale brown. When properly made, caviar eggs have the firmness of ripe huckleberries; in fact, the individual egg is known in the commercial trade as a "berry." When crunched between the teeth, a berry leaves a taste that is unique—faintly salty and nutlike. This is not true of many caviar substitutes, which we will discuss in due course, but the true product is the opening note of great gourmet dinners throughout the world. It is no longer served in the quantities available to a more opulent generation, and even generous Palm Beach hostesses are inclined to measure portions by the spoon.

Until 1966 any fish roe that could be colored black was called caviar. The whitefish, carp and paddlefish supplied large quantities of roe for the American market, and some of this "caviar" stained the customer's mouth a bilious green because of the added dye. Then the Food and Drug Administration defined the product, limiting it to sturgeon eggs. Even within the legal definition of caviar there is a wide variation in quality, since there are at least 22 species of sturgeon in the Northern Hemisphere from which roe is taken, and the eggs are processed in many different ways.

Historically, the best caviar is made from the roe of the yellow-bellied sterlet. Comparatively few people in the world have ever tasted these pearls beyond price. This delicacy was once known as the "golden caviar" of the Czars and was reserved exclusively for the Russian Imperial Court where it was ceremoniously served to music. Even if you could find it today it would cost a fortune. No doubt scarcity played some role in this regal choice. During the years when General Malcolm Beyer was president of Iron Gate Products, and the foremost caviar importer in North America, I had the privilege of attending a lunch he designed in honor of the Soviet Ambassador to the United Nations at the Hunt Room of the 21 Club. It consisted of 6 kinds of caviar—beluga, osietr, sevruga, ship, pausnaya, and Russian salmon caviar for contrast. I doubt if such an offering could ever be duplicated. It was downed with frosted thimbles of ice-cold vodka. I finally decided that osietr was the best for my taste, although I have never sampled it since, and only remember a faint vanilla fragrance and nutlike flavor.

The finest caviar exported from the Soviet Union and Iran—in sufficient quantities to supply the restaurants of the world—is made from the roe of the beluga. The giant beluga reaches a weight of 2,500 pounds. It is found through the Caspian Sea, Sea of Azov, and in the eastern Mediterranean as far west as the Danube River. The beluga is the largest sturgeon, so it produces the largest berries and commands the highest price. First-quality beluga caviar is packed as *malosol*, which in Russian means "little salt." In other words, malosol is not a brand of caviar but a type distinguished from caviar that has been heavily salted and eventually packed into the jars found on delicatessen shelves. Salt, of course, tends to shrink the egg and change its color, so the art in making caviar is knowing just how much salt to use and then keeping the product at exactly the right temperature. In round figures 1 pound of salt is sufficient for 1 *pud* or *pood* of caviar, a pud being a Russian weight unit approximating 36 American pounds.

The grotesque source of caviar is a primitive fish that probably lives to be 100 years old. Despite the precise methods of ichthyology, the accurate determination of sturgeon age is a fairly recent technique. The annuli, or growth rings, on a fish scale can be interpreted in somewhat the same fashion as the annual rings of a tree trunk. However, sturgeon do not have scales, their body covering being a series of bony plates. Eventually, Soviet researchers discovered that the first bony ray of the pectoral fin could be cross-sectioned and analyzed with accuracy. Generally speaking, it requires 9 to 15 years, depending on the species, for a female sturgeon to mature or develop the ripe ovaries that become "caviar." The beluga requires 20 years or more. This fact was unknown before 1900, which was the pivotal year in the sudden decline in sturgeon populations. Corn can be planted and harvested in a matter of months, then replanted, but a minimal 9-year-old crop was beyond comprehension.

Sturgeon are the largest fish to enter freshwater; yet this great size is sustained by the barest essentials. With the exception of the beluga, which eats other fish and sometimes seals, their diets consist of insect larvae, mollusks, worms, crayfish and plant life. Beneath the sturgeon's snout is a protractile, toothless mouth with thickened lips that operate much like a vacuum cleaner when foraging along the bottom. Seven different species of sturgeon are found in U.S. waters. Among these the white sturgeon of the West, ranging from Alaska south to Monterey, California, is the largest, reaching a weight of 1,800 pounds. Also in the Pacific is the green sturgeon, which is hardly edible, being dark-meated and disagreeable in both taste and odor—although it is a source of caviar. The Atlantic sturgeon ranges from Maine into the Gulf of Mexico, and the lake sturgeon of the Great Lakes watershed has flesh which is superior to any Soviet fish. The shortnose and pallid sturgeons are inland freshwater species of the Atlantic seaboard, and the shovelnose inhabits the Mississippi Valley.

The Atlantic or simply "sea sturgeon" was the species that for a brief period in American history was a tremendous resource. Sea sturgeon still puncture the nets of Hudson River shad fishermen not far from the George Washington Bridge, but these are mere ghosts of a horde that once existed next to an island now surrounded by sewers. When Henry Hudson arrived in 1609 he observed that "there are plenty of sturgeon which the Christians do not make use of, but the Indians eat them greedily." (Report to the East India Company of Amsterdam 1609. The sturgeon was a favorite food of all eastern riverine tribes. John Josselyn [New England's Rarities, published in London, 1672] observed that "the Indians have in their greatest request, the Bass, the Sturgeon, the Salmon, the Lamprey, the Eel, the Frostfish, the Lobster, and the Clam." He also stated that the settlers made caviare or cavialtie of the roe but it had little popularity.) In truth, the fish was largely ignored during the next 200 years. Efforts were made to popularize sturgeon as a food in America during the 1820s, but a fish of 200 pounds in size only brought 12 to 30 cents on the market and its roe was considered worthless. Then an enterprising immigrant, Henry Schacht, established a caviar business on the Delaware River near Chester, Pennsylvania, in 1873. Treated with "the finest German salt" his caviar was shipped to Europe (and often back to the U.S.) and commanded a dollar per pound. A subsequent plant built in 1880 at Bay Side, New Jersey, in which its investors poured more than one million dollars—a veritable fortune in that day—began to harvest sturgeon to the point that a thousand or more fish were always in view on its docks. The meat was shipped to Centre Market in Albany, New York, and was sold as "Albany beef" for mere pennies per pound. The market was often glutted but men continued to kill sturgeon as if the supply were limitless. In the short span of 27 years, the industry which Schacht had pioneered was virtually finished. Although futile attempts were made to propagate sturgeon artificially, the Report of the Commissioners of Fisheries of the State of Pennsylvania in 1900 clearly tells the story:

We regret to say that the sturgeon fisheries of the Delaware River are about at an end. Although we have foreseen the end for the last three or four years, it has come sooner than we expected. For the last six or seven years the catch has annually been cut in half. This year the total catch of sturgeon in the Delaware River and Bay was but 1,416 fish from which were made 308 kegs of caviar. Last year the catch exclusive of Delaware was 2,510 fish from which were made 726½ kegs of caviar. The Delaware catch last year was 700 fish approximately, from which were made exactly 200 kegs of caviar.

To keep perspective, a "keg" represented 135 pounds of caviar; the disparity between the year 1899 with a total production of about 125,077 pounds as opposed to 41,580 pounds of caviar in 1900 was indeed alarming. In 1882 caviar sold for $3 to $6 per keg, and by the turn of the century it had risen to an unprecedented $110 per keg. In this modern age that same keg would retail at about $14,850.00. During its halcyon period the Delaware River fishery produced an incredible 270 to over 674 tons of caviar per year. However, much of this was disguised as a foreign import according to the Pennsylvania report:

From 1884 to 1890 there were from 4,000 to 5,000 kegs of caviar shipped annually from the Delaware River, mostly from Bay Side, and about this time the Delaware River caviar began to dominate the market, although under the name of Russian caviar. Today it is safe to say that fully nine-tenths of the Russian caviar sold in the American and European markets is manufactured from the roe of sturgeon caught in the Delaware River.

In parallel with the collapse of our eastern sturgeon fishery the commercial fisheries in the West, notably on the Columbia River, began exploiting the species in 1888. Their peak production was reached in 1892 when 6 million pounds of sturgeon were taken from that watershed; 10 years later the total catch was a mere 100,000 pounds. Before the turn of the century the fish was virtually extinct. The highly perishable roe had been of less importance than the frozen meat which was sent by railroad to Chicago and New York, although western caviar did supplement the eastern production for a brief period. The bubbles burst almost simultaneously. Legislation was quickly enacted to protect the remaining stocks but it would take years for these slow-growing fish to recover. Thus, real Russian caviar began its costly rise to fame.

HOW TO STORE AND SERVE CAVIAR

The modern refrigerator with its compartments for below-freezing-point storage presents a problem for the storage of caviar for, once frozen and thawed, the berries will have burst; the product becomes mushy and the quality deteriorates. The proper temperature for long storage is 26°F., or 6°F. below the freezing point of water. The salt content of caviar permits this lower temperature. Stored at 26°F. caviar will retain its delicacy for many months.

Serving caviar begins with buying. The most important thing to look for is that each berry is whole, uncrushed, and well coated with its own glistening fat. Before you pay a small fortune per pound, make certain that the fat has not risen to the surface of the can during transport. This is sometimes scooped off by the purveyor for some favorite customer, leaving the uncoated berries for less-discriminating wallets. A conscientious caviar merchant sees that the tins in his refrigerator are turned frequently to keep the fat well distributed.

The best caviar is generally eaten as is, *au natural*, on a piece of freshly made thin toast, with or without butter; though the caviar itself should be fat enough not to require butter. Caviar that is more heavily salted than the malosol grade can stand a few drops of lemon juice, or it may be sprinkled lightly with some finely chopped egg white, egg yolk, onions or chives. The Russian style (usually with pressed caviar) of serving this delicacy is to heap it high on *blini* (small thin pancakes), sprinkle with onions and chopped eggs to taste, and generously anoint with very thick sour cream.

The crowning achievement of an epicurean sportsman is to serve caviar with the breast meat of cold roast pheasant minced extremely fine. It must not be ground, but knife-chopped. Each guest heaps as much caviar as he wants on a piece of dry toast or very thin black bread, then sprinkles the minced pheasant meat over the caviar. The meat shouldn't be piled on the caviar—use just the amount that will adhere to the surface. Caviar also marries well with smoked salmon; thin slices of salmon are generously spread with beluga and then rolled in a cornet shape (**Les Cornets de Saumon Fumé Astrachan**); serve with butter curls on toast points. One other accompaniment worthy of mention is the oyster, which can be sprinkled with grated onion, then garnished with fresh caviar (**Oysters Czar Nicolas**).

Naturally many chefs have tried to incorporate caviar into various dishes, but once cooked or mixed with other ingredients, the true caviar flavor is lost, although a plain French dressing made with very little and very fine wine vinegar and the best of olive oil reaches new heights when a generous amount of caviar is stirred in it. This dressing, however, is to be used only with a plain green salad such as Bibb lettuce and not in the stronger flavored, mixed-green salads.

HOW TO MAKE CAVIAR

Although the average chef, hobbyist, or professional is not likely to be faced with the task of making caviar, thousands of sturgeon are caught by anglers each year, particularly in Canada, our midwestern and western states. Frantic phone calls to *Field & Stream's* office indicate that a considerable percentage of their lucky captors don't know how to begin to use these roes. Bear in mind that the method of treating the roes is also applicable to other species of fish in making caviar substitutes such as salmon caviar or paddlefish caviar.

Caviar is made from the roes of any freshly caught sturgeon. In common with other primitive fishes such as the sharks and paddlefish, the sturgeon has a cartilaginous skeleton and its "backbone" is really a flexible sheath or notochord. When dressing a sturgeon the fish is cut around the base of the tail, then with a twisting motion the notochord is pulled free. This tough whitish sheath can be split, cleaned, air-dried, and made into a soup. After the notochord is removed the fish is bled for about an hour before butchering or removing the roe. The eggs should be washed on a fine screen with a mesh size larger than the individual eggs, permitting the eggs to fall into a tub or bowl placed beneath the screen. This is done by *gently* stirring the roe to separate the eggs from the tissue and sac. They are then tenderly washed in cold water, changing the water 3 or 4 times, and drained for not more than 10 minutes, removing any froth. After draining, the eggs should be salted, using 5 ounces of very fine-grained salt to each 10 pounds of eggs (approximately 3 percent). Immediately after this is done, the caviar should be placed in a sliplid tin or a jar, with *no* air left in the container. The caviar must be held under refrigeration at a temperature of 26° to 30°F. It will reach its peak of delicacy in 1 week, and should be served before 6 months have elapsed, for after that it may lose its delicacy and eye appeal very rapidly.

CAVIAR TERMINOLOGY

BELUGA The largest egg, gray in color, with a 3 to 4 percent salt content (malosol).
MALOSOL From the Russian; it simply means "little salt." All types of caviar can be prepared malosol and are thus considered *fresh* caviar. Due to the small amount of salt used, constant refrigeration during transport is essen-

tial, which makes any malosol caviar more expensive.

OSIETR This is the Russian word for sturgeon, but it also represents the species *(Acipenser sturio)* most sought for its eating qualities. The flesh is particularly delicious when smoked. Specimens have been caught as large as 700 pounds. The osietr produces a caviar that is golden-brown in color and has a delightful nutlike flavor.

PAUSNAYA The Russian word for pressed caviar. Not all sturgeon roe is packed whole-grain. The smaller damaged or less-firm eggs, of all types of caviar that are sieved out during the grading process, are prepared as *pausnaya*, literally "pressed caviar." Pressed caviar is usually packed in barrels of 100 pounds each, though sometimes in the same type of tin as the whole-grain caviar. When available for export, it is lightly salted and of excellent flavor. It resembles in its final state a gooey mass similar to a thick marmalade. Many connoisseurs prefer pressed caviar to the whole-grain variety.

SEVRUGA This is the smallest yet most prolific species *(Acipenser sevru)*. It may reach a weight of 100 pounds, but usually enters the fishery at 35 to 50 pounds. The eggs of its roe are small, dark gray to black in color, but of exceptionally fine flavor.

STERLET This is an almost extinct species *(Acipenser ruthenus)*, relatively small, but highly esteemed for its roe. Sterlet is the legendary "gold" caviar of the Czars and is rarely seen outside the Soviet Union.

SHIP This is a hybrid sturgeon resulting from a cross between the osietr and the sevruga. It is seldom found in areas other than the deltas of the rivers near Baku on the Caspian Sea. The roe is particularly firm and produces an excellent caviar, but it is always in short supply.

There are numerous caviar substitutes. The labeling laws in most countries today require specific identification when the word "caviar" is used in connection with roes of any species other than the sturgeon; for example, salmon caviar, lumpfish caviar, or cod caviar must appear on the label. However, many of these, which hardly resemble real caviar, are exceptionally enjoyable and can be appreciated as a distinct taste experience.

CAVIAR SUBSTITUTES

ALEWIFE CAVIAR *See under HERRING.*

CARP CAVIAR *See under CARP.*

HERRING CAVIAR *See under HERRING.*

HON-TARAKO A Japanese product made from the roe of cod which has been salted and dyed a red color.

KARASUMI A Japanese product made from the roe of mullet which has been salted.

LUMPFISH CAVIAR With the great decline in sturgeon

top, Lumpfish roe; bottom, Herring roe

stocks during the 1950s the homely lumpfish achieved stardom as a substitute in providing a "caviar" that is more familiar to most people than the genuine item. In various European translations the lumpfish is better known as henfish and sea hen because of its great fertility; a female of 18 inches in length will bear about 140,000 eggs. The lumpfish is found on both sides of the North Atlantic; in the West it ranges from Hudson Bay south to Chesapeake Bay; in the eastern Atlantic, it is found on both shores of Greenland, Iceland, the Faroes, and in the White Sea south to Gascoyne Bay, France.

The lumpfish belongs to the family Cyclopteridae, a group of small, stout-bodied fishes whose pelvic fins are modified to form an adhesive disc with which they can cling to rocks, weeds and logs; they have even been found attached inside floating barrels and boxes. Despite this unusual talent the lumpfish is covered with wartlike tubercles instead of scales and has a cartilaginous ridge along its back; its body coloration is best described as greenish, bluish, brownish and yellowish, with a splash of bright red on the belly of a breeding male. In brief, when

facing page, Beluga caviar, Iran

clinging to a rock it simply looks like a "lump." However, when lumpfish invade shallow shores (it is normally a benthic or deepwater species) in the spring to spawn, the female bears a huge quantity of eggs that are no more than 1/10 inch in diameter. This roe is the basis of a very considerable industry, particularly in Scandinavia. The egg mass changes in color from yellow to dark green as it develops and only gains its familiar black color when processed in vegetable dye.

There is very little market for fresh lumpfish in America. Its flesh, which is both rich and oily, is greatly esteemed in Denmark where cutlets of the **stenbider** are usually poached and served cold in aspic, or smoked and used as an hors d'oeuvre. The quality of lumpfish caviar is determined mainly by the amount of salt used, unlike sturgeon caviar which has variations in both egg size and flavor; many commercial products are overpreserved. Lumpfish roe, mildly salted as in Denmark, is perhaps the standard bearer by which this delicacy should be judged. (This is vastly different from cheap U.S. commercial products which are literally "jarred" in tragacanth gum and benzoate of soda.) Also known as **Seehase** or **Lumpfisch** (Germany), **Snotdolf** (Holland), **Hrognkelsi** (Iceland), **Stenbit** (Sweden), **Rognkjeks** (Norway), **Stenbider** (Denmark), **Poule de mer** (France), **Galinha-do-mar** (Portugal), **Ciclottero** (Italy), and **Dango-uo** (Japan).

PADDLEFISH CAVIAR Found only in the larger streams and connecting waters of the Mississippi River drainage and in China, the paddlefish is an ancient and primitive species distinguished by its long paddlelike snout. The paddlefish reaches a length of over 8 feet and a weight of over 200 pounds. Like the sturgeon it has a largely cartilaginous skeleton and is butchered in the same fashion. Its roe has been marketed as "caviar" in years past; however, paddlefish are not numerous enough to support a commercial industry. The flesh is excellent when smoked.

PROTEIN FRESH CAVIAR An inexpensive substitute (USSR) made from a casein and gelatin base formed into pellets, then dyed, flavored, and preserved in a saline solution. This is not a fishery product, certainly not caviar.

RED CAVIAR A trade name for salmon caviar.

SALMON CAVIAR A caviar substitute made from the roes of Pacific salmon. This product more nearly resembles sturgeon caviar and in recent years has grown into a multimillion dollar export item from the U.S. Salmon caviar originated about 1910 in the Maritime Provinces of Siberia. Its commercial preparation is a modification of the method used for sturgeon eggs. The roes are selected at Alaska, Oregon and Washington canneries in the spring season and packed in two basic styles: the American-European style requires that the berries be separated and removed from the connective tissue in the same manner that sturgeon caviar is prepared; the Japanese style differs in that the eggs are graded and cleaned in their natural casing and several layers are placed in cloth-lined wooden boxes. The boxes are held under pressure to remove all moisture, resulting in a firm product which is sliced before eating.

To be suitable for caviar, the salmon eggs must be absolutely fresh, free from blood, and of clear color and good consistency. Large eggs such as those in the female chinook do not make good caviar. Most salmon caviar is prepared from the roe of coho, pink and chum, which are best suited for the purpose. The egg sac is split and rubbed gently over a table stand with a top of 1/2-inch mesh screen. The mesh is just large enough to let the eggs drop through, separating them from the membrane. The eggs fall onto an inclined screen leading into a large shallow box. They drain on the screen and finally slide into the box. The eggs are then cured in brine testing 90° salinometer usually made from fine mild-cure salt. This is stirred occasionally with a wooden paddle to insure thorough mixing and equal absorption of brine. The brining period varies with temperature and the size and freshness of the eggs. The time required is from 15 to 30 minutes. Each packer determines the sufficiency of cure by noting the change in consistency of the eggs. The interior coagulates to a jellylike texture, but the berries must not be shrunken. After brining, the eggs are dipped from the vat, placed on wire-mesh screens, and drained overnight, or for a period of about 12 hours.

After draining, the eggs are filled into small kegs holding about 100 pounds and lined with vegetable parchment paper. The kegs are covered and allowed to stand until the eggs settle. The headspace caused by settling is then filled with more caviar, the kegs are headed, put in cold storage at 34° to 36°F., and shipped under refrigeration. The caviar is repacked in glass by wholesale dealers, usually in nappy glass jars holding 2 to 4 ounces. To obtain the maximum preservation the containers should be held at temperatures no higher than 40°F. or less than 29°F., which may keep the caviar in good condition for a year.

The processing used in the Soviet Union differs from the American method. After the eggs are separated from the membrane they are mixed in a concentrated salt brine (sp. gr. 1.200), previously boiled, and cooled to a temperature of from 13° to 18°C. (55.4° to 64.6°F.). The volume of brine is three times that of caviar. Salt requirements are the same as for sturgeon caviar. The salting time varies as follows: In the Amur district, it is from 8 to 10 minutes for the best-grade caviar; in the Kamchatka district, 12 to 14 minutes. For second-grade caviar the time is 10 to 12 minutes in the Amur area, and 14 to 15 minutes in Kamchatka.

The caviar is allowed to stand for 12 hours to cause the brine to drain off and to permit uniform penetration of salt. Dry borax and urotropine are then added and distributed uniformly by mixing. Olive or cottonseed oil is added in small amounts and mixed with the caviar to prevent the grains sticking and to give the product a more glossy, attractive appearance. The salmon caviar is then packed in barrels, which have been coated inside with a mixture of paraffin and wax. The sides and bottoms of the barrels are covered with parchment soaked in concentrated brine, then with cotton cloth impregnated with vegetable oil.

TARAKO A Japanese product made from the roe of Alaska pollock which has been salted and dyed a red color. Also known as **MOMIJIKO**.

VENDACE CAVIAR The vendace is a slender, silvery fish, rarely over 6 inches in length, which occurs in European freshwaters with the exception of Ireland and Scotland. It has been a minor item in the canning industry because the fish is flavorless and bony. However, its roe is considered a delicacy in Scandinavia, especially in Sweden. The vendace is a spring spawner, so fresh roes become available in April and May. These pink eggs are so tiny that the roes have a pastelike consistency. Most commercial semipreserved products are much too salty; the fresh flavor is fragile at best. The roe is usually served on toast points or over sliced hard-cooked eggs with grated onion. For more about the vendace *(Coregonus albula) see CISCO under WHITEFISH.* A similar caviar is made from the lavaret *(Coregonus lavaretus); see also under WHITEFISH.* In Sweden the vendace is called **Löja** and the roe made from it is **löjrom**.

Channel Bass

See RED DRUM under DRUM.

Char

A holarctic genus *(Salvelinus)* of the trout and salmon family Salmonidae, some of which are called "trout" such as the brook trout, lake trout, blueback trout and Dolly Varden trout. Technically, chars are separated from true trout by very minor characteristics and mainly on the basis of their mouth structure. In a kitchen sense however,

chars differ greatly according to species, habitat and season. The musculature may be flaky or very firm, with a wide range of color from white to deep red. As the name "char" is generally used in North America it refers to the Arctic char *(Salvelinus alpinus),* which is circumpolar in distribution *(see under TROUT).*

There are both sea-run and landlocked populations of Arctic char common to northern Canada, Baffin Island, Greenland, Iceland, northern Norway, Siberia and Alaska. Lake populations of similar char occur in Maine, southern Canada, Norway, Sweden, Finland, England, Ireland, Scotland, France, Switzerland and the USSR. These more southerly forms are smaller and lack the fine table qualities of anadromous char. Sea-run Arctic char grow to 30 pounds in size; a fat fish with firm red flesh is in my opinion infinitely superior to salmon. Only a small quantity of char is imported to the American market (40,000 to 50,000 pounds each year) from Canada but a greater amount is caught by sport fisherman.

The Arctic char is a staple among Eskimo people who use the name **Ilkalupik** for the fish but attach other names, depending on maturity and sexual differences, which reflect its edible qualities. Elsewhere the char is **Røye** (Norway), **Bleikja** (Iceland), **Röding** (Sweden), **Omble chevalier** (France), **Seesaibling** (Germany), **Paliya** (USSR), and **Windermere char** (England).

Chub

(1) The fish found in North American markets under the name "chub" is a member of the whitefish group and is correctly known as a cisco. Ciscoes are most commonly marketed in smoked form as "smoked chubs." *See CISCO under WHITEFISH.*

(2) In binomial use, e.g., blue chub, bigeye chub, silver chub, Utah chub, etc., it may refer to any of about 30 species of American freshwater cyprinids (members of the carp family), which are generally small, soft-fleshed, bony, and of little or no culinary value. These do not appear in commercial markets but are at times taken by sport fisherman.

(3) In Europe the chub *(Squalius cephalus)* is also related to the carp; it has little or no food value for the same reason as above. This species appears in French cookbooks as **chevin** or **meunier**.

Cioppino

A fish stew thought to be of early twentieth-century origin in the San Francisco area. However, *cioppin* is from the

Genoese dialect *(Dizionario moderno genovese-italiano e italiano-genovese*, etc., Gaetano Frisoni, Genoa, 1910), and is described as "a tasty stew of various qualities of fish." The word at least was introduced by Italian settlers in California. Some old recipes indicate that the U. S. version was made entirely from crab meat as distinguished from a fish soup or *zuppa di pesce*. See *FISH SOUPS AND STEWS.*

Clam

In the year 1641 the New Netherland Colony passed an ordinance to solve one of the problems confronting economists of that era. "Whereas very bad wampum is at present circulated here, unpolished wampum is hereafter forbidden, and polished wampum will have the rate of fife (five) for one stiver (an English penny), and that strung." Black wampum (actually purple), made from the heart of quahaug shells, was more valuable than white wampum made from conch shells. Wampum beads, strung into strands or belts, served for money in the eastern colonies until the end of the seventeenth century, and continued to serve for trading with western Indians until two centuries later. Then this medium of exchange lost currency as did the former Latin name of the quahaug *Venus mercenaria* or "money-conscious goddess of love." Today the quahaug is *Mercenaria mercenaria*.

However, the consumption of clams was an early American passion, and has continued to be. It doesn't take a numismatist to recognize the intrinsic value of a clam when it's shucked and swallowed in its salt fragrant glory just as it comes from the water. All clams cannot be enjoyed on the half shell as some species need to be cooked, but in any form the clam is a distinctive seafood.

Along the East Coast of North America the most widely utilized clams are the softshell (*Mya arenaria*), which is found from the Arctic Ocean to Cape Hatteras, and the hardshell, which burrows in approximately the same range. The hardshell is more properly known by its Algonquian Indian name "quahaug" or the corrupted form "quahog" (pronounced có-hog), and specifically bay quahaug, as there is a related ocean or black quahaug found in very deep water of the North Atlantic. The culinary distinction is that the hardshell is more often eaten raw and in chowder than the softshell, which is considered a delicacy when steamed or fried. Hardshell clams, which occur in shallow water, can be scooped up with a clam rake or simply by "treading" or digging them out of the bottom with one's feet. Commercial clammers often work in deepwater using hydraulic dredge boats which unearth the bivalves with high pressure jets. Of the 16 to 17 million pounds of quahaug meats consumed in the U. S. each year, New York is the source of more than 50 percent of the total landings and these are mainly from Long Island's Great South Bay. This figure does not include several million additional pounds pried from their beds by summer vacationists in the bikini littoral of the Hamptons. Quahaugs are marketed according to size, the smallest being known as Little Neck clams (named after Little Neck Bay on Long Island, once the center of the half-shell trade) when 3 to 4 years old; the next larger size is known as Cherrystone clams (named after Cherrystone Creek in Virginia) when about 5 years old. Any quahaug bigger than a Cherrystone is simply called a chowder clam as they become too overwhelming to serve on the half shell.

There are two other large eastern clams that are not as widely utilized: the razor clam, because it's difficult to "catch" and occurs in an area where the delectable quahaug is abundant; and the bar or skimmer clam, because of poor public relations; the bar clam is also called surf clam (*Spisula solidissima*). The razor clam (*Siliqua patula*) cannot be treaded by the human foot as its name very aptly describes the shells' cutting edge. Nor can it be raked as the fragile shell is easily broken. You have to learn to spot the "dimple," a small hole made by its siphon on moist sand, or a V-shaped ripple on wet sand as the tide recedes. Once located you must work quickly with a narrow-bladed shovel because the razor can dig vertically just about as fast as the average tourist. The blade of the shovel has to be pushed straight down about 4 inches from target, then the handle pulled hard in a horizontal direction to compress the sand under this fleet-footed bivalve. The pressure of the blade will slow its digging and when the shovel handle is pushed away in the opposite direction to compact the sand around the clam you should lift both sand and mollusk free. I do this from the offshore side of the dimple as the hinged part of the shell always faces deep water and if it's necessary to make a quick grab at a partially exposed clam the razor's edge is safely blunted. This requires some practice and judging by the abundance of razor clams on Long Island at least, it's a skill that disappeared in my Grandpa's era. A few ingenious baymen have devised pressure jets which work in conjunction with high-powdered outboard motors that literally "blow" razor clams loose. However, demand always exceeds supply in the New York market and on an individual level the skill is about as popular as painting pictures on the backs of turtles. The trick is not lost on our West Coast and especially around Washington's ocean beaches and inner bay areas where at favorable minus tides thousands of razor clam fans invade Grays Harbor, the Strait of Juan de Fuca, Hood Canal and Puget Sound. For that matter the sport is enjoyed all the way north to Cook's Inlet in Alaska. The serious digger uses a "clam gun" which is a metal tube about 4 inches in diameter with a closed end bisected by a lifting handle. The tube is placed over a razor clam's dimple and shoved down into the sand. Then closing off the air vent on the top of the gun a core of wet sand can be withdrawn through suction, if possible with the razor clam in it.

The bar clam on the other hand has always been considered a fine codfish bait but too big and tough for anything but a chowder. However, New England restaurateurs discovered long ago that the yellow meat of the big "skimmer" can be cut into thin strips, breaded, and deep-fried with pleasing results. They can also be put through a food chopper and made into delicious fritters or used as the base for a clam sauce with spaghetti. Many companies process this bivalve for canned "minced clams" and they are as wholesome and appetizing as the quahaug. The white adductor muscle which holds the shells shut has the texture and flavor of a scallop.

Along the Pacific Coast of the U. S., in addition to the razor and softshell clams we find the native littleneck (Protothaca staminea), no relation to the eastern bivalve which is spelled in two words, as well as the Japanese littleneck or Manila clam (Tapes philippinarium or **Asari** in Japanese). These are the most tender of the western clams and can be eaten on the half shell. The butter clam (Saxidomus giganteus), which is found all the way from northern California to Alaska, can also be downed neat provided it's very small, as they grow tough with age. I don't care much for the gaper or western horse clam (Tresus capax) although the meat can be ground and made into fritters or used as a base for chowders. Horse clams invariably contain one or more pea crabs which live inside the mantle cavity, and these commensal crustaceans are a real delicacy. California's large Pismo clam, which is found from San Francisco to southern Mexico, once so hugely abundant at market, is now almost a museum piece because of its scarcity. The even larger geoduck (Panope generosa), pronounced gooey-duck, grows to 7 inches across the shell and comes equipped with a siphon that may be six or seven times as long. Geoduck hunting is a mad sport, pursued at night after a full moon on the lowest diurnal tides. The geoduck reveals its presence by squirting water in the air like a fountain. However, it takes two people to remove this huge bivalve from its burrow, one to grab the clam's "neck" and the other to do the digging.

The geoduck is not the largest clam eaten. Among his other conquests, Alexander the Great managed to extract and consume the giant "granddaddy" clam of the Indian Ocean, a Bacchian feat which is still emulated today. The meat of this species may weigh 20 pounds and the shell a quarter ton, which is no easy shuck even by a squad of hungry Macedonians. Latter-day navigators, traveling through the tropical Pacific, discovered real giants on the Great Barrier Reef of Australia, where they grow to more than 4 feet in length. A matching pair of these shells was presented to Francis I by the Republic of Venice. Later Jean Baptiste Pigalle sculptured supports for them, and they were placed in the church of Saint-Sulpice in Paris, where they are still in use as holy-water basins.

There are other bivalve mollusks such as the ark shells, cockles and carpet shells which are generally treated as "clams" in a culinary sense and therefore are included in the section on terminology.

SOURCE AND SEASON

The most important thing to know about clams if you collect your own is the purity of their environment. Clams can be toxic depending on either the occurrence of noxious plankton blooms such as a red tide or the presence of pollution from untreated sewage. It's important to check with local health authorities in all areas where these bivalves are taken as food. Commercial stocks must pass rigid inspection; in some towns they are sterilized at depuration plants. In most states there are regulations concerning the legal season, size, daily bag limit, and approved methods of digging. The best source of this information is the local fish-and-game department as there are frequent changes in the regulations.

Clams which ingest quantities of sand, such as the softshell, razor and bar clams, should be "purged" by placing them in a container of clean seawater to which you add a cup of cornmeal. Keep the bivalves in this bath for several hours and they will expel sand and siphon in the cornmeal. If seawater is not available, place them in a salt solution (⅓ cup salt to 1 gallon water). Do not use freshwater. Discard any hardshell clams whose open shells will not close when touched, or any of the siphon clams that do not constrict their necks when touched, as these are dead and no longer edible.

Clams are marketed in three forms: in the shell, shucked, and canned. Clams in the shell are usually sold on location by the dozen, and must be alive, with their valves tightly closed, when bought. Refrigerated at

40°F., they'll stay alive for several days. Shucked clams are whole meats sold in pints or quarts. These should be plump, with clear liquor, and free of broken shell. Fresh shucked clams are sold in containers which must be refrigerated or surrounded with ice. Properly stored, they'll stay fresh for a week. Shucked clams are also available in frozen form. Once thawed they should never be refrozen. Hardshell, softshell, razor, skimmer, butter and Pismo clams are canned whole or minced either in brine or clam liquor, then heat-processed. These are packed in cans up to 64 ounces in size. Clams are also sold in smoked form, usually canned in oil. Fresh clam meats are also sun-dried in Japan and sold as **hoshigai,** skewered on slivers of bamboo.

Clam liquor extracted during the shucking operation is sold bottled in undiluted form as "clam juice" or when diluted as "clam broth." The juice is sometimes concentrated by evaporation and purveyed as "clam nectar." All three forms are useful as substitutes for a fish stock or a base in making soups and chowders.

CLAM TERMINOLOGY

ARK SHELL   *See PEPITONA.*

BAR CLAM   Also called skimmer and surf clam; this is larger than a quahaug and grows to a length of 8 inches across the shell in the waters north of Cape Cod. The shell is roughly triangular in shape and covered with a shiny brown periostracum. The meat of this clam is tough and sandy, but it can be cleansed and ground and used in chowder and fritters, or in making a clam sauce for spaghetti. The adductor muscles on the other hand are very tender and can be served raw or cooked in the manner of scallops. Use a pointed knife and insert the blade near the back of the clam where the valves are slightly irregular and offer an aperture. Slide the blade in, curving it close to the inside of the upper or lower shell, and sever one muscle. Slide the blade across and sever the opposite muscle. The clam will open readily. Drain juice into a bowl. Carefully cut out the two muscles and reserve. Discard the remaining part of the clam but save the "foot" to grind for chowder or stuffed clams. Rinse the muscles in the clam juice (never in water) to preserve their natural flavor.

BEAN CLAM   The smallest clam used in cooking is the bean clam of the Pacific Coast and the closely related **coquina** of our Atlantic shores. The average specimen is seldom more than ¾-inch long and is often smaller. These clams are extremely abundant within their range, and sufficient amounts can be collected to make an excellent broth or soup. With one exception they are too small to be utilized in any other way. Coquinas are especially abundant and popular on Florida's West Coast. The Mediterranean coquina or **olive de mer** is very similar to our Atlantic species. That half-shell treasure of Venezuela, the **chipi chipi,** is a bean clam.

BUTTER CLAM   The native delicacy of our West Coast is the versatile butter clam. The butter clam is comparatively smooth-shelled, finely etched with concentric growth lines. This clam occurs mainly on beaches having a mixture of sand and gravel, at a depth of no more than a foot below the surface from the tidal zone out to 30 feet of water. When small, the butter clam can be eaten on the half shell but the larger ones are tough. It is used chiefly in canning, but can be prepared in any manner, including frying, steaming and in chowders. It sometimes appears as a smoked product.

CARPET SHELL   This is a small clam of the genus *Tapes* found principally in the Atlantic waters of Europe, the Mediterranean and around Japan. The shells of these clams are thin and transversely ovate. The carpet shell is the **clovisse** and **palourde** of French cuisine; it is often confused with our quahaug which occurs in parts of Europe, but that is properly the **praire** in French terminology.

COCKLE   Although cockles are especially prized in Europe, particularly the genus *Cardium* which includes the common, knotted and spiny cockles, there are many species found on our Pacific Coast from southern California to Alaska which are widely utilized. Another cockle group, *Anadara* spp., is cultured in Malaysia and Thailand on a family basis like a coastal seabed farm. Along our Atlantic shores north of Cape Hatteras cockles are usually too small to be of culinary interest, but south of Hatteras the great cockle and the spiny cockle are used to some extent in making chowders; both are rather strongly flavored and do not rival the Pacific rock and hard cockles which are more tender and can be prepared by steaming or frying, or can be made into a soup.

GEODUCK   The largest American clam is the Pacific Coast's geoduck. Its shell may be 8 inches long and it may exceed 5 pounds in weight. The geoduck is nearly rectangular in shape and has such a large neck, or siphon, that it cannot be withdrawn into the shell. The shells always gape and show a brown mantle, which completely hides the body of the clam inside. In a large geoduck, the siphon can be extended 3 feet or more. This neck pumps hundreds of gallons of water daily to and from the geoduck's digestive apparatus. The meat of this mollusk is sliced into cutlets and fried, and the siphon can be skinned and ground in a food chopper to be made into a chowder.

HOW TO SHUCK A CLAM

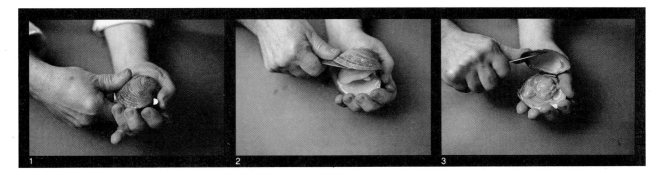

1. Grasp clam firmly with hinge part of shell
toward palm. **2.** Insert knife blade between the valves.
3. Move the blade around to sever the muscle at
the hinge and free the clam from the shells, top and bottom.

HARDSHELL CLAM A regional term for the quahaug in the eastern U. S., simply to distinguish it from the equally popular softshell clam. The shell is dingy white in color, oval shaped, and inside has a purple or violet border around the ventral margin. The bay quahaug (*Mercenaria mercenaria*) grows to 3 inches or more in length. A related ocean quahaug, which seldom occurs in water less than 50 feet deep, is larger and more elongate and the shell is black. There is also a southern quahaug (*M. campechiensis*), occurring from Virginia to Texas, which has a much thicker shell; the meat is definitely chewy and more strongly flavored, but it's used in chowders. Small quahaugs or "Little Neck" clams are mostly consumed raw on the half shell. These are not to be confused with the littleneck clams of our West Coast, which are a distinctly different species. The next larger size quahaug is called the "Cherrystone"; this is utilized on the half shell or in virtually any clam recipe. When over 3 inches in diameter, the quahaug is best relegated to chowders or to grinding to make fritters or stuffed clams.

HORSE CLAM The horse clam, also called the **empire clam** and **gaper**, grows to fairly large size with a shell up to 8 inches in length, almost matching the geoduck which it's sometimes mistaken for. Horse clams are not as popular as other Pacific species but provide quantities of edible meat. The large siphon, which has a rough outer covering, can be dipped into boiling water, then skinned, or it can be frozen and the epidermis removed with a potato peeler. The white meat of the siphon is excellent when ground for chowders, or it can be split open and tenderized by pounding, then dipped into batter and fried. The interior meat

should be split and the dark digestive gland removed; this can be utilized in the same manner as the siphon. Horse clams are rather ugly-looking as the animal appears too big for its shell which causes it to "gape" at the siphonal end.

LITTLENECK CLAMS This name (properly spelled as one word as opposed to the trade term for the small eastern quahaug or Little Neck) belongs to 2 species found in Pacific waters; these are the native littleneck clam (*Protothaca staminea*), found from California to Alaska, and the introduced Japanese littleneck (*Tapes philippinarium*), which is now distributed from California to British Columbia. These look similar, but the Japanese species is elongate and has a bright purple adductor muscle scar, in contrast to the native littleneck which is rounded and lacks the purple scar. These are not quahaugs nor really suitable raw on the half shell. Either littleneck is usually steamed, then dipped into melted butter and downed neat.

PEPITONA The pepitona or "ark shell" is a bivalve mollusk of the family Arcidae which comes in various shapes according to species—oval, oblong, elongated. There are several hundred kinds found on both sides of the Atlantic, chiefly in the Mediterranean and along the northern coast of South America. The Spanish name is used here because it's most often identified with that cuisine and the countries of South America. Although this bivalve is historically associated with the Mediterranean fishery, Venezuela is the number one consumer of pepitona in the world (annually over 5,000 tons). The bulk of this is canned and sold locally. The most important species from

SOME EXAMPLES OF CLAMS

Left, Softshell clam
center, Cherrystone clam
right, Little Neck clam
bottom, Razor clam

a culinary standpoint is the Noah's Ark, which is a wide, almost quadrangular-shaped shell with radial ribs. It's found in shallow water from Cape Hatteras south through the West Indies and also on our Pacific Coast and in the Mediterranean Sea. The Noah's Ark appears as **Arche de Noé** (France), **Arca di Noè** (Italy), **Arca de Noe** (Spain), and nonspecifically as **Castanholas** (Portugal), **Papak** (Yugoslavia), and **Calognomi** (Greece).

RAZOR CLAM Both coasts of the United States have razor clams although zoologically they are quite different and belong in different genera. The western razors are shorter and broader in the shell and have rounded ends rather than the squared ends of the eastern species. The western jackknife clam *(Tagelus californianus)* is more closely related to the eastern razor. The eastern razor is usually found in very fine sand but not in areas of low salinity (such as river mouths) or where the water temperatures are high. The razor clam is easy to identify as it has a long, thin narrow shell, which looks much like the old-fashioned straight razor. The shells are almost transparent and are covered with a shiny brown periostracum. Although the razor clam has large creamy-colored meat, it is too chewy to be eaten on the half shell, except when small. It is generally used in fritters. Eastern razors are also excellent when steamed, while the West Coast variety is most often fried.

SOFTSHELL CLAM The softshell clam is found from the Arctic Ocean south to Cape Hatteras. The bulk of our crop comes from flats in New England and Chesapeake Bay, where salinities are low. This clam was transplanted to the Pacific Coast and occurs from the San Francisco area north to British Columbia. The long siphon will jet water into the air when you walk near it, making it easy to dig out of its mud burrow. This tasty bivalve has the texture and size ideal for frying and chowders, as well as for steaming. The softshell clam can also be eaten raw with a touch of lemon juice or cocktail sauce. A popular dish is **Clams Guilford,** which is simply the clam meats dipped into an egg-milk mixture, rolled in cracker crumbs, and deep-fried. The most common method of cooking softshells, however, is steaming.

SUNRAY CLAM Also known as the **sunray venus clam** and **giant callista,** the sunray clam *(Macrocallista nimbosa)* has an elongate smooth shell, almost like porcelain; it's pink in color with radiating lavender bands crossed with bars of brown and blue. This is strictly a southern species found mainly in Florida although its range extends to North Carolina. Florida's hard clam industry is centered near the East Coast town of Grant where the bulk of the state's annual 135,000 pounds of meats are harvested. More recently an abundant population of sunray clams was discovered in Apalachicola Bay. But in comparison to the supply in the New York area clams of any kind remain a relatively minor crop in Florida. The meat of the sunray is large and tough but of excellent flavor. When ground, it can be used in any of the recipes for chowder or stuffed clams.

STEAMED CLAMS

The most succulent "steamer" is the softshell clam, but Little Necks, Cherrystones, small butter and even small razor clams can be treated in the same manner. Prepare clams for steaming by rinsing them thoroughly in cold running water to remove sand and surface dirt, and if necessary scrub them under running water with a small stiff brush to remove any foreign matter adhering to shells. Place clams in a deep pot or clam steamer with a tightly fitted lid. Pour in the liquid and seasonings your recipe calls for, but keep fluids to a minimum level—1 or 2 inches at most. Cover tightly and steam until clams on top barely open and turn off heat. Do not overcook. Prolonged steaming will toughen even the most tender small clams.

CLAMS OREGANATE

12 Little Neck clams
6 garlic cloves, puréed or minced
1 tablespoon dried orégano
2 tablespoons minced fresh parsley
½ cup fine dry bread crumbs
1 tablespoon olive oil, approximately

Open the clams, leaving each one on the half shell. Arrange in a shallow pan. Mix garlic, herbs and crumbs, and divide among the clams. Dribble a few drops of oil on each clam. Bake in a preheated 400°F. oven for 8 to 10 minutes, or in a broiler until browned. Serve hot, at once. Makes 1 main-dish serving, or 3 appetizer servings.

BABY CLAMS WITH GREEN ONIONS AND TRUFFLES

1 dozen smallest Little Neck clams obtainable
  (no more than 1½ inches across shell)
¼ cup minced green onions
2 tablespoons minced black truffle
1 lemon, quartered
6 whole green onions

Open the clams, leaving each on the half shell. Chop only the green portion of the onions; sprinkle each clam with enough of the bits to give a contrasting color, poking the greens under as well as sprinkling them over the clams. Add a pinch of truffle on top of each clam. Place clams on a tray in refrigerator for several hours to absorb the onion and truffle flavors. When ready to serve arrange the clams on a bowl of cracked ice; place lemon quarters in the center of the dish, and decorate with the whole green onions. Makes 1 serving.

NEW ENGLAND CLAM CHOWDER

4 dozen clams
5 cups cold water
2-inch cube of
  salt pork, diced
1 large onion,
  chopped very fine
4 medium-size potatoes, diced
salt and freshly ground
  black pepper
2 cups milk, hot
1½ cups heavy cream, hot

Wash clams thoroughly. Place them in a deep pan with the 5 cups cold water covering the clams. Bring to a boil, then reduce heat and simmer just until the shells open. Strain the broth through cheesecloth and reserve. Remove the clams from their shells and chop into small pieces. Combine salt pork and onion in a saucepan, and cook gently over low heat for about 3 minutes; do not brown. Add reserved broth and the potatoes. Add salt and pepper to taste. Cook until potatoes are tender. Add clams. Remove from heat and slowly add heated milk and cream. Serve immediately. Makes 6 to 8 servings.

CARTER'S CLAM SOUFFLÉ

¾ cup minced clams
½ cup strained
  clam broth, hot
2 tablespoons butter, melted
2 tablespoons flour
½ cup heavy cream
4 thin slices of onion
1 teaspoon minced parsley
½ bay leaf
dash of cayenne
3 egg yolks
4 egg whites
pinch of salt
pinch of grated nutmeg

Make a roux with the butter and flour. Gradually stir in the clam broth, cream, onion slices, parsley, bay leaf and cayenne. Cook over low heat, stirring, until thickened. Add clams and heat them, then remove pot from heat. Beat egg yolks well, then add a little of the hot sauce to them and mix. Turn into the balance of the sauce and blend well. Let the sauce cool slightly. Beat egg whites stiff with salt and nutmeg, and gently fold into the sauce. Spoon into a 4-cup soufflé dish buttered only on the bottom. Bake in a preheated hot oven (400°F.) for 25 minutes, or until well puffed and slightly browned. Serve at once. Makes 3 or 4 servings, more as an hors d'oeuvre.

CLAM SAUCE

3 dozen hardshell clams
1½ cups olive oil
6 garlic cloves, chopped

½ teaspoon hot pepper seeds
½ cup chopped parsley

Shuck the clams, saving and straining all the liquor, and chop the raw clams. Heat the oil with the garlic until garlic becomes *blond;* stir occasionally with a wooden spoon. Add the reserved clam liquor, stir well, then add the chopped clams and let all simmer for about 3 minutes. Add the hot pepper seeds, or several good shakes of crushed red pepper, and stir in the parsley. Serve at once over freshly cooked hot pasta—spaghetti or spaghettini, or linguine, or your preference. Makes enough sauce for 4 servings, using 1 pound of pasta.

If you like less garlic or less hot pepper, or more parsley, adjust to your taste.

For clam sauce with tomatoes, reduce the oil to ½ cup and add 3 cups chopped tomatoes, fresh or canned. Add the tomatoes with the clam liquor and let the mixture cook until reduced and somewhat thickened, before adding the clams. Add more parsley with the red sauce. Also, you may need to season with a little salt.

These sauces can be made with canned chopped clams, and they will be good, but not as good as when made with freshly shucked clams. Use 2 cans (7 ounces each) in place of fresh clams.

Cobia

The cobia, also known as **cabio** and **ling** on the U.S. Gulf Coast, is found in all tropical and warm-temperate waters, and occurs in the western Atlantic from Cape Cod to Argentina. This fish has no related species and is in a family by itself, Rachycentridae. The cobia is a large fish, commonly 30 to 50 pounds and has been recorded to 102 pounds. It's brown in color with a black lateral band and has a broad snout. Cobia are often mistaken for sharks when in the water as they are usually sighted near the surface and quite close to shore. They are the object of a considerable sport fishery from the West Coast of Florida to Texas, and substantial landings are made commercially.

Cobia are good foodfish. They have very tough skin with minute scales and are usually sold in skinned fillet form. The meat is firm and white and can be deep-fried in fingers and chunks. The unskinned fillet makes an excellent smoked product.

Cod

When the sad news arrived next day
In dear old St. John's town
There was crying and lamenting
On the streets both up and down
Their mothers were lamenting
Crying for those they bore
On the boisterous waves they found their graves
Where they ne'er shall see more.

from the Newfoundland ballad
Petty Harbour Bait Skiff,
John Grace

When Giovanni Caboto hoisted sail on May 2, 1497, from Bristol, England, for the New World he was, like Columbus before him, searching for the fabled western sea route to Asia. But Caboto, alias "John Cabot," a Venetian navigator sponsored by King Henry VII, returned from his first voyage to Newfoundland not with exotic spices and gems but tales of a sea so filled with fishes that "they could be caught simply by lowering weighted baskets into the water." By 1602 when Bartholomew Gosnold ventured beyond Nova Scotia seeking a source of sassafras (in the pharmacopoeia of that era it was believed to be a cure for syphilis) and named that great hook of land to the south "Cape Cod," thousands of English, French and Portuguese fishermen were already harvesting the Grand Banks. The Grand Banks are a portion of the Continental Shelf; physically a series of shoals extending for about 350 miles off the southeast coast of Newfoundland beginning with Grand Bank proper and ending at Georges Bank east of Massachusetts. The cold Labrador Current and the warm Gulf Stream join in the vicinity of the Grand Banks, creating ideal thermal conditions for plankton growth upon which fish depend directly or indirectly as a food source. This same thermal union creates a constant fog; the shallow contours of the banks (average depth 30 fathoms) which build huge seas were a mariner's nightmare.

The New England based fishing industry began with the settlement of Gloucester in northeastern Massachusetts in 1623. These early-day Gloucestermen went to sea in little Chebacco boats and, as they ranged farther offshore and eastward, worthier craft, the ketches and pinkies with their ladylike sheers raised gracefully aft, went in search of the cod, haddock, pollock and halibut. To survive the rigors of winter fishing the swiftest and most weatherly fore-and-aft rigged vessel came down the ways in 1713—the New England schooner. This was the prototype of the great ships of war in 1812. Running

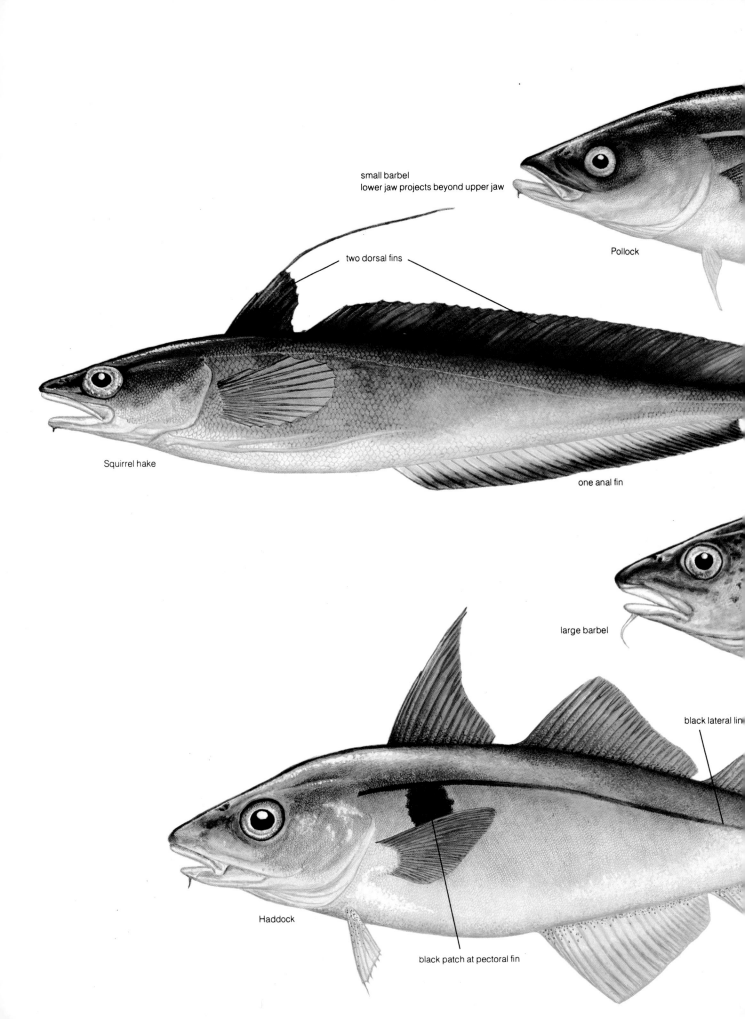

small barbel
lower jaw projects beyond upper jaw

Pollock

two dorsal fins

Squirrel hake

one anal fin

large barbel

black lateral lin

Haddock

black patch at pectoral fin

pale lateral line

tail forked

tail rounded

pale lateral line

tail slightly concave

Atlantic cod

SOME EXAMPLES OF CODS
Although color in cods is variable (there is, for example, a red phase and a gray phase in the Atlantic cod), the consistent characteristics indicated here will separate the four major members of this family.

for "market" at 12 knots in heavy swells without wetting the lee rail was a tactical exercise that Yankee fishermen learned well. The fierce Arctic gales that turn saltwater to ice, coating the vessel as she plunges to keep herself head-to-sea, can overpower modern 600- to 800-ton distant-water trawlers as the winds may last for a week and the sheer weight of ice building over the hull causes a loss of stability. On schooners it was often a brief and always dangerous life in masthead-high seas with the helmsman lashed to his wheel to keep from being washed overboard, and with nothing but bully beef, cornmeal and dark rum to warm the innards for days and sometimes weeks at a time. This life-style has changed little as, statistically, commercial fishermen are twenty more times likely to die as a result of an accident at work than all other occupied men between the ages of 15 to 44. (From *Trawler Safety:* Final Report of the Committee of Inquiry: Chairman Sir Deric Holland-Martin, London, H. M. Stationery Office, 1969 Cmd. 4114.)

In the early nineteenth century New England skippers made codfishing more profitable and at the same time even more hazardous with the introduction of dories. These small, comparatively frail craft were nested on the deck of the schooner; once the fishing grounds were reached each man went out by oar or sail, thereby covering a wider area often miles from the mother ship. A "boisterous wave" on wintry seas with a ton of cod aboard sent many a doryman to his grave, and the gray enveloping shroud of a sudden fog caused others to row over the horizon—a few even reached land. Gloucester's hero is Howard Blackburn who in February 1881 became separated from the *Grace L. Fears* during a snowstorm. Before his hands froze stiff Blackburn bent them around the oars and rowed to Newfoundland, a hundred miles away. His dorymate died. Although Blackburn lost his fingers and toes the rugged Gloucesterman survived. Rudyard Kipling's *Captains Courageous* is the classic account of life aboard a dory schooner. Despite the development of more efficient gear American dory fishing lasted until the mid-twentieth century with the final voyage of the *Marjorie Parker* which fetched ashore near New Bedford, Massachusetts, in the hurricane of August, 1954.

Men were willing to risk their lives to capture the fish that at one time filled the belly of the world. The white, flaky meat of the cod was virtually the "beef" of centuries past. It could be baked, broiled, boiled, fried, made into puddings, cakes and chowders, or preserved with salt and stored for months until ready for use with little loss in flavor or nutrition. Even its roes, tongue, air bladder and cheeks are considered delicacies and its liver

a valuable medicinal. Cod nurtured the Viking's dragon ships, the Plate Fleet of the Spaniards in their western search for treasure, and in darker days of history it was the base for "The Golden Triangle." Beginning in the mid-1600s, and for the next 80 years, cod supported the world's slave traffic as one of three valuable cargoes. A ship out of Boston would deliver salt cod to Spain or Portugal, then proceed to West Africa where the vessel took aboard slaves, before sailing on to the West Indies to exchange its human cargo for sugar and molasses to supply the distilleries of New England. The irony was that salt cod not only held the key to financing the triangle but it was also the staple item of food for the slaves; the fact that the fish was of the poorest quality, unfit for the European market, did little to discourage its ultimate popularity, as salt cod is still highly esteemed in the Caribbean and even West Africa. Some years ago, while exploratory fishing off the mouth of the Congo River, I visited the old slave port of Moanda and learned that salt cod, a comparatively expensive imported item, was in greater demand than the huge variety of fresh fish available offshore.

For centuries the cod was such a popular item of commerce that it appeared symbolically on coins, stamps, legal documents, corporate seals, letterheads, on heraldic crests and on wind vanes. The huge white-pine carving of the "Sacred Cod" which was hung in the Massachusetts Hall of the Representatives in 1784 is the most famous bit of Americana that venerates not only the state's original industry, but the source of its sea power in the war against England. It is still on display today. Inevitably, the cod became a subject of song and story both here and in Europe, but one doggerel captured the flavor of Yankee conservatism:

> *And this is good old Boston,*
> *The home of the bean and the cod,*
> *Where the Lowells talk to the Cabots*
> *And the Cabots talk only to God.*

While this may be far older, it has been attributed to Dr. John C. Bossidy, who is said to have used it as a toast at the annual dinner of the Alumni of Harvard College in 1910.

The cod assumed a religious significance in early-day Europe during the Lenten season. It was a denial food of fasting days. This did little to discourage its popularity, as abstinence from meat only made people fonder of the cod, which by choice was a festive food on holidays such as Easter, Christmas and New Year's Eve. Although most of these dishes were based on the use of salt cod which kept well during the winter, the people of

Lutefisk on display at the Norwegian Folk Museum *(Folkemuseet)* in Bygdøy, near Oslo

northern Europe utilized split air-dried cod in preparing **lutefisk,** which is soaked in a lye solution made from birch ashes. While this may sound bizarre to anyone but a Scandinavian, it was a primitive means of reconstituting a virtually moistureless fish with the texture of an oak plank. Air-dried cod can be kept in Arctic climates for years. By soaking the fish in fresh water for a week, then submerging it in a lye solution (2 cups lye to 6 quarts water) for several more days, then resoaking it in fresh water for another 2 days, the cod becomes soft, indeed so springy that it quivers when touched—a test of quality. While the nutritive value of **lutefisk** cannot be denied, it has no detectable flavor. Traditionally it's served with melted pork drippings, which does nothing to invoke a

spiritual rapport with this Viking ration.

A fresh cod is a lean fish with firm white flesh that readily flakes apart when cooked. The most popular recipes have a creamy binding base of some kind. It makes a wonderful chowder, for example, and the best I can recall were brewed on cold September mornings as we slowly headed the Cape Islander for Newfoundland's tuna grounds under a cloud of squalling gulls. We jigged up the cod with a tarred handline and sent the fish slithering into the galley. Diced potatoes and onions simmering in sea-water worked their magic in a cast-iron pot; with the chunks of cod added, a soupy marriage was consummated with pure cream, upon which golden dots of butter melted. At times we'd bring aboard a lobster and add him to the pot for texture contrast. I can never make quite the same chowder at home, at least it doesn't taste the same.

Perhaps the most universal method of cooking cod, whether in steak or fillet form, is by poaching. This is often called "boiled cod" but as explained elsewhere *(see COOKING METHODS)* something is lost in translation. I have watched chefs prepare cod in Norwegian and Swedish kitchens; while the salted water may churn violently at high heat, then and only *then* is the fish added and boiling comes to a halt. When it again begins to boil, the pot is immediately removed from the heat and the delicate cod is left in hot water for another 5 to 10 minutes, or until the meat flakes from the bone. Cod cooked in this fashion are usually served splashed with melted butter, with boiled potatoes sprinkled with chopped fresh dill, or optionally with an egg, mustard or horseradish sauce. Small (4 to 6 pounds) whole cod can be cooked in a regular fish poacher following the same procedure described for salmon. Bear in mind that the head, liver and roe are delightfully edible; the liver has no suggestion of oil in its flavor and is usually poached in salted water to which a little vinegar has been added.

SALT COD

If you ever become addicted to salt cod, which I am, the agonies of withdrawal when left in a codless land are never dispelled. Living in Florida I can now salt cero and Spanish mackerel, and these are of gourmet caliber in their own right, but I must confess that supermarket salt cod exhumed from little wooden coffins offers only a provocative memory of the past. New York City has a plentiful supply of the whole split fish in its Spanish and Italian neighborhoods and on more than one occasion I have resorted to carrying a bundle home, hoping the aircraft would arrive before that heady cod aroma permeated the cabin. Salt cod provides an essence without which there would be no **Bacalao en Salsa Verde** or **Bacalao Ligado,** or better still a creamy mound of **Brandade de Morue.**

Salt cod is not a uniform product in terms of sodium chloride content for several reasons. Fish taken far offshore and in transit for days or even weeks before curing are more heavily salted than cod taken close to land. Once ashore, weather conditions in terms of humidity and temperature are highly variable, requiring more salt in damp, frequently sunless regions such as Iceland or Greenland as compared to the more clement weather of Madeira. Thus, in Portugal the salt content of most cod products is a fairly stable 17 to 20 percent in the so-called *cura nacional,* or national cure. The two notable exceptions are a stacked and water-horsed fillet or *cura branca*

which finishes very white in color; if the salt is removed by soaking between the process of washing and drying in the *cura amarela* it results in a characteristically yellow fillet.

There are two principal methods of salting cod. The oldest is called "kench salting"; layers of fish are simply alternated with layers of salt and stacked flesh side up, in a pile. Sodium chloride extracts water and other fluids from the fish and the resulting pickle is allowed to drain off. The cod are cured for about 4 days and any superflous pickle is pressed out. Residual salt will remain on the fillet and must be removed before cooking. The other method is pickle salting; dry salt is applied to the fish, but then the cod are placed in crocks or barrels and the pickle is not allowed to drain off. This requires about 2 days and is generally used for a lightly salted product; the salt is sprinkled only in the area where the backbone has been removed as enough pickle will form to penetrate the thinner sections of the fish (the belly cavity and tail portions). However, either method can produce a heavy or light cure if desired. A heavy cure is figured at 35 to 40 pounds of salt to 100 pounds of cod and a light cure at about 15 pounds of salt to 100 pounds of cod. During the summer months a very light pickle-salted product known as the Gaspé Cure is made with 8 pounds of salt to 100 pounds of cod. This cure has always found an eager market in Italy and Spain. It has a higher moisture content (36 to 38 %) and is amber in color. In autumn when climactic conditions are favorable the Fall Cure comes in season; this is even more moist (45 %) and is whiter in color; the salt content is only 4 to 5 %, which is a marginal preservative, but fall-cured cod are usually rushed to local markets.

Both kenching and pickle-salting are essentially commercial methods where large quantities of cod are processed. Pickle-salting produces a better fillet and can be used at home. However, a third method, brine salting, is also used commercially. Brine salting differs in that the moisture content of the fish remains high and the stronger the brine, the more water the fish will retain. Usually a brine concentration of 22 to 25% salt by weight and a curing period of 5 hours will produce a good product. In the brine method salt concentrates very rapidly at the surface of the fish before penetrating deeper, which preserves its quality, but the thinner sections in the nape and tail may be overcured. Pickle salting is more precise for home use *(see under SALT FISH).*

BASIC PREPARATION OF SALT COD

Salt cod must be soaked in fresh water before cooking. The duration of this period depends, of course, on the original

Collecting salt from seawater at Alcochete, Portugal.
The salt is heaped up in pits called *salinas*. Salt boats,
salineiros, carry the salt to Setúbal and Lisbon.
There have been saltworks along this coast for centuries.

Drying and salting cod at Palhais, Portugal. The cod is dried
on racks, under netting, in the open air, but under a slatted roof to keep
it from being too hot. The pieces are flattened in a press.
Here they claim cod tastes better when naturally dried by the sun.

cure; a heavily salted product may require up to 24 hours while a lightly cured cod fillet will be restored in half that time. Size is also a factor, but generally speaking if the fish is hard as a board you can assume it underwent a heavy cure. A lightly cured cod fillet is flexible due to its greater moisture content. Most cod fillets are too large to cook whole but they can be cut into large or small pieces, leaving the rib cage area around the belly intact if you plan to make a dish that requires cod gelatin, which is essential to the sauce in **Bacalao Ligado.** This part of the cod (as well as the head if you have salted your own and reserved it) provides a delicate gelatin suitable to a number of recipes. After soaking pour off the water and cover the fish again with fresh cold water, then heat it gently on the stove. When the water begins to bubble, skim off the froth, reduce the heat, and poach for 15 to 20 minutes according to the thickness of the fish. Drain the cod and you are ready to proceed with any of the recipes.

Strictly speaking the cod is one of about 60 species in the family Gadidae. Except for the burbot which is a freshwater form, these are all marine fishes of cold-temperate and Arctic seas. The most common species other than the Atlantic cod are the haddock, pollock (known as coalfish in Europe), tomcod and various hakes. There are certain similarities in a few cods with respect to cooking but for the sake of clarity the major species must be considered individually. Due to the world popularity of cod as food a number of unrelated fish are misleadingly called "cod" of some kind. The majority of these false cods in North America are members of the scorpionfish family (Scorpaenidae), but in Latin America *bacalao* is often one of the sharks.

COD TERMINOLOGY

ARCTIC COD A small member of the cod family, seldom over 8 inches long, found in the Arctic Sea from Greenland to Siberia. Due to its range and size, this cod *(Boreogadus saida)* has no commercial value.

ATLANTIC COD The world standard bearer around which the industry is formed. Almost 7 billion pounds are landed each year by vessels of all nations. There are subspecies which differ in color and minor taxonomical details but from a food standpoint they are essentially the same fish. This cod *(Gadus morhua)* has been recorded in weights to 211½ pounds (Massachusetts, 1895), but in this modern age most fish are harvested long before attaining even a quarter that size. Cod are marketed fresh as whole gutted fish with or without heads, in skinned or unskinned fillets, and in steaks. The same cuts are purveyed in frozen

form and also in uncooked or precooked sticks or portions. They are sold air-dried (stockfish), smoked, salted and canned. Smoked cod is particularly good and is often misleadingly labeled "finnan haddie" in North America. Cod roes are marketed fresh, frozen, boiled, salted, smoked, canned, and as cod caviar in either whole-berry or pressed forms. The tongues and cheeks are usually fresh items although some tongues are salted. Cod are graded according to size in centimeters in Europe and by weight in North America.

EUROPE

Small Codling:	less than 54 cm.
Codling:	54 to 63 cm.
Sprag:	63 to 76 cm.
Cod:	over 76 cm.

NORTH AMERICA

Scrod:	1½ to 2½ pounds (less than 50 cm.)
Market:	2½ to 10 pounds (50 to 75 cm.)
Large:	10 to 25 pounds (75 to 100 cm.)
Whole:	over 25 pounds (over 100 cm.)

As found in the restaurants and markets of the world cod is also known as **Torsk** (Denmark, Norway, and Sweden), **Bacalao** (Spain), **Bacalhau** (Portugal), **Bakalar** (Yugoslavia), **Merluzzo bianco** (Italy), **Gados** (Greece), **Kabeljau** (Germany), **Porskur** (Iceland), **Kabeljauw** (Holland), **Cabillaud,** or in the form of salt cod **Morue** (France), and **Treska** (USSR).

BLACK COD A market name for the unrelated sablefish *(which see).*

BLUE COD A market name for the unrelated cabezon *(which see).*

BURBOT The only freshwater member of the cod family found in North America, Europe and Asia. The burbot *(Lota lota),* sometimes called **ling** or **lawyer** in the U.S., is not a very attractive-looking fish, being somewhat eel-shaped and often pot-bellied, with its scales embedded in a heavy skin, but it's a truly unique food. Burbot are found from New England to the Susquehanna River, throughout the Great Lakes and the Hudson Bay drainage system, and in the Columbia River. A large subspecies is found in Alaska and Siberia which attains a length of 5 feet and weights of over 60 pounds. It occurs mainly in lakes, usually in very deep water, but during its winter spawning period the burbot is found in the shallows. The flesh is white and firm, but slightly oilier than that of the saltwater cods. Due to the absence of small bones the fillets are easy to prepare in all cod recipes. Both the vitamin-rich liver and roe are extremely good eating. A popular general

Burbot, freshwater cod

recipe in Scandinavia is to stuff rolled fillets with the liver and poach in white wine; the *fumet* is then strained and made into an aspic; the rolls are served cold with horse-radish sauce. Also known as **Lotte** (France), **Donzela** (Portugal), **Lake** (Norway and Sweden), **Ferskvandskvabbe** (Denmark), **Rutte** (Germany), **Manic** (Yugoslavia), **Bottatrice** (Italy), **Nalim** (USSR).

GREEN COD   A market name for the pollock.

HADDOCK   The second most important cod from both a market and cuisine standpoint is the haddock. Except for a black lateral stripe on its body, the haddock *(Melanogrammus aeglefinus)* generally resembles a cod. However, a haddock is much smaller, usually weighing 2 to 5 pounds with the rare large one weighing over 20 pounds. This fish is found on both sides of the Atlantic, from the North Sea and Iceland to Newfoundland and Nova Scotia, southward to New Jersey, and occasionally in deep water to Cape Hatteras, North Carolina. The flesh of the haddock is softer than that of the cod and does not respond as well to the dry-salting methods. It is sold mainly in fresh or smoked form.

FINNAN HADDIE   The market name for split smoked haddock sold in fillets, and to a lesser extent in blocks or cutlets. First popularized in Findon, Scotland, by John Ross, Jr., more than a century ago. The name "haddie" is simply Scotch vernacular for the haddock. The U. S. supply of finnan haddie has never been great with only a few New England firms specializing in making this product. A limited amount is imported from Canada and Denmark.

Admirers of finnan haddie become passionate on the subject and its detractors equally so, as there is a vast difference between good and mediocre. The freshness of the fish and the curing process are critical factors. At best it's golden and moist, and has a flaky texture with a delicate oak-smoke flavor. An inferior product is fibrous, salty and dry, and at the extreme may have a sour taste. It can be as ineptly fabricated in Scotland as anywhere else. Fortunately, those specialist firms which have survived in

this age of declining haddock populations are, on the whole, quality-oriented.

Real finnan haddie is readily identifiable by its small size when split as it usually appears with backbone intact. In the common U. S. practice of substituting cod the fillet is very much larger, boneless, and is generally crosscut in chunks. When ordering what is obviously smoked cod, ask for the thick centercuts. Unless your fishmonger is generous the chances are that you won't be granted only centercuts, but at least he'll be warned away from foisting off the thin belly and tail pieces which inevitably have the texture of rope. Whether cod or haddock is used, finnan haddie is often a dyed product (either golden or lemon-colored) which is part of the curing process.

Aberdeen Finnan   In the Scotch trade it's properly called "Finnan Haddie" when the fish is hung vertically in the smokehouse, which results in a flat shape; it becomes an "Aberdeen Finnan" when smoked horizontally, thus causing the bone to curve.

Aberdeen Smokie   A very small haddock, headed and gutted but not split. Usually brined and hot-smoked.

Arbroath Smokie   Also a small haddock, headed and gutted but not split. It may be dry-salted or pickled in heavy brine (80°), then cold-smoked for several hours and finally hot-smoked. Recognized by its dark or coppery color, this process is known as the **Auchmithie Cure.**

Eyemouth Cure   A split smoked haddock in which the backbone is intact on the right-hand side of the fish. In the Eyemouth Cure the fish is only lightly smoked.

London Cut Cure   A split smoked haddock in which the backbone is intact on the left-hand side of the fish—a Grimsby "style" for the London market. Lightly smoked and never dyed, this pale product is favored among gourmets.

HAKE   There are at least a dozen species of hakes found in the world's oceans. These true members of the cod family are widely utilized by many nations. Hakes differ from other cods in having coarser, less bland-tasting flesh. However, hake can be a fine foodfish if properly handled after capture. Hake fillets should be packed in plastic bags before chilling, and should never be placed in direct contact with ice; melting ice or water storage will soften the meat to an unappetizing degree. The red hake *(Uropycis chuss)* and the white hake *(U. tenuis)*, common to the western Atlantic, are particularly palatable. In general these are small slender fish; while the white hake may reach a weight of 60 pounds, the average size is 1 to 2 pounds. As an abundant, inexpensive source of protein hake plays an important role in South American, African

Processing haddock to make finnan haddie at John Ross, Aberdeen, Scotland. The haddock is dyed to give it the characteristic golden color, then smoked, finally packaged for shipment in the familiar wooden boxes.

and Mediterranean cuisine. The **merluza** of Spanish-speaking countries is one of the hakes. Due to the characteristics of its flesh, hake is generally cooked in or served with a sauce based on tomato and onion.

During our winter months after a sudden temperature drop it's not unusual for a coldkill of hake to occur along the beaches of New York and New Jersey. Thousands of "frostfish" are washed ashore and collected by savants who dwell by the waterside. This bounty is usually harvested at night by walking the surf edge with a flashlight. Sea gulls quickly consume the frozen hake at dawn's first glow.

LINGCOD A common name for one of the Pacific greenlings which are not related to the cod. *See GREENLING.*

PACIFIC COD A look-alike relative of the Atlantic cod found in the North Pacific Ocean from Western Korea to the Bering Sea and south to the coast of Oregon. The maximum size is about 20 pounds, but this cod *(Gadus macrocephalus)* is not as numerically abundant as the Atlantic species. Nevertheless it's intensively harvested by Japanese vessels and to some extent by Soviet trawlers. The Pacific cod fishery was one of the catalysts in negotiations between the U. S. and Russia when acquiring Alaska in 1867. However, due to the long voyages necessary to reach the cod grounds and return to American ports, the total landings declined rather quickly. Presently, a few million pounds are marketed annually in Oregon, Washington and California, some in fresh form but mainly as a frozen product. These are labeled as "true cod" to distinguish them from the various related and unrelated species that have a cod name. The Pacific cod is similar in texture and flavor to its eastern counterpart and can be prepared in all cod recipes.

POLLOCK This abundant member of the cod family *(Pollachius virens)* is found on both sides of the Atlantic from Newfoundland south to Chesapeake Bay and from the North Sea to the Bay of Biscay, where it is known as **saithe** or **coalfish.** The pollock somewhat resembles an Atlantic cod, however, it has a more rounded body with a distinctly forked tail (the tail of a cod is squared) and a light rather than dark-colored lateral line. Found in shallower water than either the cod or haddock, it is caught in large numbers by both sport and commercial fishermen. Pollock reach a maximum weight of about 35 pounds but are marketed mostly in the 4- to 5-pound sizes.

POOR COD A member of the cod family *(Gadus nutus)* found in the northeastern Atlantic and the Mediterranean Sea. The flesh, is inferior to the Atlantic cod but it is popular in Italy **(Merluzzo cappellano)** and Spain **(Mollera).** This cod does not enter the American market.

TOMCOD There are two species, the Atlantic *(Microgadus tomcod)* and Pacific *(M. proximus)* tomcods. Despite their small size (seldom over 1 foot long) these shallow-water coastal fish are easily caught by amateur anglers and both are delicious. In the east, tomcod are found from Labrador south to Virginia, and in the west from central California to Alaska. Although considered marine forms, they are chiefly taken in brackish estuaries and rivers, particularly during the winter spawning season from November to February. The Hudson River directly in New York City has a faithful band of gourmets who brave chill winds to collect these miniature cod. The commercial catch is so small on either coast that tomcod is only an occasional item at market.

WALLEYE POLLOCK Usually sold as "Alaska pollock," this member of the cod family *(Theragra chalcogramma)* differs from its Pacific relatives by its very large eyes and projecting lower jaw. Although more widely distributed than the Pacific cod, the walleye pollock is taken mainly by Japanese, Soviet and Korean vessels. The fish is seldom marketed fresh but appears most often in Japan as a salted product **(Hiraki-Sukesodara)** or in freeze-dried form **(Tokan-Hin).** Fillets are sometimes cured in rice wine, and the roes are salted and colored with a red vegetable dye. The latter caviar-type product is packed in barrels or boxes and sold as **Momijiko.**

CAPE COD FISH CHOWDER

2 pounds cod or tautog fillets, cut into chunks	2 medium-size onions, peeled and diced
2 cups water	4 cups milk or half-and-half
2 cups fish stock or clam juice	1 tablespoon butter
salt	pepper
3 potatoes, peeled and diced	1 tablespoon minced
¼ pound salt pork, cubed	fresh dill (optional)

Place fish in a kettle; add water, stock and 1 teaspoon salt. Cook the fish over low heat just to the point where it can be flaked with a fork but remains firm. With a slotted spoon or spatula remove fish and reserve liquid to cook the diced potatoes. While potatoes simmer, brown salt-pork cubes in a skillet, then add onions and cook over low heat until onions are transparent. Add onions and cracklings to the liquid. Test potatoes; if done, return fish to liquid and add the milk and butter. Increase heat to bring liquid just to the boiling point, then turn off heat. Add salt and pepper to taste and dill. Makes 6 servings.

facing page, Finnan haddie with poached eggs, at Castle Cullen, Scotland

PORTUGUESE FISH CHOWDER

2 pounds cod or tautog fillets, cut into chunks	1 teaspoon salt
4 cups water	3 potatoes, peeled and diced
4 cups fish stock or clam juice	¼ pound salt pork, cubed
½ teaspoon saffron shreds	2 medium-size onions, peeled and diced
2 tablespoons vinegar	2 garlic cloves, mashed
	salt and pepper

Place fish in a kettle; add water, stock, saffron, vinegar and salt. Poach the fish over low heat until it can be flaked with a fork but still remains firm. With a slotted spoon or spatula remove fish to a platter; reserve liquid to cook potatoes. While potatoes simmer, brown salt pork in a skillet, then add onions and garlic and cook over low heat until onions are transparent. Discard garlic. Add onions and cracklings to the liquid. Test potato cubes; if they are done, return fish to liquid. Let simmer until the fish is completely cooked. Season to taste. Makes 6 servings.

BOOTHBAY FISH CHOWDER

2½ pounds haddock, cod, tautog, or black sea bass	10 onions
5 medium-size potatoes	salt and pepper
1 pound salt pork	1 quart light cream or evaporated milk

Skin the fish and cut it into chunks. Parboil the potatoes, peel them, and dice. Skin the salt pork if necessary, slice, and fry until crisp; save the rendered fat. Let the slices cool, then dice. Slice the onions and fry in the reserved salt-pork fat until golden brown. In a large kettle, about 4-quart size, arrange the ingredients in layers—fish, potatoes, salt pork, onions—sprinkling salt and pepper on each layer. Add just enough water to reach the top of the layers, then boil hard for 10 minutes. Meanwhile, heat the cream in a double boiler and add to the chowder. Serve with New England ship's biscuit. Makes 5 servings.

This recipe can be doubled if you have a kettle large enough. Frozen fish can be used in this chowder.

COD WITH EGG SAUCE

2 pounds fresh or frozen cod fillets	¼ cup flour
1½ cups milk	½ teaspoon dry mustard
¾ teaspoon salt	⅛ teaspoon white pepper
¼ cup butter or margarine	2 hard-cooked eggs, chopped
	2 tablespoons minced parsley

Thaw fillets slightly for ease of cutting. Cut into serving-size portions. Place in a single layer in a greased shallow baking dish. Combine milk and ½ teaspoon salt. Pour over fish. Place fish in a moderate oven (350°F.) and bake for 30 minutes, or until fish has lost its watery look, becoming a milky white color, and will flake easily when tested with a fork. Remove from oven. Pour off milk; use to make sauce. Keep fish warm.

Melt butter; blend in flour, mustard, ¼ teaspoon salt and the pepper. Cook and stir over low heat until bubbly. Add hot milk gradually. Cook and stir until smoothly thickened. Add eggs and parsley. Pour sauce over fish and reheat for several minutes. Or carefully remove fish to a heated platter and garnish to taste, and serve sauce separately at the table. Makes 6 servings.

PILGRIMS' COD STEAKS

6 cod steaks	2 garlic cloves, chopped fine
salt and pepper	2 cups whole-berry cranberry sauce
½ cup melted butter	parsley sprigs
2 tablespoons fresh lemon juice	lemon wedges
1 onion, chopped fine	

Preheat oven to 350°F. Sprinkle both sides of cod with salt and pepper. Place steaks in a single layer in a buttered foil-lined shallow pan. Mix melted butter, lemon juice, onion and garlic, and cook over gentle heat until onion is golden. Pour mixture over cod steaks. Bake for 30 minutes, or until fish becomes white and flakes easily. Add cranberry sauce and simmer until bubbly. Simmer for 5 minutes more, then serve cod steaks with sauce spooned over. Garnish platter with parsley and lemon wedges. Makes 6 servings.

BONAVISTA BAY CODS' TONGUES

24 cod tongues	½ teaspoon salt
½ cup milk, or 1 egg	1 cup peanut oil
½ cup flour	

In schooner days each fisherman was required to keep count of the number of cod caught and the simplest tally was to remove the tongue. The tongues were then salted in barrels and sold with the rest of the fish. Their distinctive flavor is relished by seafaring people.

Wipe the tongues with a damp cloth. If salted tongues are used, soak them in cold water for 10 minutes. Dip the tongues into milk or slightly beaten egg, and roll in salted flour. Fry in hot peanut oil for 3 to 5 minutes. Allow 4 or 5 tongues per serving. Makes 5 to 6 servings.

Cod cheeks may be cooked by the same method.

SAUTÉED COD ROE

1 large cod roe, or	4 slices of bacon, cut into
2 small roes	small crosswise strips
¼ cup flour	¼ cup melted butter
¼ cup peanut oil	¼ cup chopped parsley

If the roe is a large winter roe (before spawning), gently simmer it in boiling salted water for about 5 minutes to firm and partially cook, or the roe will burn on the outside without heating the interior. Small summer roes do not require simmering.

Roll roe in flour and brown in peanut oil. Add bacon pieces and cook until transparent. Add melted butter and continue browning until roe is crisp skinned. Arrange on a platter and pour liquid from pan over it. Sprinkle with parsley. Makes 2 servings.

MERLUZA KOSKERA
(HAKE BASQUE FASHION)
(El Emperador, Fuenterrabia, Spain)

8 skinless fillets of hake	4 tablespoons chopped
3 garlic cloves, minced	parsley
3 tablespoons olive oil	½ cup shelled green peas,
salt	blanched
flour	8 asparagus tips, cooked
12 shelled cooked shrimps	1 hard-cooked egg, sliced

Sauté garlic in oil, stirring constantly so garlic does not burn. Meanwhile sprinkle hake fillets with salt and coat with flour. Sauté hake in garlic-flavored oil for 4 minutes, then carefully turn over without breaking the fish. After this do not touch the fish but move the pan to and fro to mix the oil and flour. When the mixture thickens add a few drops of water. When hake is done, add the shrimps and sprinkle generously with parsley and green peas. Remove from heat, garnish with asparagus tips and egg slices, and serve in the pan. Makes 4 servings.

BRANDADE DE MORUE

La brandade de morue, or cream of salt cod, is believed to have originated in southwestern France in the city of Nîmes. It's one of the most famous dishes in the whole repertoire of Provençal cookery, served hot or cold, often as an hors d'oeuvre. As the word brandade implies, the cod is literally "beat up" or blended to a stiff creamy consistency; it is served in a smooth dome shape decorated with truffles (a rather expensive garnish today), surrounded by small toast triangles fried in butter or olive oil. Usually a brandade is strong on garlic, although this can be adjusted according to taste. The cod may be passed through the finest blade of a food grinder, then worked into a paste in a mortar with a pestle, but an electric blender is easier to use. Of course, salt haddock or pollock can be substituted for cod although the availability of the latter is greater. Variations of brandade de morue which eliminate the cream or milk are popular in Spain and in Italy.

1½ pounds boneless salt cod	milk (optional)
3 fresh garlic cloves,	juice and fine-grated
pressed	rind of ½ lemon
1 cup heavy cream	freshly ground black pepper
⅔ cup olive oil	toast triangles sautéed
1 large potato, boiled	in butter or olive oil
and mashed	

Soak the cod fillets in water in a nonmetal container overnight, changing the water occasionally. To begin the brandade, put cod in a suitable pot, cover with cold water, bring to a boil, and simmer for 10 minutes. Turn off heat and allow the fish to steep for 15 minutes. Drain the cod on a towel and flake with a fork. Put cod in an electric blender with pressed garlic, 4 tablespoons cream and 4 tablespoons olive oil; blend mixture to a paste, adding remainder of cream and olive oil alternately with the potato until they are completely absorbed and the mixture has a stiff but creamy consistency. Depending on the moisture retained by the cod and the size of the potato, it may be necessary to add a small amount of milk to get the right texture. Spoon the mixture into a double boiler and reheat, adding the lemon juice and grated lemon rind, and season with black pepper ground from a pepper mill. Serve hot or cold. Makes 6 servings.

BACCALÀ ALLA LIVORNESE
(SALT COD IN TOMATO SAUCE)

2 pounds boneless salt cod	2 tablespoons minced
½ cup flour	fresh parsley
½ cup olive oil	2 tablespoons minced
1 medium-size onion, sliced	fresh orégano
2 garlic cloves, minced	white pepper
1 pound ripe tomatoes,	sugar
skinned, seeded and chopped,	
or canned plum tomatoes	

Soak cod and simmer according to basic preparation (p. 78). Drain on paper towels and cut into 2-inch squares or strips. Dust cod with flour, then sauté in the oil only to brown both sides. Place fish in a flameproof casserole or glass baking dish. If there's any oil left in the pan, pass through a strainer into a measuring cup and add more, if necessary, to equal ¼ cup. Wipe the saucepan clean, add the oil, and sauté onion and garlic until pale yellow and soft. Add tomatoes, parsley and orégano. Cover and simmer for 8 minutes. Season with white pepper and a pinch of sugar. Cover the cod with the sauce. Bake in a 275°F. oven for 20 minutes. Serve hot with polenta. Makes 6 to 8 servings.

BACALAO EN SALSA VERDE (CODFISH IN GREEN SAUCE)

2 pounds salt cod	1 pound potatoes, peeled
2 onions, chopped	and sliced thin
4 garlic cloves, chopped	3 tablespoons minced
½ cup olive oil	fresh parsley, or more

Prepare cod according to basic preparation (p. 78). Remove cod from heat and bone, then return boned fish to the water in which it was cooked. Sauté the onions and garlic in the olive oil until light brown. Add potato slices and parsley, then add enough of the cod broth to cover vegetables. Let the mixture simmer, shaking pan frequently, until liquid begins to thicken into a sauce. At this point the potatoes should be about half done. Add the fish, skin side up, and cover the pan. Let everything simmer slowly until time to serve. Makes 6 servings.

BACALAO LIGADO (BLENDED SALT COD)

2 pounds salt cod	2 cups olive oil
from rib cage	4 garlic cloves

This requires a large fillet of salt cod, transparent pieces from the belly. Cut the fish into square pieces. Desalinize according to basic preparation (p. 78). Scale carefully without tearing the skin, and remove the bones while fish is raw. Place pieces of fish in skillet; cover with cold water and bring to a boil. When a slight foam forms on the surface, remove from heat; drain fish on a towel and cool; save 1 cup of the cod broth and cool it also. Meanwhile put the oil in a large earthenware pan, place pan on a metal plate over moderate heat, and fry garlic in oil until golden. Remove garlic and crush it in a mortar; add it to the reserved cup of cod broth. Let the oil become cold.

Place the cold pieces of cod in the cold oil—thicker pieces first with the thinest pieces on top. Place the pan over moderate heat. When the oil begins to boil, shake the pan, very slowly at first and then more quickly. After several minutes, add the garlic broth slowly while continually shaking the pan. The sauce will thicken in approximately 15 minutes and become blended. Reduce the heat and let the mixture cook at a slow boil until the cod is

tender, shaking the pan from time to time so the fish does not stick; pass a spatula under it if necessary. When the cod is tender (do not overcook), taste for salt. Increase the heat and shake the pan until the sauce is thick and creamy. Serve immediately, sprinkled with a generous amount of minced parsley. Some like to add a minced hard-cooked egg yolk to the broth before adding it to the pan. Makes 6 servings.

PIL-PIL

This is less a recipe than a Basque method of cod cookery. The term *pil-pil* means "simmered"; in this method the only ingredients other than salt cod are olive oil and garlic. This dish is often confused with blended cod, but true *pil-pil* is made only with clear oil, and it is made without shaking the pan, which is done with many cod dishes. This classic Basque dish should be brought to the table "with the sound of boiling." The pieces of cod are taken from the gelatinous belly section including the rib cage. The cod is desalinized by soaking overnight, then covered with fresh cold water and brought to a boil. Allow to simmer for 10 minutes, then steep in the same water for another 15 minutes. Drain the cod on a paper towel and with a fork pick out all bones, keeping the pieces as intact as possible (you don't want shreds). *Pil-pil* is prepared in a broad shallow pan or fireproof casserole. Drip in some olive oil and 2 or more minced garlic cloves—the amounts determined by the volume of cod. When the garlic is *blond* arrange the pieces of salt cod, skin side down, in one layer in the pan. Fry fish on one side, then turn over. Bring oil to a fast boil, and serve *pil-pil* immediately, in the same pan in which it was cooked.

BACALAO A LA VIZCAINA (CODFISH BISCAYAN FASHION)
(El Emperador, Fuenterrabia, Spain)

2 pounds boneless salt cod	salt
1 cup diced onion	white pepper
3 garlic cloves, minced	3 large red bell peppers,
4 tablespoons olive oil	roasted and peeled,
2 dried hot red peppers	or pimientos, cut
2 pounds fresh tomatoes,	into large strips
chopped	2 tablespoons chopped parsley

Prepare the cod according to basic preparation (p. 78); after desalinizing cut the fish into squares and poach for 10 minutes only.

Make the sauce. Cook onion and garlic in 3 tablespoons olive oil until onion is nearly brown. Add hot peppers and tomatoes, and cook until liquid has evaporated. Put the mixture through a sieve to separate tomato skins and seeds. Season the sauce with salt and white pepper to taste.

Cover the bottom of an earthenware serving dish with a layer of sauce, and place the cod squares on top. Cover with the rest of the sauce and arrange the pimiento strips around the dish. Sprinkle with the parsley and dribble remaining 1 tablespoon olive oil over all. Put in a moderate oven (350°F.) for 10 minutes, or until everything is heated through, and serve at once. Makes 6 servings.

NEW ENGLAND CODFISH BALLS

¾ pound boneless salt cod	2 eggs
1 tablespoon grated onion	flour
4 tablespoons milk	peanut oil
freshly ground black pepper	butter
3 medium-size potatoes, boiled and mashed	

Soak cod according to basic preparation (p. 78). Drain and place in a suitable pot; cover with water, bring to a boil, and simmer for 10 minutes. Remove from heat and allow to steep in hot water for 15 minutes. Drain the cod on a paper towel and flake with a fork. Combine grated onion, milk, freshly ground pepper to taste, cod and mashed potatoes. Bind with raw eggs. If mixture is too dry, add a little more milk. Shape mixture into balls. Flour them and brown on both sides in peanut oil to which a little butter may be added. Garnish with parsley and lemon. Makes 4 servings.

Conch

Although historians do not agree as to which island is the real San Salvador, in October of 1492 when Admiral Christopher Columbus made landfall in the Bahamas he observed that the gentle Arawak Indians not only thrived on conch (pronounced konk) meat but also made chisels and adz blades, trumpets and ceremonial carvings from its shell. During the next decade Spanish slave-raiding parties shipped some 40,000 Arawaks to the mines of Hispaniola, and the Bahamas remained uninhabited for more than a century. It's no longer clear who first earned the nickname "conch," whether it was the Tory sympathizers who went to the Bahamas to escape the American Revolution ("We would rather eat conch than go to war"), or the English who came to Key West in the 1880s from the Bahamas. In either case the kindred souls who settled in

the Florida Keys became identified with this mollusk for the simple reason that it was so abundant and regularly consumed. When the law finally closed the gaming and bawdy houses on Front Street in Key West its most famous madam, affectionately known as "Mom," retreated to Stock Island in a motorcade with two girls in each car, coyly peeking from under parasols. For those who bore witness, Mom rode in the lead vehicle with a loudspeaker, inviting all assembled "conchs" to her new location.

While the names conch and whelk are sometimes used interchangeably, these gastropods are in different families. The conchs (Strombidae) are a more southerly form, and the **edible pink** or **queen conch** *(Strombus gigas)* is limited in the U. S. mainly to the Florida Keys. Among people who consume large amounts of conch a careful distinction is made between "thin-lipped" conch, which is the edible pink, and the "thick-lipped" or samba conch found in the same areas of Florida and the Bahamas. However, experts believe these are the same species, the differences being the result of age and area of growth. The thin-lipped specimens are considered to be younger. The **samba** or older conch also has a pinkish interior shell but with a delft blue exterior, and it is easily recognized by the very thick lip. Various conchs can have an emetic effect, but no generalizations are appropriate. In some island kitchens "double boiling" or the practice of bringing conch meat to a boil until froth collects at the surface, then pouring the water off and cooking in fresh water, is considered a protective procedure. However, there's no mistaking the porcelainlike interior of the younger queen conch's shell, which ranges from a bright pink to a blazing sunset in color, and the banded brown and buff exterior. Other edible conchs are **Verrill's conch** *(S. Verrilli)*, which is very similar to the queen except for having 9 to 11 spines (instead of 5 to 7) on its shell and is

Pink or queen conch; left, thin-lipped; right, thick-lipped

even more colorful; the **hawkwing conch** *(S. gallus)*, which is a brilliant orange mottled with a black or brown on a lilac, pink or yellow background, and the **milk** or **ivory conch** *(S. costatus)*, which is colored yellow, pink, brown or pale mauve.

In the same geographical area we also find **helmets** of the family Cassididae which are so popular among shell collectors. Helmets are *not* conchs but are included here for the reason that these large colorful gastropods have been the source of painful gastronomic experiments due to their vague similarity to the strombids. The meats of our common helmets, the flame helmet *(Cassis flammaea)*, queen helmet *(C. madagascariensis)* and the king helmet *(C. tuberosum)* are a powerful emetic and should *not* be eaten.

While the old calypso ballad *Conch Ain't Got No Bones* is valid, the meat is tough. Like the abalone it must be tenderized. To remove the meat from the shell, with a hammer tap a hole in the third spiral down. This leads to the columellar muscle that attaches the body to the shell. Insert a sharp slender knife to cut the muscle free and the body will drop out. As with the whelks the edible part of a conch is the foot; the horny clawlike operculum must be removed and the large muscle needs to be skinned. At this stage the muscle can be pounded to tenderize, or simply passed through a food grinder, according to recipe requirements. The flavor is that of a very mild clam but distinctively a conch. It is not as strongly flavored as the whelk and for this reason is not popular in the ethnic New York market. However, about 1,300 tons of conch are consumed in the U. S. each year.

Conchs are most often made into chowders but salads, fritters and just plain fried conch (called "cracked conch") are luscious alternatives. There are as many versions of chowders and salads as there are conch aficionados. Some salad makers wouldn't consider using cucumbers or celery, and others eliminate tomatoes. The use of spices, or the amount of spices, is a tongue-searing subject in many Bahamian and Keys kitchens, and bird peppers and hot pepper sauce must be used to individual taste. Personally, I prefer the pure conch flavor which is an organoleptic experience in itself. This is best enjoyed in a "New England" style chowder with a milk or cream base. *See also WHELK* .

CONCH CHOWDER

24 conchs	3 onions, diced
½ pound butter	4 cups canned tomatoes
4 cups water	2 bay leaves
6 large carrots, diced	½ cup flour
2 green peppers, diced	¼ cup salad oil
8 potatoes, diced	salt and pepper

Grind conchs in a food grinder. Simmer the pieces in the butter until tender. Mix water, vegetables and bay leaves in a large kettle and simmer until vegetables are tender. Add conch meat and butter to the kettle and continue to simmer. Brown flour in the oil, stir the roux into the chowder, and simmer until thickened. Season to taste. Makes 8 servings.

BAHAMA CONCH CHOWDER
(Deep Water Cay Club)

12 conchs	4 cups fresh milk or
3 large mild red	evaporated milk
or white onions	3 cups diced boiled potatoes
2 small green peppers	salt and freshly ground
2 ounces salt pork	pepper
1 garlic clove, crushed	2 tablespoons butter
1 teaspoon dried thyme	2 tablespoons flour
4 bay leaves	¼ cup sherry,
2 teaspoons sugar	Madeira or Marsala

Skin conchs, pound with a mallet as if pounding veal cutlet, and cut into 1½-inch squares. Chop onions and green peppers. Render salt pork, and cook onions and peppers in fat until tender; discard pork. Cover conch meat with water in a large kettle, then add garlic, thyme, bay leaves and sugar. Simmer until conch is sweetly tender. Add milk and potato dice, stirring potato in gently. Add onions and green peppers. Season with salt and pepper to taste. Mix butter and flour to make *beurre manié* and use as much as needed to thicken the chowder. Add wine at the last. Serve with pilot biscuit, dried in the oven. Makes 8 servings.
NOTE: The trimmings from the conch can be used for stock. Strain out the bits and use the stock instead of plain water to add more flavor to the chowder.

KEYS CONCH CHOWDER

1 pound conch meat	3 medium-size potatoes, diced
2 large onions, chopped	1 tablespoon dried orégano
3 garlic cloves, mashed	½ tablespoon salt
1 green pepper, chopped	⅛ teaspoon pepper
8 ounces tomato sauce	1 bird pepper, chopped fine
6 ounces tomato paste	sherry

Put conch through a food grinder, using coarse blade, or pound with a mallet and cut into very small pieces. Cover with water and simmer for 30 min-

HOW TO REMOVE CONCH FROM ITS SHELL AND HOW TO USE THE MEAT

1. Use a hammer to tap a hole in the third spiral down. **2.** Insert a sharp slender knife in the hole and cut the columellar muscle that attaches the body to the shell. **3.** The body will drop out. **4.** The conch separated from the shell. **5.** Remove the operculum. **6.** Skin the muscle. **7.** The conch ready to use. **8.** To make conch salad, cut the meat into small bits and marinate in lime juice with onion and seasoning.

9. Mix conch with green pepper, celery and onion (see recipe on p. 92). **10.** To make conch fritters, make a batter with eggs, milk and flour, and add ground conch and seasonings. **11.** Drop batter by tablespoon into hot oil and brown on all sides. **12.** Pile up the fritters in decorative fashion, and serve with cocktail sauce (see recipe on p. 92).

utes. Add onions, garlic, green pepper, tomato sauce, tomato paste, potatoes and 3 more cups water. Add orégano, salt, pepper and bird pepper. Simmer until potatoes are tender, about 30 minutes. Add a dash of sherry to each serving. Makes 4 to 6 main-course servings, or 6 to 8 soup-course servings.

CREAM OF CONCH SOUP
(Spanish Cay)

6 conchs, bruised	¼ teaspoon dried thyme,
6 cups water	or sprig of fresh thyme
2 celery ribs with leaves,	salt and pepper
chopped	3 tablespoons butter
2 raw carrots, chopped	2 tablespoons flour
1 green pepper, chopped	2 cups heavy cream
1 large onion, quartered	¼ cup sherry
2 tomatoes, quartered	

Put the conchs in a large kettle and add the water, vegetables and thyme. Bring to a boil and simmer for 1 hour. Remove 4 conchs and set aside for another use. Grind remaining 2 conchs and reserve. Strain the broth, pressing all liquid out of the vegetables. Season the broth to taste. Melt the butter in the top part of a double boiler over simmering water. Stir in flour, then the seasoned broth and the ground conch. Mix well and continue to heat but do not let it boil. Just before serving add the cream and heat, then add sherry and serve. Makes 6 servings.

CONCH FRITTERS

1 pound conch meat	2 bird peppers, chopped fine,
1 egg	or ¼ teaspoon
⅓ cup milk	hot pepper sauce
1⅓ cups sifted flour	peanut oil for frying
2 teaspoons baking powder	
½ teaspoon salt	
½ teaspoon celery seeds,	
or 1 tablespoon	
minced onion	

Put conch through a food grinder, using coarse blade, or pound with a mallet and cut into very small pieces. Beat egg and add milk. Sift flour with baking powder and salt and add to egg mixture. Add chopped conch, celery seeds or onion, and chopped peppers or hot pepper sauce. Drop batter by tablespoon into hot oil. Brown on all sides. Drain on absorbent paper. Serve hot with tartare sauce or cocktail sauce, if desired. Makes about 3 dozen fritters.

If serving fritters as a main dish, you may prefer a less spicy flavor. Reduce the amount of bird peppers or hot pepper sauce. Make the fritters larger, about 2 tablespoons of batter for each fritter. Makes about 16 fritters. After draining the fritters of either size, pile them in a pyramid on a folded cloth napkin to serve. Garnish with parsley sprigs and lemon wedges or halves.

BAHAMIAN FISH BALLS
(Lighthouse Club, Andros Island)

2 conchs, pounded	3 slices of stale bread
½ pound grouper or snapper	3 eggs
¼ pound raw shrimps	1 tablespoon Tabasco
1 whole onion	½ teaspoon salt
1 celery rib	pepper
2 slices of pimiento	oil for deep-frying

Put conchs, fish, shrimps, onion, celery, pimiento and bread through a food grinder, using the fine blade. Stir mixture with a spoon until well mixed. Add eggs, Tabasco, salt, and pepper to taste. Roll mixture into balls, using 2 to 3 tablespoons of the mixture for each ball. Drop into oil heated to 375°F. and fry until golden brown. Makes about 24 appetizer balls.

CONCH SALAD

1 pound conch meat
1 large onion, or 3 green onions, chopped fine
6 tablespoons lime juice
¼ cup cider or wine vinegar
4 tablespoons olive or salad oil
1¼ teaspoons Worcestershire sauce
2 bird peppers, chopped fine, or
    ¼ teaspoon hot pepper sauce
1 large green pepper, chopped
2 celery ribs, chopped fine
½ cucumber, peeled and chopped fine
2 medium-size tomatoes, chopped
½ tablespoon salt
¼ teaspoon pepper

Put conch through a food grinder, using coarse blade, or pound with a mallet and cut into pieces about the size of a small green pea. Combine conch, onion, lime juice, vinegar, olive oil and Worcestershire sauce in a bowl. Mix well. Let stand in refrigerator for 3 or 4 hours, or overnight.

Add bird peppers or hot pepper sauce, green pepper, celery, cucumber, tomatoes, salt and pepper. Mix thoroughly and chill. Makes 4 or 5 luncheon servings, or 10 or 11 appetizer servings.

CONCH SALAD
(Donald P. de Sylva)

Tenderize conch by pounding the meat, then cut into ¼-inch cubes. Marinate in half water and half Key lime juice, using just enough to cover the top of the chopped conch. Sprinkle with sliced Bermuda onions and let stand for 15 minutes. Toss conch and onions together, and add salt to taste, freshly ground black pepper and bits of peppers—bell peppers, or hot Jalapeño or Havana peppers. Toss again and marinate in the refrigerator for 4 to 6 hours, stirring frequently. Toward the end of the marinating, add chopped celery.

At serving time arrange on cold shredded lettuce, spooning some of the marinating liquid over each serving. Sprinkle with chopped ripe tomato.

VARIATION: Add white wine toward the end of marinating. Or add coconut milk early in the process. Use about ¼ cup of either to each 1 cup of the lime and water mixture.

Conger Eel

A large marine eel of the family Congridae as distinguished from the freshwater eels or Anguillidae. Congers differ from the more common anguillids in several physical characters, the most distinctive being in their lack of scales. Unlike the freshwater eels of Europe and North America the conger does not spawn in a defined area (the Sargasso Sea) but lives inshore and migrates off the continental shelves to reproduce. Some species are quite large, reaching weights of 80 pounds or more. The European conger has some value as a foodfish and is marketed fresh in steak form, and hot-smoked. It often appears in *bouillabaisse* (French **congre**) and Mediterranean fish chowders. It's sold in Germany preserved in aspic as **Kochfischwaren** and is utilized to some extent in Japan **(anago).** Conger meat is generally inferior to the anguillids. *See EEL.*

Cooking Methods
DEEP-FRYING

Deep-frying is a popular method for cooking many kinds of fish. The important step, and the one often neglected, is bringing the oil to a proper temperature before adding the fish. A thermometer is necessary if one is to run the gamut from deep-frying whole large fish, which is done at lower temperatures, to cooking thin fingers or small whole fish, which is done at higher temperatures. As a rule most deep-frying is done at 360° to 380°F., the point at which oil

bubbles profusely when a dollop of batter is dropped on the surface. However, like most culinary rules, this has many exceptions. The temperature at which you deep-fry fish depends on the size or density of the pieces to be cooked and the kind of fat or oil used. In general the smaller the fish, say a baby smelt or the classic whitebait, the higher the temperature should be as the fish must brown quickly without overcooking—within 2 minutes. If the fish is thicker, and particularly if it contains much moisture, the temperature will have to be considerably lower in order to cook through and brown without burning the outside surface.

Plain butter has the lowest burning point (248°F.) and olive oil the highest (554°F.). Clarified butter will allow another 20° to 30° of heat before burning, but even clarified butter is more suitable for sautéing and panfrying than for deep-frying. Olive oil has a strong flavor and overwhelms most fish as well as Anglo-Saxon palates. Optionally then, we have rendered animal fats with a reasonable burning point (392°F.) and peanut, corn and cottonseed oils which provide a viable range to 518° without introducing a foreign flavor. Although I always favor peanut oil, most tempura kitchens, for example, use combinations of 5 or 6 oils (typically 50 percent sesame, 15 percent corn, 15 percent cottonseed, 10 percent olive oil, and 10 percent safflower oil) to maintain a high burning point while enhancing the flavor and crispness in the finished product. On the other hand, and who can argue with success, the largest "fish-and-chip" restaurant in England, Harry Ramsden's in Yorkshire, deep-fries over 400,000 pounds of fish per year (as well as 900,000 pounds of potatoes) using only the finest beef renderings or "drippings." Animal fats, including lard which is rendered from pork, impart a flavor of their own; for a bland fish such as the haddock, which Ramsden favors, rendered beef fat is eminently feasible.

One other important point in deep-frying is to let the oil or fat return to the desired temperature before adding another batch of food. Each time you lower a basket of fish into the oil, you reduce the temperature of the oil. Even a fryer with a thermostat needs to be watched for this.

Before cooking, first dip fish into milk, then into flour; or dust with flour, then dip into beaten egg and bread crumbs; or dip into a batter, roll in cornmeal, or dust with cornstarch. The oil should be deep so that the pieces of fish are completely submerged. When cooked they will rise to the surface. The fish should be drained on absorbent paper and served immediately.

Batters are usually preferable on fish for

deep-frying to achieve a crisp outside texture without loss of flavor. There are many formulas for batters, specifying various kinds of flour and differing volumes of liquid, but the basic tenet in using batters is temperature contrast. A batter must be *ice* cold when the fish is placed in hot, bubbling oil. The oil cannot penetrate the batter but instead forms a crisp coat around the fish, which literally steams inside, losing none of its flavor. If the batter is warm, or the oil at a low temperature, the fish will absorb oil and become soggy in the process. The density of the batter should also be varied according to the thickness of the product to be cooked; these can be divided into two batters—basic and thin. The following ingredients must always be in proportion regardless of the amount made:

BASIC FISH BATTER

1 egg yolk
½ cup ice water
¾ cup self-rising flour

This batter is for normal cooking periods (10 to 15 minutes) when preparing large cuts of fish in chunk, fillet, steak or finger form. These should be ½ inch or thicker. Beat egg yolk in a mixing bowl, add the ice water, and beat again until yolk is well blended. Add the flour and stir with a spoon, but do not smooth the mixture; it should remain slightly lumpy. Of paramount importance is to keep the batter absolutely cold until ready for use. It's a good idea to make the batter several hours in advance and store it in the refrigerator with the fish pieces to be cooked. When the oil is bubbling, dip the fish into the batter and drop into the pan or fryer basket. The result will be crisp and golden brown.

THIN FISH BATTER

1 egg yolk
1 cup ice water
¾ cup self-rising flour

This batter is for fast cooking (2 to 4 minutes) when preparing small whole smelts, shrimps, fillets of perch or sunfish, or fingers of larger fish such as trout, bass, walleye or salmon. These should be no more than ⅜ inch thick. Follow the same mixing procedure as for Basic Fish Batter. When blended the batter will be runny, almost liquid. Place in the refrigerator for several hours. When ready to cook submerge each chilled fish, fillet or finger in the batter and rotate by hand. Only a film of batter will adhere but this is sufficient to prevent oil penetration. The result after cooking will be a flaky crust

which does not detract from the flavor of a delicate small fish.

CHINESE BATTER
(The Mandarin, San Francisco)

1 cup all-purpose flour	1 tablespoon white vinegar
1 cup cornstarch	1 teaspoon baking powder
1 whole egg	1¼ cups cold water
½ teaspoon salt	cottonseed or sesame oil
pinch of sugar	for frying
2 tablespoons cottonseed	
or sesame oil	

This batter is for shrimps, fish fingers, or thin fillets of ½ inch or less.

Mix all ingredients with a whisk until smooth, and keep cold.

To use, sprinkle the shrimps or fish with a little sherry, then dip into batter, covering the pieces completely. Pour oil into a wok or deep-fryer and bring to high heat. Add the batter-coated pieces and reduce heat to moderate (350° to 375°F.). Cook for 2 or 3 minutes, until golden brown, turning if necessary.

Many batters have beer or carbonated water as an ingredient. This is not for flavor, because the flour absorbs the flavor completely; it adds minute bubbles to the batter, thus making it lighter and helping to give the finished coating a crisp texture. If you don't have beer, any carbonated drink will do, even ginger ale. You can counteract the sweetness with a little soy sauce if you like. *For an example of a beer batter, see Fish 'n' Chips under SHARK.*

Any other dish to be served with a batter-coated fish should be prepared and ready to serve before frying the fish or shellfish. If the fish has to wait, the crisp outer crust will become soft and the moisture in the fish will start to make the batter soggy.

DEEP-FRYING IN ADVANCE
(John Weiss)

Measure ¾ cup cornflake crumbs, or crumble 3 cups cornflakes. Mix with ¼ cup flour and 1 tablespoon seasoned salt. If more is needed, double or triple in the same proportions. Dip fish fillets into beaten egg, then roll in the cornflake mixture until there is a thick coating of crumbs. Place in a frying basket and lower into cooking oil heated to 375°F. Cook until crisp and dark brown. Remove basket from oil, drain, then drain fillets further on paper towels. When cool, place on a plate, cover with foil, and place in refrigerator overnight.

Next day place the fillets in an electric skillet,

without any additional oil, cover, and heat to serving temperature.

PANFRYING

Very small whole fish, such as yellow perch, brook trout, smelts or whitebait, are ideal panfried. The fish may be dusted with seasoned flour or cornmeal, then placed in a hot skillet in which a little butter has been brought to the foaming stage. Panfry over low heat and turn the fish to brown on both sides. When properly done the skin of the fish should be crispy, not burned, and the flesh moistly succulent. Use a large skillet so the fish are not crowded, and do not in the course of cooking use a lid—either condition will cause steam and the skin will not crisp. If the fish contain too much moisture (which is one reason why they should not be soaked in water before frying), the butter will splatter. To avoid this, invert a colander over the skillet.

Any fish over 8 inches in length if whole or over ⅜ inch thick in fillet or steak form will not crisp properly in butter alone. Butter has a low burning point and will turn black before cooking is completed. Some restaurants fake their trout *meunière*, for example, by simply sautéing one side of the fish and placing the other side under a broiler, then serving it with the crisper side up. However, this is not necessary. The average 10- to 12-inch-long trout, as well as any other species of comparable size, can be panfried in oil, starting with the oil near smoking and the fish cold. When nicely browned, drain the pan, and finish the trout in melted butter.

Do not use batters on fish that are to be panfried. The liquid ingredients become leathery and unappetizing when subjected to low heat. This is a common error in fish cookery.

SAUTÉING

The distinction between panfrying and sautéing is more observed in other cuisines than in ours, but it is a useful distinction. This process is much quicker—the food should be in and out of the pan in a matter of minutes. The French word for this *(sauter)* means to jump. Sautéing uses higher heat than panfrying, therefore the pan must be perfectly flat with even heat distribution so the fish will cook evenly. Butter alone is unsuitable, not because of the timing as in panfrying but because the heat is greater; however clarified butter is a good choice. Clarified butter mixed with a little oil, or oil alone, will serve best. The amount of oil should be very small, just enough to prevent sticking. Thin and tender pieces of fish that will be fully cooked in minutes can be sautéed. Because the time is so short, it is better to use no coating thicker than a thin layer of flour, or the fish will be cooked while the coating is still raw. It is better to season after sautéing. The pieces of fish should be dry before they are put into the sauté pan. As with panfrying, be sure not to crowd the skillet, and do not use a lid.

Sautéing is a good method for fish that has already been cooked, because it will be enough cooking to heat the food through and to brown it without drying it out.

FISH CAKES—BASIC METHOD

2 cups cooked fish	1 egg, beaten
3 cups prepared	flour
mashed potatoes	bacon or ham fat or cooking
salt and pepper	oil or clarified butter
1 teaspoon minced parsley	parsley sprigs and
1 tablespoon melted butter	lemon slices

Flake the fish and add to the potatoes. Season to taste, and add parsley and melted butter. Mix in as much of the egg as necessary to moisten the mixture; beat thoroughly. Divide into 12 portions, roll each into a ball, then flatten the tops and bottoms. Coat lightly with flour. Sauté in fat or oil or butter until golden brown.

If you prefer, coat the cakes with beaten egg and bread crumbs and deep-fry in oil heated to 375° to 385°F. until browned. Garnish with parsley sprigs and lemon slices. Makes 6 servings.

POACHING OR BOILING

With one exception "boiled fish" is a figure of speech rather than a method of cooking. Fish should *never* be actually boiled, rather poached in seasoned water or stock. This method is ideal for sections of large, firm-fleshed fish, such as salmon, cod or halibut. The fish are poached in a court bouillon or a fish stock, wine and vegetable liquor, or just in plain water and milk. The fish must be completely submerged in the liquid. Bring the court bouillon to a boil before adding the fish, or much of the flavor will be lost. The problem in poaching is to keep the fish intact. It is not difficult with small cuts, but for whole large fish you should wrap them in cheesecloth, or use a regular fish poacher which has a perforated rack on which to place the fish. When the fish are placed in the kettle, the bouillon will cease bubbling for a minute; when the boiling point is again reached, reduce the heat. If cooked too rapidly, fish will fall apart.

The singular exception to the poaching *vs.* boiling methods is the Wisconsin Fish Boil. This method

Cooked fish should flake easily when tested with a fork.

boiling kettle. When the water returns to the boil, gradually add the second pound of salt and cover the pot. Boil for 11 minutes longer.

Lift out fish, potatoes and onions, and serve with butter poured over. Makes 12 servings for men or 18 to 20 for mixed groups.

If using a single kettle, place the fish steaks directly on top of the potatoes and onions after the first 18 minutes. If you like, add bay leaves and peppercorns tied in cheesecloth when adding the fish.

Suitable fish for this method are cod, haddock, halibut, king mackerel, lake trout, red snapper, salmon, steelhead, blackfin and yellowfin tuna, wahoo, whitefish.

BAKING FISH

Baking is ideal for stuffed whole fish, which are to be cooked with skin on, or very thick cuts of fish, which might dry out under direct heat. Fatty fishes such as large mullet, bluefish and king mackerel can also be baked. Baking can be done in a very hot oven for a short period, or in a moderate oven (350° to 375°F.) for a longer time. Preheat the oven; if baking starts in a cold oven the fish tends to steam rather than bake and the exterior may be overdone when the interior is just done. Oil the baking pan so the fish does not stick. To simplify lifting out the cooked fish, line the pan with foil and oil that. According to the individual recipe, whole fish or steaks may be brushed with oil or sprinkled with a topping. Large fish may be basted during baking, and the pan juices can be used in sauce making.

PLANKED FISH

Shad, trout, snapper, whitefish, salmon, halibut and many other species are often cooked and served on a hardwood oak plank. (Do not use planks made of resinous woods, such as pine.) This is a decorative way to present a whole fish, but it can also be done with thick steaks and fillets. The plank should be a grooved one so that the juices can be retained rather than being lost in the oven. Heat the plank in the oven, then oil it thoroughly, preferably with olive oil. Season the fish with salt and pepper, and arrange it on the plank with bits of butter. Bake in a hot oven (400°F.). When fish is almost done, arrange creamy mashed potatoes or duchess potatoes around it. Broil until the potatoes are browned. Add some hot vegetables such as buttered green beans and broiled tomato slices. Garnish with parsley and lemon or radishes. This can be as simple or as elaborate as you like.

Fish can be planked for outdoor cooking also,

requires a special kettle with basket insert in which fish steaks are boiled in a brine of 2 pounds salt to 10 quarts water. This dense saline solution not only raises the boiling point but keeps the fish intact. There is absolutely no salty flavor imparted to the finished product.

WISCONSIN FISH BOIL

This method of boiling fish and potatoes together out of doors originated more than 100 years ago. Scandinavian lumbermen are said to have brought the custom to the shores of Lake Michigan. Use a special fish boil kettle, like a steamer, with an upper pot pierced with holes like a colander, or a large heavy kettle that holds 10 quarts.

12 pounds fish steaks, 1 inch thick
24 medium-size potatoes (about 8 pounds), or new potatoes
12 onions (about 3 pounds)
10 quarts water
2 pounds salt
1 to 1½ cups melted butter

Scrub the potatoes, but do not peel. Cut a thin slice from each end. Potatoes should be of uniform size. Peel onions but leave whole. Place potatoes and water in the kettle, and bring to a boil. Start timing, and gradually add 1 pound of the salt so as not to stop the boiling. Boil for 12 minutes, then add onions and continue to boil for 6 minutes longer. Meanwhile place fish steaks in the upper pot. After the 18 minutes, drop the upper pot into the but for that it will be just fish attached to the plank with wooden pegs or stainless-steel nails. The plank will be placed at an angle toward the fire and should be turned once so fish is cooked evenly. Brush with basting sauce or oil during cooking.

SPENCER HOT-OVEN BAKING

This method was originated by Mrs. Evalene Spencer of the U. S. Bureau of Fisheries in 1934, and it has since become known as "oven-frying." Its virtue is that it crisps and browns the fish, minimizes kitchen odors, and doesn't require a significant amount of cooking oil. The directions as Mrs. Spencer set them down, should be followed exactly.

2 pounds fish fillets or steaks	finely sifted bread crumbs
1 cup milk	cooking oil or melted fat
1 tablespoon salt	

Cut the fillets into portions of 3 to 1 pound, and place on the extreme left of your work table or counter. In sequence, next place a bowl containing the salted milk, then a pan containing the finely sifted bread crumbs, lastly an oiled baking pan for the cooking and a cup containing oil or melted fat, with a pastry brush or swab.

With the *left* hand put a piece of fish into bowl of milk, then toss it into the pan of crumbs. Now, with the *right* hand cover the fish with crumbs and place in the baking pan. Keep the *left* hand for the wet work and the *right* hand for the dry work. In this way the crumbs can be all used without becoming dampened, which would happen at once if the hands were interchanged.

With the portions of fish laid side by side in the pan, sprinkle each with a little oil or melted fat from the brush or swab. This is the only fat used in the cooking. The same results are not obtained if the fish is rolled in flour, cornmeal or cracker crumbs, for there is no immersion of fat to brown the covering as in deep-frying. It will be found that any of these other mediums will be browned only in splotches wherever the fat has touched them, while the bread crumbs, with the addition of a little oil or fat, will be uniformly browned.

The next requirement is a very hot oven, 500° to 600°F., at which temperature the fish will be cooked in 10 minutes. Do not be afraid of burning it and *never* add water to fish cooked in this quick-oven way. If the heat has been sufficient, when the fish is taken from the oven the pan will be quite dry underneath the fish; each piece will be beautifully browned on all sides and may be easily removed to a hot platter, with the aid of a spatula, unbro-

Fish fillets baked by the Spencer hot-oven method

ken and perfect.

A variation of the above is to use very thin strips of bacon instead of cooking oil on the fish.

BRAISING

This is a good method for lean fish and small fillets of fat fish, so that they retain their best texture and flavor. Place the fish on a bed of vegetables cut into dice (very small dice—*mirepoix*; even smaller—*brunoise*). Various additions are possible, such as salt-pork bits, herbs, etc., but simplest is often best. The vegetables can be sautéed in clarified butter first. Add a little white wine or stock or other liquid; cover the fish with a buttered parchment or foil, with a small hole in it for steam to escape. Bring the liquid to a boil on top of the stove, then place the baking dish in a preheated oven. As with baking, braising can be done for a short time at relatively high heat (425°F.) or for a longer time at moderate heat (350°F.). The fish will release some juices during the braising, and all this should be poured off to be used in any sauce. In fact, the vegetable mixture and juices can be puréed in a blender or food mill and can be thickened with *beurre manié* to make sauce without further elaboration.

This method is sometimes called "oven-poaching." A related method is cooking *en papillote*, enclosed in a sealed envelope. Originally the envelope may have been leaves or clay, later it came to be cooking parchment, cut in the shape of a double heart, folded over and crimped together. An easier material to use is foil.

Fish *en papillote* is usually served in its envelope, so all the delicious flavors will be contained until the envelope is opened at table. Cooking in plastic oven bags follows the same principle, but food is removed from the plastic for serving. Use only the plastic bags made specifically for oven use.

FISH FILLET IN OVEN BAG

1½ to 2 pounds	2 to 3 tablespoons
fish fillets	melted butter
1 tablespoon flour	1 tablespoon minced herb
1 small onion, chopped	of your choice
3 tablespoons chopped celery	salt, pepper, paprika
2 tablespoons lemon juice	

Preheat oven to 375°F. Shake the flour into a plastic oven bag and add chopped onion and celery, lemon juice and melted butter. Shake the bag to mix all together, and place the bag in a shallow baking pan. Rinse the fillets, pat dry with paper towels, and sprinkle with the herbs, and salt, pepper and paprika to taste. With a spatula slip fillets into the bag atop the vegetables; close the bag with a twist tie. With a paring knife puncture 6 or more ½-inch slits in the top of the bag to permit steam to escape. Make sure bag does not come in contact with oven walls or racks. Bake in preheated oven for 20 to 25 minutes. Remove pan from oven and allow to cool for a few minutes, then slit top of bag with knife and scissors, being careful as the steam escapes. Makes 4 to 6 servings.

A whole fish, freshly dressed, can be baked in the same fashion. Bake at 400°F. for 45 minutes.

BROILING OR GRILLING

A particularly useful method for treating the fatty fishes, such as bluefish, mullet, shad and mackerel. Fish to be broiled should be split, steaked, or filleted. Heat the oven and pan before putting in the fish so that it cooks evenly. Small delicate fish, such as snapper, flounder and trout, can also be broiled, but any lean cut should be cooked at a greater distance from the source of heat and should be basted with butter, oil or a complementary sauce. Very thick cuts of fish, such as grouper or large cod, do not broil well as the application of direct heat makes the outside leathery while the inside is barely warmed.

BROILED FISH IN CRUMB COATING

Dip boneless fish fillets into beaten egg, then coat with a prepared crumb mixture seasoned with garlic salt. Place fillets in a broiler pan and arrange thin slices of cold butter along them. Sprinkle with salt and pepper and lightly with paprika. Broil until flesh is white and flakes when tested with a fork.

BROILED FISH WITH MAYONNAISE

Arrange fish fillets or steaks on a broiler pan, season, and spread with a coating of mayonnaise. Sprinkle with paprika, or minced parsley, or snipped chives. Broil until mayonnaise is puffed and golden brown and fish is done to your taste.

BARBECUE COOKERY

Cooking over charcoal briquets, or on gas- or electric-heated units with ceramic briquets, produces the same result; the dissolving fat and juices from the fish, or oil from the basting liquid, drip on the firebed, creating a unique flavor and aroma. A barbecued product is exposed to both heat and smoke. If seafood is wrapped or sealed in foil and cooked in the same unit the result is a *steamed* product, which can be a desirable result in itself but should not be confused with the term "barbecued." Chiefly an outdoor method of cookery, the addition of moist wood chips, such as apple, hickory or maple, to the firebox adds a delectable smoke flavor to fish.

There can be no exact cooking times for barbecue recipes; heat intensity, the height of the grill over the fire, and the density of the product are extreme variables, although with experience one can accurately estimate when the cooking period is completed. I prefer a low fire and longer periods for most seafoods; this is easy to regulate on an electric- or gas-operated grill but requires considerably more attention when charcoal briquets are used. The musculature of a truly fresh fish contracts rapidly in a high heat and invariably falls apart before the skin is crisped, or in the case of steaks before the meat is cooked through.

Although a black, oily crust around the grid wires from previous use will help prevent the fish sticking, do not expect good results if lumps of crystallized foods are adhering to the metal. Keep the grid clean; lightly coat with vegetable oil before each use and burn it off before the fish is applied.

All fish should be scaled, regardless of the cut used, and brushed with melted butter, vegetable oil, or a butter- or oil-based sauce. The fish should be basted frequently while cooking to seal in its juices; use a pastry brush for this.

STEAKS The easiest cut of fish to barbecue is a steak from 1 to 2 inches in thickness such as you obtain from salmon, lake trout, halibut, mako shark, swordfish, sturgeon, king mackerel, wahoo, yellowfin or blackfin tuna.

These are firm meats and can be gently turned with a spatula one or more times without crumbling. However, it's seldom necessary to rotate steaks more than once. Marinating steaks of any species in lemon or lime juice for 20 to 30 minutes before cooking not only enhances their flavor but helps to firm the fish. Steaks should not be submerged in citrus but simply covered with juice and turned several times.

FILLETS For fish that are too small or thin-bodied to steak, the fillet is an excellent option. Do *not* use skinless fillets. In napecut form with skin on, the meat will remain intact, or the fish can be split and kited and cooked as a double fillet.

Fillets of medium-size or large fish may be the only form obtainable at market but these can be converted into boneless "butterfly steaks." This is done by making a vertical cut to the skin side of the fillet but without penetrating the skin; this first cut should be made from 1 to 2 inches from the nape end according to desired thickness. Follow with a second cut of the same thickness but now cutting completely through. You will then have two halves attached by the skin which can be opened out and formed into a steak. The balance of the fillet can be cut in the same fashion, converting all but the thin tail end into steaks.

WHOLE, DRESSED, SMALL The most difficult fish to barbecue are small ones dressed in the round if the species has a thin skin or soft musculature. Fish such as brook trout, smelt, whitefish, weakfish, Atlantic or Spanish mackerel must be treated with the greatest care to remain intact on the grill. These should not be rotated but cooked over a low fire with the unit cover in place to maintain a uniform heat surrounding the fish.

Small whole fish with thick skins such as porgies, snappers, rockfish, yellow or white perch, black sea bass or school striped bass are easily cooked over the coals and may even be turned if the skin is not scored. However, fish between 2 and 3 pounds in size cook more evenly when scored, as the diagonal slashes across the thickest portions permit uniform heat penetration.

WHOLE, DRESSED, LARGE Any whole fish of over 3 pounds in size may be considered large from a barbecue standpoint as their greater thickness requires use of the grill cover. Scoring is not recommended on very large fish as these require a prolonged cooking period in any case, and there will be a considerable loss of natural juices. Also the backbone becomes extremely fragile and often as not the fish will divide itself in pieces. This is simply a matter of allowing sufficient time on a low fire with the unit cover in place for best results. Some whole barbecued fish, such as bluefish, striped bass, salmon and red snapper, are excellent when served cold *(for recipe see under BLUE-FISH).*

LOBSTER TAILS Spiny lobster tails and the tails of lobsterettes become especially tender when barbecued, perhaps more so than when cooked in a liquid. Simply cut the back of the shell lengthwise with kitchen shears and lift all but the end of the meat free so that it rides "piggyback" on top of the tail. Place shell side down on the grill. Baste frequently with herb butter. Do not use the cover, nor wood chips as too much smoke often imparts a bitter flavor to lobster meat. Serve seated on the shell.

SHRIMPS Large shrimps, and particularly the hard-shelled rock shrimps, are delicious when barbecued. Rock shrimps are marketed in split form, and other whole shrimps should be cut lengthwise along the underside and the meats raised free except at the tail. The cooking period is short but these delicate crustaceans should be continually basted.

Crab

The coasts of North America hold a greater variety of edible crabs than any other continent, and these crustaceans play a significant role in our cuisine. Although the more popular species are localized—the King and Dungeness crabs in the cold Pacific, the stone crab in our semitropical Atlantic, and the blue crab all along our eastern seaboard—these are widely shipped throughout the U.S. in fresh, frozen and canned forms.

Crab meat varies in color and texture but it's an incredibly versatile product which can be boiled, fried, baked, made into curries, pies, croquettes, mousse, aspic, chowders, croustades, ravigote, pancakes, soufflés, and some remarkable soups. For example, **She-Crab Soup,** the spring tonic of South Carolinians, is a combination of the meat and roe of a female blue claw. The female is easily identified by its broad "apron" on the bottom side of the shell. The meat and roe, along with various seasonings, are married into a smooth white roux, made all the creamier by the roe which enhances the texture and adds greatly to the flavor. More difficult perhaps, simply because of availability, is another soup, the classic preparation **la velouté de crabes d'huître au sherry.** This velvety light cream prepared from cracked blue crabs is delicately flavored with old sherry and at the last minute fresh oyster crabs are quickly sautéed in butter and added to the soup.

Certain kinds of crabs lend themselves more readily to a particular preparation method than others.

The following encompasses our major crab species as well as some minor ones which either enter the market from time to time or may be captured by an ambulant gourmet.

CRAB TERMINOLOGY

BLUE CRAB This is the common species of the western Atlantic. It is found from Cape Cod to Florida, in the Bahamas and the Gulf of Mexico. It strays as far north as Nova Scotia and as far south as Uruguay. The blue crab also occurs sporadically in Holland, France and Denmark, and in recent years it appeared in the Mediterranean where the crab proliferated in Greece's Aegean Sea. Its scientific name *Callinectes* or "beautiful swimmer" is prophetically descriptive as the crab is now established along the coasts of Egypt and Lebanon. Like many other exotic marine organisms, this crustacean was probably transported and spread in ship's ballast. The blue crab *(Callinectes sapidus)* inhabits saltwater, as well as freshwater where chlorides exist, but its real abundance is in brackish bays and estuaries of the Gulf of Mexico and in Chesapeake Bay. A closely related species *(Callinectes bellicosus)* which differs little in appearance is found in the Sea of Cortés inside of Baja California peninsula; however, it is a very minor market item in Mexico.

The blue crab is the third most important crustacean commercially in the U.S., following shrimps and lobsters. Although many species of crabs are marketed, the blue crab is best known among seafood fanciers. It belongs to the swimming crab family (Portunidae), which is characterized by having the last pair of legs flattened into paddles for swimming. This crab is easily recognized by its oval shell which varies from a dark-blue or blue-green to brownish with mottlings of blue and cream; it's whitish or cream-colored below with scarlet markings.

Blue crabs appear inshore during warm weather, which may be as early as February in Florida waters, and remain in the shallows until winter's chill. They spawn from May to October in the middle Atlantic region, and the female which carries from ¾ million to 2 million eggs is then known as a sponge crab, cushion crab or berried crab; also as ballie, busted sook, orange crab, punk and lemon crab. The mortality among young crabs is extremely high despite this obvious fecundity. Juvenile blue crabs grow rapidly and within 12 to 18 months they reach adult size. A large blue crab would be 8 inches across the shell at an age of 3 years but these are rarely seen at table.

Lump Meat: Solid lumps of white meat from the body of the crab. This is used in recipes where appearance is

top, Blue crabs; left, male; right, mature female
center, left, Rock crab; right Jonah crab
bottom, Red crab

facing page, Steamed crabs and watermelon for a beach picnic

important such as cocktails and salads.

Flake Meat: Small pieces of white meat from the rest of the body. May be combined with some lump meat.

Claw Meat: Meat picked from the claws which in many crabs is brownish in color, therefore used in recipes where appearance is not important.

BLUE CRAB, SOFTSHELL In the process of growth all crabs must shed their shells, a necessity which provides that gourmet delight, the softshell crab. Although several species can be eaten in this state, only the blue crab is sufficiently meaty and of a size to make collecting worthwhile. Knowing *when* the crab is about to shed requires skill in reading the "sign" along a faint line on the lower or feathered edge of the next to last paddlelike finlet. To the commercial crabber at work the color of the sign determines in which of several large floating boxes the crab will be held according to market demand. If the color is white, the crab is called a "green crab"; it means that the crab will shed in 7 to 10 days and will probably be shipped in hardshell form. If the sign is passing from white to pink, the crab is called a "second." If the color is pink, it will shed in 2 days to 1 week, depending on the shade of pink. If the sign is red, shedding may occur momentarily or at most within 2 days, and this crab goes into a "buster box" for the softshell trade. When shedding occurs, the crab suddenly expands in size by one third as though it were a rubber balloon, and having "busted" the crab is immediately removed from the box. Even hardshell crabs love to eat softshell crabs, and in addition to this hazard the soft carapace will quickly toughen if not promptly taken from saltwater.

CALICO CRAB There are 2 species with this common name. *Eriphia gonagra* is known only by this name, while the other is called also sand crab and lady crab *(which see)*.

DUNGENESS CRAB This is the most popular of the western U.S. crabs and occurs from Alaska to Baja California. The Dungeness *(Cancer magister)*, one of the rock crabs, has a typical deep body and heavy carapace which is usually a pinkish green and yellow before cooking; the cooked crab as seen in markets is bright red and cream in color. Edible Dungeness crabs weigh from 1¾ to 4 pounds, and as a rule of thumb about 25 percent is edible meat. In 1973 U.S. landings of this crab amounted to 12 million pounds.

GREEN CRAB This small crab *(Carcinides maenas)* is a member of the swimming crab family (Portunidae), having more or less of an oval body and the last pair of legs flattened and with pointed tips. The shell has sharp teeth on its anterior edge, with rather short claws. The body is dark green or green with yellow mottlings. Also called "green shore crab." It occurs in European waters and in the United States from Maine to New Jersey. The species was apparently introduced here in the early 1800s, probably into the Cape Cod region. Vast quantities of soft clams are annually destroyed by green crabs in New England, and their depredations cause great economic losses to the industry. Due to its small size (seldom over 3 inches across the shell) the green crab has little commercial value, although it is utilized to some extent in Europe where it is known as the common shore crab or green shore crab. The Mediterranean species is *Carcinides mediterraneus.*

JONAH CRAB A distinctive species *(Cancer borealis).* Its elliptically shaped, roughened shell is convex, brick red above and yellowish below. Its larger size, coloration, thicker legs and scalloped shell distinguish it from the common rock crab *(Cancer irroratus)*, found from New England to Florida and Bahamas, whose yellowish shell is heavily spotted with small red dots. Only abundant in certain areas of the Northeast, the Jonah crab occurs between Long Island and Nova Scotia among the rocks at tide line and to 2,600 feet deep, and seasonally in the intertidal zone. It is principally found in clear, open waters rather than inshore, muddy bays as is the blue crab. The Jonah crab reaches 6 inches across, and is delicious to eat. Because it is relatively scarce inshore, it has never been an important commercial item. In some areas such as the south shore of Long Island the Jonah crab becomes very abundant inshore during the spring season and is readily caught by amateur fishermen from bridges and piers. It is erroneously called "mud crab" or "brown

Dungeness crab, prepared by The Mandarin, San Francisco

HOW TO REMOVE CRAB MEAT FROM COOKED BLUE CRAB

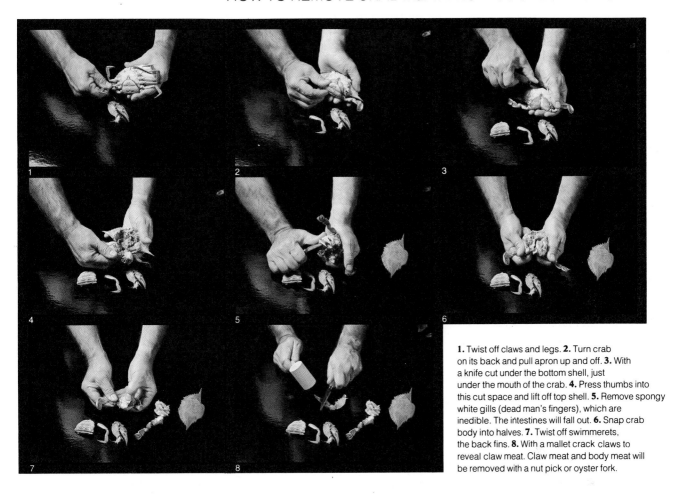

1. Twist off claws and legs. 2. Turn crab on its back and pull apron up and off. 3. With a knife cut under the bottom shell, just under the mouth of the crab. 4. Press thumbs into this cut space and lift off top shell. 5. Remove spongy white gills (dead man's fingers), which are inedible. The intestines will fall out. 6. Snap crab body into halves. 7. Twist off swimmerets, the back fins. 8. With a mallet crack claws to reveal claw meat. Claw meat and body meat will be removed with a nut pick or oyster fork.

crab." With improved methods of deepwater crabbing large populations are expected to be harvested on the Continental Shelf.

KING CRAB This large crab *(Paralithodes camtschaticus)* may weigh up to 20 pounds although the average is about half this size. Also known as the Japanese crab, Russian crab and Alaska King crab, its range is limited to the cold waters of the northern Pacific. Although the back meat is utilized in canned form, frozen King crab legs previously cooked in the shell are the principal market item. In 1973 U.S. landings amounted to 76 million pounds.

Despite its size only about 25 percent of the King crab is edible; the claws, legs and back of a 10-pound crab yield about 2 pounds of coral-streaked white meat. The peak season is in midwinter off the coast of Alaska in subfreezing and rough seas. Most vessels process the crabs aboard; in addition to maintaining live tanks, they operate cookers and freezing and glazing compartments.

The southern King crab is *Paralithodes antarctica.*

LADY CRAB This crab, also called calico crab and sand crab, is a small crab *(Ovalipes ocellatus ocellatus)* found over sand bottoms from Nova Scotia to South Carolina. A closely related variation *(O. o. guadulpensis)* extends the range of this type from North Carolina to the Gulf, to Texas. Although there is a distinct difference between the two, they can be used in the same way. The lady crab is an abundant inshore species recognized by its white to cream-colored carapace covered with bright red or purple spots. This is the crab that so frequently nips the feet of bathers along Atlantic beaches. Due to its small size, about 3 inches across the shell, the lady crab is not widely utilized as food; however, its meat is edible and of good flavor.

LAND CRAB The land crab *(Cardisoma guanhumi),* sometimes called the **white** or **mulatto crab,** is a member of the family Gecarcinidae or the group known as grapsoid

crabs. It is found in Bermuda and from southern Florida and Bahamas through the West Indies and from Texas to Brazil. The land crab is terrestrial but returns periodically to the sea to reproduce. It reaches large size and is a popular food in many countries; the meat is sweet and white, not unlike the blue crab in quality. Land crabs are particularly evident in the fall rainy season beginning in September. In Cuba, for example, they provide the annual feast where *el arribazón de los cangrejos* (the arrival of the crabs) was a celebrated event in years past. In the Cuban style, land crabs are cooked in large metal drums in a sauce composed of 50 pounds of bitter chocolate to 5 gallons of red wine; milk-soaked bread adds thickening to the sauce, which is spiced with orégano and chili peppers. However, the usual method of cooking the crabs on most out-islands is boiling in water with various seasonings.

This species was so abundant in south Florida until the 1950s that our streets were often overrun at night with migrating crabs. Evidently their place has been usurped in a changing ecology.

OYSTER CRAB This tiny crab *(Pinnotheres spp.)*, invariably less than 1 inch across the shell, lives within the cavity of oysters where it shares the food ingested by its host. A commensal animal, it does not harm the oyster since it is always in a softshell state. Only the female crab is tolerated while the even smaller free-swimming hardshelled male makes brief periodic visits for reproduction. Unfortunately, all oysters do not harbor these pale pink crustaceans and gathering a sufficient quantity for a meal is akin to looking for pearls—although the crab is more abundant. Not many oyster-packing plants collect these crabs during their shucking operation, but the few that do find a ready and profitable market for them. A related Atlantic crab lives in the mantle cavity of mussels and other bivalves. The Pacific Ocean has a similar commensal crab in the pea crab, which lives within the horse clam. Being a rather large bivalve, the horse clam is capable of supporting 2 or 3 pea crabs simultaneously, which makes collecting somewhat easier.

RED CRAB Although the red crab *(Geryon quinquidens)* was first described for science in 1879, it did not become a market item until a few years ago. This crustacean of the outer Continental Shelf generally lives at temperatures between 38° and 41°F., and at depths from 1,200 to 6,000 feet, but it has been taken from waters as warm as 47°F. and at depths of 150 to 7,100 feet. The red crab was only incidental to deepwater lobster fishing until specialized trapping methods evolved. It is taken over mud bottoms usually.

The red crab is a walking crab, with a squarish body and long slender legs. On each side of the front edge of the carapace are 5 short spines or teeth. The male crab grows to about 2¼ pounds and the female to 1¼ pounds, and one of these yields a bit less than 25 percent meat. Their natural "uncooked" color is bright red.

The pink-tinged meat of the red crab is delicious and similar in flavor and appearance to the King crab except the legs and claws are not quite as large. It is considered superior to the yellowish-colored meat of the snow crab. Due to the present scarcity of King crabs, the red crab is being substituted in its traditional recipes.

ROCK CRAB A common name for a number of crabs in the family Cancridae which includes the Jonah crab of the western Atlantic, the Dungeness crab *(Cancer magister)* of the eastern Pacific, and the edible crab of Europe *(C. pagurus)*. In 1973 European landings of the last amounted to 25 million pounds.

SNOW CRAB A market name for various spider crabs: *Chionoecetes oplilio*, also called the Atlantic snow crab and queen crab; *C. tanneri, C. bairdi* and *C. japonicus*. Japan takes over 70 million pounds of these snow crabs annually; the U.S. takes about 62 million pounds.

SPIDER CRAB The common name for a number of crabs with typically long legs and bodies covered with a dense growth of chitinous hairs, which give them a spiderlike appearance. The Japanese spider crab grows to 13 feet across the legs. The name is not marketable, and the larger edible species are sold under the names snow crab, tanner crab and queen crab. The spinous spider crab *(Maia squinado)* of Europe is very important in French cuisine; there it is known as **araignée de mer.** European landings exceeded 30 million pounds in 1973.

Spider crab

Stone crab claws are cooked after trapping, and the meat is marketed as a precooked product.

STONE CRAB A true gourmet food. The claw meat of the stone crab is rich, sweet and firm in texture. In years past it was popularly known as the "Morro Crab" of Cuba. However, the most important sources of stone crabs today are Miami and Key West, Florida, and to a lesser extent Beaufort, North Carolina, and Charleston, South Carolina. Although expensive and often in short supply, these crabs are shipped by air all over the world by Miami-based firms. *Menippe mercenaria* and another lesser known species, *Lithodes maja*, related to the King crab, are both called "stone crabs."

The stone crab is a member of the mud-crab family (Xanthidae), characterized by a hard and heavy shell which is oval in shape. The large claws have black tips, and the body grades from purplish to dark brown or reddish brown, with brownish mottlings. The legs, which are fringed with hair, have red and yellow bands and sharp points, and are not adapted for swimming as in the blue crab. The stone crab grows to about 5 inches between tips of the shell, and about 2 inches deep, giving it a more bulky appearance than most crabs. Stone crabs live for 8 to 10 years. Found from North Carolina to Texas, this crab reaches its peak of abundance and size in southern Florida, although nowhere is it as abundant as the blue crab. It is a burrower, living in deep holes of mud and sandy mud, near creeks and estuaries, as well as under rocks and among mangrove roots. In the commercial fishery stone crabs are caught with traps. Nearly all of its edible meat is in the claws and thus the Florida population, at least, has become self-perpetuating as the fishermen simply twist the claws off and release the crab to grow new ones, a process which takes about 18 months; these are called "retreads." However, retreads will never grow to the same size as they were originally. The lack of claws does not inhibit the crab's feeding as these powerful pincers are defensive weapons only, as many a careless hand can testify.

Stone crab claws are cooked by the commercial fishermen immediately after trapping, then chilled for local delivery or frozen. The "green" or uncooked claws cannot be frozen directly after capture as this causes the meat to adhere to the shell. Essentially, it is marketed as a precooked product.

Stone crab is usually served with the first and second knuckle already cracked because of the extreme density of the shell. The knuckle meat is easy to pry out with a small fork and the claw meat readily slides off the flat cartilage. Serve hot or cold with melted butter or mustard sauce.

Some attempts are being made to culture stone crabs commercially in Venezuela.

TANNER CRAB A long-legged crab found along the Continental Shelf of the north Pacific Ocean from Oregon to Alaska, also known as snow crab. A related species, found only in deep water greater than 1,500 feet in depth, occurs along the West Coast from Washington south to Baja California. Although tanner crab populations are large, this resource is not significantly utilized in the U.S. as few trawlers are equipped to operate deeper than 250 fathoms. The bulk of the catch is taken during the occasional "invasion" of tanner crabs in King crab traps in Alaskan waters.

The female tanner crab seldom exceeds 1 pound in weight; the male averages about 2½ pounds and yields a quality meat.

SEABROOK ISLAND SHE-CRAB SOUP
(Webster R. Steadman, Seabrook Island Club)

There are many versions of she-crab soup, but this recipe represents 40 years of professional experience by Chef Steadman, who has made an exhaustive study of the ingredients, and the resulting nectar is justly celebrated. It's important that no butter be used in sautéing the vegetables and making the roux; butter turns the soup yellow or streaks it. If fresh crab roe is not obtainable, the canned product is preferable to the usual substitute, the yolks of

facing page, European rock crabs at Billingsgate Market, London

Avocado stuffed with crab meat

hard-cooked eggs. Canned roe is a South Carolina specialty; it may include the gonads of either male or female crabs; the flavor is the same.

1 pound fresh lump crab meat	1 gallon milk
3½ ounces fresh crab roe	1½ cups medium-dry sherry
5 tablespoons minced celery (about ½ rib)	Tabasco
	white pepper
5 tablespoons minced onion (about 1 small onion)	3 ounces chicken soup base in fat form
2 tablespoons vegetable oil	6 ounces roux, made with
2 cups light cream	vegetable oil

Sauté both vegetables in oil until *blond* and set aside. Warm the cream and milk in the top pan of a large double boiler, then add the vegetable mixture and the sherry. Add the crab meat to the skillet used for vegetables and just heat. Check to make sure all bits of shell have been removed, then add crab meat to the milk mixture with the crab roe. Season to taste with 2 or more dashes of Tabasco and white pepper, then add the chicken base and roux. Cook over very low heat for 45 minutes. Makes 20 servings.
NOTE: Canned crab roe is difficult to find in northern states; the brand to look for is Harris's Crab Roe. The chicken soup base in fat form is also not easy to find, but Sexton's brand is sold packed in jars.

CRAB RAVIGOTE

3 cups crab meat, fresh or canned	1 tablespoon chopped parsley
½ cup mayonnaise or salad dressing	1 hard-cooked egg, chopped
	¼ teaspoon salt
2 tablespoons lemon juice	dash of pepper
2 tablespoons chopped onion	salad greens
2 tablespoons chopped sweet pickle or drained pickle relish	2 tablespoons chopped stuffed olives
	¼ teaspoon paprika
	pimiento strips

Remove any remaining shell or cartilage from crab meat. Combine ¼ cup mayonnaise, the lemon juice, onion, pickle, parsley, egg, seasonings and crab meat. Shape into a mound on salad greens. Combine remaining ¼ cup mayonnaise, the olives and paprika. Spread over crab mixture. Chill. Garnish with pimiento strips. Makes 6 servings.

AVOCADOS STUFFED WITH CRAB MEAT

3 cups crab meat, fresh or canned	¼ teaspoon Worcestershire sauce

2 tablespoons butter or other fat	2 tablespoons chopped pimiento
2 tablespoons flour	2 tablespoons chopped olives
1 cup milk	3 ripe avocados
¼ teaspoon salt	¼ cup grated cheese

Remove any remaining shell or cartilage from crab meat. Melt butter, blend in flour. Add milk gradually and cook, stirring constantly, until sauce is thick and smooth. Add seasonings, pimiento, olives and crab meat. Cut avocados into halves; remove seeds. Fill centers with crab mixture; sprinkle cheese over top of each avocado half. Place in a well-greased baking pan, 12 x 8 x 2 inches. Bake in a moderate oven (350°F.) for 20 to 25 minutes, or until brown. Makes 6 servings.

CRAB SALAD

3 cups crab meat, fresh or canned	¼ cup sliced cucumber
	¼ cup sliced green pepper
1 can (14 or 15 ounces) artichoke hearts, drained	1 teaspoon salt
	¼ teaspoon pepper
1 cup cut-up cooked green beans	¾ cup Thousand Island Dressing (p. 292)
2 hard-cooked eggs, chopped	6 large tomato slices
¼ cup sliced raw cauliflower	6 lettuce leaves
½ cup sliced celery	radish slices

Remove any remaining shell or cartilage from crab meat. Cut artichoke hearts into fourths. Combine all ingredients except tomato slices, lettuce and radish slices; toss lightly. Arrange 1 tomato slice on each lettuce leaf. Place approximately 1 cup of the salad on each tomato slice. Garnish with radish slices. Makes 6 servings.

CRAB PUFFS

3 cups crab meat,	dash of pepper
fresh or canned	1 cup milk
2 tablespoons butter	2 eggs, separated
2 tablespoons flour	¼ teaspoon paprika
½ teaspoon salt	1 cup heavy cream

Remove any remaining shell or cartilage from crab meat. Melt butter; blend in flour and seasonings. Add milk gradually and cook, stirring constantly, until sauce is thick and smooth. Beat egg yolks, and stir a little of the hot sauce into yolks; add to remaining sauce, stirring constantly. Add paprika and crab meat. Whip cream, and beat egg whites until stiff. Fold egg whites and whipped cream into crab mixture. Place in 6 well-greased, individual 10-ounce casseroles. Set casseroles in a shallow pan of hot water. Bake in a moderate oven (350°F.) for 40 to 45 minutes, or until puffs are firm in the center. Serve immediately. Makes 6 servings.

SHERRY-CRAB SOUFFLÉ

2 cups crab meat,	salt, pepper, Tabasco
fresh or canned	1 cup sliced mushrooms,
2 tablespoons butter	fresh or canned, drained
2 tablespoons flour	½ cup dry sherry
1½ cups hot milk	4 eggs, separated

Melt butter in the top part of a double boiler and blend in flour. Add milk, stirring briskly to avoid lumping; base should be thick. Season with salt, pepper and Tabasco to taste. Remove from heat. Stir in mushrooms and sherry. Beat egg yolks and add to mixture; blend well. Fold in crab meat. Let the base mixture cool completely. Beat egg whites stiff and fold in gently. Spoon into a 1½-quart casserole. Set casserole in a pan half-filled with water, and bake in a preheated moderate oven (350°F.) for about 30 minutes, or until golden brown. Makes 4 servings.

DEVILED CRAB

3 cups crab meat,	1 teaspoon
fresh or canned	Worcestershire sauce
2 tablespoons chopped onion	½ teaspoon salt
3 tablespoons	3 drops of Tabasco
melted butter or oil	dash of black pepper
2 tablespoons flour	dash of cayenne pepper
¾ cup milk	1 egg, beaten
1 tablespoon lemon juice	1 tablespoon chopped parsley
½ tablespoon dry mustard	¼ cup dry bread crumbs

Remove any remaining shell or cartilage from the crab meat. Cook onion in 2 tablespoons butter until tender; blend in flour. Add milk gradually and cook, stirring constantly, until thick. Add lemon juice and seasonings. Stir a little of the hot sauce into the egg; add egg to remaining sauce, stirring constantly. Add parsley and crab meat; blend well. Place in 6 well-greased individual shells or 5-ounce custard cups. Combine remaining 1 tablespoon butter and the crumbs; sprinkle over top of the shells. Bake in a moderate oven (350°F.) for 20 to 25 minutes, or until brown. Makes 6 servings.

CRAB LEE LIN ARK
(Mai Kai Restaurant, Fort Lauderdale)

2 cups cooked crab meat, fresh or canned
12 three-inch squares of Won Ton (recipe follows)
6 slices of American cheese
¼ pound butter
peanut oil for deep-frying

Place 1 tablespoon flaked crab meat in the center of each square of won ton. Place ½ slice of cheese encircling the crab meat. Use 1 pat of butter on top of the crab meat and cheese. Bring the ends of the won ton together in a sacklike fashion. Drop into a deep-fryer filled with peanut oil heated to 375°F., and cook for 5 minutes. Makes 12 servings.

WON TON

2 cups all-purpose flour	3 teaspoons water (if needed)
½ teaspoon salt	5 tablespoons potato starch
4 eggs	or cornstarch

Add salt to flour. Add unbeaten eggs and work well into flour. If too dry, add water, 1 teaspoon at a time. Sprinkle board with 1 tablespoon potato starch and roll out dough paper-thin. Cover the dough with a layer of potato starch, and roll up on the rolling pin. Press with the palms of the hands. Remove from rolling pin and roll again. Repeat the process 3 or 4 times, using all of the potato starch. Remove from rolling pin, and cut into 3-inch squares.

CRAB CUSTARD

3 cups crab meat,	3 cups milk
fresh or canned	4 eggs, well beaten
2 tablespoons melted butter	½ tablespoon salt
or margarine	½ teaspoon
4 slices of white bread	Worcestershire sauce
1 cup grated cheese	¼ teaspoon white pepper
2 tablespoons chopped parsley	paprika
1 tablespoon	
instant minced onion	

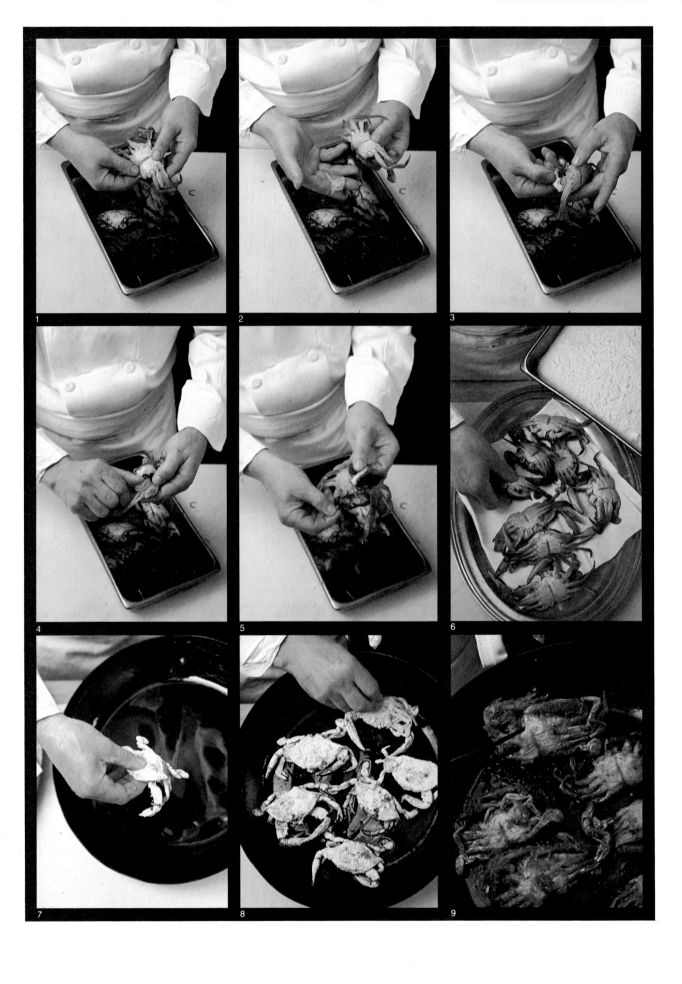

facing page, HOW TO DRESS AND PANFRY SOFTSHELL CRABS
(prepared at the 21 Club, New York City)

1. Turn crab on its back and lift up apron. **2.** Remove the apron. **3.** Lift up the flaps at each end. **4.** Pull out the spongy gill tissue. **5.** After cutting off the eyes with scissors, press above the legs and pull out the bile sac. **6.** Pat crabs dry on a towel and dust them with flour. **7.** Melt butter in a large iron skillet, and heat. Put in the crabs, underside down. **8.** Panfry over very low heat only as many as will fit in a single layer and not crowded. **9.** Turn over and panfry on the other side. Allow 5 minutes for each side.

Remove any remaining shell or cartilage from crab meat. Pour butter into an 8-inch-square baking dish, 2 inches deep. Cut crusts from bread. Place bread in a single layer in the bottom of the baking dish. Spread crab meat over the bread. Sprinkle cheese, parsley and onion over crab meat. Combine milk, eggs, salt, Worcestershire sauce and white pepper; pour over crab meat. Sprinkle with paprika. Set baking dish in a pan containing 1 inch of hot water. Bake in a moderate oven (350°F.) for 45 to 60 minutes, or until a knife inserted in the center comes out clean. Makes 6 servings.

EGGPLANTS STUFFED WITH CRAB AND SHRIMP
(Bon Ton Café, New Orleans)

1 pound shelled small shrimps	½ cup chopped celery
1 pound white lump crab meat	3 garlic cloves, chopped
6 medium-size eggplants	½ cup chopped parsley
4 tablespoons olive oil	salt and pepper
4 green peppers, chopped	2 cups fresh bread crumbs, or more
4 medium-size onions, chopped	paprika

Cut eggplants lengthwise into halves. Drop into a large kettle of boiling water and simmer until soft but not mushy. Drain, cool enough to handle, and scoop out the pulp without damaging the shells. Set the shells aside to drain. Heat 3 tablespoons of the oil in a large skillet, and cook the green peppers, onions, celery and garlic in it, stirring now and then, until vegetables are limp. Add the scooped-out eggplant pulp, cover, and let the mixture "smother" over medium heat until most of the water has evaporated. Add shrimps and cook for 20 minutes longer. Transfer everything to a large bowl and fold in the crab meat and parsley. Season to taste. Let the stuffing cool a little, then fold in as much of the bread crumbs as you need to make a rather firm stuffing. Fill the eggplant shells. Sprinkle the rest of the crumbs on top, then sprinkle with paprika. Dribble the rest of the oil on the tops. Bake in a preheated 350°F. oven for 30 minutes or longer, until heated through and browned on top. Makes 6 servings or 12 for hors d'oeuvre.

PANFRIED SOFTSHELL CRABS

12 softshell blue crabs, dressed	12 crisp toast triangles
½ cup flour	salt and pepper
½ pound butter	24 lime or lemon wedges

Pat crabs dry with paper towel. Dust with flour. Melt plenty of butter in a large shallow pan, and sauté crabs carefully over low heat for about 5 minutes on each side. If you are cooking six at one time, allow ¼ pound butter. Turn and shuffle them to prevent burning or drying out. This is an "eyeball" process. Arrange crabs on toast triangles. Optionally, pour over each crab a dollop of the browned butter remaining in the pan. Season with salt and pepper to taste. Serve with crisp watercress or spinach salad and lime or lemon wedges. I prefer the spinach salad with a sharp vinegar dressing for contrast. Makes 4 servings.

BRENNAN'S BUSTERS BÉARNAISE
(Brennan's Restaurant, New Orleans)

9 softshell crabs, cleaned and dried	6 toast triangles, buttered
1 egg, beaten	1½ cups Béarnaise Sauce (p. 289)
1 cup milk	
flour	1 tablespoon chopped parsley
¼ pound butter	

Combine beaten egg with milk and dip crabs into mixture. Drain. Dredge crabs with flour and sauté in butter over low heat until golden brown. Mount crabs on toast triangles or rounds, and cover with béarnaise sauce. Sprinkle with parsley. Makes 3 servings.

Freddie Washington in the garden at Brennan's Restaurant, New Orleans, with Busters Béarnaise and Pompano Toulouse

Crayfish

During the last week of July and through August the people of Finland and Sweden systematically attempt to consume the world's supply of crayfish. Until you have attended a *krebfest*—preferably in a moss-covered log cabin on the pine-shrouded shores of the Baltic Sea, where bone-cold aquavit, foaming golden beer and a steaming sauna are essential ingredients to the feat—you are missing one of the great events in gourmandizing. This orgy has its counterpart in the traditional Louisiana "Crawfish Boil" which may be as ancient as the Scandinavian ritual because the crayfish was not only a deified food of the fierce Houma Indians who once roamed the bayous but also their painted battle symbol. Below the equator crayfish "belong" to the Maori people of New Zealand and it was so written into their peace treaty with Great Britain.

In a charming cookbook (*Favorite Old Recipes* collected by Joseph Leiter, Lakeside Press, Chicago, 1927) Joseph Leiter's recipe for **Écrevisses Cardinalisées Monsieur Le Prieur** begins with "Have ten dozen crayfish and wash them well." Of course, Leiter is best remembered as the man who almost cornered the U. S. gold market, and presumably he had an edge on the crayfish market as well. It's a considerable task to collect a few dozen crayfish except in such disparate enclaves as our Pacific Northwest and in Louisiana, which is so abundantly blessed with these small lobsterlike crustaceans. Even Scandinavia depends to a large extent on crayfish imported from America. In 1964, Her Ernst Etter, one of Europe's most enthusiastic gourmets, celebrated the founding of the Vienna Wine and Food Society with a dinner that the city of waltz hadn't seen since Emperor Franz Josef cavorted on his summer hunting grounds below the Dachstein glacier. An ambulant collector of the exotic, Etter staggered our imaginations with a **Buisson d'Écrevisses** or "crayfish bush" that formed a brilliant red pyramid at least 4 feet high at the center of the table. It took the markets of as many countries to reach this seraphical height.

The crayfish is a small lobsterlike crustacean which inhabits freshwater on all continents except Africa. Crayfish range in size from the inch-long dwarf crayfish of America to the 8-pound Tasmanian crayfish, a culinary treasure. More than 300 species are found throughout the world, and over 250 species and subspecies are known to occur in North America. There are 29 different crayfish in Louisiana alone. Despite this numerical blessing comparatively few species grow to edible size, which is a body length of 3½ inches at minimum and preferably over 5 inches long. Most crayfish in North America can be placed in one of five genera—*Pacifasticus, Procambarus, Cambarus, Orconectes* and *Cambarellus*—and only two of these and to some extent a third produce crustaceans suitable for the table. Fortunately, for those lovers of crayfish who do not have a reliable natural source of supply, crayfish farming has commenced on a rather large scale, not only in Louisiana (which produces over 10 million pounds annually) but also in Missouri, Texas, Mississippi, Alabama and Arkansas. Most of the Pacific Coast harvest from Oregon, Washington and California is utilized locally (Jakes Famous Crawfish, a Portland restaurant, has been in business since 1892), with the remainder being shipped to France and Sweden. Three of our western crayfish species reach 6 to 8 inches in body length and most nearly resemble European crayfishes; it is postulated by some authorities that this genus *Pacifasticus* originated somewhere in Europe or Asia before the Ice Age and later migrated across the Bering Straits to North America. Along our Pacific Coast the most ideal crayfish waters are the slower-moving streams typical of the flat agricultural valleys of western Oregon. The flood plains of the lower Willamette River and its tributaries and the sloughs of the Columbia River are the locations of the heaviest harvest. However, both the Northern crayfish found from Wisconsin into Maine and the Allegheny crayfish which occurs west and north of the Allegheny Mountains reach an edible size and are worth the catching. The bulk of Louisiana's crayfish crop consists of the Red Swamp crayfish, which is found mainly in the southern portion of the state, and the White River crayfish in the north; these are both in the genus *Procambarus*, which in recent years has been spreading north and eastward through the Mississippi Valley and up the Atlantic Coast. Thousands of people make "crawfishing" a family affair. In the spring season, cars are parked all along the 80-mile stretch of Airline Highway from Baton Rouge to New Orleans. Often the water fished is nothing but an open drainage ditch. The little town of Breaux Bridge in the heart of Cajun country claims title to the Crayfish Capital of the World—*La Capitale Mondiale des Écrevisses*—and well it might be, as the crustacean appears in local cafés and restaurants in gumbos, *étouffées*, stews, pies, fried, boiled, and just about every other way it can be prepared. There is a certain irony here as the French Acadians, who first colonized Nova Scotia and were later driven south by the British, ultimately settled in Louisiana where this familiar Gallic food was found, while the British colonized New England, rich in cod, which filled the belly of the Empire.

Crayfish

Quite apart from the delicacy of its claw and tail meat, the crayfish has considerable nutritive value. It has a high phosphorus and protein content, more so in the American species than the European. The American crayfish contains more phosphorus than do fishes. Its meat averages 296.4 mg/100 g P of which the acid insoluble fraction constitutes 36.1%, inorganic phosphorus 35.5%, and ester phosphorus 28.4%. Males contained more total acid-insoluble and ester phosphorus and less inorganic phosphorus than did females. American crayfish meat contains 25.5 % more true protein than the meat of *Astacus astacus* and 19.5 % more than meat of *Astacus leptodactylus*. *(Studies on Chemical Composition of American Crayfish Meat as Related to its Nutritive Value,* Teofil Dabrowski *et al.,* Dept. of Technology of Fishing Industry, Olsziyn, Poland.)

HOW TO CATCH CRAYFISH

Crayfish can be caught in small numbers by turning over rocks in a stream bed and grabbing them by hand or snaring them with a long-handled dip net as they scuttle over the bottom. However, this can be frustrating work and the more efficient method is with traps. In waters over 10 feet deep, modified crab pots baited with fish heads are used. Floats are tied to the line to mark the trap. In shallow water lift nets and minnow traps with a funnel entrance are used almost exclusively. The bait, usually pieces of fish, beef melt or fish heads, is tied to the center of the lift net. The net is lowered into the water and raised at suitable intervals. The funnel traps are usually made of ¾-inch mesh wire and are 30 inches long. The captured crayfish are emptied through a trapdoor in the top.

Regulations concerning the capture of crayfish vary from state to state. Louisiana, for example, has no limit and no closed season and the crayfish can be captured by any legal method. Washington, on the other hand, requires a permit and then only certain specified waters can be fished with traps during the open season from April through October. So before collecting the subjects of your feast check the laws with your local conservation agency.

BASIC PREPARATION

Wash crayfish thoroughly in salted water in a large pan, letting them remain in the water for 5 to 8 minutes. With a wooden paddle stir them around gently in the water to help them get rid of grit. Lift them out of the soaking water and pour off water. Rinse any grit out of pan. Return crayfish to the pan and pour boiling water over them. Let them stand for 10 minutes. When cool enough to handle, separate the heads from the tails. Remove the crayfish fat, called the heptopancreas, from the head or cephalothorax. The fat is invariably bright orange in color but may be light if the diet of the crayfish is poor. To collect the fat, remove it with a small knife or your fingernail. Remove the shells from the tails, being careful to pull out the veins. Keep fat and tail meat separately; they are now ready to use in other recipes such as Jambalaya.

The classic *buisson d'écrevisses* or crayfish bush

BOILED CRAYFISH

Follow the procedure described for washing the crayfish. Use a large kettle or stockpot with a tight-fitting cover. Put in 3 gallons of water and 1 pound of salt. Add 1 tablespoon ground red pepper, or use 3 or 4 ounces of crab boil. Bring the water to a boil. Drop in 2 pounds of crayfish, washed but still in shells, cover tightly, and bring again to a boil. When steam appears around the edges of the cover, start counting the time. Allow 8 minutes. Lift crayfish from the water and let them cool enough to handle. The seasoned water is saved for some recipes.

CRAYFISH JAMBALAYA
(Bon Ton Café, New Orleans)

2 pounds crayfish tails	3½ teaspoons salt
½ cup crayfish fat	¼ teaspoon cayenne
2 tablespoons cooking oil	1 cup raw rice
2 medium-size onions, chopped	2 cups water
3 shallots, chopped	¼ cup chopped parsley
2 garlic cloves, chopped	

Pour the oil into a heavy-bottomed pot, and add onions, shallots and garlic. Cook over low heat, stirring constantly, for 10 minutes. Add crayfish, crayfish fat, 3 teaspoons salt and the cayenne, and cook over medium heat for about 15 minutes. With a slotted spoon lift out the crayfish and most of the vegetable bits, and set aside. Add the rice to the drippings in the pan and stir to coat the

kernels. Add water and remaining ½ teaspoon salt. Cover and cook over low heat for 20 minutes. Uncover and return the crayfish and vegetables; add the parsley. Mix well, and cook for 15 minutes longer. Makes 4 servings.

CRAYFISH BISQUE

2 gallons fine large crayfish
8 quarts water plus 2 quarts boiling water
salt
crab boil
lard
flour
3 onions, chopped fine
2 garlic cloves, chopped fine or put through a press
3 celery ribs, chopped fine
2 sprigs of fresh thyme
2 bay leaves
2 blades of mace
1 cayenne pepper pod
black pepper
2 cups crumbled stale bread
6 green onions, chopped
6 parsley sprigs, chopped
3 tablespoons butter
ground cayenne pepper
2 cups raw rice, cooked Creole style

Wash crayfish thoroughly following basic preparation, and boil them in 8 quarts of water flavored with salt and crab boil until they turn bright red. Lift crayfish from the court bouillon, and save the court bouillon. Pick the crayfish: reserve 4 dozen of the largest heads; remove and reserve all the fat from the heads; remove every particle of meat from the heads and shell the tails. Save any large claws. Reserve 2 dozen shelled tails whole and chop remaining tails. Crush all the smaller heads, still leaving the reserved 4 dozen whole. Pour 2 quarts of boiling water over the crushed heads. When water cools, pour through a strainer into a kettle with the court bouillon; the combined liquids will make the soup stock.

Make a roux with 4 tablespoons lard and 4 tablespoons flour; cook until the roux is deep golden brown. Add two thirds of the chopped onion, half of the garlic and half of the celery. Fry in the roux until onion and celery are wilted. Add the reserved whole tails and any claws. Cook for 2 or 3 minutes, then pour in the soup stock, stirring to mix well with the roux. Drop in the thyme, bay leaves, mace and pepper pod, and cook over moderate heat for 20 to 30 minutes, until the mixture thickens to the consistency of a cream soup. Season with salt and pepper to taste.

Meanwhile make stuffing for the reserved 4 dozen heads. Soak crumbled bread in enough water to moisten; add to the chopped tails with any other bits of crayfish meat. Fry remaining onion, garlic and celery, as well as chopped green onions and parsley, in the butter until vegetables are wilted. Add the chopped tails and bread and reserved crayfish fat, and cook for 10 minutes. Season with salt, black pepper and cayenne. Stuff the mixture into the reserved heads. Roll heads in flour and fry quickly in lard until they are light brown.

About 30 minutes before serving, add the heads to the kettle of soup, and heat all together. Spoon some rice into each soup plate, and ladle bisque over, serving 6 stuffed heads in each plate. The soup should be rich and creamy, with a reddish brown color, and the tails and claws should be visible. Makes 8 servings, with extra soup stock.

CRAYFISH ÉTOUFFÉE
(Bon Ton Café, New Orleans)

3 pounds crayfish meat	2 garlic cloves, chopped
¼ pound butter or margarine	1 teaspoon salt
1 large onion, chopped	½ teaspoon black pepper
2 shallots, chopped	1 tablespoon minced parsley

Melt the butter in a large heavy-bottomed pan and add onion, shallots and garlic. Cook over medium heat, stirring constantly, for 15 minutes. Add crayfish meat, cover, and cook over low heat for 20 minutes. The crayfish is smothered; it cooks in its own natural juices. Add seasoning. Remove pan from heat, add parsley, and stir well. Serve the mixture with a scoop of rice in the center of the plate; do not mix the crayfish with the rice. Makes 4 servings.

CRAYFISH PIE

3 cups cooked crayfish, tails and fat
butter
2 celery ribs
1 bunch of scallions
½ small bell pepper
4 tablespoons olive oil
salt and pepper
Tabasco
3 cups cooked rice
1¼ cups water
1 can (10½ ounces)
  condensed cream of mushroom soup
1 bay leaf, crumbled
Worcestershire sauce
4 hard-cooked egg yolks
3 slices of white bread
paprika
2 pimientos, cut into strips

Butter a large baking dish, about 2-quart size. Chop celery, including any small tender leaves, scallions, including about 1 inch of green part, and green pepper. Sauté in olive oil for about 5 minutes, then add crayfish tails and fat and sauté for about 5 minutes longer. Season with salt, pepper and Tabasco to taste. Mix with the rice, and gently stir in the water, condensed soup, bay leaf and a few dashes of Worcestershire sauce. Adjust seasoning if necessary. Pour everything into the buttered baking dish. Grate the egg yolks over the top. Remove crusts from bread and butter the bread on both sides. Cut each slice into 4 triangles, and arrange them in a circle on top of the mixture, points toward the center. Sprinkle with paprika. Bake uncovered in a 350°F. oven for about 30 minutes, until mixture is thoroughly heated and bread is toasted. Garnish with pimiento strips. Makes 6 to 8 servings.

Croaker

A member of the family Sciaenidae, or drums. There are numerous species in the Atlantic and Pacific Oceans which are important foodfish. *See DRUM.*

Cunner

Also known as **bergall,** the cunner *(Tautogolabrus adspersus)* is the northernmost member of the wrasse family, Labridae, on the East Coast of North America. It is found from Chesapeake Bay to Newfoundland but is most common in the New York to Cape Cod region. The cunner is related to the tautog but is a smaller, more slender fish with thick lips and protruding canine teeth. It grows to a weight of about 3 pounds but most of those now caught are 6 to 10 ounces in size. Cunners are abundant inshore around docks and rock pilings during our summer where they are taken in great numbers by angling. The "bergall" was a popular foodfish in the 1870s, especially from the Seventeen Fathom Bank out of New York where 2- and 3-pound fish were once hugely abundant on the mussel beds. Despite a tasty (albeit bony) flesh, it has lost currency over the years and commercial landings are now very minor. Unlike tautog, the cunner need not be skinned. It's best cooked by panfrying or ovenfrying, whole and dressed.

Bark from a particular tree is collected and pounded to a muddy paste. Lines are dyed black in the paste, and only this black fishing line is used for catching the black scabbardfish. At bottom, the catch. Facing page, the Madeira coast at Câmara de Lôbos, looking down at the fishermen at work dyeing the lines.

Cutlassfish

This unusual-looking fish with its long, silvery body and tapering filamentous tail is seldom utilized in America. It has a large mouth with sharp arrow-shaped teeth which creates a vicious appearance, but like so many "unorthodox" marine forms such as goosefish, wolffish and searobin, the cutlassfish is extremely palatable. It's consumed in large quantities by other nations, particularly Japan where the **tachiuo** is held in high esteem. The compressed and elongate body (a 36-inch-long cutlassfish weighs about 2 pounds) has evoked the common name "ribbonfish," which is misleading as this is an entirely different family of fishes.

The cutlassfish *(Trichiurus lepturus)* is found in the Atlantic and a very similar species *(T. nitens)* occurs in the western Pacific and Indian Oceans. Along our shores it ranges from Massachusetts throughout the Gulf of Mexico and south to Argentina. It's extremely abundant at times during the winter season in Florida when it occurs in dense schools, usually following our runs of mackerel or bluefish. The cutlassfish is despised by commercial fishermen because of its ability to shred nets with its sharp teeth. Sport fishermen invariably kill the cutlassfish and throw it away simply because there is no culinary tradition for its consumption. Thus, it's a potentially valuable but wasted resource.

By contrast, in Portugal the fishermen of Câmara de Lôbos have created a whole mystique around a related fish, the **espada** (pronounced Shpada). The common **espada branca** or white scabbardfish *(Lepidopus caudatus)* is taken in large quantities, but the real culinary prize is the black scabbardfish *(Aphanous carbo)*, also a member of the cutlassfish family, Trichiuridae. According to local lore, the **espada negro** is never caught anywhere else, and indeed its occurrence beyond the Madeiran coast is rare, nor can it be taken on anything but a black line and not just any black line. It requires a rather involved dyeing process, using the bark of a particular tree which is pounded to the consistency of mud. Each handmade line is 1,000 meters in length as the elusive **espada negro** occurs in very deep water. All this effort must be justified as Madeira is home base for a major cod and tuna fleet.

Cutlassfish can be prepared following any of the recipes for Spanish mackerel. The fillets are thinner, however, and cooking time should be adjusted short. The meat is firm, white, and of delicate flavor. It can be baked, broiled, panfried or smoked.

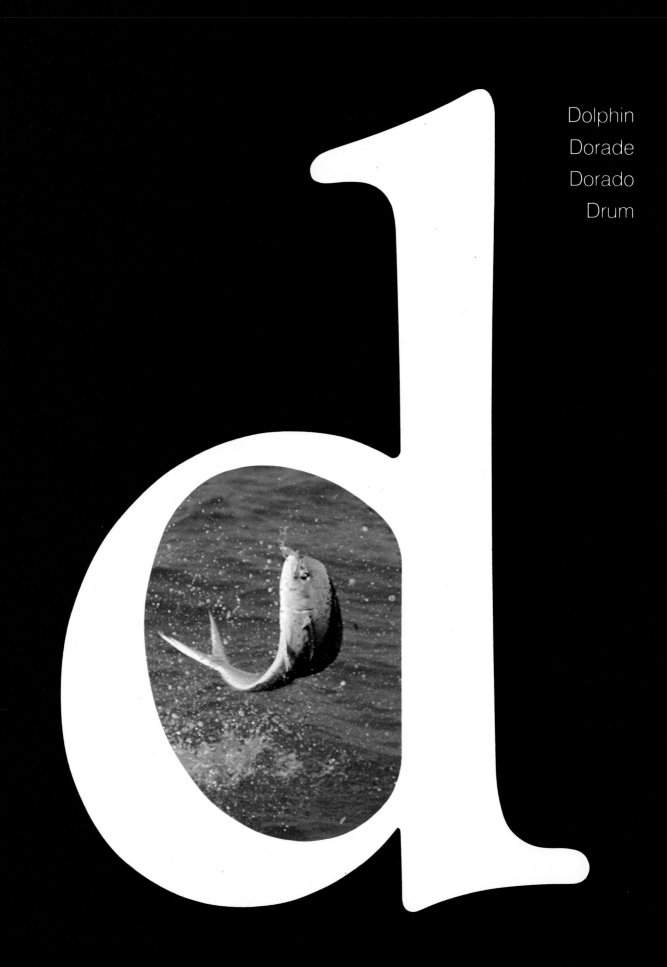

Dolphin
Dorade
Dorado
Drum

d

Dolphin

One of the most thrilling sights in offshore angling, and there are many, is a school of brilliant green and golden dolphin coming up behind the outrigger baits. These fish literally "turn on" like a neon sign when excited or feeding, and when hooked they are among the flashiest gamefish, running strong in repetitive leaps. The dolphin obviously evolved at a time when nature was in a generous mood as, apart from its beauty, it is also one of our most delicious seafoods. The meat is unique, large-flaked and sweetly moist. The roe of the female is of exquisite flavor—different from but every bit as good as shad roe. This fish incidentally bears no relation to the mammal called "dolphin," which is a member of the porpoise family.

As a commercial product the dolphin is virtually unknown in mainland U. S. markets. A swift-swimming, pelagic species, the fish is not amenable to harvesting with nets, and the relatively small amount caught with hook-and-line seldom reaches the fishmonger. Hawaii is a singular exception, where the **mahimahi** has become synonymous with island cuisine. But even at the big Market Place near Honolulu's Aala Park the dolphin is never really abundant and brings top dollar at the daily auction, even over the **ahi** or tuna. The annual landings only run about 112,000 to 114,000 pounds per year and these are taken by vessels searching for tuna and marlin using longlines. In essence the **mahimahi** is a by-product rather than a staple item, as traditionally there was never much demand for dolphin among island people. It was only with the influx of tourism since the 1950s that any market developed, and with rising prices **mahimahi** are now being imported to Hawaii from Taiwan and Japan.

Dolphin occur in all tropical and subtropical seas. They move north with the Gulf Stream in warm years and have been caught off Prince Edward Island, but their greatest abundance on our coasts is from North Carolina to Florida and through the Caribbean to Brazil. In the Pacific they range from southern California down the coast of South America. Mexico, Costa Rica, Panama and Ecuador highly prize the **dorado.** *Dorado* means "gilded" in Spanish, a name also applied to the unrelated freshwater dorado *(which see).*

For a prime quality meat it's advisable to cut the tail off each dolphin immediately after capture and bleed the fish before icing. This is hardly a "popular" procedure on most boats, particularly when the fish are coming fast but the end product is greatly enhanced and worth the effort. A fish that is not bled will be perfectly edible, but there is a marked difference in flavor. Dolphin should also be iced as quickly as possible; although they do not deteriorate rapidly, again there is a flavor loss if the dolphin are simply tossed in a fish box at warm air temperatures. The flavor disappears as quickly as its brilliant colors fade. In the words of Lord Byron (*Childe Harold's Pilgrimage,* Canto the Fourth):

> *. . . parting day*
> *Dies like the dolphin, whom each pang imbues*
> *With a new color as it gasps away,*
> *The last still loveliest, till—'t is gone—and all is gray.*

Dolphin vary in size from small "school" fish of 2 to 5 pounds, so common in late spring and summer in Florida waters, to the 40- and 50-pound fish of winter; the world's record is 85 pounds caught in the Bahamas. Dolphin are excellent eating at any size with a firm white meat of solid flake and delicate flavor. With the great disparity in size the thickness of a fillet is an important factor in cooking as these vary from ½ pound to a chunky 20-pound slab when skinned. Dolphin skin is not eaten as it's very tough; once the fillet is removed and the final incision made between the skin and meat—simply make a 3- or 4-inch cut from the tail inward to separate—then flop the fillet over and pull the skin off by hand. It will peel away clean. Cut out the dark meat along the median line. The fillet can then be trimmed into portion-size pieces if the fish is large, or left whole if the dolphin is small.

Dolphin have a tremendous growth rate, about 5 pounds per month, but a short life span of 3 or 4 years. Thus, nature compensates in their reproduction and the gourmet reaps a harvest. Unlike the spring-running shad, which spawns but once, female dolphin reproduce two or three times per year, releasing 200,000 to over a million eggs on each occasion; individual fish spawn from November to July in Florida waters, so there is an abundance of roefish available throughout most of the year. The roes vary greatly in size, from less than 8 ounces to 5 pounds or more in large dolphin. In any catch of dolphin it's easy to separate the female from the male as the former has a very rounded head profile, while the latter is blunt, almost squared off. Tourist anglers invariably select the rakish-looking male or "bull" for the taxidermist and even for cooking, much to the delight of charter-boat captains who find a ready skillet or market for the delectable orange roe. This may be treated according to all shad roe recipes. Both the fish and roe freeze well and have a minimum storage life of 90 days.

Skinned dolphin meat can be prepared in virtually any style: baked, broiled, panfried, deep-fried, barbecued, poached, served cold in aspic or made into a delicious chowder. It is excellent when smoked, but for processing the skin should be left intact to prevent the meat collapsing on the grid.

Many Palm Beach dinner parties, if the host or hostess is angling-oriented, begin with squares of dolphin marinated in lime juice and broiled to translucence in a coat of garlic butter. It may arrive as a hot hors d'oeuvre, or as a separate fish course, but in either case it always earns applause. In my own version, which is a main course, I serve crosscut fillets crowned with the cooked roe, prepared in a special way.

Dolphin; top, female; bottom, male

DOLPHIN AND ROE PALM BEACH STYLE

2 to 2½ pounds
  dolphin fillets, trimmed
  into portion-size squares
  about 1 inch thick
	¼ pound butter
	3 garlic cloves,
	  chopped fine
	1 teaspoon dried tarragon,

½ cup lime or lemon juice	or 1 tablespoon
salt and pepper	minced fresh tarragon
dolphin roe, about 1 pound	2 tablespoons minced parsley
flour	lime wedges
2 tablespoons peanut oil	
6 slices of bacon, cut crosswise into very narrow strips	

Marinate dolphin squares in lime juice for 30 minutes; turn several times. Place on greased foil in a suitable pan. Sprinkle with salt and pepper. Do not cook at this point. If the individual dolphin roe is 1 pound or more in size, simmer in cold water with a little lime juice just long enough to firm. If small, simply wash and pat dry. Dust the roe with flour. Pour peanut oil into a large skillet and simmer the bacon bits over low heat until fat becomes translucent. Add the roe and sauté until the outside becomes brown, then break the roe with a fork or cut with a knife so that it crumbles into small pieces. Add 4 tablespoons of the butter, the garlic and tarragon. When butter is melted remove pan from heat.

Bake the dolphin in a preheated 275°F. oven for 12 to 15 minutes, or until it flakes. Baste with the remaining 4 tablespoons butter. Do not brown; white is best in this case. Pour juices from the oven pan into the skillet with the roe and quickly reheat the roe, which should be in part crispy brown. Arrange dolphin squares on individual plates and pour the roe, liquid and bacon bits over each one. Garnish with parsley and surround with lime wedges. Accompany with rice and watercress salad. Makes 6 servings.

Dorade

(1) The French common name for any of the sea breams or porgies (see PORGY). In North Africa (Tunis) specifically applied to the **gilthead bream** (Sparus auratus), an important foodfish of that region.
(2) An Indo-Pacific member of the jack family (Gnathonodon speciosus) which also occurs in the eastern ocean from Panama to Mazatlan, Mexico. A valued foodfish, sometimes called the **king trevally.**

Dorado

A large freshwater fish found only in South America. The dorado is primarily sought as a gamefish and it does reach weights up to 70 pounds, but it also appears in markets and restaurants, particularly along the Paraná and Paraguay River systems. A fish of tropical and semitropical climates, the dorado is a member of the Characidae family in the genus *Salminus* which contains 4 species distributed from the Magdelena River system of Colombia in the north to as far south as the city of Buenos Aires in Argentina.

As a foodfish the dorado is very similar to our striped bass in texture and flavor. When prepared in *asado* style—usually split into halves and cooked slowly over a low charcoal fire for 2 or 3 hours and basted with garlic, herbs and olive oil—it is a mouth-watering dish. The skin is left on, unscaled, to prevent sticking to a fire grate, and the firebed itself is at least 18 inches away from the fish. Thousands of pounds of dorado are barbecued at the winter (July and August) dorado "fiestas" which are held along the Paraná River in Argentina. These social events are dedicated to catching and eating dorado, and the wine flows like Niagara as the fish steams in its own juices.

Dorado

Doré

The name in French-speaking Quebec for the walleye *(which see)*; it may appear as the **doré jaune** or **doré noir.**

Dory

See *JOHN DORY.*

Drum

Drums represent a culinary diverse family of fishes, the Sciaenidae, found in temperate and tropical seas, some of which are known as "croakers" in the Western Atlantic. They occur chiefly on the Continental Shelf, often over shallow sandy bottoms near estuaries and in the surf. Drums are so named because of their specialized "drumming muscle" which, by rapid and repeated contraction against the gas bladder, produces a distinctive sound that can be heard on land. Among some of the smaller sciaenids this is more of a grunting or croaking sound, hence the common name distinction between drums and croakers.

Another peculiarity of the drums is the presence of unusually large otoliths or "ear bones" in the skull. These extremely hard and pearllike stones are often called "lucky bones" and have a long history of superstitious folklore. The Indians used them for wampum and ceremonial purposes, and as neck charms to prevent various sicknesses. The polished and strung otoliths of freshwater drums have been found in Indian middens of the Mississippi Valley, and a necklace containing more than 25 otoliths of the white seabass interspaced with olive snail shells was found at an Indian campsite on San Nicolas Island, California.

The actual value of drums as food is greater than market statistics, as some Pacific species are not caught commercially or their sale is illegal. However, tremendous quantities are taken by sport fishermen on both the Atlantic and Pacific Coasts. As individual species these fish vary in size to the extreme, from the seldom over ½-pound star drum to the giant totuava of Mexico which reaches a length of 6 feet and a weight of 225 pounds. The totuava has for many years been on the verge of extinction. A demand for its gas bladder (sometimes called air bladder or swim bladder) by Orientals for use as a condiment in soups caused a tremendous waste of these great fish during the first quarter of the twentieth century. Although the fish was first exported to the U. S. in 1924 and reached a peak in 1928 with 1,838,000 pounds being trucked to San Francisco, by 1930 vast windrows of totuava were left to rot on Mexican beaches. The delicate and finely flavored flesh brought 10 cents per pound at market but as much as $5.00 per pound was guaranteed for the bladders which could be instantly removed from the fish and shipped in dried bundles to China. Totuava are caught mainly in their spawning season, and the population quickly declined. Protective measures have been introduced in recent years to preserve these magnificent

Red drum or channel bass or redfish

drums, but the annual landings are presently small.

Some of the better foodfishes in the drum family are the red drum, white seabass, totuava, Atlantic croaker, spotfin croaker, spotted seatrout and weakfish. Their qualitative values in texture and flavor differ greatly, with certain species in the genus *Cynoscion* having a very fragile musculature which lends itself to different recipes; for this reason the northern weakfish and its southern counterpart, the spotted seatrout, are treated separately *(see WEAKFISH)*. There is only one drum found in Europe, *Sciaena aquila* known in French as the **maigre**. However, this species ranges all the way from Norway into the Mediterranean and Black Seas and along the West Coast of Africa. In the Mediterranean it's also called **corvina** or **corbina;** in Spain and Portugal as in South America these common names are used interchangeably and in Central America, where there is a tremendous variety of sciaenids, both names are applied to any of the larger croakers. Although the deservedly famous **corvina** of Peru and Chile is a single species *(Sciaena gilberti)*, this name is simply a catchall elsewhere. The **kabeljou** of South Africa and the **mulloway** of Australia are also drums of culinary distinction.

All sciaenids are prone to trematode parasites, and this affinity is widespread throughout the world. Certain trematodes can be harmful to man; however, when present in fish they are killed with normal cooking methods. Never use any of the drums in raw fish preparations such as **seviche** or **sashimi.** If the fish is to be smoked, use the hot-smoke method and bring to a minimum temperature of 140°F. Really no different from cooking pork, in a cautionary sense.

DRUM TERMINOLOGY

ATLANTIC CROAKER   The Atlantic croaker *(Micropogon undulatus)* is the most common of the croaker species, occurring from New Jersey to Texas with its major abundance from the Carolinas to northeastern Florida and in the Gulf of Mexico. Although largely ignored as a market fish until recent years, this croaker has spiraled in sales throughout the Gulf states due to the development of a trawl fishery on the inner Continental Shelf. In Alabama alone the consumption jumped from 20,000 pounds in 1962 to 4,800,000 pounds during the first 6 months of 1972. The usual size of this species is from ½ to 3 pounds and they are sold pan-dressed (headless and gutted) and also as "flaked" croaker in 3-ounce and 4-ounce breaded portions. To make the name more attractive to the consumer, they are often purveyed as "golden croaker" which is also a common name for the larger Pacific spotfin croaker. The Atlantic croaker has lean white meat, containing about 17 percent protein.

BANDED DRUM   The banded drum *(Larimus fasciatus)* is found from Virginia southward to the Gulf of Mexico. This fish only attains a size of 1 pound and is usually caught at about ½ pound. It can be recognized by its deep, somewhat flattened body which has 7 to 9 black bands on each side. Due to its small size the banded drum has no commercial importance, but minor quantities are taken by sport fishermen.

BLACK CROAKER   This is one of the rarer Pacific drums, which ranges from Point Conception to the Gulf of California. The black croaker *(Cheilotrema saturnum)* is blue-black in color with a coppery sheen. The landings of this fish were always negligible, and only a minor amount is taken by sport fishermen.

BLACK DRUM   The black drum *(Pogonias cromis)* is found from Cape Cod to Argentina, with its center of abundance from Virginia into the northern Gulf of Mexico. It has barbels on the lower jaw and is silvery to gray-black in color. The black drum attains weights over 100 pounds. Although its flesh is coarse this drum has some commercial value, particularly the small fish of 5 to 10 pounds. However, chowder fanciers in the Carolinas prefer large black drums—the bigger the better—for their chunkier texture. Its roe is considered a delicacy.

CALIFORNIA CORBINA   The California corbina *(Menticirrhus undulatus)* is a member of the kingfish group and is highly prized by surf fishermen. On the protected list, it does not enter the commercial market. The fish is steel blue on the back shading to gray on the sides with faint crossbars or wavy lines. It occurs along sandy beaches from Point Conception to the Gulf of California. This drum grows to about 8 pounds in size and is excellent at table. The lean white meat should be filleted and panfried, poached or broiled, served with an appropriate sauce.

CORVINA   *See WEAKFISH.*

FRESHWATER DRUM   This is the only member of the drum family found in freshwater. Occurring principally in large rivers and lakes, the freshwater drum *(Aplodinotus grunniens)* is distributed from the Hudson Bay drainage of Manitoba and northern Ontario and south to the Gulf of Mexico, eastern Mexico and Guatemala. The Missouri drainage forms its western boundary. This drum has a rather oblong body with the back somewhat humped; the upper portion is pearl-gray with bronze, blue and silver reflections, the sides lighter and more silvery.

The freshwater drum has a long list of confusing market names such as sheepshead, croaker, crocus, jewelhead, white perch, gaspergou and grunter. The most commonly used name in trade is the **sheepshead.** The usual size sold runs 1½ to 5 pounds, but fish as large as 60 pounds have been caught. Otoliths of freshwater drums found in excavated Indian village sites indicate that the fish once attained a weight of 200 pounds. The annual commercial harvest varies from 5 to 8 million pounds, with the bulk of this catch coming from the Mississippi River drainage system and Lake Erie. The freshwater drum is considered a coarse fish and the quality of its lean white meat is only fair.

GOLDEN CROAKER   *See ATLANTIC CROAKER, SPOTFIN CROAKER.*

HARDHEAD   A commercial fishing name for the Atlantic croaker, which is sometimes applied in marketing.

JACKKNIFE FISH   The jackknife fish *(Equetus lanceolatus)* is distinguished by a very high dorsal fin and long tapering body which has 3 prominent black bands, one of which runs through the dorsal and across the body to its tail, giving the appearance of an open jackknife. This small drum is restricted to the Caribbean area, although it may stray to North Carolina in warm years. It's edible but of no particular culinary value.

KINGFISH   Do not confuse these drums with the king mackerel *(see MACKEREL)* which is commonly called "kingfish." There are 4 similar species of kingfish along the Atlantic and Gulf Coasts of the U. S., which differ only in a taxonomical sense. These are in the same genus *(Menticirrhus)* as the California corbina which is their Pacific counterpart. The southern kingfish *(M. americanus)* ranges all the way from New York to Argentina and to the northern Gulf of Mexico. The Gulf kingfish *(M. littoralis)* extends from Virginia to Florida and throughout the Gulf of Mexico. The northern kingfish *(M. saxatilis)* is found only on the Atlantic Coast from Maine to Florida. The minkfish *(M. focaliger)* is confined to the Gulf of Mexico. Along the Texas Coast, the southern kingfish and the Gulf kingfish are the two most common species. The former occur in the bays, although they migrate out to deep water during the coldest weather, and the latter mainly inhabit the surf.

The kingfish are of minor importance at market mainly because of their small size; they seldom reach over a foot in length. However, kingfish are good eating and are fished commercially in the Chesapeake Bay area. Large quantities are taken by anglers; in years past the northern kingfish was an eagerly pursued quarry in the New York area, particularly on Long Island. The kingfish are all similar in quality, with lean white meat and fine flavor. These should be pan-dressed and fried.

RED DRUM   This species *(Sciaenops ocellata)* is better known along the south Atlantic and Gulf Coasts as **channel bass** and **redfish.** Red drums occur along the Atlantic Coast of the U. S. from Massachusetts to Texas although their chief center of abundance is from New Jersey south. The larger red drums are usually caught along the coasts of the Carolinas where fish of 20 to 30 pounds are not uncommon; the record weighed 83 pounds. Young redfish or "puppy drum" usually of less than 10 pounds are taken mostly in Florida and in the Gulf of Mexico; big fish are rare in this area. However, many chefs consider this disparity a virtue, as the smaller red drums are preferred in most kitchens, with 4 to 6 pounds being the prime size. The Gulf Coast fishery is the largest with over 2 million pounds taken by commercials, but an additional 28 million pounds are caught by sport fishermen in a typical year, mainly in Louisiana and Texas waters. Most of these fish are harvested in the fall season when the drums are feeding heavily on crabs and shrimps and are prime for the table.

The red drum can be distinguished from the black drum by the absence of chin barbels on the former and the presence of a large black spot at the base of its tail. The body coloration is also coppery red rather than dark gray. Of the two fish, the red drum is superior at table. The best methods of preparation are in chowder form, stuffed and baked, or cut into cubes and deep-fried. The meat is firm but moist, white and heavy-flaked.

SILVER PERCH   This is not a perch but one of the commonest Atlantic drums, *Bairdiella chrysura.* In color, the silver perch is bluish-gray to olive and the sides are silvery to white, with yellow to golden fins. Occurring from New York to the Gulf of Mexico, it is most common in bays and quiet lagoons, especially around estuaries. It penetrates brackish water and even freshwater, occurring offshore in the winter and coming inshore in the spring to spawn. Although it only grows to about a foot long, it's a tasty panfish.

SPOT   A small member of the drum family, the spot *(Leiostomus xanthurus)* is found along the Atlantic Coast of the U. S., from Cape Cod into the Gulf of Mexico. Its most common occurrence is south of New Jersey. However, its greatest claim to fame is that in 1925 it appeared in such vast numbers in New York harbor that literally tons of these fish became clogged in the condenser pumps of the Brooklyn Edison Company, causing a blackout. During a previous invasion, one century earlier, their arrival coincided with a New York visit by General Lafayette; from that time on the fish was known as a "Lafayette." The spot is generally similar in appearance to the Atlantic croaker, but the body is shorter and deeper and there are no barbels on its lower jaw. Although the spot reaches a weight of 1½ pounds, the flesh is soft and often heavily parasitized. There is no commercial fishery for this species, but considerable quantities are utilized as panfish by sport fishermen.

SPOTFIN CROAKER   An excellent foodfish and popular among California anglers, it does not enter the market as it's protected from commercial fishing. The spotfin croaker *(Roncador stearnsi)* is also known as "golden" croaker. It can be distinguished by a large black spot at the base of the pectoral fins. Its high, arched body is compressed and is grayish-silver with a bluish sheen. The spotfin croaker is found from Point Conception to Baja California. It attains weights up to 9 pounds and is superior in flavor and texture to other common croakers

of our Pacific Coast.

SPOTTED SEATROUT   *See WEAKFISH.*

STAR DRUM   The star drum *(Stellifer lanceolatus)* occurs in shallow coastal waters from the Carolinas to the northern Gulf of Mexico, and can be recognized by its large eyes, upturned mouth and characteristic spongy head. It's one of the smallest drums, seldom exceeding 8 inches in length, and of no market value. However, its flesh is edible and when caught in significant numbers by sport fishermen it's utilized as a panfish.

TOTUAVA   The totuava *(Cynoscion macdonaldi)* is one of the best foodfish among the drums. It's also known as **totaba** in Mexico. This is the largest member of the family and closely related to the weakfish and corvina. It is found only in the middle and upper Gulf of California at spawning time. It appears in numbers at other seasons of the year in specific localities such as the mouth of Willard Bay in the fall and from San Felipe to the head of the Gulf in winter. The totuava is no longer abundant and only minor quantities are landed during the winter months. The totuava is best purchased in steak form and broiled, barbecued or poached, as most of the fish marketed weigh 40 to 60 pounds.

WEAKFISH   *See WEAKFISH.*

WHITE CROAKER   The white croaker *(Genyonemus lineatus)* is found from Vancouver Island to Baja California, where it schools in quiet shallow waters over sandy bottoms. It is silvery to golden in color with a pattern of faint wavy lines along the back. The white croaker grows to about 2 pounds in size, but it's only a fair panfish. The flesh is very soft and must be fried crisp to achieve any texture or flavor.

WHITE SEABASS   One of the larger drums and closely related to the weakfish of our East Coast. The white seabass *(Cynoscion nobilis)* is the most highly esteemed drum in California. Its body is elongate and the upper parts are bluish-gray with golden tints. Although the white seabass reaches a weight of 80 pounds, the usual size is from 15 to 20 pounds. It occurs from Alaska to the Gulf of California but it's more common in the southern part of this range. It can be filleted or steaked, but the latter is preferable for broiling, poaching or barbecuing with basting sauce, or small seabass can be poached or baked whole. Most of the white seabass landings are marketed in southern California and are in great demand during the summer and fall seasons.

YELLOWFIN CROAKER   The yellowfin croaker *(Umbrina roncador)* occurs from Point Conception to Baja California. It's gray green on the sides, with golden reflections and dark wavy lines and, of course, the fins are yellow. This is a popular angling species, seldom exceeding 2 pounds in weight, but a better than average panfish.

NORTH CAROLINA FISH STEW
(Joel Arrington)

This stew can be made with flounder, whiting, spot, weakfish, spotted seatrout, silver seatrout, or any fish with low oil content. Don't use bluefish or Spanish mackerel. The traditional fish is red drum. Natives of the Outer Banks prefer large drums of 35 pounds or more, but these can be tough unless cut into cubes. If you have small fish, wrap them in cheesecloth to keep the bones out of the stew. A few large vertebrae are not objectionable, but many small bones spoil the stew. Traditionally this stew is cooked in a cast-iron pot outdoors. The amount of tomatoes and Tabasco can be adjusted to your taste. Make the size of the potato pieces thicker or thinner according to the size of the fish pieces. To avoid overcooking the potatoes, some cooks simmer the fish separately for a few minutes; if you have small fish, cooking everything together works out best. This stew freezes well and is good reheated.

1 red drum, 6 to 8 pounds	12 ounces tomato purée or paste
3 pounds white potatoes	Tabasco
3 pounds yellow onions	salt and pepper
¼ pound bacon	8 eggs
4 cups canned tomatoes	

Scale the fish, cut into fillets or steaks, and then into chunks; leave the skin on the pieces; if you have steaks, leave the bones in to add flavor. Peel potatoes and cut into halves or quarters, or slices if the fish is in thin pieces. Peel and halve the onions. Brown the bacon in a large pot, uncovered. Add potato and onion pieces, fish, tomatoes and tomato purée or paste. Add Tabasco and salt and pepper to taste, and enough water to cover everything. Barely simmer the stew for about 1 hour, until the fish almost flakes. Crack the eggs and drop into the simmering stew. The yolks will be firm in about 10 minutes. Serve with hush puppies or crusty bread, to dunk into the stew, and with beer or iced tea. Makes 8 generous servings.

CALIFORNIA FISH DUGLÉRÉ
(California Wine Institute)

1 pound fish (fillet or steak of white seabass, cod, halibut, flounder, haddock, perch or sole)	½ cup drained canned tomatoes
1 tablespoon peanut oil	1 tablespoon chopped parsley
	¼ cup Riesling or other dry white wine
1 garlic clove, peeled	½ teaspoon lemon juice
1 small onion, chopped fine	1 teaspoon butter or margarine
½ teaspoon salt	1 teaspoon flour
⅛ teaspoon pepper	¼ cup skim milk

Pour oil into a 10-inch skillet. Thread garlic on a wooden pick and place in the skillet along with the onion. Season the fish with salt and pepper and arrange over the onion. Chop the tomatoes and arrange over fish, then sprinkle with the parsley. Mix the wine and lemon juice and pour around the fish. Cut a circle of wax paper, greased brown paper or aluminum foil to fit the top of the skillet; punch a small hole in the center to let steam escape. Place the paper or foil circle over the fish. Bring mixture to a boil, then continue cooking for about 10 minutes, or until the fish flakes when tested with a fork. Remove fish with a broad spatula to a heated platter. Discard the garlic. Melt butter or margarine in a small pan; blend in flour. Add milk and cook, stirring, until smooth and thickened. Pour sauce into the onion and tomato mixture and stir until well mixed; check seasoning. Spoon sauce over the poached fish. Makes 2 or 3 servings.

COLD REDFISH BAYOU
(Brennan's Restaurant, New Orleans)

1 red drum, 4 pounds, dressed, cut into large chunks	4 shallots, chopped
2 bay leaves	2 tablespoons chopped parsley
1 sprig of thyme	salt and pepper
1 celery rib, chopped	2 tablespoons unflavored gelatin
1 onion, chopped	3 tomatoes, sliced
1 lemon, cut into halves	3 hard-cooked eggs, sliced
1 can (4 ounces) chopped pimientos	1½ cups Rémoulade Sauce (p.290)

Put red drum pieces in a large kettle and cover with cold water. Add bay leaves, thyme, celery and onion. Squeeze the lemon in, then drop in the halves, rind and all. Poach for 20 minutes. Take from the heat and cool. Remove fish from cooking liquid and with a fork pick meat from the bones. Place picked fish in a dish and add pimientos, shallots, parsley, and salt and pepper to taste. Mix well. Return cooking liquid to heat, and add gelatin, softened in a little cold water. Simmer the cooking liquid until gelatin is completely dissolved, then remove from heat and strain carefully through a cloth. Place fish in a mold, barely cover with liquid aspic, and chill for 2 to 3 hours. Unmold on a platter. Garnish with sliced tomato and sliced hard-cooked eggs. Top with rémoulade sauce. Makes 6 servings.

Eel

From the eel they formed their food in chief,
And eels were called the Derryfield beef;
It was often said that their only care,
And their only wish, and their only prayer,
For the present world and the world to come,
Was a string of eels and a jug of rum.
                    —A History of Windham,
                    New Hampshire, 1719-1883
                    Leonard A. Morrison

No eel would ever win a beauty contest—if such a competition existed in the world of fishes—but perhaps that intangible is truly in the eyes of the beholder, as few marine delights are in such demand that live cargoes are airlifted daily from North America to Europe. Why the eel lost its once esteemed culinary reputation here is a mystery. But eel lovers are not offended as we can only feel remorse for the innocent who has never savored a delicately herbed **anguille au verte** or a hearty **matelote** of eel scented with Cognac. Few Italian families wait for the traditional Christmas Eve feast (made the merrier if the eel is a fat *capitone*) and find frequent reason to dine on a tomato-based **anguilla marinata** with garlic, sage, pine nuts, shredded lemon peel and white raisins in a soupy marriage of the sauce. As for smoked fillets of eel, balanced on thin slices of freshly buttered pumpernickel and downed with a foaming beer, there are few greater palate pleasers on a summer day. In Japan the Imperial dish is **kabayaki,** a split, boned and steamed eel that is dipped into a thick *tare* sauce (soy, sugar and *mirin*) then broiled and basted with more *tare*. And eel is virtually a national passion in Belgium although herring-oriented Holland runs a close second. Most of the eels delivered by Finnair from New York are off-loaded in Amsterdam.

To early settlers who lived inland among the river valleys of New England, there were two important seasons: shad time, and eel time. Autumn was "eel time" and during the month of October they were taken in such numbers on the Merrimack River that Derryfield (the old name for Manchester, New Hampshire) was synonymous

with this cold-weather staple. J. W. Meader reflected that "I have heard those say who would be good judges of the matter, that eels enough were salted down in a single year to equal to three hundred head of cattle." *(The Merrimack River: Its Sources and Its Tributaries,* J. W. Meader, B. B. Russel, Boston, 1869.)

The sea lamprey, which was considered just another kind of eel in that era, was also a popular food but not on the same plateau as the unrelated American eel. In the scientific classes of fishes, the lamprey occupies an order of its own; aside from being jawless, it is also, except for its head, boneless, a virtue which "made safe food for the children."

The city of Gloucester was under obligation to forward a dish of lampreys to the Sovereign on his accession to the throne, and annually at Christmas. King John fined the men of Gloucester 40 marks because "they did not pay him sufficient respect in the matter of his lampreys." *(The Fishes of the British Isles,* J. Travis Jenkins, Warne & Co. Ltd, 1925) Ironically, the parasitic lamprey, which is capable of boring a fatal hole in other fish with its rasplike tongue, was in such demand that as late as 1887 attempts were being made to "restore" it by stocking New Hampshire's rivers, and even a fine was levied for killing them out of season. *(New Hampshire Fish and Game Report,* 1887. The penalty: ten dollars per eel.)

Today millions of dollars are spent in research and management programs to eradicate the lamprey in our Great Lakes, which it eventually penetrated after the building of the St. Lawrence Seaway. It has a negative role in modern ecosystems, and is generally regarded as inedible—a culinary paradox in American history.

For twenty-three centuries man speculated on the origin of the eel. Failing to find roe or milt within its body the ancient Greeks named Zeus as the father of eels, as they were in the habit of assigning all children of doubtful parentage to the Sky God. Aristotle (384-322 B.C.) declared that eels rose spontaneously from mud—both in freshwater and the sea. Others believed that they originated from horsehair dropped into water. The Roman scholar Pliny the Elder (Gaius Plinius Secundus, A.D. 23-79), author of *Historia Naturalis,* postulated that young eels were produced from fragments of skin rubbed off by the adults against rocks. Through the ages Scandinavians believed that a fish, the Aalmutter *(Zoarces viviparus)* was the "eel mother," while in Italy the fishermen of Comacchio were convinced that eels copulate with water snakes. The Sardinian version was that an aquatic beetle played the role of eel-mother, and in Great Britain it was generally assumed that eels evolved from weeds. These abiogenetic myths had support until 1924 when Dr. Johannes Schmidt of Copenhagen presented facts that were as remarkable as the ancient beliefs were fantastic.

Eels are born in the southwest part of the North Atlantic in the area known as the Sargasso Sea. The young eel is ribbonlike and so transparent that print can be read through its body. In this stage it is called a *leptocephalus*, and in about a year it changes to a more recognizable form called an *elver*. During all this time the young eels have been swimming shoreward, and it is only when they near the coast that coloration begins to develop in their transparent bodies or that they begin to feed. Elvers appear along our shores in spring, entering tidal marshes and estuaries in tremendous numbers along the coast from the Gulf of St. Lawrence to the Gulf of Mexico. Most of the males remain in tidewater, while the females ascend the rivers, squirming over falls, up dams, even over damp rocks. When fully grown, the female eels, traveling mostly at night, drop downstream. They and the maturing males who have been living in the river mouths cease feeding, change from an olive to a black color, and move out to sea. Once they leave shore, the eels disappear over the Continental Shelf. Only the discovery of newly hatched larvae over the deep parts of the oceanic basin, south of Bermuda and 1,000 miles east of Florida, unraveled the mystery. On their spawning grounds, American eels mingle with the European species which have made the longer westward journey. Although the breeding grounds overlap, the larvae of the American species always work back to the west side of the Atlantic and the European to the eastern side. This trip takes about a year for the American eel, which approaches a length of 6 inches by the time it reaches the brackish waters along our Atlantic Coast. The European eel, however, takes 3 years to make its longer journey, which may be as much as 5,000 miles.

From a culinary point of view there is no distinction between the American and the European eel; they differ only in the number of muscle segments or vertebrae. There are other comparable species found throughout the world, such as the Japanese eel and the New Zealand longfin and shortfin eels, which are consumed in quantity. The conger eel is in an entirely different family (Congridae) and has a coarse musculature with an inferior flavor. It has a small popularity in Europe and is usually sold as a hot-smoked product or in fresh "steak" form cut into transverse slices. At Billingsgate Market in London they say you can't eat conger without parsley sauce and in my opinion, the sauce is better than the eel.

In America, particularly among families of Old World origin, no Christmas is complete without live eels during the preholiday fast. The tradition of fresh eels in December creates a large market for the product in many cities. This winter specialty keeps thousands of commercial fishermen at work in the principal supply points at the St. Lawrence River in Canada, Cape Charles, Virginia, and Chesapeake Bay. Weather watching is important among commercial men as winds from the right quarter will usually drive the eels into shallow water where they are netted by the tons. The eels are shipped by aerated trucks (a single truck may carry 10,000 pounds in its tanks) to such cities as Chicago, Boston and New York.

Eels are sold alive and whole, or whole and gutted, and as fillets. Special products are jellied eel in steaks or pieces, or fried and vinegar-cured, or packed in edible oil. When cooking, eels can be steamed, broiled, baked, fried, made into stews, or used as a component in a dish such as *bouillabaisse*. Steaks, pieces or flaked meat can be served cold in aspic.

When using live eels, the easiest way to kill them is to place them in a container of coarse salt. This also deslimes the eels. To remove the skin, knot a strong cord around the "neck" just below its gills and tie this off in a small loop. Drive a nail in a board and secure the loop of cord around it; cut the skin of the eel (a single-edge razor blade is ideal) just below and around the neck. The skin should be loosened with the blade, then grasped with pliers and peeled off with a quick pull. Cut off the head and dress the eel, removing fins with scissors. If fillets are desired, just cut the flesh on both sides of the backbone.

Panfrying is by far the most popular method of cooking eels; however, the meat is very firm and requires somewhat longer to cook than most other fish. The best size for frying is up to 1 pound or perhaps 1¼ pounds; if larger eels are to be used these should first be poached in water with salt and lemon juice added. Simmer for 15 to 20 minutes according to size. When panfrying, a thick section of eel will burn on the outside before it cooks through. Optionally it can be cut into fillets and pounded flat or into thin collops or steaks.

Many flavors are introduced in the panfrying process, and some are found in national dishes such as the elvers or baby eels **(angulas)** of Spain which are fried in olive oil and garlic in an earthenware pan after rubbing the bottom of the pan with a fiery *pimiento choricero* or hot red pepper. With these seasonings the eel is called **angulas en cazuelita;** in the baby eel season of spring, demand exceeds the supply. In other Mediterranean countries, basil and orégano are herb additives, while tarragon and rosemary are popular in northern France and Belgium;

naturally, dill is used lavishly in Scandinavia. The herbs may be added to the oil or fat during the final minutes of cooking or introduced in a butter sauce spooned over the fried eel. Anchovy butter is enjoyed in all cuisines.

Also known as **Ål** (Denmark, Norway and Sweden), **Aal** (Germany), **All** (Iceland), **Anguilla** (Italy), **Anguila** (Spain), **Anguille** (France), **Aal** (Holland), **Eiró** (Portugal), **Jegulja** (Yugoslavia), **Chéli** (Greece), **Unagi** (Japan).

BAKED EEL IN CREAM

3 pounds eel, skinned and cut into 3-inch sections	1 teaspoon salt
lemon juice	2 ounces butter
2 egg whites, lightly beaten	1 small onion, chopped fine
4 tablespoons flour	2 tablespoons minced dill
8 tablespoons fine dry bread crumbs	2 cups light cream

Sprinkle eel pieces with lemon juice, then brush with beaten egg white and roll them in a mixture of flour, bread crumbs and salt. Arrange the eel in a buttered baking dish and sprinkle with chopped onion and dill. Place small pats of butter over all. Bake in a moderately hot oven (350° to 400°F.) for about 30 minutes. When the eel begins to brown, add the cream and baste occasionally. Makes 6 servings.

EELS IN GREEN HERBS (ANGUILLES AU VERT)

3 pounds eels, skinned and cut into 3-inch sections	salt and pepper
4 tablespoons butter	1 cup whole watercress leaves, no stems
2 tablespoons minced onion	½ cup coarsely chopped mint leaves
2 tablespoons minced celery	
1 cup Chablis	¼ cup coarsely chopped parsley
½ teaspoon dried thyme	
1 tablespoon minced fresh tarragon	4 egg yolks
	½ cup heavy cream
½ teaspoon ground cloves	

Melt butter in a large pan and add the eels, onion and celery; cook over low heat for about 5 minutes, until the vegetables are *blond*. Add the wine, thyme, tarragon and cloves. Season with salt and pepper to taste. Bring liquid to a simmer. Add the watercress leaves, mint leaves and parsley, and cook for about 12 minutes. In the meantime, beat the egg yolks in a bowl, adding the cream and a little of the hot liquid from the eels. When blended, add this mixture to the eels, stirring in with a wooden spoon. Makes 6 servings.

JELLIED EELS

6 large eels	½ teaspoon ground allspice
4 cups water	¼ teaspoon ground cloves
2 cups vinegar	4 bay leaves
2 onions, sliced	2 tablespoons unflavored gelatin
1 teaspoon salt	
½ teaspoon pepper	¼ cup cold water

Skin and dress eels, then cut into 3-inch pieces. Do not split open. Clean abdominal sections by twisting out viscera with a small fork; then wash. Add 4 cups water, the vinegar, onions and seasonings to eel sections and simmer until meat comes away from bones. Remove meat, and put in a mold or earthenware dish. Strain the liquid in which eels were cooked. Bring it to a boil, and add the gelatin which has been dissolved in ¼ cup cold water. Simmer for 15 minutes, then pour over eel meat and chill in refrigerator for several hours, until aspic is firm. Makes 6 servings.

EEL STEW (LA MATELOTE D'ANGUILLES)

2 pounds skinned eel, cut into 3-inch sections	1 cup red Burgundy wine
flour, salt, pepper	½ teaspoon whole cloves
2 tablespoons butter	1 teaspoon black peppercorns
2 garlic cloves, crushed	
¼ cup diced onion	1 bay leaf
¼ cup diced celery	1 sprig of thyme
½ cup diced carrot	¼ cup Cognac
2 tablespoons peanut oil	beurre manié
2 cups fish stock	bread croutons
	parsley

Dust eel pieces with flour seasoned with salt and pepper. Melt butter in a large skillet and add garlic, onion, celery and carrot. Simmer until onion becomes *blond*. Add the oil and brown the eel pieces. Add the fish stock, wine, cloves, peppercorns, bay leaf and thyme. Cover and let simmer for 30 to 40 minutes. Remove the eel, strain the liquid, and add the Cognac. Thicken liquid with a little *beurre manié* and reduce by one quarter. Return eel to liquid and warm it. Place croutons in a serving dish, arrange eels in the center, and pour sauce over all. Decorate with parsley. Makes 6 servings.

Escabeche

See under PICKLED FISH.

facing page, Eel auction at Volendam, The Netherlands

Fish Soups and Stews

There are many of these in all kinds of cookery, and it's not easy to determine whether the specific dish is a soup or stew. From a restaurant point of view the availability of seasonal species at market, and the imagination of the chef in creating something distinctive, more or less determines the end result. Italy's infinite versions of **zuppa di pesce** or **brodetto,** or Spain's **sopa de pescado** and **suquillo,** often resemble a **bouillabaisse** in both ingredients and liquid volume, although a contrasting 3 or 4 kinds of fish served in a seasoned stock is essentially what one expects of a soup. Both the **brodetto** and **suquillo** (which means "little broth") are stews incorporating as many as 8 or 10 different ingredients; they include the familiar **bouillabaisse** species with the addition of squid and frequently shark meat (dogfish). If the emphasis is on mollusks and crustaceans, then we are venturing into a **cioppino** which in our San Francisco version must include clams, shrimps and crabs at a minimum. For soups or stews based on a single aquatic ingredient, see under the species name. *See also BOUILLABAISSE.*

CALIFORNIA CIOPPINO

2 dozen fresh clams in shells	3½ cups canned
1½ pounds halibut	Italian plum tomatoes
or rock cod fillets,	1¾ cups canned
cut into serving pieces	tomato purée
1 pound large shrimps in shells,	1 cup red Burgundy
split and deveined	or other dry red wine
2 medium-size	1 cup water
Dungeness crabs	2 tablespoons wine vinegar
1 medium-size onion	1 tablespoon crushed mixed
2 large garlic cloves	herbs (sweet basil, rosemary,
(optionally more)	marjoram and orégano)
6 parsley sprigs	1½ teaspoons seasoned salt
¼ cup olive oil	½ teaspoon seasoned pepper

Use a Dutch oven or a large pot with lid. Chop onion, garlic and parsley fine. Cook in oil over moderate heat until soft but not browned. Add tomatoes, tomato purée, wine, water, vinegar, herbs, salt and pepper. Bring to a boil. Reduce heat and simmer for 40 minutes. This basic sauce may be made ahead of time, to be cooled and refrigerated, if desired, but heat before adding to fish. While sauce is cooking, place clams in cold salted water (¼ cup salt to 2 quarts water) for 30 minutes. Dress the crabs, crack claws, and break into serving pieces. When sauce is completed, reserve it in a separate container. Layer all fish in the kettle, placing clams on top. Pour sauce over all. Cover tightly and cook over low heat for 20 to 25 minutes. Serve in large heated bowls. Makes 6 servings.

NOTE: Frozen rock lobster tails may be used in place of crabs; frozen shrimps may be substituted for fresh; canned clams (two 10½-ounce cans) may be used when fresh clams are not available.

BOURRIDE

1 pound skinned fillet of	4 fennel ribs, sliced
red snapper, rockfish	2 leeks, cut into julienne
or ocean perch	2 tablespoons
1 pound skinned fillet of	chopped parsley stems
tautog, sea bass or cod	1 bay leaf
1 pound skinned fillet of	1 tablespoon salt
striped bass or grouper	2 cups dry white wine
1 pound skinned fillet of	2 cups fish stock
halibut, tilefish or	4 egg yolks
white seabass	2 cups Aïoli Sauce (p. 290)
1 large onion,	12 to 16 potatoes,
sliced into rings	boiled and peeled
1 large carrot, sliced	chopped fresh parsley

The choices of fish are regional options. Use whatever is available in your area. Cut each kind of fish into 6 pieces. Place in a large deep pot. Add onion, carrot, fennel, leeks, parsley stems, bay leaf and salt. Mix wine and stock, and pour in. If necessary, add more wine and stock in the same proportions to have enough to cover fish. Bring to a boil and simmer for 12 minutes; remove from heat. Carefully remove fish to a large serving bowl. Add just enough of the cooking liquid to keep the fish moist; keep it warm. Beat egg yolks; add 1 cup of the *aïoli* sauce, and turn into a large saucepan. Strain remaining cooking liquid into the egg-yolk and *aïoli* mixture. Simmer until sauce is thick and smooth; do not let it boil. Strain into a second serving bowl. Place potatoes around fish, spoon a little of the sauce over, and sprinkle with parsley. Serve the rest of the sauce and remaining *aïoli* in separate serving bowls. Accompany with toasted or sautéed slices of French bread. Makes 6 to 8 servings.

SUQUILLO DE PESCADOR
(Los Caracoles, Barcelona)

1 pound hake fillets	1 pound Spanish onions,
1 pound haddock fillets	chopped
2 spiny lobster tails	3 tablespoons olive oil
8 lobsterette tails	1 pound tomatoes, chopped
8 large shrimps in shells	6 tablespoons almonds,
8 mussels in shells,	ground
scrubbed	2 garlic cloves, minced
½ pound squid, skinned	¼ teaspoon ground saffron
and cut into rings	1 cup seasoned fish stock

Cut fillets into serving portions and chop each lobster tail into 4 chunks. Simmer onions in olive oil until translucent. Add tomatoes and cook until soft and well mixed. Add almonds, garlic, saffron and fish stock; simmer for 20 minutes. Force through a food mill into a saucepan; keep warm. The puréed sauce, about 2 cups, is the *suquillo*, the "little sauce." Using 1 tablespoon salt to 1½ cups water, steam lobster chunks, lobsterettes and shrimps, all in shells, for 4 minutes. Add mussels and steam for 4 minutes longer. In a large shallow baking dish arrange uncooked squid and fish and steamed shellfish. Cover with puréed sauce, and bake uncovered in a 375°F. oven for 15 minutes. Makes 4 to 6 servings.

PENSACOLA FISH CHOWDER
(Manuel Francisco Gonzales VI)

A Pensacola specialty, not found in other Gulf Coast kitchens. For this chowder use red drum for choice. Failing that, red snapper, scamp or grouper. Pacific cooks can use rockfish. Use fish large enough to give chunky pieces in the finished chowder.

1 fish, 4 pounds, or 2 fish,	8 black peppercorns
2½ pounds each	2 tablespoons
salt	minced fresh parsley
ground white pepper	2 pinches of dried basil
2 large baking potatoes	2 pinches of dried orégano
1 large yellow onion	2 large bay leaves
2 large garlic cloves	2 lemons
6 scallions	⅔ cup red Bordeaux wine
⅔ cup fresh celery leaves	2 slices of bacon,
2 medium-size fresh tomatoes	or 4 tablespoons
1 medium-size green pepper	bacon drippings
¾ cup tomato paste	4 tablespoons flour
2 teaspoons	4 cups canned tomatoes
Worcestershire sauce	

Dress fish; cut off tail, fins and head, but save the head (or heads) with gills pulled out. (Add extra fresh fish heads from market if possible.) Cut fish crosswise into steaks about 1¼ inches thick. Sprinkle steaks with salt and white pepper and set aside. Put fish heads in a cloth sack and tie closed with white twine, leaving enough twine loose for a handle.

Peel potatoes and cut into 1-inch cubes. Peel and chop onion and garlic. Chop scallions, including 2½ inches of the green tops, and celery leaves, fresh tomatoes and green pepper. Put these last ingredients in a large bowl and add tomato paste, Worcestershire sauce, peppercorns, herbs, ½ lemon, unpeeled and unsliced, and ⅓ cup of the wine.

Heat a cast-iron pot, 6 to 8 quarts, or a deep iron Dutch oven. Put in the bacon slices and heat until all fat is extracted and bacon is crisp. Lift out bacon, pat dry, crumble and set aside. Gradually sprinkle the flour into the fat, stirring all the time. Cook, stirring, until roux is the color of strong coffee with cream, being careful not to scorch it. Add chopped onion and garlic and continue to cook until onion is translucent but not browned; keep stirring and don't let anything scorch. Add canned tomatoes and heat and stir until well mixed with the roux. Add boiling water to within 4 inches of top of pot. Add the bowl of chopped ingredients and seasonings, and return the bacon crumbs. Tie the bag of fish heads to the pot handle and drop into the chowder. Bring to a boil, reduce to a simmer, and cover. Let the mixture simmer for 2 to 3 hours. Stir occasionally and add a little hot water if liquid is reduced too much.

Remove fish heads and let the sack drip into a bowl to save all the juices; add juices to chowder and discard the sack. Add cubed potatoes and cook for a few minutes. Add fish steaks, and cook until potatoes and fish are just done, the potatoes still somewhat crisp and the fish still in whole pieces. Add remaining wine.

Cut remaining 1½ lemons into slices and place one in each soup or gumbo bowl. Ladle chowder into bowls, giving everyone some fish and potatoes. Add cayenne pepper or other crushed hot pepper to taste if you like. Serve with French bread, tossed green salad, Italian red wine. Makes 8 servings.

Flounder

Any one of 3 families of flatfishes representing more than 200 species in the Atlantic and Pacific Oceans. These encompass fish from the tiny dab to the giant halibut. For marketing reasons there is a considerable interchange of common names, particularly with respect to the various "soles." For purposes of this book rather than divide the

The author fishing on the Paraná River at Isla de Monos (Island of Monkeys), Paraguay; the fish is a *cachama*, a popular foodfish in tropical South America.

Order Pleuronectiformes (Bothidae, Pleuronectidae, Soleidae) taxonomically, all flatfishes of culinary importance are described under SOLE with correct common and market names. This entry is further divided in the subheads SOLE TERMINOLOGY and FLOUNDER TERMINOLOGY to include flounders more familiarly known as fluke (summer flounder), plaice or turbot. I believe this is an easier way to understand this group of fishes as it takes into account the regional designations of American and European retail outlets.

Fluke

An eastern U. S. market name for the summer flounder. *See FLOUNDER TERMINOLOGY under SOLE.*

Flyingfish

The sight of a shoal of silvery flyingfish rocketing out of the blue sea and gliding over the wave tops is particularly inspiring on a day with a freshening breeze, after you've trolled for hours without a sign of life at the baits and you come to a long weedline that often hides a school of dolphin. The swift-moving dolphin feed on these aerial acrobats and as the outrigger baits skip near great rafts of sargassum drifting before the wind the little fish rise in long graceful arcs. It's a promise that is not always kept but despite all my years of fishing I still become fascinated with their antics whether the dolphin appear or not. The fact that some fish can climb trees, or walk over land, while others fly through the air with startling ease is less an evolutionary miracle than a reminder that in nature as in life, anything is possible. I have eaten tree-walking fish in the Congo River and recently ate one of Florida's walk-

ing catfish, but the flyingfish is clearly superior if one can judge species on their nonaquatic skills. When faced with a flyingfish pie in a Barbados hotel invariably a tourist will ask do they really fly, rather than is it really edible? The answer to both questions is an unqualified "yes."

To become airborne the flyingfish swims just below the surface for some distance to gain speed, then it turns upward and spreads its pectoral fins, leaving the water except for the lower lobe of its tail. Now vigorously beating its tail back and forth in a sculling motion, it taxies across the surface to gain flying speed. Finally it extends its ventral fins and rises into the air. Its flight may cover 1,000 feet or more, but the average is much less, perhaps 100 to 300 feet. Usually it glides no more than 4 or 5 feet above the water, though it may rise higher in a strong wind, and there are records of flying fish achieving heights from 25 to 36 feet. Most flights last for 10 seconds or less but they have been observed to 30 seconds. At the end of its flight a fish may close its wings and dive gracefully into the water, or simply plop down with a splash. Often, when flying speed is lost, the fish lowers its tail, begins the sculling motion again, then takes off a second time. The fish may fly, scull, and fly again several times in succession.

From a commercial fishing point of view the flyingfish would seem like an impossible quarry, but man long ago learned that it's attracted to lights at night. They not only land on the deck of lighted boats but sometimes fly through open portholes. The oldest method of catching them in quantity was to suspend a lantern over basketlike traps although now gillnets are used. In order to locate quickly the areas where flyingfish are numerous, the boat will put over a small plankton townet to determine where its food is most abundant. Perhaps the most unusual method of capturing flying fish is to "hunt" them with a small gauge shotgun using a light skeet load, but this requires exceptional talent.

The flyingfish is considered a delicacy in some parts of the world, especially in the West Indies and Japan. It's not likely that you will ever have occasion to cook a flyingfish, but the recipes given are traditional and simple to execute.

TOBI-UO NO KAMABOKO (BAKED FLYINGFISH PASTE)

1½ pounds flyingfish fillets	½ tablespoon salt
1 egg white	crushed red pepper
1 tablespoon cornstarch	shoyu (soy) sauce
⅛ teaspoon monosodium glutamate (optional)	grated fresh gingerroot

Wash the fillets and mash to a paste. Add egg white, cornstarch, MSG and salt, and mash again until the ingredients are thoroughly mixed. Pack the paste in a buttered shallow 4-cup baking dish and sprinkle with crushed red pepper to taste. Bake in a hot oven for 15 minutes. Serve with shoyu sauce and grated gingerroot. Makes 4 servings.

BARBADOS FLYINGFISH STEW

8 flyingfish fillets	2 green peppers, sliced
salt and pepper	2 tomatoes, peeled and sliced
juice of 1 large lime	2 onions, sliced
flour	½ cup dry white wine
3 tablespoons butter	

Season fillets with salt and pepper and sprinkle with lime juice. Dip into flour and roll up each fillet, securing each piece with a wooden pick. Melt butter in a skillet; place fillets in it. Add pepper, tomato and onion slices. Pour wine over all. Cover skillet. Bring to a boil, then simmer until vegetables are tender. Makes 4 servings.

Frozen Fish

There is little doubt that a fresh fish is superior to the frozen product. However, modern-day flash-freezing techniques (accomplished with liquid nitrogen at a temperature of −290°F. which freezes most fish within 5 to 8 minutes) in large commercial plants do provide very palatable seafood, and comparable results can be obtained at home. The problem, simply stated, is to exclude all oxygen and protect the fish from moisture loss. Fish do not have an absolute freezing point. They start freezing on the outside at about 30.3°F., and the process continues to the inside. The center of the fish is the last part to freeze. Most of the water in a fish is frozen at 18°F., but a small part may remain unfrozen at temperatures below 0°F. When large quantities of fish are placed in a freezer, it takes a longer period of time for their temperature to be lowered to the freezing point. If cooling is prolonged, undesirable changes can take place in texture, color and flavor. It is important, therefore, to freeze the right amount of fish at any one time.

AMOUNT TO FREEZE

Unless the freezer is specially equipped for quick-freezing, the volume of fish to be frozen in a 24-hour period should not exceed 10 percent, and preferably 5 percent, of the total capacity. In a 10-cubic-foot unit (359 pounds) this means about 18 pounds of fish, or 35 pounds in 20 cubic feet (718 pounds). As you increase the amount to be frozen, you will decrease the *rate* of freezing and increase the storage compartment temperature during the cooling process. All freezers have areas which are colder than others; freezing should be done directly on the shelves with coils in an upright, and near the sides or wherever the chest-type freezer coils are located. Fish to be frozen should not be piled one on top of the other nor on top of other frozen foods.

STORAGE TEMPERATURE

Fish appear to be frozen solid at 20°F. Actually, their hardness has nothing to do with storage life. Oxidative changes are only retarded. Where economically feasible, fish should be kept at 0°F. to 16°F. Most fish can be stored for 6 months without developing any rancidity. However, fish with a high oil content such as steelhead, mackerel and bluefish have a shelf life of about half that time and will show a slight rancidity after 90 days.

FREEZER BURN

When frozen fish is inadequately protected against moisture loss through its packaging or storage, the surface may become dry, fibrous and discolored. This is commonly called "freezer burn." The most common cause of desiccation is improper packaging. When a fish, or any cut of fish, is wrapped in such a manner that air spaces are created within the package, moisture is transferred from the surface of the fish to the inner side of the packaging material in the form of frost. This moisture loss will cause a freezer burn.

PACKAGING MATERIALS

The selection of the proper wrap and its application are extremely important to the storage of frozen fish. Air, even freezing air, must be kept away from the fish because oxygen will cause discoloration and rancidity to develop. So the packaging material must eliminate as much air as possible and, secondly, prevent more air from entering the wrap. As a general rule, papers having a high resistance to moisture-vapor transmission are most efficient. Ordinary wax paper, for example, is not sufficient; it is not moisture- and vaporproof, and it cracks. However, wax paper can be used with a strong overwrap such as aluminum foil. A good wrapping material must also be strong enough to resist puncture, pliable enough to make a tight wrap, easily sealable, greaseproof, durable at low temperatures,

Los Caracoles, Barcelona, one of the most
famous seafood restaurants in Spain. facing page,
the owner, Señor Antonio Bofarull Ferrer;
left, a painting of him some years ago. Señor
Ferrer's grandfather started the restaurant in 1835,
and it has remained in the family ever
since. The fish specialty of the restaurant is
suquillo de pescador (recipe on page 134).
The paintings on the barrelheads represent all
sorts of fish and shellfish.

ICE GLAZING

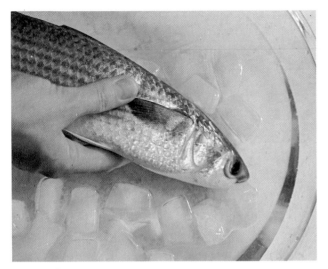

When fish is completely frozen, dip it into a
bowl of ice water large enough to submerge the fish
completely. The glaze should form at once. Repeat.
The glazed fish should be carefully wrapped. Compare
the frozen fish with a fresh fish.

and should impart no odor or flavor of its own.

There are numerous foils, films, resin-coated papers, wax papers, lacquered papers and laminated papers on the market. Of these, the most popular for freezing are transparent materials such as cellophane (Gauge Nos. 300 and 450), polyethylene, rubber hydrochloride Pliofilm, and vinylidene chloride, which is sold as Saran or Cryovac. Heavy aluminum foil is not transparent, but it is an excellent material for wrapping uneven-shaped pieces of fish because it holds tightly against the surface. When properly applied, it eliminates air pockets; by folding the edges of the foil twice or more, the package can be sealed without the use of tape or cord. Vegetable parchment is also a tough wrapping material, and being cheap it's especially suitable for wrapping large chunks of fish. However, it is not as pliable as foil.

BRINE-FROZEN FISH

Before freezing lean saltwater fish, such as cod, flounder, fluke, haddock, halibut, pollock, rockfish or whiting, it's advisable to dip them into a chilled brine. The brine prevents browning of the hemoglobin and greatly reduces the amount of drip in thawing and cooking. The fish should be immersed in a 5 percent brine solution (⅔ cup salt to 1 gallon water for 30 seconds). Oily saltwater species, such as salmon, mackerel, smelt and mullet, attain maximum storage life (6 to 9 months) when frozen in airtight containers filled with a 2½ percent brine solution (⅓ cup salt to 1 gallon water).

ICE GLAZE

Glazing is a method of freezing fresh fish that requires less freezer space for storing the frozen fish. To glaze a fresh fish, clean stomach cavity, and rinse fish thoroughly; then cut into the desired form. Place dressed fish, fish fillets or steaks in a single layer on a tray, wrap loosely with moistureproof and vaporproof material, and freeze. As soon as the fish is completely frozen, remove it from the freezer and dip each piece quickly into a bowl of ice water (33° to 40°F.) large enough to immerse the whole portion completely. If the fish is completely frozen, a glaze will form immediately. If a glaze forms, dip fish into ice water three or four times; a thin coat of ice will result from each dipping. If glaze does not form, immediately return fish to freezer and try to glaze later. Handle the glazed fish carefully to avoid breaking the glaze. Wrap the fish in airtight, moistureproof, vaporproof wrapping, and store in the freezer.

Glazing is a process used commercially to preserve the freshness, moisture and flavor of seafood.

However, since a home freezer does not meet the standards of a commercial freezer, the homemaker may need to reglaze the fish periodically to prevent moisture loss. If the fish is stored in a frost-free freezer, which extracts moisture from foods much more quickly than the conventional manual defrosting freezer, the fish may need to be reglazed within 1 to 2 months.

FREEZING IN CONTAINERS

Containers made of plastic or glass, or even glass fruit jars fitted with airtight covers, are preferable for all shellfish and bivalve freezing. Containers also provide maximum storage life for various cuts of fish when frozen in a brine solution. Their disadvantage is in the greater utilization of storage space.

To freeze fish in a container, steaks, fillets, small pan-dressed fish or chunks should be carefully packed to within 1½ inches of the top for quart-size containers and within 1 inch of the top for a pint-size. Fill the space around and between the pieces with a chilled 2½ percent brine solution until the product is covered. Remove entrapped air bubbles with a blunt knife or spatula. The lid should be screwed or pressed tightly in place to assure an airtight seal. The ice that is formed will keep air away from the fish, and the jar seal prevents loss of moisture from the contents. It is also economical and efficient to use quart- or half-gallon-size milk cartons. Cut off the lid end and place the fish inside. Fill with 2½ percent brine and freeze. When the ice block is formed, reseal the open end tightly with aluminum foil. This method will preserve small pan-dressed trout in storage for up to 9 months.

FREEZING FISH STEAKS

Certain species of fish, such as the salmon, kingfish, wahoo, halibut, swordfish, mako and tuna, are particularly good when steaked and oven-broiled or charcoal-broiled. The steaks should be cut 1½ inches thick. For convenience, wrap each individual steak in wax paper, then wrap them six to a package in freezer-weight foil. Steaks need not be completely defrosted to cook; merely allow a little longer time on the fire.

FREEZING FISH FILLETS

Firm-fleshed fish, such as the striped bass, red snapper, Spanish mackerel, black bass or walleye, are usually frozen in fillet form with all bones and skin removed. They can be frozen flat in freezer-weight foil by separating the fillets with a double thickness of wax paper, or a single thickness of silicone-treated parchment, or they can be rolled in wax paper and packed in a moisture- and vapor-proof bag. Cook frozen fillets as you would fresh fillets, allowing a little extra cooking time for complete thawing.

FREEZING CLAMS OR OYSTERS

Shuck raw clams or oysters, and freeze them with their liquor in pint- or quart-size freezer containers. For easy handling, remove the frozen blocks from the containers and wrap them in wax paper, then in a sheet of foil. When ready for use, thaw frozen clams or oysters overnight in the refrigerator. These bivalves should not be stored in the freezer for longer than 3 months.

FREEZING SCALLOPS

Scallops can be frozen in the same manner as clams or oysters; however, they can become tough and lose their delicate flavor if improperly packaged. It is better to cook scallops in court bouillon before freezing (see recipes under STOCKS) to retain quality.

FREEZING LOBSTERS AND CRABS

Live crabs and lobsters should be cooked in boiling 2½ to 5 percent brine for 10 to 20 minutes. When cool, the carapace or top shell, gills and viscera of the crab are removed and the body meat taken out with a pointed knife. Remove the meat from the claws of crabs and lobsters by cracking the claws with a small wooden mallet and shaking or picking out the meat. Remove the meat in the tail with a fork; split the tail meat for removal of the intestinal tract. Crab meat and lobster meat should be packed in jars with 2½ percent brine.

In most cases it is best to use frozen shellfish within a period of 3 to 4 months; however, a storage life of 6 months may be attained where storage accommodations are especially good and the temperature is as low as 10°F.

DEFROSTING

If possible, defrost the fish on the bottom shelf of your refrigerator 24 hours before using, or in an emergency immerse it in *cold* water. Thawing at room temperature is definitely not recommended. A greater quantity of fluid or "drip" is formed when defrosting in warm air. This fluid consists of dissolved proteins as well as minerals. Aside from the loss of food value, the spoilage process resumes at normal room temperatures. *Never* refreeze defrosted frozen fish.

Fugu

See PUFFER.

Gar
Garum
Gefilte Fish
Goatfish
Goldeye
Goosefish
Grayling
Greenling
Grouper
Grunt

g

Gar

The gar family, Lepisosteidae, contains about 10 species found in the freshwaters of North and Central America, of which 5 species occur in the U. S., mainly in our central and southern states. These vary in size from the small Florida gar which is seldom over 2 feet in length to the giant alligator gar which reaches a span of 12 feet and a weight exceeding 200 pounds. These primitive fish have long, cylindrical bodies with heavy armorlike scales, and their beaked jaws contain many sharp teeth.

Gars are edible, but the meat is soft and of little flavor. They can be made into a tasty hot-smoked product. Their greenish roes are toxic to man. Historically, the gar has been an important food of the Seminole Indians in Florida and is still preferred over other fish among the remaining tribes. This is probably due to the gar's abundance and ease of capture in the Everglades region, rather than a qualitative choice. Some attempt was made during the 1930s to develop a market for gar in Chicago and New York but it found no public acceptance. A small volume (from 5,000 to 6,000 pounds) is still sold annually.

Garum

A fermented fish sauce. This strongly flavored and aromatic product was held in high esteem by the ancient Romans who ladled it over various seafoods, particularly oysters. *Garum* is made by placing ungutted whole fish in a heavy brine solution in a container and exposing the mixture to the sun. Fermentation results through the presence of enzymes and microorganisms (actually in the fish's alimentary tract) in the presence of salt. *Garum* has many counterparts throughout the world. Vietnam or Cambodian veterans will recognize the sauce as **Nuoc Mam** or **Nam Pla**. In Japan it is known as **Shottsuru**. *See also ANCHOVY.*

Gefilte Fish

One doesn't need a Jewish mother to appreciate gefilte fish. This is one of those dishes that falls in the category of "family secrets." Jennie Grossinger, with whom I broke matzos when she ruled her fabled mountain retreat, claimed that she had the ultimate formula. To be properly made, the dish requires considerable time. The key to the whole process is the chopping of the fish to get the right texture, otherwise it cooks into rubbery balls. Gefilte fish is so popular that the Freshwater Fisheries Cooperative in Winnipeg, Manitoba, which ships millions of pounds of the species used in making the dish, has a full-time rabbi in attendance who assures that the fish are kosher.

Jewish fish cookery is traditionally limited to freshwater species such as carp, walleye (yellow pike), and whitefish. It had its roots among the people of Poland, Hungary and Czechoslovakia where variety was restricted by habitat; the affinity for carp, for example, was due mainly to the fact that this fish was most suitable for pond culture. A five-volume work, *About the Fish Ponds and Fish Living Therein* by Jan Dubravius, the Bishop of Olomouc, was first published at Breslau in 1547. This is the first known record of European fish breeding, and the text was so complete that it was translated from Latin to English, then to Polish and German, and was reissued until 1906. By the late sixteenth century, there were in Moravia and Bohemia more than 450,000 acres of breeding ponds dominated by carp as this species produced the greatest poundage per unit of feeding.

Alice Coplan, wife of the New York photographer Maxwell Coplan, taught me to make gefilte fish some 20 years ago. After a nerve-shattering job in a Bermuda hurricane Mac suggested that we repair to his home in Westchester and have Alice whip up some gefilte fish. Until that time I had eaten only commercial products in jars, which look like museum specimens waiting to be identified. Gentle Alice quickly converted me to the true Jewish fish dumpling. Her recipe is as good as any I've sampled in subsequent years. Gefilte fish has its counterpart in other cuisines such as the Norwegian **side boller,** Danish **fiskeboller,** or the German **Fischklopse.** The last are somewhat heavier and often spicier versions usually made with cod, haddock or pollock.

Gefilte fish recipes ordinarily require larger than usual amounts of fish for two reasons: it's a Sabbath or holiday dish normally served to family and friends (the chef never thinks in terms of less than 6 people); in view of the fact that it does take time to prepare with the end product having a refrigerator shelf life of several days at least, it's sensible to make more than enough. I am told that gefilte fish cut into rounds, then fried crisp and served with sweet-and-sour sauce, highlights Princess Mar-

GEFILTE FISH (prepared by Elaine Grossinger Ettes in her home)

1. Mrs. Ettes buying fish;
2. chopping vegetables for stock; **3.** making stock; **4.** chopping fish;
5. chopping vegetables to add to chopped fish;
6. adding eggs to fish;
7. mixing vegetables with fish mixture;
8. shaping large dumplings of the fish mixture;
9. cooking dumplings in stock.

facing page, Sabbath dinner in the Grossinger family home.

garet's parties at Kensington Palace; that's not a bad idea for leftovers, and it suggests various possibilities for the imaginative chef.

Remember when reading any gefilte fish recipe that the poundage indicated is in napecut skinned fillets; also, when ordering you must ask your fishmonger to reserve the heads, skins and bones as these produce not only the stock for cooking but also a fine gelatin that is usually knife-chopped and served as garnish. The selection of fish is optional. Most recipes call for carp which has a very firm flesh; however, it also tends to darken when cooked and most connoisseurs prefer a combination of walleye (marketed as "yellow pike") and whitefish. If freshwater fish are not readily available, any white-fleshed saltwater species such as cod, haddock or halibut can be substituted.

In the recipe that follows you will notice that something special is done with the skin of the fish. This is a tieback to old times when the dumplings were wrapped in pieces of skin for cooking. While this is no longer done, the addition of the skin during cooking adds richness to the broth.

Instead of making dumplings, you can shape the mixture into loaves, poach the loaves in the same fashion, and slice them to serve.

ALICE COPLAN'S GEFILTE FISH

fish bones, heads and skins	5 carrots
3½ pounds whitefish fillets	5 cups water
3½ pounds walleye	2 eggs
(yellow pike) fillets	1 tablespoon matzo meal
4 onions	salt and pepper
2 celery ribs with leaves	

Put the bones, heads and skins of the fish in a large pot but reserve one piece of skin about the size of half of a fish. Cut 2 onions, the celery and carrots into chunk-size pieces and add these to the pot. Pour in 4 cups of the water and simmer for 30 minutes.

In the meantime grind the fish fillets into a bowl, passing them through the grinder with the remaining 2 onions. When ground, add the eggs, matzo meal, and salt and pepper to taste. This mixture must be chopped. Chopping is for the purpose of getting air into the ground fish and this is the secret of the whole thing. It takes about 35 minutes of chopping, during which time you add 1 cup of cold water bit by bit, to get the texture smooth and fluffy. When the texture is correct, roll the mixture into balls. Lower the balls gently on a slotted spoon into the

broth made with the fish trimmings. The extra piece of skin should now be rolled and added also. Cook slowly for 3 hours, basting the dumplings with broth. Remove dumplings from the pot, discard the extra piece of skin, and strain the broth.

Gefilte fish can be served warm or cold. For cold service place the dumplings in a mold and pour the strained broth over them; chill. They will congeal in about 6 hours. Cold gefilte fish is usually served with grated raw carrots and lemon juice or horseradish. Makes about 36 dumplings.

GEFILTE FISH
(Grossinger's, Liberty, New York)

Skin and bone enough fish to have 3 pounds fillets. Put heads, bones and skins in a large pot along with 1 onion, 2 celery ribs and 1 carrot, all slivered or chopped. Add water to cover and simmer to make a stock. Meanwhile chop the fillets; add 1 large onion, grated, 2 eggs, and salt and pepper to taste. Mix well together, using the chopper so that the texture will be right. Shape the mixture into balls, using about ⅓ cup for each dumpling. Place the dumplings in the pot of stock, letting them rest on the vegetables and bones. Add more water to cover if necessary. Bring to a boil, then reduce heat and simmer for 1½ to 2 hours. Liquid should be reduced by half. Chill the dumplings before serving. Garnish with carrots and with the strained stock, jellied and chopped, if you like. Makes 4 to 6 servings.

VARIATIONS: 1. To stretch the mixture, add 2 slices of white bread, soaked in water and squeezed.

2. Add 1 raw carrot, grated, to the mixture with the grated onion. Add 1 more sliced carrot to the stock.

3. Do not add fish skin to the stockpot. Instead wrap each fish ball in a piece of skin for cooking. Remove skin for serving.

4. Form 3-inch flattened patties of the fish mixture. Dip into fine crumbs and panfry in oil. Or bake at 375°F. for 12 to 15 minutes.

Goatfish

The goatfishes (Mullidae), sometimes called surmullets, have a cosmopolitan distribution, being found in temperate, semitropical and tropical seas. They are distinctive in having a pair of long chin barbels resembling the whiskers of a goat. There are 5 species in American waters on the Atlantic and Pacific Coasts, but they are most common in the Caribbean, Bahamas and Florida Keys. Goatfish are rarely utilized as food here probably because of the abun-

Goatfish

dance of larger reef fish. However, a substantial amount (over 100,000 pounds per year) reaches the New York market. A Mediterranean goatfish commonly but erroneously called the "red mullet" or **rouget de roche** is famous in various cuisines of Europe. Many species of goatfish are rose to red in color and most, including our brilliantly hued yellow goatfish, will turn red when excited or killed. The ancient Romans reputedly paid for these fish by their weight in silver. All goatfish have delicate white meat and few bones.

Also known as **Salmonete** (Spain and Portugal), **Triglia** (Italy), **Trlje** (Yugoslavia), **Barbouni** (Greece), **Tekir** (Turkey), **Meerbarben** (Germany), **Mulle** (Denmark and Norway), **Mullus** (Sweden), **Chivalo** (Mexico), **Moano** or **Kumu** (Hawaii), **Himeji** (Japan), **Salmonet** (Mozambique and South Africa).

See also MULLET.

Goldeye

The goldeye is undistinguished in appearance and of no great moment when cooked in fresh form, but when smoked it is so special that the name is whispered in staid dining rooms across the border in reverent fear of its scarcity. This small freshwater fish is found from the Ohio River north to the Hudson Bay drainage system, but its historical abundance and culinary fame belong to Canada. The goldeye was a trade-goods item of the Cree Indians at Lower Fort Garry according to Bishop David Anderson (1852), but before Robert Firth's smoke process was introduced it could hardly have been wildly acclaimed, as the good Bishop further observed that "the accounts (of the fort) frequently note the buying of one or two from Indian women who came to barter."

Robert Firth was a young butcher who emigrated from Hull, England, to Winnipeg in 1886. He did a mediocre business in the meat trade, so relying on a makeshift barrel smokehouse he began curing goldeyes, which were plentiful in the Red River. A fresh goldeye is an inferior food as the flesh is soft and almost flavorless. But Firth was getting 25 cents a dozen for his cured product. One day he miscalculated the heat of his fire, and the goldeyes came out more cooked than smoked. Of course, this is the hot-smoking process, but until that time apparently nobody had tried a high-heat cycle; it magically transformed the goldeye from a mere fish to a gastronomical discovery. One nibble and Firth realized that he had found his fortune. To make the fish more appealing, he dipped them into a reddish-colored vegetable dye which remains the hallmark of goldeye to this day. In time President Woodrow Wilson and the Prince of Wales became goldeye fanciers, and business really boomed in the late 1920s when the annual production went over one million pounds. Prices soared, but the fish population went down to rock bottom. Currently, the inventory of goldeye is limited. The Canadian National Railway no longer lists the Winnipeg Goldeye on its menu, although the diehard Canadian Pacific Railway still features them—smaller and not as fat as yesteryear but goldeye nevertheless. The decline of *Hiodon alosoides* is a conservation problem which for the present is unsolved. The chief source of goldeye in years past was western Canada, but in the seldom consistent history of fishes the largest volume being received in Winnipeg today is from North and South Dakota. Much of this catch has been supplemented with the goldeye's look-alike relative, the mooneye, which is of more southerly U. S. distribution. For some reason neither fish has ever had an American processor despite the demand.

The trick in smoking goldeye is first to freeze the fish for at least 1 month. This is one of the few species that actually improves with the freezing process through moisture loss. Goldeye are defrosted in a brine solution, dyed in vats, then hot-smoked over oak logs for 3½ to 6 hours, depending on the usual variables in thermal control. The ideal goldeye weighs ¾ to 1 pound on the plate. This requires a live fish of 1½ pounds or so, because it loses 35 to 40 percent of its weight between the freezer and the kiln. Inevitably, the best goldeyes arrive at Booth's Fisheries in Winnipeg. This venerable institution was originally a Chicago firm established in Manitoba in 1896. Their average production is 150,000 pounds out of the total 200,000 pounds from all Canadian sources. Booth's may ship a few hundred pounds or so to United States restaurants, but over 98 percent of the annual harvest is quickly consumed in Canada.

Goldeye

Goosefish

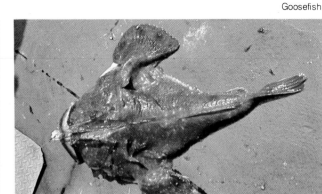

Goldeye is smoked gutted and whole. Although it can be eaten cold the full flavor is best enjoyed by steaming, wrapped in foil, for 20 minutes.

Goosefish

This ugly-looking fish, invariably discarded by American anglers, is elsewhere considered a delicacy. It is highly esteemed in Europe. It is one of the classic ingredients in a seafood paella under the name **rape** and is often included in a Mediterranean *bouillabaisse* under the name **baudroie**. In Scandinavia it appears as **kotlettfisk** which is an apt name for the "cutlets" obtained from this species. Also known as **monkfish, frogfish, sea devil** and **angler,** it is an inshore relative of the highly specialized group of deep-sea anglerfishes.

At first glance the goosefish appears to be all head with tiny eyes and a huge tooth-filled mouth. Its body, designed for hugging the sea bottom, is quite flat, and the skin, lacking scales, is thin, pliable and slippery. The most unusual feature is the modified first dorsal spine which terminates in a flap of skin; when hungry, the goosefish erects this spine and rapidly moves it back and forth to attract smaller fish. The "bait" is skillfully waved out in front of the goosefish's mouth until its prey is close, then the predator thrusts itself forward with its pectoral fins which are modified footlike structures and swallows the smaller fish. The appetite of this species is insatiable. Flounders, dogfish, skates, eels, herrings, cod and sea bass are only a few of the fishes in its diet, and sea birds, including cormorants, gulls and ducks, are part of its regular fare. Lobsters, crabs, squid and other assorted invertebrates are also taken. There are authentic records of goosefish grabbing the feet of bathers. Even wooden buoys from lobster pots have been found in the goosefish's stomach. Although the average goosefish seen in markets is fairly small, the species grows to lengths of 4 feet and may weigh over 50 pounds.

The goosefish occurs in the western Atlantic from the Grand Banks southward to North Carolina. It has also been reported from Barbados, Yucatan and Brazil. The related anglerfish of Europe has a wide distribution, and a third species appears in the western Pacific.

Only the tail section of the goosefish contains edible meat. It is white and firm, very similar to the flesh of a puffer. It is marketed in Europe in fillet form either fresh or frozen and is often hot-smoked. Small quantities are sold in the U. S., usually under the name "bellyfish." They are caught mainly by commercial cod trawlers. The Fulton Fish Market in New York purveys about 130,000 pounds each year, but demand always exceeds supply. Goosefish can be sautéed, broiled, baked, poached or cut into fingers and deep-fried tempura style.

Grayling

Up in the land where no trees grow, where the eider duck and the sandhill crane parade across the barrens, and the great white whale submerges in clots of icy foam, there are many things to make a man pause, but not even the spell of northern lights is more compelling than the sight of:

> *Rivers, bound to the Arctic,*
> *Journey many a day;*
> *A shore line girt with eddies,*
> *Where purple grayling play.*

The grayling has always had a mysterious quality about it, largely because we—in this country at least—associate it with alien places. Nobody now living can remember when this fish was so abundant in Michigan (1860-1880) that enterprising merchants hauled them away by the wagonload to feed lumber camps, or down the Au Sable and Lake Huron in the live wells of houseboats to supply restaurants of Detroit and Chicago. One

Grayling

Michigan township (formerly Crawford) adopted the name Grayling in honor of its first citizen. But this great resource which teemed in rivers of the lower peninsula disappeared shortly after the turn of the century when the virgin pine forests were gone and warming river temperatures became critical to the remaining fish's survival.

Today the grayling only appears at table when you catch your own. It is not a fish of the marketplace. Thousands of anglers fly into the Canadian wilds each season, particularly to northern Saskatchewan, the Northwest Territories, the Yukon or Alaska to seek, among other exotic species, this beautiful gamefish. Grayling vary greatly in color according to species and environment from purple to brown to silvery-gray but with reflections of lilac or gold and often with pink stripes or spots in the fins. Its unusually large dorsal fin, shaped much like a sail, has no counterpart among freshwater fishes. At its prime in Arctic waters the firm, white flesh is of delicate flavor and aroma. In the legend of the Bishop of Milan "the flower of fishes smells like wild thyme," hence its generic Latin name *Thymallus*. In Europe also the grayling remains principally a sport fish although here it may arrive in the kitchens of small country inns—on a French menu as **ombre,** in Germany and Austria as **Äsche,** in Finland as **harjus,** and in Norway and Sweden as **harr.** The grayling of Denmark or **stalling** are virtually extinct now, as its rivers have been taken over wholly for commercial trout production. The best grayling for my tastes were caught from the glacial Traun in Austria, but their quality is comparable to those found in the Great Bear River of the Northwest Territories or the Ugashik Lakes of Alaska. Yugoslavia has countless pristine grayling rivers (here the fish is known as **lipen**) although again it's a food that must be caught by angling, which is virtually guaranteed in the hatchery at Bihac in Bosnia where for a small fee one can extract his dinner from the water and have it prepared at a nearby hotel. In view of the many wild grayling available, however, the need for a captive fish is hardly necessary.

Grayling still thrive in the unpolluted rivers of England such as the Kennet, Test, Itchen, Driffield Beck, Wharfe, the Derwent of Yorkshire and the Dove. Here it's considered at its prime for table in the autumn season for, unlike the American grayling found only in rock-bottomed rivers, the European fish occurs mainly in the weedier sections of chalk streams. Izaak Walton speculated on grayling at length in *The Compleat Angler,* and it's interesting to note that his authority of the day (Aldrovandi) had already established that grayling are members of the trout and salmon family, Salmonidae. A more unlikely relationship is hard to conceive with the naked eye, except for the tiny nub of a fin called the adipose just before its tail.

"*Aldrovandus sayes, they be of a Trout kind: and Gesner sayes, that in his country (which is Swisserland) he is accounted the choicest fish. And in Italy he is, in the month of May, so highly valued, that he is sold then at a much higher rate than other fish. The French . . . call the* Umber *off the lake of Lemon,* Un Umble Chevalier; *and they value the Umber or Grayling so highly, that they say he feeds on gold, and say that many have been caught out of their famous river of Loyre, out of whose bellies grains of gold have been taken."* (Apparently the "lake of Lemon" was Lac Leman at Geneva, popularly known as Lake Geneva. There are no grayling in the lake today and none in the Loire [Loyre]. France still has three good grayling rivers, La Loue, Le Doubs and L'Ain. Walton also confused the French common names as the omble [*umble*] is a char, while the grayling is *ombre;* this is understandable as spelling was not consistent even within the English language at that time.)

"And some think that he feeds on Water-time, and smells so at his first taking out of the water; and they may think so with as good reason as we do, that our Smelts smell like violets at their first being caught; which I think is the truth."

There are numerous species of grayling; the one that prospered so splendidly in Michigan, *Thymallus tricolor,* is now a museum piece and apparently never grew much over 10 ounces in size. The American grayling *(Thymallus arcticus),* which is today found mainly from north central Canada to Alaska, attains weights up to 5 pounds as does its European counterpart *(Thymallus thymallus).* But from western Europe (with the exception of southern France, Spain, Portugal, southern Italy and Ireland) various grayling occur eastward through Siberia and northern Mongolia. In the USSR the Kosogol, Baikal, Angara and Mongolian graylings are most common, but only the Baikal grayling occurred in large enough numbers to be fished commercially in years past.

To an Alaskan the grayling is hardly exotic table fare as the state is veined with clear, cold waters, particularly in the Wood River and Igushik River systems and the Nushagak and Naknet drainages. Elsewhere in the U. S., however, one may find a small grayling on occasion in some Montana streams where it was first recorded by the Lewis and Clark Expedition (1805) as a "new kind of white or silvery trout" found in the upper Missouri River, and to a lesser extent today in Wyoming. For all practical purposes the fish is now such a rarity in Rocky Mountain waters and usually so small (less than 6 ounces) that killing one for table may be deemed a wanton act. There was only one attempt (that I am aware of) to introduce grayling to our eastern waters and that was at the old Southside Rod-and-Gun Club on Long Island in 1925. The experiment failed as the Montana form at least, could not survive in our summer water temperatures.

HOW TO COOK GRAYLING

The simplest methods are best. I prefer poaching and panfrying (in the same manner that one would treat a small trout). Grayling have larger scales than trout and should be carefully descaled, then pan-dressed. The late Charles Ritz, who made an annual trip to Bavaria just for grayling, had a share of his fish smoked, a truly incredible taste delight and reason enough to cause my visits to Paris to coincide with his triumphant return. Most recently our dinner at the Ritz consisted simply of smoked grayling accompanied by a *Grand Cru* white Burgundy, a salad, a noble Appenzell cheese, and delicate Anjou pears then in season.

Both the Marienbrucke Hotel in Gmunden on the Traun River and the Schloss Fuschl on the Fuschlamsee have long practiced the art of grayling cookery and are worth a detour if you should be near Salzburg, Austria.

Greenland Turbot

A market name for the Greenland halibut. *See FLOUNDER TERMINOLOGY under SOLE.*

Greenling

There are 9 greenlings found along the Pacific Coast of North America, distributed from Alaska to Baja California according to species. These members of the family Hexagrammidae are generally slender-bodied fishes with large mouths and sharp teeth; they vary in size from the kelp greenling, which is seldom over 2 pounds in weight, to 70 pounds or more in the lingcod. Although small greenlings enter the sport catch in considerable numbers and have good food value, they are of little commercial importance. The lingcod, however, is a popular market fish with catches ranging from ½ million to 2 million pounds annually in California alone. In recent years the landings have averaged below 1 million pounds. *See also ATKA MACKEREL, LINGCOD.*

Grouper

Groupers are members of the sea bass family, Serranidae, which is composed of over 400 species found in temperate and tropical waters in various parts of the world. However, there are many genera and only two of these are properly called "groupers" in a culinary sense, specifically those species composing *Epinephelus* and *Mycteroperca.* Groupers are particularly common around coral reefs and rock outcroppings of the inner coastal shelf which makes them less vulnerable to trawls or traps; it's essentially a hook-and-line fishery so the landings are small but relatively valuable. Groupers vary greatly in size according to species, but one, the jewfish of the western Atlantic, attains weights up to about 700 pounds. Our major grouper fishing area extends from the offshore reefs of North Carolina along the coast around Florida and in the Gulf of Mexico to Texas. Most of the Pacific groupers occur south of California with the exception of the gulf grouper, snowy grouper and spotted cabrilla, but these are caught in very minor numbers. In addition to the southern U. S., Mexico, Central and South America, the Mediterranean and South Africa have important grouper fisheries.

In Spanish-speaking countries groupers are generally known as **mero** or **cherna,** the exception being Mexico where **garopa** is often used. Mexico also differentiates with respect to the **cabrilla** (pronounced cah-*bree*-yah) which is not only applied to several grouper species but is arbitrarily used for other serranids that are not groupers. In Venezuela the name **cuna** is specifically applied to those groupers in the genus *Mycteroperca* and the more familiar **mero** to the species belonging to *Epinephelus*. The Mediterranean groupers are not outstanding foodfish when compared to those of the western Atlantic but **merou** does appear on menus in southern French ports. In Spain **mero** is commonly used, also to some extent in Portugal, but **garoupa** is generally accepted in the latter country. In Italy, the grouper is **cernia** while Yugoslavia adopts the Serbo-Croat **kirnja.** South Africa uses the names **rock cod** and **garrupa,** but the former is more common.

NOTE: Two groupers to be avoided as food in the Bahamas and West Indies are the yellowfin *(Mycteroperca venenosa)* and the misty grouper *(Epinephelus mystacinus)* as these have been implicated in ciguatera poisoning with considerable frequency; this is especially pertinent to large individuals of 10 pounds or more. As a blanket rule for all groupers *do not eat the roe.* Although the gonads are often large and invite experiment, they are not worth cooking. The roe is flavorless, pasty in texture, and has a high water content. These fish mature as females then become males as they grow older (other serranid genera are hermaphroditic), and seemingly their gonads are equally confused at any age. One also increases the risk of ciguatoxin by eating any part of the viscera of fishes in those geographic areas where ciguatera is endemic.

HOW TO COOK GROUPERS

There are differences in the texture and quality of different grouper species but they are all white-fleshed and lean. Groupers have no intermuscular bones, so they fillet perfectly. However, grouper skin is tough and strongly flavored so the fish does not lend itself to cooking in whole form or in unskinned fillets. Groupers are ideally prepared by deep-frying and poaching, and in chowders for succulent results. The musculature tends to dry out in baking and broiling. Fillets can be cut into fingers or cubes, battered, then deep-fried in peanut oil; the meat retains its moist flake and sweet taste. Deep-frying is by far the most popular method. The fillets can also be poached in a suitable stock when cut into loins or steaks according to size. None of the flavor is lost by cutting the meat into cubes and making a chowder, with the head providing a rich stock for its base. Large cartilaginous grouper heads are the "secret" of many Bahamian conch and fish chowders, and they make a wonderful stock for a *bouillabaisse.* The two largest groupers, the jewfish and warsaw, have extremely firm meat; among *savants* of the Florida Keys they are considered the finest of all chowder ingredients.

Grouper in any form is traditionally served with pigeon peas and rice in the Bahamas and West Indies.

GROUPER TERMINOLOGY

BLACK GROUPER This is a common grouper in south Florida and throughout the tropical Atlantic to Brazil. The black grouper *(Mycteroperca bonaci)* reaches weights over 100 pounds although the average at market is usually 10 to 20 pounds. The black grouper is blackish-brown in color with rectangular dark blotches over the body and irregular pale lines forming a chainlike pattern. This is a good foodfish but not comparable to the Nassau or red grouper. Also known as **cherno bonaci.**

BROOMTAIL GROUPER The broomtail *(Mycteroperca xenarcha)* is a large Pacific grouper growing to a weight of 100 pounds or more. Although a few are caught in southernmost California, it's common only along the coast of Mexico. The flesh of the broomtail is coarse but it makes a good chowder fish. Also known as **garopa jasplada.**

COMB GROUPER This grouper *(Mycteroperca rubra)* is found on both sides of the Atlantic, occurring in the Mediterranean and along the coast of Africa to Angola and in the western Caribbean to Brazil. It is brownish-gray in color with scattered white blotches over its sides and on the dorsal fin. The comb grouper reaches a weight of about 10 pounds. The **cuna negra** (not to be confused with black grouper or simply **cuna**) is of some importance as a foodfish in Venezuela.

GAG This grouper *(Mycteroperca microlepis)* is fairly

Black grouper

Nassau grouper

Red grouper

Yellowfin grouper

common from North Carolina to Florida and in the Gulf of Mexico to Louisiana. It is rare in the Bahamas or West Indies. The gag reaches a weight of about 50 pounds. It is a somberly colored fish, being an overall dull gray with darker vermiculations. This grouper has some commercial importance but lacks the quality of certain other species.

JEWFISH   This is the largest grouper *(Epinephelus itajara)*, reaching a weight of about 700 pounds. It is found in Florida and the Gulf of Mexico, and along the coast of South America to Brazil. It's also known as **guasa** (Spanish) and **giant sea bass.** A similar, though smaller species *(E. guaza)* occurs in the Mediterranean, the Canary Islands and along the West Coast of Africa. The jewfish is grayish-brown in color with scattered small dark brown spots on the head, body and fins; young jewfish also have irregular dark bars on their sides. Despite its great size, the jewfish is essentially a shallow-water species occurring inshore, in creeks and estuaries; it is often found under bridges where it systematically breaks even the heaviest tackle. The jewfish is excellent eating at any size and processed has been sold as "salt cod" in years past. The meat is firm, white and sweet. A difficult fish to skin. I have snapped tempered-steel knife blades on "small" 60- and 70-pounders. Jewfish are now rarely marketed as local demand exceeds supply.

NASSAU GROUPER   Probably the best-known grouper in southern Florida and our tropical American Atlantic, the Nassau is extremely abundant in the Bahamas and hence its name. It's one of the most common commercial fish of the West Indies. This grouper *(Epinephelus striatus)* attains weights over 50 pounds but is usually purveyed at market in the 5- to 10-pound sizes. The Nassau grouper is brownish in color with irregular dark brown bars around its body and a distinct black blotch on the "wrist" (caudal peduncle) just before its tail. It somewhat resembles the red grouper, but this species lacks the black saddle marking. The Nassau grouper is one of the very best for texture and flavor and is an important market fish in the southern U.S. when obtainable. Also called **cherna criolla** and **mero gallina.**

RED GROUPER   One of the most common groupers in southern Florida and the tropical American Atlantic, the red grouper *(Epinephelus morio)* reaches weights up to 50 pounds. It is reddish brown in color with scattered pale blotches. The inside of its mouth is red and white. The red grouper is excellent at table; an important commercial species in the Gulf area. One of the largest fisheries is based in the Yucatan Peninsula of Mexico. The red grouper is very tenacious of life; it will survive out of

water longer than other groupers even in hot weather, and withstand being held in a crowded live well. For this reason it has always been a favorite of out-island fishermen.

RED HIND   This is a small fish, seldom over 4 pounds in size and usually about 1½ pounds, but its excellent flavor and texture make it one of the more valuable groupers. The red hind *(Epinephelus guttatus)* occurs from North Carolina to Florida and through the West Indies, but is more abundant in the southern part of its range. The red hind is a colorful fish, being a greenish-yellow along the back, shading to dusky below, and the body is covered with vermilion spots. Because of the spotting it's also known in the Bahamas as **strawberry grouper.**

ROCK HIND   Similar to the red hind in appearance but with orange-brown spots and a distinct saddlelike black blotch dorsally, in front of its tail. The rock hind *(Epinephelus adscensionis)* attains a slightly larger size (to about 10 pounds) than the red hind and occurs from southern Florida to the Bahamas and into the West Indies. It's also caught in the Mediterranean and South Africa. The rock hind is almost comparable to the red hind in quality and is of some commercial importance in the Caribbean.

SCAMP   One of the smaller Atlantic groupers, the scamp *(Mycteroperca phenax)* occurs from the Carolinas to the Gulf of Mexico but is most common from Key West to Texas. Its body is pinkish-gray in color and is thickly covered with small dark brown spots. Scamp reach a weight of about 10 pounds but are usually caught in the 1½- to 2-pound sizes. A panfish of minor culinary interest.

SPECKLED HIND   The speckled hind *(Epinephelus drummondhayi)* is found from North Carolina to Mexico and is a commercial species of some importance. Although usually caught in small sizes of 2 to 4 pounds, it attains weights up to 30 pounds. It's brown in color and its body and fins are densely covered with small pearly-white spots; there is a patch of red on the lower side of its head. This is a common grouper off the Carolinas and on the Gulf snapper banks, being marketed in Morehead City, Charleston, Pensacola and New Orleans.

SPOTTED CABRILLA   This is one of several groupers bearing the name cabrilla, but the spotted *(Epinephelus analogus)* is the largest and most important. A Pacific species and common along the coast of Mexico to Panama, the spotted cabrilla is an excellent foodfish and was the most valuable species in California's grouper landings in years past. The spotted cabrilla is brownish in color with darker cross bars on its sides and is covered with small round reddish-brown spots. It reaches a weight of about

50 pounds. The consumer demand in Mexico is so great for **pinta cabrilla** that very little now appears in U. S. markets. Comparable to the Nassau grouper in texture and flavor.

WARSAW GROUPER This is a very large grouper reaching weights of at least 300 pounds, and is found in the tropical American Atlantic from Florida southward. The warsaw *(Epinephelus nigritus)* is a uniformly dark gray or gray-brown in color with a few scattered white spots. It is a deepwater species (over 200 feet) and because of its large size is not readily caught in great quantity. Nevertheless a surprising amount reaches local East Coast outlets; the Fulton Fish Market in New York handles about 250,000 pounds annually. (This landing is synonymous with "jewfish" and under that common name it has an ethnic market among Chinese people who use these similar large groupers as "steamed fish.") In Florida we catch this grouper with wire line and electrically operated reels by fishing the drop-offs along the edge of the Gulf Stream. Although difficult to skin, the meat of the warsaw is extremely firm, white and of sweet flavor. It's comparable to the jewfish when prepared in the form of a chowder. The stomachs of warsaw groupers are usually filled with crustaceans, especially crabs, which contribute to this fish's unique flavor.

YELLOWMOUTH GROUPER The yellowmouth *(Mycteroperca interstitialis)* is the most common market species in the southeastern U. S., especially in the Carolinas, but it occurs in Florida and the tropical American Atlantic. The yellowmouth grouper is light brownish-gray in color with compressed dark brown spots on the upper half of the body and yellow coloring around its jaws. This is a good grouper at table and commercially important; however, it's a small fish, seldom over 4 pounds and usually half this size.

BAHAMIAN FISH CHOWDER
(Spanish Cay)

One of the best Bahamian fish chowders I have enjoyed was prepared by Willard Hutchinson while I was a guest of Clint Murchison at Spanish Cay. Willard is a most versatile master of island cookery. His chowder differs from most Nassau chowders; he marinates and then half-fries the fish before adding remaining ingredients. The green pepper and celery in the base also lift this chowder out of the ordinary.

3 pounds grouper, skinned, boned, and cut into 2-inch cubes	1 green pepper, diced
	3 celery ribs, diced
	1 teaspoon dried thyme

¾ cup lime juice	4 cups canned tomatoes
salt and pepper	6 ounces tomato paste
½ pound salt pork, cubed	4 potatoes, peeled and cubed
1 large onion, diced	¼ cup Worcestershire sauce

Marinate the cubes of grouper in ½ cup of the lime juice, adding a little salt and pepper to taste, for about 1 hour. In a large saucepan render the salt pork. Half-fry the marinated fish cubes so that they are browned slightly. Remove the fish and set aside. Add onion, pepper and celery pieces to the pan and sauté in salt-pork fat until golden brown. Add thyme, tomatoes, tomato paste and potato cubes. Reduce heat and let the chowder simmer for about 1 hour. Add the half-fried fish cubes and cook for another 20 minutes, or until done. Just before serving, add Worcestershire sauce and remaining ¼ cup lime juice. Hardtack biscuit can be broken on top if you like. Makes about 6 servings.

GROUPER DIEPPOISE

4 fresh grouper steaks, each about ¾ inch thick	8 mushroom caps, sautéed in butter
4 cups fish stock	1 cup White-Wine Sauce II (p. 287), hot
8 mussels, steamed, with shells removed	2 tablespoons minced fresh parsley
8 shrimps, cooked and cleaned	

Bring fish stock to a boil; reduce heat. When liquid is barely simmering, lower grouper steaks into it. Simmer just until fish is opaque and separates when tested with a fork; do not overcook. When done, drain fish and place in the center of a heated platter. Strain the stock and use 2 cups to make the sauce. Arrange the mussels, shrimps and mushrooms around the fish. Pour the hot wine sauce over all. Sprinkle parsley over all. Makes 4 servings.

SAVORY GROUPER STEW

1 pound grouper fillets or other fish fillets, fresh or frozen
1 cup chopped onion
⅓ cup melted margarine or cooking oil
1 can (1 pound 12 ounces) tomatoes
2 cups diced potatoes
1 cup water
¼ cup ketchup
½ teaspoon salt
pepper
1 can (1 pound) mixed vegetables

Thaw frozen fillets. Skin fillets. Cut fillets into pieces about 1 inch square. In a 3-quart saucepan, cook onion in margarine or oil until tender. Add tomatoes, potatoes, water, ketchup, salt, and pepper to taste. Cover and simmer for 30 minutes. Add fish, mixed vegetables and vegetable liquid. Cover and simmer for about 15 minutes longer, or until the potatoes are tender and fish flakes easily when tested with a fork. Makes 6 servings.

GROUPER KIEV

2 pounds grouper fillets
¼ pound butter or margarine, softened
2 tablespoons chopped parsley
1 tablespoon lemon juice
¾ teaspoon Worcestershire sauce
¼ teaspoon Tabasco
1 garlic clove, chopped fine
½ teaspoon salt
dash of pepper
2 tablespoons water
2 eggs, beaten
½ cup flour
3 cups soft bread crumbs
fat or oil for deep-frying

Combine the butter or margarine, the parsley, lemon juice, Worcestershire sauce, Tabasco, garlic and seasoning. Place butter mixture on wax paper and form into a roll. Chill until hard. Cut fillets into 6 portions. With a sharp knife cut horizontally along one side of each portion to form a pocket, being careful not to cut completely through the portion. Cut the cold seasoned butter into 6 pieces. Place a piece of butter in each pocket and secure the side opening with a stainless-steel or wooden pick. Add water to eggs and mix thoroughly. Roll fish in flour, dip into eggs, and roll in crumbs. Chill for 1 hour. Fry in deep fat heated to 375°F. on a frying thermometer for 2 or 3 minutes, or until color is golden brown and fish flakes easily when tested with a fork. Drain on absorbent paper. Remove picks. Makes 6 servings.

OUT-ISLAND BAKE
(Jean Yehle)

3 cups cubed raw fish (grouper, snapper, rockfish, sea bass)
¼ pound butter
½ cup chopped onion
½ cup chopped celery
½ cup chopped green pepper
12 saltines, crushed
juice of 1 large Persian lime, or 2 or more Key limes
½ teaspoon ground thyme
salt and pepper

Melt butter, add onion, celery and green pepper, and sauté until vegetables are tender. Add fish, saltines, lime juice, thyme, and salt and pepper to taste. Mix well, and turn into a 6-cup casserole; cover. Bake at 350°F. for 50 minutes, then remove cover and bake for 10 minutes longer. Makes 4 servings.

Sliced tomatoes or pieces of pimiento can be added to make a more colorful dish; if you use tomatoes, add a few more saltines. Add a pinch of garlic powder if you like.

Grunt

In 1905, when Henry Morrison Flagler was building his ill-fated railroad from Homestead to Key West, these abundant and easily caught fish became a staple for the track-laying crews whose diet monotonously consisted of "grits and grunts," an expression that even today implies a basic, yet idyllic life style—one that has vanished. (The railroad, completed 8 years later, operated until 1935, when the roadbed was demolished by a September hurricane. The right of way was sold and became the present Overseas Highway.)

The grunts are a large family (Pomadasyidae) of inshore tropical and semitropical marine fishes. Many species are very colorful, especially those found in reef habitats. Their common name is derived from the grunting sound these fish make when they are taken from the water. This is produced by a fish grinding its pharyngeal teeth, a sound that is amplified by the air bladder. Anatomically, grunts are related to the snappers; like the latter, they have delicate white flesh; however, the texture is somewhat softer and the flake finer. Most grunts are small, seldom exceeding 1 pound in size; for this reason their commercial market is somewhat limited. Nevertheless, many gourmets prefer certain grunt species to the more popular snappers. They are delicious when crisply deep-fried or sautéed and can be eaten like corn on the cob if you don't mind, and can locate, the small bones. Grunts are an excellent fish to barbecue over charcoal in whole-dressed form, while basting with garlic butter. They also make a stellar addition to a **bouillabaisse, bourride,** or any fish soup.

There are about 175 species of grunts (generally known as **corocoro** in Spanish-speaking countries), but the most common to the Florida, Bahamas and Caribbean areas are the **bluestriped grunt, Caesar grunt, cottonwick, French grunt, margate, porkfish, pigfish, smallmouth grunt, Spanish grunt, tomtate** and **white**

GROUPER KIEV

1. Make butter mixture, roll, and chill. **2.** Make pockets in portions of grouper and insert a butter slice in each one.
3. Flour, egg, and crumb each grouper portion.
4. Deep-fry in hot oil.
5. Serve with parsley sprigs and carrot curls.

grunt. Of these, the porkfish (*Anisotremus virginicus*) is especially distinctive as it has fine-flaked, sweet, snowy-white meat. Porkfish seldom occur north of Florida but range southward to Brazil. It is the best of all grunts at table. Two other species are broadly distributed along our coast from the Gulf of Mexico to Chesapeake Bay. One is the pigfish (*Orthopristis chrysoptera*) which is a fairly large grunt, reaching a weight of 2 pounds, and the other, the white grunt (*Haemulon plumieri*), attains sizes up to 4 pounds. These are caught by both sport and commercial

fishermen, especially in late spring and summer months. The pigfish is mostly utilized in the North to South Carolina area and a modest amount (40 to 50 thousand pounds) reaches the Fulton Market in New York. An equal volume of white grunt is sold in the general category of "grunts" which seasonally may include other species.

The pigfish is also confusingly called "hogfish" in some areas but it is *not* related to the true hogfish (*Lachnolaimus maximus*), a member of the wrasse family (*see* HOGFISH).

Halibut
Herring
Hilsa
Hogfish

h

Haddock

A small member of the cod family. *See under COD.*

Hake

Small members of the cod family. *See under COD.*

Halibut

As a common name any of 3 species of righteye flounders—the Atlantic, Pacific and Greenland halibuts—and one member of the lefteye flounder family—the California halibut. All except the Greenland halibut have firm, bland to faintly sweet meat and can be prepared in a variety of recipes. The Greenland halibut is inferior in quality and less versatile in preparation. *See FLOUNDER TERMINOLOGY under SOLE.*

Herring

Herring were once a silvery legion that roamed the Atlantic and Pacific Oceans in uncountable billions. The name comes from late Latin *haringus*, a gray-white fish. Until recent times this clupeid was the most abundant seafood in the world. Herring bones are found among the litter of Scandinavian kitchen middens dating back to 3,000 B.C. Rich in protein and calories, the herring is a basic plankton convertor, as critical to the balance of an oceanic ecosystem as it has been to the survival of man. Herring feed on minute zooplankton called copepods by gulping down the tiny animals as they swim through the sea. These food organisms are caught in the herring's comblike gillrakers which permit the passage of water. The abundance of plankters in any one area coupled with seasonal spawning movements causes the fish to migrate extensively. In centuries past the sudden disappearance of herring shoals was attributed to the "sins and vices of inhabitants of the coast," and therefore Danish tax collectors were admonished to see that citizens in their district led a godly life. This belief was widespread. Scottish clergymen used the biblical injunction in Hosea 4, concerned with cursing, lying, theft and adultery, as supreme authority: "Therefore shall the land mourn, and every one that dwelleth therein shall languish, with the beasts of the field, and with the fowls of heaven; yea the fishes of the sea also shall be taken away." Evidently adultery was of paramount importance as effigies of women were burned when there was a "blight" on the fishing. Dr. Samuel Johnson wryly observed that "the return of the Laird of Dunvegan, after any considerable absence produces a plentiful capture of herrings; and if any woman crosses the water to the opposite island, the herring will desert the coast." (*A Journey to the Western Islands*, 1775) The herring played a more important role in the destiny of Europe as a builder of navies and empires. To eat a herring is to savor history.

In 1360 King Valdemar IV of Denmark sought to capture the Skåne fishery and was defeated by the powerful Hanseatic League within 2 years. The League gained control of the many fortresses that defended the Baltic's herring grounds and during the fourteenth century it became an economic giant. A loose confederation of merchants from each Hansa town in north Germany—such as Lübeck (whose heraldic crest was 3 herrings on a gold shield), Danzig and Stettin—the League had its own enclaves on the Scania Peninsula which thrust into the Baltic. Kolberg, for example, occupied only 48,000 square yards where its members would transact their business. In 1381 a Dutch fisherman by the name of Willem Beukelszoon invented the "rousing" method of preserving herring in barrels at sea; essentially the fish were gibbed (removing the gills and some of the viscera through an incision in the throat), then rolled in salt and packed head to tail in barrels with more salt between the layers. The barrels were topped and made airtight. This added tremendously to the League's profits, and ironically the herring went to war again as a barreled product. The "Battle of the Herrings" took place in 1429 at Rouvray, France. In the tradition of Lent, the British dispatched a supply of herring to the Duke of Suffolk's troops who were besieging Orléans. The French intercepted the convoy and the British rolled out the barrels using them as a barricade. This ingenious defense literally staved off the attack, if only for a brief period; the French army, taken in command by Joan of Arc, eventually routed the British.

The Hanseatic League collapsed early in the fifteenth century when herring suddenly ceased to spawn in the Baltic and concentrated in the North Sea. This phenomenon was more likely a result of depleting the Baltic stock rather than some unique biological condition, as historians of the time estimated that 40,000 vessels and

300,000 men were employed at the League's zenith. Nevertheless, this shift to the west pushed the balance of power to Holland in the lucrative herring market. The Dutch had 16,000 fishing vessels of all sizes by early in the seventeenth century. Every ship, no matter how small, was required to bear arms so the herring fleet became a training school for its navy. Under Martin Tromp, who destroyed the combined armadas of Spain and Portugal in 1639, the navy was invincible; but Holland's might was short-lived. Thirteen years later, in the first Anglo-Dutch War, Admiral Robert Blake was sent to annihilate the North Sea fishing fleet, and he brought Holland to heel after a protracted coastal blockade. In 1665 the Dutch burned St. John's, Newfoundland, to a cinder; they were already on the other side of the Atlantic in their search for herring. Great Britain, more concerned with the rich cod grounds of the Maritimes, declared overseas fisheries as "auxiliary to national policy" for their possession was synonymous with maritime supremacy. Thus, in 1755 His Majesty's ships entered the Seven Years War.

Hostilities continued well into the nineteenth century, often in the form of confrontations rather than declared wars. The influence of the British had by now extended to America; under the terms of the Halifax Commission Treaty of 1877, for the price of 5½ million dollars U. S. fishermen were allowed to operate within the 3-mile limit off Newfoundland and in the Gulf of St. Lawrence. The Newfoundlanders did not agree that their coast was under the sphere of Great Britain's influence and after a series of rammings between ships from Gloucester and St. John's the treaty collapsed in the Fortune Bay Riot. The Newfoundland commercials cut the American herring seines and sent the entire fleet of 22 schooners homeward at gunpoint.

It is undoubtedly apocryphal that the city of Amsterdam was built upon herring bones, but each coastal town had its golden era of prosperity, from Vlaardingen to Katwyk. The departure of the Dutch herring fleet today is from the ancient port town of Scheveningen.

Until the middle of the nineteenth century, the departure of the herring fleet took place on St. John's Day, June 24. This Catholic saint's day had been fixed long before the Dutch Reformation. Although most of the fishermen had in the meantime become Protestants, St. John's Day was still observed as the day of departure in quest of the "green" herring. This traditional and colorful ceremony attracts thousands of people on Flag Day *(Vlaggetjesdag)*, which is now celebrated on the weekend between May 15 and 20. Underlying the holiday atmosphere now is the feeling that one is attending a wake. Herring have been critically overexploited by electronically sophisticated fleets from Communist nations, and ships must venture farther from the European mainland each season. In recent years up to 250 eastern-bloc trawlers were to be seen just 12 miles out of New York Harbor during herring season. However, on March 1, 1977, the U.S. extended its control of fishing rights to 200 miles to limit indiscriminate fishing by mechanized fleets.

In 1954 the Icelandic government invited Arnold Gingrich, the publisher of *Esquire,* and myself to evaluate the possibility of developing their Atlantic salmon fishing for tourist anglers—a venture which has since become a significant part of the island's economy. None of the modern hotels and lodges that are fashionable today, existed then. We stayed in sod-roofed farmhouses except in the northernmost port town of Husavik, which had a rather ancient inn built on the waterfront, overlooking the docks. Our meals here, whether breakfast, lunch or dinner, were singular in nature—a **smørrebrød** consisting of red and rich smoked Arctic char, boiled eggs, herring in endless variety, smoked mutton, and what we both agreed was an excellent runny Brie cheese that could be layered on coarse-grained Icelandic bread. We became curious about the source of Brie at the Arctic Circle and learned that it was **hákarl** or Greenland shark in a state of controlled decay when buried in the permafrost and exhumed.

There is no real darkness at night in the latitude of northern Iceland. We had retired about 2 A.M., groggy from the damp chill of a long day on the Laxa River and overindulgence at the groaning board. While pulling the heavy comforter up to my nose, an eerie sound began. It was the distant cacaphony of horns, whistles and bells. A herring fleet was entering the fjord. These ships had bones in their teeth as the noise grew louder by the second. At least 20 boats rounded the headland at full throttle, riding low in the water, obviously loaded to the gunwales. Then, as though on cue, from over a nearby hill, charging through the fog with machete-length knives held high, came a horde of women in stout leather aprons as though to repel an invasion. From our window view it was impossible to fit motive to action. The stony-visaged females of broad-shouldered Viking stock were a formidable legion by the time they reached the docks. The din increased as thousands of sea gulls wheeled overhead. Even before hawsers were made fast the ships began unloading their cargoes of silvery herring and the women, in a ritual perhaps known to ancestors of Eric the Red, began gutting and barreling the fish. Knives flashed so rapidly that it seemed only minutes before everybody abruptly disappeared in the fog and the scrap-gorged gulls settled quietly on the bay. Whether the methods used are primitive or modern, the term "fresh" is axiomatic to the herring industry and the elapsed time between capture and preservation is the sum total of its products, more so than with other fish species.

There are 2 commercially important species of herring: the **Atlantic herring** found on both sides of the North Atlantic, from Greenland to North Carolina and from the Straits of Gibraltar to the Bay of Murmansk, USSR, and the **Pacific herring** which occurs from Kodiak, Alaska, to northern California and from eastern USSR to Japan and the Yellow Sea. Both are fish of the open ocean and travel in huge schools. They reach a length of about 18 inches and a weight of 1½ pounds; however, the average marketed is usually 9 to 11 inches long. Pacific herring differ from the Atlantic species in that the former spawn in shallow bays close to shore, while the latter breed at depths down to 100 feet. In the Pacific they gather in such vast numbers that milt ejected by the males creates great patches of "white water" clearly visible from shore. This suspended sperm not only assures fertilization of eggs dropped at random but acts as a protective screen against predatory birds.

There are 2 other species of herring which differ from the Atlantic kind in that they enter freshwater streams to spawn along the eastern coast of the U. S.: the **alewife** or "spring herring" and the **blueback herring.** Neither of these is comparable in quality to the herring taken at sea. Both are deeper-bodied fish than the oceanic form and they look so much alike that the only reliable way to distinguish one from the other is in the color of the belly cavity, which is sooty black in the blueback and pearl to pinkish gray in the alewife. Bluebacks run upstream a bit later in the season than alewives and for that reason are sometimes called "summer herring," but no real distinction is made by fishermen as they are equally limited in a culinary sense. During their spawning runs alewives are readily dipnetted in small brooks by amateur fishermen; both the roe of the female and the gonads of the male are extremely good eating. At one time in New England the roes were collected for food and the fish used as a garden fertilizer. Nevertheless, the alewife has maintained some commercial importance as an alder-smoked product, packed in barrels with brine as Corned Alewives, or packed in a vinegar cure as Pickled Alewives. There are small local markets from Cape Cod to Newfoundland but the individual product is only as good as the cure itself, and before the year 1900 a once-flourishing industry recognized the problem:

In all probability there are as many of these fish in the Delaware as the Susquehanna, yet the fishermen of the latter stream do three and four times the business in herring. This inability on the part of the Delaware River fishermen to dispose of all the herring they can catch is the stranger from the fact that Burlington cured herring, as the Delaware River curing is called, have a wide reputation for a peculiar delicacy of flavor which at one time at least caused a world-wide demand for them. It would seem as though there must be a lack of facilities for curing, such as is possessed in Baltimore, where the Susquehanna fishermen market, which is the cause for the secondary position of the Delaware River herring fishermen. It may be as claimed by the Susquehanna River and bay fishermen that while the Burlington system of curing may be excellent, the fish which enter the Delaware River are themselves without that delicate flavor and keeping qualities that those which enter the Chesapeake Bay and the Susquehanna River possess.

Unfortunately, the plump and sweet sea herring which never ventures into freshwater rivers is also marketed in the U. S. in semipreserved or preserved form. This fish is so delicate and the demand for freshly caught herring so small, that cured or pickled products are the only ones found in the average American kitchen or supermarket. Throughout Scandinavia the demand exceeds the supply; even here a large percentage of the "fresh" herring is imported from Iceland in frozen form. The world standard bearer is caught in the Baltic Sea and delivered shimmering on cracked ice at dockside. In the patois of herring fanciers a distinction is made when the herring are "fat" and therefore prime as table fare. Herring become mature between 2 and 4 years of age (at least 1 subspecies lives to be 20) and they begin accumulating large amounts of fat in their body tissues during the warmer months of the year. However, the peak season in any one country is variable as there are at least 7 subspecies of herring in the Atlantic, which are isolated geographically; these differ in several respects including their size and spawning season; some breed in the spring, others in summer, and still others in the fall or early winter. Thus, their fat content will vary from 5 to over 15 percent according to where they are caught. In the Baltic Sea, for example, there are 2 different races, a near-shore spring-spawning stock which fattens in the latter part of May and early June, and a deepwater fall-spawning population that becomes prime in late September. The same duplicity occurs with Murman, Norwegian, Icelandic, and White Sea herrings. The White Sea subspecies, formerly of great economic importance to the USSR, is divided according to the orthodox calendar; the early-

VLAGGETJESDAG, SCHEVENINGEN, THE NETHERLANDS

Flag Day, in May, is a
celebration of the departure
of the herring fleet.
One sees costumes of the
different villages, and there
are many competitions.
This is one of the great
celebrations, since the
economy of The Netherlands was
once based on the herring.

spring spawners are called **egorev** for Egorii (George) or April 23rd, and the late herring **ivanov** for Ivan (John) or June 22nd.

Herring are harvested in virtually all sizes, even 2 to 3 inches in length when they are packed as "sardines." This name is applied to a number of clupeids including the true sardines which were named after the island of Sardinia where the fishery originated. The French began packing fish in metal containers in 1850. Sardines were so popular that other countries quickly followed their lead, particularly olive oil producers such as Spain, Portugal and Italy. George Burnham of Portland, Maine, was the first American to can small herring in 1867; although he wasn't very successful, he inspired competitors who had the technical ability and the Maine "sardine" is a considerable industry today.

HERRING TERMINOLOGY

BISMARCK HERRING   This takes its name from a curing process developed in the nineteenth century. The herring is filleted with the skin left on, then cured in strong vinegar. It is packed in a milder brine of lower vinegar and salt content, usually with slices of onion with sugar added.

BLOATER   A large fat dry-salted herring marketed whole and ungutted (Great Britain). This product is usually hot-smoked but more rarely cold-smoked to obtain a golden color. It is semipreserved as **BLOATER PASTE** by grinding to a creamy texture.

BORNHOLMER   A gutted, whole, hot-smoked fresh herring from the Danish island of Bornholm off the coast of Sweden. Reputed to be caught, smoked, and shipped to Copenhagen all in the same day, the mechanics are doubtful but the product is undeniably a gourmet item. Copenhagen is virtually the only city where a Bornholmer can be sampled. This alder-smoked golden-skinned herring is usually wrapped in gold foil as a hallmark of excellence.

FLECKHERING   This differs from a kipper in being split down the back rather than the belly and not separated, then hot-smoked rather than cold-smoked. It is a German style. **Fleckhering** appears in Denmark as **Flækket Røget sild.**

GAFFELBIDDER (Norway) or **GAFFELBITAR** (Sweden)   A large fat herring, gutted, not boned, and semipreserved in vinegar, onions, sugar, salt and spices. Mild cure produces delicate flavor. In Germany it is usually ripened in barrels, then filleted and skinned before cutting into bite-size pieces.

HARD SALTED HERRING   Whole herring, gibbed or gutted, then salted in barrels. The ratio of salt to herring by weight usually runs 25 to 30 percent; salt content within the musculature is slightly more than 20 percent in the finished product. In European markets as **Hardsaltad Sill** (Sweden), **Skarpsaltet Sild** (Norway), **Hartgesalzene Heringe** (Germany), **Hareng Fortement Salé** (France), **Hardtsaltet Sild** (Denmark).

HERRING IN SOUR-CREAM SAUCE   As marketed semipreserved, these are whole fillets or bite-size pieces of salted herring, partially desalted, then marinated in vinegar. The sour-cream supplement usually contains spices and thin slices of onion or cucumber. In Europe as **Sill i sur gräddsäs** (Sweden), **Haring in Zure roomsaus** (Holland), **Hering in saurer Sahne** (Germany), **Arenque en salsa a la crema** (Spain), **Hareng à la crème** (France), **Eingelegte Heringe nach Haus Frauenart** (Germany).

HOSHI-KAZUNOKO   Herring roe immersed in sea water, washed, then air-dried (Japan).

KIPPER   A fat herring, split from head to tail but not separated, then lightly brined (7 to 10 minutes), air-dried, and cold-smoked (8 hours at 70° to 75°F). It is marketed fresh, frozen and canned. A large percentage of kippers in European markets today are artificially colored (red or yellow vegetable dye) in the brining process before smoking, but traditionalists seek the mahogany cure which requires 5 to 6 days of smoking. The term "kippered" in North America is used in connection with many hot-smoked products such as kippered sturgeon, kippered salmon or kippered black cod; this refers to the appearance of the fish in being split and golden in color.

MARINATED ROE (Japanese)   Preserved roes are soaked in water for 8 hours to remove salt. If fresh, they are simply placed in a mixture of 6 parts *mirin* (sweet sake) to 4 parts soy sauce for 8 hours to obtain flavor. The roes are then preserved in 7 parts rice-wine vinegar to 3 parts soy sauce. The product will keep under refrigeration for at least 1 month.

MATJES HERRING   Derives its name from the Dutch word for "maiden." Matjes herring represent the first catch of the year when the gonads are not, or only slightly, developed. The fish is usually skinned, filleted by hand, and given a mild cure in sugar, salt, vinegar and spices (sandalwood being the one that imparts a reddish color), and packed in bite-size pieces. In European markets as **Matjessill** (Sweden), **Matjeshering** (Germany), **Matjesstilvirket Sild** (Norway), **Matjessild** (Denmark), **Pekelmaatjes** (Holland).

MATTIE   A term applied to barrels of cured herring under the official Crown Brand Act of Great Britain which is no longer in force. A mattie is simply a herring of no less than 9 inches in length with the gut removed. In European markets Crown Branding is still practiced by individual firms to indicate the quality of their products. The other terms are as follows:

Medium: A maturing herring of not less than 9½ inches in length.

Matfull: A mature herring containing milt or roe of not less than 9½ inches in length.

Full: A mature herring containing milt or roe of not less than 10¼ inches in length.

La Full: A mature herring containing milt or roe of not less than 11¼ inches in length.

NORWEGIAN SLOE This is the large herring caught in the winter off the coast of Norway. It is subjected to prolonged dry-salting (similar to hard-salted herring). The product is distinct from **NORWEGIAN CURED HERRING** which is made from fat summer fish that are kept alive in seawater until their stomachs are empty before salting.

PICKLED HERRING An often misunderstood term in the New York delicatessen trade, where vinegar and spices create the "pickle." Internationally this is a gutted herring which is dry-salted in barrels and cured in the brine or blood pickle that is formed. This may be a mild cure (90° sal) or a hard cure (100° sal).

Variations on this are called **Alaska Scotch Cure** and **Scotch Cure.**

RED HERRING Whole, ungutted, heavily salted, and cold-smoked for a prolonged period (3 weeks) until the herring becomes deep red in color and hard. This was a popular way of preserving herring before refrigeration and is little used today.

ROLLMOPS This is simply a **BISMARCK** rolled around a pickle or onion slices and fastened with wooden picks or cloves. Rollmops are packed in mild vinegar, with sauces and other flavoring ingredients such as horseradish, tomato or mustard. When fried before packing the product is known as **BRATROLLMOPS.**

SARDINE Used here interchangeably as young herring.

SCHMALTZ HERRING Derives its name from the German word for "fat." This is literally a fat herring which does not lend itself to easy filleting, so it is skinned, cut into pieces, and pickled.

SHIO-KAZUNOKO Herring roe preserved in brine or by dry-salting (Japan).

SILD Scandinavian name for herring except in Sweden **(Sill).**

SOUSED HERRING Most popular in Great Britain, this product is salt-pickled with vinegar and spices, then the fillets (often rolled) are baked. Soused herring is sometimes colored with a vegetable dye. Also known as **Potted Herring.**

STRÖMMING In Sweden the Baltic herring subspecies is considered separate and distinct from the sea herring in a culinary sense and is given the name **Strömming** as opposed to **Sill** (all other herring).

SURSILD Norwegian name for brine-salted herring pickled in vinegar and sugar with sliced onions added. Also known as **Marinerad Sill** (Sweden) and **Sýrö Sild** (Iceland).

SURSTRÖMMING Swedish name for sour Baltic herring which are brined, then barreled and left to ferment. A sharply flavored and strong-smelling product, it is considered a delicacy. However, it is definitely not for all palates.

A VERSATILE SEAFOOD

Each nation has its own traditional herring recipes. However, combining the fish with potatoes is almost universal. In its simplest form the Scots make **Tatties an' Herrin'** with the potatoes and herring boiled in a black iron pot over a peat fire. Australia prefers **Herring Chowder** made with sliced potatoes, chopped onions, herring and milk. In England one finds, not surprisingly, that there is a **Yorkshire Herring Pie.** Sliced potatoes cover the bottom and sides of a pie plate, then herring fillets and chopped apples are arranged in layers and the "pie" is baked under a cover of well-buttered brown paper. Russian cuisine combines boiled potatoes, apples and onions with herring to bake in sour cream to create **Forshmak.** Americans found that a baked potato becomes a distinguished meal when scooped out, mixed with milk, parsley, bits of crisp bacon and chopped matjes herring; the mixture is stuffed back into the skin and browned in the oven.

Herring is the first plate at every smorgasbord—in wine sauce, cream sauce, smoked, pickled, spiced and even raw. The Italians include it in their antipasto and the Danes feature it in their reknowned **smørrebrød** (literally buttered bread). The classic is a pickled herring on dark rye bread garnished with onion rings and capers. Herring can be added to soups such as vichyssoise, made into a mousse with grapefruit segments and vegetable gelatin, used as a topping on baked squash; or it can keynote a variety of salads; **Russian Herring Salad,** for example, is a combination of mushrooms, diced boiled potatoes and beets, sliced sweet pickles and cucumber, dressed with a mixture of sour cream and mustard. Make a compound butter with puréed herring, which makes an excellent base for a canapé. Broiled or sautéed herring with scrambled eggs is an excellent breakfast or supper dish; another is herring rolled in oatmeal and broiled.

HOW TO DRESS FRESH HERRING

1. Make a ventral cut.　　　　2. Remove belly fins.　　　　3. 4. 5. Remove viscera.

6. Make a dorsal cut from nape to tail.

7. With knife point pick up skin at the nape and peel it back.　　　8. Skin both sides.　　　9. Remove head.

10. Grasp end of backbone at the nape and lift it out.　　11. You will have two boneless fillets.　　12. With knife blade remove any blood.

There are no limits to the imaginative use of herring.
How to pickle herring, see under PICKLED FISH.
How to salt herring, see under SALT FISH.
How to smoke herring, see under SMOKED FISH.

FRIED HERRING IN MUSTARD BUTTER (SENAPSSTEKT SILL)

2 pounds fresh herring, filleted and skinned	2 tablespoons heavy cream
salt	½ cup fine
2 egg yolks	dry bread crumbs
3 tablespoons prepared Dijon-style mustard	¼ cup peanut oil
	½ cup melted butter
	dill, chopped fine

Sprinkle the herring fillets with salt. In a bowl blend the egg yolks, mustard and cream. Brush each fillet with the mixture and place on a sheet of wax paper sprinkled with bread crumbs to coat the under side. Cover the top with remaining crumbs. Heat peanut oil in large skillet and fry the fillets until golden brown on both sides. Add the melted butter just before completion. Arrange herring on a hot platter and sprinkle with chopped dill. Makes 4 servings.

Hilsa

A widely distributed anadromous fish found in the Persian Gulf, Pakistan, India and east to China and South Vietnam. The hilsa *(Hilsa ilisha)* is a member of the herring family and closely resembles the American shad in appearance and habits. It supports a very large commercial fishery during the annual spawning runs into coastal rivers from January to August. The hilsa is sometimes purveyed as **Indian shad** or **palla** in the restaurants of southeast Asia, and usually appears in steamed fillet form.

Hogfish

A colorful member of the wrasse family, Labridae, erroneously called "hog snapper" and not related to the pigfish which is often called "hogfish" in North and South Carolina. The hogfish *(Lachnolaimus maximus)* is very distinctive in shape and coloration. It has a pointed snout with thick lips and protruding canine teeth. The first 3 spines of its dorsal fin extend into long filaments; the body color is usually red-orange marbled with crimson. Hogfish reach weights to 45 pounds but the average taken by fishermen is from 4 to 6 pounds.

This species is found in Bermuda and occurs from North Carolina to Brazil. It is most common on the coral reefs of the West Indies. Hogfish are particularly numerous around the Florida Keys.

Its white and firm flesh is excellent and catches are instantly sold at dockside. Hogfish are seldom caught in sufficient quantities to be a market item in the U. S. Hogfish from our coast are perfectly safe to eat but large individuals are sometimes poisonous in the waters around Cuba and ciguatoxic in the Leeward Islands.

Iahle

A species of snapper found along the coast of Africa from Liberia to Angola. The iahle *(Lutjanus eutactus)* is amber in color with a whitish belly. It grows to a weight of about 7 pounds. This is a common West African market fish comparable to our gray snapper in quality. *See SNAPPER.*

Ide

A freshwater fish of northern Europe, found in Scandinavia and from the Rhine eastward to Siberia as far as the Kolyma River. The ide *(Leuciscus idus)* is related to the carp; however, it only grows to about 8 pounds and is usually harvested in much smaller sizes. This is a fish of some culinary importance in Germany and the USSR where it's also artificially cultivated. A gold-colored mutation is popular as an ornamental species; this "golden orfe" is established in Farin Pond, near East Lyme, Connecticut. A similar species, the **Amur chebak** *(L. waleckii)* is fished commercially in northern China. Also known as **Vederbuk** (Norway), **Säyne** (Finland), **Id** (Sweden), **Aland** (Germany).

Imsella

A species of needlefish common to the Mediterranean and popular in the cuisine of Malta. *See NEEDLEFISH.*

Inconnu

See under WHITEFISH.

Jack
John Dory

j

Jack

This family of marine fishes, Carangidae, is represented in all tropical and subtropical waters of the world. A few species occur in temperate seas. Aside from those fish called "jacks" the carangids include the pompanos, amberjacks, lookdowns, threadfins and runners. Many jacks are important commercial species but their palatability ranges from poor to excellent; some are not eaten at all, and the flesh of a few (especially from tropical Indo-Pacific regions) is occasionally ciguatoxic.

With the exception of the pompano, which is clearly in a class by itself and is treated separately *(see POMPANO)* the jacks are not important foodfish in the U. S. They are mainly marketed in areas where more desirable species are not abundant or where a commercial fishery is undeveloped, as in parts of the Caribbean, Central and South America, and Africa. Hawaii is a notable exception in that several species of jacks, which attain large sizes, are highly esteemed, particularly the **black ulua** and **white ulua,** both of which may exceed 100 pounds. These jacks have very firm flesh with minimal red muscle; they are cooked in a variety of ways but they are particularly popular in the form of **sashimi.** The availability of large jacks has generally determined their utilization as in the case of early-day Florida settlers who hunted the crevalle with rifle in shallow water.

What may be said in general for the larger jacks is that they should be bled after capture by cutting off the tail. This greatly improves their flavor. Skinned fillets only should be used and these should be carefully trimmed to remove as much of the red muscle as possible. Jacks can be panfried, broiled, baked or made into a delicious chowder; the amberjack is especially versatile in this respect and in smoked form it's excellent.

JACK TERMINOLOGY

AFRICAN POMPANO   This is not a true pompano but one of the threadfins and is sometimes called **Cuban jack.** The African pompano *(Alectis crinitus)* is found on both sides of the Atlantic and along our shores from Massachusetts to the West Indies, being particularly abundant at times off the coast of Florida where fish of 25 to 30 pounds are not uncommon. The body of this fish is deep and thin; it has very tough skin with minute scales and requires a sharp knife to fillet. Essentially a chowder fish, the meat tends to dry and toughen under a dry heat.

AMBERJACK   Although there are several species of amberjacks, the largest and most important in the Atlantic is the greater amberjack *(Seriola dumerili).* It occurs along the West Coast of Africa to the Mediterranean and in the western Atlantic from Cape Cod to Brazil, although its abundance is from North Carolina (summer) south. This jack is brownish in color, with many lavender and golden tints and an amber band from eye to tail. It reaches weights up to 177 pounds. However, small amberjacks of 15 pounds or less are much the best to eat; large amberjacks are often heavily parasitized and are occasionally ciguatoxic in the West Indies. The Pacific amberjack is very similar to the greater amberjack. Smoked amberjack from Florida is a delicacy. An ideal chowder fish.

BAR JACK   This is one of the better foodfish in the jack family. Although it is not taken commercially in the U. S., the bar jack *(Caranx ruber)* occurs from North Carolina through Florida, the Bahamas, and West Indies to Panama. It's a moderately deep-bodied fish with a distinctive dark "bar" on its back extending from nape to tail. This species has firm white flesh with minimal red muscle. It is a popular food in the Bahamas. Although it reaches weights of 12 to 15 pounds, the average is much smaller, seldom exceeding 2 pounds. The bar jack can be panfried, broiled, or made into chowder. It is excellent when smoked.

BLUE RUNNER   This is one of the most common jacks *(Caranx fusus)* in the western Atlantic. It's found from Nova Scotia to Brazil and is particularly abundant in Florida and the West Indies. This is a small fish, usually less than 1 pound in weight, but it grows to about 4 pounds. It is sold commercially in Florida and is utilized to a great extent in the Leeward Islands. This is mainly a dark-meated jack but of good table value. It has a Pacific counterpart in the **GREEN JACK** *(Caranx caballus)* which is similar in size and edibility. These small jacks are usually filleted and panfried.

CREVALLE   The jack crevalle, also known as **cavally, cavalla, toro** (Mexico) and **trevally** (Australia), is found in tropical and subtropical seas throughout the world. This is the common jack *(Caranx hippos)* of Florida, where it often occurs in large schools inshore. Crevalle attain heavy sizes in excess of 40 pounds but the smaller fish of 2 to 3 pounds are best from a kitchen standpoint; these are moderately good when bled and properly filleted by re-

facing page, Bar jack

moving the dark meat.

JACK MACKEREL   The jack mackerel *(Trachurus symmetricus)*, also known as **horse mackerel,** is a true jack but it does vaguely resemble a mackerel in shape and general coloration, being dark green along the back and blending into a dull silvery below. This is a small fish, usually less than a pound in weight, although it has been recorded to 5 pounds. The jack mackerel is strictly a Pacific species ranging from British Columbia to Chile, although it's more common south of Monterey, California. The commercial catch fluctuates greatly from year to year with a low of 17 million pounds and a peak of 146 million pounds (1952). Although large numbers of jack mackerel are taken by sportsmen and fresh fish enter the market, it's more significant as a canned product.

RAINBOW RUNNER   This is a pretty jack with a bluish green back and 2 blue stripes on its sides separated by a broad yellow band. The rainbow runner *(Elagatis bipinnulatus)* is more slender than other jacks although it grows up to 30 pounds in weight. It's found in tropical and subtropical seas throughout the world. In the western Atlantic it occurs from Cape Cod to the Gulf of Mexico and through the Bahamas and West Indies. However, it's essentially a warmwater fish. This is one of the better eating jacks with considerable white muscle and a flaky texture. It can be broiled, panfried, made into chowder or smoked.

YELLOW JACK   A small member of the family, the yellow jack *(Caranx bartholomaei)* is also one of the best, having very white and sweet meat. It is found from Massachusetts to Brazil but is common only from south Florida through the Bahamas and Caribbean. The yellow jack resembles the bar jack in appearance but lacks the bluish band along its back and is suffused with yellow over the dorsal and ventral surfaces. At sizes of ¾ to 2 pounds it is excellent when barbecued. Flake off its fine scales (do not skin), score in 4 to 5 cuts on each side, and cook slowly over a low charcoal fire, basting with lemon butter until the skin turns golden brown. Small yellow jacks can also be panfried.

YELLOWTAIL   The yellowtail *(Seriola dorsalis)*, no relation to the yellowtail snapper of the Atlantic, occurs in both the eastern and southwestern Pacific, but its center of abundance on our coasts is in the San Diego area of California. The most productive grounds are the Coronado Islands of Mexico which is where most of the commercial catch is made. This is a large jack, attaining weights in excess of 100 pounds although the average is considerably smaller. Both the sport and commercial catches fluctuate to an extreme from year to year so the appearance of fresh yellowtail at market is unpredictable.

Fresh yellowtail can be baked, broiled or panfried. It is also particularly good when smoked. Canned yellowtail has declined as a product due to a limited demand.

Yellowtail is also used for **sashimi,** but the species most cultured and used for this in Japan is probably *S. quinqueradiata. S. dumerili* is also cultured there, and this was (in 1966) generally brought to the Tokyo market alive, in boxes of water, whereas the yellowtail was offered dead.

John Dory

In languages other than English, this fish is better known as **St. Peter's fish.** The John Dory has an ocellus—a large round black spot with a yellow halo on each side of its body; among early Christian cultures these spots were believed to be the fingerprints of Simon called Peter who captured the fish in answer to the biblical injunction:

Jesus saith unto him . . . Notwithstanding, lest we should offend them, go thou to the sea, and cast an hook, and take up the fish that first cometh up; and when thou hast opened his mouth, thou shalt find a piece of money: that take, and give unto them for me and thee.
                                                            Matthew 17:26-27

St. Peter held the fish so firmly between thumb and forefinger while searching for the coin that his mark has been apparent ever since. These spots are only a vague blotch on the American John Dory but otherwise it differs little from the European species. Nominally considered the Patron Saint of Fishermen (the traditional greeting among German-speaking anglers is *Petri Heil!* or "Hail St. Peter"), he is symbolically present in the blessings given by the church to commercial fishing fleets the world over.

The flesh of the John Dory is white, firm and finely flaked. It is a classic ingredient of **bouillabaisse.** In Europe it's sold mainly in fresh form but some quantity is marketed hot-smoked. Although the fish occurs in the eastern Atlantic as far north as Norway, it's more common in the Mediterranean. The American John Dory is found from Nova Scotia to Cape Hatteras, but it's not abundant enough to have commercial value. Two other closely related species occur in African waters and off New Zealand and Australia.

The fillets of this thin-bodied fish can be cooked as in any of the flounder recipes, or simply headed and gutted to be added to a **bouillabaisse.**

Also called **Saint-Pierre** (France), **Sankt**

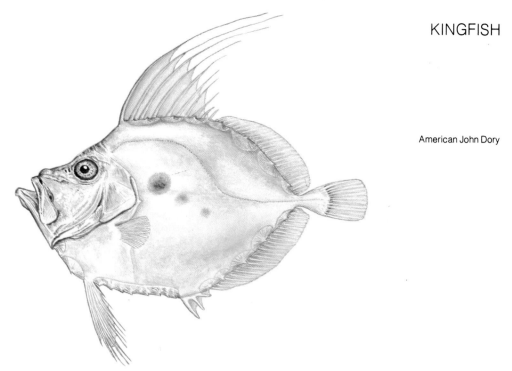

American John Dory

Petersfisk (Denmark and Norway), **St. Persfiskar** (Sweden), **Pez de san Pedro** (Spain), **Sveti Petar** (Yugoslavia), **Pesce san Pietro** (Italy), **Petersfische** (Germany), **Zonnevissen** (Holland), **Peixe-galo** (Portugal), **Petursfiskur** (Iceland).

k

Kahawai

This marine species occurs in the warm temperate waters of Australasia. A member of the drum family, a juvenile kahawai superficially resembles a salmon, which is of interest to the peripatetic ichthyophile for the reason that it's commonly called "sea salmon" and "Australian salmon," which is misleading in all respects. Before the European settlement of New Zealand and the introduction of true salmonids to its freshwater rivers and lakes (the native fauna was extremely limited), the Maori people living along the coast caught large quantities of kahawai for local consumption or for barter with inland tribes or with the sealers and whalers who cruised the North and South Islands. The kahawai were beach-seined in nets woven from the tough leaf fiber of flax plants, or caught by trolling from canoes, using wooden hooks inlaid with the iridescent blue paua (abalone) shell. Sun-dried or smoked, the abundant kahawai was for many years a Maori staple.

The only significant modern fishery for kahawai exists in Australia, where they are still an important commercial species. Almost the entire catch is canned; the flesh is dark and coarse (it improves with canning); there's little for which to recommend it, except as a gamefish on light tackle.

Kelp Bass

A Pacific member of the sea bass family, Serranidae. The kelp bass *(Paralabrax clathratus)* is most abundant from southern California to Abreojos Point in Mexico. It is commonly called "rock bass," a catchall commercial term that includes the closely related **spotted sand bass** *(P. maculatofasciatus)* and the **barred sand bass** *(P. nebulifer)*. The kelp bass is harvested mainly by sport fishermen; while available during the entire year, the heaviest landings are made from June through August. The meat of the kelp bass though firm is very bland in flavor, certainly not comparable to the rockfishes of the same area, and requires a liberal use of spices and sauces to be acceptable. Its marine habitat is among Macrocystis and Nerocystis kelps which are also frequented by the culinary superior **olive rockfish** *(Sebastodes serranoides)*. This smaller fish (to 24 inches in length) is often mistakenly referred to as a "kelp bass" and thus opinions may differ greatly on its virtues at table in view of the fact that 4 different species could be involved. *See also ROCKFISH*.

Kingfish

(1) A common name for several species of drum along the Atlantic Coast of the U. S. *See under DRUM*.

(2) A regional name for the king mackerel along the Atlantic Coast of the U. S. *See under MACKEREL*.

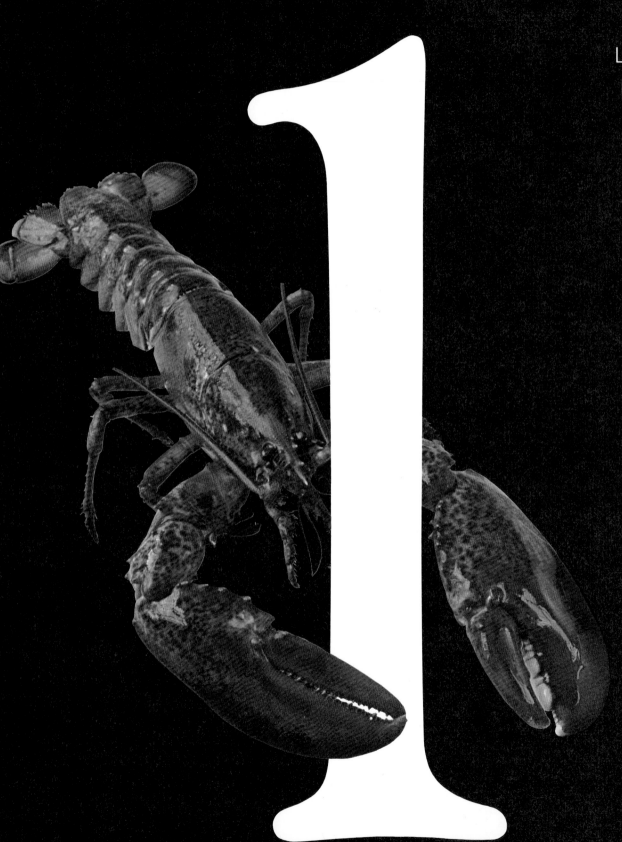

1

Lamprey
Lingcod
Lobster

1

Lake Herring

See CISCO under WHITEFISH.

Lamprey

There are about a dozen species of these eel-shaped fishes on a world basis, the most important of which is the sea lamprey *(Petromyzon marinus)*, found from Greenland to Florida and northern Norway to the Mediterranean. A marine form, the sea lamprey enters freshwater to spawn. The adult parasitizes various other fishes, attaching itself to the host's body with a sucking disc or buccal funnel, then boring a hole through the skin with its rasplike teeth. The sea lamprey has long been a problem in the Great Lakes of North America in destroying valuable commercial and sport species. Historically, it was an important foodfish in both the U. S. and Europe although it's no longer utilized to any extent in our country. Unlike the eel, which has a backbone, lampreys have a soft cartilaginous skeleton; there is no true bone present. The sea lamprey is considered a great delicacy by many Europeans and is usually baked or served in a stew. It can be cooked in any eel recipe. *See also EEL.*

Also known as **Lamproie** (France), **Lamprea** (Spain), **Lampreia** (Portugal), **Neunauge** (Germany), **Nejonögon** (Sweden), **Niøje** (Denmark), **Merinahkianen** (Finland), **Paklara riječna** (Yugoslavia), **Yatsumeunagi** (Japan).

Sea lamprey

facing page, American lobster

Ling

See COBIA.

Lingcod

The lingcod is not a cod but a member of the greenling family (Hexagrammidae). The flesh of the lingcod is often green in color; however, it turns white when cooked. A lean fish with a bland flavor, this Pacific marine species is popular in the U. S. and Canada. It is sold fresh, whole and gutted, and in fillet form. Lingcod are also hot-smoked or "kippered." The whole fish can be stuffed and baked, but a popular method is to cut the lingcod into steaks for barbecuing or broiling. Fillets can be poached, sautéed or broiled.

A lingcod has a large mouth, fanlike pectoral fins, and a long continuous dorsal fin. Unlike the true cods this fish is slender in appearance although it often grows to 50 or 60 pounds in weight. The coloration is a mottled dark gray and brown. The lingcod was a favorite food of coastal Indian tribes in British Columbia who caught them with a "hee-hee." This device, much like a shuttlecock made of wood and fibers, was pushed toward the bottom with a long 3-tined spear. When the spear was suddenly withdrawn the hee-hee spun slowly toward the surface followed by a curious lingcod. When the fish came within range it was easily dispatched.

Lobster

When the early colonists settled in New England, lobster was so abundant that depending on which historian you read, they were "a bounty to be revered, or a scourge to be abhored." As late as the 1880s lobster was so common that it was still being used as bait for cod and striped bass. Any food, no matter how unusual, may become monotonous fare by repetition, but at modern-day costs few *gourmands* will ever reach ennui with these delectable crustaceans. The ritual of eating lobster is easily learned, and to a generation already accomplished in the art of using chopsticks, the necessary manual dexterity is minimal. Perhaps the very act of breaking food by hand sets the psychological pattern to lobster cookouts and dinners, as it's a food usually shared with friends or lovers.

Our lobster from northern waters is properly called the American lobster and when compared to the European lobster it differs only in size as to culinary uses. The American species grows considerably larger. Despite all I have read about the **homard** of coastal France and the

hummer of Scandinavia, I have never found these different. In fact, a large percentage of the lobster served today in the restaurants of Paris, London and Copenhagen arrives by plane from Canada. Europe is feeling the lobster shortage and prices have skyrocketed. Our lobster is often identified with Maine as it was here that the commercial fishery began about 1840. Due to inadequate transportation for shipping live lobsters, the canning industry started a few years later, and by 1854 Maine lobster meats were being sent to foreign markets. In its halcyon period the state supplied about 75 percent of all the lobsters marketed in the U. S., but the landings in Maine dropped from 25 million pounds in 1957 to 8 million pounds in 1972. It has become such an expensive food that many restaurants no longer list it on their menus, while a few daring souls simply raised their prices and braved the uncertainty of supply.

There is very little waste in a lobster. You need only remove the intestinal tract, the spongy gill tissues, the dorsal and ventral arteries if appearance is a factor in presentation, and the stomach; the stomach is that fibrous white sac in the lobster's head but the rest of the head is to some palates, mine included, one of the tastiest portions and not to be discarded. Aside from the sweet and firm white meat, one can also eat the green tomalley, which is the crustacean's liver, and the roe or "coral" of the female lobster. The tomalley and coral have unique flavors and textures and are often incorporated in sauces. Even the shells, which people usually throw away, may be processed as containers for the next lobster feast or for any fish dinner requiring a superlative sauce. The red color of a cooked lobster is a pigment called carotene, and the shells of all crustaceans contain both this pigment and protein. With the application of heat, the carotene separates from the protein. I doubt if much food value is retained in the carapace after prolonged cooking but fortunately the flavor, in fact the very essence, and color remain; when baked in an oven for several hours to a ceramiclike texture, the shells can be broken and passed through a grinder and used in making a **Sauce Cardinal** or a **Sauce Nantua.** This is vastly superior to the canned and frozen soup substitutes so commonly disguised as "sauces." Of course, it's the proper base for a true lobster bisque.

The spiny lobster, which is generally known as "crawfish," is a very remote relative of the freshwater crayfish that confusingly bears the same common name. While they are both decapod crustaceans, so are shrimps and crabs, and any similarity lies in the fact that each is good to eat. The spiny lobster occurs only in the saltwaters of tropical and subtropical regions. From a food standpoint, the spiny lobster is equal to the American lobster but with the great handicap of seldom appearing at market in live form. This is no problem in Mediterranean countries where day boats and even divers supply the coastal villages. I recall dining at a restaurant in Guincho, Portugal, the Furnas Lagosteiras; when the chef ran out of **lagosta** it merely required downing one more glass of wine while his boys dove for a fresh supply, delivered kicking to the kitchen. At home in Florida we catch our own, or buy them direct from the fisherman, which makes a vast difference in flavor and texture, as a fresh crawfish is sweet and tender. It has a firmer musculature, yes, and unfortunately is without claws, but the tail meat lends itself to many fine recipes. If killed and held more than 6 to 8 hours from the sea before cooking or freezing, a crawfish becomes bland and rubbery. In some Caribbean island fisheries the tails may slosh around in ice water for 5 or 6 days before arriving at dockside—barely edible, and not deserving a place at table. Without a reliable source of *fresh* spiny lobster, I would put my faith in the frozen kind processed by any reputable firm from Australia, New Zealand or South Africa.

The peak of the spiny lobster season is a phenomenon known as the "crawfish march." This occurs in Florida and the Bahamas in late October and November after a period of stormy weather. This single-file mass migration involving thousands of lobsters traveling along the bottom in a chain formation is one of the most fascinating sights in the marine world. Other crustaceans such as the American lobster and the land crabs journey in groups during their breeding season but only in random movements, never with the geometric precision of the spiny lobster. To make it more puzzling, crawfish are really nocturnal animals, hiding in their dens by day, but these marches occur under a bright sun. The mass movement seems not related to reproduction as their breeding period is in the summer months. However, it is theorized that they move before the breeding season in order to redistribute the population and locate new feeding grounds, especially for the young. There is no established scientific explanation. During this critical 5 or 6 days, it is not unusual for a Bahamian fisherman to bully-net 600 to 700 lobsters per day, a largess that may well exhaust that resource in the spiraling demand for these crustaceans.

Lobsterettes, which we shall discuss in some detail *(see LOBSTER TERMINOLOGY)* occur on the continental shelves of all the world's oceans, but at present only a few shallow-water forms are taken in any quantity.

facing page, top left, Rock shrimp; top right, American lobster; bottom left, Prawn *(Macrobrachium)*; bottom right, Crayfish

These "scampi" are generically the same as the Norwegian lobster and are technically referred to as nephropids. They are smaller than the American or spiny lobsters. While their slender claws contain a mere smidgen of meat, it is the delicate tail portion that makes the "Danish Lobster," "Dublin Bay Prawn," or the various **langostinos** a gourmet item. Unfortunately, the accepted practice of substituting shrimps for lobsterettes has caused innocent diners to conclude that scampi are no different from shrimps. Many restaurants the world over make little effort to concern themselves with authenticity in seafoods; while dining in one of Dublin's distinguished hotels, celebrated for its fish and game, I ordered the local prawns, only to be served a plate of boiled shrimps—not even medium-size shrimps, or butterflied, garlicked and broiled. The management's explanation was that the local product was unavailable, and with a hint of epicurean intrigue, suggested that mine were imported from Italy. This was intended, of course, to explain why the price, if not the product, remained unchanged.

When selecting lobster recipes bear in mind that you are not dealing with a rich food, as the meat is extremely low in oil and high in protein, but rather a filling food that is made richer when served in sauces and alcohols. If you or your guests have put in a long day at the office or the backgammon table and are not *really* hungry, a cold halved lobster with herbed mayonnaise would be remedial, yet festive. A *tour de force* like **Lobster Pavillon** requires not only time in preparation but a relaxed atmosphere after a day of outdoor activity. For my part, a plain boiled or steamed lobster is the ideal, particularly when counterpointed with seasonal foods.

LOBSTER TERMINOLOGY

AMERICAN LOBSTER   This large marine crustacean *(Homarus americanus)* ranges from the Maritime Provinces of Canada, as far north as Belle Isle, to the coast of North Carolina. It is most abundant in the waters of Maine, Nova Scotia and Newfoundland. The American lobster is one of 2 generically related lobsters, a second species *(Homarus vulgaris)* being found throughout Europe. (However, only 4 million pounds are taken annually in Europe.) The lobster that made Maine famous usually weighs 1 to 5 pounds, but they grow to 45 pounds. One might imagine that so large a lobster would be tough and tasteless, but there is no loss of quality in growth. The big ones, however, are usually reserved for canning rather than boiling as few kitchens are equipped to handle a 20-pounder. Lobsters are usually trapped at depths from 10 to 200 feet, but New Jersey draggers get the monsters at depths over 600 feet in the canyons 90 miles offshore.

The color of the American lobster varies from greenish blue to reddish brown. Generally, the upper surface of the carapace is speckled with greenish black spots. This coloration differs from the smaller European species which is dark green to black and known in France as the **Prince Noir** (Black Prince). Of course, the shell of all lobsters becomes red with cooking. The 2 claws on a lobster are different: each has a heavy crusher claw and lighter biting claw, commonly called the "quick" claw as the crustacean can use it with greater speed in catching its food (or your fingers). In both the males and females about 50 percent have crusher claws on either the right or the left side. Sometimes both claws are biting claws and occasionally, though more rarely, both are crusher claws. Lobsters of all sizes are cannibalistic; when crowded together in captivity they would quickly destroy each other if their claws were not plugged or banded.

The adult lobster lives and feeds on the bottom of the sea. By means of its tail fan, its swimmerets and its walking legs, it can move rapidly from place to place. However, numerous tagging experiments have shown that populations are essentially local, migration being limited to random movements along shore. The lobster avoids sunlight and in shallow water spends the days hidden in holes among rocks or in other shady spots. In very cold water, just above freezing point, the lobster does little if any feeding. As the water warms during the spring and summer months, its appetite increases. All sedentary or slow-moving organisms such as mussels or clams, the sea urchins and starfish, worms and crabs, serve as food. Small fish are also captured and consumed. Seaweed is often found in lobster stomachs.

Also known as **Homard** (France), **Hummer** (Germany), **Astice** (Italy), **Bogavante** (Spain), **Lavagante** (Portugal), **Rarog** (Yugoslavia), **Kreeft** (Holland), **Astakós** (Greece), **Hummer** (Denmark, Sweden and Norway), **Hummar** (Iceland), **Iseebi** (Japan).

LOBSTERETTE   Any one of a number of small members of the lobster family (Nephropidae), geographically known as **Danish lobster, Dublin Bay prawn, langoustine, Norway lobster** or **Italian scampo.** Although long familiar to European tables, the domestic U.S. species were first introduced to our seafood market in 1962 by deepwater shrimp fishermen working off the East Coast of Florida, near St. Augustine. Lobsterettes inhabit the continental shelves and slopes of all the world's oceans at depths from 600 to 6500 feet. Except for their smaller size these decapod crustaceans are similar to the American lobster and European lobster in body conformation, with their large

pincers and heavily armored head and tail regions. The abdominal plates are triangular and terminate in sharp points. The fan-shaped tail is broad with numerous sharp spines along its margins. Lobsterettes are more colorful, however, often brilliantly hued in shades of yellow-orange and red, providing them with an unusual beauty not often encountered in the larger, shallow-water lobsters. The tail portion of a lobsterette supplies virtually all of the edible meat, which is comparable to the American lobster but more delicate in texture.

In the western Atlantic and Caribbean Sea there are 10 species of lobsterettes, only three of which are large enough to have any food value. These are the **Caribbean lobsterette** (*Metanephrops binghami*), the **red lobsterette** (*M. rubellus*) and the **Florida lobsterette** (*Nephrops aculeata*). The last is not to be confused with the spiny lobster, which, as already indicated, belongs to another family of decapod crustaceans. The Caribbean and red lobsterettes are distinguished from the Florida lobsterette by their large black eyes and hairless pincers. The Florida lobsterette has degenerate eyes and highly pubescent or hairy chelae. The Caribbean differs from the

red in having a shorter carapace or head region, pink rather than red chelae which are also more slender, and alternating red and white coloration as opposed to the red lobsterette's solid red to red-orange color, elongate carapace and heavy chelae. Caribbean lobsterettes have been found off the coasts of Central and South America, throughout the West Indies, Bahamas to French Guiana, including most of the Gulf of Mexico and the Caribbean Sea. The red lobsterette is distributed on the eastern coasts of Central America and the northeast coast of South America. The Florida lobsterette is found from east of New Jersey to French Guiana, in the Gulf of Mexico and the Caribbean.

ROCK LOBSTER A market name for the spiny lobster. Large quantities of South African and Australian "rock lobsters" are imported to the U. S. annually, as our demand exceeds the local supply. They are also imported from Chile and New Zealand. Although these imports represent a different genus (*Jasus*), they are of the same family and from a culinary standpoint are no different from a spiny lobster taken in North American waters.

SCAMPO In the Mediterranean the authentic *scampo* (plural, *scampi*) is the tail portion of a lobsterette. The term "scampi" in the U. S. is widely applied to a cooked dish in the form of large Gulf shrimps which are split and broiled in a garlic butter sauce. *See under SHRIMP.*

SPANISH LOBSTER This crustacean (*Scyllarides aequinoctialis*) is known by a variety of names, among them **shovel-nosed lobster, sand lobster, locust lobster, buccaneer crab, bulldozer** and **gollipop.** Prized as a delicacy but too rare to be of commercial value, it is caught in traps set on sandy bottoms in Florida and Gulf Coast waters. However, considerable quantities are being imported in frozen form by U. S. supermarkets from Thailand, Singapore and Australia under the name **slipper lobster,** and they are a good buy considering their scarcity in North America. The Spanish lobster is characterized by a rather flattened form, the absence of whiplike antennae, and the presence of paddle-shaped head appendages. Its homely appearance belies some delightful eating.

SPINY LOBSTER In the western Atlantic the spiny lobster (*Panulirus argus*) ranges from North Carolina and Bermuda to Brazil, through the southern Gulf of Mexico and the Caribbean Sea. It is most abundant in Florida, Bahamas, Cuba and British Honduras. Landings in the entire Caribbean area exceed 42.5 million pounds per year. Closely related species occur in California, the Mediterranean, South Africa and Australia. Sometimes called **crawfish,** and misleadingly **crayfish,** the spiny lobster like other members of this family (Palinuridae) has

Spiny lobster

5 pairs of legs but no claws. Thus, its tail portion provides the bulk of the meat. Compared to the American lobster its texture is coarser but of good flavor and tender when freshly prepared. Although 6 species of spiny lobster occur in the western Atlantic, the differences are taxonomical rather than culinary, and they are all generally similar in appearance; numerous spines cover the body, with 2 large, hooked horns over the eyes. The antennae, or whips, are long and jointed like the legs. The tail is segmented, and can be curled up beneath the lobster, the curling being used to propel the animal rapidly backward, although the lobster usually moves by walking forward or sideways. It is a beautifully marked crustacean with browns, yellows, orange, green and blue mottled over the upper parts and underside of the tail. Over dark bottom or in deep water, spiny lobsters are dark, while over light bottom or shallow water they are lighter. They may grow to as much as 17 pounds, but spiny lobsters over 5 pounds are uncommon. Also known as **Langouste** (France), **Langousten** (Germany) **Aragosta** (Italy), **Langosta** (Spain), **Lagosta** (Portugal), **Jastog** (Yugoslavia), **Langoesten** (Holland), **Languster** (Denmark, Sweden and Norway), **Humrar** (Iceland).

SELECTING LIVE LOBSTERS

A fresh lobster should appear lively in the holding tank, the more active the better. At a busy seaside market this is rarely a consideration as the turnover in stock is normally rapid. However, when shopping at inland markets or in areas beyond the lobster's geographical range, avoid any that appear "listless" which though safely edible may have been in the tank for some weeks; lobsters are not fed in captivity and their meat gradually shrinks away from the shell. It's disappointing to crack open a broad claw only to find a diminutive paw which seems to belong in a much smaller lobster.

If you are partial to the coral of the female lobster, then select carefully. The external features which separate the sexes among lobsters of approximately the same size are the narrow abdomen of the male as opposed to the comparatively broad abdomen of the female; the first pair of tail appendages is much reduced and modified in the female, and the openings of the oviducts at the basal segments of the second pair of walking legs of the female are "feathery" rather than firm and rigid.

The size of a lobster is no indication of its tenderness. Although so-called "chicken" lobsters of about 1 pound in weight are most popular, the meat is no better and it will probably require two of these to satisfy a real appetite anyhow. I once cooked a lobster of almost 30 pounds (which was caught by draggers off the coast of New Jersey) with a span across the claw of 18 inches; the claw meat cut into thin steaks and the tail cut into chunks were not only delicately flavored but tender as butter. In commercial grading lobsters are classed as follows:

Chicken: The smallest, about 1 pound.
Quarters: From 1 pound to less than 1½ pounds.
Large: From 1½ to less than 2½ pounds.
Jumbo: Any lobster over 2½ pounds.

HOW TO COOK LOBSTERS

The easiest way to cook live lobsters is by boiling. Measure the amount of water you will need to cover the number of lobsters to be cooked. If you are not using seawater, add 1 tablespoon of salt for each quart of water. Cover the pot and bring it to a rolling boil before dropping each crustacean in head first. Allow 10 minutes of cooking time for a 1-pound lobster and 3 minutes more for each additional pound. When the lobsters are placed in the pot the water will cease boiling for 3 to 5 minutes; this is variable depending on the number being cooked and the volume of water. Timing should begin when the water returns to a boil.

If you are using a steamer kettle with the

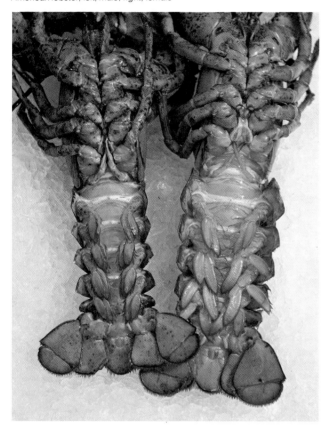

American lobster; left, male; right, female

Lobsters are one of the least parasitized crustaceans known, in fact their immunity has been a subject of research for some years. On rare occasions however, large lobsters (as well as shrimps) are attacked by microsporidia which cause the flesh to turn mushy. This has been reported from time to time in popular literature but is not a normal condition among large crustaceans. These spores are harmless to man but the cooking can be a frustrating experience when guests are waiting at table. I wouldn't hesitate to cook the biggest lobster available—when available.

HOW TO COOK SPINY LOBSTER TAILS

Spiny lobster tails can be boiled, steamed, deep-fried or broiled, or the raw meat can be removed from the shell and used in any of the prepared dishes such as curries, thermadors, newburgs or salads. Never bake it, as the musculature will tighten like a drumhead. Fast cooking is essential to a tender result. Whether the tail should be cooked in the shell is your first consideration and, more specifically, in what form? For simple boiling the tail is usually split lengthwise through the center by cutting the under shell and dividing it in two pieces; if the tail is boiled without splitting or trimming, it will be a finger bleeding struggle to pull it apart at table as the ventral carapace is extremely strong and cannot be crushed or picked apart. Optionally, to make an eye-appealing presentation, a boiled tail can be served whole by first trimming off the undershell, cutting around the edges of the carapace with a scissors, and simply lifting the shell free. Of course, the meat can also be removed by this method if a raw, whole tail is required. This is made more artful by crosscutting the base of the upper shell so that the "fan" is left attached to the meat. Small 3-ounce tails can be battered, split, and deep-fried in this form, similar to tempura shrimps.

In broiling or barbecuing, the shell lends support to the meat which results in a better appearance when trimmed piggyback style if a simple butter basting is required, or trimmed in butterfly style if a component sauce is added; with the shell in the flattened butterfly position the sauce, whether applied at some point during the cooking or afterward, will not spill off the tail.

If the lobster tails are frozen, defrost slowly in the refrigerator. These can be cooked frozen or in a partially frozen state if necessary, but in either case the result will not be as tender.

As with the American lobster only begin timing when water comes to a second boil. Use an ample amount of water in a large pot to cover the tails, and add 1

lobsters contained in a perforated top over the water, timing should begin as soon as the steam starts escaping. Use about 3 inches of water in the bottom of the kettle. Bear in mind that if you are steaming more than 3 lobsters and have to "double deck" them, the crustaceans on the bottom will cook faster than those on the top. When serving a number of people using a kettle of limited capacity, it's best to cook a few lobsters at a time as the first batch will remain warm during the short period of a second cooking. Actually lobsters have to cool a bit before you can comfortably handle them, so there's no qualitative loss. As a rule of thumb, timing from the second boiling, or the emission of steam, cook an individual lobster according to this table.

WEIGHT OF LOBSTER	TIME
1 to 1¼ pounds	10 to 12 minutes
1½ to 2 pounds	15 to 18 minutes
2½ to 5 pounds	20 to 25 minutes
6 to 10 pounds	25 to 35 minutes
10 to 15 pounds	35 to 40 minutes
15 to 20 pounds	40 to 45 minutes
20 to 25 pounds	1 hour

HOW TO PREPARE LOBSTER TAILS

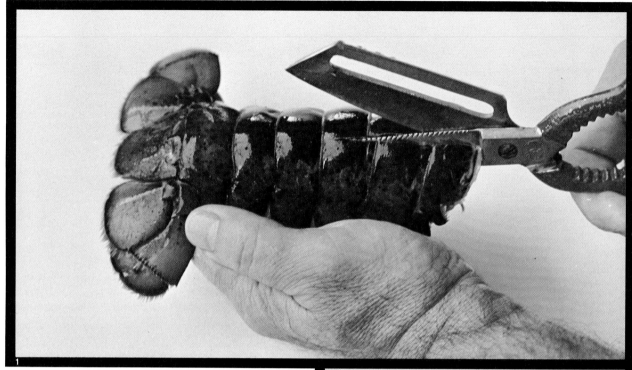

1. Cut the upper shell down the center of the back with scissors, leaving tail fan intact. Do not remove undershell. **2.** Lift uncooked tail through the slit to rest on the shell. Brush with butter and broil about 6 inches from the source of heat. This is called a "piggyback lobster tail."

3. Cut the upper shell through to the tail and press shell halves apart. Spread with sauce and broil. This is called a "butterfly lobster tail."

4. Cut off undershell, leaving the tail fan in place. Boil or deep-fry. If served in the shell, this is called a "fancut lobster tail."

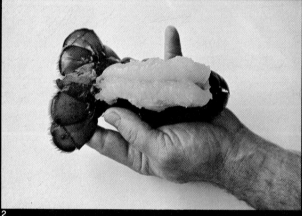

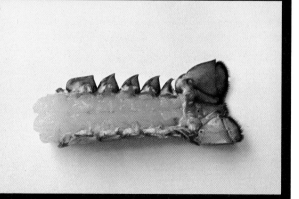

HOW TO DRESS AND SPLIT RAW AMERICAN LOBSTER

1. American lobster.

2. Cut off legs.

3. Insert knife in the abdomen.

4. Cut through undershell toward anterior.

5. then toward posterior.

6. Press lobster apart, separating halves.

7. Remove sand sac from head.

8. Remove the intestinal tract.

HOW TO SPLIT COOKED AMERICAN LOBSTER

1. Insert knife at the point where tail and body are joined, and cut toward posterior.

2. Turn lobster around and cut toward anterior.

3. The lobster split into halves. Remove sand sac from the head.

tablespoon of vinegar to each quart of water.

TAIL WEIGHT	TIME
4 ounces	5 minutes
5 ounces	6 minutes
6 ounces	7 minutes
7 ounces	8 minutes
8 ounces	9 minutes
9 ounces	10 minutes

If you are in doubt about actual weights, or if the tails vary somewhat in size, use the "5-minute rule" and test for doneness. A 5-minute period will cook the average split tail timed from the start of the second boiling. Remember, the weight in ounces includes the shell. With average 4- and 5-ounce tails, it will require a dozen to provide enough meat for 6 servings.

PRECOOKED LOBSTERS

It may be convenient to buy precooked lobsters for large supper parties, or simply as a time-saver, but always deal with a reliable fishmonger or observe the cooking personally at his shop rather than ordering by phone. Lobsters do expire in captivity and it's not uncommon for a cost-conscious dealer to refrigerate these for his precooked orders; depending on storage time, their edibility is marginal at best. To test a cooked lobster for freshness pull its tail out straight; when released it will snap back into its curled position. This indicates that the lobster was cooked while still alive. Of course, if the lobster has been sliced from head-to-tail before cooking, which is a fairly common practice, you won't be able to make the test and invariably the tomalley and coral are ruined or lost in the pot. Generally speaking, a precooked, precut lobster is not recommended.

By contrast the spiny lobster is most often sold in tail form—fresh, frozen or precooked—and with or without its shell. Within its geographic range, some live crawfish enter the market but with spiraling retail prices this product has become extremely scarce. The Bahamian fishery of a decade ago was pursued with a "tickler" and a bully net; the tickler, simply a long, metal-pointed pole, was used to flush the crawfish from its den to be quickly netted. At one time, quality-conscious dealers like Sam Sawyer of West Palm Beach wouldn't buy or deliver anything but live spiny lobsters to Florida. As demand exceeded supply, the native fishermen went back to the more expedient method of "graining" with a 2-tined spear which kills the crustacean; the tail is simply twisted off and depending on how the catch is treated (the availability of ice, freezing facilities and transportation) there is a

considerable variation in quality.

Lobsterettes or "Danish lobster" are less likely to suffer any quality loss as these deepwater crustaceans are caught in shrimp trawls. Although not marketed here in live form, they are, like shrimps, immediately iced aboard the vessel. These appear in the market whole or in tail form, fresh and frozen.

LOBSTER AMÉRICAINE McCLANE

6 pounds live American or spiny lobster (two 3-pounders or three 2-pounders)	½ teaspoon peppercorns
	1 bay leaf
	1 pound whole fresh tomatoes, halved
4 tablespoons olive oil	1 cup Chablis
2 celery ribs, including leaves, chopped fine	1 cup tomato purée
	4 cups fish stock or water, stock preferred
2 carrots, chopped fine	1 tablespoon chopped shallots
1 medium-sized onion, chopped fine	3 ounces Cognac, warmed
	butter
1 teaspoon dried thyme, or preferably 4 sprigs of fresh thyme	flour
	cayenne pepper
	salt
4 garlic cloves, crushed	parsley, chopped

Cut lobsters into halves where tail and body are joined. Split the body portion and remove the coral and liver; chop fine and reserve both. Break off the claws and crack the shells. Cut the tail portion crosswise into 4 or 5 pieces. Reserve the lobster "scraps," the remaining body portion (smash with a mallet) and legs.

Heat 2 tablespoons of the oil in a pot and sauté the celery, carrots and onion for about 3 minutes, then add the thyme, garlic and peppercorns and sauté for another 3 minutes. Add the bay leaf and lobster scraps and cover to cook over low heat for 6 minutes. When the lobster scraps turn red, add the tomatoes and mash these before adding the wine and tomato purée. Add the stock and bring to a boil, then simmer slowly, uncovered, for about 45 minutes. Strain the liquid, discarding all solids, then return liquid to the pot and reduce to about 3 cups.

Heat remaining 2 tablespoons oil in a large skillet and sauté the lobster pieces, cooking until the shells turn red, about 3 minutes. Add the chopped shallots and flame with 2 ounces of the warmed Cognac. Shake the skillet until the flame subsides. Pour the sauce over the lobster pieces and add the reserved liver and coral. Bring this to a boil, then cover the skillet, reduce heat, and let simmer for about 20 minutes. When lobster is cooked, remove pieces to serving dish.

facing page, Buoys or markers for lobster traps, Maine

Thicken the sauce in the skillet slightly with a butter and flour roux, adding cayenne pepper and salt to taste. Add remaining 1 ounce of Cognac. Pour over the lobster pieces in the serving dish and serve hot. Sprinkle with chopped parsley. Makes 6 servings.

LOBSTER THERMIDOR McCLANE

3 live American	2 teaspoons minced tarragon
or spiny lobsters,	1 teaspoon beef extract
2¼ to 2½ pounds each,	(glace de viande)
or lobsters already	2 cups heavy cream
cooked and split	beurre manié
12 fresh mushroom caps, diced	cayenne pepper
6 tablespoons butter	½ cup whipped cream
2 tablespoons lemon juice	(for glaçage)
salt	freshly grated
4 teaspoons chopped shallots	Parmesan cheese
2 tablespoons Pernod	melted butter
1 cup Chablis	lemon slices
1 cup fish stock	parsley or watercress sprigs

If lobsters are uncooked, boil them and let them cool. Split each one lengthwise and break off the claws, legs and feelers. Crack the claws to remove the meat but do not break the shell when extracting the body meat. Place meat on a cutting board. Wash out and clean each shell, then pat dry.

Dice the lobster meat into ½- to ¾-inch cubes and reserve. In a large skillet sauté the diced mushroom caps in 2 tablespoons butter, sprinkled with 1 tablespoon lemon juice and a little salt. Cook for about 4 minutes, then remove to a bowl. Add about 4 tablespoons butter to the skillet and sauté the lobster meat with 2 teaspoons of the chopped shallots. Cook for about 2 minutes, then add the Pernod. Return mushrooms to the pan and leave on back of stove or at room temperature.

In a saucepan combine the Chablis, fish stock, tarragon, beef extract and remaining 2 teaspoons of chopped shallots. Reduce this by half, then slowly add the heavy cream with constant stirring. Add *beurre manié* in order to obtain a thick sauce. Simmer for at least 3 minutes. Season to taste with remaining lemon juice, cayenne pepper to taste, and salt (optional). Reserve about one third of the·sauce in a bowl to be used for making the *glaçage.* Pour the remaining two thirds of the sauce over the lobster meat in the skillet and reheat at a simmer, then spoon the mixture into the 6 cleaned lobster shells to fill them.

Return the reserved one third of the sauce to the saucepan and add the whipped cream. Just keep the sauce warm as you quickly blend. Spoon equal amounts of this over each lobster, then sprinkle with Parmesan cheese. To prevent the cheese burning and to create a golden brown surface, dribble melted butter on the *glaçage.* Place the lobster shells under the broiler (but not close to the heat source) until a good color is obtained. Garnish with lemon slices and sprigs of parsley or watercress. Makes 6 servings.

The most famous American lobster dish, **Lobster Newberg,** was made for the first time 100 years ago at Delmonico's. It was whipped up in a chafing dish by a sea captain named Ben Wenberg. The Delmonico Restaurant, founded in 1830, is still going strong, but Wenberg's name is lost to fame except in anecdotes such as this. He and Charles Delmonico had a falling out, and the restaurant at first discarded the dish. Patrons kept asking for it, so it was restored with the name of **Lobster Newberg** or **Delmonico.** (*Delmonico's/A Century of Splendor,* Lately Thomas, Houghton Mifflin Company, Boston, 1967.) Nowadays the spelling is usually Newburg. This is the Delmonico recipe—simple, rich and delicious.

LOBSTER NEWBERG
(Delmonico Restaurant, New York City)

Cook 6 lobsters of about 2 pounds each in boiling salted water for 25 minutes. When lobsters are cold, detach bodies from the tails and cut tails into slices. Heat clarified butter in a *sautoir* and add the slices, each piece lying flat. Season with salt. Sauté lightly on both sides, without coloring the pieces. Moisten with heavy cream, reduce the cream quickly to half, and add 2 or 3 spoonfuls of Madeira wine. Bring the liquid again to a boil, then remove from heat and thicken with a liaison of egg yolks and cream. Without letting the sauce boil, heat it while incorporating a little cayenne and some butter. Toss the lobster slices lightly in the sauce. Arrange the slices on plates and pour the sauce over. Makes 6 to 8 servings.

LOBSTER NEWBURG McCLANE

6 lobster tails,	cayenne pepper
each 8 ounces	1 teaspoon beef extract
1 onion, 2 ounces,	(glace de viande), optional
chopped fine	1 teaspoon sweet paprika
5 tablespoons butter	4 tablespoons lemon juice
1 cup fish stock	12 mushroom caps, sliced
¾ cup Madeira	2 teaspoons chopped shallots
2 cups heavy cream	1 ounce Cognac
beurre manié (if needed)	2 tablespoons
salt	minced parsley

Sauté onion in 2 tablespoons butter until *blond*. Add fish stock and reduce by half. Add Madeira and reduce to half again. Slowly add the cream, stirring thoroughly, then add a little *beurre manié* to get desired thickness. Add salt and cayenne pepper to taste. Add the beef extract, if you like, and paprika, and stir to blend. Reserve. Boil lobster tails in water with 1 teaspoon salt and 3 tablespoons of the lemon juice added. Adjust the cooking time to the kind of shellfish you are using, but do not overcook. Shell tails and cut the meats crosswise into thick slices. If using freshwater crayfish leave meats whole.

In a large skillet, sauté mushrooms in 3 tablespoons butter with remaining lemon juice sprinkled over. When *blond*, add shallots and lobster slices. Sauté for about 2 minutes longer, then add the reserved sauce and the Cognac. Bring back to a bubble and spoon directly on individual plates over hot rice, toast points, or in patty shells. Sprinkle with chopped parsley. Makes 4 servings.
NOTE: In place of lobster tails, spiny lobster or slipper (Spanish) lobster may be used, or an equivalent weight of lobsterettes or crayfish. If you start with whole American lobster, use the claw meat as well as tail; add any coral, if present, to the sauce but do not add the tomalley.

LOBSTER PAVILLON

4 live lobsters,	6 ounces dry white wine
each 1½ to 1¾ pounds	4 ounces brandy or Cognac
1 small carrot	½ cup Tomato Sauce (p. 288)
1 onion	3 fresh tomatoes,
pinch of fresh or dried thyme	peeled and chopped
1 bay leaf	½ cup fish stock
1 parsley sprig	2 small garlic cloves,
4 tablespoons sweet butter	crushed
2 teaspoons salt	1 teaspoon minced chervil
pinch of cayenne pepper	1 teaspoon minced tarragon
1 cup olive oil	4 ounces port wine
4 shallots, chopped	1 cup heavy cream

Kill lobsters by cutting horizontally into halves. Prepare a *mirepoix bordelaise:* Mince the carrot, onion, thyme, bay leaf and parsley, and sauté in 2 tablespoons of the butter in a large skillet until onion and carrot are lightly browned. Cut lobster claws and tails into 4 pieces, reserving the greenish-gray liver (tomalley). Season the lobster with salt and cayenne, and sauté in very hot oil for 5 minutes. Add lobster pieces to the *mirepoix.* Add 1 tablespoon butter, the chopped shallots and the white wine, mixing well. Ignite the brandy and pour it in. Add the tomato sauce, fresh tomatoes and fish stock. Cover tightly and simmer for 20 to 25 minutes. Remove the lobster meat from the shells. Strain the sauce through a large strainer. Blend lobster tomalley with 1 tablespoon butter, the garlic, chervil and tarragon, and mix into the sauce to thicken it; do not allow it to boil. Finish the sauce with the port wine and cream. Correct the seasoning with additional salt and cayenne to taste. Pour the sauce over the lobster and serve very hot with rice pilau. Makes 6 servings.

ROCK LOBSTER SAVANNAH

12 spiny lobster tails,	1 teaspoon paprika
5 ounces each	2 eggs, separated
6 tablespoons butter	salt and pepper
6 tablespoons flour	½ cup grated
1½ cups light cream	Parmesan cheese
1 teaspoon grated lemon rind	

Parboil lobster tails in boiling salted water. When water reboils, drain immediately and drench with cold water. With scissors remove underside membrane and pull out meat. Dice meat and reserve shells. Melt butter and stir in flour. Gradually stir in cream, lemon rind and paprika. Cook, stirring constantly, until sauce bubbles and thickens. Quickly beat in egg yolks, and add salt and pepper to taste. Divide sauce into 2 portions. Add lobster to half of the sauce and spoon mixture into reserved shells. Heat remaining sauce and stir in cheese; cool slightly. Beat egg whites stiff and fold into the cooled sauce. Spoon over filled lobster shells which have been placed on a cookie sheet. Bake in a preheated moderate oven (350°F) for 25 to 30 minutes, or until puffed and brown. Makes 6 servings.

STUFFED AMERICAN LOBSTER

Have lobsters split and claws cracked. Remove intestines and gill tissue but save any tomalley or coral. For each 2-pound lobster prepare 1 cup Sauce Béchamel *(see SAUCES)* and flavor it with 1 teaspoon prepared Dijon mustard and 2 teaspoons fresh lemon juice. When sauce is thick stir in 2 tablespoons chopped scallion, including the green part, 2 tablespoons chopped red pimiento, 4 tablespoons sliced mushrooms and about ½ cup tiny fresh white-bread cubes. Add any tomalley or coral, and season with salt to taste. Gently fold in 1 cup crab meat which has been picked over carefully to remove any bits of cartilage.

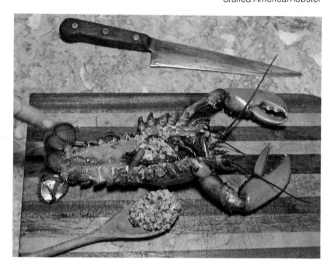

Stuffed American lobster

Stuff the lobster, rounding it on top. Cover with a thin layer of fresh bread crumbs and sprinkle with melted butter. Bake in a preheated 375°F. oven for 15 to 25 minutes. Sprinkle with a pinch of *fines herbes* and serve garnished with lemon and lime fans, or with lemon baskets filled with Green Mayonnaise or Sauce Tartare *(see under SAUCES).*

COQUILLE MAISON
(Scandia Restaurant, Los Angeles)

4 dozen small	6 drops of
lobsterette tails	Worcestershire sauce
9 tablespoons butter	¼ teaspoon salt
1 tablespoon chopped shallots	2 tablespoons flour
1½ cups white wine	3 dozen seedless
1 cup heavy cream	white grapes, peeled
3 tablespoons lemon juice	1 tablespoon chopped chives
6 drops of Tabasco	⅓ cup Hollandaise Sauce (p. 289)

Defrost and shell lobsterette tails. Melt 3 tablespoons of the butter in a heavy skillet; use several skillets if necessary; add tails and sauté, stirring, for 1 minute. Add shallots and cook, stirring, for an additional 30 seconds. Add wine, ¾ cup of the cream, the lemon juice, Tabasco, Worcestershire and salt. Heat to simmering. Soften remaining butter and combine with flour. Stir into liquid and simmer for 2 minutes. Using a slotted spoon, transfer lobsterette tails into 6 coquilles or au gratin dishes. Add 6 grapes to each dish. Stir chives and hollandaise sauce into the wine sauce. Whip remaining cream and fold into the sauce. Divide sauce among the coquilles, and brown under a hot broiler for 1 minute. Makes 6 servings.

facing page, Slatted wooden traps or pots for catching lobsters, Maine

Mackerel
Mantis Shrimp
Marlin
Milkfish
Mojarra
Mooneye
Mullet
Mussel

m

Mackerel

There are ominous connotations in the name "mackerel." One can be in a social sense "as cold as a mackerel" or the ultimate "as dead as a mackerel," and in describing a storm warning cloud formation we call it "a mackerel sky."

Mackerel scales and mares' tails
Make lofty ships carry low sails.

Less explicable to us, to a Frenchman, a *maquereau* is a gentleman who earns his money by the labors of ladies of the night. Scientifically, the name is part of a homogenous family of fishes, the Scombridae, which includes the tunas. From a culinary standpoint we will treat these 2 groups separately; the only thing they have in common in the kitchen is a sharply divided musculature with an outer lateral band of dark red meat and an inner portion, lighter in color, which cooks to white in some species. The red muscle sustains their continuous swimming, which in these pelagic fishes never ceases, and the white muscle is flexed when a burst of speed is needed. This structural peculiarity has no value in a recipe, but some scombrids have more of one than the other, and that is pertinent.

Until the year 1870 practically all the mackerel consumed in America was salted. The fish were split and gibbed and treated aboard ship. The bulk of these landings was marketed in Boston, and thus the name "Boston mackerel" became synonymous with the salted product. When the New England fleet began storing ice in pens below deck, fresh mackerel appeared at market. By 1880 the first canned product was produced at Eastport, Maine. This huge fishery, which peaked in 1885 with landings totaling 100 million pounds, went into a calamitous decline until 1910, then the mackerel population slowly expanded during the next 6 years and collapsed again. A seesaw pattern in their abundance has been observed since Colonial days and is determined by the survival of young mackerel in any given year; environmental conditions change and reproduction is not always successful.

To a European, or for that matter to any American living north of Cape Hatteras, the only worthwhile market mackerel is *Scomber scombrus*, the Atlantic mackerel. Where I live in Florida, we never see this species but are blessed with 4 others and in order of my preference, these are the wahoo, cero, Spanish mackerel and king mackerel. In my opinion, the first three are superior to the Atlantic mackerel, which may be delicious in its own right but it lacks the texture, flavor and fine white flake of these southern forms. Our wahoo and cero are never so abundant that they enter the commercial fishery, but the Spanish mackerel and king mackerel are seasonally caught in large quantities. The thing to know about any mackerel, if you catch your own, is that they must be iced within 6 hours, and preferably immediately; it's during this when the fish are exposed to ambient temperatures that the fresh mackerel flavor is lost. This is not a question of spoilage, although any delay in icing accelerates nucleotide changes in quality in subsequent storage, but a matter of the fish becoming tasteless. Properly iced, from the moment of capture, the eating quality of mackerel has been maintained to 19 days. *(Nucleotide Degradation and Organoleptic Quality in Fresh and Thawed Mackerel Muscle Held at and above Ice Temperature*, Fraser, Pitts, and Dyer, Fisheries Research Board of Canada, Halifax Laboratory, Halifax, N.S.) This is even more important in our southern waters where high ambient temperatures are the rule.

Although mackerel is generally considered an oily fish, this varies with the season and the species. Actually, a fat mackerel is much the best when fresh. Since the earliest days of commercial fishing the prime fish are taken in the fall (Atlantic mackerel) as they become thin and lean during winter and are sometimes emaciated by spring. This species does not feed, or feeds very little, from December to March. Adults which are about to spawn when they appear inshore in early summer may continue their winter fast until they have spawned, then they commence feeding greedily. (*Fishes of the Gulf of Maine*, Bigelow and Schroeder; Fishery Bulletin 74, Volume 53) Young mackerel or "tinkers" of 6 to 10 inches in length, which sometimes appear in great shoals around New England harbors and river mouths, begin foraging immediately and these fat little fish are excellent table fare. Bear in mind that both the gonads (white roe) of the male and the roe of the female are delicacies.

MACKEREL TERMINOLOGY

ATLANTIC MACKEREL This mackerel (*Scomber scombrus*) occurs from Newfoundland to Cape Hatteras in

facing page, Spanish mackerel

the western Atlantic and from Norway to the Mediterranean and the Canary Islands. The Atlantic mackerel has dark, wavy stripes on its back and shades to white on its belly. It's the most important market species in international landings. The Atlantic mackerel has a considerable amount of red muscle (from 12 to 28 percent) and a very assertive flavor. It's sold fresh, frozen, smoked, salted, canned, semipreserved and air-dried. This mackerel can be prepared by a variety of cooking methods but broiling with a contrasting sauce (usually tomato-based) is most popular.

ATKA MACKEREL This is not a mackerel *(see GREEN-LING)*.

BULLET MACKEREL Although a member of the tuna and mackerel family, the bullet mackerel and closely related frigate mackerel are tunalike in texture and flavor. These cannot be cooked in mackerel recipes. *See TUNA TERMINOLOGY under TUNA.*

CERO Also known as **pintado** (South America) and **painted mackerel,** the cero resembles the Spanish mackerel but in addition to the rows of golden spots it also has golden stripes on the sides of its body. The cero *(Scomberomorus regalis)* occurs from Cape Cod to Brazil but is more abundant from southern Florida through the West Indies. It's a big mackerel, attaining weights up to 35 pounds, but the average is between 5 and 10 pounds. In common with the Spanish mackerel it has more white meat than the Atlantic or chub mackerel and is more delicately flavored. Large cero can be steaked and are excellent when charcoal-broiled or smoked.

CHUB MACKEREL The chub mackerel or **hardhead** *(Scomber japonicus)* occurs in both the Atlantic and Pacific Oceans. This is a smaller fish (seldom over 1 pound) than other mackerels and less desirable commercially. It's similar to the Atlantic mackerel in texture and flavor and no distinction is made between them at market, except for the size. In Europe the chub mackerel is commonly called "Spanish mackerel" but bears no resemblance to our Spanish mackerel, a much superior foodfish. Also known as **Maquereau Espagnol** (France), **Spanische Makrele** (Germany), **Spansk Makrel** (Denmark), **Spansk Makrell** (Norway), **Spansk Makrill** (Sweden), **Spaanse Makreel** (Holland), **Estornino** (Spain).

FRIGATE MACKEREL *See BULLET MACKEREL.*

JACK MACKEREL This fish is not a mackerel but a member of the family Carangidae. *See JACK.*

KING MACKEREL Commonly called **kingfish,** the king mackerel is found from North Carolina (summer) to Brazil. This is the second largest mackerel, excluding the tunas, and reaches weights up to 100 pounds with an average of about 20 pounds. The king mackerel seasonally provides a considerable commercial fishery in North Carolina and Florida. It has more red muscle than the cero, wahoo or Spanish mackerel, and is a fatter fish with

Cero mackerel

a somewhat stronger flavor. Although it can be prepared as oven-broiled or baked fillets and steaks, to those of us who eat kingfish with any frequency it's infinitely superior when marinated in lime juice for a few hours, then cooked over charcoal and basted with a garlic butter or suitable sauce. The lime juice not only firms and whitens the meat but minimizes the oil flavor. The king mackerel is especially good for smoking.

MONTEREY SPANISH MACKEREL   Similar to the other Spanish mackerels, the Monterey (*Scomberomorus concolor*) resembles the sierra except that it lacks the golden spots on its sides. (Young king mackerel are similarly marked.) This species was once very common in Monterey Bay, California, but it disappeared from that area in the 1880s. Today it is found from Panama Bay to the Gulf of California. Its flesh is considered on a par with the Spanish mackerel. However, it's rarely found in U. S. markets.

SIERRA   Closely related to the Spanish mackerel, the sierra (*Scomberomorus sierra*) is essentially its Pacific counterpart in appearance. It has the same rows of golden spots along its sides. The sierra is found from San Diego to Peru, but it is quite rare in U. S. waters and is seen only in Mexican, Central and South American markets.

SPANISH MACKEREL   One of the best mackerels from a culinary standpoint, with minimal red muscle. It's leaner and more delicately flavored than the Atlantic or chub mackerel or any of the Pacific mackerels. The Spanish mackerel (*Scomberomorus maculatus*) is found from Chesapeake Bay to Brazil and in warm years may occur as far north as Cape Cod. It differs from the other Atlantic mackerels in having golden spots on its sides and no stripes. This mackerel attains weights up to 20 pounds, but market fish are more commonly from 2 to 4 pounds in size. This is our most common mackerel in Florida and Gulf waters and is caught principally in the winter and spring seasons. Broiled, baked or smoked, it rates three stars.

WAHOO   Found in tropical and subtropical seas throughout the world, the wahoo (*Acanthocybium solandri*) resembles the king mackerel in its long, slender shape but can be distinguished by prominent vertical bars on its sides when freshly caught. The wahoo is undeniably a gourmet's mackerel; it is one of the greatest of all oceanic fishes at table. Unlike most other scombrids the flesh of the wahoo is white, of fine circular flake, and delicately textured. It has minimal red muscle and is a leaner fish than the king mackerel. Although wahoo attain weights up to 130 pounds or more, the average is more nearly 25 to 30 pounds. Wahoo can be filleted for broiling or baking, or the fillets can be cut into fingers for deep-frying. The fish can also be steaked for broiling or barbecuing. Smoked wahoo is an exceptional taste treat.

Wahoo are very abundant at times in some localities, notably the Bahamas, Bermuda, around Grand Cayman, and the Pacific coasts of Panama and Costa Rica. This fish is not usually caught in sufficient quantities to be marketed with any frequency. Most landings are made by sport fishermen from North Carolina to Florida and in the Gulf of Mexico. In Hawaii, the wahoo is known as **ono** which means "sweet," an apt description.

SPANISH MACKEREL WITH MAYONNAISE SAUCE

Cover a broiling pan with aluminum foil, and wipe a little olive oil over the foil to prevent the fish sticking. Side by side, place mackerel fillets, skin side down. In a cup make a generous mixture of mayonnaise and dry vermouth, so that it remains thick but well flavored; then spread this over each fillet in a layer about ¼ inch thick. Add salt and pepper to taste, and then sprinkle each fillet with a pinch of ground fennel seed. Broil the fillets in a moderate oven for about 20 minutes, basting them with the pan juices and a few splashes of vermouth. The mayonnaise will get a golden-brown crust on the outside, but the under liquid will blend with the fish juices and become a creamy sauce.

MACKEREL FILLETS FLAMINGO

2 pounds Spanish mackerel	1 tablespoon prepared mustard
fillets	2 teaspoons
1 teaspoon salt	prepared horseradish
dash of pepper	2 tablespoons chili sauce
1 cup grated cheese	4 tablespoons butter

Cut fillets into serving-size portions. Sprinkle both sides with salt and pepper. Combine cheese, mustard, horseradish and chili sauce. Place fish, flesh side up, on a greased broiler pan about 3 inches from source of heat. Brush with butter and broil for 5 to 10 minutes, or until lightly browned and fish flakes easily when tested with a fork. Spoon cheese mixture on top of flesh. Return to broiler for 1 to 2 minutes, or until cheese melts and browns. Makes 6 servings.

MACKEREL WITH GINGER PORTED PEARS

4 fillets of Spanish	1 teaspoon lemon juice
or cero mackerel	2 tablespoons chopped
1 can (14 ounces) pear halves	preserved gingerroot
½ cup port wine	salt
½ cup syrup from pears	1 cup sour cream

Prepare the pears several hours in advance of fish preparation. Drain the pears, reserving the syrup. Combine the port and pear syrup, lemon juice, gingerroot and salt to taste in a saucepan. Bring to a boil, reduce heat, and simmer for 5 minutes. Pour over pears. Cool, then chill in refrigerator.

Broil the mackerel fillets. Center each fillet on an individual plate. Place pear halves over the mackerel decoratively, spoon on some of the sauce, and top with sour cream. Accompany with watercress salad with a light vinegar dressing for contrast. Makes 4 servings.

GRILLED MACKEREL WITH GOOSEBERRY SAUCE

(from *The Lady's Assistant*, Charlotte Mason, Dublin, Ireland, 1778)

4 fillets of mackerel	pinch of grated nutmeg
4 heaping tablespoons bread crumbs	salt and pepper
1 tablespoon chopped parsley	2 tablespoons butter
2 egg yolks	½ pound gooseberries
grated rind of 1 lemon	2 tablespoons sugar
	2 tablespoons chopped fennel

Mix bread crumbs, parsley, egg yolks, lemon rind and nutmeg together, and season to taste. Put some stuffing on each mackerel fillet, then fold over and secure. Soften 1 tablespoon butter and rub a little over each fillet. Broil gently on both sides until the fish is done. Cook the gooseberries in ½ cup water with sugar, fennel and remaining butter. Do not let the berries overcook, but just burst open. Serve hot.

The same sauce can be served with mackerel that has been poached in water with salt and lemon juice. Herrings can be cooked in the same way. Makes 4 servings.

EAST COAST MACKEREL BAKE

2 pounds king mackerel steaks	1 cup sliced mushrooms
1 teaspoon salt	¼ cup dry vermouth
¼ teaspoon pepper	¼ teaspoon crushed garlic
¼ cup flour	½ cup soft bread crumbs
fat or oil for frying	2 tablespoons butter or margarine, melted
1½ cups diced, seeded, peeled tomatoes	

Rinse and dry fish. Sprinkle both sides of fish with salt and pepper. Roll in flour. Place fish in a single layer in hot fat in a 12-inch frypan. Fry at a high heat for 2 or 3 minutes, or until brown. Turn carefully. Fry for 2 or 3 minutes longer, or until brown on the second side. Place fish in a single layer in a well-greased shallow baking dish, 12 x 8 inches. Combine tomatoes, mushrooms, vermouth and garlic in a 1½-quart saucepan. Bring to a boil, stirring constantly. Pour hot sauce over fish. Mix crumbs and melted butter and sprinkle over the top. Bake in a moderate oven (350°F.) for 20 to 25 minutes, or until crumbs are brown and fish flakes easily when tested with a fork. Makes 6 servings.

SPANISH MACKEREL WITH HEAVENLY TOPPING

2 pounds Spanish mackerel fillets
    or other fish fillets
2 tablespoons lemon juice
½ cup grated Parmesan cheese ·
4 tablespoons butter or margarine, softened
3 tablespoons mayonnaise or salad dressing
3 tablespoons chopped green onion
1 teaspoon prepared mustard (optional)
¼ teaspoon salt
dash of Tabasco

Rinse and dry fish and place, skin side down, in a single layer on a well-greased shallow baking pan, 15 x 10 inches. Brush tops of fillets with lemon juice. Broil about 4 inches from the source of heat for 6 to 8 minutes. Combine remaining ingredients. Remove fish from heat and spread with cheese mixture. Broil for 2 or 3 minutes longer, or until fish flakes easily when tested with a fork. Makes 6 servings.

SMOKY BROILED SPANISH MACKEREL

2 pounds Spanish mackerel fillets
    or other fish fillets
⅓ cup soy sauce
3 tablespoons melted margarine or cooking oil
1 tablespoon liquid smoke
1 garlic clove, chopped fine
½ teaspoon ground ginger
½ teaspoon salt

Rinse and dry fish. Skin fillets. Cut fillets into serving-size portions. Combine remaining ingredients; mix thoroughly. Place fish on a well-greased broiler pan and brush with sauce. Broil about 3 inches from the source of heat for 4 or 5 minutes. Turn carefully and brush with sauce. Broil for 4 or 5 minutes longer, basting occasionally, until fish flakes easily when tested with a fork. Makes 6 servings.

facing page, East coast mackerel bake

Mantis Shrimp

This is not a shrimp but a member of the Order Stomatopoda. There are about 200 species in the family Squillidae, occurring on both sides of the Atlantic. They are more descriptively called "mantis prawns." These crustaceans are larger than shrimps with a body length reaching 12 inches. Mantis are found from Cape Cod to the Gulf of Mexico and from the Bahamas through the West Indies. On our Pacific Coast they appear from Monterey Bay south to Mexico.

Mantis can be distinguished by a pair of raptorial claws with 3 to 6 long teeth. The carapace is somewhat flattened and of membranous texture; it has a long median ridge with deep grooves. The animal is narrow in the anterior portion but flares outward at the posterior end. The bright green eyes are mounted on narrow stalks. In some species the body is pale green or yellowish-green tinged with pink, while other species have 7 or more bright colors. The mantis shrimp bears a certain resemblance to the praying mantis insect, hence the common name.

Mantis shrimps are most active at night, and by day they burrow in mud at or below the low-water mark. There are usually several entrances to each den. They can be caught with a baited wire snare by poking it into the burrow; any small tough piece of fish, mollusk or crustacean may be used as bait. Due to the specialized method of capture mantis do not provide a commercial market in the U.S. The only way to enjoy this delicacy is to collect the crustaceans yourself. When boiled or fried, the tail is similar to that of a large shrimp. It is a popular seafood along the coast of Italy where limited quantities of **canocchie** are taken at night by net. In Hawaii they are known as **aloalo.**

Marlin

Four species of marlin are found in temperate and tropical seas: the **blue marlin** *(Makaira nigricans)* and **white marlin** *(Tetrapturus albidus)* of the Atlantic, and the **striped marlin** *(Tetrapturus audax)* and **black marlin** *(Makaira indica)* of the Pacific. Blue marlin also occur in the Pacific, but at present it has not been determined whether this is a distinct species or subspecies. Marlins belong to the family Istiophoridae, which also includes the sailfish and 4 or 5 species of spearfishes. Both the blue and black marlin reach weights up to 1 ton, although the usual in most areas is 300 to 400 pounds. Characterized by a long spear or bill, marlins superficially resemble the swordfish, which is the sole member of a separate family (Xiphiidae).

In the U. S., marlin are considered gamefish rather than foodfish, and comparatively few are landed at dockside by big-game anglers. It's common practice for sportsmen to release rather than kill a marlin after bringing it to boat. Those fish which are killed are unfortunately wasted, as there's no tradition of marlin cookery in American cuisine. The quantity taken by market fishermen in the period 1925-1935 when marlin was included in the "swordfish" catch of California was insignificant. It's illegal now to sell fresh marlin as well as sailfish in this country, a well-intentioned but impotent ruling in terms of conservation. The marlins are an extremely important foodfish in Japan, both in the form of **sashimi** and to a great extent in the making of fish sausage. The black marlin is particularly esteemed and about 1 million pounds per year are used in the sausage industry alone. These are caught on specialized gear known as "longlines," which are usually 50 to 70 miles long, mounted with 1,000 hooks and buoyed at the surface. Intensive longlining has caused a considerable decline in the world's billfish stocks for some species. Many countries operate these fleets in all seas, including North American waters.

HOW TO COOK MARLIN

Marlin are highly regarded as food in Cuba (the subject of Ernest Hemingway's *The Old Man and the Sea*) and in Mexico, Central and South America. All marlins are delicious when smoked, baked or broiled. A special delicacy is smoked marlin with scrambled eggs and chopped chives. It's a leaner meat than swordfish, and tends to dry out unless basted and cooked just to the point of "done." In the Azores both marlin and tuna are treated in the same fashion—quickly braised in olive oil, with orégano, garlic, parsley and pepper. However, marlin can be used in any swordfish or tuna recipe. White and striped marlin have pink to pale red flesh, while black marlin and the blue have meat of a deeper red color. Some variation does occur, apparently resulting from local food habits. Each species is of excellent flavor, although the white and striped marlin are more delicate and can be used in cold dishes such as aspic or salads.

Large marlin do not lend themselves to ordinary methods of dressing a fish, as the skin is very tough. The best method at dockside with the fish laid flat is to use a saw to make the initial deep cut vertically, just below the dorsal fin to a point behind the pectoral fin. Then, with a heavy sharp knife make an incision from gill to tail parallel to the back, and another incision arching over the

White marlin at Chub Cay, Bahamas, caught by J. R. Laing from his boat the *French Leave*

rib cage, then paralleling the ventral surface. The skin can then be worked free by prying it loose with the knife at the original cut, and peeling it off by hand much as you would skin an eel. Steaks can then be cut out of the thicker portions.

Also known as **Marlin** (Spain, Mexico, South America), **Madaire** (France), and **Kurokawa, Shirokawa, Makajiki** and **Kajiki,** according to species (Japan).

Merlan

The French name for hake. *See HAKE under COD.*

Milkfish

An important foodfish of the Indo-Pacific region. The milkfish *(Chanos chanos)* resembles a herring in shape but is more colorful and considerably larger, growing to nearly 5 feet and a weight of 50 pounds. Milkfish are found from the Red Sea and East Africa to Japan, the Philippines, northern Australia, Hawaii to central California and the Mexican coast. Although the soft white flesh is of no great moment in the kitchen, their cultivation in ponds is ancient, and they provide a ready source of protein. Milkfish are primarily algal feeders inhabiting coastal estuaries. While some adults are taken in nets and traps, the major fishery is for the fry which are stocked in tidal ponds and left to grow to marketable sizes. Milkfish is not utilized in the U. S., but it is sold in restaurants in the Far East as **bangos, bangdong, bangdeng** and **bangdang,** and in Hawaii as **awa.** The Hawaiians use milkfish in making fish cakes and also serve it raw in the form of **sashimi.**

Mojarra

Small silvery fishes of the family Gerridae, which are unimportant as market fish although the mojarra (pronounced Moe-ha-rah) does enter our commercial catch statistics. There are at least 9 species in Atlantic waters, from Cape Hatteras south to Brazil, and several in the eastern Pacific. Only one of these, the yellowfin mojarra which attains a size of about 1 foot in length, is utilized as food. It's an edible but somewhat bony panfish. Mojarras have compressed bodies and large smooth scales. They are erroneously called "shad" in south Florida and the Bahamas where no true shad exist. The resemblance in appearance or table quality is also illusory.

Mooneye

A small freshwater panfish of the family Hiodontidae found, but not abundantly, from Hudson Bay to Lake Champlain and west through Lake Erie to the Mississippi drainage system. The flesh of the mooneye is dry and full of tiny bones. It's a palatable product when smoked but inferior to the closely related goldeye *(which see).*

Mullet

The mullet represents a galaxy of distinguished seafoods on a world basis which are extremely nutritious and abundant. Supply has always exceeded demand in the U. S. In an attempt to arouse public interest, the state of

Florida chose the seemingly romantic Spanish name *lisa* to promote sales of the fish. This was no more comprehensible than a plague of bullfrogs. The consumer invariably asked, what is a lisa? and when the retailer explained that it's a mullet, nothing was accomplished except to suggest that the fish had to be disguised. Of course, to anybody who knows seafood and particularly the bayou countryfolk who live on the Gulf of Mexico in Florida, Alabama, Louisiana and Texas, mullet needs no explanation. Split and broiled or smoked in sweet bay or hickory, it has few peers. It's one of the most important foodfish in Hawaii, where **ama'ama** has been pond-cultured for years. Both the white gonads of the male and the orange-colored roe of the female are sumptuous dividends.

Now, to muddy our waters, the official market name used by the Canadian Government for the meat of various suckers is "mullet." This comes to the American wholesaler in numerous forms including fillets, boneless blocks, and in tray-pack breaded fish portions. There is nothing wrong with the sucker as a food. Admittedly, its correct name doesn't pique the average palate, but the soft-textured, lean white flesh of a sucker can hardly be used in recipes designed for the fat, firmly flaked meat of a mullet. So beware at the outset. There are no mullets swimming in Canadian seas. If you seek recipes in translated cookbooks of European origin, or for that matter in American works on European cookery, inevitably you will meet the red mullet.

In our culinary world the red mullet of the Mediterranean is a superstar; a **rouget de roche grenobloise** at the Ritz in Paris, or a **rouget grillé au fenouil** at Lei Mouscardins in Saint-Tropez, or in the genre of back-alley no-nonsense classic seafood cuisine a **trlja od kamena** at the Restaurant Prijeka in Dubrovnik, would get my vote. Few tourist ichthyophiles returning from Europe fail to sing the praises of red mullet. But alas, the red mullet is not a mullet at all; it belongs to the family of goatfish or Mullidae, and watch the Latin—mullets are members of the Mugilidae. Semantics are important, as goatfish of one kind or another range all the way from New Jersey to Rio de Janeiro. In warm years they wander as far north as Cape Cod. They are also found around Bermuda. On our side of the Atlantic goatfish are almost never utilized as food except in a few areas of the Caribbean. In Hawaii the **kumu** goatfish commands a top price at market and bears the same reputation locally as the red mullet in Mediterranean countries. Even the French name **rouget** does not have international currency; in the Cajun French of New Orleans it usually means red snapper, which is hardly a demeaning option; however, we have wandered a long way from mullet cookery.

More than 100 species of mullet are found throughout the world, of which a half dozen are distributed along our shores from Maine to Texas and southward from central California. The chief center of their abundance is from the Carolinas around the Gulf of Mexico. The 2 important commercial species are the **striped** and the **silver mullet.** In Europe, various "grey" mullets (which include our striped mullet) occur from the British Isles through the Mediterranean. In a culinary sense the chief difference between species is that some contain more fat than others; our silver mullet, for example, common to the East Coast of Florida, is a leaner fish than the striped mullet which is more abundant on the West Coast. During the fall season when the fish are particularly numerous and in roe, large quantities of striped mullet are split and dry-salted or smoked.

Mullet feed on microscopic plant and animal food taken from the surface of bottom sediment which is digested in a gizzardlike stomach. Like other basic converters such as the herring or anchovy, the mullet is rich in minerals and protein and has a very high iodine content. The white flesh is mild and has a nutty flavor. When freshly caught, it's especially good broiled, baked or pan-fried. It does pose some problem in freezing, however, and should not be packaged in-the-round unless the fish is to be used within 2 to 3 weeks. The white flesh freezes well and has a shelf life of about 6 months with no trace of oxidative rancidity. However, the dark lateral band, which in addition to fatty acids contains a high amount of heme pigments, is extremely unstable and does not tolerate storage—90 days at most but seldom over 2 months. About one third of a mullet fillet consists of dark meat; this portion should be sliced off and eliminated for long-term freezing; there will be less waste as the white meat stays firm and sweet.

Mullet roe has long been a delicacy of the Florida "cracker" on cattle ranches, in hunting camps, and especially in the West Coast fishing villages. It's usually served fried with scrambled eggs for breakfast, or accompanied by a heart-of-palm salad and sweet orange slices at lunch. Despite an annual catch of some 35 million pounds of mullet in the Gulf of Mexico, the roe rarely appears in restaurants—an oversight that may change in the near future. A heretofore wasted by-product in the U. S., mullet roe commands $48 to $50 per pound (1974) in the retail outlets of Tokyo. This is sold in salted and dried form known as **karasumi.** It's estimated that the Japanese consume well over 12 million pounds per year. A similar product known as **bottarga** is popular in Italy, in North Africa as **botargo,** and in the Middle East as **batrakh.**

BAKED MULLET WITH SHRIMP STUFFING

6 whole fresh mullets,	1 tablespoon dried orégano
each 1 to 1¼ pounds	½ teaspoon salt
celery salt	dash of pepper
6 slices of bacon, diced	1 cup chopped cooked shrimps
½ cup chopped onion	2 eggs, beaten
¾ cup chopped celery	oil or butter or margarine
1 cup soft bread crumbs	(optional)

Scale and dress mullets, dry, and rub inside and out with celery salt. Make the stuffing: Fry bacon slowly until golden brown. Add onion and celery, and cook over low heat until tender. Add bread crumbs and seasonings. Mix shrimps and eggs and stir into stuffing to blend. Stuff each fish cavity with some of the mixture, and sew or skewer openings. Place fish on a sheet of greased heavy foil or brown paper on a baking sheet or pan. Bake in a preheated 500°F. oven for 10 minutes, or until browned. Reduce oven to 425°F. and bake for 30 minutes longer. West Coast Florida mullet is a fat fish and requires little basting during cooking, but East Coast mullet is lean and brushing with cooking oil or melted butter or margarine during baking is essential. Serve with horseradish or tomato sauce. Makes 6 servings.

SMOKY SEAFOOD SALAD

1½ pounds smoked mullet	⅓ cup mayonnaise
6 cups salad greens	or salad dressing
1½ cups drained	1 tablespoon sugar
cooked peas	¾ teaspoon salt
1 cup julienne-cut	¼ teaspoon pepper
Swiss cheese	¼ cup crumbled cooked bacon
1 cup thin red onion rings	6 cherry tomatoes

Remove skin and bones from fish. Flake fish. Combine salad greens, peas, cheese, onion rings and fish. Combine mayonnaise, sugar, salt and pepper. Pour dressing over salad. Toss lightly. Chill. Before serving sprinkle with bacon. Garnish with cherry tomatoes. Makes 6 servings.

Mussel

I have lived near rivers or the sea for most of my life and probably spent more time aboard boats than riding in an automobile. As a result fish or any other kind of seafood has, for the most part, a childhood genesis. I can remember the first time I ate an eel because my grandfather made me catch horseshoe crabs to bait the pots; these odd-looking marine relatives of the scorpion were no less puzzling than the eel itself, which though skinned and dressed managed to wiggle out of my grandmother's frying pan. There was literally nothing that came in its aquatic season that didn't have a role in her kitchen—with the exception of mussels. Seemingly the only reason for collecting these mollusks was to catch flounders. To this day, although mussels are abundant in New England and eastern Canada they have never enjoyed the popularity accorded in European cuisine. The mussel has for centuries been an ethnic food and in terms of American cookery of interest only to more sophisticated generations. When one

Blue or edible mussel

realizes that over 80,000 tons of **moules** are consumed in France alone each year, with Great Britain, Holland, Belgium, Spain, Portugal and Italy demolishing proportionately large amounts, the blue-bearded bivalve is an old-world passion. Number one producer of mussels is Spain, with 140,000 metric tons per year. In second place is Holland with 98,000 tons, mostly collected from the parks in the Waddenzee. All of the significant Spanish production comes from the Galician *rías* (bays, inlets), especially the Ría de Vigo. The culture grounds are spread out in 10- to 50-acre plots. France and Italy follow, with the U. S. far at the bottom, producing only 3,000 tons worth only $66,000.

Mussels are bivalve mollusks belonging to the marine family Mytilidae. There are other families occurring in freshwater, however only certain species of sea mussels are suitable for eating; by far the most common species is the **blue** or **edible mussel** *(Mytilus edulis)* which occurs in Europe and eastern North America as far south as North Carolina. The blue mussel has been introduced to our Pacific Coast where it supplements the California mussel *(M. californianus)*. The blue mussel can be recognized by its smooth shell which is generally dark blue in color, covered by a black epidermis, and the inside of the shell is pearly and margined in violet. Recent research shows that *M. edulis* is probably a worldwide species, with minor ecological variations or races. It is present in polar to cool temperate waters everywhere. The smaller scorched mussel *(M. exustus* or *Brachidontes exustus)* and hooked mussel *(M. recurvus* or *B. recurvus)* and the large horse mussel *(Modiolus modiolus)* are barely edible and vastly inferior to the common blue.

Two important species in the Mediterranean, *Mytilus galloprovincialis* and *M. edulis*, are exploited in Italy. *M. smaragdinus* or *M. viridis* is distributed throughout the western Pacific and Southeast Asia. In Thailand this **green mussel,** noted for its beautiful blue-green shell, is cultured for duck food; it is said that this mussel is used to feed the famous Peking ducks before preparation. In the Philippines it is known as **tahong,** and is used in soups and salads. It is also popular in Indonesia and Singapore. There are 12 species on the west coast of Australia alone.

Saltwater mussels are found in large colonies on gravel, rocks, seawalls—literally on any surface that will support them in the intertidal zone of all temperate seas. Along the North American Coast the mussel is particularly abundant in New England. The blue-black bivalves are bound to their beds with silken anchor threads. These byssus threads are secreted by the mussel and are composed of a protein which hardens upon contact with seawater. In ancient Greece the threads of the mussel were collected and woven into byssus gloves for the hands of fishermen. These gloves had to be kept wet or they would lose their durability. They were stored in buckets of seawater, and lasted so long they were handed down from generation to generation. They were truly indestructible, more so than any man-made fiber. Like the oyster, however, the mussel begins life as a free-swimming "spat" before settling down to community living.

Mussels are cultivated on a large scale in Europe. There are 2 widely used methods of growing these bivalves—by suspension between the surface and the sea bottom, and on the sea bottom by seeding. In the Mediterranean, particularly along the coast of France and Spain where there is little variation in tide, mussels are grown on ropes suspended from rafts or wooden frames built over the water. In the *bouchot* method stakes are driven into the sediments of shallow coastal beds where tide variation is not too great and where algae are present for mussels to feed on. The stakes rapidly become covered with mussel spat. This method was accidentally devised by an Irish sailor, one Patrick Walton, who was stranded on the coast of France in 1235. The stakes are tended and the mussels collected by shallow narrow boats called *acons,* which can be moved by a foot hanging over the side.

In Holland, the bottom method is used exclusively and the seed mussels are planted in "parks" which are essentially diverted ponds of 10 to 30 acres in size. The parks are built in rows at right angles to a channel to allow free water circulation without exposing the mussels to strong waves and tidal currents. Even a thin layer of shifting sand can suffocate these mollusks.

The flavor of the blue mussel is tangy, almost smoky, and the meat is extremely nutritious, containing about 12 percent protein, 2 percent fat and 4 to 8 percent carbohydrate. A mussel is relatively rich in vitamins, particularly A, and minerals such as iron, copper, calcium and phosphorus. However, these figures are correct only for the seasons when the mussels are in prime condition, i.e., not in post-spawning condition. As with clams and oysters, mussels can be toxic if taken from polluted water or when feeding on dinoflagellates such as the red tide plankter *Gonyaulax.* However, mussel beds are monitored, and shellfish beds are closed to fishing during those periods when harmful organisms are most likely to occur. In general the "off" season is during the warm months of the year when mussels are not really prime as a food in any case. Mussels are usually at their peak for eating during the fall, winter and early spring. In late spring and early summer they spawn and as a result are lean and watery, though still edible.

PREPARATION OF MUSSELS

The rules for preparing mussels are simple. Live mussels usually keep their shells tightly closed so when collecting your own discard those with open shells. However, mussels will "gape" if exposed to temperature changes (removing from refrigerator to room temperature); to test these for freshness, hold the mussel between your thumb and forefinger and press laterally as though sliding the 2 shells across one another. If the shells move the mussel is not fresh. A live mussel will remain rigid. Each mussel must be thoroughly scrubbed with a wire brush or plastic pot scrubber to remove the mud and grass that clings to the shells as well as the byssus or "beard." After cooking discard any mussels that have *not* opened their shells on the off chance that you overlooked a dead one.

Mussels are usually served in their shells, either whole or half shell, and the easiest way to eat them is with a small fish fork. The number to serve depends on the size of the mussels and their status in the meal, whether as soup, appetizer or main course. As an entrée in the common steamed *à la marinière* recipes, allow 18 to 24 per person if small and a dozen if large.

BILLI-BI (MUSSEL SOUP)

2 quarts mussels	1 tablespoon minced parsley
2 cups dry white wine	1 teaspoon freshly ground
6 tablespoons butter	white pepper
2 tablespoons	2 cups heavy cream
chopped shallots	¼ to ½ cup Hollandaise Sauce
1 tablespoon minced onion	(p.289, optional)

Scrub mussels, remove beards, and discard any that are open. Place mussels in a large saucepan with

the wine and steam until mussels open. Stir once to help all mussels open. Discard any mussels that have not opened. Discard shells, put the mussels aside for another dish, but turn all the juices into the pan. Strain juices through a cloth-lined sieve into another pan. Heat the butter and cook vegetables in it until they are tender but still pale. Add the mussel broth, pepper and cream and place over low heat, without boiling, until well mixed and hot. If necessary to thicken, add hollandaise sauce just before serving. Makes 6 servings.

Although billi-bi is traditionally served without the mussels, you can add the mussels just before serving if you like.

MOULES MARINIÈRE

4 dozen mussels, well scrubbed
4 cups white wine
1 medium-size onion, chopped fine
4 garlic cloves, chopped fine
4 whole fresh basil leaves, or 2 tablespoons dried basil
3 parsley sprigs
1 tablespoon fresh lemon juice
1 teaspoon coarse salt
1 teaspoon coarse black pepper
4 tablespoons butter
4 teaspoons minced parsley

In Anglo-French cuisine shallots are generally used instead of onion and garlic, and thyme with bay leaf is the herb essence in place of basil. However, this recipe is popular among Mediterranean fishing families.

Place the mussels in a large kettle with all ingredients except the butter and minced parsley. Bring to a boil, then cover and simmer until the mussels have opened. Remove the bivalves with a slotted spoon, discarding any that have not opened. Add butter to the liquid and raise the heat to reduce the liquid by half. In the meantime arrange the mussels in their open shells in warm bowls or soup plates. When the liquid is reduced pass it through a fine sieve into a smaller pan, then warm again over low heat and pour some directly over each portion of mussels. Sprinkle 1 teaspoon parsley over each serving. Accompany with crisp French bread. Makes 4 servings.

MOULES PROVENÇALE

Follow the recipe for Moules Marinière, but substitute 2 cups red wine and 2 cups tomato purée for the required white wine. A robust dry red such as Gigondas is favored. In addition to the parsley, grate Parmesan cheese over the mussels.

Mussels and other seafoods prepared in traditional ways, exhibited at the Norwegian Folk Museum (Folkemuseet) in Bygdøy, near Oslo

left, Seamen's church in Fanø, Denmark
right, top and bottom, Preparing needlefish
facing page, Poached needlefish in Jensen's Inn, Fanø

n

Needlefish

These elongate fishes with multitoothed beaks are not generally considered as a seafood in American cuisine, but they are very popular elsewhere in the world. The **hornfisk** is especially esteemed in Denmark where it is most often served fried, covered with a **Sauce Verte** and with boiled potatoes. It is also poached or marinated and served cold in aspic. Needlefish have green bones which may cause some apprehension on the part of the diner, but the flesh is lean and sweet.

There are several needlefish species in the Atlantic and also the tropical Pacific and Indian Oceans. Although common in the warm waters of the West Indian region, the Atlantic needlefish is abundant along the eastern seaboard of the United States as far north as Cape Cod.

It often penetrates freshwater. The related California needlefish of the cool waters of the eastern Pacific ranges as far north as Point Concepcion, California. The largest and most heavy-bodied of the needlefishes is the houndfish. It reaches a length of 5 feet and a weight of about 10 pounds.

Due to their slender shape, needlefish are skinned and cut into sections in the manner of preparing eels. They can be used in eel recipes. I have tried smoking needlefish, but being low in fat the end product is dry. Either the frying or poaching methods are recommended. Also known as **Horngjel** (Norway), **Hornfiskur** (Iceland), **Näbbgädda** (Sweden), **Hornhecht** (Germany), **Geep** (Holland), **Aguja** (Spain), **Aguglia** (Italy), **Peixe-agulha** (Portugal), and **Aiguille de Mer** (France).

Nelma

See INCONNU under WHITEFISH.

Norway Haddock

No relation to a haddock but a market name for the ocean perch. *See ROCKFISH.*

Ocean Perch
Ocean Pout
Octopus
Oyster

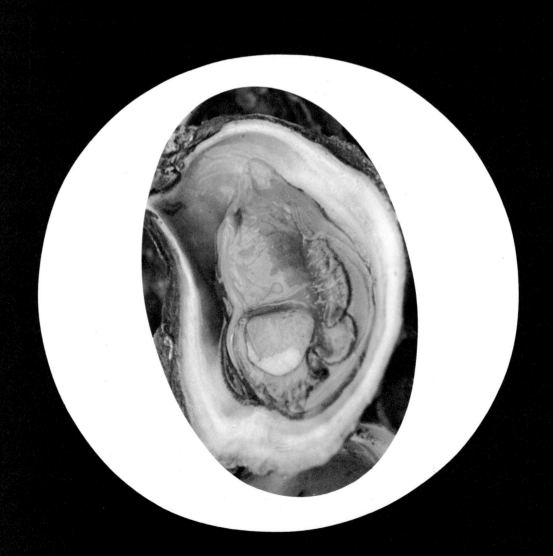

Ocean Perch

An important commercial species in the North Atlantic from the Gulf of Maine to Northern Labrador and in the eastern Atlantic from Iceland to Norway. As much as 200 million pounds are caught by American trawlers in one year, most of which is used in the frozen food trade, sold mainly as fillets and fish sticks. Also known as **sea perch, red perch, redfish, rosefish** and **Norway haddock,** the ocean perch *(Sebastes marinus)* is an Atlantic member of the rockfish group in the family Scorpaenidae. There is also a Pacific ocean perch *(Sebastes alutus)* which differs little in table quality. Neither species is a "perch." *See ROCKFISH.*

Ocean Pout

The ocean pout *(Macrozoarces americanus)* is a member of the eelpout family (Zoarcidae) which consists of about 18 species found mainly in the Pacific Ocean. This most common Atlantic representative resembles an eel in appearance but is easily distinguished by its larger mouth and the presence of small vertical fins attached to its throat in front of the large pectoral fins. It's usually brown to muddy yellow in color and sometimes identified as **yellow eel** and for no apparent reason a **muttonfish** or **congo eel.**

The ocean pout occurs from the Gulf of St. Lawrence south to Delaware Bay and occupies a wide range of depths to 500 feet. It migrates inshore during spring and offshore with the beginning of cold weather. Ocean pout attain weights to 12 pounds, but most of those caught by anglers are 1½ to 5 pounds in size. Large quantities are taken by commercial trawlers but the species is largely underutilized despite past and present attempts at its popularization.

The flesh of the ocean pout is sweet and white, and has few bones. It can be poached, made into chowder, or battered and deep-fried. Direct heat cooking tends to dry out the meat.

Octopus

The commercial catch of octopus is of minor value in the U. S., largely because of the "horror" movies and much maligned reputation of this relative of the snails, clams and oysters. Our market is limited to people of Chinese, Japanese, Spanish, Portuguese, Italian and Greek descent, who consider the octopus a rare delicacy. There is some demand for octopus in New York and San Francisco, especially around the Christmas holidays when small quantities are shipped from southern California and imported from Portugal. These octopuses generally run three to a 10-pound box, which is considerably smaller than the Hollywood kind.

The octopus is actually a mollusk in the class Cephalopoda. Like the squid, an octopus can discharge clouds of ink which take the shape of a dummy or "phantom" octopus, an illusion used to fool its attackers. It has a flexible, nearly globular body with 8 long arms covered by suction cups, and these tentacles are used to capture crabs and lobsters or to pry loose abalones. Octopuses also eat clams and scallops. With such a selective diet inevitably the meat of the octopus is equally flavorsome and is generally compared to chicken. Its meat is very valuable and is one of the more costly seafoods elsewhere in the world. A great deal of research is being done to cultivate the octopus artificially as at least some species grow very rapidly, having a life span of less than 1 year which makes their mariculture commercially feasible.

Octopuses are caught by many methods but the most common trap is the "devilfish pot," a deep, cone-shaped wicker basket with a mouth in the shape of a funnel. These pots are usually baited among rocks about a mile offshore in 100 to 200 feet of water in the California fishery. Practically the entire commercial catch consists of the common Pacific octopus *(O. dofleini)* which is found from Baja California to Alaska and east to Asia. The Atlantic octopus *(O. vulgaris)* occurs along our coast from New England to the Gulf of Mexico. This is a worldwide species and found in all tropical and warm temperate seas. It provides a vast trawl fishery off the northwest coast of Africa where Japanese and Spanish refrigerator ships buy most of the local catch. In Hawaii, where both the **puloa** and the **he'e** are popular foods, these octopuses are taken at night by torch fishing and during daylight hours with a lure made from a cowrie shell.

Octopuses are marketed in fresh and frozen forms, usually gutted with the eyes removed. In raw form the firm and delicate white meat is an integral part of **sashimi.** They are also sun-dried in Japan as **hoshi dako** or pickled in vinegar after boiling as **sudako.** Japan is the world's largest consumer, incidentally, utilizing 72,000 tons of octopus per year. Some of this is smoked and canned as an export product (obtainable in the U.S.), but it is too often rubbery in texture and tasteless. In Spain and Portugal the octopus is cut into chunks and stewed (if not literally) in a wine sauce, then served over saffron rice. It's also prepared in the style of **seviche,** known in this case as **pulpo vinagrete,** with bite-size pieces marinated in lime juice, vinegar and spices, to which chopped onions and peppers are added. Most Mexican recipes require that the octopus be cooked in its own ink, and in fact the dried ink sacs are purveyed separately as a seasoning for other seafood dishes.

OCTOPUS PRELIMINARIES

An octopus at market is invariably predressed. If you have caught your own, invert the octopus (it can be turned inside out like a sock) and cut away the beaks in the mouth region, removing these with the viscera. Remove or leave the ink sac according to recipe. The skin is perfectly edible. Bear in mind that like all cephalopods, octopus is *not* tough despite the fact that some people feel it necessary to tenderize the meat by pounding it. The Spanish method of dipping the octopus into boiling water assures a perfect result; hold the octopus by the mantle and dip the body and tentacles into boiling water for several seconds, then lift it out to cool slightly. A minute or so later, dip it again for 4 or 5 seconds and withdraw it once more. When it has cooled a second time, lower the octopus into the pot in water to cover and reduce the heat to simmer. Allow to cook for 1 hour. The octopus, which is now tender, can be cut into chunks or pieces according to recipe requirements. This process of dipping, as opposed to submerging the octopus in boiling water, denatures the protein gradually and when left to simmer it will not toughen.

Also called **Poulpe** (France), **Pulpo** (Spain), **Polvo** (Portugal), **Polpo di scoglio** (Italy), **Octapodi** (Greece), **Ma-dako** (Japan), **Ahtapot** (Turkey).

Oyster

He was a bold man that first eat an oyster.
—Jonathan Swift,
Polite Conversation,
Dialogue II

Over 70 million pounds of oysters are ingested by brothers of the raised elbow each year; however you prorate this sum of lip smacking, the vitamin-charged bivalve is clearly a national habit. Worldwide consumption in 1973 for all oysters was a whopping 1.67 billion pounds! The American record for oyster consumption belongs to Bobby Melancon who downed 188 bivalves in the 1-hour time limit allowed at the Louisiana State Oyster Festival held at Galliano in 1972. Louis XIV was said to consume a hundred or so at one sitting. Casanova reputedly ate fifty or more every evening. According to legend that noted glutton, James Buchanan Brady, once downed 156 Cape Cods before dinner, with the result that Broadway dandies concluded that oysters were the secret of success. So the ancient belief of virility on the half shell made the rounds. Actually, this concept of raw seafoods has existed among primitives for centuries. The Indians of British Columbia still eat the gonads of male salmon, just as our East Coast tribes once consumed the oyster. Doubtless a headcandler could find the association, but clinical researchers will only admit that the oyster is a healthier appetizer than powdered rhinoceros horns or beetles of the genus *Lytta.*

To my grandfather, an oyster was a delicate bud in the field of papillary joy. As a sailing man he knew the sea intimately, and when he settled down to his life on Shinnecock Bay in the 1920s it was with a wry wisdom about things that grew under water. He was hopelessly lost in a dirt garden, but he had aquatic gardens, clam and oyster beds, and submerged wooden pastures for the blue crabs and lobsters. These were crops he understood. Grandpa's idea of relaxation was to sit on the end of our dock with a pail of freshly raked oysters, shucking and swallowing until the sun went down. I don't know whether Brady debauched his bivalves with ketchup or not, but Grandpa was a purist. He elevated them neat, with the slow elbow salute of a man who knew the good things in life. We always had pearly mounds of fat Shinnecocks on the table. The bay bottom directly in front of our house was ideal bedding ground, being firm and sandy and easy for Grandpa to work. Some parts of the bay, especially down toward Ponquogue, were quite muddy, and here the oysters would sink vertically and grow into long, narrow shapes which the old man cared little about. And Grandpa never let his oysters crowd on the shell bed because then they grew small and distorted; he raked them apart about once every 3 months. The shells he originally used for bedding came from a scrubbed and sun-dried mound which had collected behind our boat shed over a period of years. These shells were the pivotal point in the whole operation in that the "spat" or larva of an oyster must arrive on a clean, hard surface or else they are unable to attach themselves and they die quickly. In a month, the larvae become seed oysters about ¼ inch long; many marine farmers buy year-old seeds when starting new beds instead of leaving breeding to chance.

The cultivation of oysters began more than 2,000 years ago when Romans collected the bivalves at Brundisium (Brindisi), which is located on the Italian "boot" near the mouth of the Adriatic Sea, and transplanted them to the region of Lucrino. The Japanese are often credited with pioneering oyster culture, but the first historical record is from Hiroshima in 1620. The stone and bamboo branch culture methods began some time between 1624 and 1643. However, the Japanese did pioneer in cultivating clams, working at this as early as 746 A.D.

The Romans had such a passion for oysters that they imported them from all over the Mediterranean and European coasts. These were shipped in special amphorae containing seawater, and in the second century they began packing oysters in ice. Oysters do not prosper on the ocean bottom but in bays and river mouths where the salinity of the water has been diluted to some extent by tributary streams or rivers. The bivalve flourishes best in brackish water (a salinity of less than 18 parts per thousand on the Brunelli scale) because in higher salt concentrations it becomes subject to predation, particularly by starfish and oyster drills, and disease. But growth is relatively slow in brackish water so the commercial farmer uses the low saline areas for his seed stock and plants this in saltier water; under optimum conditions Gulf oysters, for example, will grow from the larval stage to 5 inches across the shell in 11 months. The average life span is about 3 years, although some oysters do survive to 10 to 12 years. In colder temperate waters, the American oyster may live to 20 years. In northern waters where the growing season is shorter, such as the Cape Cod area, the technique of "off-bottom" oyster culture is to suspend the bivalves on nylon strings which are tied to racks. The string is initially threaded with scallop shells which catch the oyster larvae. The spat grow to market size in suspension above the bay bottom safely away from predators. This produces a meaty thin-shelled oyster in 2 to 3 years as opposed to the usual 4 to 5 years. Depending on water temperature and food source, they may reach market size in 1½ to 2 years.

Natural oyster beds are found in varying depths; they grow through the intertidal zone, and in subtropical areas they even grow on the aerial roots of mangrove trees and marsh grass where they are only covered by water at high tide. There is a mangrove oyster (*Crassostrea rhizophorae*), called the **Caribbean cupped oyster,** or in Venezuela *Ostras mangles*. The small and delicate **chipi chipi** of Venezuela is a mangrove product, but it is not an oyster. *C. rhizophorae* is somewhat similar to the **coon oyster,** once abundant in Florida where they

are known as coon oysters because, like Samuel Johnson's cat, the raccoon is a four-legged oyster fiend. This proximity to freshwater determines the flavor of the oyster to a large extent, because the bivalve is a vegetarian; its main food source is minute one-celled plants known as diatoms. In feeding, an oyster pumps and filters as much as 25 gallons of water every 24 hours. The diatoms, like other marine plants, are nourished by various minerals in the water, such as copper, iron and iodine, which are reflected in the oyster's food value, flavor and color. In France, oysters in the Seudre River estuary ingest large quantities of the diatom *Navicula ostrearia* which tinges the meat green. This *Navicula* is cultured in small ponds called *clairières*, where the oysters are fattened and greened for the market. At first this may seem a bilious color but their flavor is so esteemed that green oysters bring the highest possible price on the Paris market. They are known as **Marennes,** which is the name of a coastal village where the bivalves are bedded. (Marennes oysters are protected by special provisions of French law wherein the bivalves must come from a carefully defined area of beds to be so labeled. This *Appellation Contrôlée* inspired a group of wine experts who were lunching in Marennes to discuss the confused labeling in their own industry to apply the same authentication to wine labels. For some years with the exception of Alsatian wines and Champagne all others had to be printed in green (no longer enforced) in honor of the Marennes oyster. —Charles Gauthier, Personal Communication) But no matter where you seek an oyster, there are none better than those found on our own Atlantic Coast, along which this rich Lucullan fare grows under the influence of countless rivers. In world production the U. S. leads, producing 301,000 metric tons according to the latest figures. Next in production comes Japan, followed by France, Denmark, Netherlands and Canada. The U. S. production peaked in the 1920s when over 100 tons of *meats* were taken. Maryland had until recently the largest oyster harvest of any state in the Union, with an annual production of 3 million bushels; this is probably not so today as there have been many failures of the oyster crop of the East. Nearly 3,500 boats work Chesapeake Bay.

The oyster native to Pacific waters is the small one known as the **Olympia.** It rarely reaches 2 inches in length, and is regarded as a real delicacy. The other oyster in this region is a much larger one. The **Pacific** or **Japanese oyster** attains a shell length of a foot or more; because of its greater tolerance to very salty waters, it is often bedded far from the influence of rivers. Its natural habitat is the intertidal region. This Pacific oyster doesn't breed easily in the cold water of the Northwest, consequently young or seed oysters are imported annually from Japan to maintain the stock. The end product, however, is of no great moment to the gourmet; in flavor and appearance these imports are decidedly inferior to Eastern oysters, which are airlifted daily to West Coast markets. What appears to be one of the few successful mariculture operations in the U.S. is located in northern California. They are culturing "Long Island Blue Points" from spat shipped from New York. Some years when the mean summer temperature is low, Japanese oysters retain their spawn and become unpalatable.

Although all oysters are edible during their spawning season or the months without an "r" in them, the production of glycogen (an animal starch) is excessive at that time, giving the meat a milky appearance and a *blah* taste. Northern oysters are at their best in the fall and winter months, while Gulf bivalves are firm and ripe from December onward.

The ideal way to eat an oyster, and certainly the first way a toddling child must be taught to know them, is on the half shell. Preferably, it should be a crisp fall day when the wind is stirring the marsh grass and the old man has let you put out the decoys for the first time. You sit together and watch the banks of low scudding clouds from daylight until breakfast. Just when you decide to eat, the black ducks come across the horizon flashing creamy white under their wings. They bank toward the decoys with their bright orange feet lowered for a landing and then in a wave of suspicion they flare up and the old man says, "Now," and you both stand to take them passing high. He spills a pair and that's it. The old man says that the real flights will start later, so he gets a rake and a pail out of the skiff and tongs the shell mound under the decoys. Dumping the rough clutch in the skiff bottom, you sort out the bivalves that have been fouled by sponge and jingle shells and knock loose the clean ones. They must not be too big. Big "box" oysters belong in the oven. Half-shell oysters are no longer than the span of your palm. There's a box of soda biscuits and 4 lemons in the game bag. While the old man runs a dull, thin blade through each oyster, you set up 2 rows of crackers and lemon wedges on the stern seat. When you separate the shells, their pearly insides are fragrant with the nectar of a salt marsh, the meats firm yet tender, with just a suspicion of sweetness. A splash of lemon to brighten their flavor and down they go. Maybe they're the vigorous **Tangiers, Patuxents, Chincoteagues, Kent Islands, Blue Points, Cape Cods, Albemarles,** or the grand seigneur **Abascon.** It doesn't really matter at this moment.

Although the purist will take his oysters *au naturel*, an urban palate jaded by months of steam-heated living looks to the bivalve as a prelunch catalyst. There is some justification in this, insofar as the consumer is in no condition to appreciate a fresh oyster and the oyster is seldom in a condition that fulfills his destiny. In effect, one has become as dull as the other. The compromise is met in a spicy sauce designed to revitalize both. For my part this can be eliminated completely. The gentleman who avoids "cocktail sauce" is a chevalier dauntless in the tottering cause of gourmandizing.

OYSTERS AT MARKET

There are 10 species of oysters which enter the world's markets in volume, but only four are found along the shores of North America. Of these, by far the most common is *Crassostrea virginica*, variously known as the **Blue Point, Cape Cod, Chincoteague, Apalachicola, Kent Island,** *ad infinitum.* The best of all for my palate is the **Indian River oyster** of Florida; it is without peer, but unfortunately its beds are so small that it hardly supplies local demand. Estuarine environments in terms of habitat and food supply influence the shape of an oyster, its ultimate size, and the characteristics of the meat. In its natural state an oyster may grow large or small, with the shell flat or deep and rounded; the color of the meat will vary from pearly to beige or in another spectrum from pale gray to green, with a flavor from neutral to sweet and even acidly sharp. Thus, oysters are identified by locality. Europe, for example, has 2 species of oysters, the most common being the **Flat** or **Plate oyster** *(Ostrea edulis),* which in the British Isles is marketed as the **Whitstable, Colchester, Pyefleet, Helford,** and so on. In addition to the **Marennes,** France has its **Belons** from Britanny, which is probably the finest oyster in that country, but again we are still speaking of *O. edulis.* The second and distinctly different species of Europe is the **Portuguese oyster** *(Crassostrea angulata),* which though common at market is not as refined in taste as the Marennes or Belons. The flat or plate oyster is native to Brittany and was eaten there for many years. The Portuguese oyster was more popular but unavailable. In 1868 a ship with a cargo of *C. angulata* seed, for planting in more northern waters, was forced to wait out a storm at the mouth of the River Loire. Here they decided, as a matter of expediency, to dump overboard dead and dying oyster seed. Hence, a bed of the oysters was established, which has flourished since, outperforming the flat oyster by far, and becoming the greatest producer of oyster meats in the area. Today Brittany is known for its Portuguese oysters. When cultivated in fattening ponds or *clairières* the oysters may also be designated as

Blue Point

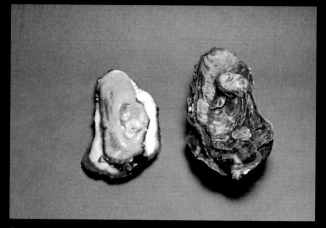

Chincoteague

Cotuit

Belon

Apalachicola

SOME EXAMPLES OF OYSTERS

Kent Island

Malpeque

Box

New Orleans

Wellfleet

Claires or *Spéciales.*

Species is less of a factor than origin and season as far as the U. S. is concerned. Our native Pacific oyster, the **Olympia oyster** *(Ostrea lurida),* and the introduced **Japanese oyster** *(Crassostrea gigas)* are not harvested in a volume to be marketed on more than a local level; in fact our East Coast variety is shipped to major western markets to supplement the demand. There are other species of *Ostrea* found in western South America, Australia and New Zealand, which are regionally important. Other important species are the **slipper oyster** *(C. eradelis)* of the Philippines and the **Sydney rock oyster** *(C. commercialis).*

Oysters are marketed fresh in the shell, or as shucked meats iced in containers, frozen shucked meats, sun-dried (China and Japan), smoked and canned in edible oil, fresh meats packed in brine and canned, and in the form of soup, stew and bisque, either frozen or canned.

By size oysters are usually sold in the U.S. as small, medium or large, but in Europe they are often marketed in a numerical system according to individual weight. The lightest oyster is designated as a No. 5 to 0 with the heaviest oysters at 00 000. Nobody except a local expert really understands this system as shell weight doesn't always indicate the size of the meat.

HOW TO SHUCK AN OYSTER

Oysters are lamentable travelers; to be palatable they must be perfectly fresh, with the shells firmly closed. They should be stored at a temperature of 41° to 48°F. If you buy them without shells the liquor should be clear. If the natural juice is milky in color do not use them. A fresh oyster, according to Montaigne, has the faint smell of violets; anybody with even rudimentary nostrils can detect a "bad" oyster. To shuck an oyster, hold it firmly with the hinge part of the shell in the palm of your hand. Push the blade of a thick, round-nosed oyster knife between the shells near the hinge and run it around until you cut the muscle that holds both valves together. If you shuck the oyster over a strainer placed on a bowl, the liquor that drains through can be used for cooking. The strainer will catch those tiny particles of shell which inevitably break loose. Admittedly, shucking is a skill that requires practice, so much so that the Irish recognize it as a sporting event. I once interviewed the so-called World's Champion Oyster Shucker, Johnny Commins, at Paddy Burke's Pub just outside of Galway.

Despite its being camouflaged behind two gas pumps, Burke's purveys the finest oysters in the Ol' Sod. While munching hot-from-the-oven coarse-grained bread,

lathered with freshly churned butter and heaped with strips of oak-smoked salmon, which we washed down with dark, frothy Guinness stout, Mr. Commins demonstrated how he achieved his record 50 bivalves in 2 minutes, 42 seconds. He uses a razor-sharp penknife instead of the orthodox dull-bladed oyster knife; although he bleeds occasionally, Commins explained that everybody gets punctured when working against the clock. A hint of blood on an oyster, he added, brings minus points. The best shuckers are the Belgians and the French, according to the champ. Next to the Irish, of course. This annual vendetta held in the village of Clarinbridge is cause for a week-long festival. A ton of oysters is a mere appetizer and with all that virility on the half shell, everybody goes home feeling like a Charles Atlas.

In the 1975 oyster-shelling championship in Paris, sponsored by The Intercontinental Oyster Growers Committee and Club Prosper Montagné (named after the compiler of *Larousse Gastronomique* and author of many books on cookery, a club naturally devoted to gastronomy), the winner, a Breton in his sixties, opened 100 Breton oysters in 4 minutes and 8 seconds. However, the record for shelling 100 oysters is 3 minutes, 37 seconds! We don't know the age of this master.

OYSTERS ON THE HALF SHELL

Fresh oysters on the half shell should be served on crushed ice in bowls or oyster plates. They are best when served absolutely cold. The standard mixture or dip is made with 2 teaspoons prepared horseradish, 3 tablespoons tomato ketchup, ½ teaspoon salt, 2 tablespoons vinegar, 4 tablespoons lemon juice, and ¼ teaspoon Tabasco. Mix these ingredients thoroughly and serve in small shallow glasses—if you must.

If your wallet can accomodate eccentric impulses, the best way to dress a bare oyster is with caviar. My first introduction to **Oysters à la Czar Nicholas** was through actor Guy Kibbee. He was a trencherman of the first rank, manning the kitchen with an economy of motion that reflected years of outdoor cookery. The one great luxury he allowed himself was caviar-wiped oysters. Nothing excited his circumvallate papillae like the clear ambrosial meat of an oyster married to delicate sturgeon eggs. Guy's favorite stand was the Grand Central Oyster Bar; he reasoned that New York's temple of transportation did such a volume of business their bivalves had to fresh. To make Guy's Caspian answer to ketchup: Bed your half-shell oysters in dishes of cracked ice and put them in the freezer while you grate an onion. Remove chilled dishes and sprinkle a bare teaspoon of grated

HOW TO SHUCK AN OYSTER

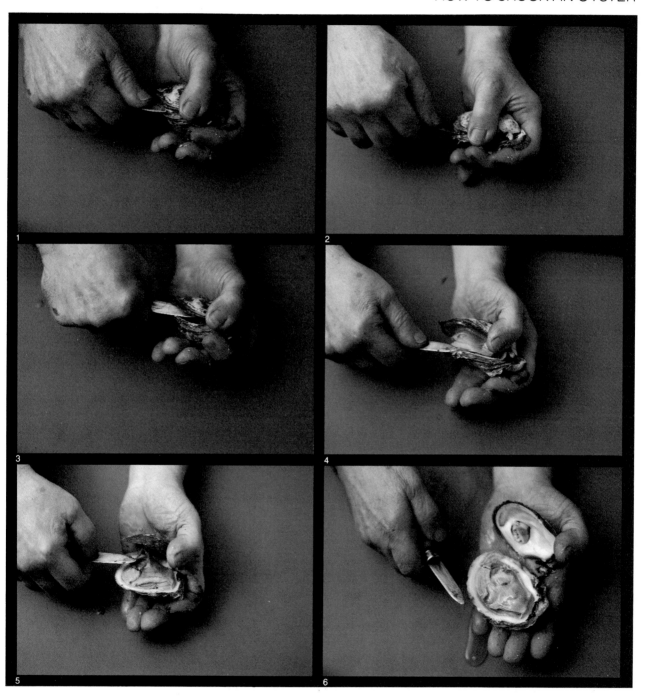

1. Hold oyster firmly with hinge part of shell
in palm of hand. 2. Push the blade of a thick oyster
knife between the shells near the hinge.
3. to 5. Run the knife around until you can cut the muscle
that holds the valves together. 6. The oyster opened.

HARVESTING OYSTERS ON THE GULF COAST

Oysters are brought up in an oyster dredger,
which is opened on board to release the catch. Shells are
often stuck together and need to be knocked apart.
facing page, Oysters are graded and bagged.

onion on each oyster meat, then a teaspoon of caviar over the onion. Garnish each dish with wedges of lemon or lime, which you will use sparingly over the caviar.

HOW TO COOK OYSTERS

The common tendency is to overcook oysters. Assuming that you start with large fresh ones, always bear in mind that an oyster should be removed from the heat just as its edges start to curl. Working from the basic premise that a cooked oyster must have a complementary meat or vegetable to enhance its texture, most recipes are developed primarily around the use of chopped greens and bacon. This can be varied, with the use of chicken, veal, turkey or chicken livers, but the great secret in making any cooked oyster dish on the half shell is in how you prepare them before they are put into the oven. The answer is pans of coarse salt. I use ordinary round baking tins filled with salt on which I place the oysters. The salt keeps the shells upright so that they retain all juices, and it keeps the shells hot to the moment of eating.

The first cooked oyster dish that amateur chefs usually attempt is **Oysters Rockefeller.** French Quarter *vivants* of old New Orleans will remember this as **Huîtres à la Montpellier.** The Rockefeller appellation was conceived because of the supposed richness of the ingredients. Actually, **Oysters Rockefeller** are not overbearing in the butterfat sense, but the combination of vegetables provides a full measure of body. The oyster permeates New Orleans cuisine; aside from Rockefeller, which originated at Antoine's, there are also **Oysters Ellis, Oysters Roffignac, Oysters Bienville** and **Oysters Grand Lake Style.** Sharing the wealth of this seafood oasis are restaurants such as Galatoire's, Brennan's French Restaurant, Dunbar's, Kolb's, Manale's, and a galaxy of Gallic halls of gastronomy. New Orleans has a magnetic attraction for the gourmet; bear in mind when you visit Louisiana that this part of our coast creates not only exceptional oysters, but a symphony of regional delights in her shrimps, sea trout, pompano and crayfish. The critical ichthyophagist will avoid such foreign items as clams or scallops, because these are usually shipped from the north. Both are found in Gulf waters, but they are inferior when grown beyond their coldwater habitat. The oyster, however, is an exception. The great bayous emptying into the Gulf feed their particular diatoms to a large distinctive bivalve, which Creole cooks worship in Grand Lake style. The ingredients are somewhat more piquant than those used in the Rockefeller, which is in keeping with Creole cookery.

PENSACOLA OYSTER GUMBO
(Manuel Francisco Gonzalez VI)

This ancient dish is special to Pensacola, but it is also made in Mobile. It has been handed down from generation to generation. It is a winter gumbo, more influenced by Spanish and Indian cookery than the gumbos of Louisiana.

1 quart shucked small or medium oysters in their liquor	6 scallions
	7 black Java peppercorns
	9 allspice berries
1 fowl, 7 pounds, with giblets	6 parsley sprigs
salt	3 tablespoons bacon fat
white pepper, Malabar preferred	1 bacon slice, minced
	3 tablespoons flour
1 yellow onion, 6 to 8 ounces	1 cup dry red Bordeaux wine
4 large garlic cloves	3 tablespoons fresh gumbo
1 red Spanish onion, or white Bermuda onion, 4 ounces	filé powder

Cut up the fowl; pull out and discard any lumps of fat; mince the giblets (liver, heart, gizzard). Sprinkle cut-up pieces with salt and white pepper and set aside to reach room temperature. Chop the yellow onion and 2 garlic cloves, and set aside in a bowl.

Chop the red onion and remaining garlic cloves. Trim scallions, leaving 1½ inches of the green top on each one; chop. Set remaining green tops aside. Put the red onion, 2 garlic cloves and chopped scallions in a second bowl. Add to the second mixture the peppercorns, allspice and minced giblets. Tie the parsley sprigs and half of unchopped green scallion tops in a piece of cheesecloth. (Remaining scallion tops are not used for this recipe.)

Put bacon fat and minced bacon in an 8-quart cast-iron pot. Bring a kettle of water to a boil. Put the iron pot over medium heat; the heat is critical as the roux must be as hot as possible without being scorched. Heat the pot until the bacon pieces are shriveled; then gradually shake in the flour, stirring all the while. Keep heating and stirring until the roux reaches the color of strong coffee with cream, 2 to 3 minutes. If the roux seems about to scorch, lift the pot from the heat for a moment, but never stop stirring. Add the bowl of yellow onion and garlic and keep stirring. When onion is translucent but not wrinkled, add the chicken pieces and keep stirring until the pieces are all brown and the roux absorbed. Each chicken piece should brown on the bottom of the pot for part of this step. All this while be sure that nothing is scorched. Pour enough boiling water into the pot to more than cover the chicken; keep stirring. Add the contents of the second bowl—red onion, garlic and scallions—and ⅓ cup of the wine. Tie the cheesecloth bag to the pot handle so that it dangles in the liquid. Add more water, almost to the top of the pot, stir, and bring to a boil. Let everything boil hard for 30 seconds, then reduce to a simmer and cover the pot.

Let the gumbo simmer until the chicken is tender, but not falling off the bones, about 2 hours. Stir occasionally. Meanwhile check the oysters to be sure they are free of shell particles, and taste one to check on the saltiness. Let oysters reach room temperature. When chicken is tender, add oysters and their liquid. Reduce heat further, to a bare simmer. Adjust seasoning if necessary. Add the rest of the wine, then slowly sift in the filé powder, stirring thoroughly all the while so there are no little lumps of filé but all is mixed in. Turn off the heat.

Serve on fluffy white rice in deep bowls, with red Bordeaux wine. Accompany with gazpacho salad and bowls of very hot fresh peppers. Let each person add hot peppers to taste to the gumbo. Makes 8 servings with seconds.

NOTE: Filé, or gumbo filé powder, is made from dried young leaves of the sassafras tree. Originally made by Choctaw Indians, the powder has long since become basic to Creole cookery. It adds a faint herby flavor, but the main use is to add thickening to gumbos. The French word comes from the verb meaning "to spin," and filé powder can become stringy if gumbo is boiled after the powder is added. For this recipe "fresh" is specified—powder that has been freshly made, not packed in a tin to lose its flavor on the market shelf; not easy for cooks to find outside the Gulf area.

MINCED OYSTERS

4 dozen oysters with liquor	1 tablespoon flour
1 tablespoon butter	3 egg yolks
parsley, chopped fine	2 cups light cream
chives, chopped fine	or rich milk
thyme, chopped fine	6 large croutons,
1 can (4 ounces)	buttered
sliced mushrooms	

Scald the oysters in their own juice. Drain, reserving some of the juice, and mince oysters but not too fine. Put the butter into a saucepan; when melted, add parsley, chives and thyme to taste, and the mushrooms. Mix the flour smooth in some strained oyster juice, and add to the herbs. Mix thoroughly, then add the minced oysters and stew gently until the sauce is absorbed and the mince forms a thick batter. Be careful not to scorch. Re-

move from heat and add the egg yolks mixed with cream. Return the pan to the heat for about 1 minute, then serve on large buttered croutons, with garnish of lemon and parsley. Makes 6 servings.

OYSTER FRY

1 pint shelled oysters,	⅓ cup flour
fresh or frozen	2 cups soda cracker crumbs
2 eggs	5 tablespoons
2 tablespoons	butter or margarine
evaporated milk	5 tablespoons cooking oil
¼ teaspoon salt	lemon wedges

Thaw frozen oysters; drain. Beat together the eggs, evaporated milk and salt. Dip oysters into egg mixture, then lightly into flour. Dip into egg mixture again, then roll in cracker crumbs. Let stand for 5 to 10 minutes before frying. Heat butter or margarine and oil in a large frypan over moderate heat. Fry oysters, turning once, for 5 to 7 minutes, until lightly browned. Garnish with lemon wedges. Makes 6 servings.

OYSTERS WITH CHICKEN LIVERS EN BROCHETTE

2 dozen large oysters	4 slices of crisp toast
1 dozen chicken livers	1 teaspoon lemon juice
7 tablespoons butter	2 teaspoons chopped parsley
salt and pepper	lemon wedges
4 slices of bacon	

Drain oysters, saving the juice. Sauté livers slightly in 3 tablespoons of the butter seasoned with salt and pepper. Crisp the bacon and put aside. Arrange livers and oysters alternately on skewers and broil until the oysters curl. Cover each slice of toast with livers and oysters. Make a sauce in the sauté pan by adding oyster juice to taste, the lemon juice and remaining butter. Pour this over oysters and garnish with bacon, parsley and lemon wedges. Makes 4 servings.

OYSTERS À LA POULETTE

2 dozen oysters	salt and pepper
1 cup milk or light cream	cayenne
for each ½ cup	nutmeg
oyster juice	2 egg yolks
1 tablespoon butter	½ teaspoon lemon juice
2 tablespoons flour	parsley, chopped

Shuck oysters, saving all the juice. Heat the oysters in the juice. As they commence to boil, turn them

LOUISIANA STATE OYSTER FESTIVAL, GALLIANO

facing page, Who can eat the most oysters in one hour?
Even the fishing boats are decorated for the festival.

into a strainer, keeping the liquor in the pan. For each ½ cup of oyster juice add 1 cup of milk or cream. Add butter and flour, mix well, and season with salt, pepper, cayenne and nutmeg to taste. Beat the egg yolks and add a dash of milk or cream to them. Put the oysters in the sauce over heat, then add the egg mixture and stir diligently. In about 3 minutes over low heat, the sauce will thicken, so remove immediately to prevent separating. When ready, add the lemon juice. Serve with a border of boiled rice, and garnish with chopped parsley. Makes 4 servings.

ANGELS ON HORSEBACK

4 dozen large oysters, shucked
24 thin slices of bacon, cut into halves
2 cups Thin Fish Batter (p. 94)
peanut oil
toast triangles, buttered
12 lemon or lime wedges
parsley

Wrap each oyster in a half-slice of bacon and skewer with a metal or wooden pick. Dip oysters into the batter and deep-fry in peanut oil heated to 375°F. for about 4 minutes, until batter is golden brown and oysters cooked to your taste. Serve arranged on a platter, with buttered toast triangles, lemon or lime wedges, and parsley garnish. Makes 6 servings.

BAKED SCALLOPED OYSTERS

Scalloped oysters should be puffy and moist, crunchy on top. Use only fresh oysters; to keep them big and juicy, arrange them only 2 layers deep in a shallow aluminum baker. A good dish for a special but easy-does-it Sunday-night supper.

1½ pints oysters
  with their liquor
¼ pound butter, melted
2 cups medium-coarse
  cracker crumbs
pepper

½ cup light cream or half-
  and-half, approximately
½ teaspoon salt
¼ teaspoon
  Worcestershire sauce
dash of Tabasco

Drain the oysters, but save the liquor. Pour the butter over the crumbs and toss together lightly with a fork. Butter a shiny 8-inch layer-cake pan 1¼ inches deep. Spread one third of the crumbs on the bottom, and cover with half of the oysters. Sprinkle with pepper. Add another third of the crumbs, the rest of the oysters, and another sprinkle of pepper. Combine saved oyster liquor and enough of the cream to make 1 cup. Stir in salt, Worcestershire and Tabasco; pour over oysters. Top with last third of crumbs. Bake in 350°F. oven for 40 minutes. Serve at once, very hot. Makes 4 servings.

OYSTERS ROCKEFELLER

36 large oysters, shucked
rock salt
1½ cups tightly packed
  fresh spinach
¾ cup tightly packed
  parsley leaves
¾ cup chopped scallions,
  including green tops
6 shallots, chopped

3 tablespoons chopped
  fresh fennel leaves
½ pound unsalted butter
2 tablespoons anchovy
  paste
Tabasco
1 cup fresh bread crumbs
½ cup Pernod or Ricard
salt and black pepper

Drain oysters, saving and straining the liquor. Scrub and dry deep halves of shells and arrange in 6 pans filled with rock salt. Place an oyster in each shell. Put vegetables through a food grinder or purée in a food processor. Melt butter over low heat and cook vegetables for 5 minutes. Stir in anchovy paste, several dashes of Tabasco, and bread crumbs. Cook, stirring, until well mixed and thick. Add oyster liquor or more crumbs to adjust thickness. Add Pernod, seasoning to taste, and more Tabasco if you like (this is a hot dish). Spread sauce over oysters. Bake in a preheated 450°F. oven for about 5 minutes and serve at once. Makes 6 servings.

Pacific Pompano
Paddlefish
Paella
Pasteurized Fish
Pavon
Perch
Periwinkle
Pickerel
Pickled Fish
Pike
Pompano
Porgy
Prawn
Prickleback
Puffer

Pacific Pompano

The Pacific pompano *(Peprilus simillimus)* is not a pompano but a member of the butterfish family, Stromateidae. It is found from British Columbia to Lower California and is sometimes called **California pompano.** It is the Pacific counterpart of the Atlantic butterfish *(Peprilus triacanthus).* As the common name implies, butterfish are quite fat; while delicious in their own right, they are not comparable to the true pompano in texture and flavor. Butterfish make an excellent smoked product.

Paddlefish

When Hernando de Soto discovered the Mississippi River in 1541, "there was a great store of fish in it of sundry sorts, and most of it differing from the fresh water fish of Spain." Members of the expedition, fishing with nets, included in their catch "the Pelefish, destitute of scales, and with the upper jaw extended in front a foot in length, in the form of a peel or spatula." *(Journal of Travels in the Arkansas Territory in the Year 1819*, with occasional observations on the manner of the aborigines, Thomas Nuttal, Palmer, Philadelphia, 1821) The paddlefish, and its Asian counterpart found in the Yangtze River system of China, are the only living representatives of a group of fossil fishes that thrived in the Eocene period. The American paddlefish *(Polyodon spathula)* is somewhat sharklike in appearance, with a skeleton composed chiefly of cartilage and a flattened snout that grows larger with age. However, the paddlefish is a harmless creature as it simply swims about with its mouth open, straining water through its gills to collect planktonic crustacea and other small animals on which it feeds. Except for a very small patch of scales on its tail, the paddlefish is smooth-skinned. Although it can attain a length of 8 feet and weight of 200 pounds, the usual fish caught is about 4 feet long and 20 pounds in size. The commercial fishermen of the Mississippi usually refer to the paddlefish as a "spoonbill cat," but it's not related to the catfish; as a food, it more closely resembles the sturgeon.

Paddlefish are still found in the Mississippi drainage system, although they have declined in the upper river where the slow currents created by a series of dams have silted their former spawning grounds. They are more numerous in the Missouri River into Montana, and in the large impoundments of both Missouri and South Dakota where extensive gravel bars and flowing water in large tributary streams provide suitable areas for reproduction. Many thousands are caught each year by "snagging," a legal and strictly controlled method, since they do not take a bait.

The meat of the paddlefish is comparable to sturgeon, being very firm with a beeflike rather than a fish texture. It's most delicious and can be baked, broiled or smoked. The greenish-black eggs of the female have been used extensively as a caviar substitute *(see CAVIAR).*

Paella

The paella of Spain is a dish that is always subject to argument as to contents. Few Spaniards agree on what the components are in a "correct" paella, as it's a regional preparation and some provinces include large amounts of seafood. A **Paella Valenciana,** which curiously enough appears on menus throughout the world, is never made with fish in Valencia, despite its being a seaport town. I say "never" in the formal sense, as the local classic only permits the addition of snails to the basic chicken, rice, green peas and beans. There is always somebody willing to throw in a rabbit, squid or eel as the appetite demands. While salmon and trout fishing in Spain, I've had the pleasure of sampling paellas from one coast to the other; although I can't recall but one or two that married poorly, it would be impossible to say that the ingredients were always alike. Half the fun in making and eating a paella is the contrast of textures and flavors among foods that are not ordinarily combined. Traditionally, paella is cooked on a wood fire and there's even some dispute as to the *kind* of wood to use. Pine is obligatory, but whether the Aleppo, Corsican or stone pines provide a more subtle smoke flavor is beyond my palate. For that matter, Spanish cedar, evergreen oak and beech are used in the mountain provinces by choice or chance.

Although a paella can be made in any large iron skillet, it's infinitely better when "constructed" in that wide, shallow pan designed for the job also called *paella*, or *paellera*. These are sold in a variety of sizes; the most practical is one big enough to contain a sufficient volume of ingredients for 8 people, as paella is a classic party dish. (Spanish *paellas* or *paelleras* can be found in import shops and in gourmet cookware shops made of

facing page, Scup, a porgy

HOW TO MAKE PAELLA (prepared by Chef José Luis Rojo at La Barraca Restaurant, Madrid)

1. Assemble ingredients.　　**2.** Cut grouper into chunks.　　**3.** Cut goosefish tail cutlets into chunks.

4. Cut squid into rings.　　**5.** Prepare spiny lobster, lobsterettes and shrimps.　　**6.** Cut lobster into medallions.

7. Slice and dice ham.　　**8.** Slice veal and pork and cut into chunks.　　**9.** Roast red peppers and peel off skins.

10. Cut peppers into slices.　　**11.** Cut chickens into 8 pieces.　　**12.** Fry chunks of pork and veal in olive oil.

13. Sprinkle rice into paella pan.

14. Sprinkle peas over rice.

15. Place chunks of fish, whole shrimps and squid rings on the rice.

16. Ladle pork, veal and ham pieces over all.

17. Pour tomato sauce and cooking liquid over.

18. Bring liquid to a boil.

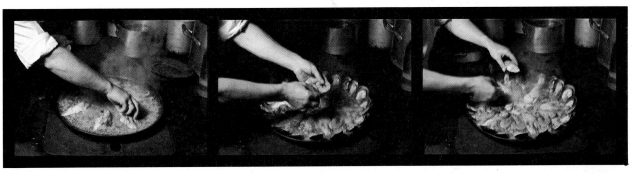

19. Arrange chicken pieces in the pan.

20. Place mussels around the edge and add lobsterettes.

21. Add medallions of spiny lobster.

22. Add red pepper rings.

23. Pour in rest of tomato sauce.

24. Bake for 15 minutes.

various materials—copper, steel, aluminum, iron; however, a large gratin dish of stainless steel or ceramic-coated cast iron or sheet steel will serve. Any substitute pan should have heatproof handles.)

In theory one could make an authentic seafood paella in an American kitchen. The 7 ingredients of aquatic origin occur around our shores and enter the market. However, the range of the goosefish (which see) or at least its centers of abundance does not overlap the grouper in the western Atlantic and no similar species occurs in the eastern Pacific. With luck both fish might be found in a worldwide market, like the Fulton Fish Market in New York, but it's easier to consider the options. What the grouper and goosefish have in common is that they are both very firm white-fleshed fish. Soft-fleshed fish do not hold up well in making a paella, and oily species tend to overpower the flavor of the meat ingredients (pork, veal, ham and chicken). So the American regional alternatives would be cod and halibut, grouper and snapper, tilefish and cod, or any combination thereof.

One of the most outstanding seafood paellas is made at La Barraca Restaurant in Madrid. Chef José Luis Rojo has prepared for us this classic version:

PAELLA

(La Barraca Restaurant, Madrid, Spain)

2 pounds mero (grouper)	½ ounce saffron shreds
2 pounds rapes (goosefish)	2 tomatoes
2 pounds mussels	2 large garlic cloves
2 pounds fresh shrimps	2 cups olive oil
1 pound squid	1 ounce paprika
1 large langosta (spiny lobster)	1½ pounds uncooked rice
1 pound langostinos (lobsterettes)	
1 pound ham	
1 pound veal	
1 pound pork	
2 small chickens	
½ pound sweet red bell peppers	
½ pound fresh green peas	

Prepare the ingredients and set everything aside until later. Fillet grouper, wash, and cut into medium-size chunks. Remove tail cutlets of goosefish and soak in water; cut into medium-size chunks. Scrub mussels. Shell and devein shrimps; leave them whole. Clean squid and cut into rings. Boil spiny lobster and let it cool. Smack the shell with a heavy knife to crack it; peel off shell, and cut lobster meat into chunks. Boil whole lobsterettes, let them cool, and shell them.

Slice ham thick and cut into squares. Slice veal and pork and cut into small chunks. Cut chickens into 8 pieces. Roast red peppers, and peel off skins; cut peppers into slices. Cook green peas in water, and drain. Put whole saffron into ½ cup hot water and let stand. Slice tomatoes, and peel and slice garlic.

Combine fish chunks, mussels in shells and shelled shrimps in 1 quart water in a large pot. Bring to a boil and simmer for 5 or 6 minutes. Remove fish and shellfish from pot and set aside. Leave water in pot. In the same water used for seafood, boil the chicken pieces for 7 or 8 minutes. Remove chicken from water and cool, but leave water in pot. Fry the chunks of pork and veal in the olive oil. When done lift out meat and leave oil in the pan. In the same oil fry the tomato and garlic slices, saffron (with liquid) and paprika. Cook to make a sauce. Put the veal and pork chunks and the ham squares into the sauce, and simmer.

When all ingredients are prepared, sprinkle rice into the paella pan, and sprinkle peas on the rice. Place chunks of grouper and goosefish, whole shrimps and rings of squid on the rice. Ladle pork, veal and ham pieces on the rice, and pour sauce over. Pour in the water used to cook fish and chicken. Put the pan over direct heat and bring liquid to a boil. Meanwhile, arrange chicken pieces, whole lobsterettes, pieces of spiny lobster, red pepper slices and mussels decoratively on the top and around the edges of the paella pan. Let the liquid boil for no longer than 4 or 5 minutes.

Place the *paellera* in a preheated 400°F. oven and bake for 15 minutes. From the moment when the paella begins to boil and the last ingredients are added, no more than 20 minutes should pass. Remove pan from oven and boil on top of the stove for 1 more minute. Makes 12 to 16 servings.

Pasteurized Fish

Fresh fish and other seafoods (especially crab meat, oysters, scallops and caviar) packed in hermetically sealed cans or glass jars and preserved by heating at temperatures below 212°F. (100°C.) to kill most spoilage bacteria. Fish may also be pasteurized by irradiation from radioactive isotopes or an electron source. Pasteurized products must be chill-stored at 33° to 35°F. (1° to 2°C.) and never frozen. The process extends shelf life while retaining some of the quality of a "fresh" product, particularly with respect to texture, as opposed to the release of free liquid from the meats during sterilization in regular canning methods.

facing page, Paella at La Barraca Restaurant, ready to eat

The author, with peacock bass, a pavon, caught on the Orinoco

Pavon

The purpose of my first trip to the Orinoco watershed in 1956 was to do some exploratory fishing for the Venezuelan government. At that time the jungle was still in a pristine state, with lush rain forests rising above the mountains and spilling their greenery down to the arid *llanos*. When I went back last year it was still as beautiful as I remembered it, with its incredible bird life and flowering trees. Herons stand patiently at their fishing while dusky skimmers do their quadrille over the sun-burnished surface. Game is not often sighted along these serpentine

streams when traveling by outboard, but the sandbars were rutted with tapir, capybara and deer tracks. Jaguar and ocelot are still numerous in the *quebradas* and huge red howler monkeys roar incessantly, sounding more like the jaguar is expected to sound than the grunt and female scream that typifies a big cat. The only disturbing sign was the tide rows of cayman carcasses where migratory Indians had camped. The Orinoco crocodile has already been almost destroyed, and the cayman, a relative of the alligator, is fast disappearing. The great majority of carcasses were from the little speckled cayman; ten years ago an Indian wouldn't bother to strip a hide much under 6 feet long, and the once common 10- and 12-foot black cayman are no longer seen. A speckled hide is worth $2.00, which buys a lot of rice and oil in port towns. Similarly fated is the manatee or sea cow, whose porklike meat was formerly an important food to the Indian. Manatees are now nearly extinct in both the Amazon and Orinoco. Even the river turtles whose eggs were once collected by the millions are feeling the pressure. A trio of Indians who stopped at our camp reported that it was a very bad year indeed, as the water level rose too early and killed the eggs warming in the sandbars. After seeing the empty beer cans bobbing in the back eddies of the Orinoco, and the new hydroelectric impoundments far to the north, the sun-bleached carcasses of the cayman symbolized an inevitability which made me sad.

For living things to exist in a hostile world, nature provides defensive mechanisms of all kinds. In the jungle, if it doesn't bite, sting, poison, puncture or fight back, it may simply fly away as in the case of the little hatchet fish. Even the common black palm is so covered with evil thorns that walking in the bush can be a painful experience for the unwary traveler. Nature was most generous in designing the piranha with its razor-edged tricuspids in jaws so powerful that the fish bites like an animated scalpel. It's not likely that you will have occasion to cook a piranha but it would be remiss not to mention these highly edible fish in the sense of a survival food. I have eaten a great many piranha, and their firm white meat is very delicate in flavor. I know of at least one resort in the interior of Brazil with the unlikely name of John F. Kennedy Hotel, situated on an island in the Aguario River, which serves deep-fried piranha to its guests quite regularly, so the experience is not unique.

In the same rivers where piranha occur we also find the brilliantly colored pavon, one of the finest freshwater fish in the world from a culinary standpoint. How the comparatively docile pavon survives among the piranha is not pertinent to a cookbook; it's sufficient to know that these basslike fish do appear to some extent in South American markets and restaurants. The problem is to identify the pavon under its various local names.

Pavon are South American tropical freshwater fishes of the family Cichlidae, also known by the Indian name **tucunaré** (pronounced too-koon-a-ray). Pavon occur from Colombia to central Brazil and principally in the Orinoco and Amazon watersheds. There are 8 or more species in the genus *Cichla*. They generally resemble a black bass in shape but are more brilliantly colored in golden yellow and red with dark bars or spots. One species known as the "peacock bass" reaches weights exceeding 25 pounds. These are all superior foodfish with very firm, white to cream-colored meat. Although pavon did appear at one time in South American restaurants they are seldom utilized now, due to overfishing and an effort to maintain the existing stocks. In 1966 I served pavon at a press reception in New York's Abercrombie & Fitch; the buffet was prepared by the kitchen of the 21 Club. Despite a large offering of many unique fish and game dishes, the pavon disappeared in a matter of minutes.

Pavon have been introduced to the Panama Canal and thrive there in large numbers. Attempts to establish one or more species in Florida and Texas—which is an ongoing project—suggest that this finest of all South American freshwater fish may possibly have a future role in our culinary scene.

Perch

As a common and market name perch is used for a number of unrelated marine and freshwater species, but specifically perch are members of the family Percidae which occur in North America and Europe. These are essentially freshwater species although some are found in areas of low salinity such as the Baltic Sea. The European perch *(Perca fluviatilis)* is somewhat larger but otherwise similar to our yellow perch *(Perca flavescens)* and may be synonymous. Other members of the perch family include our walleye and sauger and several closely related species found in Eurasia.

The so-called white perch *(Morone americana)* of North America is a member of the Percichthyidae, or temperate basses, which includes the striped bass and giant sea bass. Other species which are not perch are the ocean perch *(Sebastes marinus)* which is a popular foodfish in the U.S., and the various surfperch and seaperch of our Pacific Coast which are members of the Embiotocidae. The name **perche** is applied to numerous

snappers in coastal West Africa, while the Nile perch *(Lates niloticus)* belongs to the Centropomidae represented by the snook of Florida. *See WALLEYE, WHITE PERCH, YELLOW PERCH.*

Periwinkle

These are small snaillike mollusks belonging to the family Littorinidae. There are nearly 300 species known throughout the world but relatively few of these reach edible sizes. Winkles live in large colonies in freshwater, brackish and marine environments, clinging to rocks, pilings or wharves. They can be found from the lowest tide level to the highest as the mollusk has gills modified for breathing air. Winkles are vegetarian in habit, feeding on the thin film of diatoms and other algae covering the substrate of the intertidal zone. The shell is a conical spiral with whorls, often marked with beautiful colors. The common edible marine periwinkle *(Littorina litorea)* was originally found in the European Atlantic but has spread around the eastern coast of North America from Canada during the past two centuries, passing Cape Cod a little over 100 years ago. It now occurs as far south as Delaware Bay. This olive to gray, brown or red banded winkle grows to about 1 inch in height and diameter. Its distribution overlaps with our equally large native species, the southern periwinkle *(Littorina irrorata)*, the shell of which is yellowish in color and spotted in brown. The southern periwinkle is also edible.

Roasted in the shell, winkles were once hawked on the streets of London, and they are still purveyed both in cooked and uncooked form in Great Britain's markets. Northern European countries utilize about 5,000 tons annually. Periwinkles are generally and collectively known as **bigorneaux** (plural) in French cuisine, but provincially the mollusk is called **vignot** in Brittany and **brelin** in Normandy. Winkles are cultivated to some extent in France. A very minor quantity is harvested along U.S. shores; although available the year round, our peak season is in July and August. The bulk of landings is sold through the Fulton Fish Market in New York.

Periwinkles are delicious when simply boiled in salted water until the "lid" of the shell, or operculum, falls open. The meats can be picked out with a pin and dipped into melted butter.

Also known as **Bigorneau** (France), **Bígaro** (Spain), **Burrié** (Portugal), **Chiocciola di mare** (Italy), **Strandsnegl** (Denmark and Norway), **Strandsnäcka** (Sweden), **Strandschnecke** (Germany), **Pŭzić** (Yugoslavia), **Tamakibi** (Japan).

Pickerel

(1) In popular but erroneous use, a North American market name for the walleye and closely related sauger; both are sold as "yellow pickerel" or "yellow pike." These fish are actually members of the perch family and have finely textured flesh with few bones or none when properly filleted. *See WALLEYE.*

(2) The true chain pickerel, a member of the pike family, was a commercial species of some importance in our Boston market until the 1920s. It only appears today in the sport fishery. Pickerel have softer flesh and a needlelike bone structure which requires a special method of filleting (facing page). *See also Chain Pickerel under PIKE.*

Pickled Fish

Although the term "pickled fish" is widely used for fish cured in brine by the commercial trade, it can also be applied to those products in which vinegar is one of the major ingredients. Herring is the most common species for pickling, but practically all foodfish, both freshwater and saltwater, as well as bivalves and shrimps, can be pickled by home methods. Mackerel, mullet, alewife, catfish, pickerel, lake trout, pike, eel, carp, buffalo, as well as shrimps, oysters, scallops and mussels can be made into excellent products.

There are 3 general methods of pickling fish. The first, known as **seviche,** is really a marinated fish product with a very limited shelf life and not applicable to many species. The other 2 methods have a wider range of uses and according to the length of cure may preserve the fish for up to 6 months under cold storage. The second is the short method which is used when only small amounts, say 6 herring, are to be served within 1 week of the time they are caught or purchased. Actually many seaport restaurants around the Baltic prepare their herring in this style because of the ready availability of fresh fish in season and the rapid turnover in the amounts prepared. Usually the herring is cured for no more than 2 hours, then spiced for about 3 days. This short cure is sufficient to preserve the fish, which is consumed almost immediately after spicing.

The third or extensive method is for volume pickling when you may not have a constant supply of fish, or when you plan to use them over a period of time—from 60 to 90 days. This requires a longer cure which varies from 3 to 5 days and gives a product similar to herring found in markets. To stop bacterial growth completely, an acetic-acid content of 15 percent would be necessary, but most commercial vinegars contain 5 percent, and even this is too strong for the average palate. However, pickling solutions that contain as little as 3 percent acetic acid will retard spoilage for a week or more, and the product may be held for several months if stored at a temperature below 50°F.

Distilled white vinegar is preferred for pickling since it has a standardized acid content and does not contain any residues or seasonings that may impart odd flavors to fish. The spices used should be fresh. It's best to buy whole spices and make up the required amounts at the time of processing rather than to use already prepared mixtures.

SEVICHE

Peruvian in origin, but Latin American in popular acceptance, *seviche* (pronounced seh-*veech*-ee) is one of the simplest forms of pickling. This is usually accomplished with the citric acid of fruits rather than acetic acid and is short term in preparation and shelf life. Although the classic *seviche* of Peru is made with either corvina or bay scallops, any lean and even some fat fishes can be made into a delectable pickle. There is no standard recipe, but it's a simple dish to prepare. It consists of bite-size pieces of fish marinated in lemon or lime juice, with each layer alternated with sliced onion rings, flaked red pepper, black peppercorns and a bay leaf. Other than corvina and bay scallops an excellent *seviche* can be made from black bass, walleye, red snapper, weakfish and lake trout. Start with skinless fillets, slicing them crosswise into ½-inch strips, then cut the strips into ½-inch cubes. The amount of spices to use and the choice of seasonings depends entirely on your own taste. Some chefs add the fiery touch of jalapeño peppers or slices of red and green bell peppers or strips of pimiento for color, but the onion rings, flaked red pepper, black peppercorns and bay leaf are used in the basic original *seviche.* This is left to stand in a glass or stone container in the refrigerator for 24 hours and the citric acid literally "cooks" the fish, which loses its translucence and turns snowy white. However, if you are faced with supermarket citrus, it could be a costly process to obtain enough juice to cover even 1 pound of fish. I have both lemon and lime trees just outside my kitchen and infinitely prefer the Key lime or Persian lemon, but when fruit becomes scarce in summer I use half white vinegar and half fruit juice. There may be a qualitative difference but it's slight.

Seviche makes an excellent hors d'oeuvre, served drained and chilled in small bowls with food picks, or on shredded lettuce leaves *au naturel,* or combined with sour cream.

Chain pickerel

HOW TO FILLET PICKEREL AND PIKE

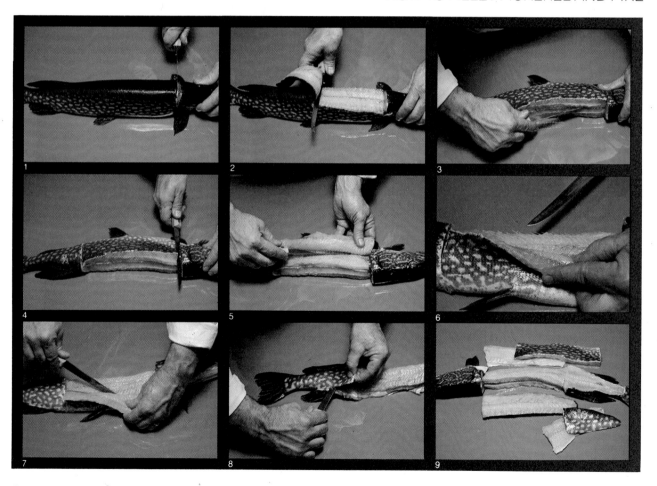

1. Scald fish to remove slime and loosen scales. (The fish in these pictures is a Northern pike; it has been scalded but not scaled.) Place fish belly down; at the back of the head make a vertical cut to the backbone. **2.** Run blade along the backbone until you reach the dorsal fin; lift up blade and remove the boneless fillet. **3.** Lay fish on its side with exposed spine toward you. Find the Y-shaped bones above the spine. Above this row of bones make a horizontal cut about ½ inch deep from head to tail. **4.** Make a vertical cut to backbone in front of the dorsal fin and a second vertical cut behind the head.

5. With the fingers lift the loosened edge; as you lift cut deeper, sliding the blade over the Y-shaped bones; continue to lift and cut until fillet is released. **6.** Turn fish over, still with the exposed side toward you, and repeat the shallow horizontal cut above the second row of Y-shaped bones. **7.** Make the vertical cuts to backbone, and lift and cut until second fillet is released. **8.** To release the smaller tail fillets, slide knife along the backbone from cut portion to tail. **9.** The bony remains with the 5 fillets. Skin the fillets. Be sure to save the liver of the pike.

EXTENSIVE METHOD

Commercial salt herring may be pickled in vinegar but fish not especially cured for spicing will be darker in color and more fibrous in texture, and often as not they will lack flavor. Assuming that you start with fresh herring, dress the fish by gutting, making certain to remove the dark strip (kidney) along the backbone. Wash the fish thoroughly in fresh water and drain. Pack the drained fish loosely in a stone crock and cover with a brine testing 80° sal (⅝ cup salt to 1 quart water) and enough vinegar to provide an acidity of 2.5 percent, which is half the amount of water used in the brine. The herring should remain in the brine at a cool temperature for 48 hours but must be removed before the skin starts to wrinkle or lose color. The length of the cure depends on the temperature of the brine and the freshness and size of the fish. As in smokehouse cookery, determining variables comes with experience but the 2-day cure is a "safe" period. The herring are next removed from the brine and soaked in cold water for 8 hours to desalinize, then drained.

The fish are now ready to process according to recipe. If they are to be stored for future use (within 2 to 3 weeks) scatter dry salt over the herring and repack in the crock more tightly. Cover the herring with a diluted brine at half the strength given. Freshen in cold water for 8 hours and drain thoroughly before using.

GLASMÄSTARSILL
(GLASSBLOWER'S HERRING)

Cut the vinegar- and salt-cured herring across the body into pieces 1 to 1½ inches long. Pack in a crock in layers with sliced onions, bay leaves and spices. Cover with vinegar diluted with water in which the sugar is dissolved. Allow to stand in a cool place for at least 24 hours before using. The cut spiced herring may be repacked in pint or quart glass jars. If packed in jars the herring may be stored in a refrigerator where they will remain in good condition for as long as 6 months. Add to each jar a few fresh spices, a bay leaf or two, and a slice of lemon at the side of the jar to give an attractive touch. Rubber jar rings cannot be used, since they are attacked rapidly by vinegar. The quantities given are sufficient for 10 pounds of herring.

vinegar	4 cups
water	2 cups
allspice	3 ounces
bay leaves	2 ounces
mustard seeds	2 ounces
black peppercorns	1 ounce
white peppercorns	1 ounce
sugar	1 ounce
cloves	½ ounce
red onions, sliced	½ pound
carrots, peeled and sliced thin	½ pound

For a smaller amount of herring using a slightly different pickle, see the recipe later in this entry.

ROLLMOPS

The vinegar- and salt-cured herring are cut into 2 fillets and the backbone is removed. Each fillet is then rolled around a small sweet pickle and fastened with a wooden food pick. The rolls are packed on end in a crock. Sliced onions, bay leaves and the spices used in the following sauce formula are scattered on the bottom of the crock and between layers:

Cook 4 cups vinegar, ½ pound sliced onions and 1 ounce sugar slowly in a pot until the onions are soft. Then add:

mustard seeds	1 ounce
black peppercorns	1 ounce
stick cinnamon, cracked	1 ounce
whole gingerroot, cracked	1 ounce
bay leaves	1 ounce
cloves	½ ounce
dill, chopped fine	¾ cup

This quantity is sufficient for 10 pounds of herring. The sauce is simmered, not boiled, for 45 minutes. The spices are strained out to pack with the rollmops. The sauce is cooled, then poured over fish until the fish are covered. Allow to stand for 2 or 3 days before using. When serving, garnish with red onion rings and dill sprigs.

RUSSIAN SARDINES

Wash and scale 10 pounds of small herring (7 to 10 inches), remove the gills and as much of the intestines as possible, and pull them out through the gill flap without tearing the throat or belly. Rinse again, drain, and pack in a crock. Cover with 3 parts distilled vinegar and 1 part water. Allow to stand for 12 hours. Make up a mixture of the following ingredients (the spices should be ground fine and thoroughly blended):

fine salt	2 pounds	bay leaves	½ ounce
powdered sugar	1 pound	cloves	½ ounce
allspice	1 ounce	ginger	½ ounce
pepper	1 ounce	nutmeg	½ ounce
saltpeter	½ ounce		

HOW TO MAKE ROLLMOPS (prepared at the Jan Schmidt Fish Market, Rotterdam, The Netherlands)

1. Ingredients are simple. **2.** Place shredded onion, a wedge of pickle and a bay leaf on a herring fillet. **3.** Roll up. **4.** Fasten with wooden food pick. **5.** Rolls ready to be placed in pickling solution. **6.** Rollmops and other fish products on display in Jan Schmidt's, which is the largest fish shop in the country.

1.

2.

3.

4.

5.

6.

After the fish have drained, coat them with the mixture and pack belly up in a crock. A small additional amount of the mixture may be scattered between the layers. The layers should be packed at right angles to each other, with the top one packed backs up. Scatter the balance of the spice-curing mixture over the top layer, and weight it so that the fish will be entirely covered when the brine forms. Some people also scatter diced onions, ground or sliced horseradish, and capers between the layers. The amount required for 10 pounds of small herring is ½ pound onions, ¼ pound horseradish and a small bottle of capers (about 2½ ounces). The fish are allowed to cure for 10 days to 2 weeks before using. Under proper storage conditions they should keep for several months or longer.

ESCABECHE

This recipe is of Spanish origin, coming down from Roman times. It's extremely popular throughout Latin America. There are many local variations in the spices used but they are all founded on this basic recipe. Mackerel, tuna and corvina are the most widely used species, but almost any fish can be made into *escabeche* provided the musculature is not too soft. The following ingredients are sufficient for 10 pounds of dressed fish:

olive oil	as required	red peppers	1 tablespoon
onions	to taste	cuminseeds	½ tablespoon
vinegar	4 cups	marjoram	½ tablespoon
bay leaves	2 tablespoons	garlic	to taste
black pepper-corns	1 tablespoon		

Cut the fish into small individual portions. Wash thoroughly, drain, and place in a 90° sal brine for 30 minutes. Wipe dry. Pour olive oil into a frying pan together with a minced garlic clove, 6 bay leaves and a few red peppers. Cook the fish until light brown in color, then remove from the pan to cool.

Add the onions to the oil and cook until yellow. Add whole black peppers, cuminseeds, marjoram and vinegar. Cook slowly for 15 to 30 minutes, then cool. When the fish are quite cold, add the rest of the bay leaves and red peppers and pack into sterilized jars. Fill with the sauce and close tightly. This preparation may be used the next day, but it will improve with storage. *Escabeche* has a shelf life of 3 weeks or more if held in the refrigerator.

PICKLED CLAMS, OYSTERS AND MUSSELS

Scrub the shells well, then steam just enough to open the shells. Save the liquor or nectar. Remove the meats from the shells; cool meats and nectar separately. When cool, pack the meats in sterilized jars with a few bay leaves, whole cloves, and a slice or two of lemon in each jar.

Strain the liquor obtained in steaming. To each 4 cups of liquor add 1 cup distilled vinegar, ½ tablespoon each of cloves, allspice and red pepper, with 1 teaspoon of cracked whole mace. Simmer for 45 minutes. When cool, pour into the jars of meats and seal. Store in a cool dark place. Pickled oysters and mussels are easily "light struck" and turn dark if exposed to the light.

PICKLED SHRIMPS

Peel, devein, and wash 10 pounds of shrimps. Make a brine of 1 gallon water, ½ cup salt, 2 cups distilled vinegar, 1 tablespoon red pepper, 1 tablespoon white peppercorns, ½ tablespoon cloves, ½ tablespoon allspice, ½ tablespoon mustard seeds and 6 bay leaves. Simmer slowly for 30 minutes, then bring to the boiling point and add shrimps. When the brine again comes to a boil, cook the shrimps for 4 minutes. Remove shrimps and allow brine to cool. Pack shrimps in sterilized jars with a few fresh spices and a slice of lemon in each jar. Fill the jars with a solution made of 4 cups water to 2 cups 6 percent distilled vinegar and 1 tablespoon sugar. Seal jars tightly and store in refrigerator.

PICKLED EELS

Clean and skin the eels, and cut into pieces about ⅝ inch long. Wash, drain, coat with fine salt, and allow to stand for 1 hour. Rinse off the salt, wipe the pieces dry, and rub with a cut garlic clove. Brush with melted butter or salad oil, and broil until the surface of the pieces is light brown. Place pieces of cooked eel on absorbent paper. When cool, pack them in layers in a crock with a scattering of sliced onion, allspice, bay leaves, mustard seeds, whole cloves, peppercorns and mace between the layers of fish. Then weight the mixture to keep it compressed. Store the crock for 24 hours. Add 6 percent distilled vinegar in proportion of 3 parts vinegar to 1 part water sufficient to cover the pieces. Cover the crock tightly, and allow to stand 48 hours before using. For 10 pounds of eels the ingredients are as follows:

distilled vinegar	6 cups	cloves	½ ounce
water	2 cups	black pepper-corns	½ ounce
allspice	1 ounce		
bay leaves	1 ounce	mace	½ ounce
mustard seeds	½ ounce		

GLASMÄSTARSILL (GLASSBLOWER'S HERRING)

3 large salt herring, cut into fillets (total weight 1½ to 1¾ pounds), or the equivalent in small salt herring	1 cup water
	12 thin slices of carrot
	12 thin slices of leek, white part only
	2 small red onions, sliced thin
1½ cups sugar	2 teaspoons mustard seeds
½ cup white vinegar	2 teaspoons peppercorns
5 whole allspice berries	4 sprigs of fresh dill
2 bay leaves	

Desalinize the herring in cold water for 12 hours. Cut the fillets crosswise into 1½- to 2-inch-thick slices. Combine the sugar, vinegar, allspice berries and bay leaves in the water in an enamelware or stainless-steel saucepan. Bring to a boil and simmer until sugar is dissolved. Let cool to room temperature.

Arrange the herring slices in layers in a large glass bowl or Mason jar. Top each layer with slices of carrot, leek and onion. Sprinkle with mustard seeds and peppercorns, and add a sprig of dill on each layer. Pour the pickling liquid over the herring and refrigerate for 48 hours. (This will keep for about 1 week.) Serve as an appetizer.

NOTE: There are many variants of Glassblower's Herring which require more or less vegetables, spices or acid in the pickling solution. The famed Solomon Gundy of the Canadian Maritimes is essentially the same concept with the difference that 3 cups of white vinegar is used and no water to ¼ cup sugar, which makes a "sharp" rather than a sweet pickle. The Norwegian version, **Sursild,** is even sharper with about 2 tablespoons sugar to the same volume of vinegar. Carrot, leek and red onion are typically Swedish.

These differences reflect the cost of sugar as well as the availability of vegetables in rural areas; most of the sea herring's range is in regions with a very short growing season where cold-resistant cabbage and cauliflower are major crops, or in regions adjacent to permafrost lands.

PICKLED EELS

3 pounds eels, skinned and cut into sections	⅛ teaspoon celery salt
vinegar	4 sprigs of fresh dill
juice of 3 lemons	1 tablespoon unflavored gelatin
2 bay leaves	sliced lemon, fresh dill or parsley for garnishing
salt and pepper	
4 whole allspice berries	

Place eels in a pot with water and vinegar to cover, using 1 part vinegar to 3 parts water. Flavor liquid with all the ingredients except gelatin and garnishing. Cook slowly till the eel is soft; remove the meat and let it cool. Reduce the broth for a few minutes, remove from the heat, and add the gelatin. Stir until the gelatin is dissolved. Strain this over the eel. Chill in the refrigerator until set.

Turn out on a chilled platter; garnish with lemon and fresh dill or parsley. Slice and serve at table. Makes 6 servings.

PICKLED WEAKFISH FORTMEYER

2 to 3 pounds weakfish fillets with skins on	4 bay leaves
	6 to 9 whole cloves
¼ cup salt	1 tablespoon pickling spices
1½ cups vinegar	2 medium-size onions, sliced
3 tablespoons sugar	sour cream (optional)

Mix salt, vinegar, sugar, bay leaves, cloves and pickling spices. Heat to dissolve the sugar and salt. Simmer for 5 minutes and cool. Cut the weakfish fillets into strips 1 to 1½ inches long. Separate onion slices into rings. Put fish and onions into a glass bowl, and cover with the cooled marinade. Refrigerate for 4 to 5 days before using.

If you prefer a sour-cream dressing, drain the fish after pickling, and cut strips into bite-size pieces; fold in as much sour cream as you like. Marinate for 2 to 3 days longer.

PICKLED OYSTERS

3 dozen small oysters	½ teaspoon ground dried chili
2 cups vinegar	12 peppercorns
12 small white onions	2 teaspoons salt
3 chili peppers, sliced	

This is a recipe that you can easily double or triple because these won't last long.

Put the vinegar in a large jar, then add onions, chili peppers, ground chili, peppercorns and salt. Place oysters in a bowl and pour boiling water over them; let them sit for about 5 minutes. Drain oysters and put them in the pickle jar. Cover the jar and leave in the refrigerator for 72 hours. Serve cold as an appetizer.

Pike

Although the pike is identified with just one classic dish in French cuisine, the much maligned **quenelles de brochet,**

Northern pike

through the centuries a "roast" pike has been synonymous with the higher arts of fish cookery. In Europe today, it's a fish of country inns where a fresh pike taken from the local river is immediately added to the *carte du jour* or reserved by the *traiteur* for some special client. Only the Baltic nations and those countries bordering polar barrens have a sufficiency of pike to purvey on a commercial level. Canada has a tremendous resource and harvests approximately 6 million pounds annually, most of which is shipped to Europe and a lesser amount to the U.S. The fact is that pike are greatly underrated as a food in North America, yet the meat is sweet, white and firmly flaked. Tremendous quantities are caught in the U.S. by sport fishermen, but comparatively few are familiar with pike cookery beyond panfrying. The three best methods are baking, poaching and smoking. "Baking" may also be read as roasting, for Izaak Walton's pike was cooked on a spit. Any of these methods should be considered before you commit the pike to a frying pan.

In the test of time, *The Compleat Angler* is one of the greatest works in the English language, having passed 340 editions since the year 1653. Izaak Walton's book is read by people who haven't the slightest interest in fishing. Washington Irving was speaking for many when he confessed that "It was Walton's fascinating vein of honest simplicity and rural feeling that bewitched me, and not his passion for angling." Charles Lamb said the book would "... sweeten a man's temper any time he read it," and Dr. Samuel Johnson, who was certainly no

fisherman, commended it purely as literature. Walton's words, penned over 300 years ago, are as relevant now as then, for his England knew a Civil War, the Great Plague, the Great Fire of London, the Execution of Charles the First—yet this simple and gentle man advised the world "... to study to be quiet and to a-fishing." Fishing, of course, is the framework for Walton's philosophy. While he wrote of silver streams that "glide merrily by"—a sight that "possessed my soul with content"—he also wrote fondly and in detail on the subject of fish cookery. The pike to Walton was "choicely good" and few can deny that his instructions are without peer.

First, open your Pike at the gills, and, if need be, cut also a little slit towards the belly. Out of these take his guts; and keep his liver, which you are to shred very small with thyme, sweet-marjoram, and a little winter-savory; to these put some pickled oysters and some anchovies, two or three ... to these you must add also a pound of sweet butter, which you are to mix with the herbs that are shred, and let them all be well salted ... These being thus mixed, with a blade or two of mace, must be put into the Pike's belly, and then his belly so sowed up as to keep all the butter in his belly, if it be possible ... Let him be roasted very leisurely, and often basted with claret-wine, and anchovies, and butter, mixed together; and also with what moisture falls from him into the pan. When you have roasted him sufficiently, you are to hold under him, when you unwind or cut the tape that ties him, such a dish as you purpose to eat him out of; and let him fall into it with the sauce that is roasted in his belly ... Then, to the sauce which was within, and also that sauce in the pan, you are to add a fit quantity of the best butter, and to squeeze the juice of three or four oranges. Lastly, you may either put into the Pike, with the oysters, two cloves of garlic, and take it whole out, when the Pike is cut off the spit; or to give the sauce a haut-gout, let the dish ... be rubbed with it. The using or not using of this garlic is left to your discretion.

The pike had its detractors as early as the fourth century, or at least Ausonius (writing in *Mosella*, his longest poem, on the Moselle River) lacked a good recipe, or frequented the wrong taverns:

> *The scourge and terror of the scaly brood,*
> *Unknown at friendship's hospitable board,*
> *Smokes midst the smoky tavern's coarsest food.*

However, the pike was favored in later centuries. H. Cholmondeley-Pennell in his *Book of the Pike* (1865) tells us that in the latter part of the thirteenth century, when Edward I regulated the prices of different kinds of fish then brought to market, "...he fixed the value of pike higher than that of fresh salmon, and more than ten times greater than the best turbot and cod." Pike were so valuable in the reign of Henry VIII that "a large one sold for double the price of a household lamb and a small one for more than a fat capon." This freshwater delicacy was only available to the landed gentry who monopolized the ponds and rivers of England and seldom allowed pike into the public market. Charles Estienne in his *Praedium Rusticum* (1554) described this fish's culinary role which appears to have originated in a dinner for Richard II in 1394:

> *Lo! the rich pike, to entertain your guest*
> *Smokes on the board and decorates a royal feast...*

By contrast, except for an occasional mention in the reports of Jesuits and other early-day accounts of the Great Lakes and Canadian fur-trading regions, there is nothing to indicate that the pike was regarded as an important foodfish in North America. The Indians held them in low esteem; among contemporary tribes such as the Crees and the Dogribs the pike is caught mainly as a dog food. In sub-Arctic areas where dogs are vital to man's survival the pike provides a readily available protein during ice-free months, as the fish is easy to catch in remote waters. The largest pike, called muskellunge, was more highly regarded by the early Indian probably because of its size as it differs little from the common pike. This peculiar name originated in the Ojibway dialect from **mas** for ugly and **kinononge** meaning fish, then bastardized by the French-Canadian **masquallongee**. In describing this species in 1818 Rafinesque indicated that settlers along the Ohio River found the muskellunge "one of the best fishes ... its flesh is very delicate and divides easily, as in salmon, into large plates as white as snow. It is called white salmon, white pike, or white pickerel and **picareau blanc** by the Missourians."

It must be said at this point that if you are looking for a recipe for "yellow pike" or "blue pike" you are reading the wrong entry. Unfortunately, these two very common market names get confused in the kitchen. Neither one is a pike; both are members of the perch family (Percidae) and are properly called walleye *(which see)*. There are considerable differences as far as preparation is concerned. The pike family (Esocidae) consists of 6 species on a world basis, five of which are found in North America, but only two of these have culinary importance; the northern pike and the muskellunge. Northern pike ordinarily weigh from 4 to 10 pounds, and muskellunge from 10 to 30 pounds. However, both fish grow to much larger sizes. These fish are similar in appearance, being elongate and having a large mouth supplied with formidable canine teeth. Their mouths are shaped much like a duck's bill. Pike are bonier than many other fish; however, this hardly detracts from the quality of the flesh. The bone problem is minimal in pike of over 4 pounds. The usually small chain pickerel, which seldom weighs over 2 or 3 pounds, can be dealt with by heavily scoring the fillets and panfrying them in hot oil, which makes the tiny bones edible. However, these Y-shaped intermuscular bones (which are also found in shad and bonefish) can be picked out easily in large fish.

SCALDING AND DRESSING

All members of the pike family have very dense slime on their bodies, and scaling these fish in the ordinary manner is a messy job at best. However, a quick bath in boiling water will coagulate the slime and loosen the scales. You can use a bucket or large washbasin, or simply lay the pike over a thick bed of newspaper and pour a kettle of boiling water on the fish, on both sides. Scalding will not "cook" the pike and the fish can be scaled quite easily. Proceed to dress the fish according to your recipe requirements.

The problem in pike cookery, if you are to roast a stuffed whole fish, is that at any edible weight a pike is *long*. A 4-pound fish, for example, may be from 22 to 30 inches in length (there is considerable variation among individual pike), and the not uncommon 10-pounder from 30 to 38 inches in length. I personally don't feel it's worth roasting a pike much under 6 pounds. Unless you have an ample barbecue pit, or an especially large oven, the fish will have to be dressed and headless if small,

Poached pike with horseradish, on the Baltic, in Sweden

or centercut or loincut if large; the centercut will give you the body cavity which can be stuffed and trussed with string. This may be a less artful presentation but it doesn't detract from the end result.

The same applies to poaching a whole fish. Fortunately, small pike are better cooked by the poaching method although I see no reason why these should not be sectioned also, as a pike's head is not particularly attractive. I think the better option is to cut the fish into portion-size pieces, or with a large pike cut it into steaks.

SOURCE AND SEASON

While there is some variation in quality due to habitat (the poorest being found in marginally warm or polluted water), generally speaking, the Esocidae are fairly uniform in texture and flavor. Pike have lean flesh and good keeping qualities both on a short- and long-term basis.

Pike appear in our American markets whole and dressed, dressed headless, in fillets, frozen fillet blocks, boneless fillet blocks and steaks. They are not taken commercially in the U.S. but are imported from Canada and available year-round in major cities. Large quantities are smoked in Scandinavia, and considerable amounts are canned in the Soviet Union. By far the greatest poundage cooked in U.S. kitchens, however, is taken by angling, especially in the spring season. They are most common in our country from New York through the Great Lakes region to Nebraska, but they do have a scattered distribution where planted in other states. The muskellunge is found in part throughout this same range. The

teeth of muskellunge have been collected in Pleistocene deposits as far south as northwest Oklahoma. It's believed that they entered the Mississippi drainage from the sea, and were isolated in the upper river during the retreat of the glaciers. Today they are most abundant in Wisconsin and southern Ontario, and in the St. Lawrence River. Due to their relative scarcity there is no commercial fishery for muskellunge, either here or in Canada.

In other cuisines the northern pike is known as **Gjedde** (Norway), **Gädda** (Sweden), **Hauki** (Finland), **Gedde** (Denmark), **Gedda** (Iceland), **Hecht** (Germany), **Snoek** (Holland), **Brochet** (France), **Luccio** (Italy), **Lucio** (Spain and Portugal), **Stuka** (Yugoslavia), **Tourna** (Greece).

PIKE AS MADE BY IZAAK WALTON

1 pike, 6 pounds, whole-dressed, or 4 pounds centercut of large pike or muskellunge	6 ounces butter
	1 cup fresh orange juice
	2 garlic cloves, minced (optional)
1 bottle (25 ounces) claret	watercress
3 anchovies, minced	orange slices

STUFFING

1 pike or muskellunge liver, minced (see Note)	½ teaspoon minced fresh marjoram
2 cups soft bread crumbs	2 anchovies, minced
1 teaspoon minced onion	6 fresh oysters, marinated in wine vinegar
½ teaspoon minced fresh savory	½ cup melted butter
½ teaspoon grated mace	salt
½ teaspoon minced fresh thyme	

Thoroughly combine the stuffing ingredients, preferably by hand, and moisten with melted butter. Season with salt to taste. Place in body cavity of fish and sew closed or truss with string.

Place stuffed fish on a greased baking pan. Pour in enough claret to come up about midway on the fish. Add the anchovies. Dot fish with 2 ounces of the butter cut into bits. Bake in a 400°F. oven for 20 minutes, then reduce heat to 275°F. and continue for another 25 minutes. Baste frequently. When done lift fish to a warm platter. Add the orange juice, remaining butter and the garlic to pan liquid, and reduce over low heat to one third of the volume. Strain and pour over pike. Surround fish with watercress and orange slices. Serves 6 "Anglers or other honest men."

NOTE: If not available at market substitute 2 heaping tablespoons of a good grade of canned *pâté de foie gras*.

BAKED MUSKELLUNGE WITH FRUIT STUFFING

5 pounds centercut of muskellunge or pike	½ cut melted butter or fat
	½ teaspoon salt
1 cup chopped unpeeled apple	½ teaspoon chopped fresh mint
1 cup chopped dried apricots	pepper
4 cups bread crumbs	¼ cup mixed water
½ cup diced celery	and lemon juice

Combine all ingredients except water and lemon juice; use pepper to taste. Fill inside of fish, and tie up in several places to hold in stuffing. Place fish in an oiled roasting pan with the water and lemon juice. Bake in a moderate oven for 10 minutes per inch of stuffed thickness, basting frequently with the liquid in the pan. Makes 8 servings.

POACHED PIKE WITH HORSERADISH (KOKT GÄDDA MED PEPPARROT)

1 northern pike, 2 to 3 pounds, whole-dressed	4 tablespoons salt
	1 bay leaf
1 fresh pimiento, sliced	½ cup melted butter
3 whole carrots, peeled	½ cup grated
2 onions, cut into quarters	fresh horseradish

This simple recipe is popular along the Baltic shores of Sweden. Place the pike in your poacher with the pimiento, carrots and onions, and add enough cold water to cover. Add the salt and bay leaf and bring water to a boil. This will take about 20 minutes. Reduce heat to a simmer and cook for another 15 minutes. Test with fork.

Arrange on serving tray and cover with melted butter and grated horseradish. Boiled potatoes and chopped eggs are the usual companion pieces. Makes 4 servings.

MOUSSE OF PIKE

(The Four Seasons, New York City)

2 pounds boneless pike	½ teaspoon grated nutmeg
3 egg whites	½ teaspoon white pepper
2 teaspoons sugar	4 cups heavy cream

Crush the pike in a mortar, then place in a bowl set in cracked ice. Add egg whites and combine. Season with sugar, nutmeg and pepper. Still over cracked ice, add the cream, little by little, and mix in. Work everything thoroughly with a spoon until the mixture reaches the consistency of a sticky batter.

MOLDED PIKE MOUSSE WITH LOBSTER AND TRUFFLES

(The Four Seasons, New York City)

Fill 8 oiled ring molds, 6- to 8-ounce size, with prepared batter for mousse. Smooth the tops, and set the molds in a baking pan containing 1 inch of boiling water. Oven-poach the molds in a preheated 375°F. oven until just done, about 20 minutes. Turn out the baked mousses onto a serving dish. Cut a cooked lobster tail into medallions, and a large truffle into slices. Arrange 2 or 3 lobster medallions on each ring of mousse, allowing space between medallions. Mask the molds with Sauce Nantua *(see under SAUCES)*, and place truffle slices between lobster pieces. Decorate with crayfish tails. Makes 8 servings.

MOLDED PIKE MOUSSE WITH LOBSTER AND TRUFFLES (prepared at The Four Seasons, New York City)

1. Crush pike in a mortar and add egg whites.   **2.** Add sugar, nutmeg and white pepper.   **3.** Add heavy cream and work the mixture to a batter.

4. Mix batter well.

5. Oil molds.

6. Fill molds with mousse.

7. Smooth the tops.

8. Pour an inch of boiling water into a baking pan.

9. Set molds in the water and oven-poach until just done.

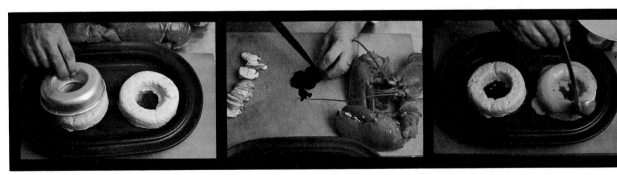

10. Unmold onto a serving platter.

11. Cut a lobster tail into medallions and a truffle into slices.

12. Coat molds with Sauce Nantua.

13. Arrange lobster medallions around the top and coat with more sauce.

14. Place truffle slices between lobster medallions.

15. Garnish with crayfish tails.

PAUPIETTES OF SALMON WITH MOUSSE OF PIKE (prepared at The Four Seasons, New York City)

1. and **2.** Place 1 tablespoon of pike mousse in the middle of each slice of smoked salmon.

3. Roll up the slices into paupiettes.

4. Place paupiettes in a buttered pan and oven-poach.

5. Transfer to a serving platter and mask with sorrel sauce.

6. Reheat and serve very hot.

PAUPIETTES OF SALMON WITH MOUSSE OF PIKE IN SORREL SAUCE
(The Four Seasons, New York City)

8 slices of smoked salmon (see Note)
8 tablespoons Mousse of Pike (p. 240)
5 tablespoons melted butter
2 tablespoons chopped shallots
1 cup white wine
1 pound sorrel, shredded
2 cups White-Wine Sauce I (p. 290)
salt and pepper

In the middle of each slice of smoked salmon place 1 tablespoon of the pike mousse. Roll the slices into paupiettes. Pour 2 tablespoons of the melted butter into a baking pan and add shallots. Arrange the paupiettes in the pan, and pour in the white wine. Bring to a boil, then cover and remove to a 375°F. oven for 15 minutes.

Place the shredded sorrel in a casserole with remaining butter, cover, and cook until dry. Add the white-wine sauce and simmer for 5 minutes. Adjust seasoning to taste. Remove paupiettes to a serving platter, pour the sauce over them, and serve very hot. Makes 4 servings.

NOTE: This dish is sometimes made with combined slices of fresh salmon and smoked salmon; this combination is much preferred by the author. In this style the recipe requires 8 slices of each.

Pil-pil

A Basque term for a method of cooking salt cod with only oil and garlic. *See COD.*

Pompano

The firm and delicate white flesh of the pompano *(Trachinotus carolinus)* is to many ichthyophiles the standard-bearer by which all other saltwater fish are judged. Whether its reputation is deserved or not, pompano is very expensive at market and certainly rates three stars at table. Although the fish may be found anywhere from Massachusetts to Brazil, its real abundance is from North Carolina to Florida and the Gulf of Mexico. The average pompano at market is from 1½ to 2 pounds in size, but occasionally we catch fish of 4 to 5 pounds. Any fish larger than this is more likely to be a small **permit** which so greatly resembles a pompano externally that only by counting fin rays can an expert distinguish one from the other. There is another related species, the **palometa** *(Trachinotus goodei)* found from Florida to Argentina and in the Mediterranean, known as **pâmpano** in Portugal, **palometa** in Spain, **leccia stella** in Italy, and **kobanaji** in Yugoslavia; however, this is an inferior fish to the true pompano of our western Atlantic, but only in the sense of being thinner in the body and therefore less versatile in preparation; it is best sautéed whole.

The silvery slab-sided pompano is one of the spookiest fish in the ocean. It's not uncommon to see a pompano "walk" across the water in a semicircular course around a running boat, and the fish may even pancake over the surface in the way children throw a flat stone to watch it skip. When approached by a boat in shallow water a pompano can streak through the air like a rocket and on several occasions I've had pompano jump aboard—an unearned but welcome dividend. This peculiarity is well known to Florida Gulf Coast commercials who often buzz the flats with a wide-open motor to locate pompano before the laborious task of hauling a seine or setting a drift gill net. Uncountable thousands of pompano are also taken by amateur fishermen from piers and bridges and in the surf. They are especially numerous from October to May in Florida; at other times they are more likely to be a frozen product.

The **permit** *(Trachinotus falcatus)* occurs through most of the same geographic range as the pompano; it is a much larger fish, running up to 50 pounds in size. It is very abundant in the Florida Keys, and on a good day it's not unusual to sight 100 permit feeding in the shallows with their backs or tails out of the water. But for all the fish you may see, very few are ever hooked and boated as they are extremely shy. Despite their parochial behavior evidently considerable numbers are netted as they appear in New York's Fulton Fish Market from time to time. For my tastes any permit of over 6 to 8 pounds is inferior to the pompano. The few really large ones I've cooked—by direct heat methods in the 30-pound class— were dry and coarse. Permit can be made into an excellent chowder, and they also retain moisture by poaching, which offers the options of serving hot with lemon butter, or cold in aspic with a mustard sauce. Captain Johnny Cass, who has made a lifetime specialty of catching permit in the Florida Keys and is also a seafood fancier of note, will admit that big permit are edible but not in the same league as the smaller pompano.

POMPANO COOKERY

The simplest ways to prepare pompano are to broil and butter-baste the fillets under an oven broiler and to split (kite) and broil in a hinged grid over charcoal, then serve with **maître d'hôtel butter** or **shrimp butter,** sprinkled with fresh lime or lemon juice. The Greek fishermen in Tarpon Springs, Florida, prefer to eliminate butter and wipe the fillets with a good grade of olive oil. This adds a somewhat robust flavor to the delicate pompano and is best enjoyed by Mediterranean-oriented palates. However, the pompano lends itself to a variety of preparations. The most famous of these is Louisiana's pompano *en papillote,* baked in a sauce of shrimps, crab meat and subtle seasonings.

Palometa

Pompano

The object of wrapping the fish in paper is to enhance the flavor by trapping the steam and savory juices inside. Modern chefs find aluminum foil much handier to use in making the *papillotes* than the traditional buttered white butcher's paper, but in either case it's the accompanying sauce which distinguishes the work of various kitchens among Creole gourmets.

BRENNAN'S POMPANO TOULOUSE
(Brennan's Restaurant, New Orleans)

1 pompano	¾ cup fish stock
salt and pepper	3 tablespoons
flour	Worcestershire sauce
6 tablespoons butter	1 teaspoon Tabasco
1 small onion, minced	2 green onions, minced
2 garlic cloves, minced	¼ cup minced pimientos
½ green pepper, minced	parsley sprigs
3 tablespoons capers	lemon baskets or wedges

Fillet the pompano; sprinkle with salt and pepper to taste; dust with flour. Broil until brown. Keep hot until served.

Melt 2 tablespoons of the butter in a large skillet. Add onion, garlic and green pepper, and sauté for 10 minutes. Add capers, fish stock, Worcestershire and Tabasco, and salt and pepper to taste; mix well. In a separate skillet melt remaining butter; add 4 tablespoons flour and cook until the roux is thick and turns light brown. Pour the roux into the other mixture; add green onions, mix well, and cook for 20 minutes; keep sauce hot. Just before serving stir in the pimientos and pour sauce over pompano. Garnish with parsley sprigs and lemon baskets or wedges. Makes 2 servings.

Porgy

There are about 15 different porgies found in the Atlantic waters of the U.S., but there are countless others on a world basis from the Mediterranean to the Indo-Pacific region. The name porgy is strictly American, derived from the Narraganset Indian word *mishcuppauog. Pauog* or *pogy* meant fertilizer, for which the fish was widely used. The name "scup" for that particular porgy also derived from this same Indian name. However, these members of the family Sparidae are more widely known as "sea bream." The most important from a world culinary standpoint are the red sea bream or **tai** and yellow sea bream or **kidai** of Japan; these have equal acclaim in Chinese seafood cookery. In the Mediterranean, the **dorade** and the large-eyed **dentex** are very popular; the latter, known as **zubatac** along the Adriatic coast of Yugoslavia, is often displayed in restaurant aquaria to be selected by the client as one would choose a lobster. On the Italian shore it's called the **dentice occhiore.** South Africa, which is particularly rich in sparids, is best known for its **steenbras** or mussel crusher, while in New Zealand the popular porgy is confusingly called "snapper"; this species (known to the Maori people as **tamure**) has always been the most important foodfish in the islands, contributing over 30 percent to the total landings annually. Their abundance attracts a considerable fleet of Japanese trawlers to New Zealand, as the **tai** which is served on religious and ceremonial occasions commands a high price in Tokyo. The **mu** of Hawaii occurs all over the tropical western Pacific. In our Atlantic waters the scup or common porgy and the sheepshead suffer by comparison to the uncommonly good dentex but they compare favorably to other sea breams.

Some 20 million pounds of porgies are marketed on the Atlantic Coast of the U.S. each year, and countless thousands are caught by sport fishermen. Like certain other popular fish such as the striped bass or red snapper, the porgy will tolerate the lack of ice, warm temperatures and delayed gutting, but the end product is what Thomas Gunn (*The Physiology of New York Boarding-Houses*, 1857) had in mind when he described "porgies purchased in their decadence from preambulatory fish vendors" in the days when fish were sold from pushcarts. The porgies may not actually spoil, but their sweet taste evaporates. All fresh porgies are fine foodfish. They have a delicate flavor, and simple preparations are best to use. Grill, panfry, or poach, and serve with melted butter.

Generally, porgies are lean and coarse-grained. The best for both flavor and texture in the author's opinion are the red and jolthead porgies (excluding European or Indo-Pacific species). However, the size of the individual fish is a critical factor in cooking. Porgies have many small, sharp bones (they were marketed in the nineteenth century as "Porgees for Poor Young Men"), and the larger fish are superior as there is a greater ratio of meat and the skeletal structure is easier to remove. A good method of preparation is to score the dressed fish and cook over charcoal; when served the meat can be lifted free of the backbone; after removal splash the porgy with an herb butter. The remaining bones in a large fish are easily picked out.

PORGY TERMINOLOGY

GRASS PORGY This is a small porgy (*Calamus arctifrons*) common to the West Coast of Florida and the Gulf of

Mexico. Its body is barred in a dark gray-green with a distinct yellow patch on its nose. This species lives among patches of eelgrass, hence the name. Most grass porgies weigh less than 1 pound but the larger ones are fair panfish.

JOLTHEAD PORGY One of our larger Atlantic porgies, the jolthead *(Calamus bajonado)* is primarily a West Indian species, but it occurs along the U.S. coast from Rhode Island to the Gulf of Mexico and is a popular market fish in North Carolina. It is also caught in Bermuda and is very common in the Bahamas. The jolthead is silvery in color

with mauve and blue reflections and handsomely marked with dark brown blotches. This porgy reaches a weight of 8 pounds or more and fish of 2 pounds are fairly common in some areas. It has a "chunky" body and the meat is of excellent flavor.

PACIFIC PORGY This is the only porgy that may enter our West Coast markets, and then in sporadic and small numbers. The Pacific porgy *(Calamus brachysomus)* is rare off California; its range is southward from Mexico to Peru where it commingles with other sparids. Although it reaches a weight of about 5 pounds, the Pacific porgy is

Jolthead porgy

only a fair foodfish and not worthy of its sometimes market name **tai.** Those porgies sold in southern California markets in years past were imported from the Mexican fishery.

PLUMA This is one of the common porgies of the Bahamas and West Indies. Although a very colorful little fish, bearing bright emerald-green spots over a silvery body with mauve reflections, *Calamus pennacula* contains more bone than meat in its usual ½-pound size.

RED PORGY This large species (*Pagrus sedecim*) is found from New York to Argentina and in the Gulf of Mexico. It has a closely related counterpart in European waters (*P. pagrus*) which is popular in Mediterranean cuisines. The red porgy is reddish silver in color with numerous tiny yellow spots that create a striped pattern on the upper half of the body. The red porgy is a deepwater sparid and attains good size, in excess of 12 pounds. A minor landing is made by sport fishermen, but mainly it's taken by commercial trawlers in southeastern U.S. waters from Cape Hatteras to northern Florida. This is an excellent porgy at table.

ROUNDSPOT This porgy (*Diplodus caudimacula*) is found in southern Florida and the Caribbean Sea. It is not a common species but occurs around many islands in cyclic periods of abundance and is a highly regarded foodfish.

SAUCEREYE PORGY This is a small, silvery porgy seldom over 1 pound in weight, occurring only in Bermuda, the Florida Keys, West Indies and parts of Central America. The saucereye (*Calamus calamus*) has limited value as a food due to its small size; nevertheless it does appear in some Caribbean markets.

SCUP This is the "porgy" of northeastern U.S. waters. The scup (*Stenotomus chrysops*) occurs from Nova Scotia to Florida but is more common from south of Cape Cod to North Carolina. Cyclic in abundance, the scup has been an important summer market and sport fish in the Boston and New York areas, but the population has declined in recent years. The scup is silvery in color with bluish and mauve reflections; it has dusky fins, often with a brownish tinge. Scup grow to 5 pounds but fish of 1 pound are closer to average. The name "scup" is derived from the Narraganset Indian **mishcuppauog** which was shortened to **scuppaug,** its common name in the nineteenth century. Scup have large, strongly imbedded scales; if you catch your own it's advisable to dress the fish as soon as possible before the scales dry and firm. Even filleting and skinning is somewhat difficult unless you use a very sharp knife.

SHEEPSHEAD This porgy (*Archosargus probatocephalus*) occurs from Nova Scotia to the Gulf of Mexico, but it's common only south of Chesapeake Bay. It is limited solely to the Atlantic and unrelated to the California sheephead *(which see)*. This fish was once so abundant in the latitude of New York that "Sheepshead Bay" in Brooklyn was considered the mother lode. Although sheepshead reportedly grow to 20 pounds in size, it's primarily a small panfish caught around bridges and docks and seldom exceeds 1½ to 2 pounds. It also enters freshwater rivers. The sheepshead is an overall dull gray in color with 5 to 7 dark vertical bars on its sides, which suggests the common name "convict" fish. The sheepshead is of minor commercial importance in the Gulf of Mexico. It's a good foodfish; however, porgies of the genus *Archosargus* have tough skin which should be removed with filleting.

WHITEBONE PORGY The most common porgy of southeastern U.S., found from North Carolina to Florida and in the Gulf of Mexico. It is not usually as large as the jolthead or red porgy but does attain 3 to 4 pounds. The whitebone *(Calamus leucosteus)* is silvery in color with dark splotches on its sides. It is similar to the jolthead in texture and flavor but often lacks the size for true appreciation.

Powan

See LAVARET *under* WHITEFISH.

Prawn

A crustacean of the order Decapoda. Prawns differ in appearance from shrimps in having more slender abdomens and longer legs but the names are used synonymously in commercial trade. Unfortunately, at market "prawn" is universally applied to any of the larger marine shrimps. The less familiar term "freshwater prawn" refers to palaemonid shrimps, specifically *Macrobrachium* of which there are more than 100 species on a world basis. The giant Malaysian prawn *(M. rosenbergii)* is perhaps the best known and is widely cultured in southern Asia as well as Hawaii and more recently Puerto Rico. The Tahitian prawn *(M. lar)* is also widely distributed in the western Pacific islands, and other species are indigenous to India, the Philippines, Africa, Central and South America. A large native form *(M. acanthurus)* is found in southern U.S. from the Neuse River in North Carolina to Texas.

Fishing dock, Maine

Prawn *(Macrobrachium);* left, a stuffed prawn; right, a cultured specimen

However, freshwater prawns are only utilized on a local level by individual fishermen at present. Strictly speaking, prawns are anadromous and not totally freshwater crustaceans, but they are harvested in rice fields, ponds and rivers.

Where cultured, prawns are usually sold at the 6 to 10 per pound heads-on count, but some species grow much larger in wild environments. Prawns are more perishable than marine shrimps and must be iced or flash frozen immediately after capture. Only the tail portion is eaten. The always sweet meat is comparable to lobster in texture and flavor. Prawns are very popular in Hawaii and Japan and bring a good price at market. *See also SHRIMP.*

Prickleback

These eellike species of the family Stichaeidae include some of the most delicious fishes found along the U.S. Pacific Coast, notably the **monkeyface eel** *(Cebidichthys violaceus)* and the **rock eel** *(Xiphister mucosus).* Although commonly called "eels," pricklebacks are not related to the anguillids and their flesh is more delicate in flavor and texture, being comparable to the meat of a crayfish tail. Pricklebacks occur in the intertidal zone and are caught by sport fishermen using special "poke poles" at low water. There are about 28 species found mainly in the Pacific (the comparatively few Atlantic forms called snakeblennies or eelblennies are small in size), but the monkeyface and rock eels which attain lengths from 20 to 30 inches are most commonly taken in California; the range of the monkeyface eel extends southward to Mexico and that of the rock eel northward to Alaska. The pricklebacks do not enter a commercial fishery.

Skinned monkeyface and rock eels are of superb flavor. Use a simple preparation—steaming or poaching; serve them in melted butter with lemon.

Puffer

The puffer or **sea squab** is one of the most delicate foodfish in the world's oceans. The creamy white meat is similar to a plump frog's leg. In Japan, where it is known as **fugu,** the fish is served in numerous forms, from a gelatin to tempura. However, it can also be one of the most toxic foods at table, a conundrum revealed in an old Japanese folk song, "I want to eat *fugu,* but I don't want to die." *(Fugu wa kuitashii, inochi wa oshishii.)* Puffer poisoning results in a number of fatalities each year in various countries, including the U.S. In Japan, where there are more than 1,500 *fugu* restaurants in Tokyo alone, the attrition among its devotees runs about 100 in a normal year and 200 in a peak year, with a 61 percent fatality rate. Yet, its popularity never wanes, in fact the demand is greater than ever, a phenomenon which Oriental psychologists explain in terms of hara-kiri gourmandizing.

Puffers, also called **blowfish, swellfish** and **globefish,** derive their name from the defensive ability instantly to inflate their bodies with air or water, expanding to the size of a baseball or a basketball, depending on the species. With skin like coarse sandpaper, the puffer's enemies are quickly discouraged, but not so man. Those mortals who crave *fugu* accept the odds, which are more favorable in the eastern U.S. if one is to be consoled by statistics. Puffers were most popular here during the period from 1950 to 1970; only a decline in their numbers shrank the market, and those currently purveyed bring top dollar.

There are more than 100 species of Tetraodontidae occurring throughout the world, and their flesh varies in degrees of toxicity. However, the gonads, liver, skin and intestines of all puffers are deadly and should never be eaten. The flesh of our northern puffer, found from Cape Cod to Georgia, is apparently the least harmful as poisonings have been extremely rare in this area. Marine biologist Paul Hamer concluded that one would have to eat more than 25 northern puffers to ingest a fatal dose of toxin. The fact that thousands of innocents have enjoyed "sea squabs" over the years, myself included, is testimony to the fact that few people have the capacity to consume the fish in large numbers. The southern puffer, on the other hand, which ranges from Florida south through the Gulf of Mexico, has been more often identified with tetraodontoid poisoning; it has never been a highly esteemed foodfish in this region, but the odds are less favorable.

One reason for the problem in Japan is that literally hundreds of thousands of pounds of *fugu* are consumed in season, from October to March, and the possibility of "error" is infinitely greater because some 30 species of puffer occur around Nippon's coasts, of which only a dozen are edible. Distinguishing each kind of puffer is a skill acquired through long experience and for the novice about as safe as a random collection of wild mushrooms on a May day in the Catskills. When the eye is deceived, *fugu* and fungi have one thing in common—it will probably be your last bite. Thus, a *fugu* chef in Japan must be licensed by the Environmental Sanitation Division of the Bureau of Health, a high-hat of office which in one respect is more demanding than a *summa cum laude* at Harvard; the applicant is required to eat those *fugu* he has cooked and certified as safe. Post-exam dinners can become post-mortems. However, most prospective *fugu* chefs are denied the ultimate test after a written examination that eliminates fully 75 percent of the applicants. He must also work under a master for 2 critical years before a license is granted.

Regardless of the source of supply and the skill of the kitchen, I cannot in good conscience recommend puffers as food.

Northern puffer; top, normal size; bottom, inflated

Rabbitfish
Rakørret
Ray
Rock Bass
Rockfish
Rock Salmon
Roe
Roosterfish

r

Rabbitfish

A common name in the southern U.S. for the smooth puffer. This species occurs in both the eastern and western Atlantic where its range extends from Massachusetts south to Argentina, including the Gulf of Mexico. This puffer is distinguished from other Tetraodontidae in its geographical range by its smooth skin (only the belly has short prickles), large dorsal and anal fins, and the concave caudal fin. The smooth puffer is not able to expand its body as greatly as the northern or southern puffers, possibly because of its larger size. It may grow to 2 feet and 7 pounds. The color is greenish-gray above, silvery on the sides and white on the belly; the fins are dusky.

Despite the potential toxicity of puffers in general, the rabbitfish has long been considered a table delicacy in some parts of our South, especially in Florida. Statistics do not indicate that rabbitfish is safe to eat, however, and its utilization is definitely a risk. It is not recommended. *See also PUFFER.*

Rakørret

A half-fermented trout (Norway) made when the fish are at their fattest. The only trout native to Norway is the fall-spawning brown trout **(ørret)** which reproduces in October, so **rakørret** is prepared in August or September. It is a national dish and extremely popular. The trout are whole-dressed, then placed in lightly salted cold water (4 tablespoons salt to 1 gallon water) for 3 hours. The skin of the trout is then scaled and scraped clean and the fish are arranged in a stone crock or wood barrel, side by side, belly up. Equal amounts of coarse salt and sugar (½ cup each over a dozen small trout of ½ to ¾ pound each) are generously sprinkled over each layer and a heavy lid is placed on top. The container must be stored in a cool place. The **rakørret** is usually ready to eat in 3 months. Fillets are served cold with crisp bread and butter.

Ray

Marine and to a lesser extent freshwater fishes of the order Rajiformes, closely related to the sharks. These flat-bodied creatures with slender whiplike tails, usually equipped with barbed spines, are found in all seas. At least one species, the manta ray, grows to a width of 22 feet across its wings and to a weight of 2 tons. Most rays are much smaller, however, and the various species which are popular as food are usually taken at weights from 8 to 10 pounds. Commercially, rays are synonymous with the closely related skates and the names are used interchangeably; the French **raie** is firmly established in seafood cookery. While skates are more commonly used as food, the word "ray" or its counterpart persists in all languages.

With the exception of the giant mantas which feed on crustaceans, fish and plankton, most other rays are dominantly mollusk consumers, a forage which is reflected in the fine quality of the flesh. The edible portions of rays and skates are the "wings," which contain a firm white meat so similar to sea scallops in texture and flavor that it has been used as a substitute for many years. The wings are punched out with an instrument similar to a cookie cutter which produces perfectly round cylinders similar to a large scallop. There are differences in quality between the various species. The **common** or **flapper skate** *(Raja batis)* of Europe is generally considered the best from a culinary standpoint. On our Pacific Coast the **big skate** *(Raja binoculata)* and the **California skate** *(Raja inornata)* are superior to other local species. On the U.S. East Coast, the **smooth butterfly ray** *(Gymnura micrura)* and **winter skate** *(Raja ocellata)* have been widely used in making "scallops." In common with sharks these fish are greatly underutilized in the U.S.; however, people of French, Italian, Japanese and Chinese descent, or countries with traditionally large markets, continue to buy the available supply. In European markets they are sold whole and gutted, or as wings cut from both sides of the disc, either skinned or unskinned. They are also prepared in hot-smoked pieces. In Japan they are often sold alive. Skate livers are a delicacy when poached and served on toast.

PRELIMINARY PREPARATION

Whether you use skinned or unskinned portions, the wings should be covered with salted or vinegared water for several hours, then drained and chilled. Use either 1 cup of salt or ½ cup of white vinegar to 1 gallon of water. If in skin, it should then be scraped with a knife to remove any excess slime; the skin can easily be peeled off after poaching, which is the most common method of cooking. If it is to be panfried or sautéed the skin must be removed before

Winter skate, a ray

cooking. Skate or ray can be held in the refrigerator for 48 to 72 hours and will improve with "age"—the texture becomes firm.

Redfish

(1) A common name for the ocean perch in the eastern and western Atlantic. *See ROCKFISH.*
(2) A regional (Southern U.S.) common name for the red drum. *See under DRUM.*

Rock Bass

(1) A small freshwater panfish found in North America, belonging to the sunfish family. *See SUNFISH.*
(2) A market name (California) for the marine kelp bass, sand bass and rock sea bass. These fish are closely related and commercially the landings are not separated but comprise a "rock bass" fishery.

Rockfish

(1) As a colloquial name, specifically in the Chesapeake Bay region, "rockfish" means the striped bass *(which see)*, but as an accepted common name in the U.S. rockfish are Pacific members of the Scorpaenidae.

Rockfish (2)

In 1869 some 65,000 Chinese laborers lay down their picks and sledges when the last golden spike was driven in the bed of the transcontinental railroad that spanned America. An industrious people, now unemployed, some wandered to New York and north to New Brunswick, others headed for British Columbia, but the majority re-

turned to San Francisco which offered the reassuring option of a boat back to Hong Kong. For the obvious reason of language they colonized, and San Francisco acquired the first Chinese restaurant in the U.S., The Canton on Jackson Street. Thus, "chop suey" became part of our American idiom and for the next century Chinese food was identified with a culinary style that originated in one city, Canton, and took its materials from an alien land. Canton, the capital city of Kwangtung (which encompasses the port city of Hong Kong) is no more representative of Chinese cuisine than say, Charleston, South Carolina, is of American cuisine. Rest assured both have superb cookery, but the full spectrum of Chinese provincial styles only began arriving on our shores in the 1960s when Fukienese, Yunnanese, Hunanese, Szechuanese and the catch-all Mandarin added their methodology to what I consider the finest cuisine in the world.

The Chinese are probably the world's most ancient fishermen, as bronze hooks were already in fashion during the Age of Shang (1766–1123 B.C.), and according to legend one Huang Ti invented boats and oars shortly thereafter in the Age of Chou. Until very recently, the fishing reel was thought to be a seventeenth-century European invention, but an angler fishing with rod and reel appears in a painting by the Chinese artist Ma Yüan whose career flourished from 1190–1225 A.D. The finest bamboo rods in the world are still made from raw cane produced in Tonkin, once part of China, now North Vietnam. Except for pond-cultured carp and mullet, the variety of fish species for culinary use found along the China Coast is not great; the golden thread, red sea bream (There are many species of "sea bream" found along the coasts of both China and Japan which appear in countless recipes. These fish are of the family Sparidae, the same as our various western Atlantic porgies, and can be substituted in translated recipes. The name sea bream is also used in Europe.), yellow croaker, ginkgofish, and seasonal migrants such as mackerel and jacks are the main market items. I have caught sailfish around the island of Taiwan which is off the coast of Fukien Province on the mainland where most of China's seafood originates, but prawns, shrimps, oysters, clams and abalone are plentiful and have a dominant role in the cuisine.

One of the tenets of Chinese cookery is to utilize virtually every organic material whether it's sharks' fins, birds' nests, sea cucumbers or ducks' feet. The rockfish was largely a neglected resource on our Pacific Coast despite the largess of more than 50 species as it is not comparable in quality to the salmon, halibut or sole. To stimulate sales the rockfish has been purveyed under a

facing page, Fishmonger in Alfama district, the oldest part of Lisbon. The fishes are European porgies.

variety of misleading and unrelated names such as rock cod, Pacific Ocean perch, black sea bass, rosefish and, totally demeaning Holy Writ, as "red snapper." The true red snapper is found only in the Atlantic Ocean and bears no resemblance to a rockfish. Legislation was passed in California to ban the practice (1972), but in a recent tour of San Francisco markets "red snapper" was still very much in evidence. Yet, with Oriental patience the rockfish can be made into an elegant dish.

In general order of importance the preferable species are the **Pacific ocean perch, bocaccio, chilipepper, canary, vermilion, yellowtail, black, olive, dark-blotched, widow, splitnose,** and **red (or turkey red) rockfishes.** While most rockfish can be kept frozen for 20 to 24 weeks, both the Pacific Ocean perch and the bocaccio have a storage capability of 30 to 32 weeks; the vermilion rockfish is, however, unsuited for freezing. Needless to say for a perfect sweet-and-sour dish the fish should be ocean fresh. If you live on the Atlantic Coast the ocean perch and black sea bass make an ideal substitute for rockfish. They are similar in flavor and texture.

When cooked in sweet-and-sour Mandarin style the rockfish has few peers. This festive seafood dinner looks difficult to prepare, but it's really one of the easiest—and made foolproof by a unique style of "scoring" which assures perfect heat penetration when deep-frying. The end result will be a crisp outside, moistly succulent inside, whole fish virtually swimming in a crimson sea with golden and paley green scales—a contrast of pickled fruits and vegetables to complement its snow-white flakes.

The cooking is simple and the decoration is fun. All you have to know is how to score the Mandarin way. Ordinarily, scoring consists of making deep slashes along the sides of a fish to expedite heat penetration. However, with a chunky body shape this is not enough. As done by Tony Ming Chan, Number One chef at Cecilia Chiang's Mandarin Restaurant in San Francisco, the fish is cut to the backbone, then the blade is pushed inward parallel to the backbone to form by repetitive scoring a series of "flaps." This provides a total surface exposure to the hot oil without losing the shape of the fish (a fish can be "squirreled" by making crisscross scores but it will no longer resemble a fish). The rockfish or sea bass should not weigh more than 3 pounds, preferably about 2½ pounds.

SWEET-AND-SOUR FISH
(The Mandarin, San Francisco)

1 whole rockfish, snapper, ocean perch, black
   sea bass or smallmouth bass, 2 to 3 pounds

1 cup cornstarch
2 quarts cottonseed or peanut oil, or sufficient
   to cover fish
1 cup pickled rinds (watermelon, cantaloupe,
   cucumber, candied gingerroot), preferably
   cut into shreds
2 large maraschino cherries
4 cups Sweet-and-Sour Sauce (p.288)

Fish should not weigh more than 3 pounds, preferably 2 to 2½ pounds. Dress and scale the fish. Score on both sides with 5 or 6 deep diagonal slashes to the backbone and inward parallel to backbone to form a series of "flaps." Coat the fish inside and out with cornstarch so that it is completely covered except for the head. Immerse the fish in a wok or deep-fryer filled with heated oil. Keep the temperature of the oil low (275°F.), otherwise the skin will brown before the fish is cooked through. Deep-fry until golden brown, about 20 minutes. Remove fish from oil and arrange on a platter in swimming position by pressing belly down with a towel. Insert cherries on food picks to create "eyes." Pour sweet-and-sour sauce over fish, and garnish its back with pickled rinds and additional cherries if desired. For a more festive presentation the author adds a bunch of green onion tops cut into inch-long sections which are poked between the flaps. Makes 4 servings.

LOTUS GARDENS ROCKFISH
(Lotus Gardens Restaurant, Vancouver)

1 whole rockfish,	½ cup water
1½ to 3 pounds, dressed	⅓ cup subgum (Chinese
and scaled	pickled vegetables)
2 quarts peanut oil	¼ cup diced leek
1 onion	toasted sesame seeds
3 tomatoes	parsley sprigs
1 tablespoon cornstarch	

MIXTURE A	MIXTURE B
2 tablespoons wine	6 tablespoons sugar
2 tablespoons soy sauce	3 tablespoons vinegar
3 tablespoons cornstarch	1 tablespoon soy sauce
3 tablespoons flour	3 tablespoons tomato sauce
	1 teaspoon salt

Preferably the rockfish should weigh 1½ to 2 pounds. Score the fish with 3 diagonal slashes on each side. Rub the fish inside and out with Mixture A. If the amount given isn't enough, whip up another batch in the same proportions. Heat the peanut oil to 275°F. and deep-

SWEET-AND-SOUR FISH
(prepared by Chef Tony Ming Chan at The Mandarin, San Francisco)

1. Score fish on one side to the backbone, making 5 or 6 diagonal slashes. **2.** Score on the other side. **3.** Cover the area inside the flaps with cornstarch. **4.** Coat the outside of the fish with more cornstarch. **5.** Deep-fry the rockfish in moderately hot oil in a wok.

DECORATING THE SWEET-AND-SOUR FISH

6. Lift fish from wok. **7.** Arrange in a swimming position on a serving platter, and insert cherries on food picks to make eyes. **8.** Pour sweet-and-sour sauce over the fish. **9.** Garnish the back with pickled rinds. **10.** Add more cherries, and serve.

fry the fish until it is golden brown, about 20 minutes. Remove fish to a piece of absorbent paper and drain by standing it stomach down so you can flatten it slightly to make the rockfish appear to be in a swimming position. Place the fish on an attractive oval platter in the oven to keep warm.

Next shred the onion and cut 2 tomatoes into sections; set aside. Mix 1 tablespoon cornstarch in ½ cup water. Heat 3 tablespoons peanut oil in a saucepan and put in Mixture B together with the tomato and onion pieces. This will quickly boil; at that point add the diluted cornstarch and stir until the mixture boils again. Remove the fish from the oven, decorate with subgum, and pour the hot tomato sauce which you made with Mixture B over the entire fish. Sprinkle some diced leek and sesame seeds over the sauce. Decorate the platter with parsley and remaining tomato cut into tiny dice. Makes 4 servings.

POACHED ROCKFISH
(Mrs. B. W. Fairbanks, Corvallis)

1 rockfish, about 4 pounds	1½ tablespoons flour, or
2 cups water	1 tablespoon cornstarch
1 teaspoon salt	2 to 3 tablespoons butter
1 bay leaf	¼ teaspoon white pepper
2 slices of onion	paprika
juice of 1 lemon	minced fresh parsley

Dress and scale the fish and place in a pot that just fits. Simmer water with salt, bay leaf, onion slices and half of the lemon juice for 5 minutes. Remove bay leaf and pour the liquid over the fish. It should be barely covered. Poach fish with liquid just below boiling point for 5 to 10 minutes, or until fish flakes readily and flesh becomes opaque instead of transparent. Carefully remove fish to a warm platter. Boil poaching liquid rapidly, reducing it to 1 to 1¼ cups. Thicken the liquid with flour or cornstarch diluted in 2 tablespoons cold water. Flavor sauce with remaining lemon juice, the butter and pepper; adjust amounts to your taste. Spoon sauce over fish, and sprinkle with paprika and parsley. Makes 4 servings.

Rock Salmon

A market name (Great Britain) for various species of fish often utilized in the popular fish and chips trade; this includes the blue shark, dogfish, wolffish and coalfish.

Rocky Mountain Whitefish

See MOUNTAIN WHITEFISH under WHITEFISH.

Roe

The gonads of fishes, properly the female ovaries but often the male testes as "white roe" or "soft roe." In cookery the term may also include the ovaries or "coral" of lobsters and scallops, the "berries" of crabs and the gonads of sea urchins. The roes of most fish are edible, but some are often toxic, including the great barracuda (Atlantic), gars, any of the puffers and trunkfishes. Among edible roes the shad, herring, alewife, salmon, vendace, flounder, mullet, sturgeon, white seabass, Pacific barracuda, cod, haddock, tuna, halibut, mackerel, paddlefish, lumpfish, carp, whitefish, cisco, tarpon, bonefish, weakfish and dolphin are widely utilized. Roes are usually cooked separately, but in the case of very small fish they are simply left in the body cavity. They can be made into sauces, creamed soups, casseroles, used as a garnish, or made into special products by salting, pickling or pressing. Roes are marketed in fresh and canned form. While edible when frozen, both the shelf life and quality are limited.

The female roe consists of 2 elongated saclike ovaries, round in cross section and covered with a membrane which is also a connective tissue. The unripe eggs or oocytes are plainly visible in a fresh roe; there should be no clouded or shriveled portions. Roes can be spoiled by careless handling in removing, washing and icing. It is especially important to eliminate all bloodstains when washing as the adjacent gall sac if broken will impart a bitter flavor. A prime roe should be intact, clean, and of uniform color. The overall color will vary according to species and maturity, ranging from pale yellow to orange but some roes are amber, or blue-gray to black. In general an immature or "green" roe which is pale in color, small in cross section and very compact or, at the other extreme, a fully ripe roe in which the eggs are ready to separate from the membrane, are both of poor flavor and texture, being too firm or rubbery. Prime roes differ in texture according to species. When cooked they range from a smooth paste to a granular consistency and vary in flavor according to the amount of protein (yolk), oil and water content.

The gonads of male fishes appear as a pair of long white sacs, somewhat flattened in cross section and much smaller than the ovaries in a female of comparable size and maturity. The immature testes are pink or reddish in color and change to white indicating the presence of spermatozoa with sexual development. This "white roe" is considered a great delicacy in various cuisines and was eaten raw by many coastal North American Indian tribes; the gonads of male salmon were held in particular

Patti McClane with a roosterfish of record size, caught off the Mexican Coast

esteem in the belief that their consumption increased virility. However, a white roe briefly poached in water with lemon juice and simply browned in butter is an extremely nutritious food of very fragile flavor. In classic French style white roe is served as **Laitances en Caisse** in baked tartlets and also in barquettes, on toast points and in the form of fritters or **Laitances en Beignets.**

Many recipes require poaching or parboiling all roe before further cooking by frying, broiling or baking; this has been construed as a means of oil reduction through separation; however, the bland polyunsaturated oil of a roe provides most of its flavor and this pretreatment has a different purpose—to firm the roe to prevent breaking, and to shorten the cooking time over direct heat when using a large roe. As a rule of thumb, if a roe greatly exceeds a 1-inch thickness it should be simmered for 5 or 6 minutes; otherwise there is no need to cook partially before some other procedure. White roe, on the other hand, is extremely fragile in all sizes and should be pretreated if the recipe requires that it remain intact. *See also CAVIAR, DOLPHIN, SHAD, SOFT ROE.*

Roosterfish

The roosterfish is a unique species; although closely related to the jacks it is in a distinct family, Nematistiidae. It occurs only in the eastern Pacific along the coast of South America from Peru to the coast of Baja California, Mexico. In Spanish-speaking countries it's known as **papagallo, gallo** and **pez gallo.** Although roosterfish are caught in all sizes, 20 to 30 pounds is ordinary and it has been recorded to 111 pounds. This is a very unusual-looking fish with 7 greatly elongated dorsal rays which gives its back fin the appearance of a long comb. Roosterfish are colorful with a greenish-black back fading to a golden-white below and many lavender tints; 2 black stripes curve downward across its body.

Roosterfish have very firm white flesh similar to the amberjack *(see under JACK).* However, the fast-swimming roosterfish is not easily caught by commercial methods and the landings are quickly sold in Central and South American markets. Small amounts are shipped to the interior cities of Mexico. At best, this is a musculature designed for a chowder. It can be deep-fried but will toughen under dry heat unless broiled or baked in a butter- or oil-based sauce.

Rouget

See GOATFISH, MULLET, SNAPPER.

Round Whitefish

See under WHITEFISH.

Sablefish	Sea Cucumber	Silversides
Sailfish	Searobin	Smelt
Salmon	Sea Trout	Smoked Fish
Salt Fish	Sea Urchin	Snapper
Sardine	Seaweed	Snoek
Sashimi	Shad	Snook
Sauces	Shark	Sole
Scallop	Sheepshead	Squid
	Shrimp	Stockfish
		Stocks
		Striped Bass
		Sturgeon
		Sucker
		Sunfish
		Surfperch
		Swordfish

S

S

Sablefish

Better known as "black cod," the sablefish is not a cod but belongs to the family Anoplopomatidae, which is a group of fishes confined to the North Pacific Ocean. Sablefish are caught in deep cold water as far down as 2,400 to 3,000 feet with pots and sunken gill nets. A large sablefish is about 3 feet in length and 40 pounds in weight. Its white flesh has a high oil content and does not lend itself to cod recipes. **Smoked Canadian Black Cod,** one of the hallmarks of discerning Pacific Northwest seafood restaurants, is sablefish at its best. It can also be barbecued with excellent results.

SMOKED SABLEFISH NUGGETS

2 cups flaked smoked sablefish	1 teaspoon grated onion
1½ cups seasoned mashed potatoes	dash of pepper
1 egg, beaten slightly	½ cup fine cornflake crumbs
	peanut oil

Combine fish, potatoes, egg, onion and pepper; beat until smooth. Chill well. Portion fish mixture with a ¼-cup measure. Shape into balls, and roll in crumbs. Fry in deep fat heated to 350°F. for 3 to 5 minutes, or until lightly browned. Serve with your favorite egg sauce or cheese sauce, hot. Makes 4 servings.

Sailfish

A marine gamefish found in the tropical and subtropical regions of the western Atlantic, Pacific and Indo-Pacific. The sailfish (*Istiophorus platypterus*) is not legally sold as a fresh product in the U.S., where it is caught by sport fishermen and usually released at the boat. However, numerous countries fish for sailfish with longlines on our Continental Shelf and these are utilized in foreign markets. Small quantities of angler-caught sailfish are processed in Florida smokehouses. Smoked sailfish is an excellent product but in fresh form sailfish is inferior to the closely related marlins. The major markets for commercially landed sailfish are in Mexico and Japan. *See also MARLIN, SMOKED FISH.*

facing page, Atlantic salmon

Salmon

The salmon is our most ancient gourmet food. Its bones have been found in the caves of Old Stone Age man in southern Europe as have the vertebrae of carp, pike and dace, but these latter fishes were probably regarded as merely edible then, as they are today. These midden heaps date back to 25,000 B.C. Troglodyte paintings indicate by their numbers that the salmon was greatly esteemed. Perhaps the most graphic tribute by a caveman is a bas-relief sculpted in the floor of the Grotto du Poisson near Les Eyzies, France, which depicts a salmon in almost taxonomic detail. The aboriginal cultures of North America (radiocarbon dating of artifacts from the Columbia River watershed indicate that Indians were probably living there about 11,000 B.C.) not only worshiped salmon as a food but gave the fish an elaborate role in their mythology. By the Middle Ages in Europe, the salmon was no longer a mere source of nourishment but a spectacular display at banquet tables where it was served whole on silver trays to the sound of trumpets—a harmonious respite between multiple meat courses. During the reign of Louis XV salmon cookery reached incredible heights, with the fish almost lost under varieties of *barquettes*, *quenelles*, sauces, and assorted accompanying seafoods. Escoffier wisely reversed the trend in saying that "salmon should be served as plainly as possible," then reached his professional nadir in suggesting that it be fried in butter.

For my taste there are three ways to know salmon at its best, and the best is simple: kited and planked, then basted and cooked by reflected heat from birchwood coals on the riverbank; or made into **gravlax;** or delicately cold-smoked in green juniper. All other methods pale by comparison; but this is a highly subjective view and of no value in the kitchen.

When speaking of salmon we are talking about 7 distinct species and a number of important variables. Recipes that work for one do not always produce comparable results with another, and depending on season or origin there are often culinary differences even within a single species.

There is only one kind of salmon native to the Atlantic Ocean. Two species occur, however, as the coho salmon has recently been established in New Hampshire waters. Six others occur in the Pacific. In addition we find related fish called "salmon" on European menus, such as the Danube salmon of Germany or the Taimen salmon found in the Soviet Union, but these members of the genus *Hucho* are inferior in quality, being coarse and lean. The Atlantic salmon and 3 Pacific species, the chinook, coho and sockeye, also occur as landlocked freshwater populations; depending on their available food supply, the end product is variable at table. Salmon from our Great Lakes, for example, feed principally on alewives, which results in an oily, ill-flavored, almost colorless meat, quite unlike that of prime salmon taken in, or recently returned from, the ocean. Landlocked salmon found in certain lakes and rivers of our New England states and the Maritime Provinces of Canada, where they feed on the delicate smelt, compare favorably to seagoing fish. I can pass no judgment on the rare landlocked Saimaa salmon isolated in the pine barrens of the Finnish-Soviet borders as I have only sampled one. Although I rushed my prize on ice to Helsinki, the salmon was so badly cooked that it was difficult to imagine how the chef had prepared it.

Atlantic salmon were once abundant in America from the St. Croix south to the Delaware River; the singular exception was the Hudson which despite its size offered few tributary streams essential to spawning. The most important rivers, on the basis of size alone, were the Connecticut, Merrimack, Androscoggin, Kennebec, Penobscot and St. John. It was in these river valleys that the Dutch and English settled beginning in the seventeenth century. One of the more famous fishing places was the falls at Amoskeag on the Merrimack River. Although salmon was not the favorite foodfish of the Indians (striped bass and sturgeon were more highly esteemed) the spring run was a time for great celebration: "At these, fishing seasons lovers' vows were plighted, marriages consummated, speeches made, and treaties formed." (The Merrimack River: Its Sources and Tributaries, J. W. Meader, Boston, B.B. Russell, 1869) By 1815, however, the proliferation of dams and pollution from sewage and textile mills had wiped out the Connecticut salmon, by 1860 the Merrimack fishery collapsed, and during the 1870s the more northerly rivers of Maine suffocated in blankets of sawdust and water-fouling effluents of the lumber industry. Although concerted efforts are being made today to restore the Atlantic salmon, they exist only as token populations in a few rivers in northeast Maine.

The malaise that blighted America had its counterpart in the industrialized regions of Europe. France and Spain once had tremendous salmon stocks; for that matter the over 800-mile-long Rhine River produced millions of pounds of the fish as late as 1885, but after the turn of the century their decline came quickly. Dominantly agricultural countries such as Ireland and Scotland managed to preserve some semblance of their former salmon populations but not in a quantity to supply even their own demand. All Atlantic salmon in U.S. markets are derived from foreign sources, chiefly from Canada in fresh and frozen forms and from Europe as a smoked product. However, many European smokehouses supplement their production with coho from Washington and Alaska. Fortunately, our Pacific salmon stocks have survived under an intensive open-sea fishery by many nations due largely to modern research and conservation programs. So the Atlantic salmon is a more costly fish at market, or for that matter even if you seek it with rod-and-reel. To pay $5,000 to $10,000 for a week of salmon fishing on an Olympian river is not unprecedented, and the torrent of gold that has poured down Norway's fjords reached flood stage in recent years. Iceland, Quebec, Labrador, Scotland and England can also provide a heady atmosphere of high finance leading one to believe that he is *buying* the river, not simply the vague promise of catching a fish. Pacific salmon, which are taken by countless thousands of people from northern California to Alaska at minimal expense, are today, as they have been historically, the more widely utilized species in American cuisine.

In 1792 a Yankee trader by the name of Robert Gray sailed into the mouth of the Columbia River, which he named after his ship. This vast river system, over 1,200 miles in length with its mighty tributary streams, was the greatest watershed in the growing boundaries of the U.S. in terms of its salmon fishery. When Lewis and Clark arrived in their overland journey by way of the Salmon River, then down the Snake to the Columbia River mouth in 1806, salmon was the principal food of the Indians. Edible roots, plants and berries contributed to a balanced diet, but "pemmican" or dried and pulverized salmon was their staple. The Indians were not avid hunters before the white man supplied them with firearms; killing an elk, deer or antelope with an eighteenth-century Shoshone bow-and-arrow required far more effort than taking salmon in baskets and dip nets. Lewis and Clark mentioned seeing 107 bags of pemmican (each weighing from 90 to 100 pounds) at one lodge, and it's estimated that over 60,000 pounds of fresh salmon were processed to make this amount.

Curing salmon by salting them in barrels and leaving them covered with the pickle that forms was the first method used by the white man along the Columbia River, not only for local use but for shipping to remote markets. In this form, Pacific salmon were sent to London, Valparaiso and the Hawaiian Islands as early as 1830 to 1840. The *lomi-lomi* salmon of Hawaii was then, and is now, no different from the product we call "lox," a salt-cured salmon that has been desalinized by soaking in

SOME EXAMPLES OF SALMONS

top, King salmon; center, Coho salmon; bottom, Sockeye salmon, male in spawning color. In spite of the attractive color of the sockeye, at this stage the flesh is watery and tasteless.

fresh water. Although the Hudson's Bay Company held a veritable monopoly on the Columbia River fishery until 1860, during the next decade American packers took over completely. With the completion of the transcontinental railroad tons of salted salmon were sent to Chicago, New York and Boston, and by ship to Europe. In 1897 S. Schmidt & Company of Astoria, and the Trescott Packing Company of Warrenton, Oregon, began using a mild cure by first dry-salting the sides (8 to 10 pounds of salt for each 100 pounds of salmon) then placing them in a 90° sal brine at a temperature of 35° to 38°F. for 20 to 90 days. This cure was in great demand for the smoked salmon trade in London and Hamburg. The mild-cured fish could be delivered by refrigerator cars as 6 cold-storage and freezing plants were already operating on the Columbia River by 1899. Initially, only chinook salmon and steelhead trout (often sold as salmon) were frozen, as large "fat" fish were preferred in European smokehouses.

SALMON TERMINOLOGY

DANISH SMOKED SALMON A U.S. market name for cold-smoked Atlantic salmon from Denmark. Denmark has no salmon rivers but harvests the waters off Greenland. For no valid reason "Danish Salmon" often commands a higher price in the American delicatessen trade as opposed to so-called "Nova" or even Scotch salmon, all of which may be the same product. Qualitative distinctions can be made on the basis of which house did the smoking.

INDIAN CURE SALMON A Pacific salmon which has been brined, then cold-smoked for a prolonged period, often as long as 2 weeks, at temperatures from 70° to 80°F. This results in an extremely firm product sometimes called **INDIAN HARD CURE.** The method was common to the coastal tribes of the Northwest for long-term storage. A kind of aquatic "jerky," it's best relegated to survival foods.

IRISH SMOKED SALMON As with Danish smoked and Scotch smoked salmon, a geographical reference to cold-smoked Atlantic salmon. Generally speaking, in terms of products sampled from various sources in Ireland, protein coagulation is the rule. The best available until recently was from Noel Huggard's Ashford Castle, where Huggard operated an electronically controlled smokehouse.

KENNEBEC SALMON An eastern U.S. restaurant idiom for the Atlantic salmon in poached steak form. Although the Kennebec River no longer supports a salmon fishery, this historic reference still appears on menus, probably for sentimental reasons.

KIPPERED SALMON This can be one of two different products: **(1)** In Europe a whole kited Atlantic salmon which has been split down the back, mildly brined, then cold-smoked. Kippered salmon was first popularized in fifteenth-century Scotland and used solely for lean, spawned-out fish or "kelts."
(2) In the U.S. a Pacific salmon in fillet, chunk or steak form that has been mildly brined and hot-smoked. Our kippered salmon is usually made from the white-fleshed chinook which is often dyed red before smoking.
LOX (1) Originally mild-cured sides of the Atlantic salmon popularized by the Russian Jewish community in London, England, beginning in 1880 and introduced to America at the turn of the century. Today, lox is more often made from one of the Pacific species for the European trade.
(2) A U.S. market name for Pacific salmon, usually mild-cured sides of the chinook. Its real distinction when properly made is a low salt content, which is bolstered by the addition of sugar in the brine. The major markets for lox are in cities with large Jewish populations where it is most often served with cream cheese and bagels.
NOVA An eastern U.S. idiom among the delicatessen trade for cold-smoked salmon. The fish may have originated in Nova Scotia, as the name implies, but considering the relatively few salmon taken in this province its probable origin includes the Pacific Ocean. Much of the "Nova" marketed is processed in Brooklyn, New York, by Vita, Acme, Marshall, and Montrose.
SCOTCH SMOKED SALMON A universal market name for cold-smoked Atlantic salmon which generally originates in Scotland. The trade in Great Britain makes a distinction because of the widespread use of Pacific salmon in Europe. The term "scotch-smoked" indicates the use of the Atlantic species as opposed to coho or chinook which are simply marketed as "smoked salmon."
SQUAW CANDY Strips cut from the sides and belly of Pacific salmon, usually salt-brined with some sugar added, then hot-smoked. Salmon with a low fat content such as the chum are preferred in making squaw candy.

POACHED WITH OPTIONS

The exclamatory panache for every buffet table is a poached and glazed whole salmon. In the hands of a master it is a work of art. For the home chef, however, there are mechanical limitations; even professionals often fumble in attempting a decorative *tour de force* with a large fish. So before perusing the recipes, let's consider the problems of a poaching method.

There are various court bouillons (*see under*

STOCKS) suitable for poaching salmon, but first you must have the correct equipment to handle a whole fish. I once cooked a 30-pound lobster to perfection in a clean metal trash can purchased for the project, but ingenuity will get you nowhere with a salmon of equal size, despite the *Farmer's Almanac* which advises poaching in an electric dishwasher at 2 cycles. The popular fish poacher for home use is 24 inches in length—suitable for a salmon about 4 pounds in weight (at this tender stage it's called a "grilse"). Preferably one should own a poacher of 36 inches in length to accommodate a typical 8- to 10-pound salmon if it is to be cooked whole, head and tail intact. However, many modern household ranges cannot support a yard-long pan even across three burners, so if both factors are negative the only option is to cut the fish into halves and cook one section at a time. The halves can then be reunited and the surgery disguised with a garniture. I saw this artfully done in one of France's greatest restaurants—Auberge Père Bise in Talloires—when Marius was confronted with an unusually large fish proudly delivered by one of his patrons just returned from Norway. Of course, size can outrun your capacity to cope with it; for example, the not uncommon 25- to 30-pound salmon has a girth that would preclude almost any poacher in existence.

If the angler has a choice, and this is a seasonal problem, particularly by late summer when small salmon are scarce, or if the fish is to be purchased at market and poached whole, select a fish of 6 to 8 pounds. Salmon of this size are easier to handle and you can obtain more uniform cooking; the finer musculature of these small fish results in a better texture. If you do not own a poacher with a removable perforated rack for lifting the fish out of the broth intact, wrap the salmon in cheesecloth, leaving about 12 to 18 extra inches of cheesecloth at each end of the fish. Twist and knot the ends (do not let these hang out of the poacher as they can easily catch fire) and use these for lifting. Remember to have somebody available to support the midsection of the fish from underneath with a broad spatula to prevent its breaking.

Alternatively, a large salmon can be cooked by slicing out a centercut to fit the poacher if you have a showcase presentation in mind such as an aspic with a traditional garniture. If it's simply a matter of eating poached fish it can, of course, be cut into steaks. It's best to dress each fish to a variety of options. For example, if you fillet the salmon you can smoke one side and barbecue the other for immediate consumption, or reserve sections of the fillets for making **sashimi** or **gravlax,** or portions can be cut into fingers to be cooked tempura style. If you prefer portions for broiling or poaching, then begin with crosscuts from the nape to the anterior insertion of the anal fin, slicing out 1-inch-thick steaks; beyond the body cavity, section it into 8- to 10-inch-wide center or "loin" cuts which can be poached, baked, or used in a variety of ways.

POACHED AND GLAZED

A whole poached salmon served in aspic *(saumon glacé)* is the ultimate centerpiece on a cold buffet table. The creative process is in 5 parts: making the court bouillon, poaching the fish, making the aspic, decorating the fish, selecting the garnitures. Aside from the poaching itself, which is the same process for any recipe, the differences in recipes are concerned with whether red or white wine or Champagne or Cognac is utilized in the court bouillon and aspic (or perhaps none of these is used) and the choice of decoration and garnitures. In brief, **Glazed Salmon à l'Impériale** is essentially the same poached fish as **Glazed Salmon à la Russe;** only the peripheral ingredients have changed. So the home chef has unlimited opportunities to create original presentations once the techniques are mastered. **Glazed Salmon au Chambertin** is not only colorful but less expensive to produce than most classics. You may use an Atlantic, coho, pink, sockeye or chinook salmon.

GLAZED SALMON AU CHAMBERTIN

1 whole salmon, 6 to 8 pounds, dressed
3 quarts Red-Wine Court Bouillon (p. 383)
2 quarts Red-Wine Fish Aspic (p. 26),
    made from court bouillon
1 cup cooked green peas
1 cup diced cooked green beans
1 cup diced cooked carrots
1 cup diced boiled potatoes
1 cup plus about 6 tablespoons mayonnaise
2 tablespoons chopped fresh dill
12 small tomatoes, peeled and hollowed
12 pitted black olives
12 hard-cooked eggs, halved lengthwise
¼ cup chopped black olives
salt and pepper
lemon slices (halved rounds) for scales
cucumber slices (halved rounds) for scales
1 small cherry tomato for eye

Measure the depth of the fish at its thickest point to determine the cooking time; allow 10 minutes to the inch. At completion the internal temperature of the fish should be 140°F. Poach the salmon in red-wine court

HOW TO DECORATE A POACHED SALMON

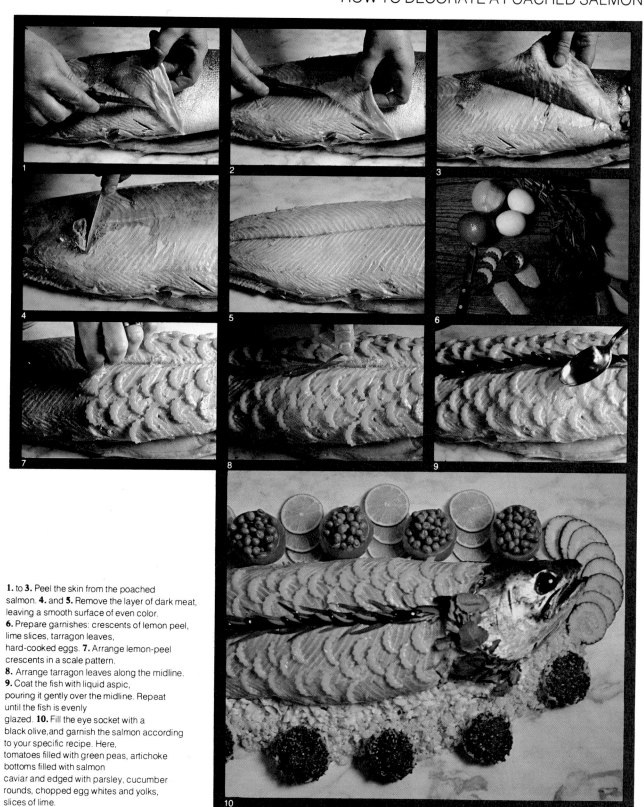

1. to 3. Peel the skin from the poached
salmon. 4. and 5. Remove the layer of dark meat,
leaving a smooth surface of even color.
6. Prepare garnishes: crescents of lemon peel,
lime slices, tarragon leaves,
hard-cooked eggs. 7. Arrange lemon-peel
crescents in a scale pattern.
8. Arrange tarragon leaves along the midline.
9. Coat the fish with liquid aspic,
pouring it gently over the midline. Repeat
until the fish is evenly
glazed. 10. Fill the eye socket with a
black olive, and garnish the salmon according
to your specific recipe. Here,
tomatoes filled with green peas, artichoke
bottoms filled with salmon
caviar and edged with parsley, cucumber
rounds, chopped egg whites and yolks,
slices of lime.

bouillon. Let fish cool in the liquid, then remove it on the poacher grid to a countertop to drain and firm. Use the liquid to make the necessary aspic, and chill the aspic until syrupy.

Remove the skin from the salmon by gently freeing the skin with the tine of a fork, then peeling it by hand, starting at tail and working toward head. Remove the salmon's eye; this will be replaced with the cherry tomato. The paper-thin layer of dark-colored meat (really muscle hemoglobin), which lies just under the skin and along the median line, is perfectly edible but for a colorful poached presentation this should be removed with a thin, dull-edged knife after the fish has "set." Carefully run the entire blade over the surface of the fish in a brushing motion following the grain of the musculature. Then gently insert the point of your knife in the median line at an angle and follow this horizontal strip from head to tail. Repeat the stroke from the opposite side at an opposing angle and the dark meat can be lifted free. The result will be an overall pink salmon which adds greatly to the eye appeal of the finished dish.

Prepare the garnishes: Mix together the peas, beans, carrots and potatoes in 1 cup mayonnaise with the dill. Fill the hollowed-out tomatoes with this mixture. Top each with a black olive. Brush the stuffed tomatoes with some of the aspic. Carefully remove the egg yolks and mash with half of their volume (about 6 tablespoons) of mayonnaise, the chopped black olives, and salt and pepper to taste. Using a pastry tube, refill the whites with the seasoned yolk mixture. Brush the eggs with some of the aspic.

Pour enough liquid aspic into a deep serving platter to form an "under layer" about ¾ inch deep. Let aspic set until firm. Place salmon on top and decorate with overlapping rows of thin lemon and cucumber slices in a scale pattern; slices can be bisected as only half of each is visible. Save the smaller end slices of both lemon and cucumber for the narrower tail portion of the salmon. Dip each "scale" into aspic to make it adhere. Insert the cherry tomato eye. Coat fish with a thin layer of aspic by pouring it gently along the midline; when this becomes firm, coat one or more times until an even glaze is obtained. Garnish the platter surrounding the salmon with the stuffed tomatoes and eggs. Keep the platter chilled until ready for table. Serve with Sauce Verte or Dill Sauce or Cucumber Sauce (see under SAUCES). Makes 12 servings.

There are various glazed salmon presentations in classic French cuisine which are considerably more expensive to assemble due to their costly ingredients. The following descriptions may give you some ideas with respect to other components which can be included.

GLAZED SALMON À L'IMPÉRIALE

Poach salmon in white-wine court bouillon and glaze with white-wine aspic. Make scale decoration from whites of hard-cooked eggs and slices of truffles. Surround the salmon on the platter with mousselines of crayfish and pastry shells filled with red salmon caviar. A very elegant presentation. Serve with cold Hollandaise Sauce or Cucumber Sauce.

GLAZED SALMON À LA RUSSE

Poach salmon in white-wine court bouillon and glaze with white-wine aspic. Decorate in rib pattern with sliced truffles along the midline and radiating tarragon leaves. The garnitures surrounding the salmon are stuffed tomatoes (as for au Chambertin), small barquettes of cucumber filled with beluga caviar, and quartered hard-cooked eggs. Serve with cold Hollandaise Sauce.

GLAZED SALMON MONSELET

Poach salmon in white-wine court bouillon and glaze with white-wine aspic. Decorate with tarragon leaves, truffles and lobster coral in floral patterns. Surround the salmon on the platter with artichoke bottoms mounded with puréed green asparagus tips, and small tomato mousses sprinkled with minced tarragon leaves.

Floral patterns are often intricate but simple to execute. For example, egg whites can be cut into the shape of flower petals with little rounds of lemon peel at the center, supported by a stem and leaves made of thin and thick strips of cucumber skin, to create a "daisy." The trick is to dip each piece into aspic as you proceed so these fragile decorations won't disassemble when the salmon is finally glazed. Other effects can be achieved by using a pastry tube filled with green mayonnaise, anchovy paste or lobster paste. Monselet is served with cold Hollandaise Sauce or Sauce Verte.

COLD POACHED SALMON À LA BREAKERS
(The Breakers, Palm Beach)

Poach salmon in court bouillon and let it cool in the court bouillon, then drain and chill it well. Coat fish on both sides with mayonnaise collée (see under ASPICS). Or coat it with green butter and decorate with stripes of mayonnaise. Garnish the platter with cucumber slices, quarters of hard-cooked eggs, gherkins and watercress.

For individual serving, cut the salmon into

serving pieces and put each on a salad plate. Garnish with Belgian endive cut lengthwise into quarters. On top of the salmon arrange several thin slices of avocado and, around the avocado, cucumber slices. Serve with green mayonnaise.

STUFFED SALMON WITH EGG SAUCE

1 whole salmon, 4 pounds, dressed
1½ teaspoons salt
1½ cups diced celery
1½ cups chopped onions
1 garlic clove, minced
1 small bay leaf, crumbled
¼ pound butter or margarine
4 cups soft bread crumbs
2 tablespoons chopped parsley
½ teaspoon dried rosemary
dash of pepper
Egg Sauce (p. 288)

Wipe 1 teaspoon of salt around inside cavity of fish. Place fish in a well-greased baking pan. Cook celery, onions, garlic and bay leaf in 6 tablespoons of the butter or margarine until vegetables are tender. Add remaining salt, the bread crumbs, parsley, rosemary and pepper; toss lightly. Stuff fish loosely; brush with remaining butter or margarine. Cover fins and tail of fish loosely with foil. Bake in a moderate oven, 350°F., for 45 to 60 minutes, or until fish flakes easily when tested with a fork. Accompany salmon with egg sauce. Makes 6 servings.

BARBECUED SALMON STEAKS
(California Wine Institute)

6 salmon steaks, each 1 to 2 inches thick
1 cup rosé wine
¼ teaspoon dried marjoram
½ teaspoon onion powder
1/16 teaspoon pepper
seasoned salt

Salmon steaks 1 inch in thickness will cook on your grill in about 10 minutes, allowing 5 minutes on each side. A 1½-inch steak requires 7 minutes, and a 2-inch steak about 10 minutes on each side. If baked or broiled in an oven the necessary time is less as the steaks cook on both sides at once. Test for doneness with a fork.

Combine the wine, marjoram, onion powder and pepper, and pour over uncooked salmon in a shallow glass or enamelware pan. The amounts of seasoning in the marinade can be increased to your taste. Use more marinade if necessary to cover the salmon steaks. Refrigerate for several hours, turning salmon once or twice. Drain well. Barbecue or broil, sprinkling with seasoned salt as the salmon cooks. Makes 6 servings.

SALMON STEAKS PROVENÇALE

6 salmon steaks, each 1 to 2 inches thick

½ cup dry white wine
celery salt
freshly ground white pepper
3 ounces butter
1 cup minced onion
2 garlic cloves put through a press
3 fresh tomatoes, peeled, drained, seeded, and minced (see Note)
1 teaspoon minced fresh tarragon
1 cup heavy cream
butter for basting
beurre manié (2 tablespoons each of butter and flour)
lemon wedges
parsley

Rub the salmon steaks with celery salt and pepper; set them aside to chill. In a saucepan melt the butter and add onion and garlic; simmer gently until onion becomes transparent. Add the tomatoes, wine and tarragon, and cook for a few minutes to blend ingredients. Add the cream; when the mixture returns to a simmer, cover the pan and turn off heat.

Cook the salmon steaks over charcoal or in the oven; baste with butter during cooking. When done set aside on a warm platter.

Bring sauce back to a simmer and add the *beurre manié* as needed, stirring constantly until the sauce is smooth and thickened. Pour sauce over the steaks either on a platter or individual dishes. Garnish with lemon wedges and parsley. Accompany with crisp steamed zucchini. Makes 6 servings.
NOTE: Use canned Italian plum tomatoes if fresh tomatoes are not of good quality.

COULIBIAC OF SALMON

BRIOCHE DOUGH
1 envelope dry yeast
¼ cup warm water (105° to 115°F.)
¼ cup warm milk
2½ to 3½ cups sifted all-purpose flour
¼ pound butter, softened
4 eggs
¼ teaspoon salt

Dissolve the yeast in the water in a large bowl. Then stir in the milk and 1 cup of the flour; mix well. Cover the bowl and let the dough rise in a warm place (75° to 85°F.) until doubled in bulk. Punch down, then add the butter, 3 eggs (save the last egg for egg wash), 1½ cups more flour and the salt. Mix into a dough and beat hard and long with an electric mixer, or beat hard with a wooden spoon. Cover and let rise again until expanded (it won't double this time). Once again punch down, turn out on a floured board, and work in enough of the remaining flour, kneading as you do, to make a soft elastic dough, not sticky. On a floured cloth, roll out the dough ¼ inch thick, thinner if possible, to make a sheet 18 by 14 inches.

COULIBIAC FILLING
3 pounds centercut salmon steaks
2 cups cracked wheat (bulgur)
4 cups boiling water
¾ pound butter
4 onions, sliced
½ pound mushrooms, sliced
6 shallots, chopped fine
⅓ cup dry white wine
salt and pepper
3 hard-cooked eggs, chopped
3 tablespoons minced fresh dill, or
    1½ tablespoons crumbled dried dill
½ cup fine bread crumbs

While the dough is rising prepare the filling. Put the cracked wheat in a heatproof bowl and pour the boiling water over it; stir, then set aside. All the water will be absorbed in about 45 minutes, and no further cooking is necessary.

Melt ¼ pound of the butter in a large skillet and simmer the onions in it until very soft and transparent, about 20 minutes. Transfer onions to a bowl and set aside. Melt 4 tablespoons additional butter in the same skillet and sauté the mushrooms over high heat for about 7 minutes, or until dry. Use 4 tablespoons more butter to coat a large ovenproof casserole. Sprinkle shallots in the casserole and arrange salmon steaks over them. Add wine, sprinkle with salt and pepper to taste, and cover salmon directly with a sheet of foil with a small hole in it for steam to escape. Bake in a 400°F. oven for 20 to 25 minutes. Let fish cool, then remove bones and skin. Save shallots and fish cooking liquid.

Mix sautéed onions and mushrooms, 4 cups of the prepared cracked wheat, chopped eggs and dill. Season with salt and pepper to taste. On the rolled-out brioche sheet, arrange half of the wheat mixture, leaving an uncovered border of dough 4 inches wide at the narrow ends and 1 inch wide at the long sides. Arrange salmon on the wheat layer, sprinkle with the shallots, and cover with rest of wheat mixture. Melt 4 tablespoons of remaining butter in the reserved fish cooking liquid and slowly pour it over the filling. Mix the egg left from the brioche ingredients with 2 tablespoons water to make egg wash. Brush some on the narrow border of the dough. Using the pastry cloth to help, shape the dough into a roll and seal with egg

wash. Trim the narrow ends if necessary, brush with more egg wash, and fold over to seal the ends. Gently roll the *coulibiac* over onto a buttered baking sheet, with the seam on the bottom. Make 2 steam vents in the pastry, or about 6 tiny slashes. Let the dough rise for 20 minutes, and preheat oven to 400°F.

Melt remaining butter and brush over the risen dough; sprinkle with the bread crumbs. Bake in the preheated oven for 35 to 40 minutes, or until the *coulibiac* is golden brown. Serve hot, cut into slices, with a bowl of melted butter, plain or flavored with dill. Makes 8 to 10 servings.

NOTES: Instead of bulgur, 4 cups of cooked rice or buckwheat (kasha) can be used.

Instead of baking the salmon, you can poach it in white-wine court bouillon. Clarify the broth and serve it in cups with the *coulibiac*.

In the original Russian dish, less of the grain was used and the mixture was thickened with *viziga*, the marrow (spinal cord) of the sturgeon. This is available in powdered form in specialty shops. If you use it, soak 4 ounces (for a *coulibiac* of this size) in cold water for 3 hours, then cover with additional water and cook for 2½ to 3 hours, until it reaches tapioca consistency. Mix with the bulgur, rice or kasha.

GRAVLAX

Any angler who has fished in Scandinavia is familiar with this raw, salt-and-sugar-cured salmon which is featured in so many country inns. It's the pure essence of the fish and a preparation for which I have an absolute craving after a cold day on the river. *Gravlax* was regularly served at the Lindström's Hotel, that ancient angling headquarters on the Laerdal River in Norway, where it was the custom among princes and kings (and Lindström's listed many among its regular guests) to start the day with a heaping plate of *gravlax* washed down with ice-cold thimbles of aquavit. Although recipes differ in the volume of salt and sugar to use, the one-half (sugar) to one-quarter (salt) ratio is typically Swedish. It's also favored by many professionals such as Arne Kesby at the Hotel Bristol, who for many years sent a weekly supply to the royal household in Copenhagen, Denmark. Some recipes require equal parts of salt and sugar, or more salt than sugar, but I believe the ratio given produces an ideal cure with only the faintest suggestion of a sweet flavor. It's important to have really pungent dill which you chop to release its full aroma.

2 pounds centercut of fresh Atlantic, sockeye,
    coho, or chinook salmon

¼ cup salt
½ cup sugar
1 bunch of fresh dill, coarsely chopped
2 teaspoons crushed white peppercorns

Scale and debone the salmon, cutting the fish into two pieces along the line of the backbone. Do not rinse the pieces but wipe dry with paper towels. Mix salt and sugar and rub the fish with the mixture. Sprinkle part of the mixture and some of the dill in a deep enamelware or earthenware baking dish. Place one piece of salmon, skin side down, in the dish and sprinkle generously with dill, crushed peppercorns, and salt/sugar mixture. Cover with the second piece of salmon, skin side up. If the pieces do not match in shape, place the thick side against the thin side.

Sprinkle the salmon with remaining salt-sugar mixture. Cover with a sheet of aluminum foil and a light weight such as a chopping board. The fish will "leach out" in about 4 to 5 hours, and the fluid should be poured off. Keep the *gravlax* refrigerated for at least 48 hours, turning the fish around at least twice during that period. It can be stored for a week and if properly chilled should keep for 2 weeks.

To serve, cut into slices free from the skin. Sauté the skin in butter in a hot skillet, roll it up and use as a garnish for the salmon in addition to sliced cucumbers, dill and lemon wedges. Serve with *gravlax* sauce.

GRAVLAX SAUCE

3 tablespoons oil	pinch of white pepper
1 tablespoon red-wine vinegar	2 to 3 tablespoons prepared mustard
1 tablespoon sugar	2 to 3 tablespoons minced dill
⅓ teaspoon salt	

Blend together all ingredients except dill. Add the dill, or serve it from a separate bowl.

HOW TO MAKE GRAVLAX

1. Use centercut, about 2 pounds of dressed salmon.

2. Cut into 2 pieces along the line of the backbone; debone and wipe dry.

3. Sprinkle salt-sugar mixture into earthenware dish and over flesh side of one piece.

4. Sprinkle with crushed peppercorns and add chopped dill under and over the fish.

5. Cover completely with a thick layer of chopped dill.

6. Place second piece of salmon on top, skin side up, thick side against thin side.

SALMON IN PAPER (PAPERI LOHI) (prepared by Chef Hannu Rikkonen at Grand Hotel Tammer, Tampere, Finland)

1. Use a boned salmon fillet with the skin still on. Cut through the flesh almost to the skin at ½-inch intervals, then cut through at each second cut, to give double slices still attached at the skin side (like the first stage in making a butterfly chop).

2. Open out the slices and place each one, skin side down, on a large sheet of buttered butchers' paper. Sprinkle with white pepper and salt.

3. Chop hard-cooked eggs and fresh dill. Sprinkle each salmon slice with egg, then with dill, then with more egg.

4. Fold the paper once over the salmon and crimp the edges together, making a package. Slide package onto a baking sheet, and bake in a very hot oven (450°F. or 250°C.) for 13 to 14 minutes.

BARBECUED GRAVLAX

When ready to barbecue, wipe the fish clean; do not wash it. Beginning an inch or two in from the tail end, skin the fillet; set the skin aside. Cut the flesh into portion-size pieces. Cup each portion on foil, leaving the top of the foil open. Cook the salmon on a charcoal grill with the lid on, to obtain some smoke flavor, until the fish flakes easily with a fork. Cut the reserved skin into strips and butter-brown to crispness in a saucepan. Serve a piece of skin with each portion, and accompany with Gravlax Sauce (p. 269) and a cold sliced cucumber salad. A 5-pound piece of salmon prepared for *gravlax* will make 6 servings.

COLLECTING DIVIDENDS

Like the cod, a salmon is about 99 percent edible. The delicately flavored gonads (white roe) of the male can be placed in water filled with ice cubes with the juice of a lemon added; after firming for about 30 minutes, dry and roll in a bread-crumb batter; sauté or deep-fry. Or gently poach the white roe and serve in pastry shells with hollandaise sauce topped with whipped cream.

The bright orange roe of the female is commonly made into a caviar substitute. *(See How to Make Caviar and Salmon Caviar under CAVIAR.)*

No matter how the fish was cooked, if the head was included, beneath the operculum (gillcover) you will find a sweet nutlike meat, which is easily pried loose with a fork. The head, bones, fins and scaled skin can be simmered into a rich fish soup or stock, or the skin can be cut into strips and crisply sautéed as in the recipe for *gravlax*. Its fat belly can be turned into a squaw candy or brined and made into lox. At Forman & Sons in London, little old ladies in soggy tennis shoes queue up in the evening on the wet cobbles to buy "leftovers" after the day's processing. They are true ichthyophiles—whether by choice or chance.

CANNED SALMON

Canned salmon is one of the most versatile seafoods on supermarket shelves but despite its popularity few buyers learn to read the labels. Five species of Pacific salmon are purveyed in canned form and individually there are de-

facing page, To serve, slide each package onto a heatproof plate, open the top of the package, and accompany with lemon.

grees of quality which can be determined in a simple kitchen test. Just as there is a difference between the finest marbled Black Angus and the beef from an old Holstein bull, so it is with most fish, and there is as much reason for a cost differential.

The industry began in 1864 when Hume and Hapgood packed 4,000 cases (each containing 48 one-pound cans) of salmon caught in the Sacramento River of California. Today, North American packers ship nearly 5 million cases of the same measure, which represents 7 percent of our total annual fish consumption. The bulk of this production consists of sockeye salmon, followed by the pink, chum, coho and chinook. This is not in order of preference but rather availability, as the delectable coho and chinook salmon command a high price in both fresh and smoked forms and demand exceeds the supply. However, quality begins with *when* the fish was caught. The word "chinook" is no guarantee that you are buying a prime fish; if it was plucked from the sea or captured in the early spring season, yes, but taken in autumn the flavor and texture wobble from good to marginal.

Salmon caught in the ocean or just prior to entering the river are firm and plump; their bright silvery bodies are in perfect condition for a migration that may extend over a thousand miles. Energy for this long journey to the spawning grounds in the form of both fat and protein has been stored in their bodies, as the adult salmon do not feed while in freshwater. During that migration the fat and protein are gradually absorbed and the flesh becomes softer and more watery. The typical red or pink color of the flesh is derived from fat-soluble carotenoids found in crustaceans such as the many shrimplike animals which salmon feed on while in the ocean. This color fades during the fasting period with a corresponding loss in food value and flavor. For racial and biological reasons, salmon from certain rivers are always of better quality than those from other waters. For example, chinooks from the Rogue River in Oregon and the Copper River in Alaska are as fine as any obtainable, being consistently fatter and of better color and flavor than chinooks from many other watersheds. In the booming new industry of salmon "farming" the fish are reared in floating net cages and fed ground shrimp shells to produce the color which is the hallmark of a prime salmon.

HOW TO DETERMINE QUALITY

You may buy a can of pink salmon and decide that pink is the greatest, only to repeat the purchase under another brand and find the pale meat of a late-run fish. If a particular label provides a good-quality salmon that's reason

Coho salmon from the Pacific Coast, in a Scottish smokehouse

enough to be loyal. Price *is* an indication of quality, and more often than not the species when identified in print will reflect the reason for its higher cost. If the label simply reads "salmon" with no species identification, the chance of finding a quality product inside is nil. However, when a can of salmon is opened in the kitchen one can use a few simple inspection criteria.

Let the can stand upright overnight in a warm place to permit the oil to come to the surface. Use a can opener that cuts the lid off cleanly so that the contents will slide out without mutilation. Upon opening the appearance of the top surface of the fish should be pink and firm. Next, the chunk of fish should be gently depressed into the can with the back of a spoon in order to permit most of the liquid to rise to the surface, so you can judge the quantity and color of the oil. Generally, the more oil and the deeper its color, the better the quality of the fish. When the contents are emptied on a plate, the interior of the can should have no offensive odor indicating spoilage. If there is skin on the cylinder of fish taken from the can, it should not show a pronounced reddish or black hue. Although there is a normal color difference between the back and belly, the naturally darker blue-green skin on the back must not be confused with the reddish or blackish discoloration which indicates sexual maturity or a late-run fish. If there are fins present or blood clots in the flesh, or if the meat is shredded, these are indications of poor quality-control in canning. When the cylinder of fish is broken apart, the color of the flesh should be uniform and not consist in part of deeply colored flesh and part very pale. In general the more vivid the color the better the product. If the packer has cooked the fish sufficiently, the backbone can be crumpled under easy pressure between two fingers. Don't waste this valuable calcium, as the bone is perfectly edible and contains significant amounts of vitamin D and phosphorus.

Since food value depends on fat and protein content, the following analysis of canned salmon (Marine Products of Commerce, Tressler and Lemon) depicts the variables among our 5 North American Pacific salmon. Protein content does not vary much but the oil, which contains a high percentage of polyunsaturated fatty acids, more than doubles between the chum and chinook. Bear in mind that all salmon are rich in vitamin A as well as niacin, riboflavin and other B-group vitamins.

NUTRITIONAL VALUE OF CANNED SALMON

Species	Total solids (percent)	Fat (percent)	Protein (percent)	Ash (percent)	Food value per pound (calories)
Chinook	36.83	15.72	17.67	1.22	991
Sockeye	35.22	11.22	20.80	1.23	860
Coho	32.51	8.49	21.08	1.21	750
Pink	30.20	6.99	20.40	0.76	696
Chum	29.96	6.69	20.67	1.02	514

HOW TO READ LABELS

CHINOOK SALMON The chinook or "king" salmon (Oncorhynchus tshawytscha) is the most highly prized of our 5 North American species. In common with all salmon, prime quality occurs when the fish is ocean-caught and has had a chance to make significant growth. The chinook is the biggest salmon (recorded to 120 pounds) and its flesh when canned readily separates into very large flakes. It is very rich in oil and is commonly sold in several grades according to color, which varies from deep red to white. Because of the large flakes and high fat content, it has a soft texture and is more suitable for eating au naturel and for salads than for cooked dishes. Often sold under the label "Royal Chinook."

COHO SALMON The coho or "silver" salmon (Oncorhynchus kisutch) is much smaller than the chinook and is fine-textured. The flake of the canned coho is pink, less often red, but always lighter than the flesh color of the sockeye. Generally speaking, it is inferior for salads but suitable for all other purposes. Coho are prime as ocean-caught fish of over 5 pounds in weight. Landlocked populations taken in freshwater such as the Great Lakes are of poor quality compared to the sea-run coho; these are not canned commercially and have little value as a home-canned product.

SOCKEYE SALMON The delicately flavored sockeye or "red salmon" (Oncorhynchus nerka) is most often a deep orange-red color; in the can it has a small flake and a considerable amount of oil. The flesh is firm and adaptable to everything from sandwiches to cooked dishes. This fish is generally found under the label "blueback salmon" and compares to the chinook in price.

CHUM SALMON An ocean-caught chum salmon (Oncorhynchus keta) is a good table fish in fresh form although it is somewhat coarse in texture. The flesh is invariably deficient in red color (it may at times appear gray) and fat content in relation to the other species, so the canned product is not highly regarded. However, the chum smokes well, and in this form was favored by coastal Indian tribes. It is a nourishing food and can be made into many palatable dishes. Its market price is lower than for the other species. The small roes of the female chum are esteemed in making salmon caviar.

PINK SALMON The pink (Oncorhynchus gorbuscha) is the smallest Pacific salmon and the flesh has a finer texture. The flakes are small and range from light peach to deep pink in color. The species has a delicate distinctive flavor and is well adapted to sandwiches, various cooked dishes and chowders. About half of the American pack of canned salmon is made up of pinks, and it can usually be obtained at a price lower than for the others—with the exception of the chum.

CANNED SALMON RECIPES

The following basic recipes are popular for the canned product and require a minimum of time in the kitchen. These work equally well with leftovers from poached, boiled or baked fresh salmon, provided the fish has not been overcooked. Hot-smoked or kippered salmon can also be used with surprisingly tasty results in recipes such as Salmon Soufflé, Salmon à la King and Salmonburgers.

SALMONBURGERS

1 pound canned salmon
2 cups chopped onions
2 cups chopped green peppers
3 tablespoons cooking oil
4 cups mashed potatoes
1 egg, beaten
1 teaspoon dry mustard

2 teaspoons
    Worcestershire sauce
¼ teaspoon pepper
½ teaspoon salt
10 hamburger buns,
    split and toasted

Drain and flake salmon; set aside. Cook onions and green peppers in the oil for about 10 minutes, or until tender. Stir in potatoes, salmon, egg and seasonings. Refrigerate until cold. Form into 10 cakes. Place cakes on a well-oiled grill and cook for 5 minutes, or until brown on one side. Turn and cook until brown on the other side. Place each burger in a toasted bun and top with a tomato slice, onion rings and sliced sweet pickles. Garnish with radishes. Makes 10 burgers.

SALMON À LA KING

2 cups canned or cooked salmon
½ cup melted butter or margarine
½ cup chopped celery
½ cup chopped green pepper
¼ cup flour
½ teaspoon salt
1½ cups liquid
    (milk combined with canned salmon liquid)
1 cup canned sliced mushrooms
2 tablespoons chopped pimiento

Break salmon into small chunks. Melt butter in a pan, add celery and green pepper, and cook over low heat until vegetables are tender. Gradually add flour and salt and stir until smooth. Slowly add liquid and cook gently, stirring, until sauce is thick and smooth. Add salmon, mushrooms and pimiento. Heat mixture and serve in a small patty shell, on toast, or over cooked rice. Makes 6 servings.

SALMON DIABLE

1 pound canned or
    cooked salmon, flaked
¾ cup sour cream
¼ cup medium-dry sherry
1 tablespoon lemon juice
1 teaspoon
    Worcestershire sauce
½ teaspoon dry mustard
2 eggs, slightly beaten

⅓ cup fine cracker crumbs
¼ cup minced parsley
1 tablespoon minced onion
salt and pepper
6 thin lemon slices
paprika

Mix sour cream, sherry, lemon juice, Worcestershire sauce, mustard and eggs. Stir in salmon, cracker crumbs, parsley and onion. Add salt and pepper to taste. Spoon mixture into 6 greased baking shells or individual casseroles. Top each with a lemon slice and sprinkle with paprika. Bake in a moderate oven, 350°F., for 30 minutes. Delicious with peas or green beans and shoestring potatoes for luncheon or dinner. Makes 6 servings.

FRUITED SALMON CURRY

1 pound canned salmon, flaked
2 tablespoons butter or margarine
1 medium-size onion, minced
½ green pepper, minced
1 garlic clove, minced
1 to 2 teaspoons curry powder, according to taste
dash of cayenne pepper
½ teaspoon salt
¼ cup flour
1½ cups liquid (milk combined with canned salmon liquid)
1 package (12 ounces) frozen melon balls in light syrup,
    partially defrosted
1 teaspoon lime or lemon juice

In a medium-size saucepan melt the butter and in it sauté the onion, green pepper, garlic, curry powder and cayenne for about 8 minutes, or until onion is tender but not brown. Stir in salt and flour and cook, stirring, until all flour is blended with curry mixture. Gradually stir in liquid and cook, stirring, until sauce is thickened. Cook over low heat for 5 minutes, stirring occasionally. Add frozen melon balls (or use fresh ones). Add salmon and lime or lemon juice; remove from heat and stir only until melon balls are defrosted if frozen, or warmed if fresh and chilled, and salmon is heated through. Serve with rice, or pile into center of a parsley rice mold. Do not let sauce cook after melon balls and salmon are added. Makes 6 servings.

SWEET AND SOUR SALMON

1 pound canned salmon, flaked
½ cup vinegar
1 cup water
1 tablespoon soy sauce
¼ cup sugar
½ teaspoon salt
1 tablespoon dark molasses
2 large green peppers, cut into 1-inch squares
1 cup thin slices of carrot
1 garlic clove, minced

1 can (13½ ounces) pineapple cubes,
  or defrosted frozen pineapple, drained
2 tablespoons cornstarch
¼ cup salmon liquid, pineapple juice or water

In a saucepan combine vinegar, the 1 cup water, soy sauce, sugar, salt and molasses; bring to a boil. Add green-pepper squares and carrot slices; simmer for 3 minutes. Add garlic, pineapple cubes and flaked salmon. Stir in cornstarch mixed with ¼ cup liquid and cook, stirring, until sauce is clear and thickened. Serve with fluffy cooked rice, additional soy sauce and hot mustard. Makes 6 servings.

SALMON SOUFFLÉ

1 cup canned or cooked salmon	½ teaspoon salt (see Note)
1 cup milk, approximately	½ cup mayonnaise
2 tablespoons butter	3 eggs, separated
2 tablespoons flour	

Butter the bottom only, not the sides, of a 1-quart soufflé dish or casserole. Drain the liquid from canned salmon into a 1-cup measure. Add enough milk to fill the cup. Discard skin and bones and flake the salmon. Melt the butter in a pan; blend in flour and salt. Add milk gradually and cook, stirring constantly, until thickened. Remove from heat; blend in mayonnaise. Beat egg yolks until light; fold into sauce which has been slightly cooled. Fold in salmon; let the mixture cool completely. Beat egg whites stiff but not dry, and fold into mixture; combine gently but thoroughly. Pour into the prepared dish, and set dish in a shallow pan of hot water in a preheated 350°F. oven. Bake for 45 minutes, or until puffed and set. *Do* serve immediately; soufflé will collapse if kept waiting. Makes 4 servings.
NOTE: Use less salt if the salmon and mayonnaise are salty.

Salt Fish

No food product has affected history more than salt fish, particularly cod and herring. When European fleets ventured into the western Atlantic seeking new fishing grounds in centuries past, the need for larger and more efficient boats created the navies of maritime nations. Cod and herring were universal coins in a trade which supported and even triggered wars—and the dark years of slavery in our own country. The intrinsic value of salt itself is very ancient for, being a precious commodity, it was taxed as far back as 2197 B.C. in the reign of the Chinese Emperor Yü. But its imagery of wealth was among the Roman legions who were issued limited quantities of salt or optionally given a *salarium* or "salt money" to buy it for themselves. Thus, the word "salary." One of the oldest roads in Italy is the Via Salaria which led to the valuable salt pans of Ostia. All countries were not rich in salt and fewer still had the pure sodium chloride that makes a prime fish product. Although sodium chloride is the dominant compound in seawater, the ocean also contains considerable amounts of magnesium chloride, magnesium sulfate, calcium sulfate and potassium chloride, all of which are undesirable in curing or cooking fish. In the complex process of manufacturing salt by solar-evaporation these contaminants can be eliminated in varying degrees with a first-grade salt containing 96 percent sodium chloride and less than 1 percent each of the undesirable compounds. Even our Yankee-wise Gloucestermen hauled salt by schooner thousands of miles across the sea from Trapani, Cádiz, and the Turks Islands to cure the New England cod. The quality of a salt-cured fish is no better than the purity of its preservative.

On a consumer level the popularity of a lightly or heavily salted product has been determined by the availability of refrigeration for retail storage and also the sodium requirements of individual cultures. It has been postulated that people living in tropical climates favor a heavy cure where other staples of their diet do not supply an adequate amount of salt. Theoretically, this would compensate for the loss of body salts through perspiration. However, there are too many exceptions in African nations and among more primitive people such as the Waika Indians of the steamy Orinoco region who find salt abhorrent due to a singular diet of roasted meats (mainly capybara, tapir and monkeys) which contain adequate amounts of sodium chloride which is preserved in the roasting method. The Waikas, with whom I have spent time, do not eat boiled foods; boiling is a process that removes salt. Other cultures maintain their body salts in hot climates through fluids; for example, the Bedouin tribes of the Hadhramaut in Arabia drink large quantities of camels' milk. The Scandinavian phenomenon of "salt starvation" is often related to the frequent use of a sauna but I doubt the validity of this premise unless one is overly hygienic. Boiled foods are most common in rural Scandinavia, particularly in Norway, and sodium chloride is a popular food preservative. Historically, it was not always obtainable in quantity, as there is little salt in the Baltic and considerable dilution from the many rivers along the Atlantic shore. The predilection for this seasoning in contemporary Scandinavia is comparable to its widespread use in the non-sauna, warmer climates of Spain and Portugal where salt fish is a national passion.

The term "salt fish," in much of Europe at least, implies a cured codfish as opposed to any other species. To this day, there is no discernible market in Spain or Portugal for fresh cod, as they prefer the **bacalao.** In a broader context, however, salt fish must include a variety of species such as mackerel, salmon (even if it *is* called lox), and certainly the herring and haddock which are traditionally preserved in this form. The method of "rousing" or salting herring aboard ship was originated by the Dutch in the fourteenth century. After removing the gills and most of the viscera through a slit in the throat the fish were sprinkled with salt and mixed or roused and packed head to tail in barrels with salt between the layers. The barrels were then topped and made airtight to prevent oxidative rancidity—exactly the same process used today.

I don't believe that pickle-cured fish is widely popular in the average kitchen, but the method has some value to fishing camps and for people living in rural areas where seasonal fluctuations in the availability of fish may be extreme. Pickle salting is done in a watertight container so that the fish are cured in the pickle that is formed. As I have already described (see COD), pickle salting differs from kenching, which produces dry-salted fish, in that the pickle is allowed to drain off, and from brine-cured fish, which results in a product with a much higher water content. It's important that pure salt be used in any cure as even very small amounts of sulfates, magnesium salts, and especially calcium salts retard the penetration of sodium chloride into the fish, and these impurities also tend to make the product bitter-tasting. Many species of fish can be pickle-cured but the most popular are mackerel, cod, herring, mullet, lake trout, salmon, alewife, pollock, rockfish, shad and striped bass. Although there is some loss of protein as well as oil from fatty fishes, the salt does have a bactericidal effect in preservation.

PICKLE SALTING

The best container for pickle-salting fish is a wooden barrel or a stoneware crock of a suitable size for the volume of fish to be processed. Lacking these, a glass or enamelware container can be substituted.

Scale and dress the fish. Small fish can be split down the back and kited (do not cut through the belly portion) but any fish over 2 pounds should be cut into 2 fillets, removing the backbone. Do not remove the "collarbone" or lug as the fillet is less likely to be damaged in handling. The fillets should be scored on the flesh side but in the thick sections only to a depth of about ½ inch at 2-inch intervals. These cuts should not penetrate the skin. Wash the fillets thoroughly in cold water, then leach in a brine made of ½ cup salt to 1 gallon water for 30 to 40 minutes, to remove diffused blood and slime. The fish should then be drained for about 15 minutes.

Fill a shallow pan with dry salt. Scatter a thin layer of salt on the bottom of the crock in which the fish are to be salted. Coat each piece of fish in the pan of salt, and rub salt into places where the flesh is scored, but minimize its application around the napes and tails. Pick up the fish with as much salt as will cling to it, and pack skin side down in the container. Arrange the pieces so that an even layer will result. Pieces should overlap as little as possible. Scatter a thin layer of salt over the layer of fish, and arrange the next layer of fish at right angles to the preceding layer. With smaller fish, it is necessary to lay 1 or 2 fish across the center to keep layers level. Stagger successive layers so that each fish rests on 2 fish of the layer below.

The amount of salt used depends upon the purity and grain of the salt; less is required, for example, if the salt is of high purity and small grain. The season of the year is to be taken into consideration; more salt is required in warm weather. Large, thick, or fat fish require more salt, and a larger amount of salt is needed for longer periods of preservation. As a general rule one tenth salt to any weight of fish, or 1 pound salt to 10 pounds fish, is minimum for a light pickle, and 3 pounds salt to 10 pounds fish for a hard cure.

Place a loose-fitting wooden cover on the top layer of fish and weight the cover. Clean bricks make good weights. The fish will form its own brine. A small fish or thin fillet will be completely pickled in 48 hours but thicker or fatter fish may take up to 10 days. At the end of this time, remove fish and scrub in fresh water with a stiff brush. The fish can then be soaked in cold water for 8 to 12 hours (depending on the strength of the cure) for immediate use, or they can be repacked for long-term storage. Apply a light scattering of salt between layers when repacking. Then fill the container with a fresh saturated brine made with 1 cup salt to 1 gallon water. Store in a cool, dark place. After a month, or at the first sign of fermentation, remove and change the brine. Fish held this way keep well, and hard-cured products may last for 9 months at low temperatures.

Sardine

In commerce "sardine" is not the name of any one fish but

rather a collective term for a number of small soft-boned species in the herring family. This may include young Pacific or Atlantic herring, blueback herring, pilchards, or sprat (which is sold as brisling sardine). The canning industry began on the island of Sardinia with a Mediterranean species *Sardina pilchardus*, thus the name has historical acceptance. However, there are some differences in texture and flavor between the various fishes and often extreme variations in the quality of the pack. During the halcyon years (1930 to 1936) of our Pacific sardine fishery, U.S. landings reached a billion and a half pounds annually. For various reasons this catch declined rapidly and today the American production is largely from the coast of Maine. Canada's major sardine fishery is in the Bay of Fundy.

Sardines are marketed fresh or lightly salted in some countries, notably Portugal, Spain and Italy, but the world trade is based on canned products. The little fish are mechanically scaled aboard swift-moving carrier boats, then washed, brined, and briefly steam-cooked at the canneries. After air-drying, the sardines are graded by size and packed manually in 3¼-ounce to 4⅜-ounce tins. Before sealing, an appropriate sauce or oil is injected by machine, and the can is sterilized in high-pressure steam ovens. The most common supplements are soybean oil, olive oil, olive oil with chili powder added, and mustard sauce. Some are fried or smoked before being packed and others are skinned and boned to be sold as "fillets of sardine." Canned sardines can be made into a variety of appetizers for the canapé tray, or used for sandwiches, salads and soufflés.

Large fresh sardines may be split and cooked over charcoal while butter basting, then served with generous splashes of lemon juice. In the Sicilian style they are baked in white wine, **Sarde al Vino Bianco,** or baked with a stuffing made from bread crumbs, anchovies, pine nuts, white raisins, onions and parsley in making **Sarde a Beccafico.**

Unfortunately, we don't have a similar sardine in U.S. waters, as its only counterpart here is our Pacific sardine *(Sardinops sagax)*, which for all practical purposes is extinct. Writing in 1873, W. C. Prime *(I Go A-Fishing)*, in his delightful sketch "Three Bottles of Claret," found the Mediterranean kind worthy of celebration which must have come as a shock to his readers, as this early American author, rightly or wrongly, considered anything swimming in the eastern Atlantic second-class:

"There are articles, of course, which are to be found in other countries superior to the same article here; but America is the only land for general good eating. One gets fearfully tired of a European kitchen, even with all the resources of Paris in the palmiest days of the Brothers. But here the varieties of fish and flesh are inexhaustible; and fruit—nowhere in the world is there a fruit market comparable with that of New York. An English sole is not equal in flavor to a flounder taken in clear water at Stonington, and a turbot is no better than a tautog. Shad, sheepshead, Spanish mackerel, red snappers, bass, bluefish—a fresh bluefish is glorious— where will you stop in the list of fish that abound on our coast, every one of which is better than any salt-water fish known on the other side of the Atlantic?"

"Excepting sardines."

"Well, I may perhaps except sardines."

"May? None of your prejudices, old fellow. There's no dish of fish to be invented equal to sardines, fried and served as they used to do it in the old San Marco at Leghorn. I lament the closing of that house with profound regret. I have gone down from Florence more than once to pass a night there just for the sake of the delicious breakfast I used to get on those sardines. No one else cooked or served them so in any town on the French or Italian coast."

"I remember fifty years ago seeing them catch sardines along the shore at Naples."

"Yes, I have sat many a morning in the window at the old Vittoria, looking out on the sea and watching the sardine nets come in, glittering with diamonds; and I have taken them with a rod at Leghorn."

In Portugal fresh sardines come packed in wooden boxes.

Fresh sardines are
salted, then grilled over
a charcoal brazier.
At a family celebration
in Cascais, Portugal,
freshly grilled sardines
are served and eaten
in the cobbled street in
front of the house.

SARDINE APPLE SALAD

2 cans (3¼ ounces each)
   sardines
1 cup diced unpeeled
   red apple

1 tablespoon lemon juice
½ cup chopped celery
⅓ cup salad dressing
lettuce

Drain sardines and cut into bite-size chunks. Sprinkle apple cubes with lemon juice to keep color bright. Combine all ingredients except lettuce. Mix gently. Serve in crisp lettuce cups. Makes 4 servings.

CURRIED SARDINES

2 cans (3¼ ounces each)
   sardines
½ cup chopped onion
2 tablespoons
   melted butter
2 tablespoons flour
1½ teaspoons
   curry powder

½ teaspoon salt
1½ cups milk
2 teaspoons lemon juice
1 hard-cooked egg,
   chopped
2 to 3 cups
   hot cooked rice

Drain sardines and cut into bite-size pieces. Cook onion in butter until tender. Blend in flour, curry powder and salt. Add milk gradually. Cook, stirring constantly, until thickened. Add lemon juice, egg and sardines. Mix gently. Heat thoroughly, then serve over rice. Makes 4 servings.

HOT SARDINE ROLLS

2 cans (3¼ ounces each) sardines
1½ teaspoons lemon juice
½ teaspoon minced onion
½ teaspoon prepared horseradish
10 thin slices of very fresh white bread
¼ cup melted butter

Drain sardines, reserving 1 teaspoon of the oil. Mash fish and add reserved oil, the lemon juice, onion and horseradish. Mix well. Trim crusts from bread and spread with sardine mixture. Roll each slice, jelly-roll fashion, and fasten at both ends with wooden food picks. Brush rolls with melted butter, then cut into halves. Place in a shallow pan and bake in a moderately hot oven (400°F.) for 10 minutes, or until lightly browned. Makes 20 appetizers.

BRUNSWICK CHEESE BALLS

2 cans (3¼ ounces each) sardines
8 ounces cream cheese
2 teaspoons Worcestershire sauce
⅛ teaspoon pepper
1 cup finely chopped nuts

Drain sardines well, and mash with a fork. Soften cream cheese. Combine cheese, Worcestershire sauce, pepper and sardines. Mix until well blended and smooth. Place in refrigerator. When mixture is sufficiently chilled, form into small balls about ¾ inch in diameter and roll in finely chopped nuts. Place a cocktail pick in each ball. Chill and serve. Makes about 30 appetizers.

HARLEQUIN SARDINE CASSEROLE

3 cans (3¼ ounces each)
   sardines
4 tablespoons butter
⅓ cup chopped onion
¼ cup chopped
   green pepper
3 tablespoons flour
1 teaspoon salt
dash of pepper
1⅔ cups milk

1 cup grated
   Cheddar cheese
1⅓ cups packaged
   precooked rice
1 tablespoon
   chopped parsley
½ teaspoon dried orégano
1 can (14 ounces) tomatoes
1⅓ cups liquid (juice
   from tomatoes plus water)

Drain sardines and cut into bite-size pieces. Melt butter and add onion and green pepper; cook until tender. Blend in flour, ½ teaspoon salt and a dash of pepper. Add milk gradually and cook, stirring constantly, until thick and smooth. Add cheese and stir until cheese melts.

Place rice in a well-greased shallow baking dish, 12 x 8 inches. Sprinkle with parsley, orégano and remaining ½ teaspoon salt. Drain tomatoes, reserving juice. Add water to juice to make up 1⅓ cups liquid. Pour over rice, stirring until all of rice is moistened. Place half of tomatoes over rice. Top with sardines. Spoon cheese sauce over sardines. Place remaining tomatoes on top of sauce, making a checkered design. Bake in a moderate oven (350°F.) for 30 to 35 minutes. Makes 6 servings.

GOLDEN SARDINE POTATO SALAD

3 cans (3¼ ounces each)
   sardines
4 cups diced
   cooked potatoes
1 small onion, chopped
2 tablespoons
   chopped parsley
1 cup chopped celery

1¼ teaspoons salt
2 tablespoons light cream
4 tablespoons
   prepared mustard
2 tablespoons vinegar
2 tablespoons sugar
dash of pepper
lettuce

Drain sardines and cut into bite-size pieces, reserving a few whole ones for a top garnish, if desired. Combine potatoes, onion, parsley, celery and 1 teaspoon of the salt. Mix lightly. Add broken sardines. Combine remaining ingredients except lettuce, to make dressing. Beat with a rotary beater or an electric mixer until light and fluffy. Pour over sardine-potato mixture; mix gently but thoroughly. Cover, place in refrigerator, and allow to marinate for about 1 hour. Serve, garnished to taste, in a salad bowl lined with crisp lettuce. Makes 6 servings.

Sashimi

A generic Japanese term for raw fish cut into various forms according to density and musculature, which is usually dipped into soy sauce and *wasabi* before eating. When perfectly fresh, raw fish does not have the texture, flavor or aroma of a cooked product but is more delicate in all respects. In common with oysters, clams, sea urchins and other foods eaten raw, *sashimi* must be prepared from fish that are no more than 24 hours from the water, and iced but never prefrozen as the thawing process leaches out the unique flavor.

Sashimi is a traditional course in any formal dinner in Japan but it's also the specialty of hundreds of small restaurants which radiate from Tokyo's Tsukiji Central Wholesale Market where the word "fresh" will divert golden streams of yen at every morning auction. Raw fish is ancient culinary history to western coastal Indian tribes and a logical basic food to the Eskimo, yet except in Hawaii it's only a recent introduction to the American scene. It is popular today because of the welcome proliferation of Japanese cuisine. The concept is no different from eating uncooked ground beef in the form of steak tartare and, in fact, there is an amazing similarity in flavor.

The skill in preparing *sashimi* rests on cutting the fish; a very firm species such as the tuna or tilefish is cubed **(kaku giri)** while less dense though still firm fish such as the striped bass, porgy and red snapper are cut into paper-thin slices **(usu zukuri),** so thin that they are literally transparent. Fish with a fragile texture, or those that would be finely flaked if cooked such as the weakfish or corvina, are flat cut **(hira giri)** into ¼-inch-thick slices, otherwise the musculature will be mushy and shredded. A thread-shaped cut **(ito zukuri)** is used on thin fillets such as the flounders, which are reduced to ¼-inch-wide strips. Mollusks such as abalone and squid, which are very firm, are usually served in small cubes or threads. Bear in mind that this is not done for presentation alone, but to make a bite-size piece of fish manageable with chopsticks. Although the honest *sashimi* chef will serve only those fish that are fresh, ordinarily several varieties are presented, decoratively arranged on the plate.

Sashimi: *wasabi* (grated green horseradish root), mackerel, tuna, shredded vegetables

HOW TO PREPARE SASHIMI (prepared at the Nippon Restaurant, New York City)

1. Porgy, cut into slices.

2. Tuna, cut into long strips;

3. then into slices.

4. Mackerel, skin is peeled off;

5. fillet is cut into long strips;

6. then into slices.

7. to **9.** Salmon is cut into slices at an angle.

10. Summer flounder (fluke)

11. Flounder is cut into very thin slices, called *hirame-usuzukuri*.

12. Flounder slices are arranged to form a flower, *hirame-hanazukuri*.

1. Squid is split open to make a large piece and scored to lie flat.
2. Seaweed is arranged on the squid. 3. Squid and seaweed are rolled up together. 4. Excess squid is cut off. 5. Squid roll is pressed to make it firm.
6. Roll is sliced to give black and white pinwheels, *ika-isobemaki*.

1. Striped bass, skin is peeled off.   2. Fillet is cut into long strips;   3. then into slices.

1. Carrot flowers: peel off outer layer of carrot.   2. Notch carrot lengthwise all around.   3. Cut crosswise slices to make flower shapes.

ARRANGEMENTS OF SASHIMI AT NIPPON RESTAURANT

Clockwise from left: squid with seaweed, flower shapes of
summer flounder, striped bass, salmon, tuna, in the center, porgy

Another flower design: Japanese pink gingerroot surrounded by flounder and salmon

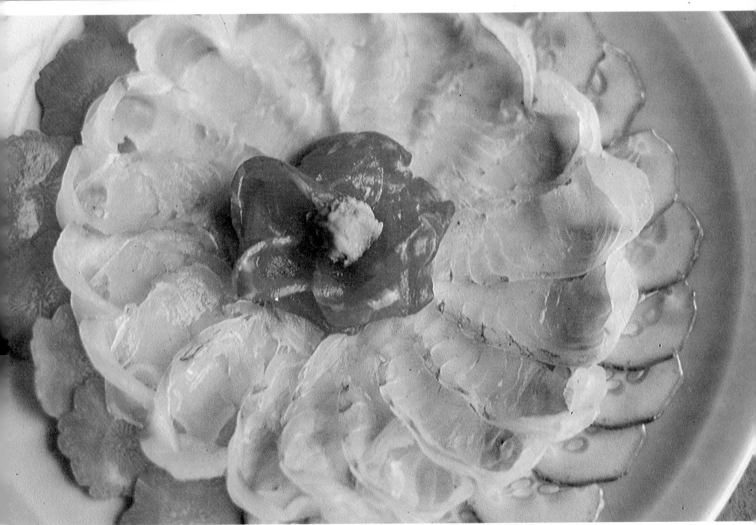

Japanese pink gingerroot in the center surrounded by salmon and summer flounder, cucumber and carrot in the outer circle.

Sashimi has a companion dish in the form of **sushi,** which is chiefly balls of vinegared rice wrapped in seaweed **(nori)** and garnished with strips of raw fish, although some cooked foods are used also.

As with shellfish the ingredients for *sashimi* must be taken from pollution-free waters. Unsatisfactory conditions can exist in the sea as readily as in freshwater, particularly in the coastal areas near large cities. Although saltwater fish can be infected with harmless-to-man parasites, freshwater species should not be used for *sashimi* because of the possibility of digenean trematode and certain cestode- and nematode-related diseases from uncooked fish. This has a parallel in eating improperly cooked pork.

Sauces

In fish cookery, the simplest sauce is a *velouté*, which is merely a white roux liquified with fish stock, then seasoned with salt, white pepper and a touch of cayenne. This homogeneous blend lends emphasis to a delicate fish flavor, particularly when poaching very bland species such as halibut, cod, sole, red snapper, whitefish or walleye. I do not suggest that a contrasting sauce, say with a tomato, mustard or cheese base, might not be appropriate, but if a rich *fumet* is available, maintaining the bland character of the fish, which is fragrantly sweet when fresh, is to me more important. One of the blandest of all fish, the sole, is subjected to every kind of sauce imaginable but this extravagance evolved at a time when transport from sea to market did not always provide perfectly fresh products. By introducing a strongly contrasting taste, any hint of staleness was effectively disguised. Actually in nucleotide degradation, a fish becomes "tasteless" before spoilage actually occurs.

On the other hand those fishes which assert their own flavor, such as the bluefish, salmon, king mackerel, tuna, herring, lake trout, mullet and striped bass, are most often presented with a contrasting sauce, usually an acidic base with vinegar or lemon juice, as fish flesh is alkaline in nature with pH values usually above 7 only declining to 6.0 and acidity if stored too long. When a natural gelling agent such as a *fumet* is not available, a sauce is generally thickened and emulsified with a starch (usually flour) and egg yolk, but these must be used judiciously to avoid a "gravy" texture. The sauce should be smooth and thin and have a natural taste. These same assertive fishes when served cold need little more than a sour-cream or homemade mayonnaise dressing to complement their texture and flavor.

The imaginative use of sauces is not limited to a singular choice as various sole presentations exploit two sauces such as a *Béchamel* and a *Nantua* in a dual role. These are spooned separately over opposite halves of the fillet—pale yellow on the left and pink on the right, or drizzled in bands across the fillet. This is perhaps more for visual appreciation, but eye appeal is a considerable factor in the enjoyment of good food.

BROWN SAUCE

½ cup red Burgundy wine 4 cups Brown Stock (p. 382)
¼ cup dry white wine Brown Roux (p. 286)
  (Chablis preferred) salt and pepper
¼ cup sherry

Never use one wine only, and especially don't use sherry alone. Pour the wines into a large saucepan and reduce over high heat to one third of their volume. Reduce heat, add the brown stock, and bring again to a boil. Add the roux in small amounts of 2 or 3 tablespoons at a time, stirring in thoroughly. The sauce must boil after the roux is added. Reduce heat, and add salt and pepper to taste. The sauce should coat the spoon. For a deep brown color caramel coloring is sometimes added, but I do not like additives and it adds nothing to fish dishes. Makes 4 cups.

SAUCE ESPAGNOLE

This name is often given to Brown Sauce, but the distinctive feature of *espagnole* (Spanish) is the use of tomatoes.

2 onions
2 carrots
2 celery ribs
2 tablespoons minced parsley stems
½ teaspoon minced fresh thyme
½ cup clarified butter or peanut oil
2 pounds ripe tomatoes, peeled and chopped
4 cups Brown stock (p. 382)
1 large bay leaf
6 to 8 tablespoons Brown Roux
salt and pepper

Peel onions, scrape carrots and celery, and chop all into small dice to make a *mirepoix*. Mix with parsley and thyme and cook in clarified butter or oil over low heat, stirring often, until the natural sugar in vegetables is released and the *mirepoix* is golden brown. Discard as many seeds from the tomatoes as possible. Add tomatoes to the saucepan and let them cook for 10 to 15 minutes, until they are beginning to liquefy. Add stock and bay leaf, stir well, then simmer over low heat, skimming as needed and stirring often, for 40 minutes to 1 hour, until reduced by one third. Put everything through a food mill, or purée in a blender and strain to discard any remaining tomato seeds. Transfer to a clean saucepan, bring again to a boil, and add brown roux, 2 or 3 tablespoons at a time, stirring in thoroughly, until the sauce is as thick as needed. Bring again to a boil, then season to taste. Makes about 6 cups.

For Sauce Espagnole in a hurry, add tomato purée to Brown Sauce. Use 2 to 4 tablespoons for 1 cup of sauce. Don't use canned tomato sauce or tomato paste as these make the sauce too acid and too strongly flavored.

BROWN ROUX

Melt ¼ pound butter in a heavy-bottomed skillet over low heat. Add 1 cup flour in small quantities and stir until blended. Place the skillet, covered, in the oven and cook at 200°F. for 1 hour, occasionally flaking it with a fork. Remove skillet from oven and let the roux stand for several hours before use.

SAUCE BÉCHAMEL (WHITE SAUCE)

Melt 4 tablespoons butter in a saucepan. The instant it is melted, remove pan from heat and sprinkle in, spoon by spoon, 4 tablespoons of flour; stir while adding and continue to stir until well blended. Slowly add 2 cups of room-temperature milk, stirring constantly. The sauce will become smooth and faintly yellow. Return the pan to the heat and stir some more. As sauce starts to bubble, add just a touch of salt and white pepper. Continue cooking over low heat until sauce thickens. Makes about 2 cups.

To make a richer sauce: separate 1 egg; use the white for something else. Add 2 tablespoons milk or cream to the yolk and beat with a whisk until blended. Then add a ladle of the hot sauce and continue whisking for a minute until the egg is blended. Turn into the rest of the sauce and heat, still over low heat and stirring all the time, till sauce is hot and thick. Makes about 2 cups.

SAUCE VELOUTÉ

2 cups Fumet de Poisson (p. 383)	2 egg yolks
	½ cup heavy cream
3 tablespoons unsalted butter	salt
	white pepper
3 tablespoons flour	1 tablespoon lemon juice

Melt the butter in a heavy saucepan. Off the heat, add the flour and mix until blended. Stir in the *fumet* and return the pan to the stove. Over low heat cook and stir for at least 10 minutes, until the sauce is smooth and somewhat thick. Beat egg yolks and cream in a heatproof bowl; still beating, add about ½ cup of the hot sauce and blend completely. Turn the egg mixture *(liaison)* into the rest of the sauce and slowly bring it to a boil, stirring all the while. Let the sauce boil for 1 second, no longer, then remove from the heat and continue to stir until the boiling has stopped. Season with salt and white pepper to taste, and stir in the lemon juice. Makes about 3 cups.

There are many other recipes for this sauce. Some add mushroom peelings and parsley stems to the flour-thickened stock and reduce and strain that without adding the *liaison.* Some use less egg yolk and cream. A velouté can be made following any of these methods, as long as it is made with good stock and is very smooth and velvety when finished.

CREAM SAUCE

1. Make 2 cups Sauce Béchamel. Add ½ cup heavy cream and reduce over low heat to 2 cups. Add another ½ cup heavy cream and heat. Season to taste, add 1 teaspoon lemon juice, and swirl in 1 tablespoon unsalted butter. Makes about 2½ cups.

2. Reduce 2 cups heavy cream by one third. If necessary, use *beurre manié,* ½ teaspoon at a time, to thicken to sauce consistency. Incorporate each amount completely before adding more. Makes about 1⅓ cups.

3. Melt 4 tablespoons butter and stir in 3 tablespoons flour off the heat. Add 1 cup heavy cream and 1 cup fish stock or chicken broth or liquid from poaching fish. Cook and stir over low heat until thickened. Makes about 2 cups.

Any of these cream sauces can be further embellished by adding 1 or 2 tablespoons of a compound butter just before serving; the particular butter should be appropriate to the dish. Or fold in whipped cream, ¼ cup for each 1 cup sauce, just before serving.

SAUCE CARDINAL

Make 2 cups Sauce Béchamel or Sauce Velouté. Adjust thickness with a few tablespoons of hot fish stock, and stir in 3 to 4 tablespoons finely minced cooked lobster and 1 tablespoon minced truffle. Just before serving swirl in, off the heat, 3 tablespoons lobster butter *(see Shellfish Butter).* Makes about 2½ cups.

SAUCE NANTUA

Make 2 cups Sauce Béchamel. Add 1 cup heavy cream and reduce the sauce over low heat by about one third, or until as thick as you like. Season with salt and white pepper to taste. Just before serving swirl in, off the heat, 4 to 6 tablespoons crayfish butter (see *Shellfish Butter*). Add a tiny bit of vegetable coloring, if necessary, to make the sauce quite pink. Makes about 2½ cups.

SAUCE MORNAY

Make 2 cups Sauce Béchamel. Make a *liaison*, as if making a Velouté, with 2 egg yolks beaten with ½ cup cream. Warm the *liaison* with some of the hot sauce, then stir the mixture into the rest of the sauce and slowly bring it to a boil, stirring. Let the sauce boil for 1 second, then transfer the saucepan to a *bain-marie* or double-boiler bottom filled with very hot water and keep stirring until boiling stops. Gently stir in 2 ounces natural Gruyère cheese and 1 ounce Parmesan cheese, both grated. Stir as the cheese melts to combine well. Do not let the sauce boil after adding cheese. Just before serving add 2 tablespoons butter and stir until melted. Makes about 3 cups.

This sauce can be made with Sauce Velouté instead of Béchamel if the stock used in the Velouté is agreeable to the rest of the dish. If you prefer, equal amounts of Parmesan and Gruyère can be used.

SAUCE VILLEROI

This sauce is used as a coating for foods to be deep-fried, usually finished with an outer layer of crumbs. It is also used as the basis for croquettes and fritters. It is a white sauce reduced to be very thick and further thickened with egg yolks. The sauces used are Velouté, Suprême or Allemande. Suprême is a development of a Velouté made with chicken stock. It is further flavored with mushrooms and enriched with more cream. Allemande is enriched with more egg yolks and even more cream.

For all practical purposes make a Béchamel with milk, or a Velouté with the appropriate unsalted stock. Reduce the sauce over an asbestos pad or over hot water, stirring often, until it is very, very thick, reduced by one third. Then add the enrichment for the Béchamel or the *liaison* for the Velouté and reduce again until the sauce is well blended and thick. Let it cool before using as a coating.

For croquettes, let the sauce cool to room temperature, then mix in the chopped fish or shellfish, and let everything chill in the refrigerator before shaping into croquettes. For fritters, coat the pieces of fish or the shellfish and place them on a flat surface, the pieces not touching. Chill until ready to fry.

Villeroi needs to be well seasoned, but it's best to do it after reducing. If it suits the recipe, add herbs or flavoring vegetables to the original sauce (onions, mush-rooms, parsley, celery essence, cuminseed, *et al*). If you start with 3 cups of the basic sauce, you should end with 2 cups Sauce Villeroi.

WHITE-WINE SAUCE I

1 tablespoon	2 tablespoons flour
chopped shallots	⅔ cup fish stock
1 tablespoon	or fish poaching liquid
chopped parsley stems	½ cup heavy cream
1⅔ cups white wine	salt and white pepper
5 teaspoons butter	

Simmer the shallots and parsley stems in ⅔ cup wine until reduced by half to a flavorful infusion. Meanwhile, melt the butter over low heat, stir in the flour to make a smooth pale roux, and add the fish stock or strained poaching liquid and remaining 1 cup wine. Cook over low heat, stirring often, until the sauce is very smooth and thick, and somewhat reduced. Strain the infusion into it, mix well, then add the cream. Continue to simmer, without allowing the sauce to boil, until it is reduced and blended to your taste. Season with salt and white pepper if you like. Makes about 2 cups.

NOTE: Other flavoring vegetables such as onion, carrot, leek or celery can be used for the infusion; a very good choice is chopped mushroom stems. A pungent herb, such as ¼ teaspoon tarragon, can be used if you find that flavor suitable for the dish. The choice of wine will also alter the taste. If you do not have fish stock or poaching liquid, use chicken stock. Clam broth is too strong in flavor for this sauce.

WHITE-WINE SAUCE II

2 tablespoons butter
2 tablespoons flour
2 cups white wine, or white-wine court bouillon,
    or liquid drained from poacher or steamer
4 egg yolks
1 teaspoon strained lemon juice

Melt the butter in a saucepan. Remove pan from heat and stir in the flour, spoon by spoon, until blended into the butter. Gradually add the white wine or court bouillon, or the cooking liquid if you have used wine in steaming or if fish has been poached or baked in wine. Let this simmer gently, but no longer than 5 minutes to prevent scorching. When ready to serve, warm the egg yolks by mixing in a cup with some of the hot liquid. Then stir the egg mixture into the rest of the sauce. Add the lemon juice, and continue stirring until the sauce thickens. Makes about 3 cups.

EGG SAUCE

2 tablespoons butter
    or margarine
2 tablespoons flour
½ teaspoon salt
dash of white pepper
1 cup milk

¼ cup half-and-half
1 tablespoon lemon juice
2 hard-cooked eggs,
    chopped
2 tablespoons
    diced pimiento (optional)

Melt butter or margarine in small saucepan. Blend in flour, salt and pepper. Stir in milk and half-and-half; cook, stirring constantly, until thick and smooth. Fold in lemon juice, eggs and pimiento; heat. Makes 1¾ cups.

CAPER SAUCE

4 tablespoons butter
4 tablespoons flour
2 cups strained fish cooking liquid
    from steamed or poached fish
6 tablespoons capers with juice

Make a roux with butter and flour, and add enough liquid, stirring as you add it, to give the consistency of a white sauce. Stir in capers. Makes 2½ cups.

CUCUMBER SAUCE

2 large cucumbers
1 small onion
2 celery ribs with leaves
½ cup light chicken or fish stock
1 tablespoon lemon juice
2 tablespoons Parsley Butter (p. 49)

Peel cucumbers and onion; wash celery ribs and trim; chop all three into small pieces. Add to the stock and lemon juice in a heavy saucepan and simmer until cucumbers are translucent and soft enough to be mashed with a spoon. Purée everything in a blender or push through a food mill. Reheat, and swirl in the parsley butter. Makes 2 cups.

For a cold cucumber sauce, see CUCUMBER CREAM SAUCE.

SZECHUAN SAUCE
(The Mandarin, San Francisco)

2 garlic cloves, sliced
1¼ tablespoons minced
    chili pepper
2 tablespoons soy sauce
2 tablespoons chicken stock

1½ tablespoons sugar
2 drops of
    sesame-seed oil
1 tablespoon vinegar

Brown the garlic slices in a wok. Add the rest of the ingredients and heat. Serve over shrimp balls. Makes ⅓ cup.

SWEET-AND-SOUR SAUCE
(The Mandarin, San Francisco)

1 cup ketchup
2 cups sugar
1 cup water
1 cup vinegar

juice of ½ lemon
1 tablespoon soy sauce
3 tablespoons cornstarch

Combine all ingredients except cornstarch in a wok or saucepan over medium heat until thoroughly blended. Mix cornstarch with a little water until fluid and pour slowly into sauce. Continue stirring to avoid lumps. When sauce is thickened increase heat for a minute to serve hot. Makes about 4 cups.

TOMATO SAUCE PAVILLON

2 tablespoons butter
1 onion, chopped
1 carrot, chopped
3 tablespoons flour
2 cups tomato purée
3 or 4 fresh tomatoes
2 cups white stock
    (fish or chicken)
2 tablespoons sugar

1 tablespoon salt
1 garlic clove
bouquet garni:
    3 parsley sprigs,
    2 celery ribs,
    1 bay leaf,
    6 peppercorns
    pinch of thyme,
    tied in cheesecloth

Melt the butter in a saucepan. Add the onion and carrot; when well browned, add the flour and let the mixture cook for a few minutes. Add the tomato purée, fresh tomatoes, white stock and remaining ingredients. Bring to a boil and let cook slowly for 1½ to 2 hours. Remove *bouquet garni*. Rub sauce through a strainer. Refrigerate any you do not use at once. Makes about 3 cups.

CREOLE SAUCE

1 onion (2 ounces)
2 green peppers
2 garlic cloves
4 large fresh tomatoes,
    or 2 cups canned
    plum tomatoes with juice
4 tablespoons olive oil
1 teaspoon brown sugar

¼ pound fresh okra,
    or ½ package (10-ounce
    size) sliced frozen okra
salt and pepper
Tabasco
2 tablespoons
    minced Italian parsley

Peel and chop onion; trim and chop green peppers; peel garlic; peel and chop tomatoes and discard as many seeds as possible, but save all the juice. Heat olive oil in a large saucepan. Push the garlic through a press into the oil; or thread the whole cloves on wooden picks if you prefer. Let the garlic cook over low heat for 1 minute, then add chopped onion and green pepper. Cook until the onion is transparent and just beginning to brown at the edges. Remove whole garlic cloves at this point. Add chopped tomatoes and sugar. Partly cover the pan and let the sauce cook until thickened and reduced; stir every few minutes so it doesn't stick. Meanwhile wash okra pods, trim the little caps, and cut the pods into ½-inch slices. When the sauce is somewhat thickened, add okra and cook for 10 minutes longer, stirring gently and often. Season to taste with salt and pepper and Tabasco, and add the parsley just before serving. Makes about 3 cups.

Creole sauce sometimes includes mushrooms, capers, and red bell peppers. Hot red peppers can be added also; if you use them, omit Tabasco.

BANANA CURRY SAUCE (for Trout)

4 tablespoons butter	2 tablespoons
4 tablespoons flour	mild curry powder
2 cups milk,	½ teaspoon ground ginger
at room temperature	1 egg yolk
½ teaspoon	2 firm bananas, quartered
onion juice	and cut into fingers

Melt butter in a saucepan. The instant it is melted, remove from heat, then sprinkle with flour, spoon by spoon, and stir in until well blended. Slowly add the milk and onion juice, stirring constantly. Sauce will become smooth and faintly yellow. Combine curry powder and ginger in a cup; add several spoons of the warmed milk and stir to make a paste. When smooth, add paste to the sauce. Put pan back over heat and continue stirring over low heat until sauce starts to thicken. Have egg yolk in a cup. Pour several spoons of now hot sauce on yolk, blend, and stir into the rest of the sauce. Add bananas and stir sauce until thick. Makes 3 cups.

SAUCE ROUILLE

1 red bell pepper, or canned pimiento
4 garlic cloves
½ to 1 cup fresh bread crumbs
¼ cup olive oil

Roast the pepper until the skin is blackened; rub off the skin and trim off ribs and seeds. Or rinse off seeds from canned pepper. Chop pepper. Peel garlic and mash in a large mortar; add pepper pieces and continue to mash until well mixed. Soak crumbs in water and squeeze

dry. Add olive oil to mashed mixture, 1 tablespoon at a time, then add as much of the crumbs as needed to make a thick sauce. For **bouillabaisse,** dilute to the consistency of cream with about 1 cup of the strained liquid from cooking the fish.

For hotter sauce, use 2 small hot red peppers instead of the bell pepper.

Use boiled potato instead of bread crumbs if you prefer. If there is liver available from some of the fish in the **bouillabaisse,** use less olive oil, or none, and substitute 2 to 4 tablespoons mashed liver.

This sauce can be served with other fish dishes; thin it with some of the poaching liquid to a suitable consistency. Strain it if you prefer. Makes about 1½ cups thick sauce.

SAUCE HOLLANDAISE

In a bowl set in hot water over low heat, beat 4 egg yolks with 1 tablespoon each of light cream and tarragon vinegar or lemon juice. Continue beating the eggs with a whisk until they begin to thicken. Add, bit by bit, ¼ pound butter and continue beating the sauce until it is thick. Should the mixture curdle, immediately beat in 1 or 2 tablespoons of boiling water in order to rebind the emulsion. Add lemon juice, salt and cayenne to taste. Set the bowl in a pan of lukewarm water until serving time. Serve with any hot or cold poached fish. Makes about 1½ cups.

SAUCE MOUSSELINE

To 1 cup hollandaise sauce add 4 tablespoons whipped cream. Fold in the whipped cream gently, then warm over low heat. Like hollandaise, this sauce is served warm rather than hot. Serve at once.

SAUCE VERTE (GREEN SAUCE)

Use the same mixture of green leaves as for Green Butter *(see under BUTTERS),* in the same proportion, or vary to your taste, but be cautious with the tarragon as it can overwhelm the other flavors. Blanch greens and drain them, then mash to a purée. Stir into 1 cup warm hollandaise sauce and keep over hot water long enough for the flavors to blend. For a larger amount of sauce, use more greens.

BÉARNAISE SAUCE
(Brennan's Restaurant, New Orleans)

4 egg yolks	2 tablespoons capers
juice of 1 lemon	¼ cup chopped parsley
2 cups melted butter	1 tablespoon
salt and pepper	tarragon vinegar

In the top part of a double boiler, beat egg yolks and lemon juice. Cook slowly over hot water, never allowing the water in the bottom pan to come to a boil. Slowly add melted butter to egg yolks, stirring constantly with a wooden spoon. Add salt and pepper to taste, capers, parsley and vinegar. Stir to blend. Makes 2 cups.

SAUCE GRÉGOIRE

4 cups fish stock	2 cups heavy cream
2 tablespoons chopped shallots	¼ cup Béarnaise Sauce (preceding recipe)
5 ounces mushrooms, chopped	few drops of Ricard or Pernod
1 bay leaf	1 teaspoon lemon juice
pinch of dried thyme	
2 cups White-Wine Sauce I (p. 287)	

Combine first 5 ingredients and reduce to two thirds. Add white-wine sauce and reduce again to half. Replace the reduction with the heavy cream. Simmer for 5 minutes more, then strain through a fine cloth. Just before serving, add the béarnaise sauce flavored with a few drops of Ricard or Pernod. Correct the flavoring with the lemon juice. Makes about 4 cups.

SAUCE CHORON

½ cup vinegar	2 tablespoons tomato purée
2 ounces shallots, peeled and minced	6 egg yolks
1 tablespoon crushed dried tarragon	1 tablespoon water
1 tablespoon crushed dried chervil	1 pound butter, melted
pinch of salt	1 tablespoon minced fresh tarragon
pinch of pepper	½ tablespoon minced fresh chervil
dash of ground thyme	dash of paprika
1 bay leaf	dash of lemon juice

Combine the first 9 ingredients in a pan and reduce to one third. Allow to cool, then add the egg yolks mixed with the water. Heat over very low heat, constantly stirring with a wire whisk. As soon as the mixture begins to thicken, add the melted butter, a little at a time, still stirring constantly. When the mixture is very smooth, strain through a sieve.

Just before serving add the minced fresh tarragon and chervil, and a dash each of paprika and lemon juice. Mix gently. Makes about 3 cups.

SAUCE COLBERT

Cream 6 tablespoons butter, and add 2 tablespoons chopped parsley, ⅛ teaspoon grated nutmeg and a pinch of cayenne. In a saucepan dissolve 1 tablespoon meat extract in 1½ tablespoons hot water, and stir in the seasoned butter, bit by bit, alternately with the juice of 2 small lemons. Add 1 teaspoon Madeira wine or sherry. Serve the sauce hot with fish. Makes about ¾ cup.

SAUCE AÏOLI

8 to 10 garlic cloves	dash of white pepper
2 egg yolks	2 cups olive oil
1 teaspoon salt	

Peel garlic cloves and push through a garlic press into the container of an electric blender. Add egg yolks, salt and pepper. Blend at lowest speed for a few moments. Drop by drop, slowly add olive oil, and blend. Sauce will be very thick. Makes about 2 cups.

DILL SAUCE

½ cup watercress leaves	2 tablespoons lemon juice
¼ cup sliced scallions	1 tablespoon Cognac
¼ cup chopped fresh dill	½ teaspoon salt
1 garlic clove, minced	¼ teaspoon black pepper
3 anchovy fillets, chopped	2 tablespoons oil
1 cup mayonnaise	½ cup sour cream

In a blender combine well all ingredients except sour cream, until creamy. Remove from blender; taste for seasoning and adjust if needed. Add sour cream and mix well. Chill before serving. Makes about 2 cups.

SAUCE TARTARE

To 1½ cups mayonnaise, add 1 dill pickle, 4 shallots and 2 anchovies, all chopped fine, 1 tablespoon each of chopped capers, parsley, tarragon and chervil, and 1 teaspoon dry mustard. Thin the sauce with heavy cream, and season it with ½ teaspoon each of lemon juice and sugar, and salt and pepper to taste. Serve with any fried fish or shellfish. Makes about 2 cups.

SAUCE RÉMOULADE

1 cup mayonnaise	½ teaspoon minced fresh tarragon
2 tablespoons water	¼ teaspoon white pepper
1 tablespoon chopped sour pickle	¼ teaspoon paprika
1 tablespoon chopped capers	¼ teaspoon Tabasco
1 tablespoon minced parsley	⅛ teaspoon salt
1 teaspoon anchovy paste	2 small garlic cloves, minced
1 teaspoon prepared mustard	2 tablespoons chopped green onion tops
½ teaspoon dry mustard	
½ teaspoon minced fresh chervil	

facing page, Seafood at Krog's Restaurant, Copenhagen, Denmark

Place mayonnaise in one bowl and water in another. Mix all the other ingredients except garlic and green onions into water thoroughly. If chervil and tarragon are dried, add another tablespoon of water. Beat the mixture into the mayonnaise, then stir in garlic and green onions. Makes about 1¼ cups.

MAYONNAISE VERTE (GREEN MAYONNAISE)

Follow the same procedure as for Sauce Verte, but stir the green purée into 1 cup mayonnaise. Add 1 drop of Tabasco and 4 drops of onion juice.

THOUSAND ISLAND DRESSING

Mince 1 canned pimiento and ¼ cup pitted green olives. Stir into 1 cup mayonnaise along with 2 teaspoons snipped chives and 3 tablespoons chili sauce. Add a dash of Tabasco or 2 dashes of Worcestershire sauce if you like. All the amounts and proportions can be adjusted to taste. If the dressing is to be used promptly, 1 fresh tomato, peeled, seeded, and cut into tiny dice, can be substituted for the chili sauce. Makes about 1½ cups.

CUCUMBER CREAM SAUCE

1 large cucumber	½ cup heavy sweet cream,
¼ cup light cream	or 1 cup sour cream
1 tablespoon lime juice	salt
10 watercress leaves,	Tabasco
blanched	1 teaspoon grated lime rind

Peel the cucumber and cut into small pieces. Discard any large seeds. Drop pieces into a blender container with the light cream, lime juice and blanched watercress leaves. Whirl until cucumber is puréed and the mixture is pale green. Whip the heavy sweet cream if you are using that. Stir the purée into whipped cream or sour cream. Season with salt and Tabasco to taste, and stir in the lime rind. Makes about 2 cups.

For a hot cucumber sauce, see CUCUMBER SAUCE.

MUSTARD SAUCE

1 cup commercial sour cream
3 tablespoons prepared mustard
4 teaspoons butter or margarine
2 teaspoons minced fresh parsley, or
   1 teaspoon parsley flakes
¼ teaspoon salt

Combine all ingredients. Heat, stirring occasionally. Do not boil. Makes about 1⅓ cups sauce.

Scallop

In Greek mythology when Aphrodite rose from the sea she skimmed over the Aegean waves on a scallop shell. This foam-borne goddess had a team of 6 seahorses to take her to the island of Cythera, and the symbol of sexual love and beauty rode in a scallop carriage. The graceful form of these shells has been reflected in art and architecture since earliest times. The scallop is the only bivalve to have a patron saint. The name *coquille Saint-Jacques*, or St. James shell, is on one hand an umbrella term for a variety of creamy scallop dishes, but it's also the name used for this mollusk in France. The apostle St. James wore the shell as his personal emblem and after being put to death by sword at the order of Herod Agrippa I (A.D. 44) it became a badge for the pilgrims who visited his shrine in Compostela, Spain, during the Middle Ages.

Beauty is not just shell deep in this pecten as the meat inside is paley sweet and nutlike with the fragrance of a freshening sea. The orange-colored coral is a delicacy in itself, and ideally one should eat a scallop fresh from the water as it's culled from the eelgrass.

There are some 400 species of scallops found throughout the world but only a dozen enter the commercial markets, and these are principally in Europe, North America, Japan, Australia and western South America. These mollusks, members of the family Pectenidae, are marine bivalves with orb-shaped shells; some are smooth but most bear radiating ribs. The shells may be orange, red, yellow, black or white in deepwater forms. Nearly all adult scallops can move freely in the water; only one genus is attached to a holdfast like an oyster. Scallops can leap in zigzag flights by forcefully opening their valves and expelling a jet of water which drives the mollusk in yard-long hops to avoid capture. This movement of the shell is achieved by the single large adductor muscle which is opposed by an elastic ligament. A scallop is able to migrate from one area to another.

The entire content of a scallop is edible but only the tender adductor muscle is consumed in North America. Unlike other bivalves, a scallop cannot hold its shells firmly closed. As a result it quickly loses body moisture when removed from water and dies. This would put a premium on rapid shipping from bay to market so only the muscle is taken by the fishermen and iced. Because they are somewhat difficult to procure in quantity, commercial distributors often put scallops through a process of "soaking" which depletes the delicate flavor of a fresh bivalve. The cream-colored meat is placed in freshwater for several hours until it has absorbed enough water to increase the bulk by about one third. Actually, this improves the appearance of the scallop in that it becomes very white, but from a table standpoint the flavor is inferior.

Of the 5 eastern U.S. species which enter our markets the **bay scallop** (Pecten irradians) is of prime importance to the gourmet. This mollusk commonly occurs in shallow water among eelgrass from north of Cape Hatteras around Florida through to the northern Gulf of Mexico. There are 3 subspecies, one found from Cape Hatteras north, another from Cape Hatteras south around Florida, and the third only in the northern Gulf. It reaches about 3 inches across the shell. There is a slightly smaller southern counterpart (Pecten dislocatus), which is abundant from North Carolina south to Florida. This shell is usually about 2 inches across and varies in color with mottlings of brown, red and yellow over a white background. Another scallop of growing commercial importance in the western Atlantic is the **calico** (Argopecten gibbus), which is particularly numerous in deep water off the Florida East Coast. The commercial market today depends on the **sea scallop** (Pecten magellanicus), which is not only large, growing to 5 inches across the shell, but more abundant than the other species. The sea scallop is concentrated off the coast of Maine but it occurs from Labrador to New Jersey. This pecten is dredged in water as deep as 900 feet. In 1973 the landings in the U.S. reached 18,000 metric tons, chiefly from Maine.

One of the most memorable feasts of scallops I've enjoyed was one that Johnny Walatka made while we were exploratory fishing in the Aleutians. We had caught a number of sea-run Dolly Varden trout that morning, their crimson and yellow dotted skins were as gaudy as circus posters, and while I fastened a kited pair to a driftwood plank, Johnny cubed and flour-dusted some big rock scallops and let them sputter in hot bacon fat. It may not sound epicurean but on that windswept coast his skillet looked like a pan of gold nuggets. The **rock scallop** (Hinnites giganteus) is a big one, from 4 to 6 inches in diameter, and is found from Alaska to Baja California.

There are two other kinds of minor importance—the **little northern scallop** and the **thick scallop** (Argopecten circularis). Commercially, the scallop has never been of great importance in our Pacific fishery. Pectens do not occur here in the abundance necessary to sustain large-scale harvesting, except for the **weathervane scallop** (Patinopecten caurinus) in the Gulf of Alaska and the Aleutian Chain. In 1968 a pioneer effort was made by skilled New Bedford fishermen to dredge the beds between Cape Spencer and Kodiak. While the initial landings of 1.9 million pounds of meats were impressive, damage to the more valuable King crab fishery by scalloping gear was so great that Alaska had to close its major grounds to commercials (Fisheries of the North Pacific, Robert J. Browning, Alaska Northwest Publishing Company, 1974).

Among the world's most celebrated pectens is the **queen scallop** (Equichlamys bifrons) of Australia and New Zealand. The queen, which goes by its Maori name **tipa,** is particularly abundant about Manukau Harbor and is only excelled by a local clam known as the **toheroa.** To visit New Zealand and not enjoy a bowl of tohero soup is a sacrilege.

In addition to the **great scallop** (P. maximus) or the **coquille** P. jacobaeus of St. James in the Mediterranean Sea, there is also a **variegated scallop** (Chlamys varius), which in French cuisine may appear as the **pétoncle.** The best of all scallops are the little Peconic Bay kind, every bit as good the **conchitas** of Peru.

During the 1960s I made a number of trips to Peru to fish out of Cabo Blanco, which was then the hottest marlin port in the world. I never did break the magic 1,000-pound mark, although one fish came close to 900. Then, almost abruptly, the Humboldt Current, in that mysterious way of the sea, shifted far offshore and the marlin disappeared. My angling memories are perhaps less provocative than the recollection of meals I enjoyed at Las Trece Monedas in Lima. When Swiss restaurateur Roger Schuler took office in 1957, the old palace at Ancash 536 was merely a plaster facade in the city's former bawdy district. The name "Thirteen Coins" symbolizes a bride's dowry, an honored custom ever since Pizarro founded Lima. Schuler's seafoods were without peer, and the tender bay scallops or **conchitas** were always "worth a detour."

COOKING SCALLOPS

Always dry the scallops very carefully if they are to be panfried or sautéed. Do not put them in butter or oil until the pan is already very hot. They should sizzle and brown almost immediately, otherwise the meats will lose their natural juices. It's much better to undercook rather than overcook scallops. Being perfectly edible raw, prolonged heating will only shrink and toughen an already tender meat. If you sauté them in butter or oil, allow only 3 minutes for bay scallops and no more than 5 minutes for the larger ones if cooked without cubing. If you are poaching scallops, which is at a lower heat, allow 1 extra minute for each of the two sizes.

Do not cook scallops ahead of time and keep them warm for later serving. Scallops must be delivered

preceding pages, Scallops; large specimens are sea scallops; smaller ones are bay scallops.

on a heated plate directly from the heat. If left for any appreciable time the moisture loss greatly diminishes their tangy flavor.

Large scallop shells are used both for cooking and serving the meats as in **Coquilles Saint-Jacques.** These shells can be purchased in specialty food shops. Although they are not affected by heat, they are somewhat fragile, so if you need 6, buy 12. They can also be used for other seafoods such as creamed crab meat or lobster, and make a decorative presentation in serving some vegetables such as peas or sliced mushrooms.

SCALLOP QUICHE

1½ pounds bay scallops,	salt and pepper
or sea scallops	pastry for 1-crust,
cut into quarters	9-inch pie, unbaked
2 tablespoons vermouth	5 eggs, lightly beaten
2 tablespoons	1 cup light cream
minced parsley	paprika
¼ teaspoon dried thyme	

Sprinkle scallops with vermouth, parsley, thyme, and salt and pepper to taste. Line a 9-inch quiche pan with pastry, and fill with the scallop mixture. Mix eggs and cream and pour over scallops. Sprinkle with paprika. Bake in a preheated 450°F. oven for 10 minutes. Reduce heat to 350°F. and bake for 25 minutes more, or until quiche is done (knife inserted in center comes out clean). Makes 6 servings.

SCALLOP SOUP
(The Mandarin, San Francisco)

⅓ pound scallops	2 ounces julienne strips
1 quart rich chicken broth	of Virginia ham
salt	1 teaspoon
1 egg white, beaten	minced fresh coriander

Heat chicken broth and keep at low simmer. Steam scallops until just done. Remove from heat and slice into julienne. Add the scallops to the chicken broth with a little salt to taste. Just before serving stir in the beaten egg white and turn off heat immediately after adding. Stir well, pour into serving bowls, and garnish with ham strips and coriander leaves. Makes 4 servings. **NOTE:** Shark fin prepared in the usual manner and cut into julienne may also be added with the scallops for an even richer soup.

COQUILLES SAINT-JACQUES

2 pounds scallop meats	2 cups Cream Sauce I (p. 286)
¾ cup melted butter	6 egg yolks

½ cup lemon juice	¾ cup heavy cream
1 tablespoon chopped	½ cup grated
shallots or scallions	Parmesan cheese
¾ cup sliced mushrooms	minced fresh parsley
¾ cup dry white wine	

Sauté scallops in ⅓ cup of the butter for 1 minute. Stir in lemon juice. Drain scallops, reserving liquid. (If sea scallops are used, cut each one into thirds.) Arrange scallops in 8 buttered coquilles or individual casseroles for main-dish serving. To serve as a first course, use twelve 5-inch coquilles. Sauté shallots and mushrooms in remaining butter. Add reserved liquid from scallops and the wine; simmer until reduced to one third. Set aside. Prepare cream sauce, then blend in mushroom and wine mixture. In a 2-quart bowl beat egg yolks with cream. Stir in cream-sauce mixture, a little at a time. Then put entire mixture back into saucepan and cook, stirring constantly, for about 2 minutes, until slightly thickened. Pour sauce over scallops; sprinkle each coquille with some of the cheese. Broil 6 to 8 inches from the heat source until lightly browned. Sprinkle with parsley, and serve with toast triangles if desired. Makes 8 main-dish servings, or 12 appetizer servings.

SEAFOOD CRÊPES

1 pound mixed cooked scallops,	2 teaspoons Dijon-style
lobster and shrimps,	prepared mustard
cut into small pieces	3 cups heavy cream
1 cup Chablis	4 tablespoons white roux
2 teaspoons	salt
chopped shallots	lemon juice
2 teaspoons	8 cooked Crêpes (p. 325)
Worcestershire sauce	grated Parmesan cheese

Pour Chablis into a heavy skillet; add the shallots and over low heat reduce the liquid to half. Add the Worcestershire and mustard, and blend thoroughly. Add 2¼ cups of the cream, then the roux, finally salt and lemon juice to taste. Bring to a boil, then reduce to a simmer and let the sauce thicken. Check to see if more salt or lemon juice is needed. Complete the sauce as quickly as possible to prevent reducing the quantity by evaporation. Reserve half of the sauce for the *glaçage*.

Add the seafood to the sauce remaining in the skillet and let the mixture barely simmer. Use a heatproof platter that will slip under the broiler; brush it with butter. Place a crêpe on the platter, spoon about 2 tablespoons of seafood in sauce on it, and roll it up. Place another one next to it and continue the operation until all crêpes are filled. Do not let the crêpes touch each other on the platter or they will break when you serve them.

Whip the remaining cream and add it to the reserved sauce for the *glaçage* at the last minute. Sauce should be warm but not too hot. (Add 2 tablespoons of hollandaise sauce to the *glaçage* if you have some available.) Pour the sauce over the crêpes, and sprinkle with Parmesan cheese. Broil under medium heat, not too close to the heat source. Makes 8 appetizer servings, or 4 main-dish servings.

To make seafood crêpes in advance: Close the ends well after you have filled the crêpes. Spoon a little melted butter on the ends to protect them when reheating. As soon as the filled crêpes are cool, cover them with foil and place in the refrigerator. Refrigerate reserved sauce, but do not add whipped cream until ready to serve.

When you are ready to serve, reheat crêpes, covered with foil, at 325° to 350°F. for 7 or 8 minutes. Test center of crêpes with fork to be sure they are hot in the center. Remove from oven. If the platter is too hot, let it cool off a little or the glaze will burn on the edges.

Warm the sauce for the *glaçage* and add whipped cream. Cover crêpes with sauce, sprinkle with Parmesan cheese, and place under broiler until brown.

PEACHY CALICO SCALLOPS

1 pound calico scallops, fresh or frozen	12 canned peach halves, drained
2 tablespoons butter or other fat, melted	¼ teaspoon each of ground cinnamon and cloves
2 tablespoons lemon juice	¼ teaspoon grated mace
½ teaspoon salt	3 slices of bacon
dash of pepper	

Thaw frozen scallops. Remove any shell particles. Combine butter, lemon juice, ¼ teaspoon salt, dash of pepper and the scallops. Place peach halves in a baking pan, 11 x 7 x 1½ inches. Combine spices and ¼ teaspoon salt. Sprinkle over peaches. Place approximately 2½ tablespoons of scallop mixture in center of each peach. Cut bacon slices crosswise into fourths. Place a bacon piece on each peach. Broil about 4 inches from source of heat for 8 to 10 minutes, or until bacon is crisp. Makes 6 servings.

SCALLOPS BAKED IN SHELLS

2 pounds calico scallops, fresh or frozen	dash of pepper
	¼ teaspoon sugar

5 tablespoons butter or other fat, melted	2 cups cracker crumbs
¼ cup ketchup	¼ cup sliced green onion
½ teaspoon salt	paprika

Thaw frozen scallops. Remove any shell particles and wash. Combine 4 tablespoons butter, the ketchup, salt, pepper, sugar, cracker crumbs and scallops. Place in 6 well-greased individual shells or 10-ounce casseroles. Combine green onion and 1 tablespoon butter; place on top of scallop mixture. Bake in a moderate oven (350°F.) for 25 to 30 minutes, or until brown. Sprinkle with paprika. Makes 6 servings.

CRISPY SCALLOP SALAD BOWL

1½ pounds calico scallops, fresh or frozen	1½ cups diagonally sliced celery
1½ cups water	6 servings of crisp salad greens
3 tablespoons lemon juice	¾ cup sliced radishes
1½ teaspoons salt	3 hard-cooked eggs, sliced
3 peppercorns	1 pint cherry tomatoes, cut into halves, or
3 onion slices	2 medium-size tomatoes, cut into wedges
½ cup tarragon vinegar	
⅓ cup salad oil	¼ pound Cheddar cheese, cut into thin strips
⅓ cup sugar	
1 garlic clove, sliced	

Thaw frozen scallops. Rinse with cold water to remove any remaining shell particles. Drain well. Combine 1½ cups water, the lemon juice, ½ teaspoon salt, peppercorns and onion slices in a saucepan; bring to a boil. Add scallops, reduce heat, and simmer for 3 to 5 minutes, or until scallops are tender. Drain scallops. Combine vinegar, oil, sugar, garlic and remaining 1 teaspoon salt; stir until sugar is dissolved. Pour over scallops, cover, and chill for several hours.

Add celery to scallops; mix. Drain, but save marinade. Arrange greens in large salad bowl. Pile scallops and celery in center of bowl, and arrange remaining foods in groups around scallops on crisp salad greens. Serve with reserved marinade or, with your favorite French or oil-and-vinegar dressing. Makes 6 servings.

Sea Cucumber

There are over 650 species of Holothurians or "sea cucumbers" found in all oceans at most depths. The sea cucumber looks like a large fat slug lying on the bottom, and its appearance is something less than appetizing. When gutted, boiled and dried, the sea cucumber shrinks

facing page, Peachy calico scallops; top, Crispy scallop salad bowl

and becomes firm, and resembles a cigar butt. It is reconstituted by soaking in water for several days until it gradually assumes its near-original size. The sea cucumber has strong longitudinal muscles so it must be cut crosswise into rings. However, to all but sea cucumber enthusiasts it has an odd, rubbery texture and flavor. Holothurians have great regenerative powers; some species can break themselves in two by transverse division, and each half will develop into a complete sea cucumber. Thus it has a mystical connotation in Oriental cuisine. For my part, it's really not worth the trouble to collect or even purchase. It is principally marketed in China as **Bêche de mer**, in Japan as **Iriko**, and in Malaya and the Philippines as **Trepang.** Also known as **Holothurie** (France), **Holoturia** (Portugal), **Cohombro de mar** (Spain), **Oloturia** (Italy), **Morski krastavac-trp** (Yugoslavia), **Sjøpølser** (Holland), **Søpølse** (Denmark), and **Seegurke** (Germany).

Searobin

This bizarre-looking fish with its homely face and huge

pectoral fins is caught in vast numbers by eastern U. S. bay and surf anglers, and invariably tossed back into the water with the thought that nothing so ugly could be edible. Yet the searobin is the same celebrated **grondin** of **bouillabaisse** fame. A bottom dweller, the searobin is at times so abundant as to be a nuisance. Searobins occur at a depth range from the tidal zone to a maximum of 450 feet; however, most species occur in shallower water, particularly in the summer months, and can be readily taken by the chef/angler. The function of its unusual fins is for walking along the bottom and stirring up sand to locate food, which consists principally of clams, squid, crabs and shrimps.

There are numerous species of searobins found in the Atlantic and Mediterranean. They are marketed in Great Britain under the name **gurnard.** All belong to the same family (Triglidae). While there are differences in body coloration and size, for culinary purposes they are essentially the same. The 2 most common species along North American shores are the northern searobin and the striped searobin. The northern searobin occurs from the Bay of Fundy to South Carolina. Like its relatives, its large head is covered with bony plates and spines. The large pectoral fins are fan-shaped, each with 2 dusky blotches. The body is reddish to red-brown or gray, with fine black markings and saddlelike blotches. It grows to about 16 inches and 1¾ pounds. Most specimens are less than a foot long. The striped searobin, a closely related species, has a distinct stripe on each side of the body, and the pectoral fin has only a single broad blotch. It grows to 18 inches and has about the same distribution as the northern.

The most common species in Europe are the gray gurnard or **Grondin gris,** red gurnard or **Grondin rouge,** streaked gurnard or **Grondin imbriago,** and yellow gurnard or **Grondin perlon.** These are marketed whole or in fillet form, both fresh and frozen, and are also canned. Between 60 and 70 thousands pounds of searobins are sold in New York's Fulton Market each year, but these only as fresh fillets. Searobins are excellent when broiled, simply brushed with melted butter and sprinkled with paprika and lemon juice. They can also be sautéed, deep-fried, poached, smoked or reserved for a **bouillabaisse.**

Sea Trout

Properly the sea trout (used as 2 words) is in Eastern Atlantic waters an anadromous brown trout—like salmon, one that spends part of its life cycle in the sea. These fish do enter some Canadian and U. S. rivers but are comparatively rare in the western Atlantic. Sea trout are most numerous in the British Isles, Scandinavia, Iceland, and to some extent in New Zealand. The name seatrout (used as one word) in America refers to several unrelated members of the drum family, totally different fish from all points of view.

The sea trout, however, can give the ambulant gourmet a migraine as they are called **peal** in the west of England, **sewin** in Wales, **white trout** in Ireland, and **bull trout** in Scotland. To make matters more complicated, small sea trout of about 1 pound in size are known as **finnock** on the East Coast of Scotland and **whitling** on the West Coast. And in the border rivers with England it may be called a **herling.**

Sea trout are caught in nets set for salmon but never in great quantities, and those that appear at table in the country inns of Great Britain are most often the result of an angler's catch. The meat is pink to red in color and every bit as good as salmon. In fact, it would be difficult to distinguish one from the other when cooked. Sea trout are generally smaller in size, usually 3 to 10 pounds, although much larger fish are taken in Sweden and Norway, often exceeding 15 pounds.

All the recipes used for salmon are applicable to sea trout.

Queen Silvia of Sweden, holding a sea trout, near the Morrum River

Seatrout

See WEAKFISH.

Sea Urchin

This spiny delicacy is unknown to the average American. A marine animal that looks like a large pin cushion 1½ to 10 inches in diameter, it can cause a painful injury if stepped on with a bare foot. Although the short-spined edible varieties can be picked up by hand if held gently, it is advisable to wear gardening gloves when collecting urchins. The demand for the cream- to orange-colored urchin roes always exceeds the supply. In the French Mediterranean, urchins are called **oursins,** while along the Pacific Coast of South America, more particularly Chile, they are known as **herizos,** and many natives of the West Indies eat them under the name of **sea eggs.** In fact they were so abundantly sold in the streets of Barbados that laws have been enacted to prevent their extinction.

There are some 500 species of these echinoderms in world distribution, and all contain edible gonads when mature; both male and female are utilized. In some areas they can be collected in huge quantities in tide pools, along shallow rocky shores, on reefs and in creeks. Gathering roe-bearing urchins is highly seasonal and dependent on water temperatures. In Florida, for example, our large Black Urchin (the one with white spines and a black "shell" or test) may commence bearing roe as early as February or as late as July. It requires local knowledge and considerable patience to savor this delicacy. Generally speaking, urchins are ripe on the East and West Coasts of North America from late summer to spring (August to April). Due to their perishability urchins are largely a cold-weather item at Fulton Market, New York, and reach their peak abundance around Christmas; the primary source in this market is the state of Maine.

The most widely distributed species is the Green Urchin, which occurs in both the Atlantic and Pacific Oceans. There is also a Brown Urchin and Purple Urchin found along the East Coast of the U.S., but these common names are misleading as the colors are quite variable. The Purple Urchin, which is found from Alaska to northern Mexico, is marketed in California, particularly at Fisherman's Wharf in San Francisco, where the local Italian population quickly absorbs the daily landings. The supply is limited, however, and orders are placed in advance.

Eating an urchin is simple. You merely cut around the bottom or "mouth" side of the shell with a scissors or break a circular section loose with a knife and shake out the viscera, which are a minor mess; underneath and firmly attached to the top side of the shell you will find the 5-branched roe, which can be scooped out with a spoon. Depending on the species and maturity, it may require 6 to 12 urchins to gather enough roe for one portion. The female ovaries are naturally more egglike whereas the male gonad has a finer texture. Heaped on crusty French bread and squirted with lemon, the only other accompaniment might be a cold glass of white wine.

Japan is an important consumer of sea urchin roes both as a fresh product and in the making of **Uni-Shiokara,** a fermented urchin paste. As a result, a profitable fishery has developed in British Columbia, Canada. The urchins are collected in waters 20 to 40 feet deep by specialist scuba divers. They rake the spiny animals into special cages that hold up to 5,000 urchins. Then the live urchins are delivered to a processing plant at Tofino where they are sliced open; the roe is carefully separated, packed in boxes, and trucked to Vancouver. The product is then airfreighted to Tokyo, arriving in less than 40 hours after it was taken from the live urchin in Canada. Also known as **Riccio di mare** (Italy), **Morski jez** (Yugoslavia), **Achinós** (Greece), **Søpindsvin** (Denmark), **Sjöborre** (Sweden), **Kråkebolle** (Norway), **Igulker** (Iceland), **Seeigel** (Germany), **Ouriço-do-mar** (Portugal), **Erizo de mar** (Spain), **Uni** (Japan).

Seaweed

Various kinds of marine algae or "seaweeds" have been utilized by man since long before the Christian era. As a food, seaweed has never had the popularity in European cultures that it does in the Orient where the abundant *Porphyra* is an important supplement to a rice diet. This aquatic plant is the ubiquitous **nori** of Japan. Although seaweeds have some nutritive value in providing vitamins (notably A, B$_{12}$ and D) and an abundance of minerals, their chief role is in supplying salt in organic form. In a culinary sense marine algae serve as a seasoning agent. Among primitive cultures such as the North American Indians, who made extensive use of *Porphyra*, the direct application of salt to food was abhorrent. Historically, the most diversified use of seaweed was made by the nineteenth-century Polynesians who recognized 75 separate marine plants as staples. Today the only known use of seaweed as a basic food is among the Seri Indians of the Gulf of California in Mexico. The Seri people make a flour from eelgrass (*Zostera marina*), which is converted into a porridgelike substance and served hot, sprinkled with sea

facing page, Green sea urchins with roe, Atlantic

Purple urchin, Pacific

Sea urchin roe on toast

turtle oil or honey.

In Europe the marine alga *(Rhodymenia palmata)* known as **dulse** or **dillisk,** and another seaweed *(Chondrus crispus)* commonly called **Irish moss** or **carragheen,** have long been a source of food for both man and cattle. Irish moss is made into a tasty dish known as blancmange when cooked with milk and flavored with vanilla and fruit. This plant is highly gelatinous when processed and is the basis for the modern carrageenin industry in stabilizing such products as eggnog, chocolate milk, whipped cream, ice cream and bakery products. It is similar to, but not the same as, agar produced from the Pacific seaweed *Gelidium,* which has broader industrial applications.

The Japanese **nori** is by far the most extensively cultivated seaweed today, with an industry that employs a half million people, harvesting over 130,000 tons annually. Chopped and dried on porous mats, the pieces of **nori** form paperlike sheets which are sorted and graded, then packaged for market. Similar products such as **wakame** made from the seaweed *Undaria,* and **kombu** which comes from the kelp *Laminaria,* are processed somewhat differently, by flavoring (usually with sweetened vinegar), dying a particular color, or drying in tangles rather than sheets. Seaweed is an integral part of many Japanese seafood dishes and most especially **sushi** *(see SASHIMI).*

For shoppers, the best places to look are health-food stores, which usually carry **dulse, Irish moss, kombu** and **wakame.** In Oriental markets, specifically Chinese and Japanese places, one can find all these as well as **nori** (laver), **hijiki, faht choy** and **gee choy,** in sheets, long strips, ground, etc. They are packed in various ways, but most kinds are available in see-through packets so the uninitiated shopper can see what each kind looks like.

Seviche

See under PICKLED FISH.

Shad

The Latin species name of the American shad is *sapidissima* which means "most delicious," a description that has been debated since before the American Revolution. In Sylvester Judd's *History of Hadley* (Massachusetts), we learn that when the English first settled in the Connecticut River valley the numerous shad were "despised and rejected"; even if you had the competency to eat shad, the act implied that one was destitute of salt pork. In 1743 a pivotal character in our history, Ebenezer Hunt, allowed that "shad are very good whether one has pork or not" and paid 3 pence for a fat fish. By the time General George Washington marched to the North River in 1776 and established a shaky position at White Plains, "some thousands of barrels of shad were put up in Connecticut for the troops," a wartime industry that would last through 4 seasons of shad runs. Whether the starving Continental Army had the competency to eat shad or not, the fish won its audience by sheer abundance. It's doubtful if many of the early English settlers had the skill to bone a shad, as this skill has escaped some of America's greatest chefs, particularly those who trained in Europe where the fish is rarely in evidence. Around the peculiar skeletal structure of the shad is a sweet white meat of distinct flavor, and the roe of the female is a delicacy in such demand that at today's prices one expects a Chablis Grand Cru to wash it down.

The American shad is a member of the herring family. (There are 27 species in the family Clupeidae found in North American waters; this family includes herrings, menhadens, sardines, false pilchards and shads. However, only 1 species, the American shad, is of culinary importance. In Europe the **Allis shad** *(Alosa alosa)* is of minor distribution and appears as a canned product in France where it is called **alose** and in Germany as **Maifisch.**) Because of its large size and distinct role in seafood cuisine, the shad must be treated separately. Shad ascend rivers along our Atlantic Coast from Northern Florida to the Gulf of St. Lawrence. These spawning runs are triggered by water temperature and as a result the season for shad extends from December in the south to late May in the north.

The shad comes into New England's rivers when the shadbush blossoms in clusters of white flowers and a mottled brown caddis or shadfly emerges in great clouds from the water to dance in a warming sun. After a harsh winter and an often monotonous diet, the early settlers swarmed to the riverbanks as "shadtime" was as important as the "eeltime" of fall. It had been wryly ob-

served that in spring people couldn't get their shirts off without help, because of the shad bones which stuck out of their skins like porcupine quills. Even the fierce Pawtucket Indians had their shad "cookouts" below the falls of the Merrimack River at Lowell, and the gregarious Winnepesaukees invited all the neighboring tribes of the Pennacook Confederacy to assemble for this joyous feast. Those shad not immediately consumed "were handed to the squaws, who stood ready, knife in hand to split the fish and hang them up to smoke for winter on the centre-pole of the wigwam or laid them out to dry in the sun." Whether the shad was ever cooked on a plank by the Indians has not been recorded, although it's probable, as using a slab of wood to hold food in reflected heat is probably as ancient as the discovery of fire. In a formal sense, the classic planked shad had its origin in this same period on the banks of the Delaware River in Andalusia, Pennsylvania.

The Fish House, which also earned a venerable reputation for its seemingly innocuous punch, concocted from the alembics of some Philadelphia citizens who formed the Schuylkill Fishing Company, was not only the first angling club in North America but probably the first gourmet society as well. It was created in 1732 for the purpose of "taking fish, shooting game, and preparing the same with their own hand." Its members met 13 times each year at a curiously churchlike 1-room wooden building, wearing aprons and straw boaters. Generals Washington and Lafayette sat at the great teakwood table while toasts were made (always in aged Madeira), and the shad sizzled on a white oak plank set at a 70-degree angle to the fire with the fillet securely nailed in place. The admonition "Gentlemen, charge your glasses!" was the opener for that Grand Prix of shaddom.

From a culinary standpoint the female shad is more desirable than the buck, not only for its roe, but also because it's a larger and fatter fish, providing an ideal fillet for all recipes. When roe and fillet are sold separately the latter, if quality, is purveyed as a "cut shad" which simply means a fillet taken from a female. Personally, I find the lean male fillet every bit as tasty although it's too thin and small after boning to be used in many preparations, and it requires more basting. A similar problem arises with the only other edible shad found on our south Atlantic Coast, the **hickory shad** *(Alosa mediocris)*. The hickory averages 1 to 3 pounds and its thin fillets are not often marketed where the American or "white" shad is available. Hickories do provide edible roes, however, and the flesh is often used in pickling—after all, the shad is one of the Clupeidae, therefore a herring.

American or white shad

SOURCE AND SEASON

Along our Atlantic Coast shad are found from the Gulf of St. Lawrence to northern Florida and enter all the major river systems such as the Connecticut, Hudson, Delaware, Potomac, Susquehanna, James, Roanoke, Ogeechee and St. Johns. Shad begin to appear in the St. Johns of north Florida during December with the peak of their run in March, whereas in the Hudson and Connecticut Rivers they begin arriving in late March and become abundant by May. Thus, fresh shad are in season for about 5 months on the East Coast. The first big run of the season which supplies major metropolitan markets such as New York and Chicago are shad from Georgia's Ogeechee River, as the St. Johns fish are not abundant enough to supply any more than the local demand.

Although indigenous to the western Atlantic, shad were introduced to the Sacramento River in California in 1871, and the fish spread during the next decade to Oregon's Umpqua and Coos Rivers, then into the Columbia, Puget Sound and the Fraser River of British Columbia. The season for fresh shad is later on our Pacific Coast, starting about April in California, with most of the market fish coming from the Columbia River in Oregon during May and June. The shad is not commercially as important here as in the East because of the much larger and more valuable fishery for Pacific salmon. However, significant quantities of shad are taken by sport fishermen.

CONNECTICUT SHAD COOKOUT

The shad cookout is uniquely a New England tradition. Edward T. Bement was the modern-day master. Mr. Bement worked for the Connecticut Board of Fisheries and Game for 30 years, and the annual cookout which he conducted for department personnel was a celebrated event. About the time shad arrived at Enfield Dam, everybody in the Nutmeg State tried to wangle an invitation to Bement's festivities.

PREPARATION

The firebox is made of concrete blocks. Bement constructs the box 3 blocks high, and the length of the box is dependent on the number of shad he has to prepare. The bottom of the box is lined with solid cobblestones, and this bed is approximately 6 inches high. This provides the proper elevation from his grates to the fire. The width of the firebox is 30 inches to conform with his grating, which is made of concrete reinforcing rods. His broilers, which are laid on the grate, are made of turkey wire using hog rings as hinges. Bement uses 30- by 18-inch broilers so that he can turn several shad at once and avoid having the fillets fall apart. Approximately 2 hours before he puts the fillets on, he starts the fire on the cobblestone bed and uses hickory or apple wood. Either wood is essential for two reasons. They are hard, close-grained and slow-burning, which allows him to make one fire and not have to add wood during the cooking process; secondly, either wood imparts just the right smoke flavor to shad.

COOKING THE SHAD

Spread out boned shad fillets, skin side down, on aluminum foil. Paint with lemon juice, using a pastry brush to cover them evenly. Add salt, pepper and paprika. Dip into a bath of flavorless cooking oil, draining off excess; then place shad on broilers. The broilers are placed on the grate so the shad are skin side up. Broil fish for approximately 12 minutes, or until light golden brown. Next turn broilers so the shad fillets are skin side down, and cook for 10 minutes on this side.

COOKING THE ROE

Lay shad roe on aluminum foil. Season with salt and pepper. Fry some good country bacon, and save the fat in dripping pans. Now place the roe in bacon fat ¼ inch deep in the pans. Put the pans on the broilers, and cook slowly with flat side of roe down until brown. Turn and brown on the other side. Roe should be served with crisp strips of bacon and parsley.

In case you are a beginner at shad fishing and can't distinguish a buck from a roe, then a simple test will dispel any uncertainty. With thumb and forefinger massage the belly toward the vent. If milt (a white substance) is extruded, it's a buck. If tiny red eggs pop out, then it's a roe. With a little experience you can identify the female visually as the vent of a roe is reddish and protrudes slightly, whereas the vent of a buck remains white.

HOW TO BONE A SHAD

It's unfortunate that boning a shad is so often considered a surgical skill requiring years of internship before a knife can be applied with confidence. For this reason many people have been discouraged from enjoying one of the most delicious fish of our spring season. Actually, boning a shad is a very simple process which demands nothing more than a sharp, thin-bladed knife and a general idea of where the "floating ribs" are located. These intermuscular bones lie in 2 rows paralleling the backbone, one row about an inch above the midline and the other about an inch below the midline on *each* fillet. As a matter of fact, if you run your finger over a fillet you can feel the tips of the bones. After filleting the shad in routine fashion, cutting it lengthwise into halves and removing the backbone, place one fillet skin side down with the tail end toward you on the work table. To remove the floating ribs "feel" their location with your finger, or if you are unfamiliar with anatomy simply start the knife at the nape end of the fish

about ½ inch in from the midline, making one long cut the length of the fillet without penetrating the skin. Now parallel this out by starting the knife about ½ inch to the right running the blade the full length of the fillet. Turn the fillet with the nape end toward you and work the point of your knife under the incised strip to loosen the end of the row of bones so you can grasp it with your fingers. Pull the strip gently back toward the tail and the entire row will come out intact. Repeat the same strokes on the opposite side of the midline to remove the second row.

Follow the same procedure with the other fillet which also contains 2 rows of intermuscular bones.

SHAD ROE

Prime quality shad roe must be fully developed but not overripe. If you catch your own shad there will be occasions when the roes from one fish will contain small eggs, while the roes from another hold eggs that are several times larger even though the ovaries are of identical size. Shad, like other species, do not all spawn precisely at the same time, and the egg diameter increases rapidly in the few days immediately prior to their release. In fact a roe can be "green" or underripe with a very firm texture and little flavor, as well as overripe, which makes them watery and also rather tasteless. Quality control is maintained in canned products by selection when packing but the fisherman will inevitably find a variety of egg diameters as roe shad of identical sizes can be at different stages of sexual development. Some other fish species spawn intermittently throughout the year, particularly in subtropical and tropical waters, and their ovaries will contain eggs of more than one size; tiny "seed" roe for future spawning and large already developed eggs for immediate spawning. However, fish such as the shad, with a well-defined reproduction period, bear prime roes for a longer time during their availability to capture and the percentage of overripe or underripe roes is not great. Ideally, the eggs are about the size of small birdshot. Roes should always be washed throughly, carefully removing all blood clots or veins, slime and the *outer* membrane. The fine inner membrane enclosing the individual lobes must be left intact. When purchasing a "set" of roes at market all this pre-preparation will have been done.

Fresh shad roe should stand in ice-cold salted water for a few minutes, then be gently simmered for another 5 minutes, or until it just firms. It can be completely cooked by simmering, to be served chopped in small pieces for certain dishes such as a soufflé or simply as an accompaniment to scrambled eggs, but if the roes are to be served whole (usually sautéed) a brief parboiling

COLLECTING ROE FROM SHAD

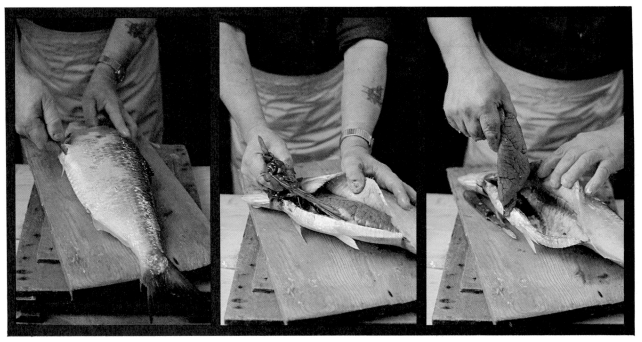

1. Cut into shad on ventral side.   2. Remove viscera from the cavity.   3. Separate roe from viscera.

makes them solid enough to handle in the skillet without breaking. The roes should then be cooled, dredged with flour, and sautéed over low heat in clarified butter to which a little diced lean bacon and, optionally, an herb such as dill, chervil or tarragon has been added. Brown the roes and serve with the pan drippings, surrounded by parsley and lemon wedges.

This basic method applies to all edible roes containing small eggs such as those of the mackerel, cod, dolphin, weakfish, seatrout, mullet, haddock, bonefish, tarpon, bluefish, corvina and whitefish. Although the roes of smaller species, such as those of the flounder, herring, alewife, smelt and capelin, are delicious, these are usually left in the body cavity and cooked with the fish; their diminutive size is not adequate even as an appetizer unless the roes are collected in a large quantity.

Fresh shad roe is also excellent when baked or broiled; in these methods the membrane has no direct contact with the heat source so they need not be parboiled. Of course, canned shad roe is a cooked product and only requires applying to the recipe.

SHAD AMANDINE

2 pounds shad fillets,
   boned
¾ cup dry bread crumbs
½ cup peanut oil

½ teaspoon salt
⅛ teaspoon pepper
½ cup milk
½ cup flour

2 tablespoons lemon juice
½ cup almonds,
   blanched and slivered
¼ pound butter

Season fillets with salt and pepper. Dip them into milk, then into flour, then into milk again, then into bread crumbs. Brown fish in oil, then reduce heat and cook for 10 minutes for each inch of thickness, turning at half time. Drain fish and arrange on a heated platter. Sprinkle with lemon juice. Sauté the almonds in butter until golden brown, and pour almonds and butter over fish. Makes 4 servings.

STEAMED SHAD WITH CAPER SAUCE

1 shad, 3 to 4 pounds,
   dressed, whole
2 celery ribs with greens,
   chopped
1 medium-size onion,
   chopped

1 lemon, sliced thin
2 bay leaves
salt and pepper
4 cups water
2 cups white wine
Caper Sauce (p. 288)

Place celery, onion, lemon and bay leaves in the bottom of a fish poacher or large roasting pan. Sprinkle with salt and pepper. Lay shad on a rack and

facing page, Ingredients for shad roe with bacon

SHAD WITH SOUFFLÉ OF ROE (prepared at The Four Seasons, New York City)

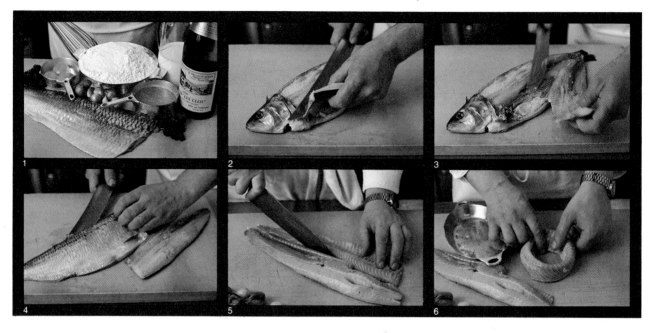

place rack in the pan. Add water and wine to the level just under rack; do not submerge fish; this may require more or less water. Cover pan tightly and steam at 300°F. for 5 hours. Do not remove lid too frequently but check at intervals to make certain that liquid is not lost through escaping steam. At the end of 5 hours the shad bones will be soft enough to be eaten. Transfer fish from the rack to a serving platter; keep warm. Pour off cooking liquid and solids from pan and strain; or remove bay leaf and purée. Use liquid or purée to make caper sauce. Serve sauce separately. Makes 4 to 6 servings.

SHAD ROE CASSEROLE WITH HERBS

4 shad roes	1 teaspoon minced chervil
2 cups dry white wine	1 teaspoon minced chives
2 cups fish stock or water	1 teaspoon minced parsley
1 teaspoon tarragon vinegar	1 teaspoon minced rosemary
salt and white pepper	1 tablespoon
¼ cup warm olive oil	chopped shallots
½ cup melted butter	¼ cup sherry

Rinse the roes carefully, and lay them side by side in a shallow earthenware casserole. Pour in the wine, fish stock or water, and tarragon vinegar; season with salt and white pepper to taste. Bring the stock to a boil, and simmer the roes gently for 12 minutes. Drain them, reserving the cooking stock for another use. Dry the roes on a paper towel, and brush them with warm olive oil. Return roes to the casserole. Season the butter with all the minced herbs and the shallots, and pour the seasoned butter over the roes. Add the sherry. Do not cover cas-

serole. Braise the roes in a moderate oven (350°F.) for 10 minutes. Serve in the casserole. Makes 4 servings.

SHAD WITH SOUFFLÉ OF ROE
(The Four Seasons, New York City)

4 shad fillets	1 ounce Pernod
½ pound shad roe	butter for baking dish
¼ pound butter	2 tablespoons
4 tablespoons flour	chopped shallots
¾ cup milk, warmed	1 cup White-Wine Sauce I
3 eggs, separated	(p. 287), made with Chablis
salt, white pepper,	6 tablespoons
grated nutmeg	Lemon Butter (p. 49), melted
flour for dusting	

Melt half of butter and blend in flour. Pour in warm milk and stir until mixture is thickened. Beat egg yolks, warm in a cup with some of the sauce, then add yolks to the balance of the sauce. Continue stirring and add salt, pepper and nutmeg to taste. Reserve.

Dust shad roe with flour and sauté in remaining butter over low heat until cooked. Flame the roe with Pernod. Cut roe into ½-inch slices and incorporate slices in the reserved sauce. Whip egg whites stiff, then fold very gently into the sauce to make soufflé mixture.

Cut shad fillets lengthwise into halves and season with salt and pepper. Butter a baking dish and sprinkle with chopped shallots. Arrange each fillet in a crown shape in the baking dish, then fill each one with some of the soufflé mixture. Pour white-wine sauce into pan. Bake in 350°F. oven for 20 to 25 minutes. Before serving splash with lemon butter. Makes 4 servings.

1. Assemble ingredients. 2. and 3. Remove fillets
on one side. 4. Make a dorsal cut and fillet the other
side. 5. Cut each fillet into halves to make
quarterfillets. 6. Curl each quarterfillet into a
turban and place in a baking dish. 7. Melt
butter in a saucepan. 8. Add flour and blend in well.
9. Pour in warm milk and stir until thickened.
10. Add egg yolks and blend well. 11. Season the
sauce. 12. Flame sautéed roe with Pernod.
13. Cut roe into ½-inch pieces. 14. Add to prepared sauce.
15. Mix in well. 16. Fold in egg whites, which
have been beaten stiff. 17. Pour soufflé batter into
the turbans of shad. 18. Bake the turbans,
with white-wine sauce in the pan, until soufflé
is puffed and brown.

facing page, Blacktip shark taken on a fly rod by Linda Drake, at Deep Water Cay, Bahamas

Shark

For aesthetic reasons sharks have never been a popular food in America, at least not under their correct name. Yet, both primitive and sophisticated cultures have utilized sharks as food since ancient times. Although the flesh of some sharks is known to have a strong purgative effect on man (the cow sharks) and in some instances may be toxic, as in the case of the Greenland shark which is perfectly edible when allowed to ferment in making the Eskimo **tipnuk** or the Icelandic **hákarl**, other species are an excellent food. The factor that prevents large-scale marketing in America is largely psychological, and not indicative of an inferior product. In 1916 the U. S. government embarked upon a campaign to promote a small shark known as the "dogfish" as a source of protein, and a substantial market existed until the end of World War I. This diminished until the period from 1937 to 1941 when an intensive commercial fishery was conducted for high-potency vitamin A shark livers. The flesh was purveyed under the name "grayfish," which did not promote sales, nor did later use of the already popular "whitefish" gain currency. Nevertheless, as much as 9 million pounds of shark was landed in one year in California alone. After being processed for liver, the edible parts were sold. This was the peak of shark consumption in the U.S.

The **mako** and **blue sharks** are perhaps the most highly prized species in world distribution. On our East Coast the mako has long been a source of "swordfish" steaks. Swordfish are comparatively rare within their range and command top prices. Makos are similar and to my taste superior in flavor and texture; being readily available, they are sometimes substituted for swordfish. The blue shark differs from the mako in that its meat is snow-white in color; it is a valuable market item in Japan where **yoshikirizame** appears in both fresh and frozen forms. One of my favorites is the **blacktip shark,** which is common to Florida and the Bahamas. The blacktip has snowy white meat and is somewhat drier than the mako, or any of the mackerel sharks, and should not be over-cooked. The best method is to cut the meat into scallop-size pieces and stir-fry Chinese style in a wok with peanut oil. Although Great Britain's popular "fish 'n' chips" is made from a variety of available species, the **spiny dogfish** and the **porbeagle shark** are its most common source. These are usually marketed as **rock salmon** in Billingsgate. **Fish 'n' chips** is virtually the hamburger of England. The delicate pieces of white fish are dipped into batter, deep-fried, and buried under a pile of French fried potatoes. This crunchy feast, which the customer sprin-

kles with salt and vinegar, is served in a cone of newspaper. The contents are eaten with one's fingers. There is some dissention as to whether it tastes better when served in the *Daily Express* or the *London Times* but it's a nourishing quick food and has been a national passion for the past century. Along the coast of Maine old salts call the dogfish **harbor halibut,** and the fact is that you would be hard pressed to tell the difference. And if you have eaten **kalbfisch** in Germany you have enjoyed hot-smoked porbeagle shark, or in the case of **spekfisch** a hot-smoked sixgill shark. Sharks rank third among the principal food-fishes in Australia, where the gummy and school sharks are highly esteemed. Norway is the major shark producer in Europe and exports fresh and frozen dogfish and porbeagle mainly to Great Britain, to help supply the demand for fish 'n' chips, and to Italy. Perhaps the best known by-product is shark-fin soup. Although one species has been so heavily utilized for this purpose that it bears the common name **soupfin shark,** my Chinese friends collect *all* fins of any shark for this purpose. When the fins are reduced, as in making a fish stock, the stock is almost flavorless but the fins provide a superior gelatin which is the base of the soup; the actual flavor is derived from chicken or pork which is introduced to the stock.

In the Pacific a major shark fishery exists in the Sea of Cortés on Isla Tiburón (Shark Island). Here, from April through June sharks migrate into the northern portion of the Gulf where the females deliver their pups. The return journey takes place from October to December when the commercials again catch them with nets, harpoons and setlines. Most of the sharks caught are the brown, blacktip and hammerhead, but the mako, tiger, bull, leopard, nurse, thresher and horn sharks also enter the fishery. After processing most of the shark meat is sold in Mexican markets as **bacalao** or salt codfish. Attending a shark butchering is a heady experience as the aroma of old carcasses blended with the ammonia smell of fillets in process permeates the beaches of Tiburón. The dorsal fins, pectoral fins and lower lobe of the tail are sliced off and sun-dried for the Chinese trade (not only in Mexico but all the way back to the Orient).

HOW TO BUTCHER A SHARK

A shark must be butchered as quickly as possible after it's removed from the water. Its meat has poor keeping qualities and cannot be left in the sun for very long. The first step is to remove the fins, then make a long incision along the back from head to tail, not deep but deep enough to penetrate the hide. Next, make circular cuts around the base of the tail and at a point just behind the head. The

hide is then pulled loose by maintaining a constant tension on it and alternately slicing at its base and peeling it free. There is no need to work all the way down to the belly as the fillet portion is the musculature along the shark's back. Like the sturgeon and paddlefish it does not have bony vertebrae but rather a tough cartilaginous skeleton located below the edible meat. The back meat can be cut into long fillets and placed in a strong brine (4 pounds salt to 10 gallons water). The Mexican commercials use large oil drums for this purpose and leave the fillets in brine for about 20 hours to leach out the uremic acid before sun-drying. The drying process is critical in preservation; the fillets must be evenly exposed to the sun on both sides and protected from damp night air.

HOW TO COOK SHARK

For osmoregulatory reasons sharks retain a high concentration of urea in their bodies. Urea becomes ammonia through enzymatic action which would render the flesh unpalatable. So the basic tenet of shark cookery is first to leach out the ammonia by soaking the fillets or steaks in a brine solution. Optionally, one can marinate shark meat in acetic, citric or lactic acids such as vinegar, lemon juice or milk, which also neutralizes ammonia. The synthetic vinegar which always accompanies fish 'n' chips, giving it that distinctive flavor, is less a seasoning than a neutralizer. When preparing the small amount of shark meat, cut into fingers or chunks, that is used in a home kitchen, all you have to do is soak the meat in saltwater for a few hours, or in milk if a deep-frying recipe is to be used, or in lemon juice if the meat is to be broiled. There will be no ammonia aroma or flavor. In fact the flesh is so moistly sweet that fish 'n' chips has the same status as Queen and Country. A large fillet would require brining at the ratio of 2 pounds salt to 5 gallons water; it should be submerged for about 8 hours, then washed.

BARBECUED SHARK

24 one-inch cubes
    of shark meat
lime or lemon juice
peanut oil
salt and pepper

24 mushrooms
8 slices of bacon, cut
    into 24 equal pieces
melted butter
parsley, chopped fine

Marinate shark in lime or lemon juice for about 20 minutes. Brush with peanut oil and season with salt and pepper. Arrange on 4 skewers alternately with the mushrooms and bacon: first a cube of shark, then a piece of bacon, puncturing the bacon near the end rather than middle, so bacon will fold over the shark, then a mushroom, and repeat. Press each mushroom tight against the bacon to hold in place.

Grill on a hot charcoal fire for about 10 minutes; time depends on heat and distance from fire but shark cooks quickly. Let dripping bacon flame up to sear the shark, then move skewers around the top of the grill to avoid burning. Skewer can be rotated after the bacon adheres to the cubes of shark. When serving, sprinkle with lime or lemon juice, melted butter and chopped parsley. Makes 4 servings.

SHARK WITH CHINESE VEGETABLES
(Joel Arrington)

Like many Chinese-style recipes, the actual cooking of this is brief, but the advance preparation takes some time and care. The preparation can all be done in advance, the cooking just before mealtime. The cooking should take no more than 15 minutes, and the vegetables should still retain a crisp texture.

2 pounds shark
2½ tablespoons
    sesame-seed oil
salt
1½ teaspoons monosodium
    glutamate (MSG)
2 cups chopped bok choy
    (Chinese chard cabbage)
1 cup chopped green onions,
    including white and
    green parts

1 cup
    sliced water chestnuts
2 cups bean sprouts
1 cup snow peas
½ cup beef bouillon
1 tablespoon soy sauce
dash of white pepper
1 tablespoon cornstarch
2 tablespoons water

Cut shark into bite-size pieces; the flesh is firm enough so that the pieces will not fall apart. Heat 2 tablespoons of the oil in a large wok (2-quart size) and in it cook the shark pieces, stirring with chopsticks or a wooden spoon, until they are cooked through but not brown. Sprinkle with a very little salt and 1 teaspoon MSG while stir-frying. With a skimmer remove shark pieces to a plate, allowing the oil to drain back into the wok. Add all the vegetables, sprinkle with ½ teaspoon MSG, and stir-fry for up to 5 minutes, until vegetables are cooked and just crisp. Add the bouillon, remaining oil, soy sauce, a little salt, the white pepper and the shark meat. Toss all together with chopsticks or forks. Dissolve the cornstarch in the water (or use some more bouillon) and quickly stir it into the mixture. When the juices are thickened, serve at once over white rice cooked quite dry. Makes 2 generous servings.

NOTES: If bean sprouts and water chestnuts are canned, drain thoroughly, rinse in fresh cold water, drain again, and pat dry before cooking. If snow peas are frozen, defrost, remove any strings or bits of stem, and pat dry. If snow peas are fresh, trim, string, and blanch in boiling water for 1 minute; drain and pat dry before using.

If you wish, MSG can be eliminated; adjust other seasonings to taste.

SHARK-FIN SOUP
(Lotus Gardens, Vancouver)

¼ pound processed
    dried shark fins
3 leeks, or 2 onions
⅙ teaspoon baking soda
15 slices of fresh gingerroot
1½ pounds pieces
    of stewing chicken

⅓ cup shredded
    boiled ham
3 tablespoons wine
2 tablespoons soy sauce
1 teaspoon salt
½ teaspoon sugar
dash of vinegar

Wash the leeks thoroughly and cut into large pieces. Place the shark fins in a large pot with the baking soda, one third of the leek pieces, 5 slices of gingerroot and water to cover. Bring to the boiling point, then remove from heat and let stand overnight. Next day drain shark fins and rinse well in cold water 3 or 4 times. Return to the kettle with plenty of water, another third of the leek pieces and another 5 slices of gingerroot. Bring to a boil, then simmer for 1 hour, drain, rinse well, and drain again.

Meanwhile, place the chicken pieces in a large kettle with about 3 quarts of water, the rest of the leek and gingerroot. Bring to a boil and boil for about 10 minutes, skimming several times, then reduce heat to a simmer and cook for 1½ hours, until chicken is very tender and the liquid reduced to about 8 cups of broth. Remove chicken pieces, bone, and shred. Simmer drained shark fins in the chicken broth for 30 minutes, then add the shredded chicken and ham and remaining ingredients. Bring soup again just to the boiling point and serve hot. Makes 8 servings.

facing page, Shark-fin soup, at The Mandarin, San Francisco

preceding pages, Fish 'n' Chips at the Portman Hotel, London.
This popular snack was formerly purveyed in cones of newspaper.

FISH 'N' CHIPS
(Portman Hotel, London)

BATTER

1 cup flour	5 tablespoons milk
1 egg yolk	5 tablespoons
4 tablespoons beer	cold water
¼ teaspoon salt	1 egg white

Pour the flour into a large mixing bowl. Make a well in the center and add the egg yolk, beer and salt. Stir the ingredients together until they are well mixed. Combine milk and water and add half to the batter. Continue to stir until the batter is smooth. Add the rest, 1 tablespoon at a time, adding only enough to give the right texture. Each batch of flour is different; for some you may need all the liquid, or even an extra tablespoon. For a light texture, let the batter rest at room temperature for at least 30 minutes, although, if necessary, it may be used at once. In either case, beat the egg white stiff—until it forms unwavering peaks on the beater when beater is lifted from the bowl. Gently and thoroughly fold it into the batter.

CHIPS

vegetable oil or shortening
2 pounds baking potatoes

Slice potatoes lengthwise into strips ½ inch wide and ½ inch thick. Heat 4 to 5 inches of oil or shortening in a deep-fryer to a temperature of 375°F. on a frying thermometer. Preheat oven to 250°F. Line a large shallow roasting pan with paper towels. Dry the potatoes thoroughly and deep-fry them in 3 or 4 batches until they are crisp and light brown. Transfer them to the lined pan to drain and place them in the oven to keep warm.

FISH

2 pounds fresh, firm white fish fillets
    such as shark, haddock or cod

Skin the fish and cut into pieces 3 by 5 inches. Wash the pieces of fish under cold running water and pat them completely dry with paper towels. Drop 2 or 3 pieces of fish at a time into the batter; when they are well coated, plunge them into the hot oil. Fry for 4 or 5 minutes, or until golden brown, turning the pieces occasionally with a spoon to prevent their sticking together or to the pan.

To serve, heap the fish in the center of a large heated platter and arrange the chips around them. Traditionally, fish and chips are served sprinkled with malt vinegar and salt. Makes 4 servings.

Sheepshead

Sheefish

See INCONNU under WHITEFISH.

Sheepshead

(1) In the Atlantic Ocean a member of the family Sparidae. *See PORGY.*
(2) In North American freshwaters a common name for a member of the family Sciaenidae, properly called freshwater drum. *See DRUM.*
(3) In the Pacific Ocean a member of the family Labridae or wrasses, but correctly as a common name "sheephead" (no s). *See CALIFORNIA SHEEPHEAD.*

Shrimp

The shrimp is our most valuable seafood product. There are about 370 million pounds landed by U.S. fishermen, and an additional 200 million pounds imported from other countries. No restaurant is too far removed from the sea to list shrimps on its menu. This ubiquitous crustacean is popular the world over as there are hundreds of species in both freshwater and saltwater. They are as common to the sweltering mammy-markets of West Africa as to the chafing dishes of the Ritz in Montreal. On the jungle shores of the Parismina River in Costa Rica I have enjoyed shrimps that ran two to a pound, and I have sampled huge tiger prawns in a fiery Bengali curry. But even the miniscule Alaskan pink shrimps, which require 160 to 180 to make 1 pound, are harvested by man. Sweet and crisp, these delicate products of a complex ecological chain are utilized throughout the world.

Shrimps are common all around the coasts of North America but our major Atlantic fishery extends from North Carolina to Florida and into the Gulf of Mexico. This is augmented by distant-water fleets based mainly in Texas and Florida which operate off the coasts of Mexico, Surinam, Guiana, and Brazil. While shrimps are found and exploited over most of our Pacific Coast, the major fishery here is in Alaska.

There are excellent prospects that shrimps will be cultured artificially. Presently they are reared in 2 ways: by allowing juvenile shrimps to be carried by the tides into coastal ponds where they grow to market size; this is the method used in India, and it has been successfully duplicated in both Texas and Louisiana; the other method is to catch gravid females at sea and allow them to spawn in ponds. There are still some problems to solve before shrimps can be held in captivity to complete their entire life cycle. Dr. Motosaku Fujinaga, a Japanese scientist who developed shrimp "farming" as we presently understand it, succeeded in growing shrimps from the egg to market size; unfortunately, his techniques are not feasible from an economic standpoint in the U. S. The cost of these shrimps in Japan is well over $10 per pound but the demand for Kuruma prawns (or "dancing" shrimps, as they are served alive) supports this price in Tokyo.

There are 7 species of shrimps of commercial importance in our Atlantic waters and the Gulf of Mexico. It really takes an expert to distinguish one from another, as anything we say about coloration is simply a generalization. For example, pink shrimps and brown shrimps are sometimes similar in color despite their different names. Usually, the **brown shrimp** (Penaeus aztecus) is reddish brown, with tinges of blue or purple on the tail and on some of the legs. **Pink shrimp** (Penaeus duorarum) seem to vary according to geographic locality; along the Atlantic Coast they are usually light brown, in the Tortugas fishery they are pink, and along the northern Gulf Coast they often resemble brown shrimps or can even be lemon-yellow. The **white shrimp** (Penaeus setiferus), found from North Carolina to the Gulf of Mexico and Texas, and the **Caribbean white shrimp** (Penaeus schmitti), are usually grayish white and are variously tinged about the tail and legs with green, red and blue. The **sea bob** (Xiphopeneus kroyeri), distributed from Cape Hatteras to Zimbros Bay, Brazil, is usually red or pinkish-red when alive but will turn black when cooked or frozen. **Royal red**

shrimp (Hymenopenaeus robustus), found from Cape Hatteras to the Gulf of Mexico, are generally deep red all over but sometimes appear pinkish-gray. The big royal red, one of my favorites, occurs mainly in deep water (from 175 to 300 fathoms) off the edge of the Continental Shelf. The **rock shrimp** (Sicyonia brevirostris), which is found from Norfolk, Virginia, into the Bahamas and Gulf of Mexico, tends to be brownish on the dorsal surface and pale on the sides; the underside and appendages are variously colored with red or purple.

The rock shrimp is a fairly recent introduction to the American market. This species has always been caught abundantly in Florida and Mexican waters during regular shrimping operations, but until 1970 it was invariably discarded; it has an extremely hard shell which complicated processing, therefore no real market existed for them. Finally, a peeling machine was designed that could handle this operation, and the demand has now reached several million pounds per year. Rock shrimp meat is firm, perhaps more lobsterlike than that of its relatives; they can be treated like miniature scampi, ideal for broiling with an appropriate sauce.

On our Pacific Coast there are 5 species of shrimps that comprise the commercial catch. The most common are the **side-stripe shrimp** (Pandalopsus dispar) and two **pink shrimps** (Pandalopsus borealis and Pandalus jordoni), which are found as far north as the Aleutians. The side-stripe is large and may grow to 10 inches in length, it, as well as the **coon-stripe shrimp** (Pandalus danae) and the **spot shrimp** (Pandalus platyceros), which are usually a bit smaller, are the "prawns" of our West Coast. There are 2 smaller species of pink shrimps which vary from 3 to 5 inches in length.

There are 11 other commercially important species of shrimps taken from Central and South American waters, and at least 10 from the Indo-Pacific region which are quite large, such as the giant **tiger prawn** (Penaeus monodon) and the **Kuruma prawn** (Penaeus japonicus). The interchange in the names "shrimp" and "prawn" has no universal recognition. In India, which is the world's largest shrimp-farming nation, all shrimplike animals are called prawns. Prawns are then divided into penaeid shrimps and non-penaeid shrimps. The genus Penaeus contains most of our marine shrimps. Correctly, we should recognize freshwater species (Macrobrachium) as prawns and all marine species as shrimps (see PRAWN). However, in commercial practice in the U.K. or the U.S., prawn is used as a name for large shrimps.

One of the most bizarre-looking aquatic creatures is a freshwater shrimp known as the Macro-

brachium. Some years ago I was crossing Pelican Bay in Lake Okeechobee when the propeller of my outboard became entangled in a heavy piece of cord. After working the cord free I discovered that it was attached to an old catfish trap that had broken loose from its buoy. Looking through the wire mesh I found myself eyeball to eyeball with a long-legged creature who appeared vicious enough to fight back. This giant freshwater shrimp measured almost 30 inches from the tip of its claw to the tail. While I didn't have the good sense to eat it, being too preoccupied with its identification, I have since enjoyed the tender lobster-like tail meat of this unusual prawn. The claws have tremendous gripping power; it is not the kind of shrimp one handles casually, as I discovered at the outset. These crustaceans are common in Florida waters and in the tropical Americas and were known to the Conquistadores. Today, the *Macrobrachium* (there are 4 species native to North America but more than 100 on a world basis) is a subject of intensive research; if successfully propagated, it could be a spectacular addition to the larder of fish cookery.

The best of all shrimps are those you catch yourself. While there are various traps and cast nets for this purpose, the simplest method is dipping. Shrimp-dipping is not the act of plunging the crustacean into a bowl of sauce but rather a nocturnal sport, especially in south Florida when chill winds, an ebbing tide and a full moon conspire to make the shrimps "run" and otherwise sane citizens do likewise. All one needs is a long-handled net and a lantern, and the endurance to stay out all night. Shrimp-dippers can be found along seawalls, docks, even in boats scooping the surface-swimming crustaceans out of the swirling currents. Shrimps are attracted to a lantern light and in a peak period during winter and spring one can catch enough to satisfy any appetite. There was a time when an even easier method provided fresh shrimps, but with spiraling costs at market "bartering" has lost most of its currency as compared to just a few years ago. After a long day on the tarpon flats we used to run southwest from Mud Key and find a trawler at anchor in the lee of one of the mangrove islands outside of Key West. For a six-pack of beer one of the crew would fill a bucket with freshly caught shrimps and lower it to our skiff—maybe 5 or 6 pounds of big pinks still salty-sweet with the Gulf's waters. For a bottle of bourbon, bucket after bucket hit the deck until we couldn't get the lid on our Styrofoam cooler. The next stop, of course, was a driftwood fire on the nearest beach where mid the panoply of gannets and willets flashing among the mangroves, and mullets flopping in a quiet lagoon, few would deny that a steamed shrimp doused in butter is one of the sea's great treasures.

HOW TO BUY SHRIMPS

Shrimps are marketed fresh and frozen, breaded cooked or uncooked, smoked, dried, canned, semipreserved (usually vinegar-cured in jars), in paste form, and in soups or other prepared dishes. In the U.S. fresh or "green" shrimps are sold by the pound, but the size designation or "count" is important as the number of shrimps supplying that weight is highly variable. In commercial grading at New York's Fulton Fish Market, for example, shrimps are boxed at 10 to 15 per pound, 16 to 20 per pound, 21 to 25 per pound, 26 to 30 per pound, and 31 to 35 per pound. What constitutes a "prawn" or a "jumbo" is arbitrary but under most definitions it's any count up to 15 per pound with 16 to 20 being "extra large." From 21 to 30 they are usually called "large" and from 31 to 40 "medium." In the small sizes almost any number is valid. With the shrimps of some 50 nations entering our present markets the old name-grading system is not uniform; shrimps now run from 3 to 160 or more per pound in the case of some sub-Arctic and European species. How many shrimps you buy depends on how they are to be used. In calculating portions remember that 2 pounds of uncooked shrimps in the shell will yield slightly more than 1 pound of meat after shelling and deveining.

Fresh shrimps are firm and smell fresh. Don't be afraid to use your nose. A stale shrimp has an offensive ammonia odor; if there's one bad shrimp in a box you can assume that they are all bad. Sometimes shrimps taste strongly of "iodine" but this has nothing to do with spoilage. Shrimps caught in brackish water (to 15 ppt salinity) rarely have this pronounced flavor as their food in low salinities does not concentrate iodine, whereas shrimps taken offshore in totally saline water (30 ppt or above) may feed on certain organisms which can produce a distinctive iodine flavor.

So-called "river shrimps," or Caridea, a tribe composed of several genera, including *Palaemon, Pandalus* and *Macrobrachium,* living in freshwater, are always iodine-free. River shrimps are common in the southern U.S.; they are of consistently sweet flavor. These are caught in small quantities and utilized on a local level.

Some countries use sodium bisulfite (illegal in the U.S.) as a preservative, and this chemical also magnifies the iodine taste. So the condition can occur at random naturally and also because of the source of supply. If you buy shrimps over a period of time which have a consistently unpleasant taste, then it's advisable to change markets. Bear in mind that shrimps generally contain the highest amount of iodine among crustaceans, but they are also high in vitamins and minerals. Based on

HOW TO PREPARE A STUFFED BUTTERFLY SHRIMP

1. Insert a knife through the shell into the back of the shrimp.

2. Cut down to the tail without cutting through to the ventral side.

3. Gently pull off the shell, leaving the tail "feathers" attached to the shrimp.

4. Butterfly shrimp, opened out and stuffed, ready for baking.

HOW TO CLEAN A SHELLED COOKED SHRIMP

  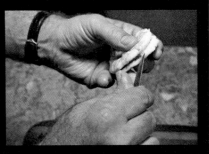

1. Pull off a narrow strip on the back of the shrimp.

2. Peel the strip down to the tail. A dark line, the intestinal tract or vein, is revealed.

3. With a small knife remove the intestinal tract; this is called deveining.

Tiny cooked shrimps, found in the waters of Northern Europe and Alaska

100 grams of meat, shrimps provide 20.5% protein (as compared to chicken 18.6%, beef 18% and pork 10.2%). (U.S.D.A. Agriculture Handbook No. 8 *Composition of Foods*, 1963)

Flash-frozen, peeled and deveined shrimps are excellent. Do not thaw these before boiling. If you use them for a special dish—**Shrimp Newburg,** for example—boil the shrimps just to the point when they turn color but are not quite opaque. Twice-cooking, as well as overcooking, makes the normally tender shrimp tough. Heating the semiboiled shrimps in a sauce will be sufficient to finish cooking them. For long-cooking dishes, such as **Shrimp Creole,** use raw shrimps, or thaw the flash-frozen ones and drain before adding.

STEAMED FRESH SHRIMPS, MY METHOD
I say "my" method, although I'm sure many other people have discovered this easy way of cooking shrimps. To me, leaving shrimps in boiling water merely makes them tough whether it's timed at 1, 3, or any number of minutes; the longer the tougher, particularly when left to stand in hot water after boiling. To make a firm but *tender* shrimp, that is to say, crisp and juicy, place whole shrimps in a pot and add enough water to cover. Use a lid that will fit tightly, but initially leave it slightly askew. Bring the water to a rolling boil and when steam is puffing from under the lid turn off the heat and clamp the lid down tight. Now, using pot holders to hold pot and lid, drain the pot by opening the lid ever so slightly and pouring the water into the sink. Close the lid again and let the shrimps sit in their own steam for 10 to 15 minutes. Do not "peek" under the lid. After the shrimps cool, then peel and devein if necessary.

TEMPURA
One of the most popular of all Japanese dishes, tempura had its origin during the period when Portuguese traders visited the islands in the sixteenth century. The Portuguese introduced their custom of eating fried shrimps during the Quatuor Tempora (the Latin term for Ember Days). The Japanese adopted the dish if not the holidays. Eschewing the heavier batter and olive oil of their visitors, they created what has almost become a cuisine within a cuisine. Although shrimp is the pivotal ingredient in Japan, a tempura may include green ginkgo nuts, tiger-lily buds, watercress, mushrooms, gingerroot, green beans, carrots, broccoli, onions, eggplant, and a variety of fishes, notably the squid and gobies (**háze** in Japanese). The cooking is ceremoniously done on a gas burner at table while the diner sits on a small cushion, as the chef artfully dips the morsels of food into hot sesame-seed oil. *(See also Deep-Frying under COOKING METHODS.)*

SHRIMP BALLS
(The Mandarin, San Francisco)

2 pounds shelled uncooked shrimps	1 tablespoon sesame-seed oil
1½ pounds water chestnuts	2 fresh scallions, green part
8 egg whites	1 tablespoon sherry
1 teaspoon salt	2 heaping tablespoons flour
dash of pepper	1 tablespoon water
pinch of ground aniseed	vegetable oil for deep-frying

Chop the shrimps fine, then mash to almost a paste texture. Do the same to the water chestnuts. Mix all ingredients except vegetable oil thoroughly, and refrigerate till firm. Heat oil in a wok over medium heat to 375°F. Form mixture into balls, the size depending on how they will be served; for appetizers or soup, they should be small. Smaller balls will cook in about 2 minutes, larger balls in 4 to 6 minutes. Drop the balls into the oil; they will sink to the bottom of the wok. When they rise and float they are done. If they are spongy, the meat inside is cooked. Deep-fry to a golden brown. Serve with Szechuan Sauce *(see INDEX).* Makes 8 appetizer servings.

HOW TO MAKE TEMPURA (prepared at the Nippon Restaurant, New York City)

1. Drop an egg into a bowl and mix well.

2. Add 2 cups ice water.

3. Beat again until egg and water are well blended.

4. Add 3 cups wheat flour.

5. Stir until batter is mixed but still somewhat lumpy.

6. Dip shrimp into batter to coat with a thin film.

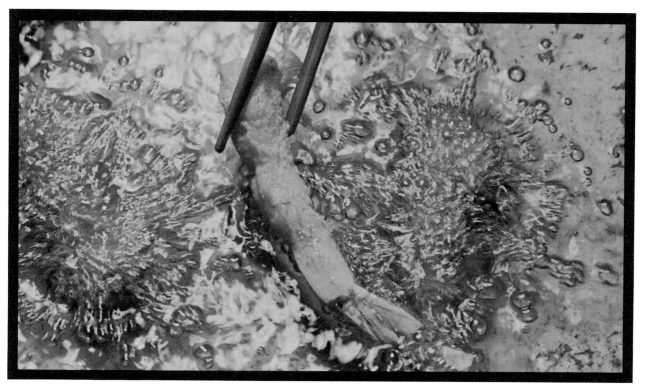

7. Deep-fry shrimp in very hot sesame-seed oil, swishing it around like a fish in water.

The *Lisa Ann* is a typical
shrimp boat working in the Gulf of Mexico.
Shrimps are an important harvest
for the fisheries of the Gulf States.

ST. HELENA ISLAND SHRIMP GRAVY
(Al Wilhelm, *Clarendon Plantation*)

5 pounds shrimps, peeled and deveined

6 slices of smoked bacon, cut into fine strips

3 medium-size onions, chopped

salt and pepper

brown gravy maker

instantized flour

Place shrimps in a large skillet, add a little water, and cook until shrimps turn red. Remove shrimps from skillet, and save the liquid, which is essential to the dish. Sauté the bacon in a skillet to extract some fat, then add the onions and cook until bacon is done and onions tender but not browned. Add to the shrimp juice. Season with salt and pepper to taste. Add a small amount of brown gravy maker (about ½ teaspoon, or to taste) for color, then thicken with instantized flour. Add the shrimps and cook in the "gravy" until done. Serve over rice. Makes 12 servings.

CURRIED SHRIMP CRÊPES

1½ pounds uncooked fresh shrimps in shells, or 1 pound flash-frozen shelled shrimps	1 apple, Greening or yellow Delicious, peeled and cored
12 cooked crêpes (recipe follows)	½ teaspoon minced fresh gingerroot
1½ tablespoons peanut oil	1 teaspoon curry powder
1½ tablespoons butter	3 tablespoons flour
1 onion, 3 ounces	1 cup chicken broth
2 green Italian peppers, 2 ounces, trimmed	1 cup plain yogurt
	½ cup heavy cream
	12 water chestnuts, sliced
	3 tablespoons minced fresh parsley

Make crêpes before starting the rest of the recipe. If using fresh shrimps, shell and devein them. If using frozen shrimps, let them thaw. Chop half of the shrimps into small pieces. Cut the rest lengthwise into halves. Put peanut oil and butter into a large skillet over low heat and turn the *halved* shrimps into the mixture for 2 minutes, no longer, until shrimps are pink. With a skimmer transfer shrimps to a plate and set aside; leave butter and oil in skillet. Chop onion, peppers and apple. Put onion and peppers into the skillet and cook over low heat, turning occasionally, until vegetables are soft and yellow, but not brown. Add apple pieces, gingerroot and *chopped* shrimps, and continue to cook until apple is soft. Sprinkle on curry powder and cook for 2 minutes, stirring.

Sprinkle on flour and stir until flour is absorbed and mixture thick. Add chicken broth; stir and heat until sauce is again thick. Turn everything into the container of an electric blender. Add yogurt and blend for a few seconds. Mixture will be somewhat lumpy. Pour off half of it into a bowl. Add ¼ cup cream to the rest and purée again to make a smooth sauce.

Add the halved shrimps, sliced water chestnuts and parsley to the lumpy sauce in the bowl and gently mix. Butter a large shallow baking dish. Spoon about 3 tablespoons of the filling into each crêpe and roll up with the seam on the bottom. Continue until all crêpes are filled. Cover the dish with foil and heat in a 375°F. oven for about 20 minutes. Meanwhile whip remaining cream to Chantilly stage and gently fold into the puréed sauce. Uncover baking dish and spoon sauce over the filled crêpes, leaving the ends uncovered for contrast. Heat again until the sauce is golden brown. Makes 12 servings for first course, 4 to 6 servings for main course.

NOTES: Instead of shrimps, crab meat or lobster can be used.

Gingerroot can be omitted; in any case do *not* use ground ginger as a substitute as that would make the sauce too spicy.

Each brand of curry powder is prepared according to the formula of the maker from a mixture of 8 or more spices; some are very mild, others almost biting. Adjust the amount on the basis of your taste. The curry should not overwhelm the shrimps.

The thickness of the sauce can be adjusted if necessary by adding less or more chicken broth or cream.

CRÊPES

1 cup unbleached flour	1½ cups half milk and half water
½ teaspoon salt	
½ teaspoon curry powder	2 tablespoons minced fresh parsley
3 eggs	2 tablespoons butter

Mix all ingredients except parsley and butter with a rotary egg beater, or in an electric blender. Cover and leave in a cool place for 1 hour. Batter will be *very* thin.

Stir in the parsley. Put a small lump of the butter in a 9-inch pan; heat. When butter is sizzling and almost ready to turn brown, pour off the butter into a custard cup. At once pour into the pan 3 tablespoons of the batter. Turn the pan to let the batter cover the entire surface. When the edges are crisp and the underneath light brown (lift with a spatula to see), turn the crêpe over and cook the other side; turn with a wide spatula, or pick up by the edge with fingertips and flip over. When the second side is speckled with brown spots, transfer the crêpe to a plate. Add another small amount of butter and continue. If you pour off excess butter as soon as the pan is well covered, this amount will be sufficient to cook all the crêpes. If crêpes are to be used on the same day, stack them up, cover, and leave in a cool place till ready to fill. If they are to be stored, separate the crêpes with a sheet of wax paper or plastic wrap, cover when thoroughly cooled, and refrigerate. Or wrap in freezer wrap and freeze. Let them reach room temperature before filling or rolling. Makes 12 crêpes.

SHRIMP-STUFFED ARTICHOKES

¾ pound	¼ cup medium-dry
cooked tiny shrimps	white wine
4 large artichokes	2 tablespoons lemon juice
1½ quarts water	½ teaspoon onion powder
2 tablespoons salt	¼ teaspoon
3 tablespoons	crushed dried basil
white-wine vinegar	2 drops of Tabasco
1 tablespoon salad oil	¼ cup mayonnaise

Rinse artichokes well, and cut off stems close to base. Place in a large kettle with water, salt, vinegar and salad oil. Bring to a boil, reduce heat, and simmer for 25 to 30 minutes, or until artichokes are tender. Test with a stainless-steel fork thrust through the base. Drain and cool. Meanwhile, combine shrimps with all remaining ingredients except mayonnaise, mix lightly, cover, and chill. Shortly before serving, spread artichoke leaves open slightly, and pull out the center tufts of leaves. With a teaspoon carefully scrape out the thistlelike "choke" in center of artichoke bottom, and discard. Scrape the tender portion from the center leaves that were removed, and combine with mayonnaise. Spoon some into the center of each artichoke. Drain shrimps, and spoon on the mayonnaise mixture. Serve at once, with additional mayonnaise, if desired. Makes 4 servings.

MANDARIN GOLDFISH ON WHITE SEA
(The Mandarin, San Francisco)

Shell and devein large raw shrimps. Chop off tail "feathers" and reserve. Split the shelled shrimps and mash each piece with the side of cleaver. Stack several together; using the blunt edges of 2 cleavers, chop the shrimps until well mashed. Using a Chinese soup spoon, shape the mashed shrimp meat into egg shapes, rounding off the top with a second spoon. Smooth off, and place on a heatproof plate. Prepare as many as will be served. Garnish each "goldfish" of shrimps with 2 peas for eyes and a thin slice of Virginia ham for a dorsal fin. Replace the uncooked tail "feathers" to make a tail for each one. Steam on the plate in a Chinese steamer for 10 minutes.

Meanwhile heat 2 cups of chicken broth. Mix cornstarch with water to make approximately ⅓ cup of a thin paste; add the paste to the hot broth together with a pinch of salt. Let cook until thickened. Just before serving stir in 2 beaten egg whites and turn off heat immediately. (Make more of the soup mixture if this is not enough to cover your serving platter.)

Pour the "white sea" soup onto a large shallow platter, and place the steamed shrimp goldfish on the surface of the soup. Garnish and serve immediately.

BARBECUED PRAWNS

1 pound prawns or	½ teaspoon
very large fresh shrimps	prepared horseradish
(about 12 per pound)	⅓ teaspoon garlic powder
⅓ cup	8 cherry tomatoes
medium-dry white wine	1 small onion,
1 tablespoon	cut into wedges
lemon juice	4 squares (1-inch size)
1 tablespoon soy sauce	green pepper

Peel and devein prawns. Combine wine, lemon juice, soy sauce, horseradish and garlic powder. Pour over prawns, cover, and marinate in refrigerator for several hours. Shortly before serving, drain well. On each of 4 long skewers thread 3 prawns, alternating them with 2 cherry tomatoes, 1 onion wedge and 1 square of green pepper. Broil over hot coals for about 3 minutes on each side, just until prawns are cooked through. Makes 4 servings.

PRAWNS À LA SZECHUAN

½ pound	1 teaspoon (or less)
shelled raw prawns	dried red chili pepper,
or very large shrimps	chopped fine
2 tablespoons vegetable oil	2 tablespoons dry sherry
½ teaspoon minced garlic	1 tablespoon ketchup
½ teaspoon grated	pinch of sugar
fresh gingerroot	1 teaspoon cornstarch
2 tablespoons	2 tablespoons water
chopped scallions	

In a wok, skillet or chafing dish (wok preferred) heat oil until quite hot. Sauté prawns, garlic, gingerroot, scallions and chili pepper. Cook for a few min-

MANDARIN GOLDFISH ON WHITE SEA (prepared by The Mandarin, San Francisco)

1. Shell large shrimps, reserving tail "feathers."

2. Mash shrimp meat with flat side of cleaver.

3. Shape mashed shrimp in a Chinese soup spoon.

4. Replace the reserved tail "feathers" to make a tail.

5. Use 2 large green peas for eyes.

6. Make a dorsal fin on each goldfish with a thin slice of Virginia ham.

7. Place goldfish on a plate and steam in a Chinese steamer for 10 minutes.

8. Serve "swimming" in white sea soup on a large shallow platter.

utes. Add sherry, ketchup and sugar; then add cornstarch mixed with water to thicken, and continue to cook, stirring and tossing constantly, until prawns are done. A few drops of sesame oil may be added. Makes 2 servings.

SPIDER-WEB PRAWNS

(The Mandarin, San Francisco)

1 cup cleaned raw prawns
peanut oil
½ teaspoon mashed garlic
½ teaspoon mashed fresh gingerroot
1 cup yellow rice wine
½ cup julienne strips of carrots
½ cup julienne strips of bamboo shoots
1 tablespoon hot bean sauce (see Note)
dash of fagara oil (see Note)
½ teaspoon cornstarch
½ teaspoon sugar

Heat a wok thoroughly, washing the sides with hot oil; discard most of the oil. Put the mixed garlic and gingerroot in the wok, add the prawns, and stir vigorously. Add the rice wine, then, always stirring, add carrots and bamboo shoots (the pieces should be matching in size). Stir-fry rapidly, then add the bean sauce, fagara oil, cornstarch and sugar. Mix well, and serve. Makes 2 servings.

NOTE: Hot bean sauce is available in Chinese markets. To make fagara oil, put bits of fagara (Szechuan pepper) in oil, heat carefully, strain, and reserve the oil. Add a dash of salt if you like. The peppers and already prepared oil are available in Chinese markets.

Traditionally, when this dish is made in China, more vegetables are used in proportion to the prawns than in this recipe.

SCAMPI PALM BEACH (SHRIMPS WITH GREEN LINGUINI)

2 pounds (18 count or 36) fresh shrimps, including rock shrimps, butterflied
¾ cup clarified butter
¼ cup olive oil
2 tablespoons minced garlic
2 tablespoons lemon juice
½ teaspoon dry mustard
1 teaspoon Worcestershire sauce
½ teaspoon crushed dried red pepper
1 teaspoon minced fresh orégano, or ½ teaspoon dried
1 teaspoon minced fresh sweet basil, or ½ teaspoon dried
1 teaspoon minced fresh tarragon, or ½ teaspoon dried
¼ teaspoon salt
4 tablespoons chopped parsley
½ cup white wine (Chablis preferred)
1 pound linguini verde
½ cup grated Parmesan cheese

This is a colorful party dish with the bright red-shelled shrimps contrasting with the green pasta, and a wonderful combination from a taste standpoint. It's my own version of "scampi" which has stood the test of many guests over the years. If the passion for garlic is unanimous the amount given can be increased, but the way to do this is by sprinkling additional freshly chopped bits over each shrimp after the sauce is applied.

In a large skillet melt butter; add oil, garlic, lemon juice, dry mustard, Worcestershire, crushed red pepper, orégano, basil, tarragon, salt and 2 tablespoons parsley. Mix well and simmer over low heat until garlic is just *blond.* Turn off heat. Take each shrimp by the tail and wipe the flesh side in the mixture so that they are thoroughly coated. After dipping, arrange shrimps next to each other, flesh side up, in a foil-lined pan. Add the wine to the skillet, bring to a boil, then simmer until the liquid has reduced by one fourth. Spoon some of the sauce over each shrimp. (This much of the recipe can be prepared in advance if you are entertaining.)

At this point you can cook the *linguini* as the time interval will be about the same as for finishing the shrimps. Set your oven at 400°F. to preheat and in the meantime bring salted water in your pasta pot to a rolling boil. Submerge the *linguini* and cook *al dente* (about 7 minutes); bake the shrimps for an equal period of time. Turn off oven and stove, drain the pasta, and return it to the pot.

Fork a small mound of *linguini* in the center of each warm plate, leaving a margin for the shrimps. Remove shrimps from the oven and arrange six, with tails pointing outward, around the perimeter of the pasta. Pour remaining sauce over the shrimps and *linguini* and decorate with remaining parsley. Sprinkle the pasta with freshly grated Parmesan cheese. Accompany with a spinach salad using a sweet vinegar dressing with no oil. Makes 6 servings.

SHRIMP RÉMOULADE

1 pound deveined, peeled, cooked shrimps, or frozen shrimps
½ cup olive or salad oil
½ cup tarragon vinegar
⅓ cup horseradish mustard
2 tablespoons ketchup
½ cup chopped green onions and tops
2 garlic cloves, chopped fine
1 tablespoon paprika
1 teaspoon salt
¼ teaspoon cayenne pepper
lettuce

Thaw shrimps if frozen. Combine all other ingredients except lettuce. Shake well. Marinate shrimps in sauce in refrigerator for several hours. Serve on lettuce. Makes 6 servings.

SHRIMP CONGA

1 pound shelled	4 ounces butter, melted
rock shrimp tails	3 ounces cream cheese
salt and pepper	1 ounce Roquefort
juice of 1 lime	or other blue cheese

Place shrimps in a baking dish. Sprinkle with salt and pepper and the lime juice. Blend butter and both cheeses together and pour over shrimps. Cover with aluminum foil. Bake in a 400°F. oven for 10 minutes. Makes 4 servings.

BROILED ROCK SHRIMP TAILS

1 pound shelled	½ teaspoon salt
rock shrimp tails	dash of white pepper
⅓ cup plus ¼ cup melted	dash of paprika
butter or margarine	1 tablespoon lemon juice

Lay shrimp tails open on broiler pan or tray. Use ⅓ cup melted butter to brush over them. Sprinkle with salt, pepper and paprika. Broil about 4 inches from the source of heat for 3 minutes; shrimps will not be brown. Warm remaining ¼ cup butter with the lemon juice and use for a dip. Makes 4 servings.

VARIATION: Mix ½ cup melted butter or margarine with

Belle Terrasse, a restaurant in Tivoli Gardens, Copenhagen, famous for seafood

½ cup vegetable or olive oil. Mix in 4 garlic cloves, minced or put through a press, ⅓ cup minced parsley, ½ teaspoon salt, and 6 peppercorns, crushed. Brush over 3 pounds shelled rock shrimp tails before broiling. Makes 8 to 10 servings.

CHARCOAL-GRILLED ROCK SHRIMP TAILS

2 to 3 pounds shelled rock shrimp tails	4 teaspoons tarragon leaves
1 cup salad oil	½ teaspoon minced chervil
1 cup lemon juice	¼ teaspoon minced basil
¼ cup soy sauce	2 garlic cloves, minced
2 tablespoons minced parsley	½ teaspoon salt
	4 peppercorns, crushed

Mix all the marinade ingredients and pour over the shrimps in a nonmetal container. Marinate for 2 or 3 hours. Arrange in a hinged wire grill, and grill over charcoal for 3 to 4 minutes on each side. Makes 8 to 10 servings.

ROCK SHRIMP MIAMI

2½ pounds peeled and deveined rock shrimps, fresh or frozen	2 teaspoons salt
	½ teaspoon white pepper
	¼ cup extra dry vermouth
½ cup olive or salad oil	2 tablespoons lemon juice

Thaw frozen rock shrimps. Preheat electric frying pan to 320°F. Add oil, salt, pepper and shrimps. Cook for 2 to 2½ minutes, or until shrimps are pink and tender, stirring frequently. Increase temperature to 420°F. Add vermouth and lemon juice. Cook for 1 minute longer, stirring constantly. Drain. Serve hot or cold as an appetizer or entrée. Makes 6 servings.

NOTE: 2 pounds white, brown or pink shrimps may be substituted for rock shrimps by increasing the cooking time in the oil, salt and pepper to a total of 6 to 8 minutes; the remainder of the instructions are the same.

Silversides

My first recollection of catching a fish of any kind occurred at the age of five or six, when my grandfather taught me to stuff pieces of stale bread in a milk bottle and sink it next to our dock. With a length of cord knotted around the bottle's neck, I simply sat and watched the "bait" until it began dancing about. My almost invisible quarry soon became so numerous that the glass sparkled like a mirror and yanking the bottle out of the water I invariably captured what would amount to an expense-account portion of whitebait in Peter Kreindler's emporium at 21 West 52nd Street. Naturally, I had no concept of their culinary stature, nor that of the tiny oyster crabs who competed with the silversides for the last bit of crust. After examining my catch I would pour them back and start over again. It wasn't until milk bottles went out of style that I discovered my **spearing,** which is their common name on eastern Long Island, were a choice food, usually reserved for fashionable restaurants where the "fishes of the king" are regally priced. In Spanish and Portuguese cultures the **pescados del rey** or **peixe-rei** are highly esteemed, and these members of the family Atherinidae reach their penultimate in the **pejerrey** of Chile and Argentina. The **pejerrey** is the largest of all silversides, attaining a length

Pejerrey, a silverside found in South American waters, a great delicacy

of over 12 inches, and is one of the most popular freshwater fishes in South America. Yet, the silversides are one of the most underutilized seafoods in the eastern U.S. Any bay or harbor from Maine to North Carolina can produce enough silversides to feed a large family in a matter of minutes by the judicious use of a short length of seine net. And if you live in southern California you can hunt for them at night with a flashlight when the grunion come on the beaches to spawn. *See WHITEBAIT.*

Smelt

The smelt was once so abundant in the Back Bay of Boston that "distinguished merchants of lower Beacon Street might be seen, at early hours, eagerly catching their breakfast from their back doors" according to the Massachusetts Fisheries Report for 1870. I can think of no finer way of starting a day, especially when the fish is delivered instantly from water to skillet because, like many other species, it offers a subtle taste experience when taken at its prime. The aroma of a smelt has been likened to that of violets or the clean smell of cucumber, much as a fresh grayling will smell of thyme. This most delicious, nutritious and inexpensive fish is more available now than ever before, thanks to modern flash-freezing, a process which preserves its soft flesh with uncommonly good results. The smelt has always enjoyed popular acclaim in Europe and its French name **éperlan** or pearly fish suggests the high esteem in which it's held. The eastern Atlantic smelt does not differ at all from our rainbow smelt; it occurs from the Bay of Biscay to the Baltic Sea and to the Penchora River of the USSR. It's widely known as **sparling** in the United Kingdom, although in marketing the names smelt and sparling are used interchangeably.

There are 9 species of smelts in North American waters and of these the most widely distributed is the **rainbow smelt** *(Osmerus mordax)*, and it's the one most people are familiar with. The name smelt is derived from the Anglo-Saxon "smoelt" which means smooth or shining. This small, smooth and shining, silvery fish occurs in the western Atlantic and Pacific Oceans and Arctic Sea, west to the White Sea. It's mostly an anadromous fish, running from the sea into freshwater during the spring season, but there are landlocked populations also, from Maine to the Great Lakes and in southeastern Canada. Large quantities of smelts are taken in harbors and estuaries of New England by "shanty-fishing" through the ice. Perhaps our largest commercial fishery is in Lake Superior, where during the approximately 10-day spawning run in late April millions of pounds of smelts are

harvested. The Duluth (Minnesota) Chamber of Commerce has received as many as 6,397 long-distance phone calls at their "smelt report" telephone exchange from amateur fishermen awaiting word that the run is on.

The second important smelt, although only utilized on a regional basis, is the **eulachon,** which is often marketed as "Columbia River Smelt." Eulachon are found from Oregon north to Alaska. They enter rivers in late winter, usually January, and continue to run until April. The Columbia River alone produces from 1 to 6 million pounds of eulachon each season, the commercial catch fluctuating as a "second choice" because of the more valuable salmon fishery in that river. The name eulachon comes from the Chinook dialect and has gone through a variety of spellings such as oolachan, ulchen, and even hooligan in Alaska. It is also known as a **candlefish,** because *Thaleichthys pacificus* is so rich in oil that the Indians would air-dry this smelt and draw a strip of cedar bark through its body to make a wick and use it as a candle. The eulachon was a staple food for many coastal Indian tribes, particularly the mighty Kwakiutl of British Columbia. To these remarkably muscular and healthy people, the oil-rich eulachon was utilized in some way with every meal, and even more so during cold winter months when summer-cut grass was mixed with eulachon fat in the form of fishcakes, a Kwakiutl staple. While making a film on salmon in Discovery Passage many years ago, my Indian guide presented me with a garumlike sauce made from decayed eulachons to be spread on a salmon steak. I must admit it was a heady experience, but the fish is too delicate to be preserved, even by freezing, and to a Kwakiutl this smelt held the same challenge as the anchovy to an ancient Roman. At market the eulachon is sold mainly in fresh and smoked form. In common with other smelts tremendous numbers of eulachon are taken by people using dip nets and baskets during the spawning runs, and "hooligan" fishing is a widely attended sport in Alaska.

The only other Pacific species that is utilized to any extent is the **surf smelt** *(Hypomesus pretiosus)*, which is a smaller and leaner fish than the eulachon; it is marketed fresh beginning in January to the peak in April. Surf smelts are seined by Indians on the coastal reservations of Washington, primarily by the Quillayute people. Other smelts of minor commercial importance found from California to Alaska are the **night smelt** *(Spirinchus starksi)*, the **longfin smelt** *(S. thaleichthys)* and the **whitebait smelt** *(Allosmerus elongatus)*, all of which are purveyed as "whitebait." The **delta smelt** *(H. transpacificus)* is taken to some extent by amateurs using nets

Surf smelt

Capelin

Eulachon

in the surf. Although the **capelin** *(Mallotus villosus)* occurs abundantly around Arctic and sub-Arctic shores in the Atlantic and Pacific Oceans, it only appears sporadically off the coast of Maine. This small smelt has some importance to Japanese, Norwegian and Soviet distant-water fleets. About 100,000 tons of capelin are used each year in Japan where the fish is known as **shishamo.** The roe-laden female is particularly valuable in the Tokyo market.

HOW TO COOK SMELTS

Smelts are sold whole or gutted when fresh, or pandressed and frozen. The best way to store smelts if you are blessed with an excess of freshly caught fish is to freeze them in blocks. Place the fish head down in suitable plastic containers and fill the container with water right up to the lid, making it airtight. When ready to have a smelt feast, remove from freezer and thaw the number of containers required. Under normal storage conditions smelts have a shelf life of about 6 months.

     The fish can be prepared in a variety of ways but frying is the most popular method. True smelt addicts eat everything but the wiggle. It is not necessary to fillet or debone a smelt as even the backbone is soft enough to eat—if you want a bonus of calcium—although I often nibble "around" that major structure as it becomes a bit filling when faced with a large platter that promises so much sweet meat. Even the heads and tails are tasty, and don't overlook the tiny roes or the male gonads. Whichever way you choose to cook them, remember that smelts must be kept completely frozen until ready for use as the fish are very perishable. Fresh smelts, of course, should be held on ice or in the refrigerator, assuming that they are going to be consumed directly. If you have the opportunity to enjoy freshly caught smelts you will notice a difference in flavor—reason enough to attend a smelt run.

     Smelts can be panfried in clarified butter as it seldom takes more than 2½ minutes to cook the fish. If the smelts are large, say 8 or 9 inches long, you can split them to minimize the cooking time. The usual method is to coat smelts in seasoned flour, then dip into beaten egg and dust once again in the flour before frying. I much prefer to use a thin batter and deep-fry them in peanut oil, tempura style. *(See Thin Fish Batter under COOKING METHODS.)* In any case, never use a heavy batter on these delicate fish as it not only hides their flavor but will require that they be overcooked in order to brown. Smelts can also be broiled or baked in a casserole with suitable sauces or grilled over charcoal and served with **maître d'hôtel butter.**

     The average size of a smelt is usually from 6 to 8 inches, requiring 10 to 12 of them to make a pound. Smelts sometimes reach a length of 14 inches; however, such fish are scarce. But large or small, they are equally good to eat. I prefer them on the small side, about 5 to 6 inches long, as they are easier to handle in the skillet or deep-fryer, they crisp more quickly, and they make a better presentation when served on a napkin or warm platter surrounded by lemon wedges and parsley.

     Smelt is also known as **Eperlano** (Spain), **Eperlano** (Italy), **Biqueirão** (Portugal), **Stint** (Germany), **Smelt** (Denmark), **Nors** (Sweden), **Krøkle** (Norway), **Kuore** (Finland), **Sifurloöna** (Iceland), and **Kyūrino** (Japan).

Smoked Fish

Although commercially smoked products are limited to comparatively few species, with salmon, trout, cod, whitefish, eel and sturgeon readily available at most fishmongers, there are countless regional specialties such as king mackerel, mullet, sailfish, smelt, shark, cobia, striped bass, grayling, searobin, sucker and catfish which are processed in local kilns. It's impossible to estimate how many amateur smokehouses are in operation, but considering the scarcity of old refrigerators in many coastal communities, especially in our salmon-rich Pacific Northwest, one may guess that this method of cooking is enjoying a renaissance period.

     While the qualities of texture and flavor vary considerably, any species of fish can be smoked; with the small portable electric hot-plate units available today, smoking is within the possibilities of backyard suburbia. Perhaps the most simplified unit is a Sterno-fueled smokebox made in Sweden, which is just big enough to hold two 10-inch-long trout. In 8 minutes it will cook and flavor the fish—an eminently practical device for camp or patio. However, this is really a "barbecued" product and the nuances of temperature control, brining and selective fuels are what smokehouse cookery is all about.

     There are two general methods of smoking foods—hot-smoking and cold-smoking. In hot-smoking a fish is processed at a temperature range from 120° to 180°F. by gradually increasing the temperature at 30-minute intervals in a period of 6 to 8 hours. The rate of increase and duration of the smoking period depend on the size and weight of the fish, their distance from the fire, and the amount of cure desired. Personally, I prefer to keep my smokehouse temperature in the midrange (140° to 160°F.) and extend the period to 10 to 12 hours. A hot-smoked product will not keep for more than a few days unless it's refrigerated, frozen or canned. This short method is most popular for a cooked product with the desirable flavor and texture in a minimum time. It differs from barbecuing, in which the fish is placed close to the heat source and cooked at temperatures of 200°F. or more; a slight smoked flavor can be imparted but its texture will not be firm—it will crumble. Hot-smoking and barbecuing produce two different results.

Cold-smoking is primarily a specialized process (salmon and trout), although it's used for many species in achieving a mild smoke flavor with minimal protein coagulation. In cold-smoking the fish is not cooked but is cured through drying at a temperature range of 70° to 90°F. for a prolonged period. Preservation depends on the strength of the brine or the amount of salt used and the length of time the fish is in the smokehouse. Today commercial operators with a rapid turnover in their products tend to minimize the brining period and seldom keep their fish in the smoke chamber for more than 36 hours. This results in a better smoked fish, moist and without excessive salt. In northern Iceland, Norway and Finland, where long-term preservation is often necessary, salmon may be smoked from 2 to 3 weeks. For our purposes, however, a fish can be cold-smoked in 36 hours.

SALT AND SMOKE

The preliminary treatment of fish before smoking is with salt, either in the form of a brine solution or direct application of dry salt. This is a preservative as sodium chloride has an inhibiting effect on spoilage bacteria. Through osmosis the salt removes body fluids from the fish and deprives the bacteria of essential water. The fluid that is extracted from the fish is partly replaced by the salt itself. The addition of smoke to the fish not only adds flavor but increases the tensile strength of the connective tissues. If the smokehouse gets too warm, for example, the fish will cook and fall apart. This is because the connective tissue becomes weakened by *moist* heat before the smoke is able to exert its curing action. Smoke, therefore, firms and with slowly applied heat dehydrates the fish. In general an 80% (80° sal) brine solution is widely used for most commercial products, but in achieving gourmet results the solution may be as low as 15% and the brining period greatly extended. A salinometer can be purchased in most hardware stores. This type of hydrometer when floated in brine will read the correct strength. Fish should be brined at a solution temperature of 60°F. after the salt has been thoroughly diluted.

The application of dry salt as opposed to brine is most popular in commercial houses where quantities of

Fishmarket and smokehouse, Cullen, Scotland

large fish such as salmon, sailfish or king mackerel are processed. It takes experience to know how much salt to use on various cuts of different thicknesses.

Only the purest salt should be used when smoking or pickling fish. The worst is common table salt which has additives to insure that it will flow freely, usually sodium carbonate or trisodium phosphate, as well as moisture-absorbing elements in the form of calcium and magnesium chloride, which cause the protein in fish to coagulate. In the amounts used for the smoke process, this results in a somewhat bitter-tasting product. *(For details see under SALT FISH.)* The best salt from a general availability standpoint is coarse Kosher salt, which is also sold as "flake" or "dairy" salt. This can be found in most supermarkets. Kosher salt is mild, almost sweet-tasting.

SMOKEHOUSE

Smokehouses are constructed in all sizes and shapes from large 40-foot vertical kilns to "walk-in" horizontal chambers of the same width. In most commercial operations these function electrically with various types of generators which feed heated air and smoke into the kiln. A smoke generator is beyond the scope of a hobbyist and unnecessary for producing the small volume of fish most amateurs process. A smokehouse need not be elaborate. Excellent results can be obtained with a large wooden barrel or even a converted refrigerator. There are available portable outdoor smokers and electric hot-plate units of various kinds, but a permanent cabinet-type smokehouse is preferable.

I have built at least a dozen smokehouses of various sizes and materials and am content now with a concrete and redwood kiln which is 8 feet wide, 4 feet deep and 5 feet high. It has a series of baffle doors in front to control the drafts and the hinged roof can be raised and folded back so it can be converted into a barbecue pit. We sometimes cook a whole wild hog or barbecue fish and fowl in volume for large dinner parties; it easily accommodates 36 Canada geese. Three tiers of ½-inch galvanized steel rods at different heights fit into slots in the cement ends and are removable; these support screen trays, racks and S-hooks for the smoking or meats for barbecuing. This is more than ample for home requirements, but the point is a smokehouse can serve for both forms of cookery and is an asset to the outdoors-oriented family.

Regardless of the structure, the unit should be vented to insure proper circulation of smoke and air. Ventilation must be controlled so the wood smolders and does not flame. It should also have racks, trays and hooks for holding the fish in such a position that smoke and heat contact all surfaces uniformly. Excessive or sudden heat must be avoided. A thermometer inserted in a cork and suspended at the top of the smoking unit is necessary for the beginner. With experience you will be able to judge the correct temperatures. If the smoker has a hot plate, it should be grounded. This can be done by running a wire from the plate to a rod driven in the ground. All smokehouses "cook" differently due to their shape and material structure, and the location of the fire. Therefore you will find it necessary to vary suggested heating cycles according to the results obtained. In general, fish to be smoked should be held at least 6 feet away from the fire if logs are used and 4 feet away when using sawdust or chips. This is variable, of course, depending on the internal temperature of the kiln under normal operating conditions.

FUEL

Any nonresinous wood can be used as fuel in smokehouse cookery. Oak, hickory, maple, beech, alder and juniper are widely available and produce a rich smoke. Fruitwood such as apple, apricot, cherry or pear makes an excellent fuel and gives an especially fine flavor to fish. The wood can be utilized in three forms: as sawdust which smolders slowly and is ideal for cold-smoking, or as chips if sawdust is not available, or as small logs which produce more heat and are commonly used in the hot-smoking process. Corncobs, coconut husks, peat, and even dry sheep dung (common to sub-Arctic lands) will also provide a workable smoke, but woods are much preferred. Some impart a very distinctive flavor, such as vine maple, juniper, sassafras, apple, apricot and hickory. It's possible to combine one with good burning qualities such as oak with a more fragrant wood like green juniper, or maple with apple, to maintain an even heat with maximum flavor. Green wood is preferable to dry wood. Always remember to remove any bark or moss from old logs as these impart a bitter taste to fish. You can keep a steady fire when using chips or logs by adding a few charcoal briquets from time to time. Briquets will burn for hours and require little attention.

PREPARATION

It is important to clean and prepare fish properly before brining. With the exception of sturgeon and goldeye, which have an extremely high moisture content and are often held in frozen storage for a month or more, the best results are obtained with fresh fish. Frozen fish can be thawed and smoked provided they have been stored under ideal conditions. However, there will always be some loss of flavor and the texture tends to be fibrous. Fish are smoked whole (in the round), gutted, in chunks, or as napecut, butterfly or kited fillets. Small fish such as brook trout or ciscoes should be gutted, while larger species like salmon or king mackerel must be smoked in fillet form, with the skin on. If the fish are very large, such as sailfish or marlin, then cut the fillets crosswise into large chunks. Fish which have a strongly aromatic skin such as northern pike or Pacific barracuda should be filleted completely with skin removed. Very small fish such as herring or smelt can be smoked whole or preferably gutted; occasionally they are smoked in gibbed form by making a small cut just below the gills and pulling out the viscera including the gills with thumb and forefinger. This leaves the belly portion uncut. I do not recommend gibbing as the fish must be suspended by the tail in order to drain properly, otherwise fluid collects in the body cavity during the smoking process, which sours and softens the flesh. Most small fish cannot be tail-hung for an appreciable length of time without dropping from the hook or nail. If using a tray or rack it's much easier to begin the smoking process with the fish on its side; at intervals rotate each one belly down to allow the collected liquid to escape. Gibbed fish are better suited to pickling.

Whether in the round or gutted, small fish are easier to handle with their heads intact. They can be spread on screen trays or racks or hung on S-shaped iron hooks, which in turn are hung over iron rods running from one side of the kiln to the other. They can also be suspended on cords tied to the rods or impaled on nail points when using smokehouse sticks. Large fillets can be treated skin side down on trays or racks but it's preferable to use 4-inch eyed iron needles by piercing these through the shoulder bony plate or "lug" and hanging them with strong cord. Eels are best hung with a cord inserted through the midsection and tied off through the head and the loop formed placed over a nail; heavy eels are especially prone to drop off without this additional support.

HOT-SMOKING—BRINE METHOD

Brining should be done in an earthenware crock or a suitable large plastic container. Do not use aluminum or other metals. The brine method is most practical for gutted whole small fish such as smelt, cisco, herring, trout, goldeye and butterfish. It can also be used for fillets of haddock, Spanish mackerel, mullet, and other species which are usually smoked in butterfly or kited form. These are first placed in a 70% (70° sal) brine solution (2 cups salt to 1 gallon water) at 60°F. for 30 minutes to leach out the blood and body fluids. Remove the fish and wash

thoroughly. Next prepare a second brine in the following proportions: to 1 gallon of water add 2 cups of salt and 1 cup of brown sugar and dissolve thoroughly. Optionally, one may include liquid onion (1 teaspoon), liquid garlic (1 teaspoon), lemon or lime juice (¼ cup), and Tabasco (1 teaspoon) to each gallon of brine for more flavor. The quantities given are on the "subtle" side and only experimentation will tell you how much seasoning produces the result you want. Tabasco gets rather heavy use in southern kilns, particularly for smoked catfish and mullet. You can also use a preboiled and chilled solution of pickling spices (1 ounce dry weight to 1 gallon of brine) added to the brine. I much prefer pickling spices when smoking dark-meated oily species in steak form, such as sailfish, king mackerel, marlin and tuna.

Leave the fish in the brine for 15 minutes to 4 hours depending on their size; small fish of 4 to 8 ounces need no more than 30 to 40 minutes total while fish of 5 to 6 pounds require 4 hours. As a rule-of-thumb the brining cycle for gutted whole fish with skin on in an 80° sal solution at 60°F. (no higher even if you must add ice cubes) is as follows:

WEIGHT OF FISH	LEACHING	BRINING
2 ounces	none	10 minutes
4 ounces	none	20 minutes
6 to 8 ounces	20 minutes	20 minutes
10 to 12 ounces	20 minutes	40 minutes
14 to 16 ounces	30 minutes	1 hour
1½ to 2 pounds	30 minutes	1½ hours
2½ to 3 pounds	30 minutes	2½ hours
4½ to 5 pounds	40 minutes	3½ hours
5½ to 6 pounds	40 minutes	4½ hours

It is not practical to use the brine method for fish of over 6 pounds in size. Large fish should be split and dry-salted. Bear in mind that if you fillet or steak a 6-pound fish, for example, into smaller pieces the leaching and brining cycle does not apply to its original weight but to the size of each portion—which may be a 2-pound fillet or a 6-ounce steak. In either case the exposed musculature is going to absorb salt more rapidly than a whole fish in skin and the time should be reduced to match the weight indicated.

After brining rinse the fish in fresh water and hang in a cool, shady, breezy place for about 3 hours, or air-dry with a fan, until a thin shiny skin or pellicle has formed on the surface. The pellicle appears as a glossy sheen over the surface of the flesh which helps to seal in the natural juices, and when the fish is properly dried it

SMOKING SALMON, JOHN ROSS, ABERDEEN, SCOTLAND

1. Dress salmon. **2.** to **10.** Fillet and
debone both sides of salmon. **11.** Dry-salt for
8 to 10 hours. **12.** After rinsing cover with
brown sugar. **13.** Sprinkle with Demerara dark rum.
14. After marinating coat with a bland oil.
15. Stretch sealer skin over salmon
(organic or artificial casing).
16. Side of salmon ready for smoking.

will feel smooth to your fingers with no trace of moisture.
If a fish is smoked before the pellicle forms the musculature will erupt in a creamy white fluid that sours in the
smoke process.

Place the fish in the smokehouse. During the
first 4 hours, the temperature should be kept low, about
110° to 120°F. A dense smoke should then be built up. The
temperature can be leveled at 160° to 180°F. for the next 4
hours, at which point the fish should be finished. They
have been completely cooked and flavored with smoke.

HOT-SMOKING—DRY-SALT METHOD

The dry-salt method can be used in either hot-smoking or
cold-smoking when processing large fish such as salmon,
striped bass, steelhead, king mackerel, cobia, sailfish or
marlin. Individual sides will often weigh 10 pounds or
more, making the brine method impractical. As a general
procedure the fish is filleted, then washed thoroughly to
remove all traces of blood. Before laying the fillet on your
work table sprinkle the skin side with enough salt to
adhere, then apply salt to the flesh side; the amount to use
depends on the thickness of the fish. A layer 1/16 to 1/8
inch deep over the thick portion of a fillet will suffice,
using much less on the thin tail portion, if the side is not
going to be hung during the cure. Brown sugar and spices
may be added (optional). Allow the side to set for 8 to 10
hours. Rinse in cold water. Air-dry for 6 hours on a rack or
screen, or preferably hung from a hook, until the pellicle is
formed. For hot-smoking the fish requires 6 to 8 hours in
the kiln with the temperature reaching 160° to 180°F.

COLD-SMOKING—DRY-SALT METHOD

Before analyzing the methods used in different countries
there are two important points which should be
explained: large fish such as salmon have a strong musculature and should not be filleted in a routine style (by
running a knife down the backbone with several strokes in
the same direction from head to tail and cut again on the
same bias). The first cut, beginning at the nape, will
penetrate short of the backbone; do not repeat this stroke
but return from tail to head. The musculature along the

SMOKING SALMON, FORMAN & SONS, LONDON, ENGLAND

Coho salmon from the Pacific are being processed.

dorsal portion is in a < shaped series, while the next layer is reversed or > shaped. A knife blade, no matter how sharp, will lift and shred the flesh on the second cut when drawn against the "grain." Cutting in alternate directions will produce a professionally clean fillet. Secondly, scoring is often overlooked by amateur smokers and it's a necessary first step when preparing a fillet of fish as large as the average salmon; 4 or 5 cuts should be made in the skin side with a sharp-pointed knife, the depth depending on thickness, but a bit less than halfway through. This is done to start the fish "sweating" when the salt is applied. It results in quicker and more uniform penetration. Do not score the posterior third of the fillet and do not salt the tail region or end quarter of the fillet; as we've already noted this much thinner area absorbs salt rapidly and when the side is hung during the cure the residual salt will drip down to the tail. Ordinarily a coating of salt about 1/16 to 1/8 inch deep according to flesh thickness is suitable, using slightly less in winter weather and slightly more in summer if working outdoors.

The general principle of cold-smoking is to dry out the product with warm smoke at temperatures not exceeding 90°F. This may take several days. The fire must not produce too much smoke during the first 12 hours if the total curing period is to be 24 hours, or for the first 18 hours if the curing period is longer. Check the thermometer occasionally. If the smoke is so dense that you can't read the thermometer put your hand inside; if the air feels "hot," the temperature is too high. When the first curing phase of the process is completed, a dense smoke should be maintained. Cold-smoking need not be a continuous day-and-night process, but it should be completed as rapidly as possible.

HOW TO SMOKE SALMON

The problem in smoking any fish is to reduce its moisture content while replacing it with salt as a semipreservative, without coagulating the protein (or cooking it) when using the cold-smoke method, yet maintaining both texture and color. The flesh of all fish differs greatly in water, protein and fat content. Also, these factors vary according to the size of the fish and the season in which it was caught. The structure of the musculature also differs in the arrangement of its fibrils and related components which we call "texture." Salmon flesh is moderately coarse despite its moist flaking when cooked, so cold-smoking is necessary if the fish is to be cut into thin slices without crumbling. Hot-smoked salmon is easier to make than cold-smoked salmon, but it is the latter product which is in greatest demand throughout the world and is pertinent here.

Like most commercial smokehouses today, Forman & Sons in London utilizes not only Atlantic salmon from the British Isles but also a large quantity of imported chinook and coho salmon from Seattle, Washington, and Kodiak, Alaska. Their average production is 1,500 salmon per week or 6,000 pounds in smoked fillets. The trade distinction is in the terminology "Scotch smoked salmon" which implies the Atlantic salmon and simply "smoked salmon" which refers to the Pacific species. The technical distinction in obtaining reasonably comparable results is in the curing process; both the coho and the chinook require a longer drying period as they contain more moisture and do not firm as readily as the Atlantic salmon. The Forman people are able to bring the coho, and to a lesser extent the chinook, to a degree of firmness that allows thin slicing without crumbling.

FORMAN & SONS (London, England)
(1) Scale and score skin side of salmon.
(2) Dry-salt for 18 to 24 hours depending on size of salmon.
(3) Rinse in cold running water to remove residual salt.
(4) Air-dry with fan for 8 to 10 hours, or longer if coho or chinook salmon is used (12 to 15 hours), until pellicle is formed.
(5) Hang salmon in smoker over oak and juniper sawdust at 110°F. (43.3°C.) for 24 hours.

A.B.S. MATTSSON (Svängsta, Sweden)
(1) Scale and score skin side of salmon, then rub with saltpeter to maintain color.
(2) Dry-salt for 16 to 17 hours.
(3) Rinse in cold running water to remove residual salt.
(4) Air-dry with fan for 5 to 6 hours or longer without fan until pellicle is formed.
(5) Hang salmon in smoker at 83°F. (28.3°C.) over alder sawdust plus green juniper branches for 36 hours.

JOHN ROSS (Aberdeen, Scotland)
(1) Scale and score skin side of salmon.
(2) Dry-salt for 8 to 10 hours depending on size of salmon.
(3) Rinse in cold running water to remove residual salt.
(4) Sprinkle with brown sugar to cover, then sprinkle with Demerara dark rum and leave to marinate for 8 to 10 hours. (Various seasonings such as juniper berries, crushed mace and bay leaves may also be placed on fish according to the requirements of Ross's customers.)
(5) Coat the salmon with a bland oil such as cottonseed oil to prevent fish from drying.
(6) Stretch a sealer skin over the salmon to retain flavoring; an organic casing such as sheep intestine was used in years past, but an artificial casing (collagen) used in contemporary sausage making is readily available.

(7) Hang salmon in smoker over oak chips and sawdust for 48 to 72 hours.
(8) No heat. Hang 40 feet up in kiln at a normal temperature of 60°F.

These three methods run the gamut from a marginal cold-smoke used by Forman & Sons to no heat at all at John Ross. In principle cold-smoking never exceeds 90°F. (30°C.) as protein coagulation increases at higher temperatures. However, to "cook" a fish its internal temperature must reach 140°F. (80°C.) when the protein is completely coagulated. So the Forman method as compared to Mattsson requires a longer period in salt, more air-drying, and a shorter period in the kiln. The Mattsson method, on the other hand, is a typical cold-smoking pro-

cess used throughout Scandinavia. Ross is most distinctive. This is the same firm that "invented" **Finnan Haddie** before the turn of the century, and their smoked products are unique. To maintain perfect translucency and yet achieve a smoked flavor Ross virtually eliminates heat. Preservation is accomplished with salt, sugar and rum; however, none of these ingredients is individually detectable. The collagen casing is permeable and allows the penetration of smoke. All three firms produce a velvety red salmon that can be sliced paper-thin on the bias. In common with other smoked fish the salmon is allowed to "set" out of the kiln for at least 24 hours to reach its peak flavor. To recognize a perfect smoked fillet at this point place your hands at the opposite sides and press ever so gently inward; tiny droplets of yellow oil will rise to the

Smoking eels at A. B. S. Mattsson on the Morrum River, Sweden

surface between the musculature at the median line. If water appears, your smoke cycle leveled too low; if *nothing* appears you have flavored a "cooked" salmon which is not all bad, but it is not a smoked salmon.

There are various recipes utilizing smoked salmon either in contrast with other fish, such as **Paupiette of Salmon with Mousse of Pike in Sorrel Sauce,** or combined with vegetable textures such as **Artichaud Pays de Caux.** If you are smoking your own fish or buying by the "slab," remember that leftover pieces can be preserved for long periods of time in screw-top jars by cutting them into thin slices, as you normally would do for serving, and covering the slices with cottonseed, peanut or olive oil. They should be stored in the refrigerator. The fish will not absorb the oil and the airproof medium retards the growth of spoilage bacteria through oxidation. I have kept smoked salmon this way in perfect condition for 6 months. It could probably be stored longer but it invariably disappears too fast to find out.

HOW TO SMOKE FLOUNDERS

This is a specialty of the port city of Esbjerg in Denmark, the home base for its North Sea fishing fleet. Smoked flounder is made into a dish called **Bakskuld,** a delicately smoke-flavored product that is quickly sautéed in butter until crisp. This plebian species becomes a gourmet delight when served spitting hot in a cast-iron cocotte. Essentially the flounder is gutted but left whole, then brined in a 70° sal solution for no more than 30 minutes, and air-dried for about 4 hours until the pellicle forms. It is finally cold-smoked over smoldering beech sawdust for 24 hours. These thin-bodied fish should never be processed closer than 6 feet from the fire. Serve with boiled potatoes, green salad and a frosty glass of beer.

This method works extremely well with Pacific sanddabs.

HOW TO SMOKE EELS

Smoked eels are very richly flavored and in great demand in Europe, particularly in Scandinavia, Belgium, Holland and Germany. Due to a widespread shortage in the eastern Atlantic a large volume of live eels is imported from the U.S. by air. Although Billingsgate Market in London still favors eels from the Irish Sea (thinner skin and better flavor) the American species is likely to appear as "Danish smoked" or "Dutch smoked" at many fishmongers. A. B.S. Mattsson on the Morrum River in Sweden produces one of the finest products in Europe but is dependent on the local Baltic Sea eel and orders far exceed their supply.

Eels are tenacious and arrive at the smoke-house alive. Optionally, one can cut their tails to bleed or, as in most commercial operations, dump the eels in a tall vertical plastic container and add 1 pound of dry salt (no water) to every 10 pounds of eels. The salt will kill the eels and deslime them to a large extent before gutting. Due to their dense musculature eels are always hot-smoked.

In the Swedish method, the eels are placed in a 15° sal brine solution and left for 20 hours. They are then rinsed in cold water for 10 minutes, then a stout cord is run through the midsection and back to the head with a large sailmaker's needle and tied back. The corded eel is then suspended in hot water, 180°F. (82.2°C.), for 3 minutes to remove any remaining slime. This can be wiped off with a piece of burlap. The head is not submerged or it would shrivel. The eels are then air-dried before a fan for 2 hours. They are smoked at 165° to 180°F. (73.9° to 82.2°C.), using beech sawdust and alder branches to maintain heat, for 4 hours.

HOW TO SMOKE SAILFISH AND MARLIN

These billfish are easy to hot-smoke and provide a very distinctive flavor and texture, quite unlike other smoked products. The sailfish and marlins have an extremely tough skin, and a sharp knife must be used to dress out the fillets. Leave the skin intact. Although the uncooked meat is dark red, it will become light pink in color after the smoking process. Crosscut the fillets into 12-inch slabs, then wash thoroughly, pat dry with a paper towel, score the skin side, and salt. Arrange slabs on your work table, skin side down, and salt the flesh side, applying a coat about ⅛ inch deep on thick cuts, less around thin edges. Let stand for 6 to 8 hours. Most sailfish fillets are 1 to 2 inches thick and in this context may be considered "thin," while the larger marlins vary from 2½ to 3 inches and are obviously "thick." If working with a 200- to 300-pound blue, striped or black marlin having fillets greater than 3 inches in thickness, it's advisable to use a brine solution (80° sal for 1½ hours) rather than the dry-salt method.

Rinse and let the slabs air-dry for 6 hours, or until pellicle is formed; these are fish of warm climates and unless a cool work room is available, use a fan to expedite drying. Optionally, you can rub or press pickling spices (in dry form) on the flesh side at this point. Hot-smoke for 8 hours but be careful not to overcook as both sailfish and marlin dehydrate and coagulate more rapidly than most other fish. Upon completing the smoke cycle, slice off an end—it should feel soft and moist between your fingers. This will firm overnight in cold storage. Serve in thin slices as an hors d'oeuvre or with scrambled eggs for breakfast or lunch.

In Sweden smoked herring is
served with green onions and egg yolks
in half shells nested in rock salt.
Everything is mixed together,
including some of the salt,
like steak tartare.
bottom, Scottish kippers resting on a
basket of smoking chips

HOW TO SMOKE TUNA

All tunas make excellent smoked products, even the so-called false albacore if properly treated.

Tuna meat provides a variety of textures and colors according to the species *(see under TUNA)* and perhaps more so when smoked. This ranges from the pale almost white flesh of the albacore and blackfin tuna to the dark red meat of a false albacore which smokes to a deep claret color and has the appearance of beef rather than fish. Essentially, the larger tuna such as school bluefins, yellowfin, albacore and bigeye tuna can be handled in the same manner as for sailfish or marlin by steaking or crosscutting the fillets into slabs and using the dry-salt method. When smoking small tuna, however, such as the blackfin, skipjack or bonito which usually run from 5 to 8 pounds, the brine method is preferable; the fish should be filleted and the dark lateral band sliced out *before* the smoke process. This lateral band turns fibrous and imparts a bitter flavor to the surrounding meat when cooked; also, it's more difficult to remove after smoking than before. These small tuna should be placed in an 80° sal chilled brine for about 1 hour when processing fillets from 5-pound fish, to 1½ hours for fillets from 8-pound fish.

HOW TO SMOKE
SMELT, HERRING, ALEWIFE, CHUB

These small thin-bodied species must be treated somewhat differently from other fish of equal length simply because they will absorb the brine solution more rapidly. In effect, the leaching and brining processes are combined. My standard procedure is to use an 80° sal solution (60°F.) and place the dressed fish in this for 10 minutes. The fish are then washed and air-dried for about 1 hour. In the smoking cycle they should be held at about 70°F. for 15 minutes and the temperature increased by 10°F. every 15 minutes until it reaches 180°F.; at this maximum they are smoked for an additional hour. It's difficult to hit each increment of increase on the button when feeding a fire by hand but don't *worry* about it; even if you come close by compensating with additional minutes the result is well worth the effort. Alternately one can use a low heat (110° to 120°F.) for 3 hours and high heat (160° to 180°F.) for 3 hours.

HOW TO SMOKE ATLANTIC, CERO AND
SPANISH MACKEREL

For best results these mackerels should be split down the backbone, the viscera removed, then carefully washed to eliminate all coagulated blood. A brief brining is preferable to dry-salting—no more than 15 minutes in a 10 percent (38.5° sal) solution for fish of 1½ to 2 pounds, and no more than 30 minutes for large fish of 5 pounds or more when processing big Spanish mackerel or cero. Excessive salt or smoke destroys the delicate mackerel texture and flavor. Although mackerel are usually classed as "fatty" fish, the Spanish mackerel and cero are leaner than the Atlantic mackerel and all three are subject to variation. Atlantic mackerel, for example, reach their peak during July to October, containing 12 to 20 percent or more of oil depending on the geographic location of capture. During the spring and winter seasons these same mackerel have a lower oil content; these "lean" periods produce a better smoked product in the sense that it's less susceptible to rancidity in storage.

Mackerel should be lightly smoked at about 100°F. for 4 hours if small, and at 150° to 200°F. for 6 hours in the larger sizes. This will provide a mild smoke flavor and a golden-brown color rather than the tarry black color found on some commercial products. Smoked mackerel are nearly as perishable as fresh fish, so for maximum shelf life in storage the product should be wrapped in a moistureproof material, frozen as quickly as possible, then stored at temperatures below 0°F. This will prevent rancidity for up to 6 months.

HOW TO SMOKE OYSTERS AND CLAMS

In raw form these bivalves are too soft to process in a smokehouse. They must first be steamed for about 10 to 15 minutes to firm the meats. Oysters and clams need not be shucked but should be simply cooked in the shell, preferably in a regular steamer. After steaming, the meats should be brined in a 70° sal solution for 5 minutes, then drained and air-dried. For easy handling in the kiln they should be arranged in one layer over fine mesh wire or screening; for regular use this can be made in the form of trays. To prevent sticking, lubricate the wire with any vegetable oil. Clams and oysters cook and absorb smoke more rapidly than fish, and the usual cycle is from 2½ to 3 hours with the heat at about 110° to 120°F. for most of that period, increasing it slightly to 130° to 140°F. during the last 30 minutes. Like other smoked products bivalves may be frozen although they can be stored in jars filled with cottonseed, peanut or olive oil at refrigerator temperatures for several weeks at least. Apple or maple wood is by far the best fuel for clams and oysters.

HOW TO SMOKE SHRIMPS AND PRAWNS

Hot smoked shrimps and prawns are not simply delicious, but spectacular. They can be used in many ways as hors d'oeuvre, or in omelets, creamed shrimp chowder, shrimp cakes, even as an ingredient for a fish stuffing. Although seldom found in retail markets, small quantities are smoked commercially in the southern U. S. and our Pacific Northwest. Unfortunately, many kilns process their shrimps in the shell, which makes them fibrous. For best results raw shrimps should be peeled, leaving the tail intact. If not peeled, excessive moisture collects between the shell and the meat during smoking, which makes the shrimps tough. Brining time will vary according to size, but the common 2- to 3-inch-long crustaceans only require 10 to 12 minutes in an 80° sal solution. They should then be washed and thoroughly air-dried and placed on fine wire mesh as for bivalves. While air-drying, the meats can be seasoned with powdered onion, garlic, ginger or any preferred flavor. The hot-smoking process will take no more than 1½ hours, beginning at 80°F. for the first half hour and gradually increasing to 140°F. in the last half hour. After the shrimps have developed an amber color at the midway point, taste one for doneness and gauge your cycle accordingly.

Fishing boats at Peterhead, Scotland, on the North Sea

SMOKED FISH SAUSAGES

Smoked sausages are not only a taste delight but can be produced from any kind of fish and presented at table as **saucisses de poisson fumé;** the "weenie" is elevated to a noble status. It's probably one of the least-known foods in American fish cookery. Unlike a fresh sausage, this one is a cooked product, in this case cooked by hot-smoking with spices and herbs. In my experience, the best are made from walleye, black bass, whitefish, albacore, blackfin tuna, red snapper and channel catfish. For a really superior product I add one quarter of the total amount in either fresh shrimps or the lobsterlike tilefish. I have also incorporated ground fresh conch meat with pleasing results and I suspect that abalone treated in the same fashion would be its equal, but that ethereal mollusk is beyond my home waters.

The smoked sausages require some time in preparation but the product has about a 2-week shelf life at ordinary refrigerator temperatures and can be held in frozen storage at −15°F. or lower for long periods. The general procedure for making fish sausages is detailed in the following table prepared by the Fisheries Research Board of Canada (*Special Products from Freshwater Fish*, A. W. Lantz). For home purposes, using an ordinary food grinder with a sausage-stuffing tube attachment, I would not suggest "fish flesh containing bones" as this is accomplished with a more sophisticated electrically operated food cutter, which rotates at 1750 rpm, capable of

homogenizing both skin and bones. Using a home-style manually operated food grinder it will also take considerably longer than 3 minutes to reduce the fish to a proper pastelike consistency. However, it's worth the effort. Sausages can be enclosed in a natural or synthetic casing, but sheep casing is preferred. This casing can be ordered at any friendly butcher shop and should be desalinized in a solution of 2 cups warm water to which 2 tablespoons of vinegar have been added. Soak the casing for several hours, then run cold water through the skins from a faucet.

The triangular steel frames used in the Canadian process are not necessary for the volume of fish sausages produced in a home smokehouse. The sausages can be linked or tied-off by hand in 12-inch lengths and hung individually on S-hooks by the string or simply draped in pairs by looping them over a horizontal rod. I am also inclined to extend the smoke period longer than the total 2 hours, 15 minutes, recommended in the table, and generally maintain a lower heat (120° to 140°F.) for 5 to 6 hours for a more aromatic flavor. I begin to test for doneness after 4 hours; the sausage should have a rich mahogany color, and though dripping with juices the skin will feel firm and the fish "set." The spice formula given is eminently tasty, but garlic powder, ground ginger and various herbs such as tarragon, dill and basil can be incorporated according to personal preference.

Fish sausages can be grilled, steamed, or panfried, then chunked and served as a hot hors d'oeuvre sprinkled with lime juice, or accompanying cold wedges of Crenshaw or Casaba melon at breakfast, or as a lunch dish with a caper, mustard or mild horseradish sauce. For a late supper try grilled sausages with scalloped potatoes and Bibb lettuce salad seasoned only with a light oil and lemon dressing.

FRESHWATER FISH[a] WIENERS   FORMULA 17

Procedure	Amount	Material or ingredients	Time	Temp
Using finest cutting blade, homogenize in food mill	1 lb	fish flesh containing bones	1 min	32 F
Using ½-inch cutting blade, coarse-cut in food mill	4 lb	boneless fish flesh	1 min	32 F
Place in food cutter; start cutter and add:	4 oz	spice formula[b]		
	2 tsp	salt		
	1 tsp	paprika		
Blend for			1 min	
Let stand for			12 hr	40 F
Return mixture to food cutter; start cutter and add:				
	12 oz	shortening		
	3 oz	breadcrumbs		
	3 oz	binder[c]		
	8 oz	crushed ice		
Blend for			2 min	
Place mixture in stuffer; extrude into casing; place stuffed casing on triangular steel frames and form wieners; place frames of wieners in smoke tunnel and smoke for			15 min	120 F
Then increase temperature by 10° every 15 min to				160 F
Increase temperature to 180 F and smoke for			60 min	180 F
Remove wieners from smoke tunnel; immediately immerse wieners in hot water			5 min	160 F
Chill wieners by cold-water immersion or cold-water spray			10 min	40 F
Peel and package wieners; plate freeze at				−40 F
Store at				−15 F

a Bullhead, whitefish, sheepshead, carp, bullhead with carp and sheepshead, chub with whitefish, chub with suckers, and suckers with carp.

b Pepper oil 17%; nutmeg oil 6%; coriander oil 9%; cloves 1½%; onion powder 4½%; paprika 21%; salt 41%.

c Commercially prepared binder preferred.

NOTE: Unless a high-speed food mill is being used, eliminate the 1 pound of fish flesh containing bones and substitute boneless fillets for a total weight of 5 pounds.

ARTICHAUD PAYS DE CAUX
(Portman Hotel, London)

18 ounces sliced smoked salmon	1 onion, 3 ounces, chopped fine
6 large fresh artichokes, 10 to 12 ounces each	pepper
1 large lemon, halved	1 tablespoon minced fresh basil
6 tablespoons flour	2½ cups milk, hot
salt	1 bay leaf
1 pound fresh young spinach	½ cup heavy cream
¼ pound butter	2 egg yolks
1 garlic clove, put through a press	4 ounces Gruyère cheese, grated

Cut the salmon into 36 pieces each about 1 inch square. Break off stems from artichokes, pull off all the outside leaves, and cut off the rest to ½ inch above the base. Trim the base all around to make a smooth surface, and rub all cut surfaces with the lemon halves. Drop the artichokes into a large stainless-steel kettle and drop in the lemon halves as well. Cover with water and stir in 2 tablespoons of the flour and 1 tablespoon salt. Bring to a boil and simmer until artichokes are tender, about 20 minutes. Test with a stainless-steel fork. Drain; when cool enough to handle, scoop out the chokes from the centers. Arrange on a shallow fireproof dish. Wash spinach, remove any coarse stems, and steam in the water clinging to the leaves until cooked but not mushy. Drain, press out water, and chop. Melt half of the butter and in it sauté the puréed garlic and half of the chopped onion until transparent, then add the spinach and continue to sauté until well mixed and tender. Season with ½ teaspoon salt, or more to taste, and a dash of pepper.

In each artichoke bottom place 3 squares of smoked salmon. Divide spinach among them, making a mound in the center, and top with the rest of the smoked salmon. Sprinkle minced basil over the top layer of salmon. Prepare the sauce. Melt remaining butter in a saucepan and add remaining chopped onion. Cook until onion is tender, then stir in remaining flour with a whisk, and add the hot milk, still stirring. Add bay leaf and simmer, still whisking, until thickened. Mix cream and egg yolks, and stir into the sauce. When well blended and very hot, stir in the cheese. Keep over heat only until cheese is melted and mixed with the sauce. Season with salt and pepper to taste, and discard bay leaf. Coat the artichokes with sauce. Glaze in a moderate oven, 350°F., until brown, or finish under the broiler. Makes 6 servings for luncheon main dish.

facing page, Artichaud Pays de Caux, Portman Hotel, London

SMOKED FISH IN MILK

3 pounds smoked fish

1 cup whole milk
    or light cream

3 tablespoons butter
    or good cooking oil

pepper

salt if needed

parsley

If the fish has been heavily salted before smoking, freshen for 1 hour or more before cooking. Drain, dry, and place skin side down on a greased baking pan or skillet. Pour the milk over the pieces, adding butter and pepper to taste, and cook slowly in the oven, or over low heat on top of the stove, for 8 to 12 minutes. Remove to a platter, and pour the liquid about the fish. Garnish with parsley. Makes 6 to 8 servings.

SMOKED FISH CROQUETTES

2 cups smoked
    fish flakes

1 garlic clove (optional)

1 cup mashed potatoes,
    hot or cold

½ tablespoon salt

⅛ teaspoon pepper

2 eggs

fine bread crumbs

2 tablespoons water

oil for deep-frying

Mash the garlic and rub over the mixing bowl. Combine fish, potatoes, salt, pepper and 1 egg, well beaten. Mix thoroughly, and form into croquettes. Roll in fine bread crumbs. Beat the second egg with the water. Dip the croquettes into the egg mixture, then drain and roll in bread crumbs again. Deep-fry in cooking oil or fat heated to 390°F. until browned. Drain and serve hot. Makes 4 servings.

SMOKED FISH POTATO SALAD

1 pound
    smoked fish, flaked

2 cups diced
    cooked potatoes

1 cup thin-sliced celery

½ cup sliced
    peeled cucumber

½ cup sliced ripe olives

¼ cup grated carrot

¼ cup minced onion

2 tablespoons
    chopped parsley

½ cup mayonnaise

1 tablespoon
    prepared mustard

1 teaspoon lime
    or lemon juice

1 teaspoon vinegar

½ teaspoon salt

¼ teaspoon celery seeds

dash of pepper

salad greens

tomato wedges

Combine the vegetables and fish in a large bowl. In a separate bowl mix the mayonnaise, mustard, lime juice, vinegar and seasonings, blending thoroughly.

Add this dressing to the fish and potato mixture and toss lightly. Chill for several hours. Serve on a bed of salad greens garnished with tomato wedges. Makes 6 servings.

SMOKED FISH SOUFFLÉ

1 cup cooked
    smoked-fish flakes, cold

2 eggs, separated

1½ cups milk

2 cups cooked rice

2 tablespoons butter

salt, pepper, paprika

Beat egg yolks until thick and lemon-colored. Add fish flakes, milk, rice, butter, and seasonings to taste. Blend. Beat egg whites until stiff, and fold carefully into the fish mixture. Pour into a 6-cup soufflé dish, buttered only on the bottom. Set the dish in a pan of hot water, and bake at 350°F. for 45 minutes. Serve with or without a tasty fish sauce. Makes 4 to 6 servings.

Snapper

Back in 1968 I was asked by the State Department to take King Mohammed Zahir of Afghanistan fishing off Palm Beach. It required a small contingent of secret service people to accompany our boat, as well as a Coast Guard vessel which hovered directly behind our trolled baits. After a few hours I realized that there wasn't a chance of getting a sailfish to strike at the surface-dancing mullet as no amount of maneuvering would keep the patrol boat off our stern. We had a deep-fishing rig aboard equipped with an electric-reel. This is not sporting gear as it's designed for steel cable line capable of hoisting 500 pounds off the bottom of the Gulf Stream in 100 fathoms of water. It's used principally in exploratory fishing for benthic species and to some extent in capturing giant groupers, which live at depths beyond the scope of ordinary fishing tackle. There are days when the great blue stream runs so fast that even a 10-pound sash-weight on the end of the cable won't touch bottom. Despite the advantage of 24 volts to turn the reel spool we sometimes hook fish that can pull a 40-foot sportfishing boat backwards. His Royal Highness was fascinated by the idea of hooking unseen monsters, but after a fruitless hour of dangling bait in 400 feet of water he said, "Your Florida fish are like good politicians . . . they know when to keep their mouths shut." The only thing that saved the day was a red snapper of about 6 pounds in size that gobbled the mullet as we drifted over a shallow ledge. This was hardly a celebrated event but the red snapper is noble fare, and indeed, baked and stuffed that night it was truly fit for a king.

The snappers are one of the more important fish families (Lutjanidae) of tropical seas, numbering about 250 species of which fifteen are found in U.S. waters from North Carolina throughout the Gulf of Mexico. Of these the most valuable from a market point of view is the red snapper which rivals the pompano in price. The red-snapper industry began in 1870 at Pensacola, Florida, where the first fish house was built by an enterprising New Englander, one S.C. Cobb. Mr. Cobb sent his live-well smacks out into the Gulf, and those snappers caught at less than 20 fathoms could be kept alive in the wells until the ships' return. In time, artificially made ice made it possible to send larger, long-range schooners to remote areas, some of them going 600 to 700 miles to the Campeche Banks west of Cuba. Today, of course, the snapper is fished by a modern fleet throughout the Gulf.

SNAPPER TERMINOLOGY

CUBERA SNAPPER This is the largest snapper *(Lutjanus cyanopterus)* known, attaining a weight of 100 pounds with fish up to 80 pounds being caught by anglers in south Florida. It ranges throughout the tropical American Atlantic. Despite its immense size the cubera is a shallow-water fish occurring in depths from a few feet to 20 fathoms. The general coloration is similar to that of the gray snapper, being dusky gray or greenish and tinged with red along the sides. Small cubera up to 20 pounds in weight are delightful eating but the flesh of larger fish is coarse and best relegated to chowders. Cuberas are seldom marketed in the U.S. due to their scarcity.

DOG SNAPPER A medium-size snapper *(Lutjanus jocu)* which reaches a weight of about 20 pounds, it's found from south Florida throughout the tropical American Atlantic. Although similar in color to the cubera snapper, it's easily recognized by its large fanglike teeth. Dog snappers have been involved in ciguatera poisoning frequently enough to be listed here as fish *not* to be eaten. This fish is not marketed in the U.S. but appears as **pargo pero** in Central America.

GRAY SNAPPER This is the most common snapper *(Lutjanus griseus)* in the western Atlantic and is found from North Carolina south to Brazil. The gray snapper also occurs in Bermuda. It is often called "mangrove" snapper in reference to its habitat. Generally gray in color with reddish tinges on its sides, this snapper becomes more red when taken from the water. It seldom reaches a weight of 10 pounds and the average is usually less than 1 pound. Because of its small size, the gray snapper is most often panfried but fish of a pound or more can be broiled, baked, used in soups and chowders. Although quite bony the meat is white and sweet. It's marketed to some extent in the southern U.S. and widely purveyed in the Caribbean.

LANE SNAPPER A very small shallow-water snapper *(Lutjanus synagris)*; it is abundant from south Florida to Brazil. The lane snapper seldom exceeds 1 pound in weight. It's a pretty little fish, rosy red in color with longitudinal yellow stripes. Its fins are red and the dorsal fin is margined with orange. There is a prominent black spot on each side of its body. Essentially a species for panfrying, but I often use it in a **bouillabaisse.** The lane is not sold in the U.S. but it's commonly found in Caribbean markets.

MUTTON SNAPPER This is a common shallow-water snapper *(Lutjanus analis)*, ranging from south Florida throughout the tropical Atlantic. The "muttonfish" usually weighs from 5 to 10 pounds but 15- to 20-pounders are not unusual, particularly in the Florida Keys and the Bahamas. A brightly colored fish, the mutton snapper has an olive-green back with orange red sides and brick-red fins. This is one of the best snappers at table, in all sizes, equaling the red and silk species in texture and flavor. It can be cooked in any manner but is particularly good when stuffed and baked, poached, or made into a chowder. Limited quantities of muttonfish enter our southern markets.

RED EMPEROR SNAPPER This is the common snapper *(Lutjanus sebae)* in the Indo-Pacific region and most abundant around the Great Barrier Reef of Australia. Essentially no different from our red snapper except for taxonomic details which have no role in the kitchen.

RED SNAPPER The best known and most popular species, the red snapper *(Lutjanus campechanus)* is found from North Carolina to Brazil. It is abundant around Florida and in the Gulf of Mexico. A fish of moderate depths (60 to 200 feet) it grows to 35 pounds although the usual red at market is from 4 to 6 pounds in size. Easily recognized by its rose-red color and carmine fins, it can be distinguished from the silk snapper by its bright red eyes. The red snapper may be cooked by any method, especially baked and stuffed, or poached and glazed in the style of salmon, or as a **rouget** done in *papillote (see recipe).*

SCHOOLMASTER SNAPPER This is our smallest *(Lutjanus apodus)*, seldom weighing 1 pound, although it has been recorded to 5 pounds in size. It occurs in shallow water from south Florida throughout the tropical Atlantic and is quite abundant in the Bahamas. The schoolmaster is a brassy-yellow in color with dark brownish vertical bars; its fins are yellow to orange. Despite diminutive size this snapper is delicious when panfried. It does not enter commercial U.S. markets but is frequently caught by

Gray snapper

Mutton snapper

Red snapper

Schoolmaster snapper

Yellowtail snapper

sport fishermen.

SILK SNAPPER This deepwater species *(Lutjanus vivanus)* occurs from North Carolina to Florida, through the Bahamas and possibly as far south as Brazil. It is seldom a large fish, never exceeding 10 pounds and usually caught at half that size. Like the red snapper, the silk is a rose-red in color but it has a bright yellow eye as opposed to the red eye of the former, and its tail is margined in black. Nevertheless it's frequently marketed as "red snapper," and there is no discernible difference in texture or flavor. It can be used in all snapper recipes.

VERMILION SNAPPER The vermilion snapper *(Rhomboplites aurorubens)* occurs from the offshore reefs of North Carolina to Brazil. This is a smaller fish than either the red or the silk snapper and less valuable in the commercial fishery. The vermilion snapper is red, with faint brown lines running obliquely forward and downward from its back, and yellow lines streak its sides. A tasty panfish, but not comparable to the larger snappers.

YELLOWTAIL SNAPPER The yellowtail *(Ocyurus chrysurus)* is a shallow-water snapper ranging from southern Florida to Brazil. It seldom weighs more than 5 pounds and the average marketed is about 1½ pounds in size. This snapper is easily recognized by a bright yellow stripe which runs from its snout to its tail. The fish is excellent eating. While other snappers can be held on ice for a reasonable period without loss of flavor, the yellowtail cannot. With this species, the fresher, the better. Yellowtail is a popular item in many Florida Keys restaurants. The fillets are usually butter-broiled or panfried, and splashed with lime juice. A different genus from most snappers, the yellowtail is white and sweet, but finer of flake. This species was long considered a "breakfast" fish among ichthyophiles. The practice had its origin in old Key West when yellowtails caught the night before were hawked on the streets in the early morning. According to Jordan and Evermann *(American Food and Game Fishes)* ". . . at the hour when one most desires to sleep, his slumbers are broken by the monotonous cry 'Yallertail—rabirubia! Yallertail—rabirubia!' first faint and distant, then growing stronger and stronger, passing under your window a distracting yell, and then gradually dying away as the peripatetic vendor of the lucious 'yallertail' vanishes down the street." I can think of no better way of starting the day.

HOW TO DRESS SNAPPERS

Some species of snappers such as the lane, schoolmaster, gray or mangrove, and yellowtail, are usually caught at ½ to 1¼ pounds in weight. These are too small to fillet and

should be pan-dressed. Bear in mind that snappers are spiny-rayed fishes and quite bony. Although the meat is soft, small snappers are very tasty when panfried or broiled. These snappers should be scaled immediately, or within a few hours after capture, as the scales will dry and "pucker," making the fish much more difficult to dress. It's advisable to trim off the spinous fins with kitchen shears before scaling to avoid accidentally puncturing your fingers. Cut away the pectoral girdle including the fins as this bony portion does not contain enough meat to salvage. When serving small snappers which have been fin-trimmed, cut the fish into halves after they have been cooked (actually you can lift it in two pieces by running the knife blade through the back and across the backbone to the belly) to reveal and remove the interior basal bones of the fins. Then lift the backbone free.

The yellowtail snapper presents less of a problem than the other small species; it is often caught or sold in filleting sizes of 1½ pounds or more. For this reason it's popular in the restaurant trade and at market. However, the lane, schoolmaster and gray snappers are much preferred by many people in Florida, the Bahamas and West Indies.

Large snappers such as the red, mutton and vermilion, which commonly weigh 4 pounds or more, are readily filleted or whole-dressed for stuffing and baking. If you are purchasing fillets at market, remember that the head, including the "throat," and the bones and skin can be made into a delicious stock, so ask your fishmonger to reserve these pieces.

BAKED RED SNAPPER AMANDINE
(The Breakers, Palm Beach)

Wipe 5 fillets of red snapper with a damp cloth. Season with salt and pepper and dredge with flour. Sauté the fillets in ¼ cup olive oil until they are nicely browned on both sides. Lay the fillets in a large baking dish and pour over them the following mixture: ½ cup shredded or slivered blanched almonds mixed with ½ cup melted butter and the juice of 1 small lemon. Bake in a hot oven for 3 to 5 minutes, or until the almonds are nicely browned. Makes 5 servings.

SNAPPER WITH CHAMPAGNE SAUCE

4 snapper fillets, ½ pound each	¼ pound butter
2 cups Champagne	½ cup heavy cream
4 shallots, chopped fine	4 egg yolks, beaten
	salt and white pepper

Place the snapper fillets in a large rectangular

pan or baking dish. Barely submerge the fish with the Champagne. Sprinkle shallots over each fillet and dot each one with 1 tablespoon of butter. Place pan over one suitably large or two small burners on the stove and bring to a boil. Immediately reduce heat and let simmer for 8 minutes. With a large spatula, carefully remove fillets to a heated platter and keep warm in oven (200°F). Reserve the pan liquid. Melt remaining butter in a saucepan over very low heat. Remove from heat and add the cream. Gradually add the egg yolks, beating steadily with a wire whisk. Place saucepan over low heat and slowly add the cooking liquid, while continuing to beat with the whisk. Do not let the sauce boil. Pour sauce over fish and decorate the rim of platter with alternate thin slices of Key lime and orange. Makes 4 servings.

RED SNAPPER FLORIDIAN

2 pounds	2 teaspoons
red snapper fillets	grated orange rind
3 tablespoons	1 teaspoon salt
melted fat or oil	dash of grated nutmeg
2 tablespoons orange juice	dash of black pepper

Cut the snapper fillets into serving-size portions. Place in a single layer, skin side down, in a well-greased baking dish, 12 x 8 x 2 inches. Combine remaining ingredients and pour over fish. Bake in a moderate oven (350°F.) for 25 to 30 minutes, or until fish flakes easily when tested with a fork. Makes 6 servings.

BAKED RED SNAPPER WITH SOUR-CREAM STUFFING

3 or 4 pounds whole-dressed red snapper
1½ teaspoons salt
Sour-Cream Stuffing (recipe follows)
2 tablespoons melted fat or oil

Sprinkle snapper inside and out with salt. Stuff fish loosely. Close opening with small skewers or wooden picks. Place fish in a well-greased baking pan, and brush with fat. Bake in a moderate oven (350°F.) for 40 to 60 minutes, or until fish flakes easily when tested with a fork. Baste occasionally with fat. Remove skewers. Makes 6 servings.

SOUR-CREAM STUFFING

¾ cup chopped celery	¼ cup diced
½ cup chopped onion	peeled lime or lemon
¼ cup melted	2 tablespoons grated
fat or oil	lime or lemon rind

1 quart dry bread cubes	1 teaspoon paprika
½ cup sour cream	1 teaspoon salt

Cook celery and onion in fat until tender. Combine with all other ingredients and mix thoroughly. Makes approximately 1 quart stuffing.

BAKED SNAPPER WITH ORANGE-RICE STUFFING

3 to 4 pounds dressed red or yellowtail snapper
1½ teaspoons salt
Orange-Rice Stuffing (recipe follows)
2 tablespoons melted fat or oil

Wash the dressed fish and pat dry. Sprinkle inside and out with salt. Stuff fish loosely. Close opening with small skewers or wooden food picks. Place fish in a well-greased baking pan, and brush with fat. Bake in a moderate oven (350°F.) for 40 to 60 minutes, or until fish flakes easily when tested with a fork. Baste occasionally with fat. Remove skewers. Makes 6 servings.

ORANGE-RICE STUFFING

1 cup chopped celery	1 tablespoon
with leaves	grated orange rind
¼ cup chopped onion	¾ teaspoon salt
¼ cup melted fat or oil	1 cup precooked rice
¾ cup water	½ cup slivered
¼ cup orange juice	blanched almonds,
2 tablespoons lemon juice	toasted

Cook celery and onion in fat until tender. Add water, juices, orange rind and salt; bring to a boil. Add rice and stir to moisten. Cover and remove from heat. Let stand for 5 minutes. Add almonds and mix thoroughly. Makes about 4 cups stuffing.

ROUGET EN PAPILLOTE
(Chef Arno Schmidt, Waldorf Astoria, New York City)

4 red snapper fillets,	1 teaspoon tomato purée
½ pound each	½ teaspoon
1 tablespoon butter	chopped fresh parsley
2 tablespoons	½ teaspoon
chopped shallots	chopped fresh chives
1 cup chopped mushrooms	¼ teaspoon
½ cup dry white wine	chopped fresh chervil
pinch of rosemary	¼ teaspoon
salt and pepper	chopped fresh dill
2 tablespoons meat glaze	melted fat or shortening
(glace de viande)	

Baked snapper with orange-rice stuffing

Butter a suitable casserole, sprinkle with shallots, and add mushrooms, wine and rosemary. Place fillets on top, and season to taste. Cover, and bake in 375°F. oven for 15 minutes. Place cooked fish on a platter, cover with a damp napkin, and set aside in a warm place. Add meat glaze and tomato purée to the mushrooms. Boil mushroom mixture over high heat until most of the moisture has evaporated and the mixture has the consistency of wet sand. Stir frequently during this cooking process. Add chopped herbs, and adjust the seasoning.

Prepare 4 sheets of ovenproof parchment paper in the shape of a heart. Butter papers. Place one eighth of the mushroom mixture on one side of each heart. Place a fillet on top. Put remaining mushroom mixture on top. Fold paper over, and crimp edges to make an airtight seal. It is very important that fish is well sealed in.

Heat 1 inch of fat or shortening in a frying pan. When smoking hot, place fish bag in fat. It will puff up like a balloon. Put in oven until paper is light brown. Serve at once. Makes 4 servings.

Snoek

(1) A common name for the pike (Holland). *See PIKE.*
(2) A common name for the snake mackerel (South Africa). This is not a mackerel but a member of the family Gempylidae.

Snook

Formerly a commercial fish of some importance, the snook *(Centropomus undecimalis)* now has gamefish status and is no longer marketed. In years past, skinned fillets were often purveyed as "red snapper" in Florida. While an expert could detect the difference in its musculature, fillets of small snook are certainly the snappers' equal in flavor. In the U. S. snook occur only in southern Florida where mangrove habitat and waters of low salinity are important to its life cycle. There has been considerable habitat destruction through dredging and filling with a consequent decline in our snook population. Today, it's a more important foodfish in Mexico, Central America, and South America from eastern Colombia to Brazil; it is generally known as **róbalo** in Spanish-speaking countries. The largest fisheries I have seen in recent years are among the coastal Indians of Colombia and Venezuela who net and handline snook in the surf. However, all of the catch is consumed locally. Almost 1½ thousand metric tons of **swordspine snook** *(Centropomus ensiferus)* is also taken annually in the Venezuelan trawl fishery. The **black snook** *(Centropomus nigrescens)* is its Pacific counterpart and is found from Baja California southward to northern Peru. It is commonly known as **róbalo preito** and is marketed to some extent throughout its range. There are several other small snook species in Florida and along both coasts of Central and South America which differ only in taxonomy.

The snook grows to more than 50 pounds in weight with a length of over 4 feet, but any snook over 20 pounds is considered a big one. I have caught quite a few big ones including several over 30 pounds; while these are of sporting interest, they have less value at table. Small snook have white, finely textured meat and are of excellent flavor, comparable to a walleye. The ideal size is a fish

Snook

of 2 to 6 pounds; as a snook grows larger its flesh becomes more coarse and loses its delicate, sweet taste. Except with the smallest fish, say 2 to 3 pounds, only skinned fillets should be used as the skin imparts an off-flavor (usually described as "soapy"). The fillets are best prepared by cutting into fingers and deep-frying. Small unskinned fillets can be panfried skin side down in a skillet with the lid on over high heat, so the meat partially steams while the skin crisps; this is a method used in Costa Rica and Panama with delicious results. In Central America fried snook is often served with slices of fresh pineapple—a delightful contrast with any delicate fried fish. Personally, I prefer snook of over 10 pounds in chowder form, although it can be made into edible dishes when baked or broiled.

Soft Roe

A European term for "white roe" or the gonads of a male fish. The soft roes of mullet, carp, herring, mackerel, salmon and various other species are widely utilized in poached and sautéed forms. Indian and Eskimo people often eat the roes raw. *See ROE.*

Sole

The story is perhaps apocryphal, but the suicide of that celebrated *maître d' hôtel* Vatel in 1671 upon learning that sole had not been delivered on the occasion of a gourmet dinner is an historical tribute to a singular fish. Vatel's peers criticized his awkward exit both for using a bacon-slicer instead of a sword and his "inability to rise above difficult circumstances." He was drummed out of the corps. Yet, the moody eccentricity of Vatel marked the birth of what has become a cuisine within a cuisine. No fish lends itself more to such a variety of imaginative dishes. One reason advanced for its popularity is that "sole doesn't taste like fish." This inaccurate distinction may please senescent palates but the other reason—that its texture and delicate flavor are ideally suited to the elaborate use of sauces, herbs, spices, fruits and vegetables as well as contrasting seafoods—is more to the point. Few fish can tolerate such a galaxy of additives without losing their identity. The anomaly is that identity is the key to sole cookery. One begins with the question: what is a sole?

The sole is the pivotal species around which European chefs created their masterpieces. Unlike flounders, which are rounded in shape, the sole is more elliptical and deeper-bodied. Its name achieved new status in the days of horse transport when enterprising wholesalers hired fast carriages to convey fish from the South Coast of England to Billingsgate Market in London. The bulk of their catch was landed at the port of Dover and soon "Dover sole" became synonymous with prime quality. When motor transport displaced the horse, inevitably all fresh soles earned the soubriquet of "Dover." Subsequently, commercial fish dealers created new sole names not simply because of the value placed on the original but to make some of the less-inspiring flatfishes more glamorous. For example, a witch flounder hardly generates gastronomic interest when purveyed under its correct common name, but when marketed as a "white sole" as it is in Ireland, or a "gray sole" as it is in the U. S. A., this very edible flounder becomes acceptable to the consumer. Thus the term "sole" encompasses any number of flatfishes in the families Bothidae and Pleuronectidae, to the extent that Dover sole and English sole are accepted common names for two Pacific flounders which bear no resemblance to the true sole. Dissimulation is important, not because the various flounders are inferior but because they differ in texture and flavor and many do not lend themselves to sole recipes. These are better prepared by other, more rewarding methods.

For example, a crisply sautéed winter flounder, small, whole, gutted but unskinned, is a plebian delight that needs no Gallic touch. The tough dark skin of a sole is virtually inedible but that of a baby "blackback" subtly complements its delicate flesh. Or, in the Danish style of **Bakskuld** an unskinned plaice is briefly brined and hot-smoked before sautéing in fresh butter—a dish fit for a king, as it became a hallmark of the Royal Court beginning in the fourteenth century. The smokehouses of the port city of Esbjerg in West Jutland still make a specialty of **Bakskuld,** and should you stray to this part of the world the Kunstpavillonen restaurant with its charming gardens and art museum serves the best. Accompanied by foaming Danish beer and a green salad these translucent gold flatfish make a delightful lunch. Smoked flounder also appears in Germany under the name **Raucherflunder,** but it seldom matches the Esbjerg variety.

There are 4 true soles in western Atlantic waters—the hogchoker, lined, naked and scrawled soles, but these diminutive members of the Soleidae seldom reach a length of over 8 inches and have very little food value. The authentic "sole" is only obtainable in the U. S. as a frozen import from England or France. It appears, of course, in posh restaurants and is usually listed as Imported English Sole or Imported Dover Sole. Some of the American flounders, however, are perfectly reliable substitutes and while they may differ in taste many people prefer these fresh fillets to the frozen original. The lemon sole, gray sole and Rex sole can be readily prepared in classic styles.

SOLE TERMINOLOGY

BUTTER SOLE A small Pacific flounder *(Isopsetta isolepis)* found from California to Alaska. Of excellent quality and marketed in fresh and frozen fillets. The butter sole compares favorably to the petrale and sand soles.

CURLFIN SOLE A small Pacific flounder *(Pleuronichthys decurrens)* found from California to Alaska. Of excellent quality but due to comparative scarcity it has been a minor market item.

DOVER SOLE (1) The common sole of Europe *(Solea vulgaris)* found from the Mediterranean to Denmark. Thick-bodied, it produces a unique fillet of fine texture and flavor.

(2) The common name of a Pacific flounder *(Microstomus pacificus)* found from California to Alaska. This deepwater flatfish reaches a weight of 10 pounds and is a major part of the western U.S. "sole" landings. It is inferior to the sand sole and petrale sole. The fish is especially slimy, so the entire catch is marketed in fillet form.

ENGLISH SOLE The common name of a small Pacific flounder *(Parophrys vetulus)* found from northern Mexico to Alaska. Of good quality but on occasion has an "iodine" aroma.

LEMON SOLE (1) The U.S. market name for a winter flounder of over 3 pounds in weight. These fish are taken primarily off Long Island, Block Island, and the Georges Banks east of Massachusetts. At the Fulton Market flounders are graded as "blackbacks" when less than 3 pounds, and as "lemon sole" if heavier.

(2) A market name in Great Britain for the lemon dab *(Microstomus kitt)*.

(3) A market name in France **(sole limande)** for the true sand sole, *Solea lascaris*.

PETRALE SOLE A large Pacific flounder *(Eopsetta jordani)* found from the Mexican border north to Alaska. Of excellent quality, and marketed in fresh and frozen fillets. The petrale sole is generally ranked first among Pacific flatfishes.

REX SOLE A small Pacific flounder *(Glyptocephalus zachirus)* found from southern California to the Bering Sea. Extremely delicate and of fine texture, it is also less numerous than other flatfishes and therefore commands a higher price. The Rex sole is too thin to fillet properly and is usually cooked whole.

ROCK SOLE A small Pacific flounder *(Lepidopsetta bilineata)* found chiefly in the offshore waters of central California. Only fair in texture and flavor, it seldom enters the market.

SAND SOLE (1) A small Pacific flounder *(Psettichthys melanostictus)* found from southern California to Alaska. Its general acceptance is second to the petrale sole.

(2) A small European sole sometimes called "French sole," or "lemon sole."

THICKBACK SOLE A true sole *(Microchirus variegatus)* found from the Mediterranean to Denmark. It is smaller than the Dover sole and a minor market item.

YELLOWFIN SOLE A small Pacific flounder *(Limanda aspera)* found from northern British Columbia to northwestern Alaska.

THE 33 CLASSICS

French cuisine has been the source of numerous seafood dishes which over the years have become more or less classic presentations throughout the world. The names used in connection with a particular fish such as **Sole Capri** or **Trout Saint-Germain** are an international language which in the first instance implies a panfried fillet of sole garnished with sugared bananas and chutney sauce, while a trout in Saint-Germain style is essentially a broiled fish covered with bread crumbs and **maître d'hôtel butter.** The ingredients are not to a rule. Many chefs add distinctive touches. An herb may be added to the sauce or a particular vegetable might be employed in the garnish; it is style of presentation much like Japanese floral decoration which, though stylized, always retains its individuality. Some of these additives are completely innocent but, cabalistically, a mark of the professional. Chef de cuisine Charles Janon of the Inter-Continental Hotel in Paris, for example, would never serve his **Sole Normande** before decorating each portion with a puff paste or slice of toast carved in the symbolic "N." This is the way it was first presented and tradition must be observed.

The following definitions are a general guide both to ordering in a restaurant and in considering the options available when deciding how to prepare a particular fish. For the most part these dishes evolved from sole cookery although the larger flounders—turbot, snapper, corvina—and other species having lean, firm white flesh can be prepared in the same manner. Fattier fishes with a coarser texture such as mackerel, striped bass or salmon are so distinctive that some of the sauces and garnishes detract from rather than enhance their flavors; these should be reviewed under their respective entries.

No one will ever agree as to the exact details of

facing page, At Sesimbra (near Setúbal), Portugal, there is a fish auction (lota) on the beach every day, all year long. In the morning and again in the late afternoon fish are unloaded directly on the beach and people arrive to bid for the catch.

these preparations, so don't be surprised to see recipes at variance in other books, or to be served a dish with a particular name and garnishes other than those listed here. Some of these preparations had a known origin, but others evolved. In your own kitchen you may devise a variation because of the fruits or vegetables in season, or the other ingredients available to you.

Amandine: panfried, splashed with slivered blanched almonds lightly browned in butter.

au Bleu: poached, in stock and vinegar.

Bonne Femme: poached, covered with white-wine sauce, garnished with sliced mushrooms and *fines herbes*, and glazed.

Capri: meunière style, garnished with fried sugared bananas and chutney sauce.

Cardinal: poached, with lobster sauce laced with brandy, garnished with button mushrooms and a lobster claw.

Castiglione: poached in white wine, covered with sauce thickened with cream and egg yolks and flavored with truffles, garnished with tomato dice and puff-pastry crescents.

Chambertin: poached whole in wine stock, then jellied.

Colbert: panfried and covered with **Sauce Colbert;** or boned, with the space filled with **Maître d'Hôtel Butter.**

Cubat: poached, covered with wine sauce made of sherry, mushrooms and finely chopped truffles, sprinkled with grated cheese and glazed.

Dauphine: rolled fillets poached in Madeira with truffles, then chilled and covered with **Sauce Villeroi** to which crayfish butter has been added; fillets are then dusted with bread crumbs and fried in clarified butter. In the exotic original Dauphine style this was served around a molded ring of pike forcemeat whose center was filled with crayfish tails, mushrooms, quenelles of pike and sliced truffles, all married in a thick **Sauce Velouté.**

Dugléré: poached in wine with chopped tomatoes, napped with the cooking liquids thickened to a sauce.

Egyptienne: poached in court bouillon, covered with white-wine sauce, bedded on fried eggplant slices, and garnished with mushrooms, truffles and parsley.

Florentine: poached, bedded on crisp cooked leaf spinach, and covered with cheese sauce.

Gondu: poached, covered with white-wine sauce, sprinkled with grated cheese, and garnished with fresh asparagus tips.

en Goujons: cut into fingers and deep-fried; served with **Sauce Tartare.**

Marguery: poached in white-wine *fumet*, covered with white-wine sauce, and garnished with cooked mussels. Shrimps, oysters and button mushrooms are sometimes added, although these were not in the original Restaurant Marguery recipe.

Maison: broiled, or poached in white wine, with pulped fresh tomato halves and mushrooms, sprinkled with *fines herbes*.

Meunière: lightly floured, panfried in butter, sprinkled with *fines herbes*, and splashed with **Beurre Noir.**

Mornay: poached in white wine and covered with **Sauce Mornay.**

Nantua: poached in white wine, garnished with meats of freshwater crayfish, and covered with **Crayfish Butter.**

Niçoise: panfried in half butter, half olive oil, garnished with tomatoes, tarragon, black olives, capers.

Normande: sautéed in half olive oil, half butter, garnished with baked apples stuffed with shrimps mixed with **Sauce Béchamel,** then the whole covered with **Parsley Butter.** An "N" shaped garnish of puff pastry or toast should lean against the apple.

Orientale: whole, deep-fried, with Chinese vegetables.

Palace: poached, covered with white-wine sauce, garnished with halved pulped tomatoes, fresh asparagus and *fines herbes*.

en Papillote: cooked in a paper bag.

Parisienne: poached in white wine, coated with white-wine sauce, garnished with truffles, mushrooms and crayfish.

Pommery: meunière style, garnished with sliced apples sautéed in butter, and splashed with **Beurre Noir.**

Portugaise: poached in white wine or broiled (the latter for oily fishes such as bluefish or mackerel), covered with tomato halves and sliced peppers.

Saint-Germain: broiled with covering of bread crumbs and **Maître d'Hôtel Butter.**

Sicilian: meunière style, splashed with **Beurre Noir,** garnished with slices of anchovy and black olives.

Véronique: poached in white wine, covered with white-wine sauce made from Sauternes and heavy cream, garnished with halved seeded white grapes.

Vert: sautéed with greens, white wine.

Walewska: poached, covered with white-wine sauce made from Marsala or dry sherry, garnished with slices of lobster, and sprinkled with grated cheese, or covered with **Sauce Mornay** and glazed.

FLOUNDER TERMINOLOGY

AMERICAN PLAICE This boreal flounder is often marketed as dab, sanddab, long rough-dab, and rough-back; it is also known as Canadian plaice. This species (*Hippoglossoides platessoides*) is found on both sides of the Atlantic from Cape Cod to the Grand Banks and southern Labrador, and in the eastern Atlantic from Greenland to Norway and south to the North Sea. It is distinct from the common European plaice; the American plaice is plain reddish to gray-brown in color on the eyed side and lacks the red spotting of the former. This is a deepwater flounder, found at depths from 120 to 2,000 feet. The American plaice grows to about 12 pounds in size but the usual market fish is from 2 to 3 pounds. It's an important commercial species taken by otter trawls on the cod and haddock grounds. Large quantities of plaice are exported from Denmark to other European countries.

A related species, the Bering flounder *(H. robustus)* occurs in the northern Pacific.

The American plaice is also known as **Balai** (France), **Rauhe Scharbe** (Germany), **Håising** (Denmark), **Gapeflyndre** (Norway), **Lerskadda** (Sweden) and **Skarkoli** (Iceland).

ARROWTOOTH FLOUNDER This flounder occurs from central California north to Alaska, west to Kamchatka and southward along the coast of the USSR. It's an important commercial species for Japanese and Soviet fishermen in the North Pacific. The arrowtooth *(Atheresthes stomias)* has been marketed here as "turbot" or "French sole" in years past, and is often mistaken for a small halibut which it resembles in shape. It's a good table fish but the flesh is somewhat soft; it should be iced and at table soon after capture. It's sold mainly in frozen form, whole and gutted. Only the simplest methods of cooking are recommended, either panfrying or broiling.

ATLANTIC HALIBUT The largest flatfish *(Hippoglossus hippoglossus)*, this flounder reaches a weight of 600 to 700 pounds and a length of over 9 feet. Today, a halibut of 300 pounds is rare. It is caught in the cooler waters of the North Atlantic from New Jersey, and occasionally to Virginia, to Greenland and along the northern European coast southward to the English Channel. A coldwater species, it is found in relatively deep water over sand, gravel or clay, rather than on soft mud or on rock. It is not an Arctic form, generally being taken in waters from about 40° to 50°F. The halibut seldom enters water shallower than about 200 feet deep and frequents waters as deep as 3,000 feet.

The halibut has firm white meat of delicate flavor. At the wholesale level it may be sold whole and gutted, either fresh or frozen, otherwise it appears in steak or fillet form (specifically in "fletches" or 4 longitudinal segments made by cutting parallel to the backbone). Halibut cheeks are considered a gourmet item. Strips of meat are also sold in dried form and small pieces with or without skin are hot-smoked.

Also called **Flétan** (France), **Heilbutte** (Germany), **Heilbot** (Holland), **Helleflynder** (Denmark), **Kybite** (Norway), **Halleflundrer** (Sweden), **Halibut** (Spain), **Alabote** (Portugal), **Heilagfiski** (Iceland).

BRILL A European flatfish *(Rhombus laevis)* closely related to the turbot. It is more oval in shape than the turbot and lacks the latter's characteristic tubercles. It occurs from the Mediterranean to the North Sea up to Bergen, Norway, and into the Baltic. Brill are smaller than turbot, reaching a weight of 15 pounds, but usually seen at 2 to 4 pounds. This flounder is not in the same class as turbot as a food but it's tasty and finds a ready market, especially in Great Britain.

Also known as **Barbue** (France), **Glattbutte** (Germany), **Rombo liscio** (Italy), **Remol** (Spain), **Rodovalho** (Portugal), **Griet** (Holland), **Slethvarre** (Denmark), **Slätvar** (Sweden), **Slettvar** (Norway).

CALIFORNIA HALIBUT A member of the lefteye flounder family, this halibut *(Paralichthys californicus)* occurs from central California to northern Mexico. It's similar in shape to the Pacific halibut. Although it reaches weights to 60 pounds, it is usually caught in much smaller sizes of 4 to 12 pounds. The meat is somewhat comparable to the Pacific halibut but much less choice. The California halibut is sold mainly as fresh boneless fillets rather than steaks unless the fish is exceptionally large.

GREENLAND HALIBUT A boreal flatfish, rather distinctive in appearance due to its elongate shape and very dark, almost black coloration on the blind side. The Greenland halibut *(Reinhardtius hippoglossoides)* ranges over a large area of the sub-Arctic and Arctic regions of the Atlantic and Pacific Oceans. It's commercially important from northern Japan to the Bering Sea and north of Newfoundland to northern Norway. During coldwater years it strays as far south as Cape Cod in the East and to southern California in the West. Historically, it has been utilized in the Japanese market as **karasu garei** or "black flounder" and in the Soviet fishery as **chernyi paltus** or "black paltus." Until 1973 it was legally sold in the U.S. and Canada as Greenland "turbot"; while that designation is no longer acceptable (FDA) the name still persists in some markets. The Greenland halibut is inferior in texture and flavor to the Atlantic and Pacific halibuts; it has a denser musculature, making it suitable for poaching or chowders, but it tends to dry and toughen under direct heat.

PACIFIC HALIBUT Except for its range this is similar to the Atlantic halibut. The Pacific species *(Hippoglossus stenolepis)* is found from central California to the Bering Sea and north to Japan. Our greatest source of supply is from Alaska. In years past the commercial landings in the

Winter flounder, dorsal view

Winter flounder, ventral view

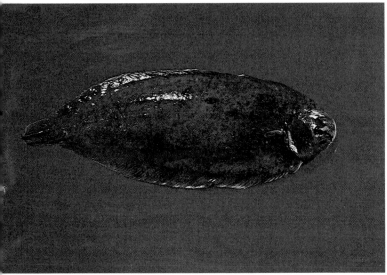

Dover sole

Turbot ▼

Brill

Summer flounder   Pacific halibut ▼

U. S. exceeded 50 million pounds. The catch today is controlled by international agreement.

PACIFIC SANDDAB A miniature but delectable flounder, the sanddab *(Citharichthys sordidus)* is found from southern California to northwestern Alaska at depths of 100 to 300 feet. It is brown in color on the eyed side and mottled with dull orange and black spots or blotches. The sanddab reaches a weight of about 2 pounds but is more often seen at 8 to 10 ounces in size. This is a tasty panfish, best prepared by gutting and removing the fins (its loose scales are easily flaked off), then panfrying or deep-frying. Sanddabs are caught the year round. Despite their very small size, they are sweet and of fine texture. Dabs are no less venerated than the petrale and rex soles by many western gourmets.

PLAICE This popular European flounder *(Pleuronectes platessa)* is easily identified by the numerous small red spots scattered on its upper or brown side. Although it attains a weight of 12 to 15 pounds, most of the plaice marketed are between 1½ and 3 pounds. Its white flesh is of fine flake and sweet and is sold mainly fresh, whole and gutted, and to a lesser extent in fillet form. Plaice are also hot-smoked, either whole or in pieces, especially in Denmark and Germany.

Plaice are found from the Barents Sea to the Bay of Biscay. The major fisheries are in the "Flemish Bight" between southeastern England and the coast of Holland, off the English Yorkshire coast, in the Irish Sea, and off Heligoland in Germany.

In French cuisine the plaice appears as **Carrelet;** elsewhere its known as **Rødspætte** (Denmark), **Rødspette** (Norway), **Rödsputta** (Sweden), **Scholle** (Germany), **Solla** (Spain), **Passera** (Italy), **Schol** (Holland), **Iverak** (Yugoslavia).

SOUTHERN FLOUNDER Unlike its close relative the summer flounder, this fish *(Paralichthys lethostigma)* is usually a plain olive color on the dark side without any mottlings or spots. It is also a much smaller flatfish, seldom attaining 3 pounds, and usually marketed at 1½ to 2 pounds. Although it's caught from North Carolina to Texas, the largest volume is harvested by shrimp trawlers in the Gulf of Mexico. In many parts of the South people catch this flounder by "gigging" with a spear at night, using a torch or flashlight.

STARRY FLOUNDER This is one of the most widely distributed Pacific flounders, ranging from Santa Barbara, California, to Alaska and westward to Kamchatka (USSR) and southward to Japan. It is sometimes called "rough jacket" by commercial fishermen. This flatfish *(Platichthys stellatus)* is abundant in the U. S. sport catch.

Although the starry flounder reaches a weight of about 15 pounds the average marketed is less than 2 pounds. It's usually retailed in fresh fillet form. Generally, the starry flounder is considered only fair at table when compared to many other Pacific flatfishes. The young or smaller ones are more desirable than large fish. It is known in Japan as **numagarei** or "swamp flounder" as it occurs there in brackish marshes, but it also enters freshwater rivers throughout its range. The starry flounder is occasionally purveyed under the catchall "sole" label in West Coast outlets.

SUMMER FLOUNDER More commonly marketed as "fluke" and easily distinguished from the winter flounder by its large oblique mouth. In color the dark side may be gray, brown or olive with more colorful tints of orange and pink, but it also has dark mottlings with small distinct spots. It is usually sold fresh, whole and gutted, and in fillets with or without skin. The summer flounder *(Paralichthys dentatus)* is comparable to the winter flounder in flavor and texture, although it's generally a larger fish at market—the average size from 3 to 5 pounds but 15- to 20-pounders are not uncommon. These big "doormats" are usually dressed in quartercut fillets and sometimes in steak form.

Fluke occur in the eastern U. S. from Maine to South Carolina. They are most available in the summer months when they frequent shallow water. During the winter they range in the 150- to 300-foot depths offshore.

TURBOT (1) A common name for several Pacific flounders—the diamond turbot, hornyhead turbot and spotted turbot. The diamond turbot *(Hypsopsetta guttulata)* is the larger, weighing to 4 pounds, but none of these species is of culinary importance.

(2) A highly esteemed European flatfish *(Rhombus maximus)* and, depending on the critic, equal or superior to the sole, or inferior only to the sole. (However, all critics will agree it is superior to its relative, brill. In *H.M.S. Pinafore* Buttercup states "Turbot is ambitious brill.") This Eastern Atlantic turbot is not in the same family as the Pacific "turbots." The turbot ranges from the Mediterranean as far north as Bergen, Norway. Its body is diamond-shaped and the dark side is covered with blunt tubercles. Turbot attain a fairly large size, over 30 pounds, although the average at market is considerably smaller. They are usually sold fresh, whole and gutted, or in quartercut fillets and steaks with skin attached.

Due to its delicate flavor and firm white meat, the turbot is usually prepared in the simplest forms, either steamed or poached, and bathed in butter. It may also appear with suitable sauces such as **Sauce Cardinal** or **Sauce Nantua.**

Also known as **Turbot** (France), **Steinbutte** (Germany), **Rombo chiodato** (Italy), **Rodaballo** (Spain), **Pregado** (Portugal), **Pighvar** (Denmark), **Piggvar** (Sweden and Norway), **Tarbot** (Holland), **Plat** (Yugoslavia).

WINDOWPANE Also called spotted flounder. The windowpane (*Scophthalmus aquosus*) is found from the Gulf of St. Lawrence to South Carolina and is particularly common in the Cape Cod to New York area. This distinctive flatfish is broadly ovate in shape, its color reddish to grayish brown on the dark side. There are some dark mottlings on the fins. However, there is no mistaking this fish as it has an extremely thin body which transmits light when held to the sun, hence the name windowpane. This flounder is edible, even sweet, but it seldom attains a pound in weight and there is so little meat in comparison to its bone structure that it's hardly worth the effort to cook. On occasion some windowpanes find their way to market.

WINTER FLOUNDER Perhaps the most important eastern U.S. flatfish from the standpoint of abundance and popular demand. The winter flounder (*Pseudopleuronectes americanus*) is generally marketed as "flounder" but sometimes as blueback flounder, blackback flounder and lemon sole (*see under Sole Terminology*). Its dark side varies in color from reddish brown to dark slate. It is usually sold fresh, whole and gutted, and in fillets with or without skin. The very sweet, fine-flaked white meat can be utilized in a variety of recipes; however, its fragile texture in small sizes (under 2 pounds) is best treated by the simplest methods such as panfrying whole fish, or broiling or sautéing fillets. The roes are excellent.

The range of the winter flounder extends along the Atlantic Coast of North America from Newfoundland and the Gulf of St. Lawrence southward to Chesapeake Bay. They are found in shallow bays and inshore coastal zones out to the deeper, offshore ocean grounds. The centers of abundance include the coasts of Massachusetts, Rhode Island and Connecticut, Long Island Sound, both shores, the eastern reaches of Long Island, and bays and coastal areas of New Jersey.

The size of the winter flounder is generally 12 to 15 inches and 1 to 2 pounds, sometimes reaching 20 inches and 5 pounds. The larger fish are often called "sea flounders" to distinguish them from the smaller bay fish. In waters off Montauk Point, New York, and around Block Island, Rhode Island, there exist populations of jumbo flounders, locally known as "snowshoes" because of their shape and size. These fish weigh up to 6 pounds or more. Similarly large flounders are taken on the Georges Banks.

FILET DE SOLE CAPRI
(Wheeler's, London)

4 fillets of sole	ground cloves
4 teaspoons lemon juice	and cinnamon
salt, cayenne pepper,	½ cup dry white wine
grated mace	4 bay leaves
5 tablespoons butter	2 tablespoons
4 bananas	Major Grey's chutney
superfine sugar	2 tablespoons sherry

One hour before cooking, brush fillets with lemon juice (about 1 teaspoon altogether), and season lightly with salt, cayenne and mace. Fold each fillet in half lengthwise, and keep cool.

Melt 1 tablespoon of the butter in a skillet. Blot the fish dry and sauté lightly on both sides, turning with care. Peel the bananas and cut into halves lengthwise and crosswise. Moisten bananas with lemon juice (about 1 teaspoon altogether), roll them in sugar, then dust them with the spices. Melt remaining butter in a separate pan; when butter bubbles, put in the bananas, cover, and brown lightly on all sides. Pour the wine over the fish fillets and arrange 1 bay leaf on each fillet. Cover fish closely with wax paper or aluminum foil and poach in a preheated 350°F. oven for 15 minutes. Remove wax paper and bay leaves and carefully transfer fillets to a hot platter; keep warm in the open oven. Arrange spiced bananas around fish. Chop the chutney to fine pieces and add to the butter left in the banana pan, along with sherry and remaining 2 teaspoons lemon juice. Simmer the sauce gently, stirring, until all is blended, thick and spicy. Pour over fish and serve at once. Makes 4 servings.

FILET DE SOLE PAYSANNE
(Wheeler's, London)

4 fillets of sole	½ teaspoon chopped parsley
lemon juice	1 cup fish stock,
salt and pepper	white wine or water
1½ tablespoons butter	beurre manié
2 medium-size carrots,	(1 tablespoon butter,
sliced thin	1 teaspoon flour)
2 medium-size onions, sliced thin	

Brush fillets with lemon juice, season lightly with salt and pepper, fold each fillet in half lengthwise, and set aside in a cool place. Heat ½ tablespoon butter in a shallow pan large enough for all the fillets in a single layer. Add carrots and onions, cover the pan, and over low heat cook vegetables until soft but not browned. Add remaining butter and arrange the folded fillets on the vege-

SOLE NORMANDE (prepared by Chef Charles Janon at the Inter-Continental Hotel, Paris)

1. Assemble ingredients.

2. Peel apples.

3. Remove cores from stem ends.

4. Mix cooked shrimps into béchamel sauce.

5. Stuff apples with shrimp mixture.

6. Place apples in a buttered casserole.

7. Dust sole fillets with flour.

8. Brown fillets in a mixture of butter and olive oil.

9. Brown on the second sides.

10. Place a baked apple on each fillet.

11. Cut an "N" from each slice of bread.

12. Arrange the "N" leaning against the apple, and pour melted parsley butter over all.

facing page, The finished dish ready to serve

FILET DE SOLE CASTIGLIONE (prepared by Chef Charles Janon at the Inter-Continental Hotel, Paris)

1. Assemble ingredients.

2. Chop mushrooms and ingredients for mirepoix.

3. Cover a baking dish with vegetable mixture.

4. Place sole fillets on vegetable bed.

5. Cover sole with mushrooms and chopped truffles.

6. When sole is cooked, pour cooking liquids into a saucepan.

7. Add cream to liquids and reduce.

8. Add remaining butter;

9. then egg yolks beaten with Madeira.

10. Beat with a whisk until all is combined.

11. Spoon vegetable mixture over the fillets, then cover with the sauce.

12. Brown until the top is golden. Serve with puff-pastry crescents.

tables. Add parsley and liquid. Cut a piece of parchment paper just large enough to cover the pan, make a tiny hole in the center, and butter it. Place buttered side down on the fish. Bring liquid to a boil, cover the pan, and simmer for 10 to 12 minutes, according to thickness of the fillets. Remove fish to a serving dish, and reduce liquid to one third of its original volume. Thicken with *beurre manié* and correct the seasoning. Pour over fish, vegetables and all. Makes 4 servings.

SOLE NORMANDE
(Hotel Inter-Continental, Paris)

8 fillets of sole	salt and pepper
with white skin intact	½ cup flour
8 sweet red apples	1 cup olive oil
2 lemons	8 parsley sprigs,
½ pound	1 to 2 inches long
cooked small shrimps	8 thick slices
1 cup Sauce Béchamel (p. 286)	of white bread
¼ to ½ pound butter,	1 cup Parsley Butter (p. 49)
melted	

In filleting a fresh sole, remove the dark skin only. Scale white skin. Wash fillets and leave under running water for 1 hour. Meanwhile peel the apples and remove cores from stem ends with a melon-ball scoop. Squeeze half of lemon juice over all the cut surfaces of apples to prevent discoloration. Mix shrimps into béchamel sauce, and stuff cavities of apples with the shrimp mixture. Place apples, cavity side down, on a buttered oven dish and sprinkle with melted butter. Cover apples and place dish in preheated 350°F. oven for 30 minutes, or until apples are tender but still holding their shape.

Dry the fillets, season with salt and pepper, and dust with flour. Brown on both sides in a mixture of half butter, half olive oil. Place browned fillets side by side on a buttered warmed serving platter. Remove baking dish from oven and *very gently* transfer apples with a broad spatula to the serving platter, placing 1 apple, stuffed side up, on each fillet. (The apples will break easily, so be careful!) Squeeze remaining lemon juice onto apples, and stick 1 parsley sprig in each. Keep the platter warm.

Cut an "N" from each slice of bread and brown in butter, or broil or toast. Place one "N" on each sole fillet, leaning against the apple. Just before serving pour melted parsley butter over the fish. Makes 8 servings.

FILET DE SOLE CASTIGLIONE
(Hotel Inter-Continental, Paris)

8 fillets of sole	1 lemon
1 pound tomatoes	salt and pepper
2 truffles	2 cups heavy cream
½ pound mushrooms	2 egg yolks
½ pound shallots	4 ounces (½ cup)
½ pound butter	Madeira wine
4 tablespoons	8 small
minced parsley	puff-pastry crescents
2 cups dry white wine	

Wash fillets in running water. Plunge tomatoes into boiling water for 12 to 15 seconds, then remove skins. Cut tomatoes into halves, discard seeds, and drain off juice. Cut the rest into small cubes and reserve. Slice the truffles and reserve. Wash mushrooms and chop fine. Peel shallots and chop fine. Drain the fillets.

Butter a flameproof platter lavishly; sprinkle with the chopped shallots, minced parsley and cubed tomatoes. Arrange sole fillets on top, and sprinkle with mushrooms. Pour the wine around the fish and squeeze the lemon over the top. Season with salt and pepper. Cover the platter with buttered foil, and bring the liquid to a boil on top of the stove (if necessary place the platter on an asbestos mat). Transfer to a preheated 350°F. oven and cook for 12 minutes.

Remove platter from oven and pour the cooking liquids into a saucepan. Simmer to reduce liquid by two thirds. Add cream and reduce again. Add remaining butter to the sauce, beating all the while. Beat the egg yolks with the Madeira and add to the sauce, continuing to beat until everything is well combined. Add the sliced truffles. Arrange the fillets on the platter, spoon the tomato mixture over them evenly, and cover with the sauce. Arrange the puff-pastry crescents around the platter, and serve hot. Makes 8 servings.

FILET DE SOLE FLORENTINE

4 fillets of sole	1½ tablespoons
2 pounds fresh spinach,	chopped parsley
or 2 packages (10	2 tablespoons butter
ounces each) frozen	2½ tablespoons flour
chopped spinach	⅔ cup half-and-half
½ teaspoon onion powder	⅓ cup white wine
1 teaspoon salt	(Sauterne preferred)
dash of white pepper	¼ cup grated
dash of grated mace	Gruyère cheese
1½ teaspoons	paprika
seasoned salt	

Wash fresh spinach well, and remove any coarse stems. Cook in the water clinging to leaves just until wilted. Drain well, and chop. Drain again, squeezing out all excess moisture. Mix with onion powder, ½ teaspoon salt, the pepper and mace. Turn into a shallow 5-cup baking dish. Sprinkle sole with seasoned salt and parsley. Roll up fillets, and place on top of spinach. Melt butter, and blend in flour. Stir in half-and-half and cook, stirring, until sauce begins to thicken. Add wine and remaining ½ teaspoon salt, and cook until sauce boils thoroughly. Remove from heat, and stir in 3 tablespoons cheese. Spoon sauce over sole and spinach. Sprinkle with remaining cheese and some paprika. Bake in a moderate oven (350°F.) for about 25 minutes, until sole is cooked through. Serve at once, from the baking dish. Makes 4 servings.

SOLE VERONICA

6 fillets of sole	1 tablespoon dry
1½ cups water	or medium-dry sherry
1 cup dry white wine	1 teaspoon lemon juice
1 tablespoon dehydrated	½ teaspoon
minced onion	Worcestershire sauce
1 bay leaf	pepper
3 or 4 whole peppercorns	1 cup fresh or well-drained
salt	canned seedless grapes
4 tablespoons butter	1 can (6 ounces) sliced
4 tablespoons flour	broiled mushrooms,
1 cup light cream	drained
or rich milk	paprika

Combine water, white wine, onion, bay leaf, peppercorns and ½ teaspoon salt in a large heavy skillet; heat to simmering. Lay fillets of sole in this liquid; cover and simmer for 4 or 5 minutes, or until fish is just tender. Drain fillets, reserving cooking liquid, and place fillets in a greased shallow baking dish or on an ovenproof platter. Strain reserved liquid; boil rapidly until reduced to ¾ cup. Melt butter and stir in flour; add cream and the ¾ cup reduced cooking liquid; cook, stirring constantly, until mixture boils and thickens. Add sherry, lemon juice, Worcestershire sauce, and salt and pepper to taste. Stir in grapes and drained mushrooms. Pour hot sauce over fish; sprinkle with paprika. Place under a preheated broiler for 1 minute, or until sauce is bubbly and delicately browned. Makes 6 servings.

SOLE VÉRONIQUE
(Hotel Inter-Continental, Paris)

8 fillets of sole	salt and pepper
½ pound butter	1 pound large
½ pound	white grapes
shallots, minced	2 cups heavy cream
2 cups dry white wine	8 small
1 lemon	puff-pastry crescents

If filleting a fresh sole, remove the dark skin only. Scale the white skin. Wash fillets and leave under running water for 1 hour. Dry fillets, and arrange them on a deep flameproof platter that has been lavishly buttered and sprinkled with shallots. Pour the wine around the fillets and squeeze the lemon over the top. Season with salt and pepper. Cover with buttered foil and bring the liquid to a boil on top of the stove. Transfer to a preheated 350°F. oven and cook for 12 to 15 minutes. While fish is cooking peel the grapes. Place them in a flat ovenproof dish and put them in a corner of the oven to warm.

When sole is cooked, pour off cooking liquid into a *sauteuse*, and reduce over low heat to two thirds. Meanwhile, place sole fillets on a clean towel and with a small knife remove the outside string of little bones. Arrange fillets close together on a warmed serving platter, and arrange grapes around the fillets.

Add cream to the reduced sauce and reduce again by one third. Remove from heat and add remaining butter in small amounts, beating all the while. Adjust seasoning to taste. Strain the sauce through a fine sieve into a warm bowl. At serving time gently cover sole and grapes with the sauce, and arrange puff-pastry crescents around the edge. Serve hot. Makes 8 servings.

FILLETS OF SOLE WITH WHISKEY
(The Four Seasons, New York City)

6 fillets of sole	1 cup White-Wine Sauce I
butter	(p. 287)
½ tablespoon	¼ cup Sauce Hollandaise
chopped shallots	(p. 289)
½ tablespoon lemon juice	½ cup bourbon whiskey
salt and pepper	

Flatten fillets with blade of a cleaver, and heat in a buttered saucepan for a moment only. Place shallots and lemon juice in a baking dish and sprinkle with salt and pepper. Fold fillets in half and arrange on top. Bake, uncovered, in a 400°F. oven for 8 minutes. Drain fillets on a towel, and place, still folded, in a buttered broilerproof dish.

Heat the sauce. At the last moment add the hollandaise and the bourbon. Strain the sauce and pour over sole. Brown quickly under the broiler. Makes 6 servings.

facing page, Filet de sole florentine

SOLE VÉRONIQUE (prepared by Chef Charles Janon at the Inter-Continental Hotel, Paris)

1. Assemble ingredients.

2. Peel the grapes.

3. Place grapes on a heatproof dish and warm in the oven.

4. Lavishly butter a deep flameproof platter.

5. Sprinkle platter with minced shallots.

6. Arrange sole fillets on top.

7. Pour wine around fillets.

8. The sole is oven-poached.

9. Remove outside string of small bones from each fillet.

10. Return fillets to platter and surround with grapes.

11. Spoon sauce over sole.

12. Complete decoration on each fillet.

facing page, The finished dish, garnished with crescent-shaped toasts and shrimp, served in the garden of the Inter-Continental Hotel

TURBOT BAKED WITH HERBS (prepared by Chef Alexandre Monnier at Hotel Okura, Amsterdam, The Netherlands)

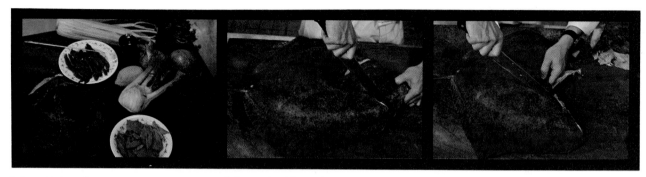

1. Assemble ingredients. **2.** Remove head from turbot. **3.** Divide turbot along the back.

TURBOT BAKED WITH HERBS
(Hotel Okura, Amsterdam, The Netherlands)

Dress the turbot: cut off the head, remove fins, skin the fish, and cut straight through along the spine, dividing the fish. Place fish with the upper (or left) side up. Cut flat anchovy fillets into halves. With a larding needle lace the fish with the anchovy pieces, putting them in at an angle to make a diamond-shaped pattern. Butter the fish generously, and cut into serving pieces. Season with salt and pepper and sprinkle with lemon juice. Broil over charcoal. Have ready a baking dish large enough to hold the turbot pieces in a single layer. Chop enough celery, fennel, parsley and onion to make a vegetable bed in the dish. Sauté chopped vegetables in olive oil until tender but not browned, and add bay leaves, thyme and black pepper. Transfer the mixture to the baking dish and arrange the grilled turbot on top. Bake in a preheated 350°F. oven for 20 to 25 minutes. Serve each portion on a layer of vegetables and garnish with a sculptured lemon. Serve with parsleyed potatoes and White Butter *(see under BUTTERS)*.

TURBOT DES GOURMETS
(Hotel Okura, Amsterdam, The Netherlands)

1 turbot, about 5½ pounds
1 pound whiting (silver hake), without skin or bones
salt and pepper
2 egg whites
2 cups heavy cream
8 ounces truffles, chopped
½ cup well-reduced Sauce Américaine
  (see Lobster Américaine, p. 182)
2 cups chopped onions
1 cup chopped mushroom stems
¼ cup chopped parsley stems
¼ cup chopped shallots
2 sprigs of fresh thyme, or 1 teaspoon dried
2 bay leaves
2 white peppercorns, crushed

2 cups white wine
2 cups fish stock (not clam juice)
4 cups light cream
½ cup Sauce Hollandaise (p. 289)

GARNISHES
8 lobster claws, cooked
8 truffle slices
16 to 24 new potatoes, cooked and rolled in Parsley Butter (p. 49)
16 shelled mussels, breaded and fried
8 large mushroom caps, fluted and poached

Dress the turbot: remove fins and the dark skin. Place fish with the upper (or left) side up. With a sharp knife cut through the length of the fish to the spine. Turn the knife flat and slide over the bones on each side, then lift out the bones. Season the inside with salt and pepper. Mash the whiting in a mortar and add the egg whites. Process the mixture through a food mill into a bowl. Set the bowl in a larger container filled with crushed ice and chill for 1 hour. Still over ice, work the mixture while incorporating the heavy cream little by little. Season this mousseline with salt and pepper to taste and add the chopped truffles and sauce américaine. Stuff the turbot with the mousseline and press the edges together over the stuffing.

Make a vegetable bed with onions, mushroom stems, parsley stems, shallots, thyme, bay leaf and peppercorns. Moisten with white wine and fish stock. Set the turbot on the vegetable bed and bake in a 350°F. oven, basting often with more wine and stock, heated. When the fish is done, in 30 to 40 minutes, transfer it to a serving platter and keep warm. Reduce the cooking liquids and vegetables, and strain. Add the light cream and reduce again, and at the last moment thicken with the hollandaise. Garnish turbot with lobster claws and truffles arranged alternately, and nap everything with the sauce. Surround with the potatoes, mussels and fluted mushrooms. Makes 8 servings.

4. Separate the pieces.   **5.** The fish divided.   **6.** Remove fins.

7., 8. Skin the fish.   **9.** Thread anchovy pieces in a larding needle.

10. Lace the fish with the anchovies, making a diamond pattern.   **11., 12.** Cut fish into serving pieces.

13. Prepare the vegetable bed for braising and the sculptured lemons for garnish.   **14.** Put vegetable mixture in a baking dish and arrange turbot pieces on top.   **15.** Serve the baked turbot with some of the vegetable mixture and garnish with the lemons.

Restaurant sign, Oslo, Norway.
Sole is enjoyed here as well as along the English Channel.

SOLE WITH GRAPEFRUIT

6 fillets of sole	2 tablespoons butter
¾ teaspoon paprika	2 teaspoons cornstarch
1 teaspoon onion salt	2 chicken bouillon cubes
½ cup chopped parsley	2 small pink grapefruits,
¾ cup white wine, not too dry	sectioned

Sprinkle sole fillets with paprika and onion salt. Sprinkle 1 tablespoon parsley over each fillet. Roll up, fasten with wooden picks, and place in a shallow baking dish. Pour on wine and marinate in refrigerator for several hours, turning once or twice, or spooning wine over fish rolls. Bake in a hot oven (400°F.) for about 20 minutes, until fish flakes easily, or poach in a covered skillet on top of the stove. Remove fish to a heated serving dish. Pour off liquid, strain, and measure. Add water, if necessary, to make 1 cup liquid. Melt butter and blend in cornstarch. Add the cup of poaching liquid and the chicken bouillon cubes, and heat to boiling, stirring constantly. Add grapefruit sections and remaining 2 tablespoons parsley, and heat a minute longer. Spoon over fillets, and serve at once. Makes 6 servings.

HALIBUT MARITIME CLUB "NAJADEN"
(R. Ringnes, Norsk Sjøfartsmuseums Restaurant)

5 pounds halibut, sole,	3 tablespoons flour
flounder, or other	4 cups well-seasoned
flat fish	mashed potatoes
1 large onion, quartered	2 tablespoons olive oil
2 leeks, quartered	3 egg yolks
½ celery knob, diced	garnishes (see Note)

4 tablespoons butter	½ cup whipped cream
1 onion, chopped	3 tablespoons grated
salt and white pepper	Parmesan cheese
1 cup dry white wine	

Fillet the fish. Put all the bones and trimmings in a large pot and add quartered onion, leeks and celery knob. Cover with at least 4 cups water and simmer for 30 minutes. Set aside. Spread 1 tablespoon of the butter in a shallow baking dish large enough to hold the fillets. Cover the dish with the chopped onion and sprinkle with salt and white pepper. Arrange the fish on top, pour in the wine, and cover with a sheet of foil with a few holes for steam to escape. Poach in the oven or on top of the stove until fish is just done. Pour all the juices from the fillets into a saucepan. Pour the stock made from the bones through a cloth-lined strainer into the same saucepan. Simmer over low heat for 1 hour, until reduced to about 2 cups.

Melt remaining butter in a saucepan, add flour to make a roux, and add the reduced stock, stirring well all the while. Cook until somewhat thickened. Beat the mashed potatoes over low heat until somewhat dried and warm, then beat in the olive oil and the egg yolks, one at a time. Adjust seasoning if necessary. Spoon the duchess potatoes, or pipe through a pastry bag, around the edges of a large heatproof china or silver platter. Place the cooked fillets in the center, and arrange the garnishes on the fillets. Fold the whipped cream into the thickened sauce, and pour about half of it over the fish and garnishes. Sprinkle the cheese on top, and heat the platter in the broiler until everything is hot and well gilded on the top. Serve the rest of the sauce separately. Makes 8 servings.

NOTE: The garnish of shellfish and vegetables can be varied according to season. Cooked shrimps, mussels and clams with mushrooms and asparagus tips make a good combination for color and taste.

HALIBUT STEAK WITH ORANGE-GRAPE SAUCE

4 halibut steaks,	½ cup cold water
¾ inch thick	2 teaspoons
2 cups boiling water	grated orange rind
2 tablespoons plus	1 can (11 ounces)
1 teaspoon lemon juice	mandarin orange
1 teaspoon salt	segments, drained
1 tablespoon cornstarch	1 cup seeded
1 tablespoon sugar	green grape halves
½ cup orange juice	

Rinse steaks and pat dry. Place steaks in a well greased large frypan. Add boiling water, 2 tablespoons lemon juice and the salt. Cover; simmer until fish flakes easily when tested with a fork, 8 to 10 minutes. While fish is cooking, prepare sauce. Combine cornstarch and sugar in small saucepan. Stir in orange juice and cold water. Cook slowly, stirring constantly, until thickened. Stir in orange rind, 1 teaspoon lemon juice and the fruits; heat. Transfer cooked drained fish carefully to a hot serving platter. Spoon sauce over halibut. Makes 4 servings.

FLOUNDER WITH CRAB STUFFING

6 pan-dressed flounder, ¾ pound each, or
  1 large flounder, about 3 pounds
Crab Stuffing (recipe follows)
¼ pound butter or margarine, melted
¼ cup lemon juice
2 teaspoons salt
2 tablesppons water
paprika

Rinse flounder and pat dry. To make a pocket for stuffing, lay the fish flat on a cutting board, light side down. With a sharp knife cut down the center of the fish along the backbone from the tail to about 1 inch from the head end. Turn the knife flat and cut the flesh along both sides of the backbone to the tail, allowing the knife to run over the rib bones. Stuff fish loosely. Combine butter, lemon juice, salt and water. Place fish in a well-greased baking pan. Pour butter mixture over fish. Sprinkle with paprika. Bake in a moderate oven (350°F.) for 30 to 40 minutes, or until fish flakes easily when tested with a fork. Makes 6 servings.

CRAB STUFFING

1 pound blue crab meat	⅓ cup melted fat or oil
½ cup chopped onion	2 cups soft bread cubes
⅓ cup chopped celery	3 eggs, beaten
⅓ cup chopped green pepper	1 tablespoon chopped parsley
2 garlic cloves, chopped fine	2 teaspoons salt
	½ teaspoon pepper

Pick over crab meat to remove any remaining shell or cartilage. Cook onion, celery, green pepper and garlic in fat until tender. Combine bread cubes, eggs, parsley, salt, pepper, cooked vegetables and crab meat; mix thoroughly. Makes about 6 cups stuffing.

Squid

Despite a relatively small market in the U.S., squids are utilized throughout the world as food. A highly specialized mollusk, the squid has 10 arms and a long cigar-shaped body with fins at the end. Squids swim backward or forward with amazing rapidity, using the funnel, or siphon, for propulsion, jet-fashion, the fins assisting in steering. A sac contains ink which may be emptied at the time of sudden propulsion, with the result that a dark cloud of ink appears as a "phantom" squid to a predator while the real squid evades capture. Some squids regularly "fly" or glide over the surface of the water.

Squids are voracious predators, feeding on small and large fishes of all types as well as on other squids. Squids as small as 1 inch travel in large schools, while giant squids, which may exceed 60 feet, evidently are more solitary. They live near the surface to depths of a mile, often coming to the top at night to feed on fishes following the migrating plankton. This nocturnal movement is the key to capturing squid. The squid schools are located during daylight hours with a depth recorder. The vessel is then anchored over the concentration and at dusk attractor lights are turned on and the squids gather at the surface. Squids can be netted or sucked directly into the hold of a ship with a large hydraulic pump.

The squid is a remarkable food in that 80 percent of this cephalopod is edible, which is an unusually large proportion when compared to finfish or most crustaceans. Its lean meat contains about 18 percent protein which makes it highly nutritious. Ironically, it's one of the most abundant marine organisms but far from overutilized; it has been estimated that the annual potential catch is within the range of 100 to 300 million tons. Squids are marketed in fresh, frozen, salted, semipreserved (pickled in vinegar after boiling), sun-dried and canned forms. The firm flesh, which turns yellow after cooking, is delicately flavored and finds its largest audience among Mediterranean and Oriental ethnic groups. Squid can be panfried, deep-fried, stir-fried, baked, boiled, and used in salads or in pasta sauces. Classically, the very small squids are cooked whole, often stuffed, while the body of larger squids is cut into rings and pieces.

The squid *Loligo opalescens*, caught in great quantities in the Monterey Bay region of California, is one of the best of all cephalopods from a culinary standpoint. Split and dressed, then dipped into a light batter, it should be cooked only until it is light golden brown. No squid is naturally tough, the flesh only becomes rubbery

HOW TO DRESS SQUID

Squid

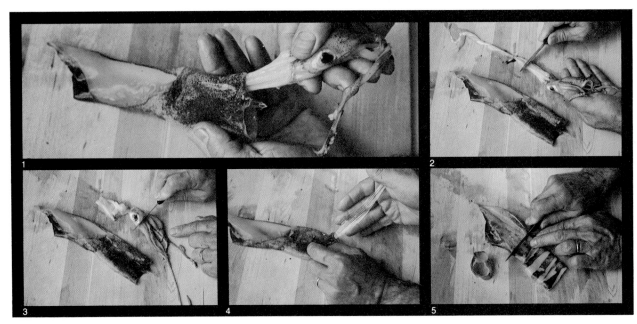

1. Separate head and tentacles from the body.
2. Remove the mantle. **3.** Separate tentacles from head, and discard the head.
4. Remove the pen (the rudimentary shell). **5.** Cut the squid into rings.

through overcooking. Sun-dried squid, which is popular in the Orient, is made tough by the drying method but in this case the squid is eaten by picking the flesh apart and nibbling on it, rather than cooking it.

Squid in its ink (**Calamare en su Tinta**) is a very popular dish in Spain, and among the Basque people (where the name for squid becomes **txipirones)** it is a national dish. According to José Luis del Val who supervised our gourmet dinner in San Sebastián, squids should be cleaned the day before cooking and allowed to "rest" for at least 12 hours to become firm and release their flavor. One person can eat several small squids (about 6 inches in body length); the larger ones are normally reserved for **paella**. Garlic could be added to the following recipe although it is not used in this simple Basque version.

TXIPIRONES EN SU TINTA
(Basque Gastronomical Society, San Sebastián, Spain)

9 small squids	2 slices of bread
3 onions	1 cup olive oil
¼ cup chopped parsley	(fine grade)
1 tomato	bread crumbs

Separate the head and the tentacles of the squids. When doing this, the pen, called the "sword" in Spanish, will come out as the head and tentacles are pulled apart. Remove purplish skin with hands. Pull off two side fins. Turn body inside out; wash with running water. (Body is white at this point.) Put aside fins and tentacles. When the head is pulled off, the ink sac will be found inside the body. Remove sac gently, and put in a cup or dish with a little water. (Ink at this point is still contained inside the sac, which has fragile skin.) Put aside.

Make the stuffing: Finely chop the tentacles and fins which were removed from the squids. Dice 1 onion, add chopped parsley, and mix together. Put aside.

Make the sauce: Peel the tomato, discard seeds, and chop fine. Chop remaining onions fine, and dice the bread. Combine all these in a pan with olive oil. Cook slowly until the mixture looks good. When done, add a handful of bread crumbs and mix in.

Fill body cavities of squids with prepared stuffing, using fingers or a spoon. Close at top with a wooden food pick. Put stuffed squids in sauce in a frying pan. Cook *very* slowly. When meat turns yellow, remove

Basque Gastronomical Society, San Sebastián, Spain. This recreational society, for men only, has existed since 1914. Fish is served at most meals, accompanied by fermented cider or a local green wine. The "honest, serious and merry" members sweeten their gastronomy with singing.

TXIPIRONES EN SU TINTA (SQUID IN ITS INK)

(prepared by Chef José Luis del Val and Gregorio Yaben at the Basque Gastronomical Society, San Sebastián, Spain)

1. Make a stuffing with chopped squid tentacles, onion and parsley. 2. Stuff the squid bodies with the mixture.
3. Close each one at the top with a wooden food pick.
4. Mix squid ink with cooked tomato sauce. 5. Strain sauce over sautéed squids. 6. Sauced squids are put back over low heat to simmer for 10 minutes. 7. Squid in its ink ready to serve.

squids from the sauce, and place in a shallow earthenware or heatproof glass dish. Mix ink, still sitting in water, with the cooked sauce. Remove pan from heat and strain sauce through a sieve directly onto the squids in the earthenware dish. (Ink bags will disappear.) Put whole dish back over very low heat and simmer for 10 minutes. Makes 3 servings.

SQUID NEAPOLITAN STYLE

2 pounds squids	1 tablespoon
1 garlic clove, sliced	seedless raisins
3 tablespoons butter	1 tablespoon
2 cups canned	chopped pine nuts
peeled tomatoes	½ cup water
salt and pepper	toast slices
12 black olives,	
pitted and chopped	

Cut squids into small pieces, and wash well. Brown the garlic in the butter in a saucepan. Remove the garlic from the saucepan and add the tomatoes, a generous sprinkle of salt and pepper, and the squids. Cover the pan and simmer for 10 minutes. Add the black olives, raisins, pine nuts and water. Cover the pan, and cook for another 10 minutes, or until the squids are tender. Arrange slices of toast in serving bowls, and spoon the squids and sauce over the toast just before serving. Makes 4 servings.

SQUID IN MUSHROOM SAUCE

2 pounds squids	½ cup dry white wine
½ cup olive oil	or dry vermouth
1 garlic clove, chopped	2 tablespoons tomato sauce
3 anchovy fillets,	salt and pepper
chopped	4 ounces canned mushrooms
1 teaspoon minced parsley	with juice

Cut squids into small pieces, and wash well. Heat the olive oil in a saucepan; then add the garlic, anchovies and parsley. While this simmers, pour in the wine or vermouth. Next, add tomato sauce, a generous dash of salt and pepper, and the mushrooms including the juice; then put in the squids. Cover the pan. Cook over medium heat for about 10 minutes. Test squid with a fork for tenderness. Makes 4 servings.

Stockfish

A term for gutted, headed, split or unsplit cod, haddock, pollock or hake, dried in the sun and wind without salt to a moisture content of about 15 percent. The product is shrunken and tough and requires prolonged soaking in a milk alkali solution before cooking. Stockfish is mainly prepared in Iceland, Norway and Sweden, where it's also called **tørrfisk.** Although the market for stockfish is not as great today as it has been in the past (Norway alone exported 50 to 55 million pounds to Africa in one recent year), it's evidently more highly regarded than it was in Shakespeare's day when Falstaff sought the ultimate expression in berating Prince Henry: "... you starveling, you elf-skin, you dried neat's-tongue, you bull's pizzle, you stockfish ... " (*Henry IV*, Part I, Act II, Scene 4).

Stocks

In fish cookery the use of stock rather than plain water will greatly enhance many recipes such as soups or chowders. Stocks also provide extra flavor when poaching fish of any kind or in cooking shellfish such as lobster or crab. When a stock is made with suitable fish trimmings, it can be clarified and reduced as a base for many sauces or made into a delicious aspic. Even a small amount of this jellied essence can be combined with white wine and cream to make a delightful sauce.

There are 2 basic cooking liquids in the seafood kitchen. The first is a court bouillon made of vegetables and seasonings which are simmered (never boiled) in water to which vinegar or wine has been added. It usually takes 40 minutes to 1 hour to obtain a good broth, after which the solids are strained out. Such a court bouillon is ideal for poaching a whole fish or large cuts that retain some skin and bone, which in turn will add their own juices to the liquid; this can be reduced to make a sauce or can be frozen for future use.

The other basic liquid is stock, which I consider extremely important—a *fumet* made by simmering the heads, bones and skins (scaled of course) of the fish with a few aromatic vegetables such as onions, leeks, carrots and celery with its greens. The key to making a flavorsome *fumet* is the fish head, as this portion contains a fine gelatin. Some species are superior to others for this purpose; the head of a red or mutton snapper, cod, grouper or striped bass produces a rich stock that can be kept indefinitely in the freezer. The only fish skins I would not use are those of the Pacific barracuda, snook and black bass, and the dark skin of soles as these impart an off-flavor.

Bear in mind that while fish trimmings make the ideal stock for sauces, beef, veal and chicken bones can be used for the same purpose. Obviously, those other ingredients will not produce a fish *fumet,* but a clarified brown stock can be used to make a **Sauce Espagnole,** for example, which is a fine contrast for many fish with an assertive flavor. Animal bones should be roasted in a hot oven until slightly brown before making a stock, because this will improve its flavor and color.

My introduction to the world of the professional *saucier* occurred at the Ritz Hotel in Paris, when my good friend Charles was kind enough to allow me to work with an apprentice. This lasted all of 3 days, at which point I never wanted to see another bone as they seemed to arrive by truck loads each morning and the heat of the ovens was equatorial. Even more discouraging was the fact that ingredients tended to run into weights such as 50 kilos of veal bones, or 20 kilos of fish bones, with volumes of liquids that defied my conversion of liters into quarts. The only thing I learned from my soggy notebook was how to make a lifetime supply of stock on a daily basis, as stocks are the "life blood" of *haute cuisine,* and a veritable river of sauces emerges from the classic French kitchen. Many recipes cannot be arrived at by "reduction," i.e., by using the measurements prescribed for 100 servings and reducing each ingredient proportionately to serve 10 people. The essential alchemy does not exist in arithmetic. The following basic brown stock is generally based on professional methods and ingredients but only after trial and error on my part to arrive at a family supply of 3 quarts, which is a practical volume to freeze and use as the occasion requires. Brown stock is, of course, converted into brown sauce and although usually identified with animal meats it has many delicious applications to fish cookery.

BROWN STOCK

4 to 5 pounds veal bones, sawed into small pieces	2 celery ribs including greens, chopped
¼ cup vegetable oil	1½ cups tomato purée
2 carrots, peeled and chopped	4 garlic cloves, crushed
1 medium-size onion, peeled and halved	2 bay leaves
1 large leek, white part only, chopped	3 cloves
	1 teaspoon whole peppercorns
	1 gallon water
	salt

Brown the bones in a roasting pan at 450°F. After they have acquired color, about 30 minutes, add the oil and vegetables and brown the vegetables with the bones for another 30 minutes.

Place the bones and vegetables in a 3-gallon stockpot and add tomato purée, garlic, bay leaves, spices and water. Deglaze the roasting pan with a little water and add this to the stockpot. Simmer, uncovered, for 12 hours. If in the last few hours it looks as if the liquid is evaporating too fast, add more water to compensate. Add salt to taste at the end of the cooking. Strain and cool the stock, then refrigerate. Discard any fat that has risen to the surface. Makes about 3 quarts.
NOTE: This stock can be frozen. 1-cup and 2-cup containers are the most practical sizes. Quart containers take too long to defrost.

WHITE STOCK

3 pounds slices of veal shin	2 tablespoons chopped parsley stems
2 pounds chicken wings	1 bay leaf
5 quarts water	2 white peppercorns, crushed
3 large leeks, thoroughly washed	1 teaspoon salt
4 celery ribs with leaves	

Put veal and chicken in a 2-gallon stockpot and cover with cold water. Bring to a boil and continue to boil for 2 or 3 minutes. Pour off the water, rinse the bones and meat, clean the pot, and return the bones and meat to the pot. Cover with 5 quarts of water. Once again bring to a boil and then reduce to a simmer. During the first hour skim the surface occasionally. Chop leeks and celery and add along with parsley stems and bay leaf. Simmer, uncovered, for 4 hours. Add more water if needed to keep the bones covered, and at this point add the peppercorns. Simmer for another hour and taste. If necessary cook longer to have the intensity of flavor you want. Add salt only at the very end and let the stock remain only delicately salted. Strain through a coarse sieve to discard all large pieces. (The veal can be retrieved and used for something else; while it is possible to retrieve some pieces from the larger section of the chicken wings, it is a lot of work and the meat will mostly be cooked to shreds.) Then strain the stock once again through a sieve lined with a moistened flannel or a triple layer of cheesecloth. Let the stock chill, and discard any fat that has risen to the top. Makes about 2½ quarts.
NOTES: This stock can be frozen; 1-cup and 2-cup containers are the most practical sizes.

To make an all-veal stock, omit chicken; but with veal alone it is better to cook this longer—6 to 8 hours. If you use a veal knuckle, which will give additional gelatin, be sure to cook for at least 8 hours. To make an all-chicken stock, omit veal and cook for 3 hours, or less.

The flavor of this stock can be adjusted by adding more of one flavoring vegetable or another, or by adding different vegetables. A particular herb—tarragon, fennel leaves or seeds, fresh dill, or various members of the thyme family—can be added to develop a particular flavor. Only remember that any flavor added at the outset will be very concentrated at the end.

WHITE-WINE FISH STOCK (FUMET DE POISSON)

2 pounds	4 cups white wine
fish heads and bones	4 cups water
3 tablespoons oil	dash of dried fennel
⅓ cup chopped onions	4 parsley sprigs
⅓ cup sliced carrots	1 bay leaf
⅓ cup sliced celery	salt and pepper

Heat oil. Cook vegetables in oil until they just begin to color. Add wine, water and fish bones. Bring to a boil. Skim. Add fennel, parsley and bay leaf. Simmer for 2 hours. Strain through cheesecloth. Season with salt and pepper to taste. Makes 3 cups.

If this is to be used for aspic, or for any other recipe that requires a crystal-clear stock, clarify it *(see under ASPIC).*

RED-WINE FISH STOCK

2 pounds fish heads,	2 garlic cloves, crushed
bones and trimmings	1 teaspoon dried thyme
8 cups water	1 teaspoon dried tarragon
4 cups red wine	1 celery rib with leaves
½ cup wine vinegar	12 peppercorns
1 large onion,	1 bay leaf
stuck with 3 cloves	3 parsley sprigs
2 carrots, sliced	2 tablespoons salt

Combine all ingredients except salt in a large pot. Bring the mixture to a full rolling boil and boil it for 5 minutes. Reduce heat to a simmer, cover the pan, and simmer for 1 hour. Strain liquid. Add as much of the salt as needed. Makes 6 to 8 cups.

This stock can be clarified *(see under ASPIC)* and can be used to make aspic with the addition of a little extra gelatin.

A court bouillon is *court* (short) because it is a bouillon without meat or fish. It can be as simple as water with crab boil, or it can have as many ingredients as a fish stock without the fish heads and bones.

Crab boil is a mixture of herbs and spices, readily available in southern states and around the Chesapeake area, and increasingly appearing in northern markets. Each packer has his own recipe, but most include chopped chilies, whole allspice berries, mustard seeds, peppercorns, broken bay leaves and some crumbled leaf herbs. Court bouillon for shrimps, crabs, lobsters and lobster tails can be made by adding 2 to 3 tablespoons crab boil and 2 tablespoons salt to 2 quarts water. Bring the water to a boil, then simmer for 15 to 20 minutes. Drop the shellfish into the simmering liquid and count the cooking time according to the kind from the moment the court bouillon comes to the boil again. For juicy shellfish undercook slightly and let them cool in the court bouillon.

Shrimps and lobster tails can be shelled before or after cooking. Uusually it's best when they are shelled first to tie the spice mixture in a cheesecloth bag so the bits do not stick to the meat. (Some companies pack their crab boil in little packets.)

Fish can also be cooked in this kind of court bouillon. Simmer the liquid until it is well flavored, then let it cool before straining it over the fish. Even with other kinds of court bouillon, the liquid should be cooled before it is poured over the fish or before the fish is lowered into it so that the fish skin is not torn or the flesh broken apart.

WHITE-WINE COURT BOUILLON

8 cups water
4 cups dry white wine
3 large onions, chopped
2 celery ribs with leaves, chopped
4 tablespoons chopped parsley stems
1 sprig of fresh thyme, or ½ teaspoon dried
2 bay leaves, broken up
6 white peppercorns, cracked in a mortar
1 tablespoon salt

Put everything in a large pot and bring to a boil. Simmer for 1 hour. Let cool, and strain before using. Makes about 2 quarts.

RED-WINE COURT BOUILLON

Follow the recipe for White-Wine Court Bouillon, but use dry red wine instead of white. Omit celery and add 2 carrots, chopped, and 2 large leeks, carefully washed and chopped. Use black peppercorns instead of white if you like.

Scottish fishing boat; baskets are used for storing and unloading fish

VINEGAR COURT BOUILLON

8 cups water

1 cup vinegar

2 large onions, sliced

2 carrots, sliced

¼ cup chopped celery leaves

4 whole cloves

4 allspice berries

6 black peppercorns,

    cracked in a mortar

1 tablespoon salt

Combine everything in a large kettle and bring to a boil. Simmer for about 1 hour. Let cool, and strain. Makes 6 to 7 cups.

The vinegar you use will make a difference. White-wine or red-wine vinegar, or cider vinegar, or an herb vinegar such as tarragon or dill vinegar, can be used. Adjust the other seasonings as you like. Fresh dill or fresh fennel can be added to this.

MILK COURT BOUILLON

Mix in these proportions: 4 cups water, 1 cup milk, 1 tablespoon lemon juice, 2 teaspoons salt, 2 white peppercorns, cracked in a mortar. Double or triple as needed.

This kind of court bouillon is used for fish with white flesh, such as members of the cod family. This can be used without simmering first.

Striped Bass

As Captain John Smith nosed the *Susan Constant* into Chesapeake Bay in the year 1607, with the *Godspeed* and *Discovery* to windward, he saw the endless horizons of the Maryland and Virginia shores where wild geese rose in great honking legions and giant sturgeons leaped in the air "forty at a time." There are more miles of coastline contained within this Bay than along the entire U.S. mainland from Maine to the State of Washington. The ship's stores were low but under their keels was a treasure trove of seafoods. From the salt-diluting currents of the mighty Rappahannock, Potomac, Susquehanna and lesser rivers the improbably pure water nurtured blue crabs, soft clams and oysters that ripened like grapes on a vine—bursting with the sweet promise of a maiden's kiss. Although the adventurer from Lincolnshire was to suffer many defeats and be tormented by his peers (the Kingdom had a more tangible wealth in mind), he correctly estimated its value: "Let not the meanness of the word fish distaste you, for it will afford as good gold as the Mines of Guiana or Potassie . . ." While the veracity of Smith's accounts was questioned on a number of subjects, as few of his countrymen shared the visionary faith in the New World, the Captain's observations on striped bass after settling at Jamestown are perhaps less an exaggeration than an impossible-to-estimate situation.

The Basse is an excellent Fish, both fresh and salte, one hundred whereof salted (at market) have yielded 5 pounds. They are so large, the head of one will give a good eater a dinner, and for daintinesse of diet they excell the Marybones of Beefe. There are such multitudes that I have seene stopped close in the river adjoining to my house with a sande at one tyde so many as will loade a ship of 100 tonnes. I myselfe, at the turning of the tyde have seene such multitudes pass out of a pounde that it seemed to me that one might go over their backs drishod.

I have seen salmon runs in remote rivers of Alaska and char migrations in the Arctic that can only be described as vast squirming masses of fish with their backs out of water as they churned over a gravel bar on a changing tide. The bounty of an unspoiled environment is awesome, and the abundance of striped bass in these early days would be difficult to imagine. Their value and inevitable depletion was prophetically realized by the colonists shortly after landing at Plymouth. When the *Mayflower* left Delfshaven, Holland, it was headed for Captain John Smith's Virginia Colony, but the 102 souls aboard suffered from *mal de mer* in the face of gales and a dwindling food supply "especially our beer." They were forced to seek a more northerly landfall and thus they arrived in Massachusetts. In the summer of 1623 the colonists finally launched a single boat, and striped bass were so abundant here that they could net enough to feed everybody for "three months space." The early settlers preferred striped bass to the princely salmon which was in great plenty at that time. William Wood observed: *The Basse is one of the best fishes in the Countrey, and though men are soone wearied with other fish, yet are they never with Basse. It is a delicate, fine fat, fast fish, having a bone in his head, which contains a sawcerfull of marrow, sweet and good, pleasant to the pallat, and wholesome to the stomach. When there be a great store of them, we only eate the heads, and salt up the bodies for winter.* (*New England's Prospects*, William Wood, London, 1634) Wood goes on to describe how the striped bass were caught with a heavy cod line, using lobster as bait. Then, lending support to Captain John Smith's estimate of this resource, he described how . . . *the English at the top of high water do crosse the creekes with long seanes or Basse Nets, which stop the fish; and the water ebbing from them they are left on the dry ground, sometimes two to three thousand at a set, which are salted up against winter.*

During the next 16 years catching striped bass accelerated, not only for food but to fertilize farm crops. The harvest consistently diminished until 1639 when the General Court of Massachusetts Bay Colony ordered that neither bass nor cod could be used as fertilizer. A subsequent act of the Plymouth Colony in 1670 provided that all income incurred annually from the fisheries at Cape Cod for bass, mackerel or herring be used to establish a free school in some town of the area. As a result of this legislation the first public school in the New World was made possible through funds obtained largely from the sale of striped bass.

Despite intensive fishing pressure in the years following, our bass population proliferated well into the twentieth century, but the giant sizes reported by Jordan and Evermann (*American Food and Game Fishes*, 1902) no longer exist. In the states surrounding Chesapeake Bay the striped bass is still called "rockfish," a misnomer, but a traditional soubriquet among tidewater commercials.

On May 6, 1896, 38,000 pounds of rockfish were landed in one haul. Among them were about 600 fish that averaged 60 pounds each, and several that weighed 105 pounds each. The roe of one fish weighed 44 pounds.

Some very large fish have been reported. Dr. Henshall saw one weighed in Baltimore which tipped the beam at more than 100 pounds; one taken in Cuttyhunk weighed 104 pounds; and Dr. Goode records an example caught at Orleans which weighed 112 pounds and which must have been 6 feet long.

In the same year that Jordan and Evermann were recording the last of the giants, this fish which nourished the early settlers and helped build their schools was now seeding the genesis of our American social scene.

As a fashionable pastime, striped bass fishing achieved status before the Civil War when Secretary of State Daniel Webster went by horse-and-carriage to what is now the Chain Bridge on the Potomac to cast a fly in its spring currents for the sporty "rockfish." In subsequent years Congressman Robert Barnwell Roosevelt and Presidents Grover Cleveland and Theodore Roosevelt became Potomac regulars after a hard day's work on the Hill. By 1870 "associations of gentlemen" were being formed in New England dedicated solely to the capture of striped bass. It was not by chance that the island of Newport off the coast of Rhode Island gave birth to Ward McAllister's now famous list of "The Four Hundred." The ancestral Stuyvesants, Tiffanys, Rhinelanders, Astors, Vanderbilts, Lorillards and related *haute monde* had simply trod the well-blazed trail of bass angling clubs which included among other outposts Point Judith, Narragansett, West Island, Cuttyhunk, Gay Head, Pasque Island, Squibnocket and Bar Harbor. It was a final touch of irony that the fish which filled the bellies of early colonists should "make" the social register.

The striped bass is an anadromous fish like the salmon, a saltwater inhabitant dependent on freshwater rivers for its reproduction. In the Atlantic, it ranges from the Gulf of St. Lawrence to the St. Johns River in northern Florida and as token population in the Gulf of Mexico from western Florida to Louisiana. The fish is most common from Cape Cod to South Carolina, a region which has suffered not only intensive commercial exploitation and pollution but a critical loss of spawning areas. The tributaries of Chesapeake Bay and the Hudson River are still major breeding grounds, and these two watersheds supply virtually all of the fish now caught along our Atlantic Coast as they migrate to and from their wintering areas. One of the more spectacular runs occurs just a few hours drive from Manhattan each autumn at Montauk Point, the easternmost tip of Long Island.

Although the summer season is bedlam today, in that October hiatus, when sunburned tourists have long abandoned the parish and the first northeaster hisses through the dune grass as rolling breakers pound against the rocks, surf casters assume their lonely vigil, whipping their baits high in an opaque sky. Sandpipers trade down the beaches while terns and gulls ceasely argue in squalling food talk. The Point was considered the end of the world when I was in short pants; deer grazed side-by-side in the bent, wind-tortured scrub oak and red foxes stalked coveys of quail around the lighthouse which was erected by order of President George Washington in 1796. Our family used to "motor" to Montauk from Hampton Bays

to gather cranberries at Fort Pond--an occasion that always included an afternoon of fishing for striped bass. Cranberries were Grandma's last cold-weather canning project for the year. Herbert Hoover was in the White House then; after not finding the promised "chicken in every pot" Grandma virtually cornered the market on Mason jars; any food that grew, wild or cultivated, had its assigned shelf in her cellar. By the time the old Studebaker returned to our salt-rimed shack late of a Saturday night, a twelve-year old boy felt like one big goose pimple. But her glowing wood stove worked its miracle as we sat down to the serious business of eating bass simmered in seawater with bay leaves and peppercorns, then bathed in what was probably 95-score butter. The world flickered silver in the magic of moonlight behind scudding clouds, and the last sounds I remember were the low boom of a gong buoy counterpointing a flight of Canadian geese as they honked along their invisible road south.

When her Majesty Queen Elizabeth and Prince Philip dined at the Waldorf in 1957, Claude Philippe, with a Gallic regard for Americana, had prepared 4,500 pounds of striped bass for the royal feast. Monsieur Philippe, who currently heads the Lucullus Circle in New York, presented the fish with a champagne sauce surrounded by golden fleurons. The bass had been caught a scant 24 hours before in the salty waters of Montauk. Her Majesty pronounced the fish a culinary masterpiece, and somehow it seemed that Captain John Smith had triumphed in the end.

FACTORS AFFECTING QUALITY

Although modern sportsmen eagerly seek trophy bass of over 50 pounds (the rod-and-reel record is 73 pounds from Vineyard Sound, Massachusetts) the anomaly is that stripers are at their peak for table in weights from 6 to 8 pounds. As the fish grows heavier, its flesh becomes more coarse; although large bass can be steaked and broiled or flaked for salads, they are not nearly as tasty as the young fish. Bass is magnificent when fresh, dressed and iced shortly after being caught, but something less than magnificent if it spends several days in transit to the marketplace. In large cities like New York, where the striper is heavily utilized by Japanese restaurants in making **sashimi**, fast delivery plus critical buying assures a prime product. The amateur angler is perhaps more inclined to mistreat his catch by leaving it ungutted and without ice in warm air. Ironically, the striper is one of few fish that does *not* require prompt field dressing to be edible. Unlike the softer-fleshed companion species such as bluefish,

mackerel or weakfish, which would quickly deteriorate under similar conditions, the firm-fleshed striper withstands abuse sufficiently to be cooked—but not enjoyed. Freshness is a quality required of all seafoods but the *degree* of freshness is commensurate with flavor in striped bass cookery. Aside from the basic tenets of judging a fish (bright unsunken eyes, red-colored gillrakers, and a firm body which allows no indentation when pressed with your fingers), a fresh striped bass should be silvery and sparkling in appearance; as the time out of water increases, the skin of the fish will become more reddish in color and ultimately a dull red-black. This is a capillary reaction.

The second factor affecting quality is the purity of the water from which the bass was caught. Fortunately to the conservationist, but unfortunately for the innocent chef, striped bass displays a considerable tolerance for polluted environments; unless you know its origin you will need senescent taste buds to enjoy the meal. It's not a question of toxicity but one of flavor. A fish taken in Jamaica Bay, the lower Hudson, or similar metropolitan wastelands may be tainted with fuel oil while a striper emerging from the cold Atlantic off Montauk or Cape Cod is sweet and unsullied.

In 1879 the striped bass was transplanted to our Pacific Coast, and its range here extends from the Columbia River in Washington to southern California with centers of abundance in Coos Bay, Oregon, and the San Francisco Bay region. Although this fish has not achieved the popularity in the West which it has enjoyed in regional eastern cookery, due to the abundance of more desirable salmon, it remains seasonally important.

There are landlocked populations of striped bass in our south Atlantic and southwestern states, notably South Carolina and Oklahoma, but in general it might be observed that their flesh quality is inferior to a prime fish taken from saltwater.

EUROPEAN BASS

From a culinary standpoint all that can be said of the striped bass applies to its close relative, the bass along Europe's shores in the eastern Atlantic and Mediterranean (also called gray bass, European sea bass, white sea perch, salmon-bass, and known in French cuisine simply as **bar** or **loup**). Both are members of the Percichthyidae. While the European bass is blue-gray and silver in color, lacking the prominent black lateral markings of our striped bass, one can find little difference in their flesh texture and flavor. Although the European bass does not grow as large as the striper (it seldom exceeds 20 pounds), the same preference is shown among gourmets for the smaller fish at table. Thus, a recipe such as **Bar en Croûte Brillat-Savarin** produces essentially the same results on both sides of the Atlantic. In Europe, the ambulant diner will find the bass on menus or in the market as **Wolfsbarsch** (Germany), **Havåbor** (Norway), **Havsaborre** (Sweden), **Bars** (Denmark), **Zeebaars** (Holland), **Roballo** (Portugal), **Lubina** (Spain), **Spigola** (Italy), **Lubin** (Yugoslavia), **Lavraki** (Greece).

OTHER TEMPERATE BASSES

GIANT SEA BASS The largest of the temperate basses, sometimes called black sea bass and jewfish but not related to either species. The giant sea bass *(Stereolepis gigas)* is strictly a Pacific form, taken mainly in the southern California to Cabo San Lucas, Mexico, area. It grows to a weight of over 500 pounds. Adult fish are dark brown to blackish in color and generally resemble the true jewfish *(see under GROUPER)*. In common with groupers the flesh of giant sea bass is white, lean, and almost bland in flavor. It is totally unlike the related striped bass in a culinary sense. A minor market item, as these huge fish are not abundant, the bulk of its landings arrive in San Diego and Los Angeles from the Mexican fishery. Giant sea bass can be treated according to any grouper recipe.

WHITE BASS The white bass *(Morone chrysops)* is a small freshwater panfish related to the striped bass. It usually runs ½ to 2 pounds but in some waters 3- and 4-pounders are caught. At the turn of the century its distribution was limited to the Great Lakes south to Missouri and from the west slope of the Allegheny Mountains to Mississippi. The extensive construction of impoundments in our southern and southwestern states has greatly increased its range and popularity. In recent years, the annual catch by anglers in Oklahoma alone has averaged about 2½ million pounds, which is comparable to the entire commercial catch in Lake Erie. The white bass vaguely resembles a small striped bass in having about 10 narrow dark stripes along its sides although it has a more compressed body and is silvery in color. It is found in large clearwater lakes as well as rivers. This is a tasty panfish that can be cut out into boneless fillets and panfried or deep-fried, or loosely wrapped in foil with butter, salt and pepper, to be cooked in the oven or on a charcoal grill. The meat is usually white but sometimes has a pinkish color.

YELLOW BASS The yellow bass *(Morone mississippiensis)* is also a freshwater panfish but somewhat smaller than the white bass, running from ¼ to 1 pound. The yellow bass is not as widely distributed as the white and is found mainly in our Midwest, from southern Minnesota, Wisconsin and Michigan to Alabama, Louisiana and east Texas. It resembles the white bass in shape but has only 6 or 7 dark stripes on its often bright yellow sides. Its flesh is considered by some anglers (this species is not taken commercially) to be superior and is often compared to the yellow perch in being firm, white and flaky. This is probably a condition of habitat, as anatomically the white and yellow bass are the same. Either fish can be used in perch recipes.

POACHED STRIPED BASS WITH CAPER SAUCE

1 striped bass,	2 cups white wine
6 to 8 pounds,	(Chablis or Sauternes)
whole-dressed and scaled	2 cups water
1 lemon, sliced thin	2½ cups Caper Sauce
1 onion, sliced thin	(p. 288)
4 celery ribs	
including leaves, chopped	

Place sliced lemon, sliced onion and celery ribs on the bottom of a poacher. Lay bass on the rack and place in the poacher. Pour the wine and water over fish, cover, and poach gently for 30 minutes, or until the bass tests done. Arrange bass on a platter and peel off visible skin. Strain the cooking liquid and use to make caper sauce. Spoon the sauce over the fish. Makes 6 servings.

BAR EN CROÛTE BRILLAT-SAVARIN

1 striped bass,	½ teaspoon dried thyme
6 to 8 pounds,	2 bay leaves, crushed
whole-dressed and scaled	salt and pepper
2 ounces fresh tarragon	Puff Pastry (recipe follows)
(1 small bunch)	1 egg, beaten

This is a *tour de force* for beginners, both in skinning the bass and making a decorative puff pastry. Begin the skinning operation with a cut around the tail, just penetrating the skin; then make a similar incision along the full length of the back or dorsal surface. Lift the skin free with a knife point, then gently pull it downward from the back, rolling the flap off without breaking it. Bone the bass by cutting through the full length of the ventral or underside of the bass but do not split the fish. The bass must remain whole. Sprinkle herbs inside of fish. Salt and pepper inside and out.

Make 2 layers of puff pastry, each ⅓ inch thick, and place the fish in between layers. Cut off excess, making the remaining pastry follow the shape of the fish. Using a knife, decorate the pastry to create "scales."

Brush pastry all over with the beaten egg. Bake in a 350°F. oven for 40 to 45 minutes. Serve with Sauce Choron *(see under SAUCES)*. Makes 6 servings.

PUFF PASTRY

1½ cups sifted flour
½ teaspoon salt
¼ cup ice water
½ pound butter, very cold

Sift flour and salt together. Stir in water with a fork, then knead dough until it is satiny smooth and elastic.

On a floured board, roll out the dough into 2 neat rectangles, each about 6 inches wide by 11 inches long.

Slice each ¼-pound stick of butter 3 times lengthwise, and put 3 slices on the upper half of each rectangle, laying them across the width and leaving a ½-inch margin. Fold the lower half of the dough up over the butter and press the edges together. Bang the dough with a rolling pin several times to flatten the butter, then roll out each packet to a sheet 18 inches long and 6 inches wide. Fold dough from one end to center, then fold the other end over that. It is important to keep rectangles with neat edges and to work quickly so that the butter does not get too soft. Wrap each piece in aluminum foil and chill for 30 minutes. Take out one piece and place on a board so that the narrow ends of the rectangle are parallel to the edge of the table nearest you. Roll lengthwise from short end to short end, again to 18 inches in length, and fold as before. Repeat with the second piece. This is called a "turn." After each "turn" the dough is refrigerated again for 30 minutes. Give it at least 5 turns. Keep in the refrigerator until ready to bake, or freeze for future use.

STRIPED BASS ON FLAMING FENNEL WITH PERNOD
(The Four Seasons, New York City)

1 striped bass,
  6 to 8 pounds,
  whole-dressed and scaled
24 dried fennel twigs
salt and pepper
1 pound butter

10 shallots, chopped
1 pound mushrooms, sliced
2 cups fish stock
2 cups dry white wine
2 ounces Pernod,
  approximately

Score bass with 3 or 4 incisions on facing side. Insert 1 fennel twig in each incision. Season inside of fish with salt and pepper and insert 6 to 8 fennel twigs in the cavity. Dot the bottom of fish cooker or large roasting pan

Striped bass on flaming fennel with Pernod, prepared at The Four Seasons, New York City with half of the butter. Melt remaining butter and reserve. Sprinkle shallots and sliced mushrooms over butter, and place the fish on this bed. Pour in equal parts of fish stock and white wine to cover bottom half of fish. Add a dash of Pernod. Pour remaining butter over top half of fish. Bake in a preheated 400°F. oven for 5 minutes. Reduce heat to 350°F. and continue baking for 30 to 35 minutes. Baste at least three times during cooking period.

Make a bed of remaining fennel twigs on a silver serving tray. Carefully remove baked fish from pan and place on top of twigs. At tableside, sprinkle twigs with Pernod. Pour a small amount of Pernod into a ladle, warm it, and ignite. Pour it flaming over the presoaked twigs; ignite the twigs. Using two large fish servers, hold the bass over the burning twigs until flames die out. Serve with Sauce Grégoire *(see under SAUCES)* and with parsleyed potatoes. Makes 6 servings.

BAKED STRIPED BASS BLOCK ISLAND

1 striped bass, 6 to 8 pounds
2 cups onion dressing, or your own favorite
salt and pepper
2 ounces salt pork
butter for pan
½ to 1 cup light cream or half-and-half

Dress the striper with the backbone remaining in the fish. Score both sides, making cuts about 2 inches apart. Put the dressing inside the fish near the nape, and sprinkle salt and pepper on both sides. Cut salt pork into strips and fasten over the scored cuts with wooden picks. Place fish in a buttered roasting pan, and bake in a 450°F. oven for 1 hour. Pour in enough of the cream to cover the bottom of the pan, and cook for 15 minutes longer, basting occasionally, until fish is light brown. Makes 6 to 8 servings.

BAKED STRIPER IN WHITE WINE

1 striped bass, 3 to 6 pounds	2 tablespoons chopped mushrooms
salt and pepper	1 tablespoon chopped parsley
juice of 1½ lemons	1 garlic clove, minced
2½ tablespoons butter	pinch each of dried marjoram and thyme
1 onion, chopped	
1 cup dry white wine	
1 cup water	dash of cayenne

Clean fish thoroughly. Rub inside and out with salt and pepper and the juice of ½ lemon. Butter a

baking pan and add chopped onion and wine. Place the fish on this bed, and dot it with small pats of remaining butter. Bake in a preheated 425° to 450°F. oven for 20 to 25 minutes, or until fish flakes when tested with a fork. Baste frequently with pan juices. Transfer fish to a serving platter and add to the baking pan the remaining lemon juice, the water, mushrooms, parsley, garlic, herbs and cayenne. Mix well with pan juices over low heat on top of the stove. When reduced to a sauce, season to taste. Pour over the fish when ready to serve. Makes 3 to 6 servings.

STRIPED BASS WITH BEURRE BLANC

1 striped bass, 6 to 8 pounds, whole-dressed and scaled	1 pound mushrooms, sliced
	2 lemon slices
	1½ cups fish stock
salt and pepper	1½ cups dry white wine
½ pound butter	1 bunch of parsley
10 shallots, chopped	12 lemon wedges

Wipe fish with a damp cloth, and sprinkle with salt and pepper inside and out. Butter a large roasting pan, and spread the bottom with chopped shallots, sliced mushrooms and lemon slices. Place the fish on this. Using equal parts of fish stock and white wine, cover half the fish. Cover top of fish with melted butter. Place fish in 400°F. oven for 5 minutes, then reduce temperature to 350°F. and cook for 30 to 35 minutes. Baste every 10 minutes. Arrange cooked fish on a platter surrounded by parsley sprigs and lemon wedges. Cover with the mushrooms from the roasting pan. Serve with Beurre Blanc *(see under BUTTERS).* Makes 6 servings.

CRANBERRY-STUFFED BASS

1 whole striped bass, 2½ to 3 pounds	½ cup whole-berry cranberry sauce
salt	¼ teaspoon celery salt
paprika	¼ teaspoon onion powder
1 small apple, peeled, cored and chopped	2 tablespoons chopped parsley
grated rind and juice of 1 lemon	1 egg, well beaten
2 cups cooked rice	¼ cup melted butter or margarine

Preheat oven to 350°F. Sprinkle fish inside and out with salt and paprika. Mix chopped apple, lemon rind, rice, cranberry sauce, celery salt, onion powder, parsley and egg. Use mixture to stuff fish. Sew or skewer opening. Place fish on a greased foil-lined shallow pan. Combine butter and lemon juice. Brush over fish. Bake for 40 minutes, or until fish is golden brown and flesh flakes easily. Place fish carefully on a platter and remove skewers or thread. Serve garnished with parsley and thin lemon slices. Makes 4 servings.

Sturgeon

An Act of King Edward II made the sturgeon a "Royal fish," and a law decreed that every sturgeon caught must be offered to the monarch. Apparently his majesty was the only ruler fond of sturgeon as the ancient prerogative was seldom enforced thereafter, although a few particularly large fish were seen at Buckingham Palace in subsequent reigns. The eventual abolition of this law hardly raised an eyebrow in Britain, as the sturgeon never attained a popularity in the restaurant trade. Nor did whales which were similarly given royal status. As a readily available source of protein the fish was prominent in Russian cuisine for centuries, primarily in a baked form or made into soup.

Although the extremely firm but delicately flavored meat of a sturgeon can be prepared in the simplest fashion such as deep-frying, the major retail market in North America and western Europe is for the smoked product, which tastes very similar to smoked breast of turkey. Like caviar it commands a comparatively high price. However, it is also marketed frozen in steaks or whole and gutted, and semipreserved in wine, vinegar and spices and packed in glass jars. Canned sturgeon usually consists of brined pieces which are cooked in tomato, mustard or other sauces, or in aspic. Smoked pieces are also canned in oil.

Both the green and white sturgeons are utilized in the Pacific Northwest; these are mainly from the Columbia River system, and they are processed in Seattle. The green sturgeon is inferior (the flesh retains a reddish color) and is sold primarily as a canned smoked product, while the white sturgeon is used in both fresh smoked and fresh steaked forms. The sea sturgeon enters major eastern ports, with the bulk of the landings at Fulton Market presently coming from Georgia and South Carolina.

Small sturgeon are the best eating, and fish of 8 pounds or less can be cooked whole. Steaks from larger fish are usually panfried, deep-fried or barbecued. When cut into chunks, sturgeon can be pickled. Otherwise follow swordfish recipes.

Atlantic sturgeon

STURGEON CÔTE D'ÉMERAUDE

(The Four Seasons, New York City)

6 to 8 pounds crosscut of fresh sturgeon	8 cups white wine
salt and pepper	4 cups White-Wine Sauce I (p. 287)
1 tablespoon dried thyme	½ pound mushrooms, sliced
2 bay leaves	
½ pound fresh fatback	½ pound mussels, shelled
4 medium-size carrots	½ pound shrimps, shelled and deveined
½ celery rib	
5 shallots	½ pound oysters, shelled
2 ounces butter	

Season the body cavity of the fish with salt, pepper and thyme, and add the bay leaves. Lard the fish with the fatback, lengthwise as much as possible. Slice the carrots, celery and shallots, and brown them lightly in butter. Place the fish with the vegetables in a baking pan, and add 6 cups of the white wine. Braise in the oven for 40 minutes, or until done. Remove the fish to a serving platter and keep warm.

Strain the cooking juices and reduce to one third. Add the white-wine sauce and reduce for 5 minutes more over high heat, stirring constantly with a wooden spoon. Strain again. Meanwhile, cook mushrooms, mussels, shrimps and oysters in remaining 2 cups white wine for 10 minutes. Add to the strained sauce, and pour over the fish. Serve accompanied with boiled potatoes or rice pilaff. Makes 8 to 10 servings.

Sucker

Suckers are among the most abundant and widely distributed freshwater fish in America. There are 57 species occurring in every habitat from small brooks to the Great Lakes. While some never achieve an edible size, many attain very substantial weights; the bigmouth buffalo, for example, has been recorded to 80 pounds. From a culinary standpoint there are 3 important groups of suckers: the fine-scaled suckers, the redhorse suckers, and the larger buffalos. When taken from cold deep lakes or clear running streams, as most commercially important species are, suckers have a firm, sweet white meat. They are all lean fish—16 to 18 percent protein and 2 to 3 percent fat; they are suited to a variety of cooking methods. The only objection to suckers as food is their numerous small bones, as the ribs, including a set of accessory ribs, are distributed from the head to the tip of the tail. This is less of a problem with fish weighing from 3 to 5 pounds, which is the usual market size. Except for the buffalo, suckers are usually marketed as "mullet" in fresh and frozen forms; these may be dressed and headless, tray-pack fillets, fillet blocks, boneless blocks or tray-pack fish portions. Suckers make an excellent smoked product, and can be turned into flavorsome fish sausages.

Suckers earn their name from the method of feeding as they use their rounded, protruding lips almost like a vacuum cleaner as they suck algae and crustaceans into their mouths. They have no teeth in their jaws, but the bones in their throats are equipped with grinders which are strong enough to crush the shells of snails or freshwater bivalves. Mollusks, the larvae of aquatic insects, plant material and small crustaceans are the sucker's principal foods. Due to this rather specialized diet, some species, like the comparatively huge bigmouth buffalo, which feeds entirely on minute animal plankton and to a lesser extent on algae, are rarely caught by anglers. Contrary to the derisive term "sucker," most species can be more difficult to catch than glamorous gamefish like the trout.

The buffalos are perhaps the best known suckers at market. Redundantly called "buffalofish," they greatly resemble carp and in fact are used interchangeably in all carp recipes. In this respect many people consider the buffalo a superior fish as the musculature contains less troublesome bones. For many years the annual catch of buffalo has amounted to about 15 million pounds, most of which comes from the Atchafalaya and Red Rivers of Louisiana.

Suckers are scored to soften the intermuscular bones. Most people do not fillet the fish, but halve it lengthwise and cut through the skin to the vertebrae. Others fillet and score from the flesh side; this takes more time, and care must be taken to keep from cutting through the skin or the fillet will fall apart. I prefer the latter method when frying suckers as the fish cooks faster and more heat gets into the intermuscular bones without overcooking.

Both the roe and white roe of suckers are edible and are considered a delicacy among mountain folk in the southern U. S. They are prepared like mullet roe, rolled in cornmeal and fried. Another way is to fry the roe about half done, then scramble with eggs.

The head of large spotted suckers is sometimes used in making chowder; it was more common some years ago. The head is skinned, exposing a great amount of meat on the sides of the skull; the head is then cooked in seasoned water. The meat is removed from the bones and the stock used in the stew.

White sucker

SUCKER TERMINOLOGY

BLUE SUCKER This species *(Cycleptus elongatus)* is found from the Missouri River in Montana east to Pennsylvania and south to the Gulf of Mexico. It occurs in rivers and deep lakes. The blue sucker attains a weight up to 16 pounds and is considered an excellent foodfish in regions where large specimens are available.

BUFFALO The "buffalofish" may be any one of 3 species, all found throughout the Mississippi Valley but seldom taken in the Great Lakes. The **bigmouth buffalo** *(Ictiobus cyprinellus)*, which also goes by such picturesque names as redmouth and gourdhead buffalo, prefers bays, sloughs and lakes rather than the swift currents of rivers. Ordinarily it is the largest of the group, the giants reaching a weight of 80 pounds. The **black buffalo** *(I. niger)*, called also the bugler, the rooter and the prairie buffalo, is most abundant in the southern part of the Mississippi Valley, usually weighs less than 20 pounds but may weigh as much as 70 pounds, and is very similar to the bigmouth in its qualities as a foodfish. Third and last of the common market species is the **smallmouth buffalo** *(I. bubalus)*, known in some localities as the highback or channel buffalo, and in the southern Mississippi Valley as the razorback. This is a fish of the rivers, at home in deep channels and turbulent currents, with a more slender body fitting it for an active existence. The smallmouth buffalo may reach a weight of 45 pounds. It is usually considered superior in flavor to the other species.

CARPSUCKER There are 2 species, the **river carpsucker** *(Carpiodes carpio)* and **high fin carpsucker** *(C. velifer)*, and both are best ignored as a food. Their flesh is extremely bony and soft, and of muddy flavor.

LONGNOSE SUCKER The longnose sucker *(Catostomus catostomus)* is abundant east of the Rocky Mountains from Alaska to Maine. It is a coldwater fish found in deep lakes, and it enters streams during the spring breeding period. The longnose is somewhat smaller than the white sucker but some fish attain a weight of several pounds. Its food value is about the same as the white.

REDHORSE SUCKER There are 10 species of suckers known as "redhorse." Some of these attain weights of 5 to 6 pounds. Various redhorse are distributed from the St. Lawrence River to the Gulf of Mexico. The **black redhorse** *(Moxostoma duquesnei)* and **golden redhorse** *(M. erythrurum)* are popular foodfish in the south.

SPOTTED SUCKER The spotted sucker *(Minytrema melanops)* ranges from southern Minnesota to Pennsylvania and south to Florida, Texas and Kansas. It occurs in large streams and lakes but only in clear water. It may grow to 6 pounds in size and is one of the better species in texture and flavor. It's popular in Georgia.

WHITE SUCKER This is the most important of the fine-scaled group. The white sucker *(Catostomus commersoni)* ranges from northern Canada south to Florida and west to Montana. Commercial fishermen have reported taking this species to a size of 8 pounds although the average fish is considerably smaller. The white sucker is actually an olive color, almost golden, and in the spring spawning season the males develop a lateral band of pink or red.

Sunfish

Of the various kinds of freshwater fish caught in the U.S. today, sunfish outrank all other species in sheer numbers harvested by sport fishermen. Although sunfish were marketed commercially in some southern states until the 1950s they are protected today. A small amount from the Great Lakes and Lake of the Woods, Ontario, reaches New York outlets; the crappie in particular is bought almost exclusively by the city's Chinese population. Most sunfish are readily caught, particularly in the spring season, and certain species attract thousands of anglers to the waterside during their spawning period when the fish are both aggressive and concentrated in shallow water. Widely known as bream or "brim" (a name adopted by early-day southern Colonists who saw a resemblance between our sunfishes and the nonrelated European bream), these are the panfish glorified by the barefoot boy, and members of the same family (Centrachidae) as the larger black bass. Dated fossils indicate that the centrachids evolved about 60 million years ago during the Cenozoic epoch, or shortly after the disappearance of the dinosaur in North America. Sunfish are not indigenous to other continents although the bluegill has been planted in waters of South Africa, Central and South America, Puerto Rico, Cuba and Hawaii.

All sunfish are edible; even the smallest ones can be dusted with cornmeal and deep-fried to a crisp. Of the many species a few are outstanding. I prefer the redear to the bluegill although both have the ideal sunfish flavor and aroma, a sweet (but subtly so) taste that suggests fresh celery. The skin of a sunfish, unlike its larger relative the black bass, is not only edible but to many palates an essential part of the flavor experience. Large sunfish can be filleted but the usual catch is too small and should be pan-dressed. Actually, there's a considerable loss of meat in the filleting process; unless you have a very large number of fish on hand it's not recommended. Sunfish are spiny-rayed species and in addition have a somewhat heavy and sharp skeletal structure. However, country boys eat a bluegill or redear in the style of corn on the cob, by holding a pan-dressed fish between the fingers and nibbling around the bones. Actually, once you discover how the interior of a sunfish is contructed it's easy to "lift" a fillet off, then pop the backbone out of the remaining half. The fillet is boneless. Problems only arise when the rib cage has been left in (it should be sliced off when pan-dressing by making an angular cut from nape to vent) and when not recognizing or removing the basal bone processes of each fin, excluding the tail. The crisply fried tail is a nutlike dividend. In brief, the sunfish will not tolerate careless work with a fork, or else bones will mix with the fillet and the transcendental pleasure of "a mess of bream" becomes literal rather than a platitude.

While deep-frying is in my opinion the best method, sunfish can be panfried and oven-fried, or even baked and broiled. In common with catfish, no meal of sunfish is complete without a platter of hush puppies and a crisp green salad. The fish should be served hot, directly from the fryer. Do not try to keep them warm in the oven as they quickly become soggy. When practical, it's best to cook and serve small amounts at a time, making certain that the oil in the fryer is still hot enough.

SUNFISH TERMINOLOGY

BLUEGILL The best known and most important sunfish, the bluegill *(Lepomis macrochirus)* is readily identified by a black spot on the posterior end of its dorsal fin and its blue-black ear flap. Bluegills have been widely transplanted from their original range in eastern and central U. S., and now occur in most states. They are very popular in farm ponds (some of which are run on a fee basis for the privilege of fishing) and are caught the year 'round. The usual size is about ½ pound, but some waters produce bluegills of a pound or more, and rarely to 4 pounds. Personally I prefer the smaller fish when deep-fried.

CRAPPIE There are 2 species of crappie, the **black crappie** *(Pomoxis nigromaculatus)* and the **white crappie** *(Pomoxis annularis)* which are known as **speckled perch** in various parts of the southern U.S., also **sac à lait** in Louisiana and **calico bass, strawberry bass, bachelor perch** and **papermouth** in some northern states. As a food, the two species can be considered as one, their table quality depending on habitat and season; the best fish are from clear waters and are prime before spawning in the spring season and again in winter. Crappie fishing is tremendously popular with small "cities" of campers and trailers rising overnight around many midwestern and southern lakes when a run is on. The sport is considered a form of spring fever in Texas, Missouri, Mississippi and Florida.

The crappie is usually larger than the bluegill, with 2-pound fish not uncommon, and recorded to weights of over 5 pounds. The flesh of the crappie is white and soft, and has a bland flavor that people become addicted to.

FLIER The flier *(Centrarchus macropterus)* or **round sunfish** is generally small, seldom exceeding 4 ounces in weight. It's found from Virginia to Texas and through the Mississippi drainage to southern Illinois. This is a pretty fish, with each scale having a dark spot forming longitudinal lines along its sides. The flier reaches a larger size in some acid-water creeks and ponds but it's a chunky little sunfish and has some food value even when small. The meat is flaky and delicately flavored. I count the flier as one of the better sunfishes at table.

GREEN SUNFISH The green sunfish *(Lepomis cyanellus)* is found from the Great Lakes region south to Mexico but not east of the Alleghenies. It's usually a dark olive-green in color and yellowish on the belly and its black ear flap has a white to pinkish margin. Green sunfish are usually small but they reach a weight of 1 pound in some waters. Regardless of size, however, the green sunfish is inferior as a food, the meat being soft and invariably muddy in flavor.

LONGEAR SUNFISH The longear *(Lepomis megalotis)* seldom grows much over 4 or 5 inches in length in its northern range, but it attains pan size in our central and southern states where it may run to ½ pound in weight. It's similar to the flier from that standpoint but, unlike the latter, the longear is not as plump and provides very little meat unless caught in 8- and 9-inch lengths. The flavor and texture is good but size is a definite drawback in this case.

PUMPKINSEED This very common and gaily colored sunfish occurs principally in our eastern and northern states. The pumpkinseed *(Lepomis gibbosus)* is a favorite quarry of small boys with cane poles. While it's generally considered a minor food, in some waters it grows to ¾ pound. The flesh is flaky and sweet, and when large is equal to the bluegill or redear. Unfortunately, small pumpkinseeds are not plump enough to provide much eating.

REDBREAST SUNFISH The redbreast *(Lepomis auritus)* also known as **robin, sun perch** and **yellow belly sunfish,** can be distinguished by its long black ear flap and bright orange-red belly. The redbreast is found in both lakes and rivers of the Atlantic drainage from New Brunswick to Florida. Although it's a smaller fish than the bluegill in northern waters, it attains pan size in our central and southern states, running from ½ to 1 pound. North Carolina especially produces large redbreasts in some

top, Fishing for bluegills, New York State;
bottom, Bluegill, the most important sunfish

Pumpkinseed, a sunfish

Black crappie, a sunfish

Redbreast sunfish

Redear sunfish

Rock bass, a sunfish

coastal rivers.

REDEAR SUNFISH The redear *(Lepomis microlophus)* also known as **shellcracker,** is my favorite sunfish at table. Its principal diet is mollusks and crustaceans which produces a firm white meat of excellent flavor. The redear is also a plumper sunfish than the bluegill and inch-for-inch is a meatier fish. The redear's original range was the southeastern U. S. but it has been introduced elsewhere. As the name implies, its ear flap is usually margined in red but can be orange. Redears run ½ pound in size but 2-pounders are not uncommon and in Florida they are sometimes taken up to 4 pounds.

ROCK BASS The rock bass *(Ambloplites rupestris)* is a chunky sunfish and is often caught in weights up to 1½ pounds with a rare maximum of about 4 pounds, which makes it a fairly substantial panfish. The rock bass is a dark olive in color, mottled with brassy brown blotches. It has bright red eyes and is sometimes called **redeye bass** or **goggle-eye.** The rock bass is widely distributed from southern Canada to Georgia and east to New England. It has been transplanted to other states. Found in both lakes and streams, it feeds primarily on crayfish, which produces a delicately flavored meat in coldwater habitats. There is some variation in quality, however, depending on the source of supply.

WARMOUTH The warmouth *(Lepomis gulosus)* or **stump knocker** is sometimes confused with the rock bass. It is similar in color, including the eyes, and has the same chunky body. However, it has 5 bluish lines on the head radiating outward from the eye. The warmouth is commonly found in sluggish and turbid waters in the eastern half of the U. S.; it is inferior to most other sunfishes as a food. The flesh is soft and often of a muddy flavor.

SUNFISH CASSEROLE

4 cups fillets of any sunfish	1½ tablespoons grated onion
4 thick slices of white bread	3 tablespoons Worchestershire sauce
1 cup milk	1 teaspoon dry mustard
¼ pound butter, melted	dash of Tabasco
1 green pepper, chopped	¾ teaspoon salt
1 pimiento, chopped	dash of pepper
3 tablespoons chopped parsley	crumbled cornflakes

Drop sunfish fillets into boiling water. Let the water come to a boil again, then remove the fish and drain; set aside. Remove crusts from bread and tear bread into small pieces. Mix with milk, butter, green pepper, pimiento, parsley, onion and seasonings. Cook for 10 minutes, stirring. Add the drained fish and cook for 5 minutes. Put in a shallow 2-quart casserole and sprinkle crumbled cornflakes lightly over the top. Brown in a 375°F. oven for 10 to 15 minutes. Makes 6 servings.

Surfperch

There are 20 surfperches in the family Embiotocidae which occur on our Pacific Coast from Alaska to Baja California. Only 2 species are found throughout this range while the others are of local importance in limited areas. Surfperch are popular among anglers along ocean beaches, but certain species remain in protected bays and harbors and are commonly called "seaperch." Exceptional fish attain a weight of 4 pounds, however, they are usually smaller, vaguely resembling a perch in shape but they are not related to the true perch *(see YELLOW PERCH).*

Of the various species those in the genus *Amphistichus* are more sweetly flavored than those surfperch classified in other genera. The best in order of importance are the **redtail surfperch** *(A. rhodoterus),* **barred surfperch** *(A. argenteus),* and the **calico surfperch** *(A. koelzi).* These are of a quality suitable for steaming and poaching whereas the species known as "seaperch" are much more bland (in some cases tasteless) and should be panfried, oven-fried, or broiled. The common **rubberlip seaperch** *(Rhacochilus toxotes)* is a filter feeder, frequenting sewage outfalls, and is not recommended as food.

The unrelated **opaleye** *(Girella nigricans),* a member of the sea chub family (Kyphosidae) found in southern California waters, is also perchlike in shape and marketed as "perch." The opaleye is superior to most surfperches at table and is unmistakable in appearance, being an olive green in color and having bright blue eyes.

Surfperch are of minor value in the Pacific commercial fishery and the entire catch is locally marketed in fresh form. *See also OCEAN PERCH.*

Surmullet

See GOATFISH.

Swordfish

I have caught very few swordfish over the years, one off Montauk, one in Mexico and four off the coast of Chile. Actually, I never put in the hours on swordfish grounds that the sport requires. While we eyeballed many out of Cabo Blanco in Peru, giant black marlin were "finning out" at the same time and from an angling standpoint this was the more desirable target. *Xiphias gladius* is not a fish that one takes casually or with any consistency as even when they're sighted basking on the surface (the scythelike dorsal fin can be seen at some distance) and baited, the odds are great that the broadbill will sound. The late Lou Marron set the world's record with a fish of 1,182 pounds but even "Uncle" Lou never caught many, and I've known people who fished them season after season before finally scoring. The Latin name *gladius* is for the short sword carried by Roman legions, and the fish sometimes uses it with stunning effect. It has rammed many ships, plunging deep into oak planking, and even attacked the research submersible *Alvin.* During World War II when merchant vessels were being sunk off the coast of Bermuda, bales of rubber frequently washed up on the beaches impaled with the broken bills of swordfish. The swordfish's proclivity for attacking ships and floating objects has long been known, as Oppian observed that:

Nature her bounty to his mouth confined . . .
gave him a sword, but left unarmed his mind.

Due to the fact that the swordfish is not readily spooked by ships, most of the fish taken by commercials are harpooned, although many are caught on longlines in the Pacific and some are trapped in tuna nets in the Mediterranean.

Swordfish are found throughout the world in tropical and temperate seas, and in the western Atlantic are taken from Newfoundland to Cuba. They are present off our coast usually from late June through the summer, then move offshore into deep water along the edge of the Continental Shelf. In the eastern Atlantic they occur from Iceland to Scandinavia to the southern tip of Africa as well as in the Mediterranean, the Sea of Marmara and the Black Sea. However, the only major European fishery is around Portugal and the Mediterranean. In the Pacific swordfish are found from southern California to Chile and from Japan to New Zealand and Australia on the west side, and in numerous locations throughout the Indian Ocean. Everywhere it occurs the swordfish is greatly esteemed and brings top prices at market. The controversial Federal ban (U.S.) on swordfish containing purported high levels of mercury has done little to discourage its popularity.

Swordfish is usually sold in fresh or frozen steak form; the season for fresh fish in U.S. waters is during the summer and fall months. The meat is very firm and of distinctive flavor. The only other fish comparable to it in texture and quality is the mako shark, which has

Mako shark steak

Swordfish steak

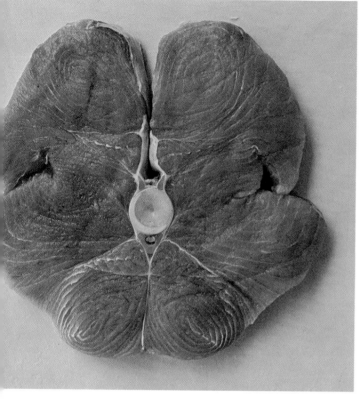

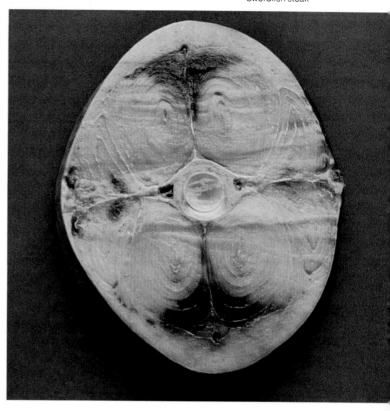

been substituted for swordfish during periods of scarcity and high prices.

OVEN-BROILED SWORDFISH STEAKS

The simplest method of cooking swordfish is by oven-broiling with a suitable butter basting, flavored with garlic, lemon, or herb. The steaks can be placed on a well-greased pan or foil and cooked in a preheated oven (375°F.) for 12 to 14 minutes. Turn the steaks just once but baste several times. The heat source should be about 4 inches from the fish. Serve with rice and a green salad.

SWORDFISH STEAKS ON CHARCOAL

Cooking swordfish over charcoal is the very best method. Being a dry, firm and lean meat, it gains flavor by marination in herbs and olive oil. The rich smoke that results from the oil dripping on the hot briquets greatly enhances the end result. In the course of cooking, turn the steaks just once by lifting with a spatula to brown both sides.

6 swordfish steaks,
  8 to 10 ounces each,
  1 inch thick
1 cup olive oil
1 tablespoon
  crumbled dried orégano
1 tablespoon
  crushed bay leaf
juice of 1 lemon
4 garlic cloves,
  chopped fine
2 tablespoons
  crumbled dried basil
1 teaspoon celery salt
1 teaspoon
  coarse black pepper
melted butter

Combine all ingredients except fish and butter in a bowl and mix thoroughly. Wipe each steak in the marinade to cover both sides and refrigerate for 2 to 3 hours. Turn once or twice to make certain the steaks are well coated. With the grid about 6 inches from the firebed, grill the steaks uncovered for 5 minutes, then turn and cook for 7 minutes on the opposite side. Baste the steaks with remaining marinade, using a pastry brush. Arrange steaks on a platter and splash with melted butter. Garnish with finely chopped parsley. Makes 6 servings.

VARIATIONS: Garlic butter may be used to splash on the cooked steaks, or an oil and lemon sauce made of equal parts of olive oil and lemon juice, well mixed, to which finely chopped parsley has been added, may be served.

For Mediterranean style swordfish, garnish each steak with 2 anchovy fillets and a halved black olive; the fillets are usually placed in the form of an **X** and centered with the olive. Use the oil and lemon sauce.

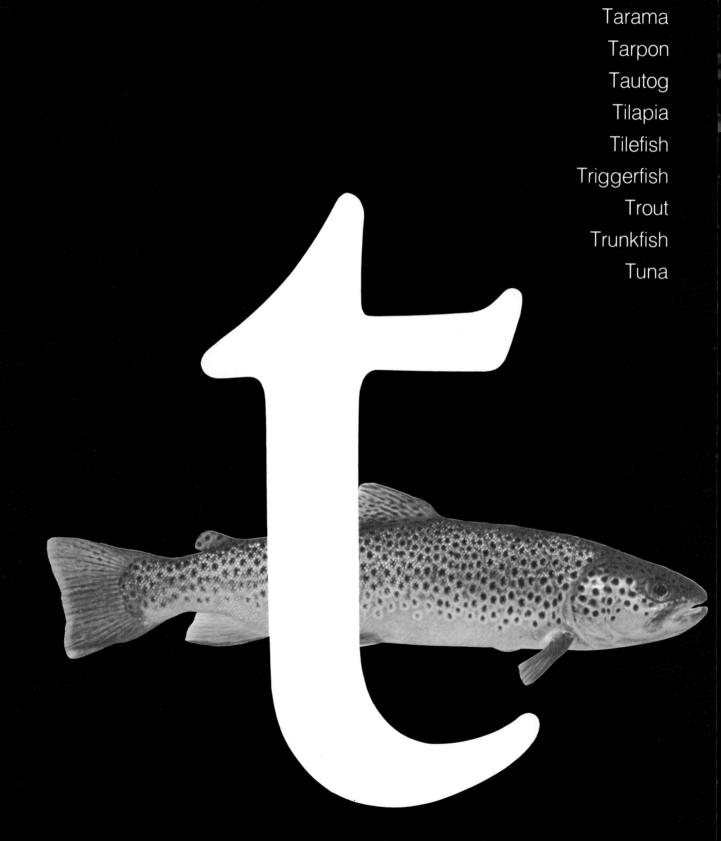

Tarama
Tarpon
Tautog
Tilapia
Tilefish
Triggerfish
Trout
Trunkfish
Tuna

Tautog

t

Tarama

A paste made from the roes of mullet, primarily a Greek or Turkish product; also called **Atarama.** Carp, mackerel and codfish roes are often substituted, but these alternates lack the flavor and consistency recognized in a quality *tarama.* The paste is made into an appetizer, *taramasalta,* which is purveyed in cans and jars as an imported item in American and European markets. However, it is easily made at home when fresh roes are available.

TARAMASALTA

½ pound fresh mullet roe (carp, mackerel or
    codfish roe may be substituted)
1½ cups olive oil
1 cup soft white bread crumbs
juice of 2 lemons
2 tablespoons grated onion
salt and pepper

Taramasalta is easily prepared in an electric blender. Poach the roe for 2 minutes to firm slightly, and remove the membrane. Drain the roe and let cool. Place the roe in the blender container and whirl at low speed, adding the oil slowly and alternating with small amounts of bread crumbs which have been moistened with lemon juice. Continue beating until oil and bread crumbs are all used, then add the onion, and salt and pepper to taste. Blend to a mayonnaise consistency.

Serve the paste chilled on toast fingers or crackers, garnished with parsley. Makes about 3 cups.

Tarpon

This great marine gamefish known as the "silver king" is almost a culinary debacle, its flesh being soft, dark and tasteless. The roes of female tarpon, however, are extremely good and are a popular food in Mexico and Central America. Tarpon roes are large (although the eggs are suitably small at the right stage) and should be parboiled before panfrying. The roe can be treated as in any recipe for shad roe.

Tautog

More commonly known in the New York area as **blackfish,** the tautog *(Tautoga onitis)* is a member of the wrasse family, Labridae. It is found from Nova Scotia to South Carolina but is most common from Cape Cod to Delaware Bay. In appearance, the tautog is a dark fish, generally dull gray or green with darker blotches on its sides. It has a plump body and thick lips. Tautog grow to about 25 pounds, but the average fish is closer to 3 pounds. This wrasse is caught along rocky shores and by partyboat fishermen around submerged offshore wrecks. The commercial fishery has never been significant although there is a ready sale for all tautog that are landed. The fish has very firm, white meat which is particularly suitable for chowders as the musculature does not flake or shred.

Tempura

See under SHRIMP.

Tilapia

The tilapia was introduced to the U.S. as a species suitable for obnoxious algae control during the late 1960s, notably in Florida, Alabama and California. There are numerous species of tilapia, which are members of the family Cichlidae, distributed throughout Africa from Egypt to the Cape of Good Hope. Easily pond cultured and a cheap source of protein, these cichlids have also been stocked in parts of Asia, the Philippines, Ceylon, Hawaii, Puerto Rico, and Central and South America. The various species range in size from small aquarium fish to weights of 5 pounds or more; most occur in freshwater but some are found in brackish water and saltwater. Tilapia gener-ally resemble our sunfish in shape and in fact are called **bream** in Natal and Rhodesia. They are also known as **mudfish** and **kurper** in South Africa. Their collective Swahili name **ngege** is widely used in central Africa where tilapia fishing is a considerabe industry in Lake Albert and Lake Rudolf.

Tilapia vary in quality from fair to good as a table fish, the better ones being the **ngege** of Lake Victoria *(Tilapia esculenta)* and the widely distributed tilapia from Lake Naivasha *(T. nigra)*. The largest tilapia *(T. nilotica)* has been reported to 20 pounds in size from Lake Rudolf, but the fish occurs all over tropical Africa and Syria; it is a foodfish of some importance.

Tilefish

Tilefish are members of the family Branchiostegidae, a small group of fishes that are widespread in tropical and temperate waters. Three species occur along our outer Continental Shelf and its upper slope to depths of over 1,000 feet from northern Nova Scotia to southern Florida and the Gulf of Mexico. A fourth species is found in the Pacific from Washington to Baja California.

The common tilefish *(Lopholatilus chamae-leonticeps)* is a gaily colored, stout-bodied fish with a bluish to olive-green back that fades to a yellow-gold and rose on its sides and belly. It is sprinkled with irregular yellow spots, and the fins vary from pink to purple with a blue iridescence. The tilefish also has a distinctive fleshy protuberance in front of the dorsal fin, which looks like a miniature rudder balanced on its head. Tilefish grow to 50 pounds or more but are usually marketed at 6 to 8 pounds. The other 2 Atlantic species, the **blackline tilefish** *(Caulolatilus cyanops)* and the **sand tilefish** *(Malacanthus*

plumieri) are southerly in distribution; the latter, a small-er tropical shoalwater inhabitant, bears no resemblance to tilefish of the other genera, nor does it have any value as food. The Pacific species *(Caulolatilus princeps)*, known as **ocean whitefish,** also enters western markets but in very minor quantities.

The first commercial catch of tilefish was made in 1879 off the Nantucket Shoals Lightship. While draggers were still looking for the mother lode in 1882, an inexplicable mortality occurred to this species which re-sulted in 4,250 square miles of the Atlantic being covered with dead tilefish. It is generally believed that a drastic thermal change virtually erased this population as they require very cold water. During the following 5 years not a single one could be found. Gradually the tilefish began to appear again, and today they are taken at the rate of 10 million pounds a year. Because of the great depths which tilefish frequent, the sport fishery is limited. Specialist party boats operating out of New York and New Jersey ports catch tilefish on the slopes of the Hudson Canyon at depths of over 300 feet, while the blackline tilefish is caught in deep water at the edge of the Gulf Stream, principally out of Miami.

Tilefish have unusually firm, yet tender flesh, which is best compared to lobster or scallop meat. Their dominant food is red crabs and other crustaceans, which is reflected in the tilefish's flavor. They can be cooked by a variety of methods including poaching, baking, broiling, deep-frying (cut into fingers or cubes), and made into chowder. The meat makes excellent **sashimi** as well as a superior smoked product. Both the tilefish of northern U.S. waters and the blackline tilefish are exceptional at table, yet often ignored in Atlantic coast markets due to their unfamiliar name. However, the Pacific species or so-called "ocean whitefish" occasionally has a harmless

Tilefish

but very bitter flavor; for this reason it enjoys little consumer confidence. This unpleasant taste evidently relates to a change in the diet of ocean whitefish when they invade shallow water; benthic or deep-dwelling populations of the same species are always of good flavor.

TILEFISH AMANDINE

2 pounds tilefish fillets	½ cup sliced almonds
¼ cup flour	2 tablespoons
1 teaspoon seasoned salt	lemon juice
1 teaspoon paprika	4 or 5 drops of Tabasco
4 tablespoons melted	1 tablespoon
butter or margarine	chopped parsley

Rinse fillets and pat dry. Cut them into serving-size portions. Combine flour, seasoned salt and paprika; mix well. Roll fish in flour mixture. Place fish in a single layer, skin side down, in a well-greased shallow baking pan, 15 x 10 inches. Drizzle 2 tablespoons melted butter or margarine over fish. Broil about 4 inches from source of heat for 10 to 12 minutes, or until fish flakes easily when tested with a fork. Sauté almonds in remaining 2 tablespoons melted butter or margarine until golden brown, stirring constantly. Remove from heat. Add lemon juice, Tabasco and parsley to almonds; mix. Pour over fish. Serve at once. Makes 6 servings.

TILEFISH FRUIT SALAD

1½ pounds tilefish fillets	½ cup slivered blanched
1 avocado,	almonds, toasted
peeled and sliced	⅓ cup mayonnaise
1 tablespoon lemon juice	or salad dressing
2 cups orange sections	salad greens
1½ cups sliced celery	

Place fillets in boiling salted water. Cover and simmer for about 10 minutes, or until fish flakes easily when tested with a fork. Drain. Break fish into large pieces. Sprinkle avocado with lemon juice to prevent discoloration. Reserve 6 avocado slices and 6 orange sections for garnish. Cut remaining avocado and orange into 1-inch pieces. Combine all ingredients except salad greens; chill. Shape the salad mixture into a mound on salad greens and garnish with alternate slices of avocado and orange. Makes 6 servings.

SEA SLAW, LOW-CALORIE

1½ pounds tilefish fillets	1 tablespoon lemon juice
1 quart boiling water	1 teaspoon salt
1 tablespoon salt	1 cup shredded green cabbage

Tilefish sea slaw, low-calorie, ingredients facing page, Sea slaw ready to serve

¼ cup low-calorie	1 cup shredded red cabbage
salad dressing	1 cup thinly sliced celery
(mayonnaise type)	6 lettuce cups
2 tablespoons chopped onion	lemon wedges
2 tablespoons	
sweet pickle relish	

Place fillets in boiling salted water. Cover and simmer for about 10 minutes, or until fish flakes easily when tested with a fork. Drain. Remove skin and bones from fish; flake. Combine salad dressing, onion, relish, lemon juice, salt and flaked fish. Chill for at least 1 hour to blend flavors. Add shredded cabbage and sliced celery; toss lightly. Serve in lettuce cups, and garnish with lemon wedges. Makes 6 servings, approximately 120 calories in each serving.

Triggerfish

These colorful reef dwellers are found in warm seas throughout the world. They are a distinctive group of fishes, with a deep compressed body and a long snout. The name is derived from an interlocking arrangement of the first 3 dorsal spines which can be held in an erect position, but if you depress the second or "trigger" spine, it unlocks the first spine. The meat of the **ocean** and **queen triggerfish** is firm and white and is often compared to frogs' legs in flavor and texture. These fish have a very tough skin with platelike scales and are difficult to dress. Optionally, they can be skinned, then cut out into fillets, or filleted and then skinned; either way it requires a strong sharp blade.

The ocean triggerfish is called "turbot" in the

Queen triggerfish

Bahamas and West Indies; while it doesn't resemble that European flounder, its culinary reputation is commensurate among island people. The ocean species occurs only in the western Atlantic, but the queen triggerfish ranges from Massachusetts to Brazil and in the warmer waters of Europe, notably the Mediterranean where you may find it as **Kostorog** (Yugoslavia), **Pesce balestra** (Italy), **Baliste** (France), or **Pez ballesta** (Spain).

Trout

I have probably caught at least a half-million trout in my lifetime. While the greatest percentage were released to lend themselves to other anglers, it still adds up to many meals from Alaska to New Zealand and across to the Arctic barrens of Finland. Trout in a collective sense are not my favorite fish at table. There are more degrees of quality than species; certainly the pink-fleshed brook trout of central Labrador and Quebec, and the crimson-meated rainbows of southern Chile and Argentina, or for that matter a fresh-run steelhead from Oregon's Rogue River, are without peer. The native cutthroat trout of the Rocky Mountains and the golden trout are especially memorable and made even more so when cooked at a campfire among the craggy peaks of the Jim Bridger Wilderness. For my part, brown trout usually rate well down the list comparatively, although the unique sea-run form taken in the frigid rivers of Iceland and Norway has an ocean-firm musculature and a flavor superior to Atlantic salmon. The Sheriff House at Stockbridge can make brown trout from the weedy Test River taste like no other fish, but that is kitchen magic and perhaps a dollop of nostalgia for Hampshire's waters. In the same genre I recall those little Catskill brook trout of my boyhood, delicate and as gaily colored as butterflies; panfried with crunchy skins, one could eat them heads and all. It was a morning ritual with a steaming mound of hot cakes splashed with butter and homemade maple syrup, but *that* appetite is as distant now as the old wood-burning stove that worked its daily miracles.

Trout are the most universally cultured fish both for the purpose of angling and for the commercial market. Their domestic propagation began in the fourteenth century when a French monk, one Dom Pichon, discovered that trout eggs could be artificially impregnated. During the next 400 years there were some minor individual contributions to trout culture, but the science did not gain momentum until 1852 when the first public-owned trout hatchery was constructed in France. The alarming decrease of trout in America due to the industrialization of our river valleys soon required their production by artificial methods here, and in 1864 Seth Green built a hatchery at Mumford, New York. Jordan and Evermann in *American Food and Game Fishes* (1902) quote a Reverend Myron Reed " . . . a noble man and excellent angler . . . " as seeing that era as the terminal point in the history of our angling. *"This is the last generation of trout fishers. The children will not be able to find any. Already there are well trodden paths by every stream in Maine, New York, and Michigan."* The good reverend went on to say that *" . . . trout will be hatched by machinery and raised in ponds, and fattened on chopped liver, and grow flabby and lose their spots. The trout of the restaurant will not cease to be; but he is no more like a trout of the wild river than the fat and songless reed-bird is like the bobolink. Gross feeding and easy pond life enervate and deprave him."*

Seth Green was a pioneer fish culturist; he helped to construct private and state hatcheries throughout New England and the Middle Atlantic states. Athough he initially reared our native eastern brook trout, then the hardier rainbow trout of our West Coast, in 1886 a German fish culturist, Von Behr, sent the first brown trout to the U.S. It was during this period that immigrants to New Zealand brought Atlantic salmon from England by ship and, failing to establish that species, began the importation of Pacific salmon and rainbow trout from California. To this day, the generic American Indian *quinnat*, which is simply the collective name for all salmon, is used in New Zealand for the chinook. The rainbow trout, however, was a phenomenal success and by the turn of the century the fish was being shipped all over the world ultimately to thrive in countries where natural populations of salmonids were unknown. Transplanted into ecological voids such as New Zealand, Tasmania, temperate South America and the high country of South Africa, the red-sided rainbow is today internationally esteemed. The species is farmed throughout Denmark, for example, where the commercial production of trout is that nation's second largest industry.

From a culinary standpoint I feel the same way about trout recipes as about salmon recipes—the simplest methods are best. My first choice is blue trout.

Next to this a smoked trout served cold Véronique in aspic with white grapes and a very mild horseradish sauce, not the fiery kind that overwhelms the trout's delicate flavor. And trout can be prepared in the same manner as **gravlax** *(see under SALMON)*, only it's called **gravöring.** A chowder made from large pink-fleshed trout with a basic milk, onion and potato base is classic, and small brook or cut-throat trout panfried are wonderful in the outdoors. A planked or **Crucified Trout** is as easy to prepare as building a fire, but limited, of course, to the riverbank. The more theatrical poached dishes such as **Glazed Trout à l'Impériale, à la Russe,** or **Glazed Trout Monselet,** can be made with fish of over 4 pounds in size, and the preparation is the same as in the recipes for salmon.

TROUT QUALITY

There are numerous species with distinct flavors and textures, and even within a species they vary depending on size and environment. Flesh color may range from white to brilliant red, the coloration deriving from dietary fat-soluble carotenoids found in crustaceans; in waters where trout consume large quantities of crayfish or shrimps or, in mountain lakes of the west, where trout feed on a large red copepod, the flesh will be more highly colored. Generally speaking, wild trout with their natural foods are superior in the kitchen to hatchery fish, although some commercial operations raise a very acceptable product indeed. With the exception of the lake trout and to a lesser extent the steelhead, all other trout in the U.S. restaurant trade are by law of hatchery origin. Wild fish legally enter most European markets although the vast majority are from fish farms in Denmark, France and Italy. By the same token wild trout can be less than perfect such as the fish in Lakes Michigan and Huron which feed primarily on alewives, resulting in a pale and somewhat oily flesh. Lakes with algal blooms (which causes a "muddy" taste in fish flesh and particularly in the skin) and rivers containing an abundance of organic material also produce trout of poor quality. Generally speaking, fish taken from high, clear mountain lakes and swift-flowing clear streams are the best eating.

Trout are marketed fresh, whole gutted or ungutted, and frozen whole gutted, boneless, and breaded. They may be hot- or cold-smoked in whole gutted or fillet form. From a quality point of view "flash-frozen" trout from many hatcheries can be superior to "fresh" trout which have been held in ice for prolonged periods.

TROUT SIZE AS A FACTOR IN COOKING

The size of a trout is a determining factor in selecting

preceding pages, The author fishing for brown trout on the Salza River, Austria

appropriate recipes. Generally speaking, whole-dressed small fish of 6 to 9 inches in length are perfect for panfrying or deep-frying; they cook and crisp quickly without loss of flavor. Whole-dressed trout of 12 to 14 inches in length are the most tolerant in being suited to all cooking methods other than frying, unless they are filleted or cut into pieces; trout of this size begin to develop a girth which requires a cooking period beyond the point when the skin becomes crispy. Some chefs "panfry" these larger trout by crisping one side, then placing the fish under a broiler to brown the opposite side while gaining the extra cooking time. This is a sensible procedure, but there are many attractive alternates in poaching, baking and broiling, either in whole-dressed, butterfly or fillet forms. Large trout of 20 inches or more (over 4 pounds) can be cut into fingers, battered and deep-fried, steaked and broiled, smoked, poached, stuffed and baked, or steaked and boiled. The boiling method is a special technique (see *Wisconsin Fish Boil, under COOKING METHODS).*

Trout have a simple skeletal structure and are easily boned, in fact the backbone and rib cage can be lifted out of a cooked fish with no residual structures to be concerned about. All trout have very small scales; those in the char group, which include the brook trout, Dolly Varden and lake trout, have such minute scales embedded in the skin that scaling before cooking is not really necessary. Trout also have a comparatively small body cavity and can be gutted simply by bending the head back, cutting the "throat latch" loose, and with forefinger extended into the stomach pulling the entrails out with the gills.

There are some species of trout of such limited distribution that they rarely enter the kitchen except on a very local basis; among these are the **Mexican golden trout,** the **marble, softmouth** and **Ohrid trout** of Yugoslavia, the **Apache** and **Gila trout** of Arizona and New Mexico, the **Sevan trout** of the USSR, and the **Garda trout** of Italy. The following are those that are most commonly marketed or caught by angling.

TROUT TERMINOLOGY

ARCTIC CHAR Although not a true trout, this close relative of the brook trout is available on occasion in the larger U.S. cities via the Canadian Eskimaux Fisheries Co-Ops. Token populations of Arctic char exist in about a dozen ponds in Maine where they are known as **blueback trout** and **Sunapee trout,** and also in Quebec where they are called **Quebec red trout.** The char is common to northern European markets (Iceland, Finland, Norway and Sweden) and to a lesser extent in the Alpine regions of western Europe. Those found in the U.K., the most famous

of which is the char in Lake Windermere, are very small fish, usually less than 1 pound in size, but they have been celebrated by gourmets for centuries either in the form of **char pie** or **potted char** (prepared as one makes potted shrimps by mashing the cooked meat into a paste, adding seasoning to taste and enough cream to make it smooth; this is pressed down firmly in a stone crock, covered with a layer of melted butter, and left to firm in the refrigerator). The flesh color of char varies from white to red according to season and location, with those fish feeding largely on capelin having white to pink flesh and those char consuming mostly amphipods and euphausids displaying more pink to red flesh. In Sweden a distinction is made between char with pink meat, or **röding,** and those with light-colored flesh, or **blattjen,** where both occur in the same lakes; the **röding** feeds inshore and at the surface while the **blattjen** is strictly a bottom forager. However, for the world's standard bearer I would choose the sea-run char of Baffin Island. Extremely rich and fine textured, its bright orange to red flesh can be prepared by all cooking methods. Fresh or smoked it is superior to Atlantic salmon. *See also as separate entry under CHAR.*

BROOK TROUT This species *(Salvelinus fontinalis)* is generally considered the finest trout at table, but there are such qualitative differences in the extremes that it's often difficult to relate one dining experience with another. The brook trout is endemic to northeastern North America from Georgia to the Arctic Circle. It has been widely transplanted to the remainder of the U. S., Canada, Argentina, and to a lesser extent in Europe. Generally a dark olive on the back with lighter sides and a reddish belly, it has red spots each surrounded by a pale blue aureole. The flesh color can be white in fish of recent hatchery origin (as opposed to pale yellow or orange in wild brook trout) to deep red-orange in some populations. Among the best for flavor, texture and color are those taken from the interior lakes and rivers of the Maritime Provinces of Canada. Brook trout in some of the larger waters of Labrador, Quebec, Ontario, Manitoba and Argentina may run 6 pounds or more, but the average in U. S. streams is usually less than 1 pound. Some hatchery fish are marketed fresh and frozen but these are not comparable to wild brook trout of the north. A sea-run form, sometimes called **sea trout** or **salter,** is inferior in having very pale and somewhat oily flesh, often poorly flavored. This is an anomaly as anadromous fish usually improve with sea feeding but the brook trout does not. The common French name for char in Quebec, France and Switzerland is **omble,** specifically **omble chevalier** for the Arctic char, and **omble de fontaine** for the brook trout; this is not to be confused with the grayling or **ombre.**

Small fish (to 10 inches in length) are usually panfried. Larger fish can be poached, baked, broiled, smoked or made into chowder.

BROWN TROUT The brown trout *(Salmo trutta)* is found from the Mediterranean basin to the Black Sea and north to Arctic Norway and Siberia. Introduced to North America beginning in 1883, then to New Zealand, parts of Asia, South America and Africa. This trout is generally an olive to golden-brown in color with large black or dark brown spots on its sides, with a lesser number of orange or red spots. As a foodfish the brown is variable in quality. The flesh color is most often white to pale orange in eastern U. S. and European waters; some crustacean-feeding populations in large lakes attain a pink to red color and may be marketed in Europe as **salmon trout** or in French

In Argentina the rainbow trout develops red flesh from eating tiny freshwater crabs, cangrejos.

Brown trout

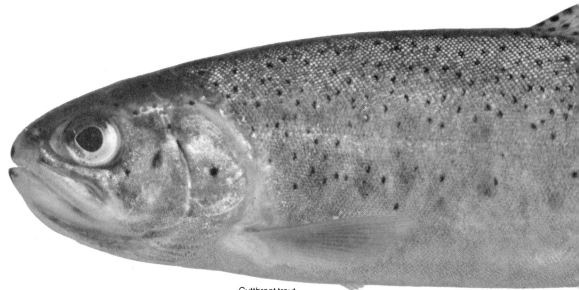

Cutthroat trout

Brook trout

Steelhead, the sea-run form of the rainbow trout

kitchens as **truite de lac** or **lake trout** as opposed to the common form of brown trout, **truite brune.** The latter often appears euphemistically on the menus of country inns as **truite de rivière** in deference to its local habitat. In either case it will have a white or very pale yellow to possibly orange meat. One race of brown trout found in some Irish lakes, known as the **gillaroo,** feeds exclusively on snails and its flesh becomes quite red in color, but not the very deep red of brown trout in some South American rivers where the fish consume quantities of freshwater crabs. Sea-run brown trout or sea trout are common only in Europe and southern Argentina, but these are superior to most inland populations. In French cuisine the sea trout or **truite de mer** is mainly an import item as there are few rivers left other than the Allier which support anadromous fish. Scotland, Norway and Iceland have many good sea trout rivers, but Sweden produces the largest fish by far with individual catches exceeding 25 pounds. Sea trout enter the Baltic commercial fishery and are often seen in Scandinavian markets. The meat of the sea trout is red-orange in color and cooks out to a bright pink. It's often superior to salmon in texture and flavor.

Although brown trout attain weights up to 40 pounds, the usual fish in river populations is 1 to 2 pounds in size with sea-run browns of 4 to 5 pounds quite common. Small fish (to 10 inches in length) from wild populations are ideally panfried. Larger fish can be poached, broiled, smoked or baked.

CUTTHROAT TROUT The cutthroat trout *(Salmo clarki)* is endemic to western North America from northern California to Alaska and inland throughout the mountain states and provinces. There are many subspecies or races which vary greatly in color, although they all have black spots to a greater or lesser extent and a distinct red marking below the lower jaw which gives this trout its common name. Among the various races are some of the most beautiful trout in the world and notably the rare **Piute trout** *(Salmo c. seleniris)*. Another variety, the **Lahontan cutthroat,** was once subject to an intensive commercial fishery from 1900 to 1925; it was sold mainly in the San Francisco market and almost became extinct. The quality of cutthroat trout at table is consistently good. The flesh color ranges from pale yellow to orange or red. Some populations feed extensively on freshwater shrimps *(Gammarus)*, which creates a firm meat of excellent flavor. Cutthroat trout attain sizes up to 40 pounds although the average caught by angling in most streams is from 1 to 1½ pounds. The sea-run form, sometimes called

Lake trout

harvest trout, seldom exceeds 5 pounds. The cutthroat is not sold commercially today but a significant quantity is taken by angling.

DOLLY VARDEN This char *(Salvelinus malma)*, or Dolly Varden trout, is found from northern California to Alaska and around the north Pacific to Japan and Korea. It also occurs inland in our western mountain states. It generally resembles the Arctic char in appearance and may have pink, orange or yellow spots on its sides, but the spots are always smaller in diameter than the iris of the eye (on the Arctic char the spots are larger). Sea-run fish are silvery in color, while some inland populations of Alaska, particularly on the Kenai Peninsula, are so brightly colored that they are called locally "golden trout" or "golden-finned trout." This fish was named after Miss Dolly Varden, a character in Charles Dickens's *Barnaby Rudge*, who wore a pink-spotted dress. The table quality varies according to habitat, but prime sea-run fish in the north have pink to red flesh and are excellent eating. However, these anadromous trout often winter over in lakes and become lean and flavorless by spring. By contrast, nonmigratory Dolly Vardens inhabiting large lakes in the southern part of their range may remain very fat, particularly in waters where they feed on Kokanee (landlocked sockeye salmon).

This trout attains weights to over 30 pounds but the usual fish is 2 to 3 pounds.

GOLDEN TROUT A remarkably beautiful trout, originally found only in the Sierra Nevada Mountains of California, the golden trout *(Salmo aguabonita)* has also been established in high-altitude waters of Wyoming, Idaho and Washington. The golden is a black-spotted trout with a brilliant yellow-gold body, often bearing a vermilion stripe along its sides. There is considerable variation in this basic color pattern according to habitat with some fish displaying much more crimson than gold (Jim Bridger Wilderness), but it's so special that one cannot confuse it with other trout. The golden is seldom found in lakes or streams below 8,000 feet elevation and essentially can only be enjoyed by anglers who pack-in on foot or by horse to the high country. This is an excellent trout in the pan, having firm pale orange to red flesh. It is fatter than other trout species (although much less so than the lake trout) and at its culinary peak when freshly caught. Golden trout do not keep well, and care must be taken if any of the catch is to be transported from remote waters. This fish can be prepared by all cooking methods according to size but is especially good when smoked.

LAKE TROUT This largest North American char grows to

100 pounds in size although the usual catch in most waters is from 10 to 20 pounds. The lake trout *(Salvelinus namaycush)*, also called "togue" (Eastern U.S.), "mackinaw" (Central and Western U.S.), and "gray trout" (Canada), inhabits deep clear lakes from Labrador across Canada, and southward in the cold waters of the U.S. from Maine to Idaho and north to Alaska. The lake trout is not as colorful as most other species. Its body is generally blue-gray or bronze-green with pale spots on its sides and back. The meat varies from white to red and is usually oilier than that of other trout.

There is considerable variation in the fat content of different lake trout populations. Lake trout analyzed in Lake Superior had a fat content (dry weight) of 6.6 to 52.3 percent; the percentage increases in proportion to the fish's size—the larger the trout the greater its fat content. ("Fat Content of the Flesh of Siscowets and Lake Trout from Lake Superior," Paul H. Eschmeyer and Arthur M. Phillips, Jr., *Transactions of the American Fisheries Society,* **94,** 1965, No. 1.) The closely related **siscowet,** considered a lake trout subspecies until recently, showed a fat content of 32.5 to 88.8 percent, which makes them difficult to prepare in most cooking methods, except by smoking. Even a 20-inch-long siscowet, which is really a prime size at table, contained 64 percent fat as compared to 23 percent for the leaner lake trout of the same length. A third form of lake trout called **humper** or **paperbelly** has a fat content midway between the lake trout and siscowet. The physical appearance of these fish is sufficiently different for commercials to identify and market separately. The siscowet and humper usually bring lower prices, but humpers are sometimes sold as lean fish when the market demand is high.

The lake trout is best treated by cutting into steaks and broiling, or by boiling or smoking.

RAINBOW TROUT The rainbow trout *(Salmo gairdneri)* is, as described earlier, endemic to western North America but has been transplanted all over the world during the last century. This species is the trout most widely cultured by hatcheries for the public market and restaurant trade. Domestic fish invariably have white flesh but wild stocks run from a pale orange to a very deep red in some rivers. The rainbow generally has a dark olive back with silvery sides and is profusely spotted in black. The common name derives from a broad reddish band which extends laterally from the gillcover almost to its tail. Although it attains weights up to 50 pounds and is often caught in large sizes on our Pacific Coast and in Chile, Argentina and New Zealand, the usual river fish of inland U.S. waters is about 1 to 2 pounds. In common with the cutthroat, the rainbow occurs in a number of races or strains which differ somewhat in appearance. The **Kamloops trout** of British Columbia, for example, is a very deep-bodied fish with a small head as compared to other more slender races such as the rainbows of the Kern and Shasta Rivers. Rainbow trout also occur as anadromous populations and the sea-run form is known as a **steelhead.** The steelhead is larger than the average rainbow found inland, and fish of 6 to 12 pounds are not uncommon. The meat of the steelhead is of excellent quality and pink in color when cooked, or similar to the Atlantic salmon.

Rainbow trout can be prepared by all methods suggested for the brook and brown trout.

SEA TROUT Properly a sea-run brown trout *(see under SEA TROUT).* The name is also applied to anadromous brook trout in northeastern North America and sometimes confused in cookbooks with the spotted seatrout which is not a salmonid but a member of the drum family *(see DRUM, WEAKFISH).*

Trout are also known nonspecifically as **Truite** (France), **Trucha** (Spain and South America), **Truta** (Portugal), **Trota** (Italy), **Pastrva** (Yugoslavia), **Péstropha** (Greece), **Forelle** (Germany), **Forel** (Holland), **Ørred** (Denmark), **Ørret** (Norway), **Tammukka** (Finland), **Öring** (Sweden), **Urrioi** (Iceland), **Masu** (Japan).

BLUE TROUT

During the summer of 1948 I made a tour of the trout streams in Normandy with that *grand hôtelier* Charles Ritz. Automobiles were still scarce in postwar France but the resourceful Monsieur Ritz borrowed an open touring car of 1924 or 1925 vintage which had originally belonged to the French police. Among other things, its brakes were virtually worthless. The car didn't have a horn, so Charles simply leaned out over the door and yodeled when we approached a busy intersection. This had a miraculous effect on otherwise indifferent citizens, and especially on the livestock in rural areas. In Niederwald, Switzerland, one learns to yodel at an early age, and the Ritz family held many local honors. Driving with Charles was a hair-raising experience even when he had a horn to blow, but the frenzied activity of motoring from river to river was assuaged by some of the finest dry fly fishing I have ever enjoyed. The trout taken from cold cress-filled waters provided many memorable meals. Among other delights I was introduced to **truite au bleu,** a dish of European origins that only found its way to American tables in recent years.

The organoleptic appreciation of trout begins with a fish done in the blue style. This dish is the pure unadulterated essence of trout. If a salmonid has any ambition whatsoever, it is to expire in a metallic burst of blue. When you achieve a *limon bleu*, a touch of the fork will loose rivulets of ambrosial nectar, clear and heady as a summer brook. The very color tells you that the sweets of the river are locked in the fish. Its belly skin may be the shade of a blushing cardinal, or yellow spring butter, but once the trout enters the court bouillon, its mayfly fat is sealed under the regal robe. Since the day Philogenes of Leucas recited the ground rules of purist cookery, the trout has worn this color with unparalleled majesty. Ernest Hemingway, who was a man of lusty appetites, described it best in one of his columns for the *Toronto Star Weekly (By-Line: Ernest Hemingway*, edited by William White, Charles Scribner's Sons, 1967) written while he was fishing in Switzerland.

It is not a well-known dish at the hotels. You have to go back in the country to get trout cooked that way. You come up from the stream to a chalet and ask them if they know how to cook blue trout. If they don't you walk on a way. If they do, you sit down on the porch with the goats and children and wait. Your nose will tell you when the trout are boiling. Then after a while you will hear a pop. That is the Sion being uncorked. Then the woman of the chalet will come to the door and say, "It is prepared, Monsieur."

Then you can go away and I will do the rest myself.

Blue trout recipes invite a turgid flow of metaphor from European cooks, but they always fail to explain where the color originates. There are no plums in plum pudding, no duck in Bombay duck, and no blue coloring in a trout's skin. The color comes from the same lubricant that makes a fish slippery—the film that keeps our trout waterproof. Without it he would drown and without it there can be no blue. Consequently, the idea has existed that the trout must be cooked alive. Something is always lost in translation, but this calculated sadism grew out of the French phrase, "in a live condition," meaning that the trout should *not* be washed or scaled before going into the vinegar bath. A fish that is handled too much or one that has been frozen will not color, simply because the slime has been removed. Bear in mind that all trout have almost microscopic scales and the skin is an important source of flavor as well as nutrition, which we try to preserve in all cooking methods; it is removed usually for decorative purposes in preparations such as trout in aspic. Actually, your fish should be quite dead, but killed and gutted an instant before bluing. All good restaurants which serve this have a holding pool in the dining room from which the trout are removed with a dip net. Part of the dogma handed from kitchen to kitchen also reveals that more than one restaurant has made a practice of using trout that are not exactly fresh. Numerous recipes suggest running a cord through the trout from mouth to tail, or piercing the fish's head with a toothpick and trussing him tail to head. The idea is to serve curved trout, but the final gesture of a *freshly killed* trout is to curl, and he will do this with no help from the chef. String and toothpicks are dubiously necessary only when the fish has been dead for many hours and the muscle tissue will no longer contract. The actual preparation of the fish is easy.

Virtually all blue trout recipes require that the fish be cooked in what amounts to vinegared water; this inevitably results in a trout that tastes like vinegar. To retain a delicate flavor I prefer a two-step procedure which produces instant bluing and more aromatic poaching.

COURT BOUILLON FOR BLUE TROUT

2 quarts water	1 onion, quartered
1 cup dry white wine	few parsley sprigs
1 tablespoon lemon juice	1 tablespoon
2 celery ribs,	fresh tarragon,
cut into small pieces	or 1 teaspoon dried
large fistful of	3 bay leaves
celery leaves	6 peppercorns, bruised
1 large carrot,	salt
cut into chunks	

Put all the ingredients in a large kettle, bring to a boil, and let it bubble merrily for 30 minutes. Strain to remove the solid parts, and return the liquid to the kettle. Bring again to a boil.

tarragon vinegar
water
trout

In another kettle mix one third tarragon vinegar with two thirds water and bring to a boil. With large kitchen tongs grasp each trout firmly by the lower jaw and lower it into the hot vinegar mixture. When properly blue, place the trout in the boiling court bouillon. The bouillon will cease bubbling for a few minutes, but when it comes to a boil again, remove the pot from the heat and cover. Let this stand for 15 to 20 minutes and your trout are cooked. Remove the fish carefully with a large spatula, and drain them.

Classically, blue trout are served with marble-size new potatoes bathed in butter and garnished with parsley. There should also be a side dish of garden-fresh asparagus smothered in mousseline sauce (hollandaise mixed with an equal part of stiffly whipped cream). After the cream has been added to the hollandaise, heat it very carefully and stir until the sauce is hot. A dry white wine would be the proper mate to such rich fare. A watercress salad is a must.

The way they did trout in the old days out of Willie Pollock's Antumalal Lodge on the Trancura River in Chile would be hard to duplicate but it should be recorded before the formula is lost. You would begin at dawn when snow-capped Andean peaks gleamed like helmeted sentinels, with a skilled *botero* maneuvering the craft over foaming rapids. Wherever he gentled the double-ender into smooth currents behind piano-sized boulders you could make a few casts to the rainbow trout that lay in these calm eddies. Often as not, a fish would rush the fly, then you bounced down through swift water following its furious leaps. By noon on a good day the count was 40 or 50 released fish. The *botero* always saved two of a size suitable for his grill. Then, he would pull up on a gravelly bank in the shade of the forest and begin his ritual by chilling the wines behind a cofferdam of river stones. While you gathered dry wood, he spitted a lamb on a long iron rod. After much calculation with respect to its position over the fire, the rod was angled into the ground, and the grill balanced on rocks of a proper height below the lamb. When the flame seared its fat, the crimson-fleshed trout, now in fillets, were laid skin side down on the grill where the lamb sprayed hot droplets over the fish like an atomizer until a golden crust sealed their juices inside. The trout was served first, washed down with a cold *vino blanco*. Next came the pink lamb with a pot of brown rice and crisp green asparagus followed by those incredible succulent pears that grow only in Chile. One could also pick the huge blackberries growing profusely in the volcanic ash along the stream bank. Soon it was siesta time and you dozed by the sound of the Trancura's rapids before getting on with the fishing.

WATERCRESS PURÉE WITH RED TROUT (PURÉE DE CRESSON AVEC TRUITE ROUGE)

A soup called a purée is one that is thickened or given body by puréeing all the ingredients. Often potatoes are added and the mixture is made smooth by blending them into the liquid at the end of the cooking process. (Some starchy vegetables such as lentils or split peas do not require potatoes for thickening.) I created this recipe while living on the Beaverkill River in Turnwood, where we had an abundance of watercress growing in the stream back of our kitchen, both a bland and a spicy species. The name "red trout" refers to its flesh color, which is not common on the Beaverkill. One needs a big native brown trout that has been feeding on crayfish in sufficient quantity to "blush" amid the emerald green watercress. Fresh coho, sockeye or Atlantic salmon, or a brilliantly hued brook trout from Quebec or Labrador, provide an ideal *visual* contrast. However, the dish is equally *flavorsome* with white-fleshed trout, or any of the firm chowder species such as halibut or cod; even fillets or walleye and black bass can be used with great success.

2 pounds trout fillets, skinned and chunked
4 cups fish stock or clam nectar
5 tablespoons butter
4 bunches of watercress, stems included, chopped
1 large leek, white part only, chopped
1 medium-size onion, chopped
salt
4 cups chicken consommé
1 pound medium-size potatoes, peeled and halved
juice of ½ lemon
¾ cup heavy cream
white pepper
½ bunch of watercress sprigs for garnish

Melt 3 tablespoons of the butter in a large pot and add the chopped watercress, leek and onion. Salt lightly. Cover the pot and let the vegetables combine their juices over low heat for about 10 minutes. Add the fish stock, consommé and potatoes, bring to a boil, reduce heat, and cook for about 1 hour, until potatoes are done. Do not cook too fast or the soup will become too thick.

While the purée is cooking, poach the trout in a separate pan in lightly salted water with a little lemon juice added. Poach the fish just to the point where it looks cooked but is still firm. Remove from heat and cover. It will continue cooking in the warm water.

When the purée has simmered for 1 hour, pour it into a blender container, in several batches unless your blender is very large. Add the cream and remaining 2 tablespoons of butter. Blend thoroughly until the potatoes are smooth. Return the purée to the pot and reheat but do not boil. Season with additional salt if needed and white pepper. With a slotted spoon or spatula remove trout from the pan and arrange chunks in individual serving bowls. Pour the purée over the fish, leaving some of the trout chunks exposed above the surface. Garnish with sprigs of watercress. Serve hot or cold. Makes 4 main-dish servings, or 6 soup-course servings.

facing page, The author fishing for trout on the North Fork of the Shoshone River, Wyoming

HOW TO DECORATE A POACHED TROUT (prepared by Chef Charles Janon at the Inter-Continental Hotel, Paris)

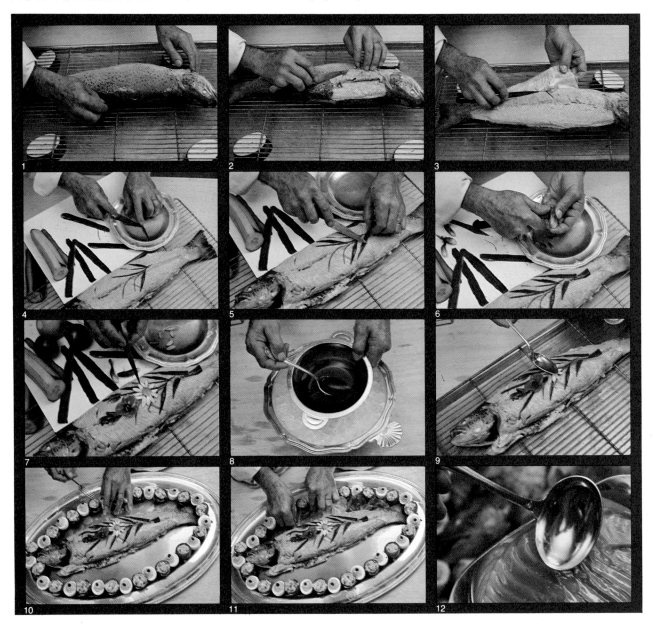

1. The poached trout. 2. With the point of a knife
loosen the skin. 3. Peel off the skin, leaving a smooth
surface of uniform color. 4. Cut a thin strip from
cucumber peel and dip it into liquid aspic. 5. Arrange
on the trout in a leaf design. 6. Cut red radishes
into long slices, retaining the red skin. 7. Arrange
radish pieces on the trout like blossoms, and
make a large daisy from cooked egg white and lemon peel.
8. Chill the aspic in a pan filled with cracked ice.
9. Spoon the aspic gently over the decorated trout.
10. Arrange trout on a platter and surround with small
tomatoes filled with salade russe and
stuffed hard-cooked eggs decorated with capers.
11. Arrange small lettuce leaves around the dish.
12. Serve with green mayonnaise.

facing page, Trout ready to serve, presided
over by Chef Charles Janon

TROUT MEUNIÈRE

The term *meunière* or "miller's wife" indicates dusting the food with flour and panfrying in clarified butter. For smaller fish or thin skinless fillets of fish such as sole, flounder or perch this is easily accomplished, but with a ½-pound trout it is difficult to achieve a crisp skin before burning the butter. The use of a light oil for browning is recommended. Freshly caught trout within 6 to 8 hours from the water will "curl" with the application of heat to the point that they become impossible to brown evenly and the skin will rupture; scoring a small trout will simply dry out the fish. A curled or broken fish doesn't matter in camp, but for an artful dinner presentation hold the trout, already dusted with seasoned flour, overnight in the refrigerator. The chilled fish will not only cook in shape but will achieve a crispier skin.

6 whole 8-ounce trout, dressed	½ cup flour
¼ pound sweet butter	peanut or cottonseed oil
1 teaspoon salt	12 parsley
½ teaspoon pepper	or watercress sprigs
	2 lemons, quartered

Clarify the butter and discard the milky solids at the bottom of the pan. Set aside. Mix salt and pepper with the flour. Wash the trout under cold running water and drain thoroughly but do not pat dry. Dust each fish inside and out while still damp with the seasoned flour so that it's lightly coated. Pour oil into a heavy skillet, using enough to keep trout from sticking—about ¼ inch deep—and bring to a high heat. Add trout, two or three at a time, cooking at a moderate temperature (about 350°F.) for 4 to 5 minutes on each side, or until golden brown. The tails should be crisp. Remove trout to absorbent paper.

Reheat the clarified butter until it's brown in color, but do not burn. Arrange trout on warm individual serving plates or a serving platter and pour hot butter over each fish. Garnish with the lemon wedges and sprigs of parsley or watercress. Makes 6 servings.

TROUT WITH ALMONDS

4 whole 12-ounce trout, dressed	juice of ½ lemon
1 cup blanched almonds	1 cup seasoned flour
½ pound butter	8 lemon wedges dipped into minced parsley

Knife-chop the blanched almonds. Melt 6 tablespoons of the butter in a small frying pan until very light brown. Add the almonds and sauté over low heat until they are golden. Add the lemon juice to the pan.

Flour the trout as for Trout Meunière, and panfry them, two at a time, in remaining butter in a large frying pan. Shake the pan a little as they cook to prevent sticking. Cook for about 5 minutes on each side and remove to a hot platter. When all are cooked and arranged on the platter, pour the almond mixture over them and garnish with the parsley-coated lemon wedges. Makes 4 servings.

TROUT GRENOBLOISE

This is similar to the recipe for Trout Meunière but the cook adds some good lemon juice, or lemon pulp cut into tiny cubes, and capers to the melting butter before pouring it over the fish. This creates a more piquant flavor, but the result depends on the quality of the lemons. If the only fruit available is the small highly acidic supermarket variety it's best to minimize the citrus. A sweet Mexican or Key lime is much the better option. There is no way of stating how much juice should be used; it's best judged by taste. Allow 1 tablespoon of capers for each fish and decorate the sides with fluted lemon or lime slices.

SHERIFF HOUSE TROUT
(Sheriff House, Stockbridge, England)

4 trout, 12 ounces each, kited and boned	⅔ cup fresh heavy cream
1 pound sole fillets	sea salt and white pepper
3 egg whites	butter

Pound sole fillets in a mortar and rub through a fine wire sieve; repeat until sole has the texture of cream. Break egg whites with a fork and beat into sole, a little at a time. Sieve once again. Gradually beat the heavy cream into the mixture and season with salt and freshly ground pepper to taste. Spread some of this stuffing on the inside surface of each trout. Reshape the fish and arrange in a fireproof casserole dish which has been well buttered. Wipe exposed parts of trout with more butter. Bake at 350°F. for about 20 minutes. Cover with Sheriff House Sauce. Makes 4 servings.

SHERIFF HOUSE SAUCE
2 shallots, chopped fine
2 tablespoons butter
½ cup white Burgundy wine
1 ounce Cognac
1 tablespoon minced fresh parsley

This sauce can be made while the trout are cooking. Sauté shallots in butter just to soften, then add wine and boil for a few seconds. Reduce heat, and add the Cognac and parsley. Bring to a boil again while stirring, then pour over trout.

facing page, Trout with almonds

TROUT STUFFED WITH CRAB MEAT

4 trout, 12 ounces each, kited and boned	1 tablespoon minced parsley
8 ounces crab meat	1 teaspoon dried orégano
3 stale rolls	juice of ½ lemon
1 cup milk	½ teaspoon Worcestershire sauce
1 whole egg	dash of Tabasco
1 extra egg yolk	salt and pepper
⅓ cup chopped raw bacon	melted butter
⅓ chopped onion	paprika

Prepare the stuffing: Soak the rolls in milk, squeeze dry, and add eggs. Sauté the bacon and onion until onion is limp and amber in color but not brown. Add the crab meat and sauté for 5 minutes. Add to bread mixture and then stir in remaining ingredients except melted butter and paprika. Add seasoning to taste. Spread some of the stuffing inside each trout and fold over other halves. Brush the top of each trout with melted butter and sprinkle generously with paprika during the last few minutes of cooking. Bake in a 400°F. oven for 20 to 25 minutes, or until skin is brown and crisp. Makes 4 servings.

TROUT PORTUGAISE

1 trout, 16 ounces, dressed	orégano
3 tomatoes, quartered	1 stuffed green olive, sliced
3 green peppers, quartered	3 black olives, halved
¼ cup melted butter	6 anchovy fillets
¼ cup fine-grade olive oil	1 teaspoon grated lemon rind
	salt and pepper

Lay trout in a baking dish. Arrange tomatoes and pepper quarters around fish. Combine melted butter and olive oil and pour about half of the mixture over all. Sprinkle with orégano. Bake at 350°F. for 15 minutes. Remove from oven and with a fork gently lift off top side skin of trout. Place a green olive slice in the eye. Arrange black olive halves and anchovy fillets in "backbone and rib" pattern. Pour remaining butter-oil mixture over fish and sprinkle with more orégano, the grated lemon rind, and salt and pepper to taste. Put back in oven for 10 more minutes, or until done; test with a fork. Accompany with boiled rice. Makes 2 servings.

BAKED TROUT MONTBARRY

4 whole 12-ounce trout, dressed	1 teaspoon fresh tarragon
	½ cup melted butter
salt and pepper	4 egg yolks
1 tablespoon minced parsley	2 ounces brandy
1 teaspoon minced onion	5 tablespoons bread crumbs
1 tablespoon minced chives	5 tablespoons grated Swiss cheese (Emmental)
1 teaspoon minced chervil	paprika
3 tablespoons minced mushrooms	

Season the trout with salt and pepper inside and out. Line a well-buttered baking dish with the parsley, onion, chives, chervil, mushrooms and tarragon leaves. Put the fish on top and pour the melted butter over them. Cover the dish with foil, and bake in a 400°F. oven for 10 to 12 minutes. Beat the egg yolks with the brandy. Remove the foil from the fish, pour the egg and brandy mixture over them, then sprinkle with the bread crumbs mixed with the Swiss cheese and a little dusting of paprika. Return to the oven and bake until the crumbs are golden brown. Makes 4 servings.

TROUT PARMESAN

4 trout, 12 ounces each, boned and butterflied	peanut or vegetable oil for deep-frying
4 eggs, beaten	2 cups milk
½ pound Parmesan cheese, grated	4 tablespoons flour
salt and pepper	4 tablespoons butter
	capers

Dip trout into beaten eggs. Place half of the grated cheese on wax paper. Press the trout into the cheese to coat heavily. Salt and pepper generously. Deep-fry trout in peanut or vegetable oil until they are crisp.

To make sauce, heat milk to the boiling point and blend in flour and butter. Stir over low heat until thick. Add remaining cheese and the capers, and blend thoroughly. Pour over the fish before serving. Makes 4 servings.

TROUT IN BANANA CURRY SAUCE

4 whole 12-ounce trout, dressed	2 cups Banana Curry Sauce (p. 289)
1 cup evaporated milk	fresh or dried grated coconut
1 cup cornflake crumbs	2 hard-cooked eggs, mashed with fork
melted butter	
2 cups boiled rice	

The method of cooking the trout is optional; poaching or baking produce different but savory results. If baking, dip trout into evaporated milk and dust with

facing page, Trout Parmesan

CRUCIFIED TROUT (RISTIINNAULITTU SIKKA)
(prepared by Helvi Kaartinen at the Rustholli Restaurant, near Tampere, Finland)

cornflake crumbs. Place fish belly down on foil in an oven pan, drizzle with melted butter, and cook at 350°F. for about 20 minutes, or until nicely browned. Arrange fish over a bed of rice in "swimming" position. Pour hot banana curry sauce over each portion. Ring with grated coconut and sprinkle mashed egg over sauce. Makes 4 servings.

TROUT IN ASPIC

1 whole 2-pound trout, dressed
6 cups Court Bouillon for Blue Trout (p. 423)
tarragon leaves
pimiento strips
black olives, pitted and halved
1 cherry tomato half
4 cups liquid White-Wine Aspic (p. 25)

Poach the trout in the court bouillon used for making blue trout. It is not necessary to blue the fish; however, it is an artful touch. When the trout is cooked, 15 to 20 minutes depending on size, transfer the fish with a large spatula from the poacher to a dry towel.

When trout is cool enough to handle, carefully peel off skin on both sides. Place trout on a deep serving platter and decorate as desired; tarragon leaves or pimiento strips can be arranged to simulate "ribs" interspersed with halved black olives, and a halved cherry tomato can be used to create the "eye." Slowly pour the liquid aspic over the fish on the serving platter to cover the fish. Let chill until aspic becomes firm. Makes 4 servings.

CRUCIFIED TROUT

1 trout, 2 pounds or more   brown sugar
¼ cup melted butter   paprika
dry mustard

Split the trout but not through the skin. Do not kite or debone after splitting as the bones will keep fish intact. Nail fish around edges to an oak, hickory or similar hardwood plank. Brush with melted butter and dust lightly with dry mustard, a bit more heavily with brown sugar, and finally with paprika. Cook fish by reflected heat from wood fire. This takes about 20 minutes depending on size of trout. Bones can be lifted free with fork. Makes 2 or more servings.

1. The trout is split, with the halves remaining joined at the belly, and dry-salted. **2.** The fish is nailed to a birch plank. **3.** A fire of birch is built. Mrs. Kaartinen is holding the handles of the planks. **4.** The trout is cooked by the reflected heat of the fire. **5.** The dish ready to serve, garnished with dill and lemon. In this case the head of the trout has been added for an extra fillip.

POACHED STEELHEAD

1 steelhead trout,
 6 pounds whole-dressed
2 quarts water
2 onions, sliced
1 celery rib
2 parsley sprigs
1 tablespoon salt
12 peppercorns

4 whole allspice berries
1 bay leaf
2 cups medium-dry
 white wine
lemon wedges
radish roses
carrot curls
watercress

Combine water, onions, celery, parsley, salt, peppercorns, allspice, bay leaf and wine in a fish poacher. Simmer, covered, for 30 minutes. Place whole steelhead in the poaching liquid, bring liquid back to a simmer, and cook for about 30 minutes, until fish is done. Remove trout from poaching liquid, and carefully remove skin. Serve warm or cold, garnished with lemon wedges, radish roses, carrot curls and watercress. Makes 8 to 10 servings.

Trunkfish

Trunkfish

A small family (Ostraciontidae) of fishes found in tropical and subtropical seas usually occurring in shallow water. The trunkfishes are unique as their heads and bodies are covered with a hard shell composed of rigid hexagonal or polygonal plates instead of scales. Gaps exist at the mouth, nostrils, gills and fins so the fish can swim and feed. The body is square, pentagonal, or nearly triangular in cross section; being boxlike in appearance, the various species are often called **boxfish.** Trunkfishes are usually seen sculling slowly along over sandy flats where they feed on marine plants, sea urchins, starfish and crabs. The average fish is between 1 and 2 pounds in size, but the common **scrawled cowfish** (Acanthostracion quadricornis) attains a weight of about 5 pounds. The cowfish has 2 forward-projecting preopercular spines on its head which resemble a pair of horns—hence the specific common name; it is also known as **toro** in Central and South America, and **chapin** in Puerto Rico.

The carapace of trunkfish holds a toxic substance; however, the epidermis is inedible and only the musculature of the back and ventral surface is utilized. Trunkfishes are one of the most highly esteemed seafoods in the Bahamas and West Indies, to the point that those caught by commercial fishermen are invariably reserved for personal use. The boneless, long-grained meat is similar to a chicken breast in texture and of very delicate flavor. The meat of the cowfish with its liver is made into a popular soup in coastal South America, but the liver gives the dish an unappetizing bluish color. I do not recom- mend the consumption of trunkfish livers, nor the soup, as the presence of epidermal toxin suggests that its viscera, and especially the liver, are potentially dangerous.

The capture of a large boxfish at the Chub Cay Club in the Bahamas is cause for a festive dinner. No better recipe is available than a stuffed and baked version presented by comanagers Bill and Penny Turtle.

STUFFED BOXFISH
(Chub Cay)

Dress the boxfish by making an incision along the entire length of its ventral surface. Remove viscera with a spoon (the shell edges are rigid and somewhat sharp). The body cavity is small and easily emptied.

Make a suffficient amount of your favorite poultry dressing to fill the cavity, incorporating some finely chopped onion, green pepper and tomato.

Wrap the boxfish in heavy foil and bake in a preheated 350°F. oven for 45 minutes. Remove foil and "crack" the shell of the fish with the back of a knife; it will readily fall away.

The meat can be forked out and dipped into melted butter, much as you would eat lobster, or served with an appropriate sauce.

Tullibee

See Cisco under WHITEFISH.

Tuna

They say that the Phoenicians, inhabitants of the city of Cádiz, travel for four days with winds from the East, beyond the pillars of Hercules, until they arrive in certain desert

facing page, Mr. and Mrs. Harry Serlis at their home in California. Mr. Serlis was formerly the President of the California Wine Institute. The dish is a poached steelhead garnished with carrot curls and stuffed whole artichokes.

places, full of seaweeds and drones, which are covered by the ebb and are uncovered by the flow of the tide. There they find an extraordinary number of tuna fish of an incredible size. When they catch them they preserve them, they put them in jars and take them to Carthage. The Carthaginians not only export them but they also use them because they are so good.

De Mirabilis auscultationibus

Aristotle

Among the ancient peoples of the Mediterranean and Black Seas the tuna was not merely an epicurean delicacy roasted on a spit while basted with oil and spices but a catalyst in the growth of civilization. Its value in trade is engraved on the oldest Punic coins from Carthage, Cádiz, Carteia (now Gibraltar) and the Eastern Empire of Byzantium. The tuna grounds were below those coastal cliffs where watchmen could sight great migrations from elevated platforms, then give cry inviting the fishermen to row out and spread their nets. Thus, the cities of Eregli, Cisira, Eritria (on the island of Euboea in the Aegean), Naxos (Greek colony on Sicily), the Aegean island of Icaria, the Ionian islands Cephalonia and Zante, Tenedos (at the entrance to the Dardanelles), Tunis, Tripoli, the Sicilian cities of Syracuse, Cefalù, Palermo, Trapani and Messina, Taranto on the Italian heel, the islands of Elba and Sardinia, the Terra Cetaria stretching from Segeste to San Vito, Cetabriga and Cetabora (today Setúbal) on the Portuguese Coast—all had their genesis around crude spruce observation posts or *tinnoscopi* before the birth of Christ. Many ancient place names derive from the root word *cete*, meaning a fish of great dimensions but also, specifically, locations where tuna were caught.

Although Aeschylus (525–456 B.C.) in his tragedy *The Persians* likened the massacre of the Persian Navy by the Greeks at the Battle of Salamis to the butchering of tuna, indicating that it was already an established trade, it was Aristotle (384–322 B.C.) who first wrote at length about the species, establishing a mythology that would survive for over 1,000 years through scholarly repetition. Aristotle believed that tuna grew to a weight of 15 talents (1,200 pounds) and that the fish lived for 2 years, becoming fat to the point of exploding. According to the master, all tuna spawned in the Pontus or Black Sea, which the fish arrived at by keeping land in sight with their stronger right eyes. He further observed that tuna sleep so soundly at night that they will not move at the blow of a harpoon; it was believed that the fish slowly sank to the bottom while sleeping, then floated to the surface again and repeated their somnambulant descent. In his opinion small tuna were difficult to catch but the large ones were excited by a small worm or *assillo* which attached itself to their fins at a certain time of year (during the heat of summer and until the star Arcturus rises, which not unexpectedly coincides with the peak spawning run) and therefore became more vulnerable to capture.

Polybius of Megalopolis in Arcadia (205–125 B.C.) in his *Historiarum Reliquiae* agreed with Aristotle, but he was the first author to state that tuna feed on acorns, and so the fish became known as *porco marino* or "sea pig." The nutlike fruit that Polybius believed to be an acorn comes from a plant *(Posidonia caulinii)* which occurs in Mediterranean and Iberian Atlantic waters, and it's often found in windrows on beaches, especially after a storm; but not one has ever been discovered in the stomachs of tunas.

The Greek geographer Strabo (60 B.C.–25 A.D.) elaborated on its acorn diet, describing in detail the mythical oak trees that grow in the sea "whose fruits litter the beaches in and out of the Pillars of Hercules (Straits of Gibraltar)," and provided the tuna with an even more remarkable eyesight, bearing economic implications: *After passing the promontory of Cianee (on the Black Sea near the Bosphorus), when they see from the Chalcedonian coast a certain white rock, they are taken by terror and turn immediately to the opposite coast. At this point, carried away by the precipitous course of the waters, the nature of those regions, lead by the currents toward the Horn of Byzantium (the Golden Horn) and pushed by their natural impetus, they become an easy catch and abundant profit for the Byzantines and the Romans. The Chalcedonians, by contrast, who are on the other coast, do not enjoy these riches because not even one pelamyd reaches them.* (Chalcedon was a separate kingdom belonging to the Bithynians until Rome claimed it by force in 74 B.C.)

The pelamyd in many ancient manuscripts implies young bluefin tuna, but it is unquestionably one of the smaller scombrids and probably the Atlantic bonito. Aritotle refers to a pelamyd with stripes on the upper body and, later, Pliny calls this fish *sarda* (fish of Sardinia), which describes the bonito *Sarda sarda*. In Greek, young tunas were called *cordili* and adults *orcini*.

In subsequent works, Pliny the Elder (23–79 A.D.) repeated everything Aristotle had said and added a few fables of his own, notably a confrontation between the fleet of Alexander the Great and an immense school of tuna which isolated the vessels, requiring them to fight the fish off in "battle order." But Pliny did recommend the fat of fresh tuna to cure ulcers and the ashes of tuna heads mixed with salt and honey "to keep away boils or pimples from the parts of which we are ashamed." During the next century, Plutarch and Galen added little to man's knowledge of tuna, but Oppian of Anabarzuz in Cilicia (there were two Oppians and the work of the one from Cilicia was known to the second who copied the former's style in a treatise on hunting) became fascinated by the "persecution" of tuna and swordfish by the *assillo*.

> *He runs after tuna and swordfish*
> *the damned companion, whom they*
> *cannot rid themselves of, the cruel assillo.*

The *assillo* was described as wormlike by Aristotle and like a spider or scorpion in shape by others. In the light of present knowledge it was actually a parasitic copepod *(Brachiella thynni)*, which is more common in swordfish than tuna and may appear in different shapes at various stages in its development. However, this parasite is comparatively rare in terms of infestations as modern-day researchers handle thousands of tuna without finding a single copepod. Oppian's observation was nevertheless repeated and embellished by later authors.

The first suggestion of fact in the life history of tuna is found in the work of Claudius Aelianus. Aelian (170–235 A.D.) taught rhetoric while producing an encyclopedic work of 17 volumes *De natura animalium.* He listed 110 species of fish and 40 of these were not described by Aristotle, which indicates some original effort. In book IX he observes that ". . . tunas have the property of feeling the effects of the change of seasons and they know with precision the solstices (also mentioned by Plutarch) and can compete in this matter with the most knowledgeable person on the subject of sky phenomena." Aelian was unaware of the pineal apparatus situated at the base of the tuna's brain under a translucent skull membrane which, like a photographer's exposure meter, is capable of measuring light; but his hypothesis was correct. Migratory orientation is not a question of the tuna's seeking land (which it cannot see in any event) but to some extent a matter of responding to the phenomenon of changing light intensity at various seasons of the year.

While philosophers and naturalists speculated on the mysteries of tuna, poets sang its praises as a food. Theophrastus, Archestratus, Theodoride, Enbulo, Aristophanes, Strattide, Eriso, Aristofonte, Antigonus, Menandeo and Ovid rejoiced at the fish which the Greeks dedicated to Artemis (Diana). Ovid's enthusiasm was probably a result of his living in a Black Sea fishing port; among his unfinished works was the 132-line *Halieuticon*, a treatise on fishing.

In the earliest recipes, according to Archestratus and Salviani, fresh tuna was often seasoned with cinnamon, ground coriander, vinegar and honey, then cooked in olive oil with chopped onion. Apicius favored cuminseed and mint, and in various preparations added black pepper, mustard, thyme and raisins. Giovio and Aldrovandi prepared their tuna in the style Ligurians named *azemino*, with wine, oil, garlic, pepper and onions. The smaller pelamyds, according to Platina, were best when fried with orange juice and parsley. Tuna not eaten in fresh form was salted and dried in small cubes as *cibio* or cut into squares which resembled wooden blocks and were called *melandrio* after the European black oak *(Melandria).* Pickled in brine for 8 to 10 days and packed in barrels, any cut of tuna was known as *salsamentum sardicum*, but the meat was graded as choice *(sorra)*, second quality *(netta)*, or lowest quality *(businaglia)*. Tuna roe was considered a supreme delicacy and was preserved by salting, pressing, and drying in the form of *bottarghe* (ovaries) or *lattumi* (testes). But the mystique in tuna cookery was the recognition of specific parts of the fish for their superior table qualities.

Both Vitellius and Apicius, for example, celebrated for their culinary skills, considered *sorra* the most delicate cut and preserved it in large crystal vases for their sumptuous banquets. The butchering of tuna was a high art in Mediterranean cultures and it continues to be today in many countries, although it's virtually unknown in America, where canned tuna is a compacted steamed product and the fish is relatively uncommon in fresh form. The only part of a tuna not utilized by ancient fishermen was the tail, but even a dried caudal fin had its purpose when nailed over a doorway to protect the home from evil spirits. In so large a fish with a well-defined musculature various "cuts" of meat can be recognized for their quality. In the opinion of Francesco Cetti: "At every spot, at every different cavity at which the knife penetrates this meat is different: firm in one spot, tender in another; here it looks like veal, there like pork." (An eighteenth-century writer, Cetti's natural history of Sardinia, *Storia naturale della Sardegna*, 1777, was still supporting the acorn myth.) Thus, a tuna vocabulary or *vocabolario tonnaresco* evolved from several languages: much of it is still used today and has a modern Japanese counterpart, but the classic terminology is from old Mediterranean cultures which predated the Oriental fishery.

The tuna was divided into 2 parts with a vertical cut from the back to the anus. Both the tail portion and the trunk were next incised laterally at the midline to distinguish and separate the dorsal-lateral from ventral-lateral musculature. The first portion removed was the *cozzo* (also known as *zuffo*) or "shoulder butt" from in front of the dorsal fin between the interneural and occipital bones. The remaining dorsal or back meat provided

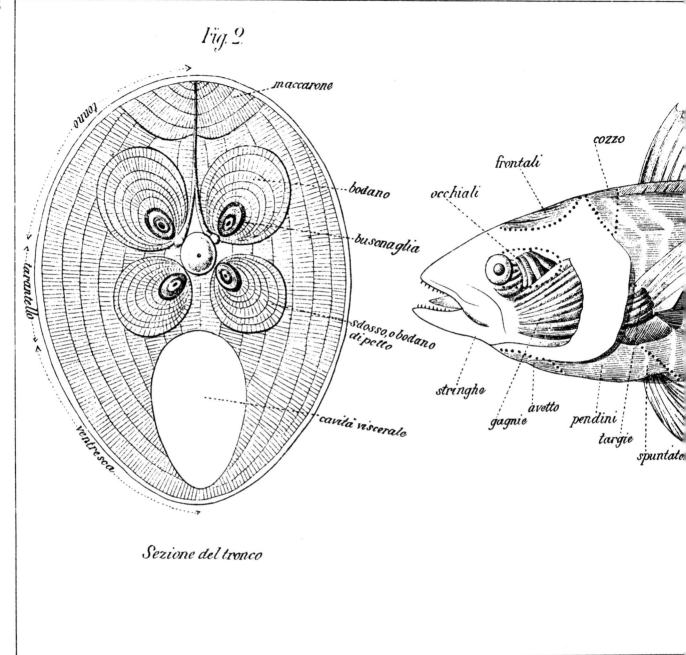

Fig. 2

maccarone

tonno

bodano

occhiali

busonaglia

frontali

cozzo

tarantello

sdosso, o bodano di petto

cavità viscerale

ventresca

stringhe

gagnie

avetto

pendini

targie

spuntato

Sezione del tronco

tonno, which are the thin superficial muscles, some of which serve as "elevators" for the fins and cover the spaces between the bones of the dorsal fin; this thick layer of meat above the backbone is known as *maccarone*. The innermost portion paralleling the backbone dorsally, consists of coarse and dark meat or *busonaglia* (or *saigacho* in Portuguese) which is the poorest quality. This is surrounded by the *bodano* (or *bodino* in Sicily). The master of the knife next removed portions of the belly or *sorra;* first the lower most lateral-oblique muscle of which the fattest part was considered "choice," the *ventresca* or *sorra bianca.* This is the part of the abdomen in which the muscles divide into lamellae separated by fatty inclusions. Just above the *ventresca* is the *tarantello* (named after the Gulf of Taranto, a famous tuna center in the

Roman era), which was cut and squared off with the knife. Then we have the cones of inner red meat with longitudinal fibers paralleling the abdomen on either side, called *sdosso* or *badano di petto (sdosso* has the same root as the verb "to undress" and *petto* means "breast"). The *sdosso* is lifted out in a whole piece or sometimes cut into strips.

The unequal small pieces that are left are separated, and are called *scorcilli;* thè snippets of the *bodino* form the *bodinella;* the points of the *sorre,* at the front of the ventral fins, or the lower front part of the belly, the side muscles of the trunk, are called *spuntature* or *mondezze,* and the smaller pieces and the scraped parts near the bones are called *mollicaglie* (crumbs). The last part left is the *schinale,* the spinal column, with the *interspinosi* (portion between the bones) of the dorsal fins,

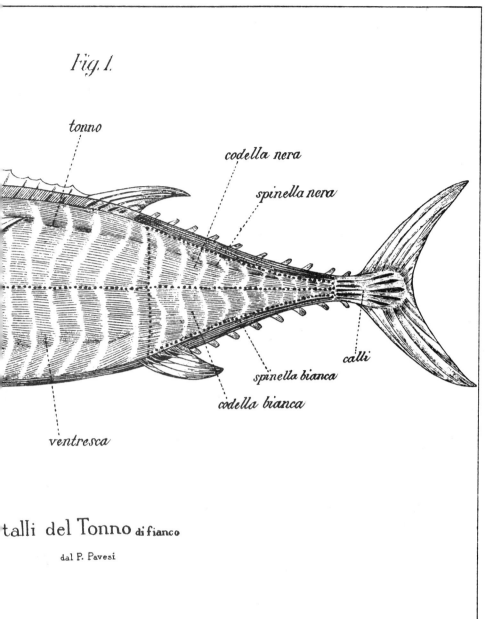

Fig. 1.

tonno

codella nera

spinella nera

calli

spinella bianca

codella bianca

ventresca

...talli del Tonno di fianco

dal P. Pavesi

DIVIDING THE TUNA

left, Cross section of tuna
right, Side view of tuna
Each section of the fish is
separated for a particular
usage determined by its
quality. The Italian names
of the various parts
are explained in the text
(pp. 437 to 439). The
diagram by P. Pavesi
is reproduced from *Il Tonno e
la Sua Pesca* (the tuna
and its fishery), by Corrado
Parona, Venice, 1919.

and some muscles.

The fragile lower muscle, which is called *spinella bianca*, on the belly side, and the fragile upper muscle on the back side, which is called the *spinella nera* (*bianca* is white, *nera* is black), are separated from the tail by 4 lengthwise incisions, two by two, parallel and close to each other. The major portion of the tail is subdivided on the anterior; the superficial side muscles are called *fimminello* (Sicily) or *codella* (Sardinia). This is cut again into 2 portions: the white and the black parts; and each is again cut into 4 pieces. From the back are cut out the *calli*, or those inner muscles found in the tail fin, called by the Sicilians *codarchi*. From the head the cutters skillfully take out with their knives the *frontali*, meat found in the sides of the interparietal bone or superoccipital bone at

the end of the *zuffo* (shoulder butt). They take out the eyes with all their muscles, and the maxillary and palatal muscles. They take out the *pendini*, or muscles of the membrane of the gills, finally the *gagnie* (Sardinia) or *gargie* (Sicily), other muscles of the operculum (gillcover), until nothing is left but the skull.

Tunas are members of the mackerel family (Scombridae) but they are so unlike other mackerel from a kitchen standpoint that we will treat these two groups separately. There are 6 species of tuna which come to market in fresh, frozen and canned form, and each is distinctly different in color, texture and flavor. The *light* meat pack for the canning industry comes from the yellowfin tuna, skipjack and small bluefin, whereas the *white* meat tuna pack is derived only from the albacore. Generally speaking, flesh color is a reflection of quality in the sense that the darker tunas tend to be less delicately flavored. Tuna is also sold as salted fillets, air-dried, smoked, and in a variety of prepared forms such as sausages, wieners, in tuna paste and tuna loaf. The roe is also salted and air-dried, also canned in some countries. In the U. S. tuna is dominantly a canned rather than a fresh product, although large quantities are taken by sportsmen in our northeastern waters and in the Pacific.

American commercial fishermen did not pursue tunas in the western Atlantic until about 1960. Minor landings of bluefin and skipjack tuna were made but essentially the fishery in this ocean was on the European side where bluefin and albacore were traditionally important foods. The yellowfin, bigeye, skipjack and albacore had been caught, again in minor amounts, off the coast of Africa, but at the beginning of that decade a dramatic change took place. The French and Spanish fleets appeared in force off West Africa, followed by the Japanese longliners who eventually spread their operation all over the tropical and subtropical Atlantic. The U. S. tuna fleet confined its operations mainly to the Pacific where it had been rooted historically. The IATTC (Inter-American Tropical Tuna Commission) quota on yellowfin encouraged Pacific and Puerto Rico based seiners to work Atlantic waters—first the northwest Atlantic, now more off Africa. In a single decade the tuna landings of the Atlantic almost doubled from 180,000 metric tons in 1955 to 330,000 metric tons in 1964.

One of the most ancient large-scale fisheries in the world, which has existed in the Mediterranean and its approaches since the early Christian era, is the fixed trap for bluefin tuna. These traps, variously known as *almadraba* in Spain, *armacoa* in Portugal, *tonnara* in Italy and the *madrague* to French fishermen, are set near the coasts and depend on the spawning migration of bluefin traveling eastward in their "arrival" run during May and June and westward in July and August on their "return" run. Where catches were measured in thousands of tons in years past, the fishery has declined to a few hundred fish in recent seasons, and in many areas the traps are closed. For a variety of reasons the giant Atlantic tuna has been greatly reduced.

Until recently, the bluefin tuna never had any commercial value in eastern U. S. waters. There were no processors comparable to the well-organized California canning industry with its far-ranging tuna fleet. Since this fish is most common at the size of a baby elephant, it's hardly the kind of fish that one can bring home after a

day's sport. I have seen 600- to 700-pound bluefins towed from weigh stations and dumped at sea when the petfood and fertilizer markets were at low ebb. Even the smaller "school" tuna of 40 to 50 pounds pose a transportation problem, not to mention dressing and icing. For years, tuna was generally downgraded as a food mainly through the lack of knowledge concerning its preservation and cooking. To cultures elsewhere in the world this species is greatly esteemed, particularly in Japan where paper-thin slices or cubes of a fat bluefin dabbed with *wasabi*, a fiery green horseradish sauce, is fit for the Emperor. As with so many other fish the amount of fat in a tuna varies greatly from season to season, almost month to month. This is a total preoccupation on the part of Japanese markets because of the great demand for **sashimi.** At auction in Tokyo's Tsukiji Central Wholesale Market the tails of tuna are cut off and the caudal peduncle notched to reveal the color of the flesh, with the pink or fatter meat or **toro** commanding a higher price than the dark or lean meat. A lean fish may be used for **sashimi** in lesser restaurants or rolled in seaweed with rice for **sushi,** but most of it goes into smoked fish sausages or **tsuna hamu.** Although Japanese longliners capture tuna all over the world and are concentrating of late in the Mediterranean, our bluefins from the coast of New England were bringing over $1.00 a pound to American fishermen in 1973 (from 5 cents a pound the year before), and these were iced and airlifted to Tokyo where the cost to the retailer was more than $3.00 per pound. *(Trends in Bluefin Tuna Catches in the Atlantic Ocean and the Mediterranean Sea, Frank J. Mather III, Woods Hole Oceanographic Institution, 1974)* Special freezer ships docked in Maine and anchored off Massachusetts also purchased giant bluefin for the Japanese **sashimi** market, sometimes directly from the catching vessel (including harpooners, rod trawlers, and at least one seiner). This abundance of fat tuna off our Northeast coast is a phenomenon common to all the world's oceans, but it must be understood in a time context.

Much of our western Atlantic run of giant bluefin originates off the coast of South America and enters the Florida Straits by way of the Bahamas. After spawning in that area these are all lean fish. By the time they have passed Montauk they are eager to fatten up on shoals of herring and squid, and reach their peak condition like an Alsatian force-fed goose in the waters of New England and eastern Canada during late summer and fall. On occasion at least a portion of the Bahamian school heads directly for Norway, as tuna tagged off Cat Cay and Bimini have been recaptured 50 to 120 days later, and

facing page, Landing the tuna catch at Funchal, Madeira

BIGEYE TUNA ON THE BEACH AT FUNCHAL, MADEIRA

Tuna boats moor 40 to 50 feet offshore.
Men and boys in smaller boats row out to bring in the catch.
Whole tunas are strung together by a thick rope
through the mouths and in groups of ten or more they are towed
in by the rowboats. Tunas are hauled up on the
beach and eviscerated, then carried up the stone steps
to be weighed and distributed.

preceding pages, Carrying a bigeye tuna, which may
weigh 300 pounds, up the steps from the beach at Funchal

Fish market, Funchal, Madeira. While other species
are sold here, tuna is the most important. It is being cut into
steaks and prepared in various other ways.

these arrived in Europe as *very* lean fish. On the other hand tagged tuna recaptured 3 months later, indicating that they had made the same journey in a previous year and fed in European waters, were in a normal fat condition. This has a parallel in the stocks of fish entering the Mediterranean; those tuna arriving in the spring, known as *tonno di corsa*, are leaner than the fall-migrating tuna, or *tonno di ritorno*, which are leaving the Mediterranean after spawning and fattening. For this reason, ever since ancient times prime fall fish are always allowed more cooking time in traditional recipes.

Bluefin tuna undergoes a change when it's cooked. When raw it does not even have a fish flavor but is more nearly like a fine slice of roast beef and even more softly textured. Yet cooked it becomes very firm and has a stronger flavor, not at all unpleasant but one that people either like or dislike. In Spain, Portugal and Italy the bluefin is an important market fish and here cooked dishes are the rule. These older cuisines have learned to treat the tuna by brining and chilling to get a perfect result. An ancient and classic dish in Madeira, for example, a garlicky creation which explains how Portuguese navigators found their way home, is **Atum de Escabeche** *(see recipe)* which is usually made from small bluefin or "school" tuna, although at times chunks of giant tuna (400 pounds or more) are used. The dark-meated bluefin requires soaking in salted water, and Madeiran fishermen are quick to point out that the fish is both heavy and oily if eaten *immediately* after cooking. For best results the tuna should be cooked one day, refrigerated overnight, and served hot or cold the next day.

Dried bonito or skipjack tuna become **katsuobushi,** one of the most versatile seafood products in the Orient. Strips of the fish are repetitively roasted and dried, then defatted by enzymatic action to the point that they become as hard as wood. In fact **katsuobushi** has to be shaved with a very sharp blade or a special planing tool to be made edible. These flakes not only retain their food value but are used as a seasoning to be sprinkled on vegetables and rice, or to provide the base for a delicately flavored soup called **dashi.** The flakes can be bought in specialty shops in the U.S., and a fairly good dehydrated version of the soup is available. A similar "knot" or **bushi** of fish is made from Pacific mackerel and is known as **sababushi,** but it lacks the refined flavor obtained with skipjack.

A MODERN TUNA SAGA

The most critical hour in a lifetime of angling is difficult to measure when one has the choice of a cap-

sized boat in a sub-Arctic river, a plane crash in Alaska, an earthquake in Peru, a revolt in the then Congo and sundry other events that inevitably occur when journeying off beaten paths. But the cliff-hanger that always comes to my mind concerns a 585-pound Newfoundland tuna, not big since tuna grow over twice this size, but a powerful amount of muscle capable of speeds up to 40 miles per hour.

We had hardly left the dock that morning when my tuna came up and wolfed a herring bait. For the first half hour the fish acted like all the other bluefins I had caught, making gut-busting runs that jolted my shoulders. About the time I was getting my second wind the fish turned from deep water and headed for a public bathing beach on the west shore of Conception Bay. It was less than a mile distant. The skipper tried to gun the old Cape Islander to head the bluefin off, but the great squat lady couldn't get her stern moving fast enough to intercept the fish. I had visions of a quarter-ton beast rocketing through innocent bathers, cleaving their heads off with a 120-pound test line. Locked in my harness I shouted for a knife to cut the line, but the captain had his own problems. As we approached the beach, the boat had full headway and reverse engines merely left her wining and churning as we went aground like a stranded whale. When the hull hit bottom I nearly went through the back of a fighting chair. The impact tossed a cod chowder off the galley stove and smoke billowed from below decks where the buttery liquid had splashed over hot iron. The mate coped with the "fire" while the captain futilely worked the throttle, a scene that stopped traffic on a highway beyond the beach. In minutes there must have been a hundred bewildered people gathered around my bluefin who was squirming in a few inches of water as helpless as a guppy on a wet floor.

TUNA TERMINOLOGY

ALBACORE The albacore *(Thunnus alalunga)* is found in both the Atlantic and Pacific Oceans, in tropical and temperate waters. This is the most valuable species to the U.S. canning industry and the only one labeled "white-meat tuna." Albacore migrate back and forth between North America and Japan and are in season along our West Coast from July through October. Although comparatively small quantities enter our fresh-fish markets, significant amounts are taken by sport fishermen. Water temperature plays a key role in the occurrence of albacore with the fish commonly found at 60° to 66°F. Colder or warmer currents tend to divert the schools farther offshore and both sport fishing boats and commercials operate from several to 100 miles from land in clear blue water at various points along the coast. Albacore is delicious when poached in a loin cut or barbecued in steak form. The steaks can also be panfried. A poached loin served cold on the following day with a dill or cucumber sauce makes a delightful entrée. There is no need to brine albacore before cooking. In French cuisine the true albacore is known as **germon** whereas the name **albacore** means the yellowfin tuna.

BIGEYE TUNA One of the larger tunas, the bigeye *(Thunnus obesus)* attains weights exceeding 400 pounds. This fish is found in all tropical and semitropical seas. The major fisheries for bigeye are in Chile and Peru, and around the Azore Islands. This is a very popular fish in the Azores, where 200-pound tuna are common. The meat of the bigeye is not as light as in the albacore, nor as dark as the bluefin. It's highly prized in Japan where it's known as **mebachi.** Brining this fish is optional, but it may improve the flavor somewhat. Although simply called **atún** in Spanish-speaking South America, in Spain it's the **patudo** and the same name is used in Portugal.

BLACKFIN TUNA The blackfin *(Thunnus atlanticus)* seldom enters U.S. markets, but of all the tuna it's my favorite. Found only in the western Atlantic from Cape Cod to Brazil, the blackfin grows to about 60 pounds although the average we catch in Florida waters is usually 8 to 10 pounds. The meat is firm and very light in color when cooked. It's a delicately flavored fish, perfect when stuffed and baked and a great addition to the smokehouse. No need to brine before cooking.

BLUEFIN TUNA The largest of all tunas, the bluefin *(Thunnus thynnus)* is found in temperate and subtropical seas. It probably attains a weight of 1,500 pounds, and fish of 400 to 600 pounds have been common until recent years. The skin of this fish is steel-blue in color with lavender and greenish reflections when fresh. Formerly of minor value in the U.S., it's highly esteemed in other countries, notably in Europe and Japan. Fresh bluefin can be used in all tuna recipes but it's best brined before cooking. The meat is intermediate in color and marginally classed as light. Most canneries go by color, but usually fish over 120 pounds are too dark for the "light" classification.

BONITO There are 3 species of bonito, all similar in size and food value. The Atlantic bonito *(Sarda sarda)* occurs off our coast and is found in the Mediterranean and Black Seas, while the two other bonitos range along our Pacific shores with one occurring as far south as Chile and the other as far west as the Indo-Pacific region. Bonito can be recognized by the prominent oblique stripes on the upper half of the body. These are considered the least valuable tunas and cannot legally be labeled as "tuna" in the U.S. The meat is dark and strongly flavored. It must be brined before cooking.

BULLET MACKEREL Although the **bullet mackerel** *(Auxis rochei)* and the **frigate mackerel** *(Auxis thazard)* are separate species, they differ only in the number of scale rows under the second dorsal fin, a taxonomic rather than a culinary distinction. Both are called "bullet mackerel" by commercial fishermen. Bullet mackerel are found worldwide in tropical and semitropical seas. They seldom exceed 2 pounds in size. Bullet mackerel are tunalike, similar to the bonitos and are not adaptable to mackerel recipes. The meat is dark and strongly flavored.

LITTLE TUNNY Better known in the U.S. as **false albacore** or more confusingly as "bonito," the little tunny is easy to recognize as it has a patch of scattered spots, usually 4 to 6, just below its pectoral fin. The little tunny *(Euthynnus alletteratus)* is found only in the Atlantic Ocean and the Mediterranean Sea, but there are two very similar species which occur from southern California to Peru and another from Hawaii to the Indo-Pacific region. All are small tunas seldom reaching a weight of 15 pounds and averaging about 4 pounds. The little tunny has very dark meat even after cooking and is strongly flavored unless it's brined. However, this is an edible fish and utilized in other parts of the world, notably Hawaii where it's known as **kawakawa.** It's excellent when smoked *(see SMOKED FISH).*

SKIPJACK TUNA Also called **oceanic bonito, watermelon,** and **Arctic bonito,** this generally small tuna *(Euthynnus pelamis)* is recognized by dark longitudinal stripes on its lower sides. Large specimens can weigh as much as 40 pounds, but the average is usually 6 to 8. The skipjack is found in all tropical and semitropical seas. This is one of the most important commercial species in the Pacific, particularly in Japan where it's called **katsuo,** and in Hawaii where it's known as **aku.** The skipjack has light-colored meat comparable to the yellowfin. It's popular as **sashimi** but is also fried, baked and broiled. In dry form it's commonly served with the Hawaiian poi. For American palates the skipjack should be brined before cooking.

Also known as **Listado** (Spain), **Barrilete** (Chile and Peru), **Gaiado** (Portugal), **Tonnetto striato** (Italy), **Trup prugavac** (Yugoslavia), and **Palamida** (Greece).

YELLOWFIN TUNA This is the most gaily colored tuna with long bright yellow dorsal and anal fins and a stripe of golden yellow on its sides. Yellowfin tunas *(Thunnus albacares)* are found throughout the world in tropical and subtropical waters although they occur as far north as

Raw fresh tuna resembles raw beef.

New Jersey in the Gulf Stream during summer months. This species provides the major landings of our California-based tuna industry. The meat of the yellowfin when cooked is not as light as albacore nor quite as dark as the bluefin but comparable to the blackfin. It's an important foodfish in Hawaii as **ahi** and in Japan as **shibi.** This tuna need not be brined before cooking.

Also known as **Rabil** (Spain), **Albacore** (France), **Atún amarillo** (Mexico to Chile), **Tonno albacora** (Italy), **Albacora** (Portugal), **Tonnos macrypterus** (Greece).

PRELIMINARY SUGGESTIONS

In all fresh tuna recipes I'd advise removing the midlateral strip of dark meat. This accumulation of myoglobin is rich in stored carbohydrates and is an energy reserve for the tuna, but it's bitter in flavor when cooked. In other countries and especially Japan the **chiai** is sometimes eaten raw; however, this is more for its nutritive value than for epicurean reasons. All tunas are unusually bloody fish, but the bonitos and little tunny (false albacore) are even more so. The initial step if you are catching your own is to bleed the fish by cutting it a few inches above the tail immediately after capture. Fillet the tuna and discard the dark meat, then wash the remaining strips in running water until the water flows clear and there is no trace of blood. Place the fillets on ice and brine at home.

Throughout ancient times, in fact as late as the 1865 edition of Eliza Acton's *Modern Cookery for Private Families* in which she gave advice on "how to sweeten tainted fish" (rub it with vinegar if it's bad, or disinfect with chloride of soda if it's "in a worse state"), occasional mention was made of the sometimes toxic properties of tuna meat. In the warm climate of the Mediterranean it was inevitable that scombroid poisoning would occur. It's a tribute to the skills of those early-day fishermen in butchering and brining without ice or refrigeration that such poisoning was not a daily event. Unlike other types of ichthyosarcotoxic poisoning (in which poison is contained within the flesh such as ciguatera or tetrodotoxin), scombroid poisoning is seldom severe; the symptoms occur within 1 hour of consumption and are dissipated in 8 to 12 hours. *A toxic tuna, whether fresh or canned, has a distinct peppery taste, sharper than any normal use of pepper as a seasoning would suggest.* In hot weather amateur fishermen are often careless about tuna because of their large

After soaking in brine, the blood is leached out and the tuna whitens.

size, leaving the fish exposed to the sun for long periods, which is not a safe procedure.

Fillets or steaks can be processed in a pressure cooker with about 2 inches of water, under full pressure for 20 minutes. When completed the meat will be in flaky chunks. These can be placed in suitable containers and covered with resultant juices and frozen for future use. Or they can be chilled to be made into tuna salad or tuna loaf, or can be simply dusted with flour and panfried, basting with butter and lime juice. Tuna processed in this manner lends itself to a variety of recipes.

Tuna can be made into a unique sauce by crumbling the meat and beating it into a smooth paste with olive oil, cream, egg yolk and lemon juice; served over slices of roast veal it becomes the classic **vitello tonnato.** In my own style—over rice with additional chunks of tuna added to the sauce and sprinkled with chopped fresh basil leaves—it's a taste delight.

ATUM DE ESCABECHE
(Hotel Quinta de Penha de Franca, Funchal, Madeira)

3 pounds fresh tuna, cut into large chunks	2 small onions, cut into chunks
1 cup salt	½ cup olive oil
6 garlic cloves, crushed	

Dissolve salt in 2 quarts of water. Chill this brine, and soak tuna in it for about 1 hour. The meat will whiten as the blood is leached out. Remove fish and quickly wash. Place tuna, garlic, onions and olive oil in a kettle with enough water to cover. Bring to a boil, then reduce heat and poach with the lid on for about 45 minutes, or until the fish flakes with a fork. Arrange chunks of tuna on a serving platter and refrigerate for 24 hours. When ready to serve pour on the dressing, also made the previous day. Makes 6 to 8 servings.

1 cup olive oil	4 garlic cloves, pressed
1 cup vinegar	1 small hot red pepper, sliced into rings
1 bunch of parsley, chopped fine	

Mix all ingredients together well, but remove the rings of red pepper before serving. Makes about 2 cups.

The traditional Madeiran **Atum de Escabeche** is accompanied by boiled potatoes with skins on, which have been cooked with branches of orégano (the Madeiran variety is called *uregos).* Orégano leaves also garnish the potatoes when served. Olive oil is a taste which sometimes overwhelms all but Mediterranean palates. For a milder version I prefer blending cottonseed or peanut oil half-and-half to make the amounts given. This dressing must be poured over thoroughly chilled tuna.

MARMITAKO

(Basque Gastronomical Society, San Sebastián, Spain)

A traditional Basque dish, a tuna stew cooked by fishermen at sea.

8 pounds fresh tuna
11 pounds potatoes
2 large onions
6 or 7 green peppers
12 garlic cloves
1 cup olive oil
1 pound whole tomatoes, peeled

Peel the potatoes and cut into large square chunks. Drop chunks into a large pot of cold water. Mince onions, chop peppers, and sliver garlic. Pour the oil into a huge pot (about 12-quart size), and add onions, peppers and garlic. Sauté until onions are golden. Add whole tomatoes and continue to cook, mashing the tomatoes with a wooden spoon to reduce the whole mixture to a purée. When the tomatoes are partly reduced, add the potato chunks and mix well so the sauce gets into the potatoes. Add enough water to reach 2 fingers above the level of the sauce and potatoes. Bring to a boil, then let the stew simmer gently.

Meanwhile, skin the tuna and remove any bones. Remove the red part of the meat around the center bone. Cut meat into large chunks. When the potatoes are tender and the sauce reduced to a purée, but *not* to a thick paste, add the tuna chunks. Cook over high heat for 5 minutes. Remove pot from stove, cover it, and let stand for 30 minutes. Makes 12 servings.

BRAISED FRESH TUNA WITH RED WINE

2 pounds fresh tuna (6 small steaks)
2 tablespoons plus 1 teaspoon salt
3 tablespoons olive oil
4 large scallions
2 green Italian peppers (about ½ pound)
¼ cup chopped flat Italian parsley
freshly ground pepper
4 teaspoons fines herbes

1 cup dry red wine (Chianti, Burgundy, et al.)
3 tablespoons tomato purée (optional)
beurre manié
2 teaspoons capers

If tuna steaks are large, halve them. Dissolve 2 tablespoons salt in 4 cups water and soak the tuna steaks in this brine for about 1 hour. Rinse tuna and pat dry. Pour the olive oil into a flat baking dish large enough to hold the steaks in a single layer. Chop the scallions, including the green part, and peppers. Mix with the Italian parsley and arrange this *mirepoix* in the baking dish. Sprinkle with 1 teaspoon salt and a little pepper. Place tuna steaks on the vegetable bed and sprinkle them with a little pepper and the *fines herbes.* Pour the wine around the tuna steaks. Oil a sheet of foil and cover the dish, placing the oiled side down; make a few holes for steam to escape. Braise in a preheated 375°F. oven for about 40 minutes. Remove from oven and gently transfer the tuna steaks to a serving platter; keep warm. Pour the liquid and vegetables into the container of a blender and reduce to a purée that is still a little lumpy. (Or force through a strainer or food mill.) Return the purée to a saucepan and add the tomato purée if you wish. (Sauces made with red wine have an unexpected purply color that may be disagreeable to some; the taste is fine, however.) When the sauce is hot, add as much *beurre manié* as needed, 1 teaspoon at a time, to thicken it; or use the purée without thickening further. Spoon over the tuna and sprinkle with capers. The fresh tuna tastes somewhat like veal and the texture and appearance are very like veal. Accompany with steamed Italian rice, or with small shell pasta, and broiled fresh tomatoes coated with crumbs and Parmesan cheese. Makes 6 servings.

This dish is perfectly good served at room temperature, which makes it good for a buffet, or cold the next day. If you are planning to serve it cold, do not thicken the sauce. It will form a thin jelly after refrigeration.

CANNED TUNA

Canned tuna is packed in three basic styles: (1) solid pack or "fancy" (2) chunks or "standard"; and (3) salad or "flakes."

The fancy pack usually consists of large pieces of solid meat with no small fragments. In a standard pack, three pieces of solid meat are placed in each can, with sufficient small fragments to give the desired net weight. The common practice in packing "standard" tuna is to fill in 25 percent flakes but some packers use no more than 15 percent. Flake tuna consists entirely of small crumbs or

facing page, Atum de escabeche, poached fresh tuna served cold in a dressing flavored with hot peppers, a traditional Madeiran dish; prepared at the Hotel Quinta de Penha de Franca, Funchal, Madeira

finely divided meat, packed down into a more or less solid cylinder. If a standard pack is being canned, it will use practically all the flake material. Flake tuna is usually packed when "fancy" tuna is being canned. Meat going into the flake pack is of the same quality as in "fancy" or "solid-pack" tuna and is by no means a secondary grade product. If the meat is tender and brittle, the amount of flakes will be greater than if the tuna is firm and dry. More flakes are obtained when the tuna are of the smallest sizes.

Species is a factor in establishing the quality of a pack. Albacore has been considered the finest tuna and is the only variety which can be marketed as "white-meat tuna." With the world decline in the catch of albacore, more attention has been paid to developing fancy packs from other species of tuna. Much of the fancy pack is prepared from yellowfin tuna. The catch of this species is larger and more consistent than that of albacore. On the other hand, the popular Italian *tonno* is solid dark meat (usually from the bluefin or skipjack), which is heavily brined and packed in olive oil; this stronger flavor has some demand in the Italian-American market.

From a kitchen point of view it's unnecessary to buy the more expensive fancy tuna if it's going to be made into sandwiches, croquettes or salad by breaking or mashing the solid pack, when flake tuna would serve that purpose. The solid pack and chunk tuna are best utilized in casseroles or the latter in salads that require large pieces of fish. Tuna may be packed in brine, or in cottonseed, olive or corn oil, and certain products are brined with tomato sauce added, also packed in aspic or in sauces with spiced vegetables. Obviously, the brine pack is the most "neutral" and more suited to recipes which do not require oils or other seasonings. In a pinch, the oil can be drained by putting the tuna in a colander or sieve and flushing it out with water and gently squeezing the meat, or by passing it through a potato ricer.

SALADE NIÇOISE

This salad is arranged on a flat platter, round or oval, rather than in a salad bowl. Peel 4 ripe firm tomatoes and cut them into thick slices. Discard as many seeds as possible. Sprinkle slices lightly with salt and set aside to drain. Drain 2 cans (2 ounces each) flat anchovies and soak the fillets in water to remove some of the salt. Allow about 30 minutes for these steps. Wash, drain, and pat dry 2 heads of Bibb lettuce (or use 1½ heads of Boston lettuce or 1 head of romaine). Arrange the lettuce leaves on the platter and circle the edge with the tomato slices. Pat the anchovies dry and arrange one on each tomato slice. Fill the center of the platter with slices of 3 green peppers, 2 cans (7½

ounces each) water-packed tuna, drained and separated into large chunks, and 4 hard-cooked eggs, each cut into 4 wedges. Arrange 24 oil-cured black olives on the tuna. Spoon about ¾ cup vinaigrette, made with olive oil and red-wine vinegar, over the salad, and grind black pepper over everything. Sprinkle with 2 tablespoons minced fresh basil and 2 tablespoons minced fresh parsley. An excellent summer salad for luncheon or supper. Makes 8 servings.

u

Ufsi

The name for pollock (Iceland). *See under COD.*

Ukha

A Russian fish soup made from a basic stock and featuring one or more species of fish, usually including sturgeon, and in its most famous version, the sterlet. Small sterlet of 5 to 6 pounds are often poached whole for this purpose and presented as a companion piece to the soup, which is strained and served separately as a clear broth. There is no standard recipe for an *ukha* as the general concept is to use any fresh fish available by first simmering onion, parsnip, bay leaf and peppercorns for about an hour, or until a mildly flavored stock is obtained (fish heads and bones are sometimes added for a stronger flavor), then introducing the fillets, chunks, or whole fish with salt to taste and poaching until these are cooked. This soup has a counterpart in almost all cuisines. *See also BOUILLABAISSE; FISH SOUPS AND STEWS.*

Ulua

There are several important ulua in our Hawaiian fishery, notably the **black ulua** (Caranx stellatus), **white ulua** (Caranx ajax) and the **striped ulua** (Caranx ignobilis). Both the black and striped ulua are broadly distributed in the Indo-Pacific region, occurring from Hawaii to East Africa, but the white ulua is limited to the Hawaiian Islands. Ulua are members of the jack family which in general is not a distinguished group of foodfish, but these are exceptions to the rule. The black and white ulua grow to about

150 pounds and are popular market species. Ulua have firm pink flesh which turns white after cooking; they are usually baked, broiled or fried and make excellent **sashimi.** Young ulua or **papio** of ½ to 2 pounds are considered among the best of Hawaiian foodfish. *See also JACK.*

Uo-Miso

A fermented fish paste made from dried cod **(uo).** The meat is boiled, then kneaded and mixed with soybean paste **(miso),** mirin wine and sugar. It also appears as **tai-miso** when made from sea bream. Sometimes sold as a canned product.

Usuba-Aonori

An edible seaweed (Japan), specifically green laver *(Enteromorpha linza). See under SEAWEED.*

U'u

The u'u or red squirrelfish *(Myripristis murdjan)* is a small tropical Pacific reef fish of great popularity in Hawaii and Tahiti. Although it seldom weighs much over 1 pound, the u'u brings a high price in local markets. This bright red fish is nocturnal in habits, living in coral holes by day and foraging in open water at night. U'u are taken by angling, with nets and by spearfishermen.

Uvak

The name for Greenland cod or fjord cod (Sweden) as opposed to cod, **torsk.** The Greenland cod *(Gadus ogac)* is a smaller, less desirable market species.

V

Vairon

The common minnow *(Phoxinus phoxinus)* of Europe, found from Great Britain to the Amur River in Siberia. Although usually an inhabitant of freshwater streams and lakes, the vairon also occurs in brackish habitats such as the Baltic Sea. The vairon is finely scaled and its body is bronze in color with faint vertical bars and minute dark spots; it seldom exceeds 4 inches in length. Although Izaak Walton gave a recipe for "Minnow Tansy" in which the little fish were fried with cowslips, primrose and tansy, it has been more traditionally an item of French cuisine where it's treated in the style of whitebait **(vairons frites).** However, the flesh is not as delicate nor as sweet as the whitebait species. There is no large scale commercial fishery for vairon except in northern USSR, although it appears on the menus of European country inns where caught locally. Also known as **Elritze** (Germany), **Centibocca** (Italy), **Oerekyt** (Norway), **Elriste** (Sweden), **Krasavka** (USSR).

Vendace

See CISCO under WHITEFISH.

Ventresca

In Mediterranean cuisines the abdominal sections of various tunas are in some demand for their oil content and stronger flavor. The fat belly strips of albacore are packed in Italy as *ventresca.* This product is usually cooked in brine and packed with olive oil and canned. It's recognized by the same name in Spain and Portugal. Similar cuts from the bluefin tuna are sold as *tarantello.* These products are occasionally marketed in specialty shops in New York and San Francisco.

Viziga

The spinal cords of sturgeon (USSR) served as an hors d'oeuvre, or sold dried and powdered in Europe as a gelling agent. A classic ingredient in making a **coulibiac** of salmon. *Viziga* in powder form is available in specialty shops in large population centers in the U.S.

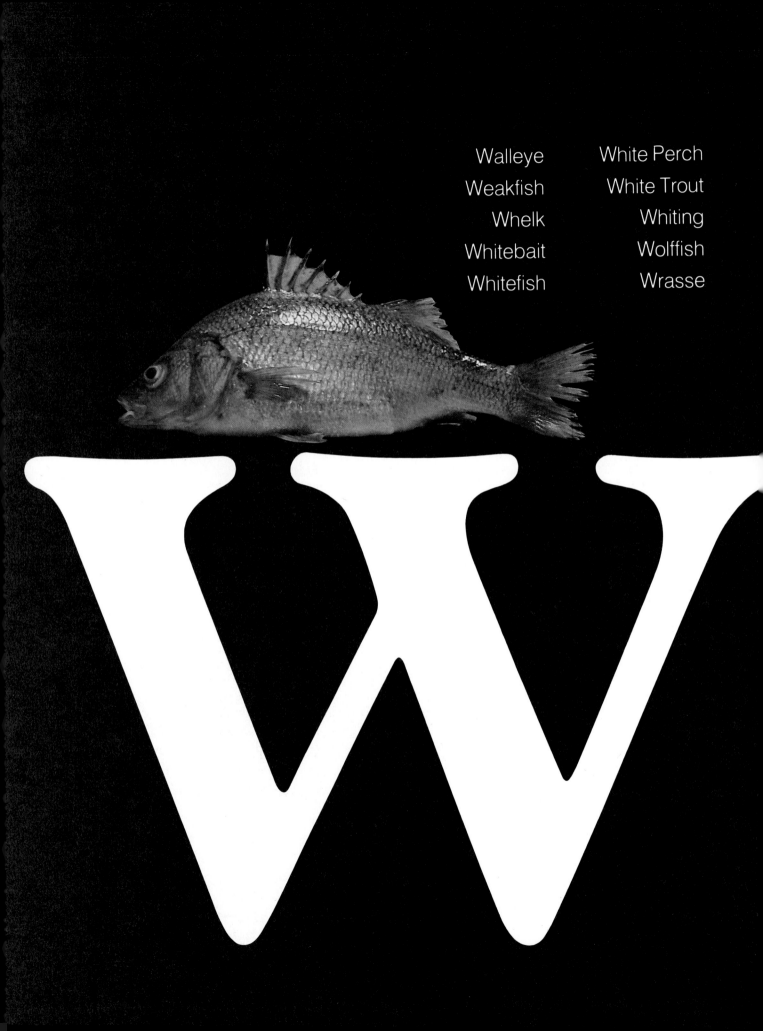

Walleye   White Perch
Weakfish   White Trout
Whelk   Whiting
Whitebait   Wolffish
Whitefish   Wrasse

W

Walleye

One of the rules in judging the freshness of a fish at market, that it must display "bright" eyes, can be ignored here as the name walleye is an oblique reference to the Latin *vitreum* or glassy. The walleye *(Stizostedion vitreum)* has eyes like opaque moon marbles, an adaptation to dim light because it's primarily a nocturnal forager. Despite its otherwise commonplace appearance, this fish and a European counterpart are among the most esteemed in the culinary world. To me, the walleye brings to mind a thousand wilderness campfires, when the first chore of the day was to catch a few for lunch—even before considering the pursuit of a noble trout. Seldom will an American or Canadian sportsman deny that the walleye is an incomparable foodfish; its meat, snowy white, fine of flake and sweetly flavored, may well be considered the "sole" of freshwater, not in a literal sense as their textures differ and their respective flavors when fresh lie somewhere between a mature Chablis and a flowery, young Gewürztraminer. The walleye is so versatile that a fillet can be prepared following the whole galaxy of sole recipes. In common with the sole it thrives in a tangle of names. The important one to recognize in U.S. markets is **yellow pike.** This fish is not really a pike at all but a member of the perch family, Percidae, and closely related to the yellow perch. Nevertheless, the pseudonymous yellow pike is firmly established in trade. On Canadian frozen and packaged products it's often labeled "walleyed pike" although the only remote similarity to a pike is that both fish have sharp canine teeth. In the French-oriented restaurants of Quebec the walleye will appear as **doré,** which is descriptive of its brassy-gold coloration. That it could be called a "salmon" by the early settlers of Pennsylvania was a tribute to the quality of its flesh.

The walleye was not native to Pennsylvania. While records are vague, apparently a Jesuit priest stocked a "wagon load" in the Chemung River, a tributary to the North Branch of the Susquehanna at Elmira (then the village of Newton), New York, in 1812. This was not unusual as the church was ever mindful of its fishes. Even that Puritan cleric Cotton Mather often cited fishing methods to point up his sermons. (In one sermon Mather noted that some ministers were like rod fishermen in that they spent too much time on individual cases. Nothing like the net, he advised, whether you are fishing for souls or trout.) The reproduction of these walleyes was so successful that they literally swarmed in the pools and eddies of the entire river system, and "Susquehanna salmon" were soon in greater favor than shad. This gave rise by 1830 to the often confusing clause in labor agreements "that salmon should not be given (to hired help) more than two or three times a week." The fact that it was called a salmon, as was the striped bass in the early settlement of New York, led some historians to conclude that Atlantic salmon once occupied both the Hudson and Susquehanna Rivers. (Several attempts were made in the nineteenth century to establish Atlantic salmon in the Hudson and also the Delaware River, but these projects failed. The natural range of the species never extended farther south than the Connecticut River.) Whether the clause was designed to protect palates from an overexposure to walleye or to conserve the household supply is not clear, as the fish always brought a high price at market and was so eagerly pursued that its population dwindled almost to extinction before the turn of the century.

The walleye is found from Connecticut to North Carolina, westward to Wyoming and Montana, and north to Hudson Bay. It only assumes commercial importance in the Great Lakes region of the U.S., with most of the fish at market coming from Manitoba, Ontario, Saskatchewan and Alberta. The major Canadian fisheries are most active in winter months, using gill nets set under the ice. The fish are sold in the round, whole-dressed, pan-dressed, as napecut fillets, skinless fillets, cooked and breaded fillets, and in frozen 1-pound packs. In addition to the 12 to 13 million pounds purveyed in our markets, an equal amount is harvested by anglers. On the Wolf River in Wisconsin, for example, walleyes migrate a hundred miles upstream from Lake Winnebago, and to the thousands of people who attend this run (at which time the fish are easily caught in sunlight or dark) it's the first harbinger of spring. There are many comparable migrations in midwestern waters, northern New York and in our southern impoundments, particularly in Kentucky and Tennessee (which produced a record walleye of 25 pounds). Through a portion of the walleyes' range from the Great Lakes to Tennessee, west to the upper Missouri and north to the Assiniboine River, we find a second and very similar percid, the **sauger** *(Stizostedion canadense).* A third member of the family which differs from the walleye in coloration is called the **blue pike** *(Stizostedion v.*

Walleye

glaucum), but this deepwater form is only taken commercially in Lake Erie and Lake Ontario. All three are excellent foodfish, although the walleye and blue pike are generally considered superior to the sauger. Unlike a pike, the walleye has a simple skeletal structure without Y-shaped intermuscular bones, and there's little loss of meat in dressing the fish as it has a small abdominal cavity. Even in warm weather the lean walleye does not degrade rapidly, and it has a long shelf life when frozen.

The walleyes of Europe are closely related to the percids of North America. Of course "walleye" doesn't have international currency and the most important species *Stizostedion lucioperca* is widely known as the **zander** or **pike perch**. It occurs over most of Europe and any qualitative distinctions are a matter of environment. The best fish at table are usually taken from clear cold rivers or deep oliogotrophic lakes such as Balaton in Hungary—a habitat comparable to our Great Lakes or waters of the Canadian Shield. Those zander caught in diluted salinities such as the Aral, Baltic and Black Seas are perhaps a shade less than perfect, but the comparison is a matter of individual taste. Although the **fogas** of Lake Balaton is a standard bearer, fish of equal quality are caught in Sweden's vast inland lakes such as Vänern, Mälaren and Hjälmaren. Another but smaller species, *Stizostedion volgense*, is found in eastern Europe notably in the Volga, Don and Dnieper, but it has little importance as a commercial fish.

The walleye can be prepared by any method. All sole recipes are adaptable. It can be baked, broiled, deep-fried, panfried, poached or served cold in aspic. As "yellow pike" it's a common ingredient in gefilte fish and also in **quenelles de brochet.**

Also known as **Sander** (Sweden), **Kuka** (Finland), **Sandart** (Denmark), **Sandre** (France), **Sandra** (Italy), **Zander** (Germany), **Smud** (Yugoslavia), **Fogas** (Hungary), and **Ssandart** (USSR).

Weakfish

It's unfortunate that the weakfish (*Cynoscion regalis*) didn't retain its original Narraganset Indian name **squeateague.** Admittedly, various coastal tribes had differing versions such as **squit, succoteague, squitee,** even **chickwit,** but an Anglicized sobriquet hardly describes this handsome gamefish which deserves three stars at table. The only discernible reason for the label "weak" is its fragile mouth structure which, to the chagrin of many a fisherman, permits a hook to tear out rather easily. Although members (there is more than one weakfish as we shall discuss presently) of the drum family, this particular group differs greatly from the red or black drums, the croakers, whitings or related species.

In addition to the northern weakfish, there is a southern form called the **spotted seatrout** (*C. nebulosus),* which is seldom found in quantity north of

Spotted seatrout, the southern form of weakfish

Virginia but is common as far south as the Gulf of Mexico. This fish is not related to the true trout, although it superficially resembles one with its bold black spots. For that matter the northern form is sometimes marketed as "gray trout." There is also a **sand seatrout** *(C. arenarius)* and a **silver seatrout** *(C. nothus)* in the Atlantic, but these are small fish, seldom exceeding a foot in length and of no market value. In this same genus the Pacific species are the **white seabass** and various **corvinas.** The corvinas are dominantly Central and South American and highly esteemed as food. It's rather amusing to hear people who live in Atlantic weakfish country rave about the fabulous corvina they had in Panama or Peru as the difference would only be of interest to a taxonomist. In 1958 I interviewed Luis Firpo for a story in *Esquire* magazine. Gene Tunney told me that "The Bull of the Pampas" was the strongest man he ever met in the ring. I asked Firpo (who in a previous bout had knocked Jack Dempsey through the ropes for that famous "long count") to what he owed his great strength.

"Corvinas" he replied. "I eat corvina every day of my life since I can remember. Even when I fought Tunney I had corvina shipped to America. It makes muscle and pleases my stomach."

At the time we were sitting in La Cabaña, the most famous steak house in Buenos Aires, and Luis Firpo *was* eating corvina.

For the past few years, weakfish have been giving themselves up to their joyous captors in such numbers that the casual observer would think the northeast Atlantic was paved with them, yet no fish has such extreme highs and lows in its abundance. Historically, we know that **squeateague** were available at Fraunces Tavern when George Washington was President, but some time prior to 1800 the fish vanished completely. According to Henry B. Bigelow and William C. Shroeder in *Fishes of the Gulf of Maine,* when a stray specimen was taken at Provincetown in June 1838, the fishermen were so unfamiliar with it that it was sent to Boston for identification. This disappearance evidently involved the whole northern range of the species, for weakfish vanished from the Nantucket and Martha's Vineyard region about the same time, and didn't appear again until 1870. Then in 1881, one of the largest waves of weakfish ever recorded made *The New York Times*:

A GREAT CATCH OF FISH—WHAT
THREE STEAM SMACKS CAUGHT OFF ROCKAWAY
    A great catch of weak-fish was made yesterday about two miles off Rockaway Beach, by the steam smacks "E. T. DeBlois," Captain J. A. Keene; "Leonard Brightman," Captain Elijah Powers, and "J. W. Hawkins," Captain J. W. Hawkins. These smacks were engaged in the menhaden or "moss-bunker" fishery for the oil-rendering and fish-scrap works on Barren Island, and were cruising off Rockaway yesterday in search of schools. About noon a vast school of

what fishermen supposed at first to be menhaden was discovered stretching along the coast for miles.

To borrow their language, "The water was red with the fish, but they didn't break the surface as menhaden always do." The boats were lowered, the seines spread, and then it was discovered that the school was of Weak-fish and not menhaden. "I have been in the business for twenty years," said the mate of the Brightman, "and I never saw anything like it before."

The fish varied in length from one and one half to three feet, and in weight from three to seven pounds. The "De Blois" took over 200 barrels, the "Hawkins" 150 barrels, and the "Brightman" 350 barrels. The entire catch was estimated at something over 200,000 pounds, which, at the ordinary market price for Weak-fish—seven cents a pound—would amount to $14,000.

But, of course, the market price could not be maintained in the presence of such a catch as this, and it was said yesterday afternoon that a strong effort was being made by the whole-sale fish dealers of Fulton Market to prevent the greater part of the fish from being put on sale . . .

A crowd speedily gathered about the boat, and the fish sold almost as fast as they could be handled at twenty-five cents a pair. The pressure of the crowd became so great at one time that police assistance was invoked, and Officer William Brown, of the steamboat squad, was detailed to stay on the boat.

While Owens was selling the fish at twenty-five cents a pair, an attempt to break the price was made by two well-known "longshore" characters, Jack Sullivan, the shark-catcher, and T. Long, alias "Blindy," who bought one thousand pounds of the fish at one cent per pound, and stood on the street retailing them at twenty cents per pair.

Fish-dealers say that there will be no difficulty in selling all the fish this morning at from one to three cents per pound. Friday morning, they say, is the best in the week for the sale of fish. Tons of ice were cracked last evening and put on the fish to keep them fresh until to-day.

During the years shortly after World War II fleets of charter boats and commercial seiners were unable to more than dent the vast schools of "tide-runner" weakfish that invaded eastern Long Island from late April to July. Sport fishermen often reported 150 to 300 fish on a single tide. The waste was enormous. Landings for market reached over 2 million pounds in 1945 and dropped to less than ½ million pounds in 1949. Off the more extensive coast of Virginia, the 1945 catch was 22 million pounds with a drop to 6 million pounds by 1949. Then the weakfish virtually disappeared in the early 50s and showed no sign of recovery until 1972.

FACTORS AFFECTING QUALITY

The flesh of weakfish is white, sweet, lean and finely textured. Because of the texture it's also fragile and must be iced immediately after capture to retain its natural elasticity and flavor. Serious anglers, both in the north and south, always have an ice chest aboard when fishing for "trout" as quality diminishes very rapidly; the fish remains perfectly edible after a few hours at normal outdoor temperatures without icing, but it will not taste the same.

Weakfish roe is exceptionally good and can be treated in any of the recipes for shad roe. As a rule this isn't available in metropolitan markets (as the fish should be gutted and on ice in transport), but seaside dealers often receive the day's catch in-the-round, and when purchasing freshly caught weakfish be sure to ask for the roes. The angler, of course, will dress his catch as quickly as possible and reserve the roes on ice. These roes freeze perfectly, and can provide a long series of "gourmet" evenings during the winter months.

WEAKFISH MEUNIÈRE
(Galatoire's Restaurant, New Orleans)

Melt ½ pound butter in a large flat pan. Wash weakfish fillets in saltwater, then season with salt and pepper to taste. Dip into cool milk and sprinkle lightly with flour. Sauté in butter until well browned, approximately 20 minutes. Arrange on a serving platter. Brown the butter left in the pan and add 2 lemons cut into pieces; pour over the fish.

WEAKFISH CHEF FARFANTE
(Spanish Park Restaurant, Tampa, Florida)

6 weakfish, each 2½ to 3 pounds	3 tablespoons plus ¼ pound butter
6 large shrimps, cooked	4 tablespoons flour
½ pound cooked lobster meat	6 egg yolks
1 large onion	6 anchovy fillets
¼ pound almonds, toasted	1 pound cracker meal
1¼ cups milk	6 whole eggs, beaten
	½ cup dry sherry
	juice of 1 lime

Fillet the weakfish; chop up the shrimps and lobster; chop the onion very fine. Pound the almonds in a cloth with a wooden mallet until crushed. Scald the milk. Sauté the onion in 3 tablespoons butter until brown; add shrimps, lobster and flour. Add the scalded milk and stir until creamy; keep stirring, and add the egg yolks as the mixture thickens. Divide into 6 portions and add 1 anchovy fillet to each part. Arrange 1 portion of this mixture between 2 weakfish fillets, as if making a sandwich. Roll the sandwich in cracker meal, then in beaten eggs, finish-

WEAKFISH AND BROCCOLI ROLL-UPS

1. For each serving prepare a skinless weakfish fillet, about ½ pound. Score fillets to facilitate rolling, and season. Blanch 2 broccoli florets for each fillet; they should still be crunchy and bright green. **2.** Place 2 florets on each fillet, stem ends toward center. Roll up fillets, starting at head end, and fasten with skewers. Place in a saucepan, half-cover with poaching liquid, and cover the pan. Poach in oven or on top of stove for 15 to 20 minutes. **3.** Garnish each roll-up with 2 pimiento strips. Serve with poaching liquid thickened to a sauce, or with Sauce Mornay.

SAUCE FOR POACHING
Melt 4 tablespoons butter and in it sauté 2 tablespoons each of chopped green onion, celery leaves and parsley until vegetables are tender but still bright green. Add ¾ cup each of fish stock and dry white wine, ½ teaspoon salt and pinch of dried tarragon. Cool sauce to lukewarm before pouring it over roll-ups. After fish is cooked, reduce liquid and thicken with *beurre manié* for a sauce.

---

ing with another roll in the cracker meal. Prepare the rest of the fillets and stuffing in the same way. Bake at 325°F. for 24 minutes, 12 minutes on each side. Melt remaining ¼ pound butter in the sherry; add lime juice and crushed almonds. Pour hot almond sauce over the fish, and serve. Makes 6 servings.

MONTAUK WEAKFISH CHOWDER

This is a recipe for field trips or boating trips. Except for the fresh fish, all other ingredients are canned or packaged.

3 to 4 pounds fresh weakfish fillets
6 slices of canned bacon
8 to 10 tablespoons dehydrated minced onion
2 cans (16 ounces each) small whole potatoes
1 tablespoon celery seeds
1 tablespoon dried parsley flakes
2 or 3 dashes of Tabasco
salt and coarse-ground black pepper
1 can (11 ounces) evaporated milk
4 cups milk made from nonfat dried milk powder

Wash weakfish fillets in saltwater and dry on paper towels. Dice the bacon and fry. Mix the dehydrated onion with 1 to 1¼ cups water to make the equivalent of 3 large onions, diced. When bacon is done, add onions to bacon and place in a large pot. Drain the liquid from canned potatoes and set liquid aside. Cut the potatoes into quarters and add them to the pot mixture. Season with celery seeds, parsley flakes, Tabasco, and salt and pepper to taste. Add enough water to the liquid from the potatoes to make a total of 1½ cups; add to the chowder. Stir the ingredients, cover, and simmer for 10 to 15 minutes. While the pot simmers, cut the weakfish fillets into 1-inch cubes. Add to the chowder and cook for an additional 10 minutes, or until the fish chunks are tender. Add the evaporated milk and the mixed powdered milk slowly to the chowder, cover, and bring to a gentle simmer. Serve hot with saltines or pilot crackers, plus celery and carrot sticks. Makes 6 servings.

WEAKFISH ROE PÂTÉ

Simmer fresh weakfish roes in salted water until they are cooked through, approximately 7 minutes. Drain and chill in the refrigerator. When thoroughly chilled, remove them from the refrigerator and discard the thin membrane that sheathes the roe. Blend the roes with mayonnaise, a dash of salt and pepper and Worcestershire sauce. For 1 pound of roes add approximately 1 tablespoon of fresh lemon juice. Garnish and serve.

FRIED WEAKFISH ROE
(Bambi Meyer)

Clean weakfish roes, removing the blood with light pressure from thumbnail or the back of a knife blade. Rinse roes in saltwater. Dip into flour seasoned with salt and pepper to taste so that a light and even coating is formed on the roes. Panfry in enough margarine to cover the bottom of the pan, over low heat so roes do not burst, until done—when they are light brown and crisp on the outside. Serve as a first course, or with salad and French bread as a full meal.

SEATROUT QUENELLES

These are mousseline quenelles, closely related to the Mousse of Pike and quite different from the lyonnaise type illustrated by Quenelles of Black Bass.

1 seatrout (weakfish), about 2½ pounds
2 whole eggs
2 egg whites
2 cups heavy cream
½ teaspoon salt
1/16 teaspoon ground white pepper
⅛ teaspoon ground coriander
2 cups seasoned chicken or fish stock
2 cups dry white wine, Bordeaux type
peel of 1 orange
2 cups Cucumber Sauce (p. 288)
grated rind of 1 orange
½ teaspoon orange bitters
3 tablespoons minced fresh parsley

Have the seatrout filleted; the 2 fillets should weigh about 1½ pounds. Rinse them, pat dry, and place them skin side down on a chopping board. With a chef's knife scrape the fish from the skin, starting at the tail end, 1-inch section at a time. Discard the skin. There should be about 1 pound of semipuréed fish. Purée fish in a food processor, then add the eggs and egg whites beaten together. Or purée in 3 portions in an electric blender, using the beaten whole eggs and egg whites as the liquid. Or put through a food grinder and mix with the eggs in a large mortar. Put the purée through a food mill; this is the only difficult step, but don't skip it; when you finish all the little bits of sinew and connective tissue will be left in the mill, giving you a perfectly smooth purée. Chill the purée for several hours or overnight.

With an electric mixer set at whipping, beat the cream into the fish, adding the seasoning as you go. (You can use more salt and other seasoning if you prefer but this amount gives a delicate taste.) Chill the whole mixture again for several hours.

Pour stock and wine into a large deep skillet and bring to a simmer. Adjust the heat to keep the liquid at that temperature. Using a cream-soup spoon (with a round bowl), scoop up mounds of the cold batter and lower them into the stock. They will flatten out slightly. Make only as many as will fit in a single layer and not crowded. Don't let the stock-wine mixture boil; while the quenelles won't inevitably fall apart, they will get frizzled on the edges like fried eggs dropped into very hot fat, and the tops will become beige-colored and less tender than they should be. There will be 16 to 20 quenelles. Cover the skillet and let the quenelles cook gently for 10 minutes. With a skimmer or two wooden paddles gently turn them over and cook for 5 to 7 minutes longer. Lift the cooked quenelles with a skimmer to a serving dish with a cover. (If you are not serving these at once, place them in a buttered shallow ceramic baking dish. In spite of the delicacy of these, they can be made a day ahead. Pour a little of the cooking liquid over them, cool, cover tightly with a plastic wrap, and refrigerate. At serving time discard plastic, cover with foil instead, and reheat in a 300°F. oven.)

Meanwhile make the sauce. Cut the orange peel into julienne slivers about the size of matchsticks. Boil in water for 10 minutes, then drain; repeat twice; cool in ice water, then drain on paper towels. Make the cucumber sauce as far as the puréeing; don't purée to complete smoothness but leave tiny chunks of cucumber. Stir the grated rind and orange bitters into the sauce, and reheat. Spoon about half of the sauce over the quenelles in their serving dish, then sprinkle the orange peel slivers and parsley over all. Serve the rest of the sauce separately. Makes 4 to 6 servings.

Whelk

Although whelks appear in the kitchen middens of North American Indians with some frequency, scholars have debated whether they were processed as food or in making wampum. The convoluted shells of both the knobbed and the channeled whelk were filed into elongate beads and had the same currency in trade as properly crafted quahaugs. It would seem likely that whelks were used for both purposes by East Coast tribes. The only historical suggestion that these gastropods had a culinary value is in the use of the word "periwigge" in William Wood's *New England's Prospects* (London, 1634), when describing the kinds of shellfish then in favor.

facing page, Weakfish lends itself well to this recipe; to prepare it amandine, simply add blanched almonds sautéed in butter to the recipe for weakfish meunière.

The lucious Lobster, with the Crabfish raw
The Brinish Oister, Muscle, Perriwigge,
And Tortise sought for by the Indian Squaw,
Which to the flats daunce many a winters Jigge,
To dive for Cockles, and to dig for Clammes,
Whereby her lazie husbands Guts she cramms.

The "periwigge" or periwinkle is of course a common article of food in Europe, but the edible species *Littorina litorea* has only migrated to the northeast coast of America during the last century. This species is most popular in Northern Europe, where 4,800 metric tons are consumed annually. The few already established species of whelks would hardly have been considered as a food by the Indian who had an abundance of large mollusks, as these only grow from ½ to 1 inch in size. Periwinkles are in a different family (Littorinidae) from whelks (Buccinidae), but there is sufficient physical similarity in the conical spire of the shell with its whorls and round aperture to conclude that both are periwinkles. Not surprisingly, in Scotland today periwinkles are called "whelks" or "buckie" (from the Mediterranean trade in **buccin, buccino** and **bocina),** and it's obvious that in William Wood's time no distinction was made.

Whelks are mollusks with thick-walled shells, which are distantly related to the conch and abalone. The meat of the whelk is delicious, in my opinion, although not as refined as our southern and western gastropods, but this is subjective. Our Italian markets spurn all save the whelk for its stronger flavor in making **scungilli,** a Roman dedication that I must defer to in its garlicked form. As with other gastropods it's the large foot of the mollusk that is used as food. The color of the meat varies according to species, ranging from white to yellow. In the case of the waved whelk the meat is white but blotched and streaked with black. The most common whelk found on both sides of the Atlantic and circumpolar in distribution is the **waved whelk** *(Buccinum undatum),* occurring as far south on our coast as New Jersey. It's most abundant from Maine to Massachusetts. It is the edible whelk of northern Europe and the British Isles; there it is marketed fresh in the shell, as shelled cooked meats, semipreserved in vinegar and salt, and also canned. It is consumed in greatest numbers in the U.K.; 2,900 tons are downed each year.

The **knobbed whelk** *(Busycon carica),* sometimes called the giant whelk, is a large snail growing to 9 inches long; it's found from Cape Cod to Texas. It is pear-shaped and generally gray in color, and the aperture is brick-red. Although equally good to eat, the knobbed whelk is not sold in any numbers as it cannot be trapped as easily as other whelks. Whelks are taken in baited traps

similar to lobster pots.

The **channeled whelk** *(Busycon canaliculatum)* is not quite as large as the knobbed; it grows to about 7 inches. The shell is yellowish gray in color with a yellow aperture. It's common along the shores of Long Island Sound but is found from southern New England to northern Florida.

There are other but smaller species of whelks and related moonshells which are all edible, but the waved, knobbed and channeled are the ones that enter our markets, and even then only in minor quantities. In the U.S. whelks are almost entirely purveyed at Italian fishmongers in our larger cities. The Fulton Fish Market in New York sells an average 126,000 pounds of meats each year during the spring to fall season, mainly from the waved whelk taken in Narragansett Bay, Rhode Island, around Long Island and along the New Jersey shore.

Also known as **Buccin** (France), **Buccino** (Italy), **Bocina** (Spain), **Buzio** (Portugal), **Bourou** (Greece), **Wulk** (Holland), **Buckie** (Scotland), **Konksnegl** (Denmark), **Kongsnegl** (Norway), **Valthornssnäcka** (Sweden), **Beitukongur** (Iceland), **Bai** (Japan).

SCUNGILLI MARINARA
(Sloppy Louie's Restaurant, Fulton Fish Market, New York City)

1½ pounds whelk meat, parboiled, sliced thin	2 tablespoons tomato sauce
3 tablespoons olive oil	½ teaspoon salt
2 garlic cloves, mashed	½ teaspoon dried orégano
1 small onion, sliced thin	½ teaspoon dried basil
1 celery rib, minced	2 bay leaves
2 cups Italian plum tomatoes	¼ teaspoon hot pepper seeds

Place the oil, whelk, garlic, onion and celery in a large skillet and brown. Discard the garlic and add tomatoes, tomato sauce and salt. Cover and cook slowly for 5 minutes, then add the orégano, basil, bay leaves and hot pepper seeds. Cook for 5 minutes longer. Discard the bay leaves. Makes 4 servings.

Whitebait

A seafood dish resembling a plate of fried minnows. Whitebait is considered an Epicurean delight both because of its scarcity and its unusual texture. Correctly made, it requires 5 or 6 species of saltwater fish in the immature stage. Whitebait had its origin in England about 1780. The man credited with its invention was a Thames fisherman named Robert Cannon. In subsequent

facing page, top, Seining whitebait; bottom, the catch, Atlantic silversides

years, his heirs assumed the purveying of whitebait, and during the 10-year reign of King George IV they supplied the royal household every day of the season (from February through August). The esteem in which whitebait was once held is reflected in the annual Ministerial Whitebait Dinner which some observers believe helped formulate the British Constitution. Greenwich, Blackheath, Lovegrove and Quartermain were great whitebait centers, according to Victorian epicures. The original dish consisted of juvenile herring, sprat, sand launce, smelt, stickleback and pipefish, all being dusted in fine flour and instantly deep-fried to a crisp succulence. Preferably, each fish is no more than 2½ inches in length. In New Zealand whitebait encompasses at least 5 species of juvenile *galaxias*, the choicest one being the **inanga**. This same genus occurs in both Chile and Argentina and is the South American gourmet item called **puyen**. In North America juvenile herrings, anchovies, silversides, sand launce and Pacific surf smelts are all marketed as whitebait. A combination of **sand launce** (commonly called "sand eel") and **silversides** (sometimes called "spearing") is by most standards the ultimate in flavor. Whitebait appears seasonally in seafood restaurants such as the Gloucester House in New York and Gage & Tollner in Brooklyn.

Due to the small size and delicacy of the fishes in a whitebait composition, they are marketed and cooked whole and ungutted, whether fresh or frozen. Ideally, whitebait should be enjoyed fresh from the water, a feat that is remarkably easy to accomplish by any summer vacationist at the seashore. A simple haul seine (a 10-foot length of net with a fine mesh) is all that's required to gather the ingredients. Virtually any saltwater bay along the East or West Coasts of America will provide a whitebait dinner. Both Long Island and Cape Cod, for example, are abundantly blessed with silversides and sand launce. Also known as **Blanchaille** (France), **Bianchetti** (Italy), **Seioi** (Iceland), **Bliek**, or **Witvis** for freshwater species (Holland), **Shirasu** (Japan), and **Puyen** (Argentina, Chile).

Whitefish

My travels through the Arctic have for the most part been under comfortable circumstances with the advantage of modern aircraft to get out at the first snowfall, and ample supplies of food to support a month's stay when necessary. Most of these journeys were to fixed camps where a bunk and potbellied stove provided the creature essentials that assure survival. However, other trips have been exploratory in nature, along the coast of Labrador, the east and west shores of Hudson Bay, around Baffin, Victoria and Banks Island, often camping with Indians south of the Circle and with Eskimos on the roof of the world. On several occasions I've been stranded for a few days by an early winter and each time I lived on whitefish. It was hardly coincidental as this species is common to the North country, and its delicate, almost sweet, snow-white meat does not suffer under repetitive dining. My record is nine meals in a row.

The name "lake" whitefish is somewhat confusing because the fish is not necessarily caught in lakes, but let me emphasize the word as there are numerous species of whitefish which differ greatly in quality. The king of them all is *Coregonus clupeaformis*, and it is found in deep cold waters from New England to the Great Lakes to Hudson Bay and northwestward to Alaska. In North America whitefish have decreased in number, but as transportation facilities expand toward the Arctic into remote lakes the market haul has increased. When the northland is frozen and the ice on Great Slave Lake is 4 feet thick, whitefish are gillnetted by an ingenious method of running the mesh between spud holes, then hauled away in heated snowmobiles. Canada produces the largest catch in the world (20 million pounds), mainly from northern Saskatchewan into the Northwest Territories. A considerable sport fishery exists in streams such as the Kanuchuan River and Gods River in Manitoba as well as the tributaries of Lake La Ronge, Reindeer Lake and Cree Lake in Saskatchewan. Some angling possibilities exist in the northeastern United States also. Maine has many lakes which are not exploited. The common whitefish is abundant in Moosehead, Chamberlain, West Grand and Sebago Lakes where they provide excellent fishing on small dry flies in the spring of the year. Do not confuse the Menominee whitefish with the larger lake species in this region; the Menominee is a round whitefish, common to New England, which, though good, differs considerably in quality.

After easing the *Half Moon* into New York Harbor in 1609, and exploring the upper reaches of its major river in the vicinity of what is now the city of Albany, Henry Hudson concluded that this channel was no shortcut to China. A year later he ventured far north into that great inland sea of Canada which also bears his name. After a mutinous uprising, Hudson and eight others, including his young son, were set adrift in a small boat never to be seen again. During the next two centuries, expedition after disaster-prone expedition went seeking the fabled Northwest Passage, including the "elite of

Cisco, a member of the whitefish family; when marketed in smoked form it is known as chub. The fish in the photograph were caught in northern Manitoba.

Maritime England"—109 men led by Sir John Franklin, all of whom disappeared. The final irony was the murder or suicide of Thomas Simpson in 1840. Seemingly this would be unrelated to our subject, but young Simpson had in a span of three years solved the geographic riddle of the northern route. Upon his death, Governor George Simpson (a cousin), in the calculating way of empire, wrote him off in favor of a whitefish.

Early next morning I received occupation enough for one day at least. A boat from our establishment brought me the journal and other papers of my late lamented relative, Mr. Thomas Simpson, whose successful exertions in arctic discovery and whose untimely end had excited so much interest in the public mind. By the same conveyance we got a supply of whitefish. This fish, which is peculiar to North America, is one of the most delicious of the finny tribe, having the appearance and somewhat the flavor of trout. (Narrative of a Journey Round the World during the Years 1841 and 1842, George Simpson, London, 1847)

At a time when the world was demanding news comparable to the first moon landing and receiving several widely different versions of the demise of its greatest hero, Governor Simpson was musing on the culinary value of whitefish! This distraction was probably less gastronomic than economic, as the Governor was subsequently responsible for establishing on the Columbia River the first commercial salmon fishery for the Hudson's Bay Company, which shipped its products all over the world.

Whitefish are members of the salmon and trout family (Salmonidae) as they have a fleshy or stubby adipose fin just before the tail and an axillary process at the base of each pelvic fin. This detail is far removed from their culinary relationship which bears little resemblance. Unlike other salmonids the flesh of all whitefish is white, of larger flake, and more delicately flavored. Whitefish have small mouths and weak jaws; many species have filamentous gillrakers which adapt them to feeding on plankton and bottom organisms such as mollusks, insect larvae and crustaceans. There is seldom enough variation in their diet to affect the quality of the fish. The roes of the female contain thousands of tiny

Round whitefish

eggs which can be prepared in the style of shad roe or processed as a caviar substitute. Trout eggs, on the other hand, reach a large size at maturity and become rubbery in any cooking process.

WHITEFISH TERMINOLOGY

CISCO Any one of a number of small lake-dwelling members of the whitefish group of which six are marketed as **chub** in the U.S., or **tullibee** in Canada. Other names include lake herring, bloater and grayback. They are all related to the lake whitefish but are smaller (usually sold at from less than 1 pound to 2 pounds) and have a finer and more sharply boned musculature. Ciscoes are taken both commercially and by sport fishermen. Tremendous quantities of smoked chub appear in all major metropolitan markets. They are rarely sold in fresh form except in the locale where caught, but like the larger lake whitefish (*Coregonus clupeaformis*) ciscoes have a delicate white flesh for which poaching is the ideal cooking method. These fish occur from New England to the Great Lakes and north into Canada. The name "tullibee," which was used by the early fur traders in the Prairie Provinces of Canada, indicates the lake herring.

Cisco or lake herring	*Coregonus artedii*
Deepwater Cisco	*Coregonus johannae*
Longjaw Cisco	*Coregonus alpenae*
Shortjaw Cisco	*Coregonus zenithicus*
Shortnose Cisco	*Coregonus reighardi*
Blackfin Cisco	*Coregonus nigripinnis*

There is one species of cisco in European waters *(Coregonus albula)* which is found from the British Isles to northern Germany and Poland, and from Scandinavia to Siberia. It's better known as the **vendace** in Great Britain, **löja** or **siklöja** in Sweden, **mikku** in Finland, **merkii** in the Soviet Union. Although the fish is sold to a minor extent in fresh, frozen and smoked forms, its chief value is for the roe which is a caviar substitute. The Finnish specialty **Kalakukko** is made of tiny ciscoes combined with strips of salt pork and sealed in a rye dough pastry. By slow cooking at a low heat the bones become soft and edible.

HUMPBACK WHITEFISH The humpback whitefish (*Coregonus pidschian*) is common along the Arctic border of Russia through Siberia and extends into Alaska. It also occurs in the Alpine regions of Europe, notably in Lake Constance and in Southern Sweden. The species name *pidschian* is the name used by the Ostjaks of Siberia. Although the humpback attains good size, due to its isolated range and scattered distribution, it never enters American or most European markets.

INCONNU In French, *inconnu* means "unknown," a name applied to this largest member of the whitefish group by the early-day voyageurs when they first penetrated the Mackenzie River system. It was an unfortunate choice. The only alternate is the Eskimo **sheefish** (the *shee* a phonetic adaptation of the Eskimo word), which is no more comprehensible from a modern marketing point of view. In a peak year only 50,000 to 60,000 pounds of inconnu are shipped to the U.S. from Canada, as buyers are reluctant to purchase an "unknown" fish. Yet, its delicate oil-rich white steaks are exceptional when broiled and bathed in lemon butter, and few fish are its equal when smoked.

There are two forms of inconnu, a landlocked or strictly freshwater population which inhabits large northern lakes such as Great Slave, and the anadromous or migratory form which goes out to sea. The landlocked inconnu may reach weights of 20 to 30 pounds, but the seagoing fish have been recorded to twice that size in North America. These are equally palatable. The inconnu is a winter staple of the Eskimo in various watersheds of the Northwest Territories, Yukon and Alaska. It also occurs in Arctic rivers of the USSR and in the Caspian Sea. Inconnu (Russian **nelma**) are an important commercial fishery in the Soviet Union.

LAKE WHITEFISH Found from New England to Minnesota and north to Canadian Arctic drainages, this species (*Coregonus clupeaformis*) is commercially our most valuable whitefish. Although it attained sizes of over 20 pounds in Lake Superior many years ago, the average today is very much smaller; any fish over 4 pounds is considered a "jumbo" by market fishermen.

In Europe and Asia another species (*Coregonus nasus*) is identical to our lake whitefish in all respects and is considered by some taxonomists as conspecific with *C. clupeaformis*. In any event the minor physical differences are of no importance from a culinary standpoint. This whitefish has a wide range from Lake Vättern in Sweden and along the coast of the Arctic Ocean where it ascends all the great Russian rivers. In the Soviet Union it's known as the **tschir**. It also occurs in many Alpine lakes of Europe.

LAVARET Also known as **houting, skelly** and **powan** in the U.K., this is one of the more valuable whitefish—*Coregonus lavaretus*. It is found from the British Isles (Loch Lomond and Loch Eck) through northern Europe to the Bering Straits. This species encompasses many forms—migratory and nonmigratory as well as lake, riverine and marine populations which vary greatly in size and quality. The only historical fisheries are in the English Lake District, the Baltic Sea and Siberia, but lavaret has been reared artificially in northern Germany and central Europe.

MOUNTAIN WHITEFISH Also known as the **Rocky Mountain whitefish,** this species is in a different genus (*Prosopium williamsoni*) from either the lake whitefish or ciscoes. While its flesh is not quite as delicate, it's a fine foodfish nevertheless. The mountain whitefish occurs in lakes and streams on the western slope of the Rocky Mountains from northern California to southern British Columbia and along the east side to the headwaters of the Missouri and Saskatchewan Rivers. This is not a market species but vast quantities are taken by sport fishermen and consumed locally. The mountain whitefish superficially resembles the lake species but its body is more cylindrical as in the round whitefish. Although it grows to weights of 5 pounds, the majority caught weigh less than 2 pounds. Mountain whitefish eat considerable quantities of algae during the summer months and for this reason are really prime as table fare in the clear waters of winter. In rivers which have minor algal blooms, however, such as the Gallatin or North Platte, this is a negative factor. These whitefish can be panfried, but they are superior when poached or smoked and served with a dill, mustard or horseradish sauce.

ROUND WHITEFISH Sometimes called the **Menominee whitefish** and closely related to the mountain species, the round whitefish (*Prosopium cylindraceum*) occurs from New Brunswick to the Great Lakes to Alaska and the Arctic Ocean. This species is very abundant in the deep, cold lakes of Maine. Its firm white flesh contains less oil than the lake whitefish, and being of a smaller size (usually 1 to 3 pounds) it has never been a significant commercial fish. Substantial catches are made by angling, however, and I would rate it above the ciscoes at table. Like the mountain whitefish, it's best poached or smoked.

White Perch

(1) A market name for the freshwater drum, which is not a member of the perch family. *See DRUM.*

(2) A small freshwater panfish belonging to the family Percichthyidae, or temperate basses, which includes the striped bass and giant sea bass. The white perch (*Morone americana*) is found from Nova Scotia to North Carolina and inland to the Great Lakes. Essentially a freshwater species, the white perch also occurs in brackish water and saltwater. It enters rivers in large spawning runs during the spring and early summer from Cape Cod to Chesapeake Bay. Although commercial landings are

Lake whitefish

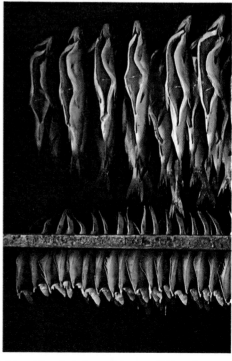

left, Whitefish prepared for smoking; right, Whitefish and flounder in the smokehouse at Esbjerg, Denmark

top left, Flag of state, a white perch surrounded
by stars; bottom left, Frying the perch, the
test of a new member; right, The Company's emblem,
the white perch, presides over the dining area;
both Washington and Lafayette dined here.

SCHUYLKILL FISHING COMPANY, PENNSYLVANIA

small or little utilized, this fish is taken in quantity by
sport fishermen.

The white perch has firm white flesh and is
delicately flavored. It can be prepared by any cooking
method but panfrying, poaching and oven-frying are most
popular. This fish makes an excellent chowder.

No panfish has more historical significance
than the white perch. Fishing and hunting were formally
recognized as sports in America in 1732 with the formation of the Schuylkill Fishing Company, near Philadelphia, the oldest club of its kind in the world in continuous
existence. This social concept had been introduced at an
earlier date in England, but these organizations did not
survive 243 years. Founded as the Colony in Schuylkill
(pronounced School-Kill, which means hidden stream in
Dutch), it had its own flag of state, emblazoned with a
crown and three perch in white against a red background.
While faithful to his Majesty George III, when the American Revolution began, the flag was changed to red, white
and blue with thirteen stars and stripes. Symbolically, the
stars surrounded the silhouette of a white perch. This
gregarious and delicious fish was so abundant in the
lower Delaware and its tributaries that it appeared at
every meeting, which included meals of fish and game

freshly killed for the occasion. Although the Company
could lay claim to the origin of planked shad (see under
SHAD) the perch, carefully fried, was the display piece of
all festive boards. Indeed, to qualify as a citizen of the
Company one was required to fry a half dozen in a long-
handled iron skillet and turn the lot simultaneously by
flipping them into the air, a manual feat that even its
present-day members are pressed to learn. According to
Company records any but the following procedure would
be contra regulam et rationem:

The fish are fried in the best butter of the market,
to a brown color, and never shapelessly broken by turning;
but in regularly laid rows and adhering to each other, and not
to the pan. They are dexterously tossed in the same compact
form, with great ease, after a little practise, to the surprise
and admiration of spectators.

Again drawn or melted butter is made in perfect
purity, without any of the usual additions of flour and water
forming an unpalatable compound of liquid, batter and oil.
The pound (butter) is reduced in a vessel by gradual heat and
slow turning, and retains its original taste and color without
being transmitted to oil. However, according to the old
proverb "everyone to his taste" and use reconciles us to
abuse. This is not considered a departure from ordinary

economical practises at the Castle though it may be deemed so in a private family.

White Trout

A market name (U.S. Gulf Coast) for the sand seatrout *(Cynoscion arenarius).* The sand seatrout occurs from Florida's West Coast to Texas and Mexico. A relative of the weakfish but a small species, seldom exceeding 15 inches in length, it is of minor commercial value. *See WEAK-FISH.*

Whiting

A common market name for the hakes which belong to the cod family Gadidae. The name whiting is most often applied to the silver hake *(Merluccius bilinearis). See HAKE under COD.*

Wolffish

This odd-looking fish occurs in the North Atlantic and North Pacific. Its compressed elongate form varies in color from slate blue to purplish brown, with 10 or more transverse bars. The wolffish has a large head and strong jaws equipped with sharp canine teeth as well as vomerine molars for grinding clams, whelks, mussels and other mollusks, which results in an unusually firm white flesh. There are 4 species of wolffish, but one cannot distinguish any culinary differences.

Wolffish are caught here from southern Labrador to Cape Cod and occasionally as far south as New Jersey. In Europe they are taken from western Greenland to Iceland, the Faroes, Spitzbergen, and in the White Sea to the Bay of Biscay. They live in moderately deep water (200 to 500 feet) and are apparently a solitary species as they are caught in the same areas at all times of the year. Annual landings of about 1½ million pounds are made in the Gulf of Maine and on the Georges Banks. As a food the wolffish is most popular in Norway, Denmark, France and Spain. It grows to a length of about 5 feet and a weight of about 40 pounds. A small amount is sold in the U.S. under the totally confusing name "ocean catfish." In European markets it's known as **Lobo** (Spain), **Loup** (France), **Zeewolf** (Holland), **Katfische** and **Wasserkatze** (Germany), **Havkat** (Denmark), **Steinbit** (Norway), **Steinbitur** (Iceland), **Bavosa Lupa** (Italy), **Gata** (Portugal).

Wrasse

A large family (Labridae) of marine fishes, comprising about 450 species found mainly in tropical waters but with some members occurring in the temperate zone. The vast majority of labrid fishes are small, colorful reef dwell-

Wolffish

ers of no food value. Only 4 species found along the North American coast attain good size and are of culinary importance: the **tautog, hogfish, cunner** and **California sheephead** (*see under individual entries*).

The **ballan wrasse, rock cook** and **rainbow wrasse** are common labrids of the Eastern Atlantic and Mediterranean; their flesh is soft and flavorless.

Yellow Perch

Our kitchen at home in Florida has played host to some huge fish over the years, so when we rented a summer house on Cape Cod one summer, my wife's request for a dozen yellow perch seemed reasonable. After all, it was a common sight to see small boys and gaunt cats dragging strings of perch along the back road. My neighbor's 5-year-old son assured me that a red worm and a bent pin was adequate equipment, but the wisdom of this young realist escaped me. He didn't know about our kitchen. It was like telling Einstein how to correct algebra papers. Being in a confident mood, I selected the lightest fly tackle to give the perch a sporting chance and repaired to Gull

Pond, a bowl of white sand scooped out of scrub oak and pine. Here and there, a fat perch drifted under the lily pads looking like a figure in a Japanese print—a miniature Samurai warrior in his barred jade and yellow mail balanced on flame orange fins. I aimed each cast to bring my artificial fly enticingly over the fish, confident of a quick success. Obviously, this was the wrong fly, so I tied on another. The second was no better than the first, and the third was no better than the second. To be ignored by a salmon or spurned by a marlin is not without some glory. To muck one's way around a pond for 2 hours futilely chasing our dinner was shattering. Resorting finally to the advice of my young compatriot I managed a cracker crumb revenge before dark. In angling, big is not always smartest, and in the skillet big is not always best. Few mortals would deny that a yellow perch taken from a clear cold pond is a supreme taste experience. Ausonius described it centuries ago:

Nor let the Muse, in her award of fame,
Illustrious Perch unnoticed pass thy claim.
Prince of the Prickly cohort, bred in lakes,
To feast our boards, what sapid boneless flakes
Thy solid flesh supplies! though overfed,
No daintier fish in ocean's pasture bred
Swims thy compeer.

Fortunately, yellow perch are readily caught, indeed taken by the uncounted millions throughout the year on the simplest of equipment, and especially in the spring and winter seasons when the fish are prime. This is a true perch, a member of the family Percidae, which includes the North American walleye and sauger. The

Fish market at Fiumicino, Italy, at the north mouth of the Tiber, on the Tyrrhenian Sea

Yellow perch

yellow perch *(Perca flavescens)* is so closely related to the European perch *(Perca fluviatilis)* that there is some question whether they are separate species; from a culinary standpoint there is no detectable difference except that the perch of Europe grows to a somewhat larger size. Both are highly esteemed foodfish, having a white and unusually firm musculature, so much so that it becomes elastic if overcooked. While sharply spined in the dorsal fin, perch have a simple skeletal structure and the boneless and skinless fillets make a valuable commercial product.

In North America, yellow perch are found from Nova Scotia to South Carolina, north to central Canada and westward almost to Great Slave Lake, and east to Quebec. They are one of the most abundant fishes in the Great Lakes and have been the subject of a large commercial fishery, particularly on Lake Erie. Although the average fish caught weighs about ½ pound, spring runs of "jumbo" or "jack" perch weighing from 1 to 2 pounds and occasionally larger are attended by hundreds of thousands of amateur anglers in our midwestern states. Perch also provide a tremendous winter fishery for the cold-foot clan who fish through the ice, both here and in northern Europe where the perch grows to 4 pounds or more. This is a valuable market fish around the Baltic where boatloads of **ahven** are landed each morning in Finnish ports while fresh **abborre** is purveyed by Swedish fishmongers. These local catches are quickly sold and are usually out of stock before the pike, herring and walleye.

Z

Zander

A member of the perch family (Percidae) originally limited in distribution to the lakes and rivers of central Europe and the USSR. The zander *(Stizostedion lucioperca)* is related to the North American walleye. In 1887, a small quantity of live zander was shipped to England by the ninth Duke of Bedford. For many years the fish remained in a few lakes of Bedfordshire but in recent decades it has become more widespread; it now occurs in the Great Ouse watershed and the reservoirs of Essex. The zander is a famous foodfish in Hungary, where it is known as **fogas.** *See also WALLEYE.*

Zubatac

An Adriatic member of the porgy family known in English as the large-eyed dentex. This fish is especially popular in Yugoslavia and Greece. *See PORGY.*

CONVERTING FROM U.S. CUSTOMARY SYSTEM TO METRICS

U.S. CUSTOMARY SYSTEM

a few grains	= less than $^1/_{16}$ tablespoon
a pinch	= less than ⅛ teaspoon
½ tablespoon	= 1½ teaspoons
1 tablespoon	= 3 teaspoons or ½ ounce
⅛ cup	= 2 tablespoons or 1 ounce
¼ cup	= 4 tablespoons or 2 ounces
⅓ cup	= 5 tablespoons plus 1 teaspoon
½ cup	= 8 tablespoons or 4 ounces
⅔ cup	= 10 tablespoons plus 2 teaspoons
¾ cup	= 12 tablespoons or 6 ounces
1 cup	= 16 tablespoons or 8 ounces
2 cups	= 1 pint
2 pints	= 1 quart
1 imperial pint (Canada)	= 2½ cups
1 imperial quart (Canada)	= 5 cups
4 quarts	= 1 gallon

OUNCES TO GRAMS

¼ ounce	= 7 grams
1 ounce	= 28.35 grams
2 ounces	= 56.7 grams
4 ounces	= 113.4 grams
6 ounces	= 170.1 grams
8 ounces (½ pound)	= 226.8 grams
16 ounces (1 pound)	= 453.6 grams or 0.4536 kilogram

CONVERSION FACTORS:
ounces to grams: multiply ounce figure by 28.3 to get number of grams;
pounds to grams: multiply pound figure by 453.59 to get number of grams.

VOLUME MEASURES BASED ON THE WEIGHT OF LIQUIDS
(WATER, MILK, BUTTER, SUGAR)

¼ teaspoon	= 1.17 grams
½ teaspoon	= 2.34 grams
1 teaspoon	= 4.7 grams
1 tablespoon	= 14.3 grams
2 tablespoons (1 ounce)	= 28.35 grams
4 tablespoons (¼ cup)	= 56.7 grams
8 tablespoons (½ cup)	= 113.4 grams
12 tablespoons (¾ cup)	= 170.1 grams
16 tablespoons (1 cup)	= 226.8 grams
32 tablespoons (1 pint)	= 453.6 grams or 0.4536 kilogram
64 tablespoons (1 quart)	= 946.35 grams or 0.9463 kilogram

OUNCES TO MILLILITERS AND LITERS

1 ounce	= 29.57 milliliters
4 ounces	= 118.29 milliliters
8 ounces (1 cup)	= 236.59 milliliters or .237 liter
16 ounces (1 pint)	= 473.18 milliliters or .473 liter
32 ounces (1 quart)	= 946.35 milliliters or .946 liter
128 ounces (1 gallon)	= 3785.4 milliliters or 3.79 liters

In cooking it is generally possible to substitute 1 quart for 1 liter and vice versa, since a liter measure holds only a little more than a quart measure.

VOLUME MEASURES BASED ON WEIGHT OF DRY INGREDIENTS
(USING ALL-PURPOSE FLOUR AS THE STANDARD)

1 teaspoon	= 3 grams
1 tablespoon	= 9 grams
¼ cup	= 36 grams
⅓ cup	= 46 grams
½ cup	= 72 grams
¾ cup	= 108 grams
1 cup	= 144 grams

Each dry ingredient has its own weight, which is not necessarily the same as the weight of an equal volume of flour. These equivalents, therefore, are only approximate for any other dry ingredient, and the gram measure can also vary slightly for different kinds of flour.

INCHES TO CENTIMETERS

½ inch	= 1.27 centimeters
1 inch	= 2.54 centimeters
2 inches	= 5.08 centimeters
5 inches	= 12.7 centimeters
10 inches	= 25.4 centimeters
15 inches	= 38.1 centimeters

CONVERSION FACTOR:
multiply the inch figure by 2.54 to get the number of centimeters.

TEMPERATURES—FAHRENHEIT (F.) TO CELSIUS (C.)

	° Fahrenheit		° Celsius
freezer storage	− 10	=	− 23.3
	0	=	− 17.7
water freezes	32	=	0
	50	=	10
room temperature	68	=	20
	100	=	37.7
	150	=	65.5
water simmers	205	=	96.1
water boils	212	=	100
	300	=	148.8
	325	=	162.8
baking	350	=	177
	375	=	190.5
	400	=	204.4
	425	=	218.3
	450	=	232
broiling	500	=	260

CONVERSION FACTOR:
subtract 32 from the Fahrenheit figure, multiply by 5, then divide by 9.

CONVERTING FROM METRICS TO U.S. CUSTOMARY SYSTEM

METRIC SYSTEM

1 gram x 10	=	1 decagram
1 gram x 100	=	1 hectogram
1 gram x 1000	=	1 kilogram
1 gram x 100,000	=	1 quintal
1 centimeter x 10	=	1 decimeter
1 centimeter x 100	=	1 meter
1 centimeter x 1000	=	1 kilometer
1 kilogram	=	1 liter = 1000 cubic centimeters

GRAMS TO OUNCES

1 gram	=	.0353 ounce or $1/28$ ounce AVDP
10 grams	=	.353 ounce
28 grams	=	1 ounce
100 grams	=	3.5 ounces
200 grams	=	7 ounces
500 grams	=	17.5 ounces or $1^1/8$ pounds
1000 grams	=	2.205 pounds or 1 kilogram

CONVERSION FACTOR:
multiply gram figure by .0353 to get the number of ounces; or, if it's easier this way, divide the gram figure by 31, but the second method will not be as accurate as the first method.

CENTIMETERS TO INCHES

1 centimeter	=	.39 inch
2 centimeters	=	.78 inch
5 centimeters	=	1.95 inches (almost 2 inches)
10 centimeters	=	3.94 inches (almost 4 inches)
15 centimeters	=	5.89 inches
20 centimeters	=	7.99 inches
100 centimeters (1 meter)	=	39.37 inches (longer than our yard)

CONVERSION FACTOR:
multiply centimeter figure by .39 to get number of inches.

TEMPERATURES—CELSIUS (C.) TO FAHRENHEIT (F.)

	° Celsius		° Fahrenheit
	− 20	=	− 4
	− 10	=	14
water freezes	0	=	32
	10	=	50
	20	=	68
	50	=	122
water boils	100	=	212
	150	=	302
	175	=	347
	200	=	392
	225	=	437
	250	=	482
	275	=	527
	300	=	572

CONVERSION FACTOR:
multiply Celsius figure by 9, divide by 5, then add 32.

The temperatures given for boiling in both columns apply only at sea level. Liquids will boil at lower temperatures as you go higher. For each 550 feet the boiling temperature will be reduced by 1°F.

METRIC TONS TO SHORT TONS (FISHERY STATISTICS)

1 metric ton	=	2,204.6 pounds
100 metric tons	=	110 short tons
500 metric tons	=	551 short tons
1,000 metric tons	=	1,102 short tons
10,000 metric tons	=	11,023 short tons
50,000 metric tons	=	55,115 short tons
75,000 metric tons	=	82,673 short tons
100,000 metric tons	=	110,231 short tons
200,000 metric tons	=	220,462 short tons
300,000 metric tons	=	330,693 short tons
400,000 metric tons	=	440,924 short tons
500,000 metric tons	=	551,155 short tons

CONVERSION FACTORS:
metric tons to short tons: multipy the metric figure by 1.1023112; short tons to metric tons: multiply the short figure by .90718486.

For complete tables, with fractions and multiples, consult *Units of Weight and Measure,* National Bureau of Standards, U.S. Department of Commerce, Miscellaneous Publication 286, Washington, D.C.

Acknowledgments

We wish to thank the following individuals
and organizations who contributed directly or indirectly in
compiling the materials in this book:

ANTONIO ALONSO, Spanish National Tourist Office, New York City
JOEL ARRINGTON, Department of Economic Resources,
          Raleigh, North Carolina
JAMES AVAULT, Louisiana State University, Baton Rouge, Louisiana
CRISTALLERIES DE BACCARAT, Paris, France
PETER BALAS, Inter-Continental Hotel Corp., Paris, France
PACE BARNES, Executive Editor, E. P. Dutton & Co., Inc., New York City
BASQUE GASTRONOMICAL SOCIETY, San Sebastián, Spain
GARY BEARDSLEY, Miami Marine Laboratory, Miami, Florida
HENRY W. BEARDSLEY, Inter-Continental Hotel Corp., New York City
BELLE TERRASSE RESTAURANT, Copenhagen, Denmark
L. BERNARDAUD, Paris, France
SERGIO BETANCOURT, Pan American World Airways
MALCOLM K. BEYER (GEN.), Iron Gate Products Co., Inc., New York City
BILLINGSGATE MARKET (THE FACTORS), London, England
ANNIKA AND LENNART BORGSTROM, Svängsta, Sweden
GEORGE BRAUN OYSTER CO. INC., Cutchogue, New York
BRENNAN'S RESTAURANT, New Orleans, Louisiana
JEROME BRODY, Oyster Bar & Restaurant, Grand Central Terminal,
          New York City
RAY BROOKER, Freshwater Fish Marketing Corp., Winnipeg, Manitoba
BURDINE'S, West Palm Beach, Florida
CALIFORNIA DEPARTMENT OF FISH AND GAME, Sacramento, California
CALIFORNIA WINE INSTITUTE, San Francisco, California
CANADIAN DEPARTMENT OF FISHERIES AND FORESTRY, Ottawa, Ontario
CECILIA CHIANG, The Mandarin, San Francisco, California
ORFÈVRERIE CHRISTOFLE, Paris, France
HOWARD COOPER, East Hampton, New York
HOTEL d'ANGLETERRE, Copenhagen, Denmark
DONALD P. DE SYLVA, Rosenstiel School of Marine and
          Atmospheric Sciences, Virginia Key, Florida
BRENDA DICKINSON, Merchandising Specialist, Department
          of Natural Resources, Tallahassee, Florida
GILBERT DRAKE, Deep Water Cay Club, Bahamas
GILBERT DRAKE, JR., Key West, Florida
ELDRED TROUT PRESERVE, Eldred, New York
A. J. ESTAY, New Orleans Shrimp Company, Baton Rouge, Louisiana
DORIS FLEMMING, Louisiana Tourist Board, New Orleans, Louisiana
W. A. FLICK, Department of Natural Resources, New York State College of
          Agriculture and Life Sciences,
          Cornell University, Ithaca, New York

OLGA FORBES, Chub Cay Club, Bahamas
FORMAN & SONS, London, England
PETER FRENCH-HODGES, British Travel Association,
        London, England
HARRY GONZALEZ, Palm Beach, Florida
GRAND HOTEL TAMMER, Tampere, Finland
LARRY GREEN, Northwest Field Editor, *Field & Stream*
ANDREW GLAZE, British Tourist Authority, New York City
HAMMACHER SCHLEMMER, New York City
HOLMENKOLLEN TURISTHOTELL, Oslo, Norway
CHARLES JANON, Inter-Continental Hotel, Paris, France
JAN SCHMIDT FISH MARKET, Rotterdam, The Netherlands
JENSEN'S INN, Fanø, Denmark
JOHN ROSS, JR., LTD, Aberdeen, Scotland
PAUL KALMAN, New Orleans, Louisiana
KONTIKI RESTAURANT, Bygdøy, Norway
PAUL KOVI, The Four Seasons, New York City
PETER KREINDLER, 21 Club, New York City
KROGS FISKERESTAURANT, Copenhagen, Denmark
STANLEY LEEN, Leen's Lodge, Grand Lake Stream, Maine
ELEANOR LESLIE, Inter-Continental Hotel Corp., New York City
DONALD E. McALLISTER, National Museums, Ottawa, Canada
TONY MADEIRA (Heyward Associates), Portugal National Tourist
        Information Office, New York City
FRANK J. MATHER, III, Woods Hole Oceanographic Institution,
        Woods Hole, Massachusetts
HUGH J. MEETER, Holland Herring Council
CHARLES R. MEYER, Southold, New York
ROBERT W. MINNERS ASSOCIATES LTD, New York City
MONTE LEONE HOTEL, New Orleans, Louisiana
NAJADEN RESTAURANT, Bygdøy, Norway
STATE OF NEW HAMPSHIRE DEPARTMENT OF FISH AND GAME,
        Portsmouth, New Hampshire
KURT NIELSON, Danish National Tourist Office, Copenhagen, Denmark
NIPPON RESTAURANT, New York City
NORWEGIAN FOLK MUSEUM, Bygdøy, Norway
CARL NYBERG, Manager, Finnair, Helsinki, Finland
ARTHUR OGLESBY, European Editor, *Field & Stream*
HOTEL OKURA, Amsterdam, The Netherlands
WILF ORGAN, Director, Development and Extension Services,
        Winnipeg, Manitoba
CLAUDIUS CHARLES PHILIPPE, New York City
JOHN RAYNER, Fisheries Director, Oregon State Game
        Commission, Corvallis, Oregon
ED REDDY, Palm Beach, Florida

UNIVERSITY OF RHODE ISLAND, MARINE ADVISORY SERVICE,
        Providence, Rhode Island
CHARLES C. RITZ, Ritz Hotel, Paris, France
ROSEDALE FISH & OYSTER MARKET, New York City
RUSTHOLLI RESTAURANT, Tampere, Finland
SVEND SAABYE, Copenhagen, Denmark
EARL OF SEAFIELD, Cullen, Scotland
HARRY SERLIS, San Francisco, California
RICHARD SHOMURA, Director, Honolulu Laboratory,
        National Marine Fisheries Service
SCOTT SIDDAL, Rosensteil School of Marine and Atmospheric
        Sciences, Virginia Key, Florida
DEBRA K. SIMS, Seafood Specialist, Department of Natural Resources,
        Titusville, Florida
C. L. SMITH, AMERICAN MUSEUM OF NATURAL HISTORY, New York City
REX SMITH, Frigidaire, Dayton, Ohio
STATE IN SCHUYLKILL FISHING COMPANY, Andalusia, Pennsylvania
HANS STERNIK, President, Inter-Continental Hotel Corp.
L.B.E. THUNG (COMMANDER), Royal Dutch Navy, The Hague,
        The Netherlands
PENELOPE TURTLE, Chub Cay Club, Bahamas
VERA LINENS, INC., New York City
JOHN VON GLAHN, The Fishery Council, New York City
HENRY WARREN, The Breakers, Palm Beach, Florida
ALEYNE WHEELER, British Museum (Natural History), London, England
FRANK WOOLNER, Editor, Saltwater Sportsman
HERBERT N. WYATT, Fisheries Biologist, Tifton, Georgia
Y.E.B. YATES, Factor, Seafield Estates and Sportings Club,
        Cullen, Scotland

Our grateful appreciation to GEORGE MORFOGEN
of the Oyster Bar & Restaurant, Grand Central Terminal, New York City,
for his help with specimens and his generous gift of time and expertise.

To WILMA WALKER DEZANGER our gratitude for her help
in arranging photographic trips and collecting recipes,
and for styling food pictures, and our appreciation
to JOHN FORASTE, MELISSA HUBNER, ANN BRODY and
ROBERT DEZANGER for their photographic assistance
in various parts of the world.

Special thanks are due to INEZ M. KRECH for her superlative
editorial assistance in the preparation of the manuscript, and
for preparing captions and index.

Index

The system of alphabetization follows that of the encyclopedia; each entry, whether a one-word entry or not, is read as one word. Therefore Blackfin and Blackfish come between Black drum and Black grouper. References to the left column of each text page are shown by means of the letter "a" following the page number, thus: 106a. References to the right column are shown by means of the letter "b" following the page number, thus: 106b.

All common names, foreign names and scientific names given in the encyclopedia are listed in the index. While all pages concerned with Crab are listed following the general entry Crab, for particular species one must consult the common name (Blue crab, Dungeness crab, Lady crab, Spider Crab, etc.) in its alphabetical place under B, D, L, S. In the encyclopedia most of the information on Flounder falls under the entry Sole; these pages are listed following Sole, but there is also an index entry Flounder, showing all relevant pages, as well as separate entries for particular species called flounder (Arrowtooth flounder, Summer flounder, Winter flounder), as well as entries for flounders called Brill, Halibut, Turbot.

Page numbers referring to illustrations are set in boldface, thus: **41.** References to illustrations for identification follow the main heading (Crab), the common name of the species (Jonah crab), and the scientific name (*Cancer borealis*); they are not shown following the foreign names of the species.

Dishes that are merely mentioned, described or pictured are listed in this part of the index. Page numbers for full recipes and their illustrations are listed in the second part of the index, along with cooking information.

Recipes and Cooking Information